STEPHEN'S COMMENTARIES
ON THE
LAWS OF ENGLAND

VOLUME III

EDITORS FOR VOLUME III

CIVIL PROCEDURE

BY

R. SUTTON, M.A.
One of His Majesty's Counsel
READER IN COMMON LAW TO THE COUNCIL OF LEGAL EDUCATION

EDWARD F. IWI
Solicitor of the Supreme Court (Honours)
AN ASSISTANT EXAMINER TO THE LAW SOCIETY

WITH CHAPTERS 1–3 ON THE ORGANISATION OF THE COURTS BY

W. H. D. WINDER, M.A., LL.M.
Of Lincoln's Inn, Barrister-at-Law
FORMERLY LECTURER IN LAW IN THE UNIVERSITY COLLEGE OF WALES

THE LEGAL PROFESSION

BY

T. G. LUND, C.B.E.
SECRETARY, THE LAW SOCIETY

E. H. V. McDOUGALL
UNDER-SECRETARY, THE LAW SOCIETY

CONSTITUTIONAL AND ADMINISTRATIVE LAW

BY

F. H. LAWSON, D.C.L.
Of Gray's Inn, Barrister-at-Law
PROFESSOR OF COMPARATIVE LAW IN THE UNIVERSITY OF OXFORD

H. J. S. JENKINS, B.C.L., M.A.
Of the Inner Temple, Barrister-at-Law
DIRECTOR OF LEGAL STUDIES IN THE
UNIVERSITY COLLEGES OF SOUTH WALES AND MONMOUTHSHIRE AND OF SWANSEA

WILLIAM O. HART, C.M.G., B.C.L., M.A.
Of Lincoln's Inn, Barrister-at-Law
FORMERLY FELLOW AND TUTOR OF WADHAM COLLEGE AND UNIVERSITY LECTURER IN LAW
IN THE UNIVERSITY OF OXFORD

STEPHEN'S COMMENTARIES

ON THE
LAWS OF ENGLAND

TWENTY-FIRST EDITION

Editor-in-Chief
L. CRISPIN WARMINGTON
Solicitor of the Supreme Court (Honours)

VOLUME III

CIVIL PROCEDURE

CONSTITUTIONAL AND ADMINISTRATIVE LAW

LONDON
BUTTERWORTH & CO. (PUBLISHERS) LTD.

AUSTRALIA :   BUTTERWORTH & CO. (AUSTRALIA) LTD., SYDNEY, MELBOURNE AND BRISBANE
CANADA :   BUTTERWORTH & CO. (CANADA) LTD., TORONTO
NEW ZEALAND :   BUTTERWORTH & CO. (AUSTRALIA) LTD., WELLINGTON AND AUCKLAND
AFRICA :   BUTTERWORTH & CO. (AFRICA) LTD., DURBAN

1950

PRINTED IN GREAT BRITAIN

MADE AND PRINTED IN GREAT BRITAIN BY WILLIAM CLOWES AND SONS, LIMITED
LONDON AND BECCLES

TABLE OF CONTENTS
TO VOLUME III

PAGE

SUMMARY OF CONTENTS OF VOLUMES I–IV   ... xiii

BOOK I
CIVIL PROCEDURE

PART I
ORGANISATION OF THE COURTS

CHAPTER 1. THE EXISTING COURTS   3

CHAPTER 2. THE SUPERIOR COURTS   7
  Section I. The Supreme Court of Judicature ...   7
              (i) The High Court of Justice   ...   7
              (ii) The Court of Appeal   ...   11
  Section II. The House of Lords   12
  Section III. The Judicial Committee of the
      Privy Council   14
  Section IV. The Palatine Courts   15

CHAPTER 3. JURISDICTION OF THE HIGH COURT   17

CHAPTER 4. THE JUDGES AND OFFICERS OF THE
            SUPREME COURT   23

PART II
PROCEEDINGS IN THE HIGH COURT

INTRODUCTION TO PART II   35

CHAPTER 5. PROCEEDINGS IN THE KING'S BENCH
            DIVISION   36
  Section I. Commencement of Action   36
  Section II. Pleadings   42

v

PAGE

Section III.   Interlocutory Proceedings   ...   57
Section IV.   Advice on Evidence   70
Section V.   Trial   72
Section VI.   Taxation of Costs   76
Section VII.   Execution...   77
Section VIII.   Appeal   83
Section IX.   Specially Indorsed Writ   86
Section X.   The Commercial Court   90

CHAPTER 6.   PROCEEDINGS IN THE CHANCERY
DIVISION   93
Section I.   Writ of Summons   93
Section II.   Originating Summons   101
Section III.   Petition   103

CHAPTER 7.   MATRIMONIAL CAUSES   104
Section I.   Proceedings in the Probate, Divorce,
and Admiralty Division of the High Court   106
(a) Divorce   106
(b) Bars to Divorce   110
(c) Procedure in the High Court   114
(d) Judicial Separation and Restitution of
Conjugal Rights   130
(e) Nullity   131
(f) Recognition of Foreign Divorce Decrees   133
Section II.   Proceedings in Courts of Summary
Jurisdiction   133

CHAPTER 8.   PROBATE PROCEEDINGS   137

CHAPTER 9.   ADMIRALTY PROCEEDINGS   141

CHAPTER 10.   EVIDENCE AND ESTOPPEL   150

PART III

OTHER PROCEEDINGS

CHAPTER 11.   PROCEEDINGS IN THE COUNTY COURTS
AND OTHER COURTS   171
Section I.   Proceedings in the County Courts ...   171
(a) Constitution   171

PAGE

(b) *Jurisdiction* 172
(c) *Procedure* 175
Section II. *Proceedings in Other Courts of
Limited or Special Jurisdiction* 182

CHAPTER 12. PROCEEDINGS IN BANKRUPTCY ... 189

CHAPTER 13. ARBITRATION 224

PART IV

THE LEGAL PROFESSION

CHAPTER 14. SOLICITORS 235
Section I. *How to become a Practising Solicitor* 237
Section II. *Offences by Solicitors and Un-
qualified Persons* 243
Section III. *A Solicitor's Work, Privileges, and
Disabilities* 248
Section IV. *Solicitors' Remuneration* 252

CHAPTER 15. BARRISTERS (" COUNSEL ") 259

BOOK II

CONSTITUTIONAL AND ADMINISTRATIVE LAW

PART I

GENERAL INTRODUCTION

CHAPTER 1. THE SCOPE AND SOURCES OF CONSTITU-
TIONAL AND ADMINISTRATIVE LAW 267

CHAPTER 2. THE THEORY OF GOVERNMENTAL
POWERS AND DUTIES 271

CHAPTER 3. THE KING'S PLEASURE 284

CHAPTER 4. THE SOVEREIGNTY OF PARLIAMENT ... 288

PAGE

CHAPTER 5.   THE ROYAL PREROGATIVE   294

CHAPTER 6.   THE DOCTRINE OF STATE NECESSITY
              AND ACT OF STATE...   309

CHAPTER 7.   THE DEVELOPMENT OF CABINET
              GOVERNMENT AND THE CONVENTIONS
              OF THE CONSTITUTION   315

CHAPTER 8.   SUBORDINATE LEGISLATION AND
              ADMINISTRATIVE JURISDICTION   ...   321
    Section I.   Introduction   321
    Section II.   Subordinate Legislation   322
    Section III.   Administrative Jurisdiction   ...   328

CHAPTER 9.   THE SEPARATION OF POWERS AND
              THE RULE OF LAW...   333

PART II

PARLIAMENT

CHAPTER 10.   THE CONSTITUENT PARTS OF PAR-
               LIAMENT   347
    Section I.   The Title to the Crown   347
    Section II.   The House of Lords   350
    Section III.   The House of Commons   352

CHAPTER 11.   DISQUALIFICATIONS FOR MEMBER-
               SHIP OF PARLIAMENT   354

CHAPTER 12.   THE ELECTION OF MEMBERS OF THE
               HOUSE OF COMMONS   359
    Section I.   The Parliamentary Franchise   ...   359
    Section II.   The Process of Election   366

CHAPTER 13.   THE ASSEMBLING, ADJOURNMENT,
               PROROGATION AND DISSOLUTION
               OF PARLIAMENT   372

CHAPTER 14.   THE POWERS OF THE CONSTITUENT
               PARTS OF PARLIAMENT   375
    *Section I.   Conditions for the Validity of an Act
    of Parliament*   375

PAGE

Section II. The Parliament Act, 1911...   ... 377
Section III. King, Lords, or Commons, acting
    separately   380
Section IV. The Law and Custom of Parliament 381

CHAPTER 15. THE PROCEDURE OF PARLIAMENT ... 389

PART III

CENTRAL AND LOCAL GOVERNMENT

CHAPTER 16. THE ORGANS OF CENTRAL GOVERN-
        MENT   403
Section I. The Prime Minister, the Ministry,
    and the Cabinet   403
Section II. The Civil Service 408
Section III. The Central Government Depart-
    ments 410

CHAPTER 17. THE NATIONAL BUDGET   423

CHAPTER 18. FOREIGN AFFAIRS 443

CHAPTER 19. THE ROYAL FORCES...   446
Section I. The Army   446
Section II. The Royal Navy   449
Section III. The Royal Air Force   450
Section IV. The Central Departments   ... 450
Section V. The Status of Members of the Armed
    Forces   451

CHAPTER 20. THE ORGANS OF LOCAL AUTHORITIES 455
Section I. Introduction 455
Section II. Local Authorities (outside London) 459
Section III. London   467
Section IV. Local Government Elections   ... 469
Section V. Other Bodies...   472

CHAPTER 21. THE FUNCTIONS OF LOCAL AUTHORI-
        TIES 477
Section I. Rating and Valuation   477
Section II. Police   479

PAGE

Section III.   Highways   483
Section IV.   Public Health   490
Section V.   Housing   494
Section VI.   Town and Country Planning   ...   497
Section VII.   The Licensing Laws   498

CHAPTER 22.   CENTRAL CONTROL OF LOCAL GOVERN-
                MENT   503

PART IV

CHURCH AND STATE

CHAPTER 23.   THE CHURCH OF ENGLAND...   ...   509
Section I.   The Establishment   509
Section II.   Holy Orders   512
Section III.   Officers of the Church   512
Section IV.   Representative Assemblies of the
                Church   516
Section V.   Ecclesiastical Courts   519
Section VI.   Meaning of Ecclesiastical Law   ...   522

CHAPTER 24.   OTHER RELIGIOUS BODIES...   ...   523

PART V

THE SUBJECT

CHAPTER 25.   THE CONSTITUTIONAL POSITION OF
                THE SUBJECT   529
Section I.   The Duties of the Subject   529
Section II.   The Rights of the Subject   534
Section III.   Interferences with the Fundamental
                Liberties   552

PART VI

THE JUDICIARY

CHAPTER 26.   THE CONSTITUTIONAL FUNCTIONS OF
                THE JUDGES   565
Section I.   Introduction   565

PAGE

Section II.   Remedies against the Crown   ...   568
Section III.   Remedies against other Public
    Authorities   571
Section IV.   Orders in Lieu of Prerogative Writs   573
Section V.   Limitation of Actions against Public
    Authorities   581

PART VII

THE COMMONWEALTH AND EMPIRE

CHAPTER 27.   THE COMMONWEALTH AND EMPIRE   585

Section I.   The British Islands   585
Section II.   Colonies   588
Section III.   Protectorates and Protected States   595
Section IV.   Mandated and Trust Territories...   596
Section V.   The Dominions   596
Section VI.   The Unity of the Empire   600

SUMMARY OF CONTENTS
OF VOLUMES I TO IV

VOLUME I

Book I. THE SOURCES OF THE LAW OF ENGLAND
AND HISTORY OF ENGLISH LEGAL
INSTITUTIONS

Book II. THE LAW OF PROPERTY
Part I.   Land Law
Part II.   The Law of Pure Personalty
Part III.   Trusts and Trustees
Part IV.   Transfer of Property Peculiar to
Pure Personalty
Part V.   Transfer of Property on Death
Part VI.   Transfer of Property : Conveyanc-
ing
Part VII.   Disabilities
Part VIII.   The Death Duties

VOLUME II

Book I. THE LAW OF CONTRACT
Part I.   General Principles
Part II. Particular Contracts and Quasi-con-
tract

Book II.   THE LAW OF TORTS

Book III. NATURAL PERSONS

Book IV. ASSOCIATIONS OF PERSONS

xiii

VOLUME III

Book I. CIVIL PROCEDURE

    Part I.   The Organisation of the Courts
    Part II.   Proceedings in the High Courts
    Part III.   Other Proceedings
    Part IV.   The Legal Profession

Book II. CONSTITUTIONAL AND ADMINISTRA-
           TIVE LAW

    Part I.   General Introduction
    Part II.   Parliament
    Part III.   Central and Local Government
    Part IV.   Church and State
    Part V.   The Subject
    Part VI.   The Judiciary
    Part VII.   The Empire

VOLUME IV

Book I. CRIMINAL LAW

    Part I.   The General Nature of Criminal
            Liability
    Part II.   Particular Crimes
    Part III.   Evidence
    Part IV.   Procedure

Table of Cases
Index

BOOK I
CIVIL PROCEDURE

PART I

THE ORGANISATION OF THE COURTS

SUMMARY

PAGE

CHAPTER 1. THE EXISTING COURTS   3

CHAPTER 2. THE SUPERIOR COURTS   7

CHAPTER 3. JURISDICTION OF THE HIGH COURT   17

CHAPTER 4. THE JUDGES AND OFFICERS OF THE
                    SUPREME COURT   23

THE EXISTING COURTS

The short history of legal institutions in Volume I of this work touched on the diverse origins and modes of operation of the courts which have existed at different periods. At the present day it is true to say that all courts of justice in England are now derived, mediately or immediately, from the power of the Crown ; and in all courts the King, as the fountain of justice, is supposed, in contemplation of law, to be always present, being represented by his judges, whose power is only an emanation from his royal prerogative. Justice is administered by a variety of courts, some with a limited, others with an extensive jurisdiction ; some constituted to determine in the first instance, others upon appeal and by way of review ; some of record, others not of record ; some superior and others inferior. But certain rules apply to all courts, to whichever of these cross-divisions they may happen to belong.

Unless there are special circumstances the public have the right to be present at the sittings of all courts (*Scott v. Scott*, [1913] A. C. 417). Lord HEWART, C.J., said in *R. v. Sussex Justices, Ex parte McCarthy*, [1924] 1 K. B. 256, at p. 259 : *Justice is administered in public.*

> " . . . a long line of cases shows that it is not merely of some importance but is of fundamental importance that justice should not only be done, but should manifestly and undoubtedly be seen to be done."

The present Lord Chief Justice (Lord GODDARD) amplified this in *R. v. Caernarvon Licensing Justices, Ex parte Benson* (1949), 113 J. P. 23, at p. 24, where he said :

> " . . . that is one of the main reasons why all courts of justice are open to the public—so that the public may see justice done—and justice must be done in a way which will satisfy the minds of the public that it is not only being done but is obviously and clearly being done."

There are, however, exceptions in which this fundamental principle gives way to the paramount duty of securing that justice is done ; and, where it can only be done by a court sitting *in camera*, this course will be followed. The principal exceptions in practice are : (i) decision of questions affecting wards and lunatics, where the jurisdiction of the court is " parental and administrative " rather than contentious ; (ii) " litigation as to a secret process, where the effect of publicity would be to destroy the subject-matter " ; (iii) any other case in which the presence of the public would make the administration of justice impracticable, and where the interests of the state might be prejudiced by the trial being held in public, *e.g.*, particularly in time of war. The mere fact that the evidence is likely to be unsavoury does not justify a sitting *in camera*.

Of course, an Act of Parliament may direct or empower a court to exclude members of the public upon the trial of cases of a particular character, *e.g.*, the Children and Young Persons Act, 1933, s. 37, though under this section *bonâ fide* representatives of newspapers may not be excluded ; in suits for nullity on the grounds of incapacity, the evidence as to sexual capacity is heard *in camera* unless the judge in the interests of justice directs otherwise (Supreme Court of Judicature (Amendment) Act, 1935, s. 4).

Protection of judges.

On the other hand, although the members of courts are in general not trusted to do their work other than in the full blaze of publicity, they are accorded a peculiar privilege. It is a rule of law, which applies to all judges alike, and is established to secure their independence of all external influences, and especially of all unworthy fear of the consequences of their acts, that no action may be brought against a judge in respect of acts done within his jurisdiction, even though they are alleged to have been done maliciously and without reasonable and probable cause. There are, to be sure, methods, some more difficult than others, of removing a judge who is corrupt or inefficient, and all judicial officers are bound by the oath which they take " To do right to all manner of people after the laws and usages of this realm without fear or favour, affection or ill-will."

The existing courts may be classified in several different ways. First, there is an ancient distinction which runs through the whole judicial system and is still of importance. Some courts are courts of record, and others not of record. A court of record is one whose acts and judicial proceedings are enrolled for a perpetual memorial and testimony ; and the rolls are called the records of the court. These records are of such high authority that their truth cannot be called in question in any court. But this rule does not prevent the judge from making inquiries in certain cases, and, if there appear any mistake of any officer of the court in making up the record, the judge will direct him to amend it. And in general, all slips in legal proceedings (including records) may be amended by an order of the court. The records of a court of record eventually find their way into the Public Record Office to be kept there for all time.

All courts of record are the courts of the King, in right of his crown and royal dignity ; and they comprise both superior and inferior courts, a classification which is described below. The characteristic of a court of record is that it has power to fine and imprison for contempt of its authority, so that if a new court possessing this power is set up it *ipso facto* becomes a court of record. But in some courts of record, *e.g.*, in county courts, this power is limited to contempts committed *in facie curiæ ;* that is to say, to wilful insults to the judge, or to any juror or witness, registrar, or other officer of the court, during his attendance in court, or in going to or returning from the court, and to wilful interruptions of the business of the court, and to wilful misbehaviour in court. On the other hand, the superior courts of record have a far greater jurisdiction in contempt of court, *e.g.*, any person who publishes, no matter where, any matter likely to prejudice the just course of proceedings before them, may be fined and imprisoned for contempt.

In the second place, courts may be classified according to whether they are superior or inferior courts. Some courts are of an inferior or limited jurisdiction, while others are of a superior and universal authority. This is an important distinction ; inasmuch as an action brought in any of the former class is always liable to a plea of want of jurisdiction, while no such plea can, with rare exceptions be urged in a superior court. Moreover, the superior courts have a coercive or restraining jurisdiction over the inferior ; not merely by way of appeal, but by way of order of prohibition to forbid proceedings in any matter beyond the jurisdiction of the inferior courts, or by way of an order of *certiorari* (p. 579) to remove the proceedings from the inferior to a superior court.

An account will be given of the superior courts in the next chapter. Of the inferior courts of civil jurisdiction the most important are the modern county courts. These courts were first set up by statute in 1846, it having been found by experience that the administration of justice had become too centralised without facilities afforded by local courts with a limited jurisdiction to determine small claims expeditiously and cheaply. The county court system is fully explained in Chapter 11 of this Book. The more important of the other existing inferior courts of civil jurisdiction are dealt with in the same place.

Civil and criminal courts.

A third classification of courts is into those which are of civil and those which are of criminal jurisdiction. Criminal courts have as their object the conviction and punishment of offenders against the criminal law while the function of civil courts is to give monetary or other forms of redress to the individual. The various kinds of criminal courts is a matter for detailed exposition in Volume IV, Chapter 14. It may here be observed that certain courts possess both a civil and criminal jurisdiction. The most comprehensive example of this duality of function is found in the courts held by the justices of the peace or other magistrates. These courts, for example, have power to make affiliation orders and orders in proceedings between husband and wife. A special Section is devoted to this jurisdiction in the chapter on Matrimonial Causes which forms Chapter 7 of this Book.

CHAPTER 2

THE SUPERIOR COURTS

SUMMARY   PAGE
Section I. *The Supreme Court of Judicature*   7
       (i) *The High Court of Justice*   7
      (ii) *The Court of Appeal*   11
Section II. *The House of Lords*   12
Section III. *The Judicial Committee of the Privy Council* ...   14
Section IV. *The Palatine Courts*   15

The superior courts of civil jurisdiction with which this chapter deals are the following :

> the Supreme Court of Judicature (consisting of the High Court of Justice and the Court of Appeal),
> the House of Lords,
> the Judicial Committee of the Privy Council, and
> the Chancery Courts of the Counties Palatine of Lancaster and Durham.

Section I. THE SUPREME COURT OF JUDICATURE

The Judicature Acts, 1873 and 1875, which were re-pealed and replaced by the Supreme Court of Judicature (Consolidation) Act, 1925 (called in the following pages, for brevity, the " Judicature Act, 1925 "), created and constituted a court called the Supreme Court of Judicature, consisting of the High Court of Justice and the Court of Appeal. *(margin: Supreme Court created by Judicature Acts.)*

(i) THE HIGH COURT OF JUSTICE. To the High Court of Justice was transferred all the jurisdiction which in 1875 was capable of being exercised by (*a*) the High Court of Chancery, (*b*) the Court of King's Bench, (*c*) the Court of Common Pleas at Westminster, (*d*) the Court of Exchequer, (*e*) the High Court of Admiralty, (*f*) the Court of Probate, (*g*) the Court of Divorce and Matrimonial Causes, (*h*) the Court of Common Pleas at Lancaster, (*i*) the Court of Pleas at Durham, and (*j*) the *(margin: The High Court of Justice.)*

courts created by the Royal commissions of assize issued to the judges proceeding on circuit.

The Divisions of the High Court. For the more convenient distribution of business, the High Court was, however, organised in Divisions. At first there were five Divisions, namely,

> the Queen's Bench Division,
> the Chancery Division,
> the Common Pleas Division,
> the Exchequer Division, and
> the Probate, Divorce, and Admiralty Division ;

and to each Division was assigned, speaking generally, the class of business which before 1875 was within the special or exclusive cognisance of the court or courts from which the particular Division took its name. The business which was common to all the common law courts was (by inference) left to be dealt with indifferently by the Queen's Bench, the Common Pleas, or the Exchequer Divisions. In 1880 the three Common Law Divisions of Queen's Bench, Common Pleas, and Exchequer were united into one Division, then called the Queen's Bench Division and now, the King's Bench Division ; and in 1884 the bankruptcy business of the London Court of Bankruptcy, a purely statutory tribunal under a chief judge, which had been established in 1869 to deal with bankruptcy business, was assigned to that Division under the provisions of the Bankruptcy Act, 1883, whence, in 1921, it was transferred to the Chancery Division. The Lord Chancellor now has power to redistribute business among the Divisions.

There are, therefore, at the present day, three Divisions which divide the work of the High Court between them. The explanation for the grouping of the multifarious titles of Probate, Divorce, and Admiralty in the same Division is mainly a historical one. The law relating to these matters was originally based, to a greater or less degree, on the Roman or Civil Law, either directly or through the medium of Canon Law, and it was customary for practitioners known as civilians to specialise in Civil Law in whichever court it might be followed. Although it is now uncommon for Civil Law to be cited in court the occasion for such citation is still far more likely to arise in the Probate, Divorce, and Admiralty Division than in the other Divisions of the High Court.

The judges of the High Court will be considered in detail later (p. 23). They are distributed among the three Divisions of the High Court. At present the Chancery Division, nominally presided over by the Lord Chancellor who in practice rarely sits there, has not less than five puisne (or junior) judges ; the King's Bench Division, presided over by the Lord Chief Justice, has not less than seventeen ; and the Probate, Divorce, and Admiralty Division, presided over by the President of the Division, has not less than three. *Judges of the High Court.*

The High Court has both original and appellate jurisdiction. Actions commenced in (or transferred from a county court or other inferior court to) the High Court are tried before a judge alone, if they are tried in the Chancery Division ; or by a judge alone or with a jury in the King's Bench Division or on the Probate or Divorce sides of the Probate, Divorce, and Admiralty Division ; or by a judge assisted in certain cases by nautical assessors, if tried on the Admiralty side of the last-named division. *How court constituted.*

The plaintiff may, within certain limitations, bring his action in any Division he chooses. If he brings in one Division an action assigned by the Judicature Acts to another Division the judge has power either to retain it, or to transfer it to the Division in which it ought to have been commenced ; and where it can be more conveniently dealt with. But it is one of the essential principles of the Judicature Acts that all Divisions of the High Court are competent to conduct all kinds of business ; and, therefore, the judge ought not to dismiss any proceedings for want of jurisdiction. *All Divisions of equal competence.*

It is to be observed that judges, when they decide cases on circuit, are exercising the jurisdiction of the High Court no less than when they sit in the Law Courts in the Strand ; but although they are usually members of the King's Bench Division, the courts which they hold are not courts of that Division. And in fact they are now empowered to try certain matrimonial causes at *Judges on circuit.*

the assizes, and in doing so must follow the practice of the Probate Divorce, and Admiralty Division in such matters.

Interlocutory proceedings. The interlocutory proceedings in an action, that is to say, the various proceedings on summonses which take place between the issue of the writ and the trial, are, as we shall hereafter see, generally conducted in chambers ; usually before an officer of the court known as a Master or Registrar, but sometimes before a judge.

Divisional Courts. An important part of the jurisdiction of the High Court is exercised by special sittings of the judges of a particular Division called Divisional Courts, consisting of two or more judges sitting together. A Divisional Court of the King's Bench Division exercises (subject to any Rules being made to the contrary) both original and appellate jurisdiction. For example, it has jurisdiction on motion to order a person to be attached or committed for contempt of court, or to make orders of mandamus, prohibition, and *certiorari*, and to order the issue of a writ of *habeas corpus ;* it determines questions of criminal law on cases stated by quarter or petty sessions, and hears appeals from an inferior court, except county courts, appeals in proceedings relating to election petitions, parliamentary or municipal, and certain appeals from a judge or Master in Chambers.

Appeals in bankruptcy matters from county courts having bankruptcy jurisdiction are at present assigned to a Divisional Court of the Chancery Division.

A Divisional Court of the Probate, Divorce, and Admiralty Division hears appeals from separation or maintenance orders made by courts of summary jurisdiction : and appeals from a Wreck Commissioner's report to the Board of Trade cancelling or suspending the certificate of the master, engineer, or mate of a ship for misconduct.

The judgment of the Divisional Court of any Division upon an appeal from an inferior court is final, unless leave to appeal to the Court of Appeal is given by the Divisional Court or by the Court of Appeal. In a criminal cause or matter a decision of a Divisional Court is, however, final and no appeal lies to the Court of Appeal.

When we come to deal, in the following chapters, with the details of procedure in the High Court, we shall have frequent occasion to refer to rules of procedure which regulate these details. Here it is sufficient to say, that, as regards the rules of procedure and practice to be followed in the Supreme Court, the Judicature Act, 1925 (s. 99), gives power to a Rule Committee, consisting of certain judges of the Court and two practising barristers and two practising solicitors, to make Rules of Court for the purpose of carrying the Acts into effect. In pursuance of similar powers contained in the earlier Acts, Rules have been made called the Rules of the Supreme Court, 1883. These Rules regulate the practice in all proceedings in the Supreme Court ; but the Judicature Acts, and Order LXXII of the Rules, provide that the procedure and practice in force before the Acts came into operation in 1875 shall remain in force, where no other provision is made by the Acts or the Rules, and so far as they are not inconsistent with the Acts or the Rules. Thus, in probate matters, the practice is still largely regulated by the Probate Rules of 1862, made under the Court of Probate Act, 1857. In divorce business the practice was until 1938 regulated by rules made under earlier enactments, but is now regulated by the Matrimonial Causes Rules, 1947. *Rules of Court.*

(ii) THE COURT OF APPEAL. To the other branch of the Supreme Court of Judicature, namely the Court of Appeal, was transferred, by the Judicature Act, 1873, all the appellate jurisdiction of all courts hearing appeals from superior courts of first instance within England and Wales. *The Court of Appeal.*

The Court of Appeal has, in general, jurisdiction to hear and determine an appeal from (*a*) any judgment or order of a Divisional Court, as explained above ; (*b*) any final judgment or order of the High Court in a civil proceeding ; (*c*) any interlocutory order of a judge in chambers in matters of practice and procedure, subject, in most cases, to leave to appeal being given ; (*d*) any decision or order of a county court judge on a question of law ; and (*e*) the judgments of certain other courts such as the Mayor's and City of London Court, the Liver- *Jurisdiction.*

pool Court of Passage, and the Courts of the Counties Palatine of Lancaster and Durham.

Over any matter brought on appeal before the Court of Appeal, the court has all the power and jurisdiction of the High Court, and may make any order which ought to have been made in the court below, or such further order as the justice of the case may require.

Judges of the Court. The Court of Appeal consists of certain *ex-officio* judges, namely, the Lord Chancellor, Lord Chief Justice, the Master of the Rolls, and the President of the Probate, Divorce, and Admiralty Division, and every person who has held the office of Lord High Chancellor, and of eight Lords Justices. But any judge of the High Court may, if so required by the Lord Chancellor, also sit as a judge of the Court of Appeal ; and any Lord of Appeal in Ordinary who, at the time of appointment as such, was either a member of the Court of Appeal or qualified to be a member, may if he consents, upon the request of the Lord Chancellor to do so, sit and act as a judge of the Court of Appeal. Of the *ex-officio* judges only the Master of the Rolls usually sits.

Three judges constitute the Court. As a rule, three judges are required to constitute the Court of Appeal, and, generally speaking, the Court of Appeal sits usually in two divisions, but sometimes in as many as four ; but the only limit to the number of divisions in which it may sit is the number of judges ; and any division may deal with any appellate business which is within the jurisdiction of the court. It is to be observed that the divisions in which the Court of Appeal sits do not correspond to the Divisions of the High Court, nor do they have any particular name. The Court of Appeal is an undivided tribunal exercising appellate jurisdiction over all three specialised Divisions of the High Court.

Section II. THE HOUSE OF LORDS

Jurisdiction of the House of Lords. It is expressly provided by the Appellate Jurisdiction Act, 1876, that an appeal shall lie to the House of Lords from any order or judgment, either of the Court of Appeal in England, or of any of the Scotch or Irish Courts, from which error or an appeal lay thereto at or immediately before the commencement of the Act. Leave to appeal is necessary, whether the order appealed against is final or interlocutory. The setting up of the Irish Free State, as it was then called, resulted in a withdrawal of appeals from the courts of the Irish Free State to the House of Lords, and transferred them to the Judicial Committee of the Privy Council. Eire, however, passed legislation which abolished the right of appeal to the Judicial Committee of the Privy Council. Appeals from the courts of Northern Ireland still go to the House of Lords.

In theory, every member of the House of Lords has a right to be present and vote at the hearing of an appeal; but, by a convention of the Constitution, this right is no longer exercised. It is provided by the Appellate Jurisdiction Act, 1876, that no appeal may be heard and determined, unless there be present not less than three specially qualified persons, known as Lords of Appeal. This class of peers comprises the Lord Chancellor, Lords of Appeal in Ordinary, and such peers as are for the time being holding, or have held, " high judicial office," as defined by s. 25 of the Appellate Jurisdiction Act, 1876, and s. 5 of the Judicature Act, 1887. *Judges of the Court.*

With regard to the Lords of Appeal in Ordinary, it is enacted that, in order to aid the House of Lords in the hearing and determination of appeals, His Majesty may appoint by patent two (now nine under the Appellate Jurisdiction Act, 1947) qualified persons, who shall hold office during good behaviour, and notwithstanding the demise of the Crown, but who shall be removable on an Address of both Houses of Parliament. The qualification for such an appointment consists of holding or having held " high judicial office " for two years, or having practised for fifteen years as a barrister in England or Ireland, or as an advocate in Scotland. Each of such Lords of Appeal is entitled during life to rank as a baron, and, even after his retirement or resignation, to a writ of summons to attend, and to sit and vote, in the House of Lords; but his dignity is not hereditary, though his children are entitled to the courtesy prefix of " Honourable." It would appear that he lacks the essential quality of peerage, namely, " ennoblement of blood." *Lords of Appeal in Ordinary.*

Each member of the court as constituted for the hearing of any appeal has the right to deliver a separate judgment, or " speech " as it is technically called ; and usually several are delivered.

The House of Lords may sit as a Court of Appeal during the prorogation of Parliament, and even during the dissolution of Parliament, should His Majesty think fit, by writing under his sign manual, to authorise the Lords of Appeal to hold sittings during such dissolution. The House of Lords does not possess the necessary machinery for executing its decrees in judicial matters ; and, accordingly, a decree of the House of Lords is usually made (in England) an order of the High Court.

Section III. THE JUDICIAL COMMITTEE OF THE PRIVY COUNCIL

The Judicial Committee of the Privy Council.

Judges of the Court.

This is a body of very miscellaneous composition and includes all privy councillors who hold or have held high judicial office in the United Kingdom, in particular the Lords of Appeal in Ordinary and certain ex-judges of the Supreme Court of Judicature ; certain judges and ex-judges of the superior courts of the Dominions and India ; and certain other persons specially appointed under statutory powers. All must be members of the English Privy Council. This is a fundamental condition, notwithstanding the Statute of Westminster, 1931, which gave to the Dominions equality of status with England. Provision is made for the attendance, as assessors of the committee on the hearing of ecclesiastical cases, of archbishops or bishops of the Church of England. The greater part of the work of the committee is in fact done by persons competent to hear appeals in the House of Lords, and so the two final courts of appeal, though theoretically distinct, tend more and more to become identical in composition.

Jurisdiction.

An appeal lies to the Judicial Committee (*inter alia*) in England—

    (i) from the ecclesiastical courts, but only in certain cases ;

    (ii) from the Prize Court ;

and, outside the United Kingdom,

(i) from the Channel Islands and the Isle of Man ;

(ii) in certain cases from the highest courts of some of the self-governing Dominions, and other colonies and possessions generally. This right was completely abrogated by Eire, even before, as the Republic of Ireland, she ceased to be part of the Empire, and is partially abrogated by some of the Dominions in pursuance of the power granted by the Statute of Westminster ; and

(iii) from certain courts established in foreign countries under the Foreign Jurisdiction Act, 1890.

An appeal to the Judicial Committee is brought by way of petition ; but where there is no appeal as of right, it is necessary first to petition for leave to appeal. The Committee, after hearing the parties, and, usually, after taking time for deliberation, delivers a single written judgment through the mouth of one of its members, in the form of reasons for humbly advising His Majesty to allow, or (as the case may be) dismiss, the appeal. Differences of opinion between the members of the Committee are not officially recorded. A judgment of the committee is technically only a resolution or advice offered to His Majesty, and, therefore, strictly speaking, has binding authority only on the courts from which an appeal lies to it. In practice, however, such a judgment is regarded by the High Court and Court of Appeal, as carrying almost as much binding authority as a judgment of the House of Lords. *Procedure.*

Section IV. THE PALATINE COURTS

The counties palatine of Lancaster and Durham were for centuries to a large extent independent of the central government of the realm, and in particular each of them possessed a fully developed judicial system of its own. Thus there was a Court of Common Pleas at Lancaster and a Court of Pleas at Durham. These were abolished *Chancery Courts of Lancaster and Durham.*

by the Judicature Act of 1873, and their jurisdiction merged in that of the High Court of Justice. But each county palatine possessed in addition a Court of Chancery, and in both counties this court has preserved its jurisdiction in full, and does most useful work. The Chancery Court of Lancaster is presided over by a Vice-Chancellor. He ranks immediately after the High Court judges and is appointed by the Chancellor of the Duchy of Lancaster, who is now usually a Minister of the Crown and often a member of the Cabinet. The Palatine Court of Durham is presided over by the Chancellor of the county palatine.

Their jurisdiction

These courts have jurisdiction in all cases within the competence of the Chancery Division of the High Court where the person of the defendant is within the county palatine ; this is an application of the principle that Equity acts *in personam*. But though clearly differentiated from the High Court by the fact that they exercise only local jurisdiction, they are not limited in their jurisdiction by any considerations of the importance or value of the subject-matter of a case, and are, therefore, courts of superior jurisdiction. An appeal lies direct to the Court of Appeal and thence to the House of Lords.

CHAPTER 3

JURISDICTION OF THE HIGH COURT

In speaking of the inferior courts it has been assumed that their jurisdiction is different in point of quality from the jurisdiction of the superior courts in that the latter is unlimited. Now in one sense of the word this last statement is true, for only the superior courts themselves can decide judicially whether they are acting within their jurisdiction or not. If, then, a superior court should wrongly decide that to be within its jurisdiction which is not, it merely commits an error in point of law or fact which can only be corrected on appeal. And the jurisdiction of the Court of Appeal and the House of Lords is in respect of such a matter no greater than that of the superior court itself. There is nothing, so far as the superior courts are concerned, corresponding to the orders of prohibition and *certiorari* by which inferior courts are kept to their proper limits ; the Court of Appeal and the House of Lords exercise no authority over the other superior courts by the issue of these or similar orders.

It follows from the fact that superior courts have jurisdiction to decide whether they have jurisdiction or not in respect of any given case that a judge of a superior court can never be said to be acting outside the limits of his jurisdiction. Accordingly he can never be sued at all in respect of anything done by him in his judicial capacity.

But beyond this point it is quite untrue to say that the superior courts exercise an unlimited jurisdiction. It is easy to see that the Chancery Courts of Lancaster and Durham have a limited jurisdiction ; but the same is no less true of the High Court of Justice. This is clearly the case if an Act of Parliament withdraws a matter from the cognizance of the High Court. The court must then obey the statute and decline to deal with the matter. But there are also common law limits to its jurisdiction,

Marginal notes:

Distinction between superior and inferior courts as regards jurisdiction.

Superior courts do not possess unlimited jurisdiction.

of such importance and of so peculiar a nature that they are usually made the subject of independent study. They form part of that branch of the Law of England which is called by some authors Private International Law, by others International Private Law or Jurisprudence, and by others again the Conflict of Laws, and which is concerned with those cases that contain some foreign element. We can explain the general nature of this branch of law by the following illustration :

Foreign element cases.

> Let us suppose that M. Dubois, a Swiss manufacturer, meets in Amsterdam M. Meyer, of Paris, and agrees to sell and deliver to him in Paris a certain quantity of silk. Then let us suppose that the silk is delivered in Paris, but, on the instructions of M. Meyer, who has now transferred his residence to London, it is rejected on the ground that it is not equal in quality to the sample. M. Dubois denies the purchaser's right to reject the silk.

Now it must be obvious to everyone that here is a pretty problem. According to what law is M. Meyer's claim to reject the silk to be tried ? French, Swiss, Dutch, or even English ? That problem must be solved by reference to Private International Law. Only when the preliminary question has been decided, by what law the case is to be tried, can the real point at issue, namely, whether M. Meyer is in law entitled to reject the silk, come before the court.

But in reality yet another question must be answered before it can be decided what law is applicable. In what country should M. Dubois sue M. Meyer for refusing to accept the silk ? In France, in Switzerland, in Holland, or in England ? In other words, which country's courts have jurisdiction ? That is the other great division of Private International Law.

Nature of Private International Law.

It is clear that in consequence of the international character of modern trade, such questions as these must arise every day ; and it is no less obvious that ideally the rules by which they are decided should be the same in whatever country they come before the courts. But, in spite of its name, Private International Law is no true international law, and, unfortunate though it may be, the rules of Private International Law vary from state to state. It may well be that the French Courts claim exclusive cognizance of a matter which according to the English rules should be decided in England, and the courts of different states may easily apply different laws in a given case. The English theory is that Private International Law, as applied in the English courts, is not international law at all, but a branch of the law of England, in exactly the same way as the law of property or the law of torts. Its principles must be discovered in the usual way from Acts of Parliament or other subordinate legislation, or from the decisions of the courts. But the courts recognise the value of uniformity, and will accordingly listen with respect to the views of foreign jurists and foreign courts.

So Private International Law raises these two questions, first, has an English court jurisdiction to try a case which contains some foreign element ; and secondly, if it has jurisdiction, what system of law must it apply in deciding that case ?

We are only concerned here with the question of jurisdiction, and the illustrations that we propose to give will serve to show that the jurisdiction even of the Supreme Court is not unlimited. *Jurisdiction over a case containing a foreign element.*

In the first place, an English court has no jurisdiction to hear an action which relates to foreign land, even though the parties are in England, unless there is some personal equity binding upon the defendant, which entitles the court to invoke the principle that equity acts *in personam*. It cannot, for instance, entertain an action for a trespass committed on French land, but if the defendant is bound by a valid trust to deal with the land in a certain manner, and if he is personally present in England, the English court, as a court of conscience, acting *in personam* and not *in rem*, can order him to do what is necessary in France in order to carry out the trust. *Jurisdiction in case of foreign land.*

Again, an English court generally has no jurisdiction to entertain a suit for divorce unless the parties are domiciled in England at the time of the suit, but this *Divorce jurisdiction.*

question is more fully discussed in Chapter 7 of this Book.

Further, it has at common law no jurisdiction in respect of a personal action, such as an action for breach of contract or for trespass to the person, unless the defendant is actually present in England at the time of the action. The reason is that the necessary preliminary to an action is the service of a writ of summons upon the defendant. The rule at common law is that this writ must be served upon the defendant personally within the realm, so that if he happens to be abroad, it is impossible for the English court to acquire jurisdiction over him, even though he may be a British subject, or if not a British subject, may be domiciled in England. The maxim is *actor sequitur forum rei*.

Now it is obvious that this limitation of the court's jurisdiction has its inconveniences, for it enables a defendant to escape responsibility for wrongful acts by removing himself from the country, even though he possesses property here that might be seized. Nevertheless,

the general principle that jurisdiction depended upon service of a writ upon a defendant in England remained unaltered until the Common Law Procedure Act, 1852. That statute, which is now replaced by the Judicature Act, 1925, and the Rules made thereunder, permits a person, *in certain cases*, to be served with a writ or notice of a writ even though he is out of the country, and the effect of such service is to give the English court jurisdiction over him (see also p. 39, *post*).

But we should be giving a false impression if we omitted to state that in personal actions at least any defendant can submit to the jurisdiction of the court. By so doing he makes the court fully competent to deal with the case, even though it belongs to a category of actions which do not come within Order XI, rule 1, *i.e.*, the Order which specifies the various cases in which the court may make an order giving leave to serve the writ or notice thereof out of the jurisdiction. It is in practice not uncommon for parties to agree, when they make a contract, that any question arising out of it shall be tried in the High Court, and to provide for an address within the jurisdiction of the High Court at which proceedings can be served. But certain proceedings, notably petitions for divorce, do not admit of such a submission. It is never in the power of the parties to divorce proceedings to choose their court.

No action may be brought in an English court against a foreign sovereign, though he may himself **bring** an action in England and in that case by invoking the jurisdiction submits to it. This immunity from suit attaches not only to the sovereign State in its public capacity, but also to its head in his private capacity, and it seems that there is no difference in this respect between a crowned head and an elected president. Whether or not the State is in fact sovereign, is a question not for the jury, but for the judge, who is bound to accept the opinion put before him by the Crown in its executive capacity ; for, as it lies with the Crown to recognise or not to recognise the sovereign character of a foreign State, any information furnished by the Crown on such a question is the best evidence of recognition. Some of these points are well illustrated in the case of the *Duff Development Co.* v. *Kelantan Government*, [1924] A. C. 797. *Immunity of foreign sovereigns.*

The same immunity attaches to the property of a foreign sovereign, so that, for instance, no ship belonging to a foreign sovereign can be arrested and made the subject of an admiralty action *in rem*.

Ambassadors and members of their suites enjoy the same immunity from process as the sovereign by whom they are accredited. Consuls are not so favoured, although they have certain privileges which are deemed necessary to the efficient and independent performance of the duties connected with their office ; for instance, their official papers cannot be seized. Moreover, members of an ambassador's suite lose their immunity if they engage in trade. *Ambassadors.*

The ambassador's house is for many purposes treated as though it were a part of the territory of the state by which he is accredited. Accordingly it is not subject to the jurisdiction of the English courts ; and the ambassador is not liable to pay rates or taxes in respect of it.

An ambassador may, with the consent of his sovereign, waive his own immunity, and that of any member of his suite, but it is probable that he alone has that power ; a subordinate official cannot waive his own immunity without the consent of the ambassador or his sovereign.   The immunity extends for a reasonable time after the ambassador's recall.

We have spoken only of ambassadors for the sake of brevity, but it should be understood that these immunities attach also to Ministers, Charges d'Affaires, and all other diplomatic representatives accredited to and actually received by the Government of this country.

Criminal jurisdiction.   The jurisdiction of the High Court in a criminal cause or matter is described in Volume IV, Chapter 14.

THE JUDGES AND OFFICERS OF THE SUPREME COURT

In order to understand the procedure of the Courts, which will be discussed in Part II of this Book, it is important to appreciate who are the various officers of the Court responsible for the conduct of business in the various divisions.

The Lord Chancellor is appferred by the King on the advice of the Prime Minister, and is a member of the Cabinet. He is the President of the Court of Appeal, but he seldom sits ; he is also the President of the Chancery Division. Amongst his duties it falls to his lot to advise the Crown in connection with the appointment of all puisne judges and subordinate officials in the Supreme Court, except those in the Probate, Divorce, and Admiralty Division. His chief duty is to preside over the deliberations of the House of Lords when it is sitting either in a judicial or legislative capacity. Like all judges of the Supreme Court he is addressed as " My Lord." *The Lord Chancellor.*

The Lord Chief Justice of England is appointed by the King on the advice of the Prime Minister. He is President of the King's Bench Division and also of the Court of Criminal Appeal. When he sits in the Court of Appeal he takes precedence immediately after the Lord Chancellor. In addition to being a member of the Privy Council he holds the office of Supreme Coroner of England. He appoints, in rotation with the Lord Chancellor and the Master of the Rolls, the Masters of the King's Bench Division. The Lord Chief Justice of England is responsible for the due administration of the Courts. *Lord Chief Justice.*

The Master of the Rolls is appointed by the King on the advice of the Prime Minister. The Master of the Rolls is the virtual head of the Court of Appeal, because the Lord Chancellor and the Lord Chief Justice seldom *Master of the Rolls.*

23

sit in the Court of Appeal. He ranks immediately after the Lord Chief Justice. All the records at the Public Record Office are in his custody. As head of the solicitors' branch of the legal profession he directs the Law Society to admit suitable and qualified persons to the Roll of Solicitors. By virtue of his office he has a general jurisdiction over the Law Society, and all appeals, except from the orders and findings of the Disciplinary Committee, are heard by him.

President of Probate, Divorce, and Admiralty.

The President of the Probate, Divorce, and Admiralty Division is appointed by the King on the advice of the Prime Minister. He ranks immediately after the Master of the Rolls and in the absence of the Master of the Rolls would, if he sat in the Court of Appeal, preside. He sits in Court as a judge of first instance and he appoints the Registrars and subordinate officials of the Probate, Divorce, and Admiralty Division and has the general control over the work of that division.

The Lords Justices.

The Lords Justices are appointed by the King on the advice of the Prime Minister. If appointed direct from the Bar they must be barristers of not less than fifteen years' standing, and hold office upon the same tenure as the judges of the High Court. They sit in the Court of Appeal and take precedence in order of appointment. All the Lords Justices, when exercising jurisdiction under the Lunacy Acts, are collectively termed " the Judge in Lunacy," although in non-contentious matters this jurisdiction is exercised by one Lord Justice subject to an appeal to all the Lords Justices. When requested they sit as additional judges of the High Court.

The Puisne Judges.

The Puisne Judges of all divisions are appointed by the King on the advice of the Lord Chancellor ; they rank amongst themselves according to the date of the appointment and immediately before the Vice-Chancellor of the County Palatine of Lancaster. They must be barristers of not less than ten years' standing.

Duration of office.

All the judges of the High Court and of the Court of Appeal, with the exception of the Lord Chancellor, hold office during good behaviour and can only be removed by the King on an address by both Houses of Parliament. In order that their independence may be preserved their salaries are paid out of the Consolidated Fund, and consequently are free from all parliamentary control, which they would not be if voted annually by Parliament.

Subject to a few exceptions, all the judges of the High Court have equal power and jurisdiction, and may legally sit in any Division and, at the request of the Lord Chancellor, in the Court of Appeal ; while the Lord Chancellor has power to request any person who has been a judge of the High Court or of the Court of Appeal to sit and act as a judge either of the Court of Appeal or of the High Court.

Two of the judges of the High Court, usually the two junior judges, are selected at the commencement of each long vacation for the hearing in London or Middlesex, during vacation, of all such applications as may require to be immediately or promptly heard. The appointment is for one year. The vacation judges may sit either separately or together as a Divisional Court as occasion shall require, and may hear and dispose of all causes, matters, and other business, to whichever Division the same may be assigned. *The Vacation Judge.*

Special commissioners who are county court judges, King's Counsel or other persons holding judicial office (*e.g.*, a Metropolitan Magistrate) may be appointed to try nullity and divorce cases, either in London or the Provinces. When they are sitting they have all the powers of a judge of the High Court. *Special Commissioners.*

The Clerk of the Crown in Chancery and Permanent Secretary to the Lord Chancellor is an official appointed by the King on the advice of the Lord Chancellor. He is responsible for the continuity of policy in the Lord Chancellor's Department, as, unlike the Lord Chancellor, he does not vacate office on a change of Government. Amongst his duties are to administer the oaths of office to the new Lord Chancellor and to compile the Coronation Roll, *i.e.*, an official record of the coronation proceedings which is afterwards preserved in the Public Record Office. *Clerk of the Crown in Chancery.*

The Chief Taxing Master is in charge of the Taxing Office. He is assisted by the Taxing Masters. They tax all costs in matters resulting from litigation in all divisions except the Probate, Divorce, and Admiralty Division. *Taxing Masters.*

In addition they tax solicitors' bills of costs rendered by them in contentious and non-contentious work. The taxation is subject to review by a judge. The Taxing Masters are solicitors of at least ten years' standing, and are addressed as " Master ".

The Official Solicitor. The Official Solicitor acts on behalf of all persons concerned in litigation who are of unsound mind and in proceedings in the High Court for the adoption of children under the Adoption of Children Act, 1926, and generally protects their interests in all proceedings. One of his duties is to see that persons who have been committed to prison for contempt do not languish in prison indefinitely, and from time to time he urges them to purge their contempt. If they have no means he will apply to the Court on their behalf for an order discharging them from prison.

The Tipstaff. The Tipstaff is the Constable of the Supreme Court, whose duty it is to arrest persons who have been committed to prison for contempt of Court.

Solicitors of the Supreme Court. A solicitor, unlike a barrister, is an officer of the Court, He is liable to receive the Court's displeasure and be committed to prison for contempt of Court if he omits to fulfil an undertaking that he has given to the Court, *e.g.*, if he omits to enter an appearance to a writ the service of which he accepted on behalf of his client when he undertook in writing to appear (see as to solicitors generally, Chapter 14, *post*).

The Chancery Registrars. The Registrars are practising solicitors of ten years' standing whose duty it is to attend the Court of Appeal and the judges of the Chancery Division and to draw up the judgments and orders of the Court of Appeal and the Chancery Division. The office is more ministerial than judicial, because the Registrar has no power to include in the judgment or order any terms that the Court have not ordered. The correct method of address is " Sir ".

The Chancery Master. A Chancery Master is a practising solicitor of ten years' standing, and he is attached to the chambers of a group of judges. All summonses are heard in the first place by the Master. The Master can deal with certain cases, but otherwise, after satisfying himself that the form of summons and the evidence in support (which is given by affidavit) are in order, adjourns the matter to the judge for

The Master
of the
Court of
Protection
(the Master
in Lunacy).

The
Examiner.

The Master of the C rister of at least three
as the Master in Luna reside at the examina-
It is closely allied to give their evidence
appointed by the Lord ners may be either
barrister of ten yea s, or special—someone
Assistant Masters, ressed as " Sir ".
"Master". The func harge of the District
orders vesting in rec are in effect " branch
unsound mind, ment e Supreme Court and
on the grounds of ill t the same powers as
after their own affa ch Division. Most of
directions of the Mast d Wales have district
patient is properly ca are addressed as
safeguarded during hi e judge in chambers in

The District Registrars.

King's
Remem-
brancer.

The King's Remem
of the King's Bench ranks as one of the
administrative side of on and must have the
judicial functions in s in the King's Bench
charge of the revenue n Office is in charge
He is addressed as " N This Department is

The Master
of the
Crown
Office.

The King's
Bench
Masters.

The Masters of the is in the King's Bench
of at least ten years a rota of associates to
in rotation by the Lor Master of the Crown
and the Master of the King's Coroner and
in the King's Bench D o with the office of
in the first instance. o the Royal Palaces),
cery Division, whose gistrar of the Court of
the King's Bench M e he is assisted by an
before them jurisdic
against their decision the directions of the

The Chief
Associate
of the
Crown
Office.

The Central
Office.

The Central Office arranges " the lists,"
the Chief Master's Dep of the King's Bench
Filing Department, K arranges the Court of
and the Crown Office a rrange their own list ;
by clerks under the c don leave this work to

The Official
Referee.

The Official Referee
to whom cases inv r the judge and take
accounts, and other gment in their books,
for trial. He is ad e Court and which are
appeal lies on a poin Record Office. The
order to the Court of nable the successful

The
Associates
of the
Crown
Office.

litigant to sign judgment, *i.e.*, to convert the judge's directions into an order of the Court (see p. 75, *post*). The Associates are empowered to administer oaths and they do so to witnesses at the trial. Amongst their duties is to keep a register of the exhibits put in evidence by the parties at the trial and to number each document and to issue a certificate of all exhibits tendered as evidence. It is their duty to take objection to a document on the grounds that it is insufficiently stamped—an objection which counsel usually does not and is not supposed to take.

The Clerk of Assize.

The Clerk of Assize is now appointed by the Lord Chief Justice. He superintends the arrangement of the work of the Assizes and is responsible for the indictments. The Records of the Assize and the Royal Commission for holding the Assizes which he reads on the "Commission day," *i.e.*, the first day of the Assizes, are in his custody. which in due course he transmits to the Public Record Office. He must now be a barrister or solicitor of not less than five years' standing.

The Clerk of Arraigns

The Clerk of Assize, formerly had the assistance of the Clerk of Indictments or Arraigns. This office, together with that of "Associate on a Circuit" (who was responsible for the civil business of a circuit) has been abolished (without prejudice to the existing holders) by s. 2 of the Supreme Court of Judicature (Circuit Officers) Act, 1946 ; the duties of these officers now form part of the business of the Central Office of the Supreme Court.

Probate and Divorce Registrars.

There are seven Probate Registrars, of whom the Senior Registrar is in charge of the administrative side of the Probate, Divorce, and Admiralty Division. The functions of a Probate Registrar are similar to those of Chancery Masters in that they consider the papers before the cases come on for hearing in Court in connection with probate and divorce. (There is a separate Registrar of the Admiralty Court, see p. 31, *post*.) They issue grants of representation, *i.e.*, Probate or Letters of Administration, in non-contentious cases, and they are responsible for the taxation of costs in litigious matters in the Division. They are appointed by the President of the Probate, Divorce, and Admiralty Division, and must be a barrister or solicitor of ten years' standing, or a district probate registrar of five years' standing, or have served for ten years as a clerk in the principal probate registry. Like the King's Bench Division the Probate Division has " branch offices " at the principal cities in England and Wales known as District Registries, which are under the jurisdiction of a District Probate Registrar, for whose appointment five years' standing, or ten years as a clerk in the Principal or a District Probate Registry suffices. These District Probate Registrars have jurisdiction in non-contentious probate matters only. Functions in regard to divorce matters are exercised by the District Registrar of the District Registry of the King's Bench Division.

The Clerk of the Rules arranges the daily cause lists of the Probate, Divorce, and Admiralty Division. His duties are similar in this division to the functions of the Chief Associate in the King's Bench Division. In addition to these duties he sits beside the judge in chambers of the Probate, Divorce, and Admiralty Division and draws up the orders made by the judge. The Clerk of the Rules is appointed by the President of the Probate, Divorce, and Admiralty Division.
The Clerk of the Rules (Probate and Divorce).

The Medical Inspector of the Court is a duly qualified medical practitioner whose duty it is medically to examine parties in nullity cases where impotence is alleged or at the request of the parties where wilful refusal to consumate the marriage is alleged, and to report the result of his examination in writing to the Court. He is appointed by the President of the Probate, Divorce, and Admiralty Division.
The Medical Inspector.

The King's Proctor is responsible for making inquiries in order to ascertain if a divorce case is improperly prosecuted. For this purpose if directed by the Attorney-General he may intervene in a suit either before or after the granting of a decree *nisi* to prevent it being granted or made absolute as the case may be.
The King's Proctor (Probate and Divorce).

The Registrar of the Prize Court is a barrister of at least fifteen years' standing. He is appointed by the President of the Probate, Divorce, and Admiralty Division.
The Registrar of the Prize Court (Admiralty).

Admiralty
Marshal.

The Admiralty Marshal is the constable of the Admiralty Division whose duty it is to arrest ships ordered by the Court to be arrested, until such time as the owners enter into a bond in a sum fixed by the Court.

The Regis-
trar of
the
Admiralty
Court.

The Registrar of the Admiralty Court is a barrister who is appointed by the President of the Probate, Divorce, and Admiralty Division. In regard to the interlocutory proceedings in an Admiralty action his duties are similar to those of a Master of the King's Bench Division. He, with the assistance of one or more merchants selected by him from a list approved by the President, assesses the damages when a ship has been in collision.

BOOK I
CIVIL PROCEDURE

PART II
PROCEEDINGS IN THE HIGH COURT

SUMMARY

INTRODUCTION TO PART II   35

CHAPTER 5. PROCEEDINGS IN THE KING'S BENCH
            DIVISION   36

CHAPTER 6. PROCEEDINGS IN THE CHANCERY
            DIVISION   93

CHAPTER 7. MATRIMONIAL CAUSES   104

CHAPTER 8. PROBATE PROCEEDINGS   137

CHAPTER 9. ADMIRALTY PROCEEDINGS   141

CHAPTER 10. EVIDENCE AND ESTOPPEL   150

INTRODUCTION TO PART II

We now come to a subject intimately connected with Object of this Part. the foregoing. As we have described the constitution of the Courts which administer the law, so now we are to describe the method by which cases are brought before them, how the issue is settled which they are to decide, the modes of trial, and the way in which execution is levied on a final judgment. The subject of civil procedure is very large and complicated and no more than an outline has been attempted. The opening chapter is confined to proceedings in the King's Bench Division of the High Court. Subsequent chapters describe the procedure in the Chancery, and Probate, Divorce, and Admiralty Divisions, and give a short description of county court procedure. Since the passing of the Matrimonial Causes Act, 1937, proceedings in a Court of Summary Jurisdiction for a separation order is sometimes a forerunner to proceedings for divorce. It may be objected that any discussion on Matrimonial Causes in the High Court should not strictly include the proceedings before the justices—as the justices are not part of the High Court. But as this book is written for the purposes of assisting students it is thought desirable that a purely scientific treatment of the matter should give way to expediency, and accordingly all proceedings before justices relating to matrimonial causes, whether leading ultimately to divorce or otherwise, are dealt with here. Probate is dealt with in outline and so is Admiralty.

The reader is reminded that before certain proceedings, or certain steps in proceedings, can be taken, the leave of the Court must be obtained under the Courts (Emergency Powers) Act, 1943. The restrictions imposed by this Act are temporary, and it has been decided for that reason not to incorporate them in the text.

CHAPTER 5

PROCEEDINGS IN THE KING'S BENCH DIVISION

SUMMARY				PAGE
Section I. Commencement of Action ...	...	...	...	36
Section II. Pleadings	...	...	...	42
Section III. Interlocutory Proceedings	...	...	...	57
Section IV. Advice on Evidence ...	...	...	...	70
Section V. Trial	...	...	...	72
Section VI. Taxation of Costs ...	...	...	...	76
Section VII. Execution...	...	...	...	77
Section VIII. Appeal	...	...	...	83
Section IX. Specially Indorsed Writ ...	...	...	...	86
Section X. The Commercial Court ...	...	...	...	90

Section I. COMMENCEMENT OF ACTION.

Writ of summons. An action in the King's Bench Division is commenced by the issue of a writ of summons, which in its completed state runs as follows :

Precedent
of writ.

1948, C., No. 105.

IN THE HIGH COURT OF JUSTICE.
KING'S BENCH DIVISION.

Between   Edward Coke

Plaintiff

and

(L.S.)   William Blackstone

Defendant

GEORGE THE SIXTH, by the Grace of God, of Great Britain, Ireland and the British Dominions beyond the Seas, King, Defender of the Faith, To William Blackstone,
of 10 Cheapside
in the City of London.

WE COMMAND YOU, That within Eight Days after the Service of this Writ on you, inclusive of the day of such Service, you do cause an Appearance to be entered for you in an Action at the Suit of Edward Coke ;
And take Notice that in default of your so doing, the Plaintiff may proceed therein, and Judgment may be given in your absence.

36

Witness, WILLIAM ALLEN VISCOUNT JOWITT, Lord High Chancellor of Great Britain, the 12th day of April in the year of Our Lord One thousand nine hundred and forty-eight.

N.B.—This Writ is to be served within TWELVE Calendar Months from the date thereof, or, if renewed, within SIX Calendar Months from the date of the last renewal, including the day of such date, and not afterwards.

The Defendant may appear hereto by entering an Appearance, either personally or by Solicitor, at the Central Office, Royal Courts of Justice, London.

A defendant appearing personally may, if he desire, enter his appearance by post and the appropriate forms may be obtained by sending a Postal Order of 2s. 10d. with an addressed envelope, foolscap size, to the Controller of Stamps, Royal Courts of Justice, London.

The above will appear on the face of the writ, and the following upon the back.   *Precedent of indorsements of writ.*

THE PLAINTIFF'S CLAIM IS FOR damages for wrongful dismissal.

THIS WRIT was issued by Kenyon Ellenborough and Co. of and whose address for service is 25 Park Lane in the City of Westminster.
Solicitors for the said Plaintiff, who resides at 20 Prince Henry Street in the City of London.

THIS WRIT was served by me at 10 Cheapside in the City of London,
on the Defendant William Blackstone
on Monday the 19th day of April 1948.
Indorsed the 19th day of April 1948.

(Signed) JAMES MANSFIELD
(Address) 15 Tooting Common, London, S.W.

The modern writ should not be confused with the old "original writ" which it now supersedes. The modern writ, as was the old "original writ," is issued in the King's name, but whilst the "original writ" was a command to the sheriff to procure the attendance of the defendant in Court, the modern writ is a command from the King direct to the person to whom it is addressed to "enter an appearance," usually within eight days of the day of service inclusive of that day, and he is warned that, if he fails to do so, judgment may be given in his absence. Before the writ is issued, the spaces left blank on the face   *Object of writ.*

of the form of writ provided must be filled in by the plaintiff or his solicitor with the names and addresses of the parties to the action ; and the writ must be indorsed at the back with a statement of the nature of the claim which the plaintiff makes against the defendant.

No one who is under an incapacity can invoke the law without the mediation of a third party. Hence an infant or a person of unsound mind can only institute proceedings if the consent in writing of another person known as " the next friend " is filed at the time the writ is issued, and the name of the next friend must appear on the writ. A woman may now be " the next friend."

Form of indorsement. In every case the writ may be *generally* indorsed, whatever be the nature of the claim. In all actions except claims for damages for libel, slander, malicious prosecution, false imprisonment, seduction or breach of promise of marriage, and in actions in which fraud is alleged by the plaintiff, the writ may be *specially* indorsed. The object of a special indorsement is that proceedings may be taken by the plaintiff at an early stage in the action to ascertain whether the defendant has any real defence by issuing a summons for summary judgment and thus forcing the defendant to put his defence on oath as a condition precedent to the Court granting him leave to defend the action. Proceedings of this nature will be discussed latter.

A general indorsement consists of a very short statement of the nature of the claim made, or the relief required, in the action ; *e.g.*

> the plaintiff's claim is for :
>   " damages for breach of contract," *or*
>   " £x for the carriage of goods by railway," *or*
>   " £x for the use and occupation of a house," *or*
>   " damages for slander."

Issue of writ. The next step after settling the contents of the writ is to issue it. For this purpose, two forms must be filled up and taken to the writ department of the Central Office of the Supreme Court, or to a District Registry, where they are marked in the top right-hand corner with a letter, being the first letter of the plantiff's surname, and number of identification, and are sealed by the officer. If the writ is issued out of a District Registry the name of the District Registry appears on the face of the writ immediately beneath the words " King's Bench Division." One of the forms is stamped with an impressed stamp for thirty shillings, and filed by the officer ; the other is not stamped, but is sealed and returned to the person issuing it, and becomes the writ in the action. If for any reason further sealed copies are required application is made to the Court to issue " Concurrent writs."

This writ must be served on the defendant. This is done by handing to him a true copy of the writ and leaving it with him and at the same time showing him the original writ if he desires it. The seal of the Court is shown on the copy for service by the letters " L.S." Service may be effected anywhere within the jurisdiction at any time of any day, except Sunday. When prompt personal service is impossible, leave may be obtained from one of the Masters—who deal, in the first instance, with most matters of procedure—for " substituted service," *i.e.*, service on the defendant's agent, or by advertisement, or by sending the defendant a copy of the writ in a registered letter, or by some mode of bringing the issue of the writ to the defendant's knowledge otherwise than by personal service.

Service of writ.

Substituted service.

Care should be taken to indorse the writ with a memorandum of service, whether personal or substituted, within three days of the date of the service of the writ. This is important if subsequent proceedings become necessary as a result of the defendant omitting to enter an appearance to the writ.

Service on the defendant, however, may be dispensed with when the defendant's solicitor undertakes in writing to accept service and to enter an appearance on his behalf. It is usual to indorse a memorandum to this effect on the face of the writ. The solicitor should never give this solemn undertaking unless he has instructions from his client, because having once given this undertaking he is bound to carry it out and enter an appearance, otherwise he is liable to be committed to prison for contempt of Court.

Acceptance of service.

If the defendant is a British subject and is resident abroad it is necessary to apply to the Master for leave to

Defendant abroad.

serve the writ out of the jurisdiction.   If the defendant is
not a British subject and is resident outside the British
Dominions the writ itself is not served on him, as the
King's writ does not run in a foreign country against
someone who is not a British subject, and consequently
notice of the writ and not the writ itself is served on the
defendant.   The granting of leave to serve the writ or
notice of the writ out of the jurisdiction is a matter of
discretion, but leave cannot be given unless the case
falls within the circumstances specified in Ord. XI, r. 1
(consider *George Monro, Ltd.* v. *American Cyanamid and
Chemical Corpn.*, [1944] K. B. 432 ; [1944] 1 All E. R.
386).   In order to avoid any international complications
the service of the notice of the writ is arranged by the
Foreign Office through the usual diplomatic channels.
When the defendant is abroad the time limited for his
appearance is of course extended beyond the usual period,
but the Court must now have regard to any Air Mail
service in operation in fixing the time within which the
defendant must appear.

Entering appearance.

Appearance.   After service of the writ, the defendant
must enter an appearance in accordance with the form
hereunder.

1948, C., No. 105.

IN THE HIGH COURT OF JUSTICE.
KING'S BENCH DIVISION.

Between   Edward Coke
Plaintiff
and
William Blackstone
Defendant

Enter an Appearance for William Blackstone the Defendant in
this Action.
Dated the 23rd day of April 1948.

(Signed) FERRET & Co.

of and whose address for service is 260 Lombard Wall in the City
of London.

Solicitors for the said Defendant.

Entry consists of delivering at the Central Office, or the
District Registry out of which the writ was issued, a
memorandum in writing containing the name of his
solicitor, or a statement that he defends in person, and

giving his address within the jurisdiction for service of notices or other documents in the action. Notice of his appearance is sent to the plaintiff's solicitor or the plaintiff if he is acting in person. A defendant in person may enter an appearance through the post.

A defendant who does not reside or carry on business within the jurisdiction of the district registry out of which a writ has been issued has the option of entering an appearance to the writ either in that district registry or at the Central Office. If the defendant elects to enter the appearance at the district registry all interlocutory proceedings take place in that district registry, but if the appearance is entered in the Central Office the memorandum must state that the defendant neither resides nor carries on business within the district, and the action is then given a new distinctive number and the proceedings are then transferred to the Central Office and the action continues as if the writ had been issued originally out of the Central Office.

District registry.

If the defendant is a person of unsound mind an appearance should be entered as though he were of sound mind and an application made to the Court for the appointment of an independent adult to act as " guardian *ad litem*." Until a guardian has been appointed no further steps can be taken. If the defendant is an infant he cannot enter an appearance except by his " guardian *ad litem*," but in this instance no order of the Court for the appointment of such guardian is necessary. The solicitor who is desirous of appearing on his behalf must file an affidavit to the effect that the " guardian *ad litem* " is a fit and proper person to act as such and has no interest in the matters in question in the action adverse to that of the infant, and the consent of the guardian to act must be filed at the Court.

Person of unsound mind.

Infant.

Judgment in default of appearance. If the defendant does not enter an appearance within the time stated in the writ, the plaintiff may search for an appearance and, after filing an affidavit of service, enter judgment against the defendant. Where the writ is for a debt or other liquidated sum, that is to say, where the amount of money claimed is certain, and nothing more remains to be done in order to ascertain it, the judgment is final ;

Interlocutory judgment.

but where the claim is for unliquidated damages, or for the recovery of a chattel, the judgment is " interlocutory," and an order is made for the assessment of the damages or the value of the chattel by a Master or Official Referee, or by the Sheriff under a writ of inquiry. After interlocutory judgment has been entered, the defendant cannot, apart from the procedure indicated in the next paragraph, deny his liability ; but he may dispute the amount for which he is liable, and for that purpose attend in person or by solicitor or counsel, and give evidence, if he chooses, as to the assessment of the damages. The plaintiff may sign final judgment for the amount of the damages so assessed. If the action is for the recovery of land, the plaintiff may, in default of appearance, enter judgment for recovery of possession.

Where judgment may be set aside.

In any case in which judgment has been entered in default of appearance, the Court has a discretionary power to set aside the judgment on such terms as it may think fit. The terms are usually the payment of all costs incurred by the plaintiff, and payment into Court of the amount claimed, but, subject to that, upon showing any reasonable cause, such a request by the defendant is usually granted if the Court is satisfied that he has a *prima facie* defence to the action on the merits.

Section II. PLEADINGS

Nature and object of pleadings.

The main objects of pleading are, to ascertain what are the questions of fact or law at issue between the parties, and to give each party notice of the case which the other intends to set up at the trial. To attain these objects, certain rules of pleading have been provided, of which the fundamental rule is that every pleading shall contain only a statement in a summary form of the material *facts* on which the party pleading relies for his claim or defence, as the case may be, and *not the evidence* by which they are to be proved, nor *the law* which the party pleading will seek to apply to the facts. For full precedents of pleadings reference should be made to that admirable book " Common Law and Chancery Pleadings " by Benas and Essenhigh. Every pleading must be signed by the bar-

Pleadings contain Facts : not Evidence nor Law.

rister or solicitor who settles it, or by the party himself;
in the specimen statement of claim " Colin Blackburn "
represents the name of the junior barrister who settled it.
King's Counsel are by virtue of their position prevented
from settling pleadings. If the document exceeds ten
folios (*i.e.*, 720 words) it must be either printed or litho-
graphed. For this reason each document contains,
immediately above the names of the parties, a statement
of the number of folios, thus : " Fos. 3." It should be
noted that pleadings are exchanged between the parties
and are neither delivered to nor filed in Court. In
order to discourage litigation during the summer vacation
the time for delivery of pleadings does not run during this
period and pleadings cannot be delivered during the long
vacation without leave of the Master. Before the action
is set down for trial neither the Master nor any official of
the Court will see the pleadings unless some point is raised
upon them. The document must at the foot give the
date on which it is delivered and also the name and
address of the solicitor delivering it.

Statement of Claim. In the hypothetical action, of
which we have given the writ of summons (p. 36), the
Statement of Claim might run somewhat as follows :

1948, C., No. 105.   Precedent of
Statement
of Claim.

IN THE HIGH COURT OF JUSTICE.

  KING'S BENCH DIVISION.

  Writ issued 12th April 1948.
  Fos. 3.

Between   Edward Coke

Plaintiff

                and

        William Blackstone

Defendant

Statement of Claim

   1. The Plaintiff is a commercial traveller.

   2. The Defendant is a clothing manufacturer, carrying
on business at 20 Prince Henry Street in the City of
London.

   3. By an agreement in writing dated the 21st January
1946 and made between the Plaintiff and Defendant, the
Defendant agreed to employ the Plaintiff and the
Plaintiff agreed to serve the Defendant as a traveller for

a term of 3 years certain as from the 28th January 1946 at a yearly salary of £500 payable monthly.

4. The Plaintiff duly entered upon the said employment in pursuance of the said agreement: yet by a letter dated the 20th February 1947 and written by the Defendant to the Plaintiff the Defendant wrongfully and in breach of the said agreement dismissed the Plaintiff from his service forthwith.

And the Plaintiff claims damages.

Colin Blackburn.

Delivered the 30th day of April 1948 by Kenyon Ellenborough & Co. of 25 Park Lane in the City of Westminister, Solicitors for the Plaintiff.

Contents of Statement of Claim.

The Statement of Claim must set out the material facts on which the plaintiff bases his claim, and the precise remedy or relief which he seeks to obtain. As the general indorsement on the writ does not comprise a statement of the precise ground of complaint, or the precise remedy or relief to which the plaintiff considers himself entitled, the claim may be altered, extended, or modified by the statement of claim without amending the indorsement on the writ, provided that this does not entirely change the cause of action. The Statement of Claim may be delivered at the same time as the writ is served, but if not so delivered it must be delivered within ten days of the defendant's appearance unless the time is extended either by an order of the Master made on a summons for an extension of time or by a consent in writing given by the defendant or his solicitor.

Object of the Defence.

Defence. Now, after the delivery of the Statement of Claim, the defendant knows exactly the case he has to meet, for, unless the plaintiff amends his claim, he cannot make any further allegations at the trial. But the plaintiff does not know how much he will in fact have to prove; he does not know precisely what is the point in issue. It is the function of the Defence to resolve his doubt. Where the defendant makes a counterclaim (see p. 45, *post*) this forms part of the same document as the defence. The defendant must deliver his defence within fourteen days from the time limited for the appearance or from the delivery of the Statement of Claim, whichever shall be the later, unless the time is extended either by an order of the Court or the written consent of the plaintiff or his solicitor is obtained. If the writ is specially indorsed with a Statement of Claim and the plaintiff has in the meantime served a summons on the defendant for summary judgment, the latter need not deliver his defence until ordered by the Master.

The form of defence (and counterclaim, if any) should be on these lines (the student should refer continually to the Statement of Claim set out on pp. 43–44) :

Precedent of Defence and counterclaim.

1948, C., No. 105.

IN THE HIGH COURT OF JUSTICE.
KING'S BENCH DIVISION.
Fos. 8.
Between   Edward Coke

Plaintiff

and

William Blackstone

Defendant

Defence and Counterclaim

1. The Defendant admits paragraphs 1 and 2 of the Statement of Claim.

2. The Defendant does not admit that the terms of the agreement of the 21st January 1946 are sufficiently set out in paragraph 3 of the Statement of Claim and will refer to the same when produced at the trial for the full terms and conditions thereof.

3. It was an express term of the said agreement that the Plaintiff should at all times and in all ways use his best endeavours to promote the welfare of the Defendant's business.

4. The Plaintiff on the 10th October 1946 sold subject to the confirmation of the Defendant goods of the Defendant to the value of £800 to a company of the name of C. A. & S. Ltd. of T. in the County of K.

5. The said company at the time of the said sale was to the knowledge of the Plaintiff insolvent : yet the Plaintiff falsely and fraudulently represented to the Defendant that the company was a sound company with which it would be advantageous for the Defendant to do business.

6. On the 15th January 1947 the said company was wound up and a final dividend of 5s. in the pound was paid to the creditors, including the Defendant.

7. In consequence of the said default and fraud of the Plaintiff the Defendant dismissed the Plaintiff from his employment as he lawfully might, which is the wrongful dismissal complained of in the Statement of Claim.

8. Save and except as hereinbefore expressly admitted, each and every allegation made in the Statement of Claim herein is hereby denied as though the same were here set out and specifically traversed.

Counterclaim

9. The Defendant repeats paragraphs 4 to 7 of his defence.

10. Relying upon the said representations of the Plaintiff the Defendant confirmed the said sale and delivered on credit to the said company the said goods to the value of £800 and by reason thereof has suffered damage.

Particulars of Special Damage

To the value of the goods sold and delivered £800.

To amount received by way of final dividend at the rate of 5s. in the £, £200.

And the Defendant counterclaims £600 damages.

J. S. WILLES.

Delivered the 12th day of May 1948 by Ferret & Co. of 260 Lombard Wall in the City of London, Solicitors to the Defendant.

Rules applicable to Defence. In settling the defence, the main rules of pleading to be borne in mind are : that it is not sufficient for the defendant merely to deny his liability, but that he must deal specifically with every allegation of fact in the statement of claim of which he does not admit the truth ; and that he is generally taken to admit every material fact alleged in the statement of claim, unless he denies it, specifically or by implication, or states that he does not admit it. To these rules there is this important exception, that no denial as to damages claimed or their amount is necessary ; for an allegation of damage is deemed to be put in issue in all cases, unless expressly admitted.

Courses open to defendant. In answering the statement of claim, the defendant may take one or more of the following courses :

1. *Traverse* : that is, he may deny every or any allegation of fact made in the statement of claim. In addition to thus dealing with the allegations in the statement of claim the defendant may and should plead any facts which constitute an answer to the claim.

All equitable or statutory defences, *e.g.*, the Statute of Frauds or the Limitation Act, 1939, must be specifically pleaded.

2. *Objection in point of law* : that is, he may say that, even assuming the facts alleged in the statement of claim are true, they do not entitle the plaintiff to the relief or remedy claimed. When a point of law is raised an order

is sometimes obtained that the question of law be tried as a preliminary point before the trial of the other issues in the action.

There are cases where this is the most convenient and expeditious course, as the determination of the question of law may settle the dispute between the parties. Usually, however, the facts have first to be ascertained and in those cases this procedure ought not to be adopted.

Another step which sometimes serves the same purpose as an objection in point of law, but is more drastic and peremptory, is an application to the Court under Ord. XXV, r. 4, to strike out an opponent's pleading on the ground that it discloses no reasonable cause of action or answer, or that the action or defence disclosed in the pleading is frivolous or vexatious ; whereupon the Court may order the action to be stayed or dismissed or the defence to be struck out, and give judgment accordingly. For instance, if your client was a member of either House of Parliament, and was sued for damages for slander contained in a speech made in the course of debate in Parliament, you could apply for the statement of claim to be struck out, on the ground that, speeches in Parliament being absolutely privileged, no cause of action was disclosed ; and that would be an end of the matter. But as was said by Fletcher Moulton, L.J. (*Dyson* v. *Attorney-General*, [1911] 1 K. B. 410, at p. 418), in speaking of this rule :

Application to strike out pleading.

> " the power of arresting an action and deciding it without trial is one to be very sparingly used, and rarely, if ever, excepting in cases where the action is an abuse of legal procedure."

In addition the Court has power at any stage of the proceedings to strike out any pleading

> " which may be unnecessary or scandalous or which may tend to prejudice, embarrass, or delay the fair trial of the action " ;

and the Court has an inherent jurisdiction to stay proceedings and strike out claims or defences which are frivolous or vexatious or an abuse of the process of the

Court. The High Court may also, upon the application of the Attorney-General, make an order that a person

> " who has habitually and persistently instituted vexatious legal proceedings without any reasonable ground "

shall be prevented from instituting proceedings in any court, except by leave of the High Court.

Amendment. If for any reason it is desired to amend any portion of the writ other than the indorsement the Master's leave must be obtained. If the plaintiff is desirous of amending the indorsement of the writ or his pleadings he can generally amend them once without any leave. The defendant can amend his defence and any subsequent pleadings if he obtains an order from the Master for that purpose. It is usual to allow the party seeking to amend to do so if he pays the costs occasioned by his amendment. It is usual to show the amendment by making the alterations to the original document in red ink, a different colour being used to show any subsequent amendment. Every document that has been amended must be re-delivered to the opposite party to the litigation, who considers whether the amended document served on him makes it desirable for that party to make alterations to his pleadings.

It is usual for Counsel to settle the proposed amendments when the original document has been originally settled by Counsel.

If Counsel settles the amendment he must re-sign the pleading in the same colour ink as the amendment.

Discontinuance For a variety of reasons a plaintiff may desire to cease the litigation that he has begun or the defendant not to proceed on his counterclaim if he has delivered one. At one time a plaintiff could at any time before verdict elect to be non-suited, the effect of which was to bring the proceedings to an end so far as that action was concerned. The plaintiff if he wished could subsequently bring another action on the same facts, though he had to pay the costs of the first action. At the present day there is no such thing in the High Court as a " non-suit," but a plaintiff is still entitled to discontinue his action. If he wishes to do so he must serve a notice of his intention so to do upon the defendant, and the defendant is thereupon entitled to tax his costs. If this notice is served at an early stage of the proceedings (*e.g.*, at any time before the receipt of the defence) the plaintiff need not ask the leave of the Court to discontinue and he will be entitled to bring a fresh action on the same facts, though if he has not paid the defendant's costs of the discontinued action the Court will stay all proceedings in the subsequent action until he has done so. When once, however, such a step as setting down the action for trial has been taken the plaintiff cannot discontinue as of right, but must obtain the leave of the Court to do so. This leave is obtained on an application under the " liberty to apply " reserved in the order for directions (see p. 62), and on hearing the application it is open to the Court to refuse the leave asked or to grant it only on the condition that the plaintiff bring no further action on the same facts ; in any case the plaintiff must pay the defendant's costs of the discontinued action.

A defendant is not in the same position with regard to the withdrawing of his defence as the plaintiff is in regard to withdrawing his claim. A defendant can only withdraw his defence or discontinue his counterclaim with leave of the Court. If the Court gives the defendant leave to discontinue his counterclaim the defendant, of course, is liable to pay the costs.

Payment into Court. In an action for debt or damages, the defendant may, at any time after appearance upon notice to the plaintiff, pay into Court a sum of money in satisfaction of the claim or if more than one claim, in satisfaction of all or some of the claims ; in the latter case the notice to the plaintiff must specify in respect of which claims the money is paid in and the amount paid in in respect of each, otherwise the payment in will be of no advantage to the defendant. No reference is now made in the defence of any sum paid into Court, except where a defence of tender has been pleaded ; and no statement is now made in the notice of payment as to whether the payment is made with or without a denial of liability. Where the defendant has paid into Court a sum of money, if the plaintiff, within seven days of receipt of the notice of payment in, gives notice in writing to the defendant

Payment of money into Court.

that he accepts the money so paid into Court all further proceedings will be stayed, and the plaintiff can take the money out of Court. Unless the action is for defamation, no further steps can be taken by the plaintiff, except that he may proceed to tax and recover his costs. If he proceeds with the action and does not recover more than the amount paid into Court he will, as a rule, be ordered to pay the defendant's costs incurred subsequent to the date of payment in. If he recovers less than the amount paid in, the balance will be repaid to the defendant (*Bonitto* v. *Fuerst Brothers & Co., Ltd.*, [1944] A. C. 75).

Money may be paid in either as an attempt at a compromise, or as a necessary condition of the defence of apology and amends afforded to a newspaper or other periodical publication in an action for libel by the Libel Acts, 1843 and 1845.

In actions for damages for libel and slander when money is paid into Court, if the sum paid into Court is taken out the action does not automatically abate, but the plaintiff can apply to the judge in Chambers to settle a statement to be read in open Court setting out the circumstances of the case. The costs of the application to the judge in Chambers, and the subsequent appearance in Court are at the discretion of the judge before whom the statement is read in open Court. The object of allowing a statement to be read in open Court is that it gives the plaintiff an opportunity of clearing his name ; a right which he would not have in the usual way, because taking the money out of Court paid therein in every other type of action automatically brings the proceedings to an end, so that there are no proceedings before the Court upon which the Court can permit the plaintiff to be heard.

Tender.

Tender. If, before action brought for a liquidated claim, the defendant has offered to pay the amount claimed, he may plead a *tender*, *i.e.*, that he offered unconditionally the exact sum due in legal currency ; but, if so, he must pay into Court the sum so tendered. If the plea is upheld at the trial, the defendant will be entitled to his costs of the action. Tender, in the cases where it is appropriate, is a defence, and not a mere attempt at a compromise, as payment into Court usually is.

For the requisites of tender see Volume II, p. 80.

Set-off. Where the claim is for a debt or other liqui- Set-off.
dated amount, and the defendant had at the date of the
plaintiff's writ a cross-claim against the plaintiff, the
defendant may set up this cross-claim in his defence.
This is known as pleading a " set-off." At law only a
cross-claim for a debt or other liquidated amount could
be set-off, but now in accordance with the rule in equity
the defendant may set-off an unliquidated claim for
damages if it arose out of the same facts as the plaintiff's
claim. Where the set-off is established, it operates as a
good defence to the action, if it is not less than the
amount of the claim ; and it reduces, *pro tanto*, the
amount of the judgment if it is less than the claim. But
if it exceeds the amount of the claim, the defendant
cannot recover the balance unless he also counterclaims
for such balance. Claims cannot be the subject of set-off
unless they exist between the same parties and in the
same right. For instance, a debt due from the plaintiff
personally may not be set off against a claim made by a
plaintiff who sues in a representative capacity (*e.g.*, as
executor of the will of a deceased person). But a defendant can set-off a debt originally due from the plaintiff
to a third party, which the third party has assigned to
the defendant before the issue of the writ. Set-off is a
defence, and should be pleaded as such.

Counterclaim. The defendant may admit the plaintiff's Nature of
counterclaim.
claim in his defence, subject to a counterclaim ; or he
may dispute the claim in the defence and also set up a
counterclaim. A counterclaim is in the nature of a cross-
action, which the defendant is entitled to set up against
the plaintiff, to the same extent as if he had brought a
separate action against the plaintiff for the purpose. The
subject-matter of the counterclaim need not be of the same
nature as the claim, nor need it even arise out of the same
transaction, or have any relation or analogy to it. Any
cause of action or claim of any nature or amount, which
the defendant may have against the plaintiff, may be set
up by way of counterclaim ; subject to the plaintiff's
right to raise the objection that the claim made by the
defendant cannot be conveniently tried by the same Court

or at the same time as the plaintiff's claim, and ought to be disposed of in an independent action. On this ground, the Master has power to strike out the counterclaim, and leave the defendant to bring an independent action. What is pleaded in the defence as set-off may also be set up by way of counterclaim ; but the converse is not true. Counterclaim is wider in its scope than set-off ; but set-off is a defence, and, whenever the same claim can be pleaded either as a set-off or as a counterclaim, it will generally be found advantageous to plead it as both.

Claim and counterclaim independent actions. For most purposes, the claim and counterclaim are treated as independent actions, combined for the purpose of determining all the matters in difference between the parties. Thus, if the plaintiff discontinues his claim, the defendant is still entitled to proceed with the counter-claim. Where the defendant recovers more on the counterclaim than the plaintiff recovers on the claim, the Court has a discretion to order judgment to be entered for the defendant for the balance ; but the more usual practice, where the plaintiff succeeds on the claim and the defendant succeeds on the counterclaim, is that two judgments should be entered, one for the plaintiff on the claim with costs, and the other for the defendant on the counter-claim with costs. Where both plaintiff and defendant fail, judgment is entered for the defendant on the claim with costs, and for the plaintiff on the counterclaim with costs ; the costs being set-off, and an order being made for the payment of the balance. The same rules as to pleading and particulars apply to a counterclaim as to a statement of claim. In cases where the defendant merely pleads a " set-off " but does not counterclaim there is only one action before the Court, and if the defendant fails in his defence of set-off, judgment will be entered for the plaintiff with costs, but he does not get a separate order against the defendant for costs on the issues of "set-off."

In our hypothetical action the defence of tender is not available, nor is a set-off possible, for the claim is not for a debt or liquidated amount.

The defendant's real defence is that he was justified in dismissing the plaintiff on account of the plaintiff's misconduct. Accordingly, while putting the plaintiff to the proof of his case, the defendant pleads this fact as an answer to the plaintiff's claim. And, as he claims to have actually suffered pecuniary loss from the plaintiff's misconduct, he carries the war into his enemy's camp by counterclaiming.

In this imaginary action " J. S. Willes " is the barrister who settled the defence.

Now the result of the pleading up to date is that the plaintiff knows that he must formally prove his allegations and in particular produce the agreement on which he relies, and must be prepared to deal with the allegations made by the defendant. The defendant, however, has also set up a cause of action himself, and this is based on allegations which must in their turn be answered. But first we must mention the topic of particulars.

Particulars.—The object of particulars is to narrow the issues of fact so as to save expense, or bind the party giving the particulars to definite details or incidents, or to explain vague or general allegations in the pleading which cannot be properly answered by the other side without more specific information. Thus, particulars must always be given by a party who relies on any misrepresentation ; or fraud ; or negligence, undue influence, or any general charge of misconduct ; or who claims special damage. _{Object of particulars.}

A party may give no particulars in his pleading, or he may give some, but insufficient particulars. The party who is not satisfied owing to the absence or insufficiency of the particulars given in his opponents pleading, should, in the first instance, apply to the opposite party by letter for such particulars or " further and better " particulars as he thinks he is entitled to have. The letter should state clearly the matters of which particulars are required. If the request is refused or he is dissatisfied with the answer given, he may apply to the Master on summons, or on the hearing of the Summons for Directions (*post*, p. 59) or at a later date by notice under the Summons for Directions (which is, so to speak, kept alive for this and similar purposes) for an Order compelling his opponent to deliver such particulars.

If an order is made the particulars should be given in the following form :

1948, C., No. 105.

IN THE HIGH COURT OF JUSTICE.

KING'S BENCH DIVISION.

Fos. 4.

Between   Edward Coke

Plaintiff

and

William Blackstone

Defendant

*Particulars of paragraph 5 of the Defence
and Counterclaim*

*Delivered in pursuance of an Order of Master Blank,
dated the 21st day of May 1948*

1. The Plaintiff acted fraudulently in that, in his letter transmitting the order of C. A. & S. Ltd. to the Defendant he wrote the words " I hope you will deliver promptly, for this is a fine opening," meaning thereby that the company was a sound company with which it would be advantageous for the Defendant to do business.

2. At the time that the Plaintiff wrote the said letter the said company was not a sound company but insolvent.

3. The Plaintiff knew when he wrote the said letter that the said company was insolvent.

4. Relying upon the representation contained in the said letter the Defendant supplied the said company with the said goods to his loss.

J. S. WILLES.

Delivered the 1st day of June 1948 by Ferret & Co. of 260 Lombard Wall in the City of London, Solicitors for the Defendant.

It will be noted that the Particulars are signed by the person drawing them, be he counsel or solicitor, or the party in person.   This is so because the Particulars are a part of the pleading.

An order for particulars, however, is not usually made before the defence is delivered, unless it appears necessary to enable the defendant to plead.   A party may, if he be so minded, apply at once to the Master without previous letter to his opponent, but, in that event, he may be ordered to pay the costs of the application. On the other hand, a wrongful refusal of particulars on an application by letter from the other side, may lead to an order that the party refusing shall pay the costs of the necessary application to the Court. Such costs would be awarded to the party entitled " in any event," that is to say, whatever the ultimate result of the action. In any application to the Court that is reasonably justifiable, the costs would generally be made " costs in the cause," that is, they would ultimately be paid by the unsuccessful party. The costs of interlocutory matters are generally dealt with in this way and thus made to form part of one bill to be dealt with when the action is over.

The proper course is undoubtedly for the party to supply the necessary particulars, either in the pleading itself or annexed thereto or in a separate document delivered therewith.

Reply and Defence to Counterclaim. After delivery of the defence, the plaintiff may deliver a reply and ought to do so if he wishes to set up facts dealing specifically with allegations in the defence or to raise an objection in point of law or to deny some only of the facts alleged in the defence while admitting others. If there is no counterclaim and the plaintiff merely denies the allegations in the defence, no reply need be delivered, for if there is no reply all material facts alleged in the defence are deemed to be denied. Where, however, there is a counterclaim the plaintiff must answer it. In this case the pleading is usually called a " Reply and Defence to Counterclaim." The rules applicable to a defence apply to the plaintiff's answer to the counterclaim. In our case the pleadings end with a reply and defence to counterclaim as follows :

Reply.

1948, C., No. 105.

Precedent of reply.

IN THE HIGH COURT OF JUSTICE.
KING'S BENCH DIVISION.

Fos. 3.

Between   Edward Coke
                                        Plaintiff
                    and

                William Blackstone
                                        Defendant

          REPLY

1. The Plaintiff as to the Defence says that he joins issue with the Defendant thereon.

2. The Plaintiff as to the Counterclaim says that, save that the Plaintiff admits that it was a term of the written agreement of the 21st January 1946 that the Plaintiff was at all times and in all ways to use his best endeavours to promote the welfare of the Defendant's business, and that at the winding-up of C. A. & S. Ltd. a final dividend of 5s. in the pound was paid to the Defendant, the Plaintiff does not admit any of the allegations contained in the Defendant's counter-claim.

3. If the Company C. A. & S. Ltd. was at the time of the sale complained of insolvent, which the Plaintiff does not admit, the Plaintiff was unaware of the insolvency.

4. The Plaintiff never at any time expressly or impliedly represented to the Defendant that the said company was solvent, or alternatively never made any such representations without believing the same to be true.

COLIN BLACKBURN.

Delivered the 9th day of June 1948 by Kenyon Ellenborough & Co. of 25 Park Lane in the City of Westminister, Solicitors for the Plaintiff.

The time for delivering a reply is seven days from delivery of defence, and when a counterclaim is pleaded, fourteen days from delivery of defence and counterclaim, but the period may be extended by agreement. If the defendant refuses to extend the time, an application may be made to a Master.

The pleadings are generally closed at this stage ; but it is possible, with leave, to have a " rejoinder," a " surrejoinder," a " rebutter," and a " surrebutter."

Thus both parties know that all the important allegations made by the defendant must be proved, for the plaintiff has traversed them. The defendant will have to establish the insolvency of the company at the time of the sale, the plaintiff's knowledge of it, and the writing of the letter and its contents. But he must go further than that ; for in order to succeed in his defence he must show that the default of the plaintiff amounted to a failure to use his best endeavours to promote the welfare of his business, so that he was justified in dismissing him from his employment. And to succeed on his counterclaim he will have to prove not only that the letter amounted to a fraudulent representation that the company was solvent, but also that his loss was attributable to his belief in the truth of the representation.

Section III. INTERLOCUTORY PROCEEDINGS

The issues having been defined in the pleadings, the next matter for consideration is the machinery to bring on the action for trial.

It must be apparent to the student that cases do not come on for hearing before the Court without some measure of control and direction being exercised during the preliminary stages. It is this measure of control and direction which we propose to discuss under the heading interlocutory proceedings.

Normally the control and direction is exercised by the Masters in Chambers, who in effect direct what is to be done and fix the time in which it is to be done. To enable the Master to exercise his jurisdiction it is necessary that a summons or notice of application should be issued in the action and that it should be served on the other party. When the summons or notice of application comes on for hearing, the Master then makes an order, subject always to the right of a litigant who is dissatisfied with the Order of the Master to give notice of appeal to the Judge in Chambers. In addition to exercising control and direction to which we have referred the Masters also decide, subject to a right to appeal to the Judge in Chambers, points of dispute that arise in the action relative to the trial, *e.g.*, whether certain documents are privileged from production or whether certain questions ought to be allowed in interrogatories. *[marginal note: Master in Chambers.]*

If a plaintiff omits to comply with an order of the Court, *i.e.*, a Master in Chambers or the Judge in Chambers, within the time limited by the order, for example, to file an affidavit of documents within the prescribed time, the defendant may either apply to attach the plaintiff and have him committed to prison for contempt of Court, or, as is more usual, apply to the Court to dismiss the action for want of prosecution. If the defendant is in default the plaintiff can apply either for attachment or to strike out the defence and for leave to enter either interlocutory or final judgment as the circumstances admit. The remedy of attachment, however, is but rarely resorted to. *[marginal note: Failure to comply with order.]*

Affidavits. Before proceeding with the next stage of the action it is desirable to consider the form and contents of an affidavit, which is a document on oath, since if the document does not comply with the rules it cannot, without leave of the Court, be used or filed.

It is illegal to swear statements on oath, except in legal proceedings. In extra-judicial matters, *e.g.*, a declaration that a conveyance has been lost, the statements are made in a Statutory Declaration. The effect of making a false statement in either case may amount to perjury.

Form of affidavit.

It is not proposed to go into the technical details as to the form of the document except to draw attention to the fact that it must be made in the first person and must be divided into numbered paragraphs. The affidavit is sworn before a Commissioner for Oaths who is usually a practising solicitor of five years' standing who derives his commission from the Lord Chancellor. If the affidavit refers to any documents these must be " exhibited " or annexed to the affidavit and the Commissioner for Oaths identifies them with the affidavit by marking them with his signature.

Filing.

In matters in the Chancery Division the original affidavit is first filed and retained in the Court archives and an office copy is obtained from the Court. It is this copy that the Court uses in the proceedings and the original is not usually referred to.

In the King's Bench Division the original is not filed before it is used, it is handed in to the judge or Master, and after it has been read by him he sends it to the filing department and the affidavit is filed ; if required in the future the original is bespoken from the filing room and later returned.

An affidavit once filed cannot be removed from the file unless the Court so orders.

Exhibits are not filed, but are retained by the solicitor and must be produced by him when required.

Purpose of third party notice.

THIRD PARTY PROCEDURE. Occasionally a defendant may think that some other person is liable to indemnify him against the plaintiff's claim or at least bound to contribute something towards it, and in these circumstances he is entitled to bring in the person against whom he makes such a claim as a party to the action. He does this by obtaining the leave of the Master to serve upon that person a third party notice.

The effect of a third party notice is that if the third party does not enter an appearance to the third party notice or deliver his defence he will be deemed to admit the validity of, and will be bound by any judgment given in the action between the plaintiff and defendant, whether by consent or otherwise and to admit his liability to contribute or indemnify. *Effect of notice.*

If the third party enters an appearance, the defendant, after serving notice of the intended application on the plaintiff and the third party, should apply to the Court or judge for directions.

To enable the third party, when once he has been brought into the proceedings, to prepare his own defence the rules provide that he is to be entitled to receive copies of all documents that have passed between the plaintiff and the defendant. *Pleadings of third party.*

Other machinery exists for bringing in a third party when the defendant raises a counterclaim against the plaintiff and another.

THE SUMMONS FOR DIRECTIONS. In our imaginary action we reached the stage at which the pleadings were closed and the issues determined. When a pleading subsequent to a reply has not been ordered, the pleadings are deemed to be closed at the expiration of seven days from the delivery of the defence or reply (if any). It is now necessary that the action should be disposed of. To enable this to be done the plaintiff must within seven days after the pleadings have closed issue a summons for directions which is " returnable " before the Master. The expression " returnable " means in effect that the summons comes on for hearing before the person named. If no summons has previously been issued since the action commenced the action is then assigned to a Master ; if a summons has already been issued the action is allocated to the same Master. The object of this is to enable the same Master to deal with the action throughout its stages, as is *Summons returnable before Master.*

obviously convenient. The Master always sits in Chambers, *i.e.*, in a private room in the Law Courts as opposed to open Court, in the morning to dispose of summonses attended by solicitors, and in the afternoon to take summonses attended by counsel.

Attendance of counsel.

Care should be taken when instructing counsel to attend the hearing of the summons to instruct him to apply to the Master at the time he makes his Order to exercise his discretion and grant a certificate for counsel, because unless this is granted at that time the successful party may not be able to recover the costs of counsel's attendance later from his opponent. It is not usual to instruct counsel to attend the hearing of a summons for directions unless it becomes apparent that some matter of importance is likely to become contested.

It is usual, in cases where the Master grants a certificate for counsel, if the other party appears by a solicitor, for the Master to make an order for a " special allowance " for the solicitor. The effect of this order is that the solicitor is entitled to a fee of £1 6s. 8d. for attending before the Master in place of the usual fee of 13s. 4d.

Purpose of summons.

The summons requires the defendant to attend to enable the Master to give the necessary directions for the purposes of clarifying the issues and bringing the action on for trial. It is usual to ask in the summons that directions should be given for discovery of documents (*post*, p. 65) and for inspection. In actions involving personal injuries, it is usual in order to save the expense of doctors attending Court to ask that medical reports should be exchanged and, if the doctors agree, to dispense with their attendance at the trial, but if the doctors are unable to agree, then to limit the number of doctors called at the trial. In furtherance of the policy to keep down the cost of litigation it is usual to limit the number of expert witnesses and, where applicable, to agree photographs and a plan of the *locus in quo*, and, sometimes, to limit any appeal to the Court of Appeal. The Master directs the mode of trial, *i.e.*, whether by judge and jury, judge alone, or an Official Referee. If he orders it to be tried with a judge alone and if the case is likely to

The lists.

exceed four hours he directs it to be entered in the long
non-jury list—if more than two hours, but less than four
hours in the short non-jury list, if under two hours in
the short cause list.

The reader can well imagine the difficulty of all concerned in attempting to forecast the length of the trial
of an action before discovery of documents has taken place
and notice to admit facts has been given.

The tendency at the present time is for the Court to
order actions to be entered in either of the non-jury lists
or the short cause list, and thus avoid taking away from
their daily labours hard-working citizens who, until the
Juries Act, 1949, came into operation on October 1, 1949,
were not paid (as members of a "special jury," see below). *Juries.*

Where the claim is for damages for libel, slander,
malicious prosecution, false imprisonment, seduction or
breach of promise of marriage, either party is entitled to
have the action tried by a jury, and in cases where fraud
is alleged, the party against whom it is alleged is entitled
to have the action tried by a jury.   But in any case where
the Court is of opinion that the trial thereof requires any
prolonged examination of documents or any scientific
or local investigation that cannot conveniently be made
with a jury, it may order the action to be tried without
a jury.   In other actions the Court has a discretion
whether it will order the action to be tried by a jury.

Until the end of September, 1949, there were two
forms of jury—the common jury and the special jury.
The property qualification of a special juror was higher
than that of a common juror, and either party could
apply for a special jury.   Special juries were abolished
by the Juries Act, 1949 (except the " City of London
special jury " in commercial causes, see p. 92, *post*), and
the expression common jury is accordingly no longer to
be used. *Special jury.*

The Master decides the place of trial ; whether at the
Royal Courts of Justice in the Strand, or at Assizes.
There is no hard-and-fast rule that is applied by the
Court to determine this ; the convenience of the parties
and the witnesses are considered, but the action is usually
ordered to be heard either where the cause of action arose *Venue of trial.*

or the place where the defendant resides. Where a claim is within the county court jurisdiction the action may be transferred to the county court for trial.

Trial by Master. If the parties consent the Master may try the action in his private room.

Other matters. The Master can also make an order on any other matter that the parties desire to be determined which would otherwise require a separate application.

" Liberty to apply." The parties are usually given, by the order, " liberty to apply " to the Master for further directions.

Variation of Master's Order. Formerly the Master had power to vary his order if at a later date it became apparent that the original order required the adjustment of some of its terms in order to do justice to the parties, but the Master now has power to reverse his order. This power has been given to the Master who makes an order for directions to cover a case where later it is found that the order should never have been made, because the action should have been transferred to an official referee and ought not to have been set down for trial in one of the non-jury lists. In these circumstances the whole of the order for directions ought to be set aside to enable the official referee to make such order as the circumstances require.

Cases where plaintiff must give security. *Security for Costs.* The general principle is, that a defendant cannot compel a plaintiff to give security for the defendant's costs in the event of the plaintiff failing in his action and having costs awarded against him ; but there are exceptions to this rule. Thus a plaintiff may be ordered, on the defendant's application, to give security for the costs of the action if the plaintiff is ordinarily resident outside England, Scotland, and Northern Ireland ; or is an insolvent person suing, as nominal plaintiff, for the benefit of a third party ; or is a limited company and there is reason to believe that the company will be unable to pay the costs of the defendant if he is successful. When the order is made proceedings are stayed until it is complied with. But the mere fact that the plaintiff is insolvent or without visible means is not sufficient ground for granting the application.

Transfer to County Court. Where, however, in an action of tort the plaintiff is without visible means of paying the costs of the action in the High Court, if he should fail, the defendant may apply for an order that, in default of the plaintiff giving security as fixed by the Court the case be transferred to the County Court. The application for security or transfer to the County Court must be supported by affidavit, setting out the facts relied upon, except in cases where it appears from the writ itself that the plaintiff is ordinarily resident out of the jurisdiction (County Courts Act, 1934, s. 46).

When once an order for security has been made, the party entitled to demand the security can apply from time to time for further security. The reason is that the Court does not usually make an order for a large sum in the first instance.

A defendant who is not counterclaiming cannot be compelled to give security for the plaintiff's costs.

APPEALS TO THE JUDGE IN CHAMBERS. If a party is dissatisfied by a decision of a Master he can appeal to the Judge in Chambers without leave either of the Master or of the Judge in Chambers. All the judges who sit in the King's Bench Division are on rota to sit as Judge in Chambers.

Unless the time is extended by the judge, the notice of appeal, whether against the whole or part only of the Master's order, must be given and entered so as to come on for hearing within five days from the date of the order. It is the duty of the party who has given notice of appeal to serve it on his opponent, and he is responsible for seeing that all the affidavits that were before the Master when he made the order are before the Judge in Chambers. It is uncertain how far the recent rule that a Master can now reverse his own order is going to affect appeals to the Judge in Chambers. It may in due course become clear whether a dissatisfied party should now ask the Master to revise his order made under the Summons for Directions or whether notice of appeal to the Judge in Chambers should be served.

Notice of appeal.

When the appeal comes on for hearing by the Judge in Chambers, he may either dismiss the appeal, allow the appeal, or make such order as is necessary. Usually an appeal lies to the Court of Appeal with the leave of the

Judge in Chambers, or if he refuses it with the leave of the Court of Appeal granted on an application made to it for that purpose ; where the judge grants the defendant unconditional leave to defend on a summons for summary judgment (see p. 89, *post*), the plaintiff is not allowed to appeal to the Court of Appeal. If, however, the judge refuses to make an order giving the defendant unconditional leave to defend, the defendant can then appeal to the Court of Appeal without leave.

Appeal from
Judge in
Chambers.

SETTING DOWN FOR TRIAL. When the pleadings are closed and the place and mode of trial determined, the action may be entered for trial. This is primarily the duty of the plaintiff ; for it is to be supposed, since he began the action, that he is anxious to have it tried. If the plaintiff neglects to set it down the defendant may do so or apply to have the action dismissed for want of prosecution. No notice of trial need be given in an action which the Court has ordered to be set down for trial on a specified date ; in other cases ten days' notice of trial must be given before the action can be entered in the list and come on for hearing. The latter is the more usual procedure. If the action is to be heard in London it is set down for trial at the Crown Office Department. To enable this to be done copies of the writ and pleadings, including particulars, and further and better particulars (if any) are stitched into a bundle, and two of such bundles, one stamped with an impressed stamp of £2, are duly lodged and upon production of the original order for directions it is entered by the Crown Office Department in the appropriate list for trial. If the action is ordered to be tried at the Assizes, the original order for directions is produced to the Associate of the Circuit (p. 30) and the pleadings are left with him. The stamped copy of the pleadings is for the Court records, the unstamped copy is for the use of the judge at the trial. When the action is thus set down it takes its place in the list of actions to be tried and as the actions before it are disposed of, so the day of trial will draw near. If the matter is to be disposed of at Assizes it will come on at the next Assize unless that be due to begin within seven days. During this time the parties

Notice of
trial.

have to " prepare " for trial.   This consists of two courses Preparation
for trial.
of preparation :

   (*a*) collecting and arranging the material in the party's
       own knowledge and possession,

   (*b*) obtaining from the opponent such information as
       the law allows.

It is with the latter that we are now concerned, though
both are equally important in order to secure the success
of an action.

Within certain limits, a litigant is allowed, before the Discovery of
documents
and facts.
trial, to see certain documents which are within the pos-
session or power of his opponent, and to find out certain
facts which are within his opponent's knowledge.   The
former of these objects is obtained by " Discovery of
Documents " ; the latter " Discovery of Facts."

DISCOVERY OF DOCUMENTS. If any document is Rights of a
party with
regard to
documents.
referred to by a party in any of his pleadings, or in any
affidavit or answers to interrogatories sworn by him or on
his behalf, it must, as a rule, on notice being given, be
produced for the inspection of the other party giving the
notice.   But, in addition to this limited right of *discovery*
each party is usually entitled to general inspection of all
documents in the possession or power of his opponent
which relate to any of the matters in question in the
action.

Mode of Discovery. Application for general discovery Affidavit of
documents.
of documents is usually made on the summons for direc-
tions ; and, in a suitable case, an order is made by the
Master directing each party to make discovery on oath.
In order to save the expense of affidavits the Master will,
if the parties agree, order a " list of documents."   The
parties usually consent if it is believed that they are likely
to be as frank in disclosing their documents in an unsworn
list as they would be if the list was on oath in the form of an
affidavit.   Discovery is made by an affidavit or list of
documents, in which the party sets out in two schedules
to the affidavit or list three lists of documents.   The first
schedule is divided into two parts, the first part containing a description of all the material documents in his

possession or power which the party is willing to produce, and the second part containing those documents which he objects to producing.

In the second schedule are set out those documents which the party once had, but no longer has, in his possession. If discovery is by list, the three lists contain the same three classes of documents.

The grounds of objection to produce the documents described in the second part of the first schedule must be stated in the body of the affidavit. It must clearly be understood that all material documents must be enumerated in the schedules to this affidavit ; even though the party making the affidavit may object on proper grounds to produce some of them. The validity of his objection is for the Court to determine.

Privileged documents.

The following classes of documents are usually privileged from inspection :

1. Written communications passing between the party and his solicitor or other legal professional adviser in his professional capacity, or between his solicitor and counsel, for the purpose of legal assistance, whether litigation is pending or not.

2. Documents which have been prepared solely for the purpose of litigation, such as proofs of witnesses, instructions to counsel, briefs, or written statements prepared by any servant or agent of the party for the use or assisance of the solicitor in advising in the conduct of existing or contemplated litigation (not necessarily *the* litigation in which the question of privilege has arisen).

3. Documents of title to any property, if they contain nothing which can assist in establishing the alleged title of the opponent.

4. Documents not in the sole possession of the party or held by him on behalf of some other person, for instance, as agent or trustee.

5. Documents which would tend to incriminate the party producing them.

6. Documents the production of which is contrary to public policy or detrimental to the public service.

The validity of the claim of privilege is usually decided upon the application of the other party to a Master for an order compelling his opponent to produce the documents in his possession or power.

The affidavit of documents, if drawn up in proper form, is *prima facie* evidence that the party making it has no other relevant documents in his possession ; but the other party, if dissatisfied with it, has two courses open to him. First, he should write to his opponent and request him to disclose certain documents which are referred to in the documents disclosed, or in the pleadings, as being or having been in his possession ; if he fails to comply with this request, application should be made to the Master under the power given in the summons for direction, commonly known as " liberty to apply," for an order and, if successful, the party succeeding will usually be awarded the costs of the application in any event. Secondly, he should write a letter stating that in his belief the other party has, or has had, in his possession, custody, or power, certain particular and relevant documents or classes of documents, which he must specify or indicate, and in default of satisfaction he should swear an affidavit of the facts and apply to the Master, who must make an order and the party against whom the order has been made must then deal with the allegations in the order, and if the documents or some of them are in existence, he must file a further and better affidavit and disclose and state where they are, or if they do not now exist, he must state this information in his affidavit and disclose what has become of them, and if the documents never existed he must swear to this effect in the affidavit.

Option of party who is dissatisfied with opponent's affidavit.

After making an affidavit, the deponent must give the other party inspection of those documents the possession and relevancy of which he has admitted, and for which he has not claimed privilege ; and must give or allow copies to be made of any of the documents so inspected upon payment of the usual charges for this purpose. It must be pointed out that the provisions for further discovery previously indicated only apply when discovery is made on affidavit of documents and not when lists are exchanged. If a party does not make complete disclosure in his list of documents, all the Court can do is to order that the party in default should make discovery on

Inspection of documents.

an affidavit of documents, because until this has been done the Court cannot deal with the matter. This is the distinction between discovery on lists of documents and discovery on affidavits of documents.

Discovery of documents against the Crown. As a result of the Crown Proceedings Act, 1947, the Court can now make an order for discovery of documents against the Crown. Production or indeed disclosure, however, can be prevented if the Minister of the Crown swears that either the disclosure of the existence of the document or production of the document would be injurious to the public interest. Once the Minister of the Crown has sworn the affidavit it is final and conclusive and the Court is powerless to inquire further into the matter or to enforce the disclosure of the existence of the document, or to order its production.

Production of original. *Proof at Trial.* As a general rule, the contents of a private document can only be proved at the trial by production of the original. A party, therefore, who intends to rely on a document in the possession of his opponent, must serve him before the trial with a notice to produce it. **Secondary evidence.** If at the trial the party refuses to produce a document which he has had notice to produce, the party relying on the document is allowed to prove its contents by what is called secondary evidence—that is, by means of a copy, or even by oral testimony. This notice to produce documents at the trial must not be confused with the notice to produce documents referred to in your opponent's pleadings or affidavits.

If the original of the document is in the possession of the party relying on it, not only should it be referred to in his affidavit of documents, but notice to inspect and admit it ought to be given to his opponent before the trial. If a notice to admit documents is served by a party on his opponent and no notice of non-admission is served on the party serving the notice to admit, the effect of the failure to serve the counter-notice is that the documents referred to in the notice to admit will be deemed to be admitted unless the Court shall otherwise order. If a party does not admit (within reason) he may have to pay the costs of proving the document at the trial. If the document relied on is in the possession of a stranger to the action, who is within the jurisdiction, he should be served with a *subpœna duces tecum*, summoning him to attend at the trial and produce the document.

INTERROGATORIES. Where a party to the proceedings wishes to ascertain, before the hearing of the action, whether certain facts exist, which are within the knowledge of his opponent, and which he would not be able to prove himself or by his witnesses at the hearing, interrogatories may be ordered by the Court in order to clarify the position. Interrogatories are questions in writing to be answered in writing on oath, that is to say by affidavit, by the opposite party, to the best of the knowledge, information, and belief of the party swearing the affidavit. Leave to administer interrogatories must be obtained from the Master, upon the summons for directions or on notice under the summons ; and a copy of the proposed interrogatories must be supplied to the other side, and another submitted to the Master, so that, on the application for leave, any objections to them may be dealt with. *(Discovery of facts.)*

The object of interrogatories is to obtain information on material facts which are within the knowledge of the opposite party and not of the party interrogating, or to obtain admissions which will save the expense of calling witnesses, or to ascertain with greater precision the case which the other side intends to set up at the trial.

The Master, in deciding whether to allow the particular interrogatories proposed, will consider whether their object can, more conveniently or at less expense, be attained by other means ; and he will take into account any offer made by the opposite side to deliver particulars, or make admissions, or produce documents relating to the subject matter of the interrogatories.

Objection to Interrogatories. The party interrogated may object to interrogatories on a variety of grounds, some of which are similar to those already mentioned in connection with the production of documents for inspection. The objections most frequently made are, that the particular question objected to is directed to facts which are not relevant to the matters in issue, or is oppressive *(Grounds of objection.)*

or vexatious, or is " fishing," *i.e.*, is put with reference to facts which may possibly have occurred but are not definitely alleged, on the chance of discovering something which may assist the party interrogating to make out some case against his opponent.   It is also an objection that the question seeks to discover not merely facts, but the evidence by which they are intended to be proved.

Evasive
answers. *Further and better answers.*   If interrogatories are allowed, and are insufficiently or evasively answered, the party interrogating may, on application to the Master, obtain an order for " further and better answers," or even for a *viva voce* examination.   At the trial, the party by whom the interrogatories have been administered, may put in all or any of the answers as evidence, or rely on them for purposes of cross-examination ; but, if he relies on part of an answer, he must usually put in the whole of it.

Section IV. Advice on Evidence

The next step in the proceedings is to obtain advice on evidence.   Advice on evidence is given by the junior counsel concerned in the case, who also will have drawn all the pleadings, and, except in special circumstances, have been solely responsible in all the interlocutory matters.   The procedure, which entails in this case no application whatever to the Court, is for the solicitor concerned to set out in writing what evidence and documents are available, supplying counsel with all the documents. These documents will be the correspondence and other documents in the client's possession and copies of documents in the possession of the opponents that have been disclosed on discovery by them.   Counsel will usually advise which of the documents before him ought to be copied and delivered with the brief, and counsel will also advise which of the documents ought to be copied for the use of the judge at the trial in order to keep down to a minimum the costs for making unnecessary copies. " Proofs " of witnesses intended to be called, that is to say statements of the evidence each witness is prepared to give, and copies of all pleadings, opinions, and interlocutory orders should also be supplied to counsel.

Counsel's duty is to consider these carefully and advise whether the evidence thus disclosed is sufficient and what further evidence, if any, it is necessary to obtain. It is the duty of the plaintiff's solicitor to provide the Court with copies of all the necessary documents that are common to both parties, *i.e.*, the documents disclosed in the affidavits of documents by both parties which counsel has advised should be copied. The usual procedure is that the respective solicitors meet at the office of the plaintiff's solicitors and " agree " a bundle for use of the judge, and they further agree as to the page numbering of it. This enables counsel for both parties and the judge to have bundles of documents that are paged in the same order, a course that assists in the smooth running of an action. Careful attention to this stage of the preparation of an action is very essential, as the duties of both solicitor and counsel during the actual trial require great concentration and alertness, and the dislocation caused by a sudden necessity of summoning an additional witness or securing an additional document is apt to throw the whole presentation of the client's case into confusion. If a leading counsel is briefed at the trial, a copy of the advice on evidence given by the junior counsel should be supplied to the leading counsel with his brief. This will assist him when reading his brief and papers to decide what evidence is required to deal with the issues raised in the pleadings.

To enforce an unwilling witness to attend, a subpœna Witnesses. is issued. This is the King's command to his subject to attend Court, either to give evidence as a witness or to produce documents. If the subpœna is to attend Court and give evidence, it is known as a *subpœna ad testificandum* or a " *subpœna ad test.*" If the subpœna is to attend Court to produce documents, it is known as a *subpœna duces tecum*. A person duly served with a subpœna, if paid sufficient money to bring him from his house to the Court (this is called " conduct money ") and not attending, may be either fined or committed to prison for contempt of Court and, moreover, he may be liable to an action for damages at the suit of the party who issued the subpœna.

Section V. TRIAL

Jury sworn.

THE HEARING. We now pass to the trial or hearing of the action. If the action is to be tried with a jury, the jurors are called and sworn. But before they are sworn, they are liable to be " challenged " (or objected to) by either party on a variety of grounds, though in civil cases the right of " challenge " is not often exercised, and when exercised it is limited to objecting to individual jurors on suspicion of bias or partiality.

Case opened for plaintiff.

The plaintiff has, as a rule, the right to begin ; because on him usually lies the burden of proving at least one of the facts which are necessary to entitle him to the relief claimed and are not admitted in the defence, *e.g.*, the amount of unascertained damages claimed. Accordingly, when the jury is ready, the pleadings are opened, by the junior counsel for the plaintiff, with a brief statement of their effect ; and then the case is opened, usually by the plaintiff's leading counsel, with a statement of the facts relied on and the evidence intended to be produced in their support, and an explanation of the issues to be decided.

Case opened for defendant.

After the opening statement is finished, the evidence for the plaintiff is given. When this has been done, the case is opened on behalf of the defendant. If evidence is produced in support of the defence, his counsel is entitled to sum it up. The plaintiff's counsel, if he began, is then heard by way of reply ; but no reply is allowed, except on behalf of the Crown, unless witnesses have been called or documents put in for the defence. If the defendant does not call any witnesses or put in any documents, counsel for the plaintiff sums up his evidence at the close of the plaintiff's case ; and then counsel for the defendant replies.

Summing up by counsel, and reply.

The procedure for the giving of evidence and the three examinations which every witness is liable to undergo are described in Chapter 10, *post*.

No mention must be made of the fact that money has been paid into Court ; and no facts must be stated by counsel which are not admitted or intended to be proved.

Judgment or verdict.

After the speeches of counsel, the judge, if the action is tried without a jury, delivers *Judgment* ; and if the action is tried with a jury, he sums up the case to them, and the jury then considers its *Verdict*. The general rule in England is that the jury must give a unanimous verdict, thus differing from the Scottish and Continental practice. If the jurors cannot all agree on the verdict, they are discharged ; and then a second trial before a fresh jury will be necessary, unless the parties consent to accept the verdict of a majority.

In every witness action an official shorthand note is now taken for the benefit of the judge if he desires a transcript, and also for the use of the Court of Appeal, if the case eventually go there. Shorthand note.

Normally, the evidence must be given in English, unless the judge is satisfied that the witness does not understand English, in which circumstances an interpreter can be secured and the witness can give the evidence in his native language. In regard to the use of the Welsh language doubts existed whether it was legal to use the Welsh language in Courts in Wales, but these doubts have now been removed. The Welsh Court Act, 1942, enacted that any party or witness, although he understands English, may give his evidence in Welsh, if he considers that he would be at any disadvantage in a Court in Wales, if he were not allowed to use the Welsh language. This right, however, does not extend to a Welshman giving evidence in a Court in England. Courts in Wales.

The Associate must number every document handed in in evidence and must mark the same with a distinctive number and sign, to show whether the same was put into evidence by the plaintiff or by the defendant. At the conclusion of the trial the exhibits are handed back to the parties and in the event of an appeal they must be produced to the Court of Appeal. An office copy of the list of exhibits must be obtained from the Associate and produced to the Court of Appeal. The original certificate of the exhibits is attached to and forms part of the pleadings, which are later filed on entering judgment (see p. 75, *post*). Exhibits.

The judge may leave the jury to return a *general verdict* for the plaintiff or for the defendant ; or he may direct a *special verdict*, by putting to the jury certain questions to General and special verdicts.

answer.   In the latter case, he afterwards decides what is
the legal result of the answers.   When the damages
claimed are unliquidated, they are assessed by the jury.
The judge then gives *Judgment* according to the findings
of the jury, and decides all questions with regard to costs.

Where an
appeal
is desired.

Stay of execution after trial.   If the unsuccessful
party desires to appeal, an application may be made for a
stay of execution, *i.e.*, for an order that the judgment given
against him shall not be enforced by seizure of his goods
or other compulsory means.   If this application is granted,
it is usually granted on the terms of payment of any damages awarded into Court or occasionally to the plaintiff,
and of notice of appeal being given within a fixed time,
and, as regards costs, that they be taxed and paid to the

Stay of
execution.

successful party's solicitor, on his understanding to return
them, if so ordered by the Court of Appeal.   But the
Court's discretion as to the terms upon which it will grant
the stay are not fettered by any fixed rules.

Unless a stay of execution is granted either by the Court
of Trial or the Court of Appeal the judgment can be executed forthwith, and the serving of a notice of appeal
does not of itself operate as stay of execution of the judgment.   This rule applies to any order or judgment,
whether interlocutory or final, and therefore a party
desirous of appealing against a judgment on which execution can be levied should always apply for a stay of
execution.

COSTS.   The costs of the action are in the discretion of
the judge (Judicature Act, 1925, s. 50, Ord. LXV, r. 1).
The principle is stated in the speech of Viscount Cave,
L.C., in *Donald Campbell & Co.* v. *Pollak*, [1927] A. C. 732,
at p. 811.

" A successful defendant in a non-jury case has no doubt,
in the absence of special circumstances, a reasonable expectation of obtaining an order for the payment of his costs
by the plaintiff ; but he has no right to costs unless and
until the Court awards them to him, and the Court has
an absolute and unfettered discretion to award or not to
award them.   This discretion, like any other discretion,
must of course be exercised judicially, and the Judge ought
not to exercise it against the successful party except for some
reason connected with the case.
Thus, if—to put a hypothesis which in our Courts would

never in fact be realised—a judge were to refuse to give a party his costs on the ground of some misconduct wholly unconnected with the cause of action or of some prejudice due to his race or religion or (to quote a familiar illustration) to the colour of his hair, then a Court of Appeal might well feel itself compelled to intervene. But when a judge, deliberately intending to exercise his discretionary powers, has acted on facts connected with or leading up to the litigation which have been proved before him or which he has himself observed during the progress of the case, then it seems to me that a Court of Appeal, although it may deem his reasons insufficient and may disagree with his conclusion, is prohibited by the statute (the Judicature Acts) from entertaining an appeal from it."

The same principle applies to actions tried with a jury.

If the action is of the kind which could have been brought in a County Court, then, unless the judge certifies that there was sufficient reason for bringing it in the High Court, or that the defendant objected to the transfer of the action to a County Court, the plaintiff, though successful, will be entitled to no costs, or to costs only on the County Court scale, according to the nature of the action and the amount recovered.

ENTERING JUDGMENT. The Court having directed judgment to be entered, the successful party now takes the next and all subsequent steps to convert the judge's direction into an Order of the Court. To enable this to be done the successful party obtains from the Associate a certificate as to the Court's directions, the original copy of the pleadings, stamped £2, endorsed with the actual periods occupied in the hearing of case, and the list of exhibits. He then draws up the judgment in accordance with the Associate's certificate.

It depends on the actual length of the trial what Court fees are to be paid on the signing of the judgment. If the case lasts over five hours, which does not include the time occupied in adjournments, an additional fee for every hour or part thereof over five hours is payable.

The Associate's certificate, together with the stamped copy of the judgment and the pleadings, is filed at the Central Office, and the other copy of the judgment is handed back duly sealed by the Court to the successful party.

During the nineteenth century solicitors were rather

neglectful with regard to filing the pleadings when drawing up the judgment ; at one time inducements were held out to persuade them to do so, but without result. To overcome the problem, the rules were altered to provide that no judgment was in fact to be sealed unless the pleadings had been filed, and a note of this was endorsed on the judgment.

A copy of the judgment as sealed by the Court is served on the losing side.

It is important that the date shown in the seal should appear on the copy of the judgment which is served. The time for appealing against the judgment runs from the date when the judgment was sealed and not from the date when the judge pronounced his findings in Court, and directed judgment to be entered in accordance with his findings.

Section VI. TAXATION OF COSTS

Party and party costs.

The order almost always directs that the costs shall be taxed. Within seven days of the sealing of the judgment the successful party must obtain " a reference for taxation," *i.e.*, he must get the matter allotted to one of the Taxing Masters to tax the costs. When a Master has been assigned from the rota the successful party must lodge at the Chambers of the Taxing Master a copy of the judgment and a statement of the parties to the action and produce the office copy judgment. If this step is not taken within the time before mentioned, then unless he has good cause to show for the omission, he may be penalised by certain costs not being allowed, and he may also be penalised if he omits to leave the bill of costs and all documents referred to therein within the time directed by the Master's clerk. The solicitor for the party who has obtained an order for costs, then delivers his bill at the Master's Chambers and the bill is then provisionally taxed by one of the clerks in the absence of the parties, and items which are obviously improperly charged in the bill are taxed off. The bill as provisionally taxed is returned to the successful party and notices of taxation are sent to the parties. The party lodging the bill sends a copy thereof as provisionally taxed to his opponent. This bill is then taxed by a Master, or in certain cases by his chief clerk, who, after hearing the objections of the other party, disallows or reduces such items as he considers unreasonable or excessive. Either party can carry an objection in writing to the Master's taxation. The Master then considers the specific matters raised in the objections and gives his reasons in writing. If the party is dissatisfied with the Master's decision on a matter of principle he can issue a summons before the judge to review the Master's certificate, but if the dissatisfaction is one that goes to a question of quantum, *i.e.*, the Master has not awarded a sufficient sum for instructions for brief, the Master's decision, after he has given his answers to the objection, is final. When the bill has been finally taxed an appointment is taken to " vouch the bill." Vouchers for counsel's fees paid and all other disbursements must be produced before the Master certifies the amount due. The certificate of the Master fixing the total amount of the costs is called the " allocatur." The costs so taxed are known as *costs as between party and party*. As a rule, the amount allowed on taxation is all that can be recovered by the successful party ; and he has to pay his own solicitor the extra costs disallowed on taxation, in so far as they are reasonable and proper charges as between himself and the solicitor, or *costs as between solicitor and client*, as they are called. The judge cannot (in matters usually dealt with in the King's Bench Division) award that costs to be taxed as between the solicitor and client shall be paid by the other side, unless there is an express statutory provision enabling him to do so. The parties may agree as a term of a settlement that the costs are to be taxed as between solicitor and *own* client—which includes items for work done which are not covered by a taxation of costs on a solicitor and client basis. The Taxing Master's certificate is then filed, and the amount so certified is entered on the judgment.

Solicitor and client costs.

Section VII. Execution

Execution is the process by which a judgment is enforced. There are many modes of execution ; but the following are those usually adopted to enforce a judgment for the payment of money. Before execution can be issued for the payment of a sum of money the following conditions must be complied with. First, there must be a judgment or order directing the party in default to pay a sum of money ; secondly, the sum of money must be certain, *e.g.*, costs that have already been taxed ; thirdly, the sum must be due. In the absence of special circumstances to the contrary the money is payable forthwith ; and lastly, execution on the judgment or order must not have been stayed, as until the stay of execution has been removed the Court will not allow the judgment or order to be enforced.

Execution against goods. 1. *Writ of fieri facias.* This is the most common form of execution ; and it is directed against the goods and chattels of the judgment debtor. The writ (commonly called a writ of *fi. fa.*) is issued by the judgments department if the proceedings are in London, or by the District Registry if the proceedings are pending in the Registry. It is addressed to the sheriff, and authorises him to seize and sell sufficient of the goods and chattels of the judgment debtor, to satisfy the amount of the judgment together with interest at the rate of four per cent. The writ when issued is sent to the under-sheriff of the county where the judgment debtor's goods are to be found ; and the under-sheriff, after noting on the writ the time when he receives it, issues his warrant to his officer in the debtor's district. The reason why the time is noted is that all goods of the debtor at the moment the sheriff receives the writ are liable to be taken in execution. If the writ is handed to the deputy-sheriff in London he does not time the writ, but sends it to the under-sheriff, who times the writ when he receives it. The officer, who is usually an auctioneer, makes the seizure. He must seize the chattels of the judgment debtor only. It is also necessary to impound, *i.e.*, take the goods into the custody of the law. Seizing and impounding are essential formalities. Touching a chair as representing all the furniture in a room is sufficient. The goods can now be impounded on the premises although the judgment debtor has the right to have them removed to a public auction room for sale.

If the goods are not properly seized and impounded the sheriff's deputy cannot validly sell them, and a purchaser gets no title to the goods. Under this writ, the sheriff may sell a lease belonging to the debtor, or his growing crops, but not any freehold interest, nor fixtures, nor any equitable interest in land or goods, unless (at any rate in the case of goods) the whole beneficial interest is vested in the judgment debtor. The sheriff may also take under a writ of *fi. fa.* any money, bank-notes, bills of exchange, or other securities for money, belonging to the judgment debtor, and may sue upon them in his own name, and pay over to the judgment creditor the money which he recovers. The wearing apparel and bedding of the judgment debtor or his family, and the tools and implements of the debtor's trade, are exempted from seizure up to a total value of five pounds.

If the officer executing the warrant seizes goods of a third party, *i.e.*, goods that do not belong to the judgment debtor, the third party may claim the goods from the sheriff. If the claim is admitted by the judgment creditor the sheriff releases the goods of the third party ; if not, the sheriff usually seeks the protection of the Court by taking out an *Interpleader Summons* (Ord. LVII), which is served on both the claimant and the execution creditor, and calls on them to appear in chambers and state the nature and particulars of their claims, and either to maintain or abandon them. On the hearing of this summons, the Master may (amongst other courses open to him) dispose of the merits of the rival claims to the goods, and decide them in a summary manner, or direct an issue to be tried between the claimant and the execution creditor, for the purpose of determining which of them is entitled to the goods, or, in certain cases, transfer the proceedings to a County Court. *[margin: Sheriff's interpleader.]*

The same Order (LVII) regulated another kind of interpleader commonly called " Stakeholder's Interpleader," to distinguish it from the Sheriff's Interpleader already discussed. A " stakeholder " is a person who is " under liability to any debt, money, goods, or chattels," and from whom the debt, money, goods or chattels are being claimed by two or more adverse claimants. For example *[margin: Stakeholder's interpleader.]*

A has a wireless set on loan from B. C informs A that
it is C's property and demands its return. B claims
the wireless set as his property and demands its return.
A the stakeholder, as he is called, claims no interest in the
subject matter of the dispute (other than charges or costs),
and merely wants to be told who the person is who is
lawfully entitled to recover the wireless set. Accordingly,
under this order he may take out an interpleader summons, but unlike the sheriff he has to swear an affidavit of
the facts. On the hearing of the summons any action
which may have been begun against him will be stopped ;
and the adverse claimants B and C will be directed to
fight out the issue between themselves.

Execution against land.   2. *Writ of elegit.* Under this writ the sheriff can
deliver to the judgment creditor all land, including lease-
holds, legally in the possession of the judgment debtor,
or held solely in trust for him under a bare trust, to hold
until the judgment is satisfied. Thereupon the judgment
creditor becomes *tenant by elegit* for a period long enough
to enable the debt and costs to be paid off. He can, if he
wishes, by taking appropriate steps, obtain possession of
the land ; or he may, after a writ or order for enforcing
the judgment has been registered, apply, by originating
summons in chambers in the Chancery Division, for
an order for the sale of the debtor's interest in the
land.

Attachment of debts due to judgment debtor.   3. *Garnishee Order.* Debts " owing or accruing " to
the judgment debtor cannot be seized under a writ of
fieri facias ; but they may be attached by means of
garnishee proceedings. The judgment creditor may
obtain, on *ex parte* application to the Master in Chambers,
supported by an affidavit of the facts, an order that any
debt owing from any person within the jurisdiction who
is indebted to the judgment debtor, and who is called
the *garnishee*, be attached to answer the judgment,
together with the costs of the garnishee proceedings, and
that the garnishee appear in Chambers and show cause
why he should not pay to the judgment creditor the
debt due from him to the judgment debtor. This order
(called a " garnishee order *nisi* ") must be served on the
garnishee, and also on the judgment debtor. As soon as

it is served, it binds the debt in the hands of the garnishee; and he must not pay his debt to the judgment debtor.

If the garnishee admits his liability, he may pay the debt into Court or wait until the order is made absolute and pay the judgment creditor in pursuance thereof ; but it is not safe for him to pay the judgment creditor until the order *nisi* has been made absolute. If he disputes his liability he should appear, for if he does not appear the order may be made absolute in his absence and execution may be issued against him to enforce it. If the garnishee appears, the Master may direct an issue to be tried between him and the judgment creditor ; and if that issue be decided in favour of the garnishee the order will be discharged, if in favour of the creditor, it will be made absolute. Payment by a garnishee into Court after service of the order *nisi*, or to the judgment creditor when the order has been made absolute, is a valid discharge of his debt to the judgment debtor. It is perhaps interesting to note that the word " garnish " comes from the same root as the word " warn." A garnishee is therefore a person warned to pay his debt to the judgment creditor.

4. *Charging order*. On the application of the judg- ment creditor to the Master, an order may be made charg- ing stock or shares belonging to the judgment debtor with payment of the amount of the judgment debt. The order must be served on the company, bank, or corporate body, whose stock or shares are charged ; and its effect is to prevent the judgment debtor from transferring such stock or shares until the order is discharged. The creditor may bring a separate action in the Chancery Division to obtain an order for the sale of the stock or shares comprised in the charging order.

Charge on stock or shares.

5. *Receiver*. In cases where the debtor has an equit- able interest in land or other property, which cannot be taken in execution by any of the modes above mentioned, but which is properly available for payment of his debts, an order may be obtained appointing a receiver to receive the debtor's interest in the property and so make it avail- able for satisfaction of the judgment. This is commonly called " equitable execution."

Equitable execution.

Judgment for recovery of land.

6. *Possession of land.* A judgment for the recovery of land is enforced by a *writ of possession* by which the sheriff is ordered to enter on the land, and cause the person named in the writ to have possession of it without delay. This form of execution applies where an action for the recovery of land has been brought and it must not be confused with the seizure of land under a writ of *elegit* already described, which is a means of satisfying a judgment for the payment of a sum of money. Before a writ of possession can be issued it is necessary to obtain leave from the Court to proceed on the judgment for possession. Before the Court will give leave it must be shown to the Court that all persons in actual possession of the whole or any part of the land of which possession is sought by virtue of the judgment have received such notice of the proceedings as may be considered sufficient to enable them to apply to the Court for relief or otherwise. This application is made *ex parte* to the Court by the plaintiff, who swears an affidavit in support of the application.

Judgment for recovery of chattel.

7. *Possession of chattel.* A judgment for the recovery of a chattel may be enforced by a *writ of delivery*, by which the sheriff is ordered to distrain the defendant by all his lands and chattels, till he delivers the particular chattel. If it is intended that the defendant should have the option either of restoring the chattel or paying its value, the plaintiff applies for a writ of delivery ; if the plaintiff seeks to recover the particular chattel detained without giving the defendant that option, he applies for a writ of delivery *absolute*, and, if the defendant still refuses to deliver, a *writ of assistance* may be obtained to enable the sheriff to seize the chattel.

Imprisonment.

8. *Attachment and committal.* This is the remedy for contempt of Court by disobedience to its order. A judgment or order directing the defendant to do some specific act other than to pay money, or to abstain from doing some act, may be enforced by a writ of attachment or order of committal. In these cases the defendant is sent to prison until he " purges his contempt," by making an apology and satisfying the Court that he is prepared to obey its orders. It is a condition precedent to obtaining a writ of attachment or a committal that the party in

default should be served with a copy of the order endorsed with a notice addressed to him by name stating that if he fails to obey the order he may be liable to attachment for contempt of Court.

9. *Sequestration.* A judgment or order to pay money into Court, or to do any other act within a limited time, may also be enforced by a writ of sequestration against the rents and profits of any real estate, and against all the personal estate, of the person who disobeys the order. This is an additional remedy for contempt. The writ is directed to persons called sequestrators, and authorises them to enter on the lands of the disobedient person and receive the rents and profits, and to take possession of his personal property until he obeys the order ; and, by leave of the Court, the sequestrators may sell the personal property, and pay the proceeds into Court, to be dealt with as the Court may direct.

Seizure of rents and profits, and personalty.

10. *Bankruptcy.* Whilst bankruptcy is not strictly a form of execution, yet it is a popular method employed by creditors to obtain the fruits of their judgment by serving on the debtor a bankruptcy notice. This, if he neglects to comply with it within the time specified in the notice, is usually followed by a petition to the Court requesting the Court to make a receiving order, whereby the official receiver is constituted receiver of the property of the debtor, who must when the debtor has been adjudicated bankrupt hand the same over to the bankrupt's trustee in bankruptcy. For a fuller discussion, see Chapter 12 of this Book, *post*, p. 189.

Bankruptcy notice.

Section VIII. Appeal

An appeal, or application for a new trial or to set aside a verdict, finding, or judgment, lies to the Court of Appeal from every final judgment of the King's Bench Division, whether the trial was with or without a jury. The appeal or application in all cases is by notice of motion, which must state whether the whole or part only, and, if part only, what part of the verdict, finding, or judgment, is complained of.

Notice of motion.

Where the trial was with a jury, the notice of appeal must also state the grounds of the application ; but where the trial was without a jury it is not necessary to ask specifically for a new trial, or to state the grounds of the appeal. The notice of motion in the case of a final judgment is a fourteen days' notice, and must be served within six weeks from the trial, or, where the trial has been adjourned for further consideration, within forty-two days from the date when the judgment was entered and sealed, notwithstanding the fact that the judge might have delivered judgment many days earlier. During the long vacation time does not run. The Court of Appeal has power to extend the time for appealing beyond six weeks.

Grounds for application. *Application for new trial.* The grounds for the application for a new trial are generally one or more of the following :

1. That the judge misdirected the jury.
2. That the verdict was against the weight of the evidence, that is to say, that the verdict was perverse, and such that no reasonable men could on the evidence have found.
3. That there was no evidence to go to the jury, that is, that the evidence was insufficient to make out a *prima facie* case for the party tendering it, and should not have been left by the judge to the jury.
4. That the conduct of the jury or their verdict was irregular for any reason, such as that they tossed up a coin or drew lots to relieve them of their duty to form a decision.
5. That the damages are excessive or inadequate, that is to say, so large that no reasonable men could have given them, or so small that the jury must have left entirely out of consideration some substantial element of damage, or made some mistake in calculating the figures.
6. That the judge wrongly admitted or rejected material evidence.
7. That a substantially wrong verdict was given owing to one of the parties being taken by surprise.
8. That fresh and conclusive evidence has been discovered since the trial, which could not reasonably have been discovered before it.

Where the action was tried by a judge alone and an appeal is brought to reverse or vary his judgment the foregoing grounds, if proved, or one of them, so far as they are applicable to an action tried by a judge alone, are sufficient either to reverse the judgment or for the Court of Appeal to order a new trial.

But there can be no direct appeal from the verdict of a jury, in respect either of the finding of fact or of the amount awarded as damages.

The appeal or application for a new trial must be heard by not less than three judges, except by consent of the parties. The Court of Appeal has all the powers and jurisdiction of the High Court, and can give any judgment or make any order which ought to have been given or made in the Court below. It has full discretion over the costs of the appeal ; but, as a rule, the costs follow the event. If a new trial is ordered, the costs of the first trial generally abide the order made on the second as to costs, but the costs of the appeal usually go to the successful appellant in any event. If the judgment of the Court below is reversed, the appellant usually gets the costs of the action. The appellant's solicitor must leave with the Clerks to the Lords Justices three bundles of all the necessary documents which were used by the judge of first instance, together with the documents that have come into existence since the trial and three indices of the documents that are so left. Omission to do this may have serious consequences to the appellant's solicitor, because if the appeal comes on before the Court for hearing and these documents have not been lodged within a reasonable time before the hearing of the appeal, the hearing of the appeal may be postponed and the appellant's solicitor may be ordered to pay the costs of the adjournment personally. *(Powers of Court.)*

When the appeal is concluded, the successful party attends at the Crown Office and obtains the order, and if the order gives him costs, he proceeds to tax them as before described.

An appeal lies from the Court of Appeal to the House of Lords, by leave of the Court of Appeal. If the Court of Appeal refuses leave to appeal an application must be made to the Appeal Committee of the House of Lords. *(Appeal to House of Lords.)*

The Court of Appeal or the Appeal Committee of the House of Lords sometimes impose terms on the proposed appellant before granting him leave to appeal to the House of Lords, *e.g.*, when the proposed appellant is very wealthy and the successful litigant in the Court of Appeal might be seriously embarrassed by the costs of an appeal to the House of Lords. Leave in those circumstances is usually granted on the terms that the proposed appellant should pay the costs of the appeal to the House of Lords whatever may be the result of the appeal. The appeal, if leave is granted, is brought by way of petition. The appellant, unless suing *in forma pauperis*, is required to give security or to pay to the account of the Security Fund Account of the House of Lords the sum of £200 as security for the costs of the appeal. The appellant and the respondent each lodge a printed " case " setting out shortly the nature and main facts of the dispute, and the proceedings in the Courts below, summarising the judgments, and stating reasons why the judgment of the Court of Appeal should be reversed or affirmed.

(margin: Security of costs.)

(margin: Lodgment of " case.")

The cases are bound in a volume, together with an appendix, which contains the pleadings, the documents put in at the trial, the judgments delivered, and the orders or decrees made in the Court below. The appeal must be brought within six months from the delivery of the judgment appealed from. On the hearing of the appeal, each of the parties is entitled to speeches by two counsel ; and the appellant's counsel is also entitled to be heard in reply. The House of Lords may dismiss or allow the appeal, or vary the judgment appealed from ; and it has full power to deal with the costs of the appeal, and of the proceedings in the Courts below.

(margin: Hearing of appeal.)

Until 1947 an appellant or respondent suing or defending *in forma pauperis* was described in the title of the suit, as " Jones a pauper." An order has now been made that the expression " pauper " is now never to be used to describe a party to an appeal to the House of Lords.

Section IX. SPECIALLY INDORSED WRIT

The procedure above described is applicable in general to actions commenced by a writ *generally* indorsed. A writ may, however, be *specially* indorsed. We have not burdened the student by giving frequent references to the Rules of Court ; but the Rules applicable to the procedure connected with special indorsements have become such household words in the profession that he should be familiar with them. The Rule regulating special indorsements is Ord. III, r. 6, and generally writs are not specially indorsed unless advantage is going to be taken of the summary procedure provided by Ord. XIV.

Except in actions for libel, slander, malicious prosecution, false imprisonment, seduction, or breach of promise of marriage, and actions in which fraud is alleged by the plaintiff, the writ of summons may, at the option of the plaintiff, be specially indorsed with or accompanied by a statement of his claim, or of the remedy or relief to which he claims to be entitled. *When writ may be specially indorsed.*

Thus a special indorsement is a statement of claim ; and, without a special order, no further statement of claim can be delivered after it except by way of amendment. Hence, a special indorsement must state concisely all the material facts necessary to constitute the cause of action relied on, and must contain particulars sufficient to enable the defendant to make up his mind whether to admit liability or to resist the claim. It must be drawn in the form of a pleading under the heading of the words " Statement of Claim," and be signed by the solicitor or counsel settling it. *Contents of special indorsement.*

The following is a simple precedent of a special indorsement : *Precedent.*

STATEMENT OF CLAIM

THE PLAINTIFF'S CLAIM is for the price of goods sold and delivered to the defendant.

PARTICULARS

1948		£	s.	d.
29th January.	20 quarters of wheat at 55/-	55	0	0
21st February.	30 quarters of barley at 32/-	48	0	0
25th March.	40 quarters of wheat at 57/6	115	0	0
		218	0	0
1948				
20th April.	Paid	60	0	0
	Balance due	158	0	0

(Signed) KENYON ELLENBOROUGH.

And the sum of £5 8s. 6d. (or such sum as may be allowed on taxation) for Costs ; and also, in case of the Plaintiff obtaining an order for substituted service, the further sum of £3 3s. 6d. If the amount claimed be paid to the Plaintiff or his Solicitor or Agent within four days from the Service hereof further proceedings will be stayed.

This Writ was issued by Kenyon Ellenborough and Co. of and whose address for service is 25, Park Lane in the City of Westminster, agents for A. Goodfellow of Long Melford in the County of Suffolk, Solicitors for the said Plaintiff who resides at 20, Prince Henry Street in the City of London.

Indorsement to be made within 3 days after Service.

This Writ was served by me at 10 Cheapside in the City of London on the Defendant William Blackstone on Monday the 17th day of July 1948.

Indorsed the 19th day of July 1948.

(Signed) JAMES MANSFIELD

(Address) 15 Tooting Common, London, S.W.

Advantages of special indorsement. The main advantage of a specially indorsed writ is that, on the defendant entering an appearance, the plaintiff may apply to the Master by summons for summary judgment under Ord. XIV.

It is generally assumed that there is little or no defence to such an action, though, as we shall see later, provision is made for the case where this assumption is ill-founded. The object is then to avoid the long wait that would be necessary if the case had to await its turn in the general list of actions, only to be disposed of in a few moments as an undefended case. To effect this the plaintiff who has specially indorsed his writ may apply to the Master for summary judgment. In support of his application, the plaintiff or someone on his behalf who is authorised by him and has personal knowledge of the facts must make a formal affidavit verifying the cause of action, and stating that in his belief there is no defence to the action. To enable the summons to be taken out the appearance must be produced at the time the summons is issued. A copy of the summons, with a copy of the affidavit, must be served at the defendant's address for service four clear days before the day named for hearing of the summons. There are several courses open to the Master upon the hearing of the summons :

Summary judgment under Ord. XIV.

No defence.   1. If it appears to him that there is no defence, he will make an order empowering the plaintiff to enter final judgment for the amount claimed, and interest, if any, or for the recovery of the land, as the case may be, and costs.

2. If the defendant has any defence to the action, he may, and generally does, make an affidavit showing cause against the plaintiff's application ; and the Master may (but rarely does) order the defendant to attend and be examined on oath and produce books or documents. Thereupon the Master, unless satisfied that the alleged defence is a sham, set up merely for the purpose of delay, or that the facts alleged by the defendant do not amount to a defence in law, should give leave to defend as to the whole or part of the claim to which the defence goes. And where there is a triable issue of fact or a doubtful point of law to be decided, the defendant is entitled to unconditional leave to defend ; even although the Master may think that the defence is not likely to succeed. The function of the Master is to assume that every word in the defendant's affidavit is accurate and to ask himself might that answer be a defence to the claim ; if so, he must give unconditional leave to defend. The Master must not question the genuineness of the defendant's affidavit, otherwise he would on the hearing of the summons be in effect trying the action which he has no power to do except by consent. An appeal from a decision of the Master lies to the Judge in Chambers. If the Judge in Chambers grants the defendant unconditional leave to defend this is final, and the plaintiff cannot appeal, but if he refuses to give the defendant unconditional leave to defend the defendant may appeal without leave of either the judge or of the Court of Appeal to the Court of Appeal. *Unconditional leave to defend.*

3. Another course open to the Master is to give conditional leave to defend, *i.e.*, conditional on the defendant giving security or bringing money into Court ; but the condition of bringing money into Court or giving security ought only to be imposed where the defence set up is so vague and unsatisfactory, that the Master is practically certain that there is no defence, but has sufficient doubt to enable him to exercise his discretion in giving leave to defend subject to the conditions, instead of making an order for judgment. *Conditional leave to defend.*

4. Where the defendant has no defence to the claim, but *Counterclaim.*

sets up a plausible counterclaim, judgment is sometimes given for the plaintiff on the claim, with a stay of execution as to so much of the claim as is covered by the counterclaim, till the trial of the counterclaim.   But if part of the claim only is admitted, and the counterclaim is for a larger amount, the plaintiff is, as a rule, not entitled to any judgment till the trial.

Trial by Master.

5. With the consent of both parties, the Master may either refer the action to another Master for trial, or he may finally dispose of the matter himself in a summary manner.

Treated as summons for directions.

In the event of leave to defend being given, whether conditional or unconditional, the Master usually treats the summons as a summons for directions, and gives the necessary directions for the further conduct of the action.

Transfer to County Court.

If the amount in dispute does not exceed £100 the action may be transferred to the County Court for trial, and if the action is transferred to the County Court for trial it is usual to leave the question of costs to the County Court judge's discretion.

The order.

The plaintiff in any event draws up the order.   The affidavits which are read by the Master at the hearing are sent for filing by him, but care should be taken in drawing up the order to insert in the order all affidavits read by the Master, otherwise the plaintiff will lose costs even if he ultimately succeeds.   A copy of the order when drawn up is served on the defendant.

When the action is transferred to a County Court for trial the plaintiff arranges for all the necessary documents to be lodged at the County Court, and he then enters the action for trial.

Section X. THE COMMERCIAL COURT

Trial of commercial cases expedited.

In 1895 the judges of the Queen's Bench Division, acting under powers conferred by the Judicature Act, 1873, enabling them to make arrangements for the disposal of business in their Division, issued a notice containing certain provisions.   The effect of the notice was to create in the division a Court which is generally called the " Commercial Court " ; in which a judge of the division, familiar with mercantile law and the methods of business men, sits for the disposal and trial of commercial causes.

Although the judge is bound by the rules of evidence and procedure applicable to every division of the High Court and to every Court of each division, these rules are so applied as to secure, as far as is practicable, the speedy and economical trial of commercial actions.

Transfer of action to Commercial Court. If it is desired that an action should be tried in the Commercial Court, the writ should be issued out of the King's Bench Division in the ordinary way, and an application be made by summons to the judge of the Commercial Court to transfer the action to the Commercial List. The application may be made by the plaintiff or the defendant, at any time after the service of the writ ; and if the action is a commercial cause, the judge has a discretionary power to grant or refuse the application. *(margin: Application by summons.)*

If an order for transfer is made, the action is placed in the Commercial List, and the words " Commercial List " thenceforward appear upon all the papers in the action, while interlocutory matters pass out of the hands of the Master, and the summons for directions, and all subsequent applications under it, are heard by the judge in Court, instead of by the Master in Chambers, as in an ordinary action in the King's Bench Division. The main object of proceedings in the Commercial Court is, that the judge (and, to some extent, the same judge) should have the control of the action as soon as possible after its commencement, and of all its stages, down to and including the trial, and give such directions as will enable him to dispose, with as little delay and expense as possible, of the real controversy between the parties. The judge is supplied from a rota containing three or more names of judges of the King's Bench Division, each in turn sitting in the Commercial Court for two or three months at a time. The frequent applications made to a Master in an ordinary action, which often cause expense or delay not commensurate with the benefit derived by the litigant from their results, are discouraged in the Commercial Court. *(margin: Greater control of judge.)*

Advantages. Thus, pleadings may be dispensed with where the facts are substantially undisputed ; and the *(margin: Pleadings shortened.)*

action is then ordered to be tried on mutual admissions, or on a joint statement of facts. The pleadings are described as *points of claim* or *points of defence*, to emphasise the desire (not always, however, realised) for brevity and conciseness of pleading ; and applications for particulars are not encouraged. When the case involves a question of law which may dispose of the whole action,

Preliminary point of law. it is frequently ordered to be tried as a preliminary point of law. Instead of the ordinary affidavit of documents, an order is usually made that the solicitors for the respec-

Documents. tive parties prepare *lists of documents*, exchange the lists, and give inspection of the documents set out in their respective lists. In actions, however, against underwriters on policies of marine insurance, the plaintiff is generally required to make an *affidavit of ship's papers*, which is more stringent in form than an ordinary affidavit

Interrogatories. of documents. Interrogatories are rarely allowed in the Commercial Court.

Admissions. To avoid the expense of proving documents strictly, or of examining witnesses abroad on commission, or of calling witnesses to prove facts which are not seriously disputed, the parties to an action are encouraged to admit as evidence documents or affidavits which would be inadmissible except by consent, and to make admissions of facts. Pressure may be indirectly brought to bear upon a party to make such admissions, by means of the discretionary power of the judge to order him to pay the costs occasioned by his refusal to make admissions which the judge at the trial, after hearing the evidence, considers

Fixed date for trial. that he ought to have made. A day is fixed for the trial, in order that the parties and their witnesses may make their arrangements for attendance, and be saved the inconvenience of uncertainty as to the date when the case will be reached. When a commercial case is tried by a judge with a jury (which does not happen very often), the jury is summoned from the City of London, and is usually a special jury. This is known as a " City of London Special Jury " ; for this purpose only the special jury still exists, having been abolished in all other cases by the Juries Act, 1949.

CHAPTER 6

PROCEEDINGS IN THE CHANCERY DIVISION

SUMMARY   PAGE

Section I. *Writ of Summons* 93
Section II. *Originating Summons*   101
Section III. *Petition* 103

In the King's Bench Division proceedings are usually commenced by writ of summons. In the Chancery Division it is possible for proceedings to commence in three ways. First, where the parties are antagonistic or the facts are in dispute the usual method is by writ ; secondly, where the facts are agreed and the parties are on friendly terms, *e.g.*, a matter of construction of a will, the proceedings are usually commenced by originating summons ; and last, in certain cases where payment out of Court of moneys exceeding £1,000 is sought the procedure is by petition. *Introductory Note.*

Section I. WRIT OF SUMMONS

Where an action is commenced by writ of summons there are, generally speaking, the same stages as we have just gone through in treating of an action in the King's Bench Division ; but there are some variations of considerable importance, which we must now consider. *Commencement by writ of summons.*

Commencement of Proceedings. The cause must be assigned to one of the judges of the Chancery Division, which is done by ballot in the Writ Department of the High Court before the issue of the writ, and the judge's name is written on the original writ and copies ; except that where a cause or matter has been once assigned to one judge, every subsequent writ, summons, or petition relating to the same cause or matter, or so connected therewith as to be conveniently dealt with by the same judge, must be assigned by certificate to the same judge. The *Indorsements.*

indorsements of claim required on every writ of summons vary with the nature of the equitable relief that may be sought, and include claims as a creditor, or as a legatee, to have the estate of one who is deceased administered or to have the accounts of certain partnership or mortgage transactions taken or that certain trusts may be carried into execution or that a certain deed may be set aside or rectified or for the specific performance of contracts, and a great many others. But it must not be supposed that these examples by any means exhaust the business of the Chancery Division; and indeed there is high authority for the proposition that almost any variety of action which might have been brought in Common Law Courts can now be brought in the Chancery Division. It is important to observe that in any proceedings taken by a mortgagee to enforce his security, even suing on the covenant for repayment of the principal moneys and interest, must now be instituted in the Chancery Division.

Action which must be brought in Chancery Division.

In particular, actions in which an injunction of some kind is claimed form a large part of the business of this division. It is specifically provided that in all cases of ordinary account, as, for instance, in the case of a partnership, executorship, or ordinary trust account, where the plaintiff, in the first instance, desires to have an account taken, the writ of summons must be expressly indorsed with a claim that such account be taken. The writ is served in the same manner as a writ issued in the King's Bench Division, and the indorsement of service must be duly completed.

Default of Appearance. In an action of the nature usually assigned to the Chancery Division, there is no judgment in default of appearance to the writ; but if the defendant does not appear, the plaintiff files at the Central Office the usual affidavit of service, and a copy of the statement of claim. A certificate from the plaintiff's counsel is lodged in the Appeal and Cause Clerks Department that the case will not last more than ten minutes and is therefore fit to be marked " Short," together with minutes of the proposed judgment and a notice of motion. It is then entered in the judge's list and comes on for hearing in open Court when the judge next takes " Motions for

Judgment," and the plaintiff may be given such judgment
as the judge considers the plaintiff to be entitled to upon
the statement of claim.

Specially indorsed writs are not uncommon in the
Chancery Division. Under Ord. XIVA, the Chancery
Division's counterpart of the King's Bench Ord. XIV,
in cases where an action for specific performance is brought
in respect of a contract *in writing* for the purchase or
sale of any property, then if an appearance is entered
the plaintiff may swear an affidavit as to the facts and
may issue a summons for securing summary judgment,
which is returnable before the Master. When the summons comes on for hearing before the Master the procedure
is similar to that described on the hearing of a summons
under Ord. XIV in the King's Bench Division (see p. 88,
ante).

Interlocutory Motions. Motions for temporary relief,
pending the trial of the action, hence called "interlocutory" motions, are of everyday occurrence in the
Chancery Division; their object being most commonly
to obtain either an injunction or the appointment of a
receiver. Interlocutory relief may be granted either
(1) upon an *ex parte* motion, or (2) upon a formal notice
of motion. If an interlocutory injunction is desired it
is essential that the writ should be indorsed with a claim
for an injunction.

(1) *Ex parte.* In cases of extreme urgency, where the
applicant can satisfy the Court that the delay caused by
proceeding in the ordinary way would or might entail
irreparable or serious mischief, interlocutory relief may
be granted *ex parte*, *i.e.*, on the application of one of the
parties without notice to the other, by an order commonly
known as an *interim* order. But in such cases the Court
usually grants relief only until the first day for which a
formal notice of motion can be given. Applications of
this kind may be made immediately after, but not before,
a writ has been issued; and must be supported by
evidence in the form of an affidavit showing a *prima facie*
case of threatened injury. But, in such cases of apparent
urgency, the strict rules of evidence are frequently
relaxed; even to the extent of admitting a mere hearsay

Specially
indorsed writ.

Object of
interlocutory
motions.

Relief granted
on application
of one party in
urgent cases.

affidavit, *e.g.*, that of the plaintiff's solicitor, based on a letter or telegram received from his client. The defendant, on the other hand, is protected from improper use of this process by the practice of the Court, which almost invariably grants this relief only upon the terms of the plaintiff giving an " undertaking in damages," whereby he is required to undertake, by his counsel, to abide by any order which the Court may make as to damages, in case the Court should thereafter be of opinion that the defendant has sustained any injury by reason of the order made. The application for an *ex parte* order is made in open Court, to the judge to whom the case has been assigned.

Undertaking in damages.

Owing to the urgency of the matter no time is available to file the original affidavit and to obtain an office copy prior to counsel making the application. If the order is made the Registrar requires counsel's brief and the writ to enable him to draw up the order. He will not hand this out to the plaintiff unless he receives an office copy of the affidavit which had been read in open Court to obtain the order, thereby assuring himself that the original has been filed. Immediately the judge grants the injunction every modern means of communication should be used to bring it to the defendant's notice. A copy of the injunction duly indorsed with a penal notice to the effect that if the defendant fails to obey the order he may be liable to attachment for contempt of Court is served on the defendant, together with a copy of the writ and a copy of the filed affidavit and exhibits. If counsel has asked for leave to serve a notice of motion with the writ, a copy of the notice of motion is also served.

Relief where no immediate urgency.

(2) *Formal notice of motion.* In all save the most urgent cases, interlocutory relief, where necessary, is obtained on ordinary motion, notice of which may, by special leave of the Master obtained *ex parte*, be served together with the writ, or before the time limited for appearance ; or, without leave, at any time, after the defendant has entered appearance to the writ or after the time limited for appearance has elapsed ; two clear days are required (in the absence of special leave of the judge to the contrary) to elapse between the service of the notice

and the day named for hearing the motion. The motion must be supported by evidence given by affidavit ; and the defendant usually obtains an adjournment to enable him to file evidence in opposition. But the Court may refuse such an adjournment except upon terms ; as, for example, that the defendant gives an undertaking, until the further hearing in the terms of the notice of motion, to discontinue the acts complained of. At the hearing of the motion a stamped copy impressed with a 10s. stamp must be handed up to the judge, otherwise he will not hear the motion. In the Long Vacation the notice of motion must be set down for hearing in the list.

When the evidence is complete, the Court may either grant the relief asked, or dismiss the motion ; or, if it appear that the matter in dispute cannot conveniently be decided on affidavit evidence, or without pleadings, may order the hearing to stand over to the trial of the action. On the other hand, it may, and frequently does (especially in actions where an injunction is the principal relief claimed), appear that justice can be done by treating the motion as the final trial of the action without pleadings ; and this is effected by consent of the parties, the hearing of the motion being then disposed of, or sometimes adjourned to a convenient day, either with or without the condition that either party shall be at liberty to cross-examine the witnesses who have made affidavits on behalf of his opponent. As a condition of obtaining an interlocutory injunction, the plaintiff is in all ordinary cases required to give an undertaking in damages in the terms indicated above for an *ex parte* application. Courses open to Court.

Statement of claim and defence. The rules as to delivering the statement of claim and the defence which have been described in connection with procedure in the King's Bench Division are with some minor variations applicable to proceedings in the Chancery Division. When the defence has been delivered the summons for directions is then issued. Pleadings.

Summons for directions. Special directions with regard to the place or mode of trial are most unusual, inasmuch as in the ordinary course all actions in the Chancery Division are tried by a judge sitting in the Royal Courts of Procedure.

Justice in London, without a jury. Though cases which may be brought in either division are sometimes ordered to be tried at the local Assizes, *e.g.*, a right of way case in Yorkshire, in which several old inhabitants will be called to give evidence, no action, cause, matter or issue assigned to the Chancery Division is to be fixed for trial at Assizes without an order of the judge in person.

As in the King's Bench Division, any defendant may, by leave of the Court, bring into the action by means of a " third party notice," any person, not a party to the action, against whom he claims any right of contribution or indemnity.

Date for hearing. The date for the hearing of a witness action in the Chancery Division is fixed by the Master in Charge of the Chancery witness list, upon information supplied by the solicitors to the parties as to number of witnesses, probable length of trial, and like matters.

Trial.

Trial and Evidence. For practical purposes, it may be assumed that the plaintiff who institutes an action in the Chancery Division generally desires that it may be tried by the only method usually employed by that division, that is to say, by a judge sitting without a jury, as explained above ; and it is expressly provided that all actions which are specially assigned to the Chancery Division shall be so tried, unless the judge shall otherwise order.

Evidence.

As regards what is and what is not evidence, the admissibility of evidence, the weight of the evidence when admitted, and generally as regards all the rules of evidence, the Chancery Division is nominally in entire agreement with the King's Bench Division ; though it may be doubted whether the rules are generally applied as strictly in the former division–where juries are unknown–as in the latter.

Judgment.

Judgment and consequential proceedings. There is usually a considerable difference between a judgment or order of the Chancery Division and a King's Bench judgment ; the latter judgment being, usually, for the recovery of a specified sum of money, or the possession of specific land or chattels, whereas, in the Chancery Division, the judgment must be adapted to the nature of the relief sought, which is seldom of so simple a character. And first it is to be noted, that there is nothing in the Chancery

Division corresponding to the practice of " Signing judgment " in the King's Bench Division ; or at least there is no such thing as an order giving leave to sign judgment. The decision of the Court, whether pronounced at the trial of the action, or on motion for judgment, or otherwise, is finally recorded by means of a single document drawn up in the manner which we are about to explain. But, first, it is convenient to remark, that the principal cases in which judgment is obtained on motion, as distinguished from the trial of the action, after the defendant has appeared to the writ, are (*a*) in default of defence, and (*b*) on admissions in the pleadings.

The judgment is drawn up by the Registrar, who is present in Court on the day when it is delivered or made, and takes down a note of it in his book. Very frequently, for the assistance of the Registrar in more complicated cases, the judge directs the junior counsel for the plaintiff to sign " minutes " of the judgment ; and, in any case, the solicitor of the successful party " bespeaks " the judgment by leaving at the Registrar's office within three days after the judgment is pronounced, his counsel's brief, indorsed with a note of the decision, and the " minutes," if any, which have been signed by the direction of the judge. The Registrar then issues what is sometimes called " minutes," but is in reality the draft of the judgment or order ; a copy being furnished to each solicitor engaged in the case. This draft is "settled" by the Registrar in the presence of the solicitors ; and any party not satisfied therewith may on motion " speak to the Court on minutes," and the judge who tried the case then settles the minutes of his own judgment. *{How drawn up.}*

Subsequently, the judgment or order is " passed "—*i.e.,* the engrossment, after being duly stamped, is examined by the solicitors to the parties and signed by them in pencil and initialed by the Registrar in ink. It is then deposited at the " entering seat " ; and an official duplicate is issued to the solicitor of the successful party. The judgment must, unless otherwise ordered, be drawn up and entered within fourteen days from the date thereof and if this is not done the Registrar reports the matter to the judge. With the exception of certain simple orders *{Procedure.}*

of procedure, made and drawn up in the judge's Chambers, all orders made in the Chancery Division are drawn up in the manner just explained. It is to be noticed, moreover, that it is the practice of the Chancery Division to state precisely upon whose application the order is made, and all the parties in whose presence it is made, accounting for any parties to the action who may not have been represented on the application. The common practice of the King's Bench Division, of merely prefacing the order with the recital that it is made " upon hearing counsel " (or the solicitors as the case may be) " on both sides," or " for all parties," is never followed in the Chancery Division. Within seven days of the order being sealed the successful party should, if costs are ordered to be taxed, proceed to obtain a reference for taxation ; the procedure in connection with this matter has already been described (p. 76, *ante*).

Accounts and inquiries. In many cases the judgment, thus delivered and recorded, finally disposes of all matters in dispute ; but it frequently happens, both at the trial of an action and also on motion for judgment, that, before justice can be completely administered, accounts, and inquiries of varying degrees of complexity have to be taken and made, and often also real or other property sold. And indeed in some classes of actions (*e.g.*, foreclosure and redemption among many others) some such accounts and inquiries are almost inevitably necessary. In all cases, the judgment directs the necessary accounts and inquiries to be taken and made, specifying them clearly in numbered paragraphs, and proceeds to direct that the further consideration of the action be adjourned, until the result of the accounts and inquiries has been ascertained and certified. **Summons to proceed.** The party having the carriage of the order, usually the plaintiff, then issues a summons returnable before the Master to proceed. This summons is served on the other parties, and the Master then proceeds to carry out the directions contained in the order. It is usual for the summons to be adjourned from time to time until the Master has completed his task. The accounts, having been taken by the Master, will again be brought into Court for " further consideration." that is, to settle the final order. In simple cases this order will have been agreed between the parties and will merely require the assent and approval of the Court ; and it will only be in cases of some complication, or where infants or persons under disability are concerned (as to the protection of whose interests the Court must always be satisfied) that any lengthy consideration will be necessary. The Court then gives effect to the Master's certificate and makes it an order of the Court, and directs the taxation of costs. This order is also drawn up by the Registrar and the matter is referred back to the same taxing Master to tax the further costs.

Section II. ORIGINATING SUMMONS

As has already been mentioned, where the facts are agreed and the parties on friendly terms, proceedings are often begun by originating summons. This occurs especially when the proceedings are, as is often the case in that division, of an administrative rather than a judicial character. Such are, for example, applications for the appointment of a new trustee, or for advice in the management of infants' estates. But the procedure by originating summons is also most convenient where the point in issue between two parties is purely one of law, *e.g.*, a question of construction arising under a will or other instrument. *When originating summons used*

Form of Summons. The following is a simple precedent for an originating summons. *Precedent of originating summons.*

1948, S., No. 15.

IN THE HIGH COURT OF JUSTICE.
CHANCERY DIVISION.

MR. JUSTICE BLACKSTONE.
   In the matter of the trusts of the will of
      John Scott, deceased.

Between   William Scott   *Plaintiff*
                     AND
       Lancelot Shadwell, John Leach,
         and Thomas Plumer   *Defendants.*

Let Lancelot Shadwell, of Sparksfield Manor in the County of Middlesex, John Leach of Fritlingsea House in the County of Essex, and Thomas Plumer of 115 Long Lane, Salden, in the County of York, who claim to be entitled as beneficiaries under the will of John Scott, deceased, within Eight Days after Service of this Summons on them respectively, inclusive of the day of such Service, cause an Appearance to be entered for them respectively to this Summons, which is issued upon the Application of William Scott, of Old House, Newcastle, in the County of Northumberland, the executor of the said will for the determination of the following questions :

1. Whether upon the true construction of the said will, the defendant Lancelot Shadwell is entitled to a legacy of one thousand pounds or not.

2. Whether upon the true construction of the said will, the legacy to the defendant John Leach should be paid free of duty or not.

3. Whether the defendant Thomas Plumer is in the events which have happened entitled to one-third share of the legacy to the surviving nephews and nieces of the testator or not.

4. How the costs of this application are to be borne.

And that, if necessary, the order may be made for the execution of the trusts of the said will.

Dated the 15th day of March in the year of Our Lord one thousand nine hundred and forty-eight.

This Summons was taken out by Thurlow Wedderburn and Co., Solicitors for the above-named William Scott.

The Defendants may appear hereto by entering Appearance either personally or by Solicitor at the Central Office, Royal Courts of Justice.

NOTE.—If the Defendants do not enter appearance within the time and at the place above-mentioned, such order will be made and proceedings taken as the Judge may think just and expedient.

Under this procedure there are no pleadings (and it is apparent from the precedent above that none are necessary), and the evidence is always given on affidavit (though in special cases provision can be made for the cross-examination of witnesses). In a case like this the plaintiff, who is in fact only concerned to find out what is the law on the subject, and to protect himself in the discharge of his office, would put in the will and an affidavit, giving all the facts, including, for instance, the relationship of the defendants, who are competing beneficiaries, to the deceased, where that has any bearing on the matter in issue.

When the proceedings are brought by originating summons, the summons is allotted to a judge and in due course an appointment is taken before the Master attached to the particular judge. When the defendants have answered the plaintiff's affidavit, if they are advised so to do, and all the documents are in order, to the satisfaction of the Master, the case is put into the judge's list to come on for hearing either in open Court or in Chambers.

There are certain rules which determine the Master's choice in these matters. If any party desires to brief counsel before the judge, the case is put into counsel's list. When the matter comes on before the judge he will make an order which will be drawn up by the Registrar, and the procedure previously described will be followed.

If the matter is decided in open Court an appeal lies as of right to the Court of Appeal. Before one can appeal from the judge in Chambers in the Chancery Division application must be made to the judge to adjourn the matter formally into Court, and an appeal then lies to the Court of Appeal.

In Chancery proceedings it is usual to ask the Master to mark the attendance of the solicitor in his notes ; this he does by entering a fee on his notes. If the Master omits to do this the solicitor will not get his attendance allowed on taxation.

This procedure is comparatively simple, cheap, and expeditious, and is very extensively used in the Chancery Division.

Section III. PETITION

Proceedings by petition are rare and, as has been stated, are used to obtain payment out of Court of money exceeding £1,000.

If it is desired to tax a bill of costs which has been delivered by a solicitor to his client, it is usual to ask the Court to do this on a " petition of course."

Apart from the general procedure and jurisdiction of the Chancery Division, a petition is also required in matters connected with companies and bankruptcy. With regard to companies, where a company is desirous of reducing its capital or an application is made concerning the alteration of its objects set out in the memorandum, as distinct from its articles of association, or proceedings are instituted for a compulsory winding-up order, the procedure is to present a petition to the Court, which must be duly served on the company and advertised. A petition is used to obtain a receiving order in bankruptcy. The procedure in such matters is, however, governed by special rules (see Chap. 12).

CHAPTER 7

MATRIMONIAL CAUSES

SUMMARY   PAGE

Section I. *Proceedings in the Probate, Divorce, and Admiralty Division of the High Court* 106

(*a*) *Divorce* 106
(*b*) *Bars to Divorce* 110
(*c*) *Procedure in the High Court* 114
(*d*) *Judicial Separation and Restitution of Conjugal Rights* 130
(*e*) *Nullity* 131
(*f*) *Recognition of Foreign Divorce Decrees* 133

Section II. *Proceedings in Courts of Summary Jurisdiction* 133

Historical outline.

Before 1858 matrimonial relief was granted by the Ecclesiastical Courts and included; (i) A divorce *a mensa et thoro* (which was equivalent to the present-day decree of judicial separation) on the ground of adultery, cruelty or unnatural offences, (ii) A decree of restitution of conjugal rights on the ground of desertion, and (iii) A decree of nullity of marriage on various grounds, such as, the close relation of the parties by birth or marriage, impotence, mental incapacity or prior and subsisting marriage with another person. But, acting under the influence of the canon law, the Ecclesiastical Courts would not grant a divorce *a vinculo matrimonii*, or as we say to-day—a divorce decree. To obtain a complete divorce a private Act of Parliament was necessary and that very few petitioners could afford. Far-reaching and important changes were effected by the Matrimonial Causes Act, 1857. This Act transferred the jurisdiction of the Ecclesiastical Courts in matrimonial matters to a newly created secular Court called, "The Court for Divorce and Matrimonial Causes"; substituted for a divorce *a mensa et thoro* a decree of judicial separation and conferred on the new Court the power to pronounce a decree declaring a marriage to be dissolved (a divorce decree) on the ground that since the marriage the wife had been guilty of adultery or the husband had been guilty of adultery coupled with cruelty or desertion, or, after the Matrimonial Causes Act, 1884, failure to comply with a decree of restitution of conjugal rights. By the Judicature Act, 1873, the jurisdiction formerly exercised by the Court for Divorce and Matrimonial Causes was assigned to the Probate, Divorce and Admiralty Division of the High Court of Justice, which for convenience, we shall refer to in this Chapter as the Divorce Court or the Court.

After the Matrimonial Causes Act, 1923, a wife could be granted a divorce on the ground of adultery committed by her husband since the marriage without coupling another matrimonial offence with the adultery.

Finally, the Matrimonial Causes Act, 1937, made cruelty, desertion or incurable unsoundness of mind, grounds for divorce and introduced additional grounds for obtaining a decree of nullity of marriage.

Four principal decrees are pronounced by the Divorce Court : **Decrees.**

(1) *Dissolution of marriage* (popularly known as a divorce).—The effect of this decree is to end the marriage between the parties, who cease to be husband and wife and are free to remarry.

(2) *Judicial Separation.*—This decree renders it no longer obligatory for the party obtaining it to cohabit with the other party to the marriage. They remain, however, husband and wife.

(3) *Restitution of Conjugal Rights.*—This decree orders the party to the marriage against whom it is made to return, and render conjugal rights to the other party. Disobedience to the order is a ground for instituting a suit for judicial separation. The parties remain husband and wife.

(4) *Nullity of Marriage.*—This decree pronounces and declares the marriage to be and to have been absolutely null and void, and frees the party obtaining the decree from all bond of marriage with the other party.

A decree for divorce or nullity of marriage is in the **Decree** first instance a decree *nisi*, which is not made absolute **nisi.** until the expiration of six weeks from the decree *nisi* being pronounced.

Marriage
and matri-
monial relief.

With the exception of certain suits for nullity of marriage where the so-called " marriage " was void *ab initio* as it would be, for example, if either party to the marriage ceremony was under the age of sixteen years, or was previously married and is still married to another person (Vol. II, p. 479), the Divorce Court cannot pronounce the decrees we have mentioned, unless the parties have validly contracted a marriage that ordains " the voluntary union for life of one man with one woman to the exclusion of all others " (*per* Lord Penzance in *Hyde* v. *Hyde and Woodmansee* (1866), L. R. 1 P. & D. 130) and that marriage is still subsisting. In a recent case Lord Greene, after referring to *Hyde* v. *Hyde and Woodmansee,* said :

> " At any rate, rightly or wrongly, the courts have refused to regard a polygamous marriage as one which entitles the parties to come for matrimonial relief to the courts of this country " (*Baindail* v. *Baindail,* [1946] P. 122, at p. 126; [1946] 1 All E. R. 342, at p. 345).

Section I. Proceedings in the Probate, Divorce, and Admiralty Division of the High Court.

(a) Divorce

Dissolution
of marriage.

Having considered the fundamental conception of marriage, so far as matrimonial relief is concerned, we now proceed to discuss how it may be brought to an end, by a decree for divorce. In order to obtain a divorce :

(1) There must be a valid and subsisting marriage.

(2) The Divorce Court must have jurisdiction to entertain the suit for divorce.

(3) The suit must be founded on the commission of a matrimonial offence which is a ground for divorce.

(4) At the date of the presentation of the petition for divorce three years must have passed since the date of marriage.

Validity of
marriage.

1. *Valid marriage.* The requirements for a valid marriage in English law are : (i) that the parties have the capacity to contract marriage, and (ii) that certain forms and ceremonies are observed. Both requirements have been discussed in Volume II of these Commentaries;

the capacity to marry on pages 480, 481, and the forms and ceremonies on pages 483—490.

2. *Jurisdiction.* The jurisdiction of the Divorce Court Domicil. in suits for *divorce* rests on the domicil of the parties in England or Wales at the institution of the suit (*Le Mesurier* v. *Le Mesurier*, [1895] A. C. 517). The meaning of the term " domicil " has been explained in Volume II., pages 474—478. The domicil of the parties means the domicil of the husband when any question arises concerning the jurisdiction of the Court in matrimonial suits. There are two statutory exceptions to this rule.

(*a*) Where a wife has been deserted by her husband, or where her husband has been deported from the United Kingdom under any law for the time being in force relating to the deportation of aliens, and immediately prior thereto he was domiciled in England or Wales, notwithstanding the change of the husband's domicil since the desertion or deportation the Court can nevertheless hear the petition (Matrimonial Causes Act, 1937, s. 13). The application of this section is not limited to divorce proceedings, and extends to proceedings for nullity, judicial separation and restitution of conjugal rights.

(*b*) The other exception applies to a marriage celebrated on or after September 3, 1939, and before a day to be appointed by Order in Council, *and* at the time of the marriage the husband was domiciled outside the United Kingdom, *and* immediately before the marriage the wife was domiciled in England, *and* proceedings are commenced not later than five years after the appointed day, *and* since the celebration of the marriage the parties have not at any time resided in the country in which the husband is then domiciled. If these circumstances exist, the Court has jurisdiction in proceedings brought by either party to the marriage for divorce (or nullity) as if both parties were domiciled in England (Matrimonial Causes (War Marriages) Act, 1944). It will be noticed, that the second exception unlike the first is a temporary measure.

3. *Matrimonial offence.* Any one of the following Grounds for divorce. five groups of offences constitutes a ground for divorce (Judicature Act, 1925, s. 176, as substituted by the Matrimonial Causes Act, 1937, s. 2.)

(*a*) Adultery committed since the celebration of the marriage.

(*b*) Desertion without cause for a period of at least three years immediately preceding the presentation of the petition. It is very important to notice, that this period of at least three years is not any period of at least that duration. The period must be " immediately preceding the presentation of the petition " and it is spoken of as " desertion for the statutory period."

Therefore, if desertion, which may have lasted for ten or more years, is terminated during the statutory period, for example, by the deserting party becoming insane and incapable of forming the intention to continue the desertion, or by the parties entering into a mutual agreement to live separate and apart, or by an unjustifiable refusal of the deserted party to accept a genuine offer by the deserting party to resume cohabitation, a petition for divorce (or judicial separation) could not be granted.

Though there can be no desertion while the parties are living apart under a valid and subsisting separation agreement, if one of them repudiates the agreement, and the other " accepts " the repudiation and is willing to resume cohabitation, the repudiating party may be guilty of desertion without cohabitation being resumed (consider *Pardy* v. *Pardy*, [1939] P. 288 ; [1939] 3 All E. R. 779). There is no desertion while a decree of judicial separation is in force ; or while a separation order made in a Court of Summary Jurisdiction is in force for the order contains a clause known as a " non-cohabitation clause," which relieves the innocent spouse of the necessity of cohabiting with the guilty spouse (p. 134, *post*). The mere refusal of sexual intercourse by one of the spouses, while in all other respects the spouses continue to live together as a normal married couple, does not constitute desertion by the refusing spouse (*Weatherly* v. *Weatherley*, [1947] A. C. 628 ; [1947] 1 All E. R. 563).

Adultery committed by the *deserted* party will not prevent the continuance of a period of desertion, if the *deserting* party is ignorant of the adultery, or the intention of the *deserting* party to desert is uninfluenced by knowledge of the adultery (*Herod* v. *Herod*, [1938] P. 11 ; [1938] 3 All E. R. 722).

(c) Cruelty since the celebration of the marriage. Cruelty as a ground for divorce (or judicial separation) may be defined in the legal sense as, conduct that causes danger to life, limb or health, bodily or mental, or gives rise to reasonable apprehension of such danger (*Russell* v. *Russell*, [1897] A. C. 395).   In this case Lord Davey said :

> " The general idea which I think underlies all these decisions is that while declining to lay down any hard and fast definition of legal cruelty, the Courts acted on the principle of giving protection to the complaining spouse against actual or apprehended violence, physical ill-treatment or injury to health " (at pp. 467–8).

Conduct that creates mental distress or anxiety is not legal cruelty unless thereby causing injury to, or reasonable apprehension of injury to, bodily health. The intentional acts of a spouse may constitute cruelty, though the acts were not done maliciously or with the intention of harming the other spouse (*Squire* v. *Squire*, [1949] P. 51 ; [1948] 2 All E. R. 51).

(d) That the respondent is incurably of unsound mind and has been continuously under care and treatment for a period of at least five years immediately preceding the presentation of the petition.   A person of unsound mind is deemed to be under care and treatment : (a) while detained in pursuance of any order or inquisition under the Lunacy and Mental Treatment Acts, 1890 to 1930, or of any order or warrant under certain Acts of Parliament affecting the services, or is being detained as a criminal lunatic (for which expression the Criminal Justice Act, 1948, substitutes " Broadmoor patient ") or in pursuance of an order made under the Criminal Lunatics Act, 1884 ; (b) while he is receiving treatment as a voluntary patient under the Mental Treatment Act, 1930, being treatment which follows without any interval a period of such detention as aforesaid ; and not otherwise.   Temporary releases (spoken of as " absences on trial " under the Lunacy Act, 1890, s. 55), of a patient to see whether recovery has been effected are methods of taking care of and treating the patient, so if later the patient returns to a mental hospital the absence does not operate to prevent the period of time of five years from being continuous, which is essential if the petition is to be successful.

(*e*) That the husband has since the celebration of the marriage been guilty of rape, sodomy, or bestiality.

Postpone-
ment of
proceedings.

4. *Period required before proceedings can be commenced.* No petition can be presented to the High Court for divorce within three years of the date of the marriage, unless a judge of the High Court is satisfied that the case is one of exceptional hardship suffered by the petitioner or of exceptional depravity on the part of the respondent (Matrimonial Causes Act, 1937, s. 1). When special circumstances exist of the type indicated an application may be made to a judge of the Probate, Divorce, and Admiralty Division by originating summons for leave to file a petition within three years of the date of the marriage. Before giving leave the Court will inquire into the prospects of a reconciliation. The respondent can be heard without either entering an appearance or filing an affidavit in reply to the allegations.

(b) Bars to Divorce

The reader will find it convenient, if at this stage we discuss the bars (or defences) to a suit for divorce before we explain the procedure governing the conduct of the suit.

These bars are either *absolute* or *discretionary*. If absolute a decree cannot be granted ; if discretionary the Court may in its discretion grant or refuse to grant, a decree.

Absolute.
bars.
Collusion.

Let us examine first the *absolute* bars.

(1) *Collusion.* This means an agreement between the parties as to the presentation or prosecution of a petition whereby they make a bargain as to the withholding or the disclosure or the manufacture of evidence in the case ; as, for example, that the respondent shall abstain from defending the suit. But the mere fact that both parties want a decree of dissolution of marriage does not amount to collusion, nor does the supplying of existing evidence,

even for reward. Collusion is an absolute bar whatever may be the ground of the petition.

(2) *Connivance.* This means an actual corrupt in- Connivance. tention on the part of the petitioner of promoting or encouraging beforehand the respondent's adultery—mere knowledge that adultery will take place and a passive acquiescence in it do not without more amount to connivance. This bar applies where the ground of the petition is adultery.

(3) *Condonation.* This is a " forgiveness of the con- Condonation. jugal offence with the full knowledge of all the circumstances ; and is a question of fact, not of law." It is a " blotting out of the offence, so as to restore the offending party to the same position he or she occupied before the offence was committed " (*Keats* v. *Keats and Montezuma* (1859), 1 Sw. & Tr. 334) ; but subject to a condition, express or implied, that there shall be no further matrimonial offence. But *any* subsequent matrimonial misconduct which is sufficiently serious for the Court to regard it as a substantial breach of conjugal duty, though not of itself sufficient as a ground for a decree, revives the previous offence, which has been conditionally forgiven. Thus adultery if condoned, is renewed by desertion although the desertion may be for less than three years (*Beard* v. *Beard*, [1946] P. 8). Mere forgiveness is not condonation ; it is necessary that there should be a resumption of cohabitation so as to restore the offending party to his or her former position, and this there may be without a renewal of sexual intercourse. On the other hand, if there be absolute and unconditional forgiveness of a matrimonial offence which has been already committed (a clause to this effect being not infrequently inserted in separation deeds) the doctrine of revival on the commission of a subsequent offence has no application and relief cannot be granted in respect of the forgiven offence.

Condonation is an absolute bar to a petition founded on adultery or cruelty.

On a petition for divorce it is the duty of the Court to Onus of inquire, so far as it reasonably can, whether there has proof. been any connivance or condonation on the part of the petitioner and whether any collusion exists between the parties. If the Court is not satisfied with respect to any of these matters, it must dismiss the petition (Matrimonial Causes Act, 1937, s. 4).

The effect of this provision appears to be, that if the circumstances of the case give rise to a reasonable suspicion of connivance or collusion or (presumably) condonation, the onus rests on the petitioner to satisfy the Court that the suspicion is without foundation (*Churchman* v. *Churchman*, [1945] P. 44 ; [1945] 2 All E. R. 190).

Discretionary bars. *Discretionary Bars.* Having discussed the three absolute bars, we now proceed to discuss the five discretionary bars, of which the first three apply whatever may be the ground of the petition. If any of these are found to exist the Court has a discretion whether it will make a decree or dismiss the petition. The discretionary bars are as follows :

Petitioner's adultery. (1) *Adultery of the petitioner.* The adultery must have been committed subsequently to the marriage. The discretion, which is conferred on the Court by statute, must be exercised cautiously, and if possible consistently, having regard to the parties themselves and the interest of the community at large. But, the Courts have refused repeatedly to lay down strict rules governing the exercise of the discretion, and the " utmost that can be properly done is to indicate the chief considerations which ought to be weighed in appropriate cases as helping to arrive at a just conclusion " (*Blunt* v. *Blunt*, [1943] A. C. 517, *per* Viscount Simon at p. 525 ; [1943] 2 All E. R. 76, at p. 78) as, for example, the interest of the children, the prospect of the future marriage of the petitioner to the person with whom he or she committed adultery, the prospect of a reconciliation between the husband and wife.

Where both spouses ask for a decree for divorce, and both ask for the discretion of the Court, the Court can grant one a decree, or dismiss both petitions or grant each a decree.

Delay. (2) *Unreasonable delay in presenting or prosecuting the petition,* which means an unreasonable delay after the discovery of the existence of the offence for which the divorce is claimed.   Unless a satisfactory explanation can be given of such delay, the petitioner is not entitled to a divorce.   Want of means, however, is generally considered a satisfactory explanation, though in view of the increased facilities for litigation by " poor persons," this excuse would appear to be of declining importance.   Consideration for the feelings of others or for the welfare of a child may also suffice.   It has been said, that delay as a discretionary bar means " culpable delay, something in the nature of connivance or acquiescence."

(3) *Cruelty towards the other party to the marriage.*   Conduct that constitutes legal cruelty has been described on p. 109.   The general, but not inflexible, rule is, that the cruelty in order to constitute a bar to a decree of dissolution must have been such as to lead to the misconduct complained of in the unsuccessful party. Cruelty of petitioner.

(4) *Desertion.*   Where the ground of the petition is adultery or cruelty, if the petitioner has without reasonable excuse wilfully separated himself or herself from the other party before the adultery or cruelty complained of the petition may be dismissed.   Desertion by the party alleging it, when pleaded as a bar, need not have continued for any specific period.   The act relied on as desertion must, however, in all cases have been done in opposition to the wishes of the person who alleges it. Desertion.

(5) *Wilful neglect or misconduct.*   Where the ground of the petition is adultery or unsoundness of mind or desertion, if the petitioner has been guilty of such wilful neglect or misconduct as has conduced to the adultery or unsoundness of mind, or desertion, the petition may be dismissed.   The principle on which the Court acts is, that the neglect or misconduct, to operate as a bar, must directly conduce to the adultery or unsoundness of mind complained of. Neglect by petitioner.

It is scarcely necessary to add, that if the Court is not satisfied on the evidence that the case for the petition has been proved, it must dismiss the petition. Case not proved.

(c) *Procedure in the High Court*

THE PETITION.   The proceedings are instituted by presenting a petition.   Here is an example of a petition :—

IN THE HIGH COURT OF JUSTICE.
PROBATE, DIVORCE, AND ADMIRALTY DIVISION
    (DIVORCE).

To the High Court of Justice.

The 1st day of June 1948.

THE PETITION of Mary Orange, SHEWETH :

1. THAT on the 28th day of March 1934 the Petitioner Mary Orange then Mary Lamb, Spinster, was lawfully married to Lemon Orange (hereinafter referred to as " the Respondent ") at the Tower of London in the County of London.

2. THAT after the said marriage the Petitioner lived and cohabited with the Respondent at 1 Blossom Square, Bloomsbury, in the County of London and other places, and there are now living issue of the said marriage two children only, namely Michael John Orange born on the 27th day of March 1937 and Peter David Orange born on the 16th day of June 1940.

3. THAT the Petitioner is domiciled in England and now resides at 30 Clements Road, Westbury, in the County of Middlesex.

4. THAT the Respondent is a Commercial Traveller, he is also domiciled in England and now resides at 10 Rabbit Warren, Hampstead, in the County of London.

5. THAT there have not been any proceedings previous hereto with reference to the said marriage or the said children of the marriage in the High Court, in any County Court, or in any Court of Summary Jurisdiction by or on behalf of either of the parties to the said marriage.

6. THAT the Respondent has frequently committed adultery with Polly Flinders.

7. THAT on the night of the 27th–28th March 1947, the Respondent committed adultery with the said Polly Flinders at the Black Lion Hotel, Tawcaster in the County of Wessex.

8. THAT the Petitioner has not been accessory to or connived at or condoned the adultery alleged in this Petition.

9. THAT this Petition is not presented or prosecuted in collusion with the Respondent or with the said Polly Flinders.

10. THAT the Respondent is a Commercial Traveller and earns as such an income of £12 per week and is possessed of property, the extent of which is not known of the Petitioner.

THE PETITIONER THEREFORE PRAYS THAT THE COURT WILL
    DECREE :

1. That her said marriage may be dissolved.

2. That she be granted the custody of her said children.

3. That the Respondent be ordered to pay to the Petitioner such sums by way of alimony pending suit as may be just.

4. That the Respondent be ordered to secure to the Petitioner such gross or annual sum of money for her life by way of maintenance as may be just.

5. That the Respondent be ordered to pay to the Petitioner during their joint lives such monthly or weekly sums of money for her maintenance as may be reasonable and that provision be made for the maintenance of the children of the marriage.

6. That the Respondent be ordered to pay the costs of this suit.

That such further and other relief be granted to the Petitioner as may be just.

WILLIAM SYKES.
(*Signature of Counsel*).

IN THE HIGH COURT OF JUSTICE.
PROBATE, DIVORCE, AND ADMIRALTY DIVISION (DIVORCE).

IN THE MATTER OF THE PETITION OF MARY ORANGE.

FOR DISSOLUTION OF MARRIAGE

I, Mary Orange of 30 Clement's Road, Westbury, in the County of Middlesex, the Petitioner in this cause make oath and say as follows :

1. That the statements contained in paragraphs 1, 2, 3, 4, 5, 8, 9, and 10 of this Petition are true.

2. That the statements contained in paragraphs 6 and 7 of this Petition are true to the best of my knowledge, information, and belief.

Sworn at 15 Clement's Road, Westbury,
in the County of Middlesex this 1st day
of June, 1948.   MARY ORANGE.

Before me, THOMAS ATKINS.
A Commissioner for Oaths.

As will be seen from the form of petition it is addressed to the High Court and sets out amongst other matters : Contents of petition.

(*a*) The place and date of the marriage and the name and status of the wife before the marriage.

(*b*) The principal addresses where the parties have cohabited within the jurisdiction, or, if be the case, that there has been no address of cohabitation within the jurisdiction.

(*c*) Whether there are living any children of the marriage, and, if so, the names and dates of birth and ages of such children and, if it be the case, that the parentage of any living child of the wife born during the marriage is in dispute.

(*d*) The occupation of the husband and the residence and domicil of the parties to the marriage at the date of filing the petition.

(*e*) Whether there have been in the High Court, County Court or a Court of Summary Jurisdiction any, and if so what, previous proceedings with reference to the marriage or the children of the marriage by or on behalf of either of the parties to the marriage, the date and effect of any decree or order made in such proceedings, and, in the case of proceedings with reference to the marriage, whether there has been any resumption of cohabitation since the making thereof.

(*f*) The matrimonial offence charged giving particulars of the acts relied on. If desertion is the matrimonial offence which is charged in the petition full particulars of the acts relied upon by the petitioner supporting the allegation of desertion must be given in the body of the petition.

(*g*) Whether the petitioner has in any way been accessory to or connived at or condoned the offence.

(*h*) Whether the petition is presented or prosecuted in collusion with the respondent or any of the co-respondents.

Wife petitioner. A wife petitioner may include in her petition a claim for alimony pending suit, maintenance of the children, maintenance or a secured provision, in which case the petition shall contain a statement in general terms of her husband's income and property in so far as she is aware of them.

Prayer for the relief claimed. The petition concludes with a prayer setting out particulars of the relief claimed including :

(*a*) The amount of any damages claimed against a co-respondent in a husband's petition ; and any claims for :

(b) custody of the children of the marriage (including a legitimated child (*M*. v. *M*., [1946] P. 31)) ;

(c) maintenance of the children ;

(d) alimony pending suit (in a wife's petition) ;

(e) maintenance or secured provision (in a wife's petition) ;

(f) costs ; and

(g) in appropriate cases a prayer that the Court will exercise its discretion to grant a decree *nisi* notwithstanding the adultery of the petitioner during the marriage.

If the petitioner is the husband praying for a dissolution of his marriage on the ground of his wife's adultery, every alleged adulterer must be made a co-respondent ; unless the Court gives leave to proceed without doing so on " special grounds " being shown by the husband.   And if damages are claimed, the alleged adulterer must be served with the petition, unless the Court directs otherwise.   If the wife is a petitioner praying for a dissolution on the ground of adultery, the woman accused by the petitioner of adultery with the husband must be made a respondent, if a claim for costs is sought against her ; if this is not done and the woman named (as she is called) failed to intervene, costs could not be awarded against her, as she would not be a party to the suit (p. 126, *post*). *[margin: Co-respondent.]*

It is essential that the petitioner should ask the respondent for the name and address of the woman, if adultery was committed with a woman unknown, so that the woman can be named in the petition and the petition served on her.   The Court is very reluctant to grant a decree in the case where adultery is alleged with a woman unknown, and accordingly the petitioner's solicitor is under an obligation to the Court to take every step and make every inquiry possible to obtain the name and address of the woman. *[margin: Woman unknown.]*

The petition is signed by the solicitor or counsel who settled it, or by the petitioner if acting in person.   The petitioner swears the affidavit which is at the end of the *[margin: Affidavit.]*

petition verifying the facts set out in the petition and the petition together with the marriage certificate, are filed either at the Divorce Registry, Somerset House, or at a District Registry.

Petitioner an infant or person of unsound mind.

An infant or person of unsound mind petitions by his next friend, who must sign a written authority attested by a solicitor who certifies that the proposed next friend has no adverse interest in the proceedings.

Service of the petition.

A copy of the petition accompanied by (i) a notice to appear, (ii) a form of acknowledgement of service (set out below), and (iii) a memorandum of appearance in duplicate (example set out below) must be served personally (but not by the petitioner), or by registered post on every respondent and co-respondent named therein.

IN THE HIGH COURT OF JUSTICE.

PROBATE, DIVORCE, AND ADMIRALTY DIVISION (DIVORCE). *

Between   Mary Orange   *Petitioner,*

                             and

                  Lemon Orange   *Respondent.*

I am the person named as Lemon Orange the respondent in the Petition.

I have received a copy of the Petition filed in this Suit.

Signed Lemon Orange.

Dated June 7th, 1948.

To the Petitioner
    or her Solicitor.

Appearance.

The person desiring to appear or his solicitor must, within eight days of the receipt of the notice to appear, leave or send by post to the Divorce Registry the memorandum of appearance in duplicate. The form of the memorandum varies in the cases of husband respondent, wife respondent and co-respondent or person named. The following is a memorandum of appearance by a husband respondent.

IN THE HIGH COURT OF JUSTICE.

PROBATE, DIVORCE, AND ADMIRALTY DIVISION
(DIVORCE).

Between	Mary Orange	*Petitioner*,
	and	
	Lemon Orange	*Respondent*.

1. A copy of a Petition by your wife for divorce is delivered herewith.
2. Have you received and read the copy of the Petition ?
3. On what date and at what address did you receive it ?
4. Are you the person named as Respondent in the Petition ?
5. Do you intend to answer the Petition ?

NOTE.—If you intend to defend you must within 22 days after receiving the Petition, send or deliver an Answer to the Divorce/District Registry, together with the prescribed fee (2s. 6d.), and in addition within twenty-four hours thereafter send a copy thereof to the Petitioner's solicitor, or, if she is not represented by a solicitor, to the Petitioner.

6. The Petitioner also claims :

(1) Costs.
(2) Custody of the children.
(3) Alimony pending suit.
(4) Maintenance of the children.
(5) Maintenance.
(6) A secured provision.

Even if you do not intend to defend the Petition you may wish to be heard as to these claims or you may wish to apply for access to the said children. If so, state below on which of the claims you desire to be heard, and if you desire access to the children.

I desire to be heard on claims numbered ——.

If you desire to be heard as to the claim(s) for alimony, maintenance of the children, maintenance and/or a secured provision, in addition to sending this form of appearance you are required within 22 days after receiving the Petition to send or deliver to the Registrar an affidavit giving full particulars of your property and income, together with the prescribed fee (2s. 6d.) and at the same time to send a copy thereof to the Petitioner's solicitor, or if she is not represented by a solicitor, to the Petitioner. If you allege that your wife has property or income, you should so state in your affidavit.

7. What is the address to which any communications for you should be sent ?

DATED the 7th day of June 1948

(Signed) LEMON ORANGE.

The Registrar on receipt of the memorandum enters an appearance and sends by post to the petitioner or his solicitor one copy of the memorandum sealed with the seal of the Registry and delivers or sends by post a notice of entry of appearance to the person entering an appearance. But, in general, an appearance may be entered at any time.

An infant or a person of unsound mind defends or intervenes by his guardian *ad litem* and there are elaborate rules dealing with service of documents, appearance, and other matters in these cases. The Official Solicitor, if he consents, will be the guardian *ad litem* of a person of unsound mind.

If the woman with whom the husband is alleged to have committed adultery is not made a respondent (p. 117, *ante*) by serving her with a copy of the petition accompanied by, *inter alia*, a notice to appear, the copy petition served on her must be accompanied by a notice that she is entitled to intervene by entering an appearance, and she will then become a party to the suit if she appears.

Answer.

The next step is for the person who has appeared to file an answer to the petition, which must be done within fourteen days after the time limited for the entry of appearance, by sending it by post to, or leaving it at, the Registry. Within twenty-four hours thereafter he must send to the petitioner, or the petitioner's solicitor, a copy of the answer. The answer is signed by the counsel or solicitor who settled it or by the party if acting in person.

If the answer contains more than a simple denial of the facts stated in the petition, by, for example, asking for relief in respect of cross-charges, and is filed by a husband or wife, it must state the existence or otherwise of collusion, connivance or condonation, and whether he or she was accessory to any adultery as in the case of a petition and at the end of the answer there must be an affidavit supporting it. A co-respondent, though admitting the adultery alleged against him, may deny the claim for damages.

A form of answer to the petition on p. 114 is as follows :

IN THE HIGH COURT OF JUSTICE.

PROBATE, DIVORCE, AND ADMIRALTY DIVISION (DIVORCE).

The 21st day of June 1948.

Between	Mary Orange	*Petitioner,*
	and	
	Lemon Orange	*Respondent.*

The Respondent Lemon Orange by Ferret & Co. of 260, Lombard Wall in the City of London, his Solicitors, in Answer to the Petition filed in this suit says :

That he is not guilty of adultery as alleged in the said Petition.

Wherefore the Respondent prays that the Court will reject the Petitioner's prayer and dismiss the Petition.

The petitioner is not allowed to file a reply without leave unless the answer claims relief, in which case a reply may be filed without leave within fourteen days from the delivery of the answer. Reply.

It should be noted, that a respondent or co-respondent who has appeared, but not filed an answer is entitled to be heard on any question as to costs and damages and a respondent spouse on any question of custody of or access to any children of the marriage, but without leave a co-respondent will not be heard as to damages unless he appears before the Registrar's certificate (p. 122, *post*) is granted. Right to be heard though no answer filed.

Provision is made in the Rules for obtaining particulars of allegations and statements in the pleadings. Particulars.

Before a petition can proceed to trial or hearing the respondent and every co-respondent or person named in the petition must have entered an appearance or returned to the petitioner's solicitor an acknowledgement of service. If neither of these courses has been taken, an affidavit must be filed showing that the petition was served personally (or in accordance with an order for substituted service) and stating the means of knowledge of the identity of the person served. This may be done by means of a photograph of the party served being identified by the Appearance or non-appearance.

petitioner at the hearing, or by the petitioner being present at the service of the petition and identifying the person served.

Registrar's certificate.

Setting down for trial. The pleadings having been delivered the next step is to apply to the Registrar for his certificate which states : (*a*) that the petition has been duly served ; (*b*) whether an appearance has, or has not, been entered, and, if an appearance has not been entered, that the time for entering an appearance has expired ; (*c*) if an appearance has been entered, that the time for filing an answer or any subsequent pleading has expired, and for the Registrar's directions as to the place of trial. There are comprehensive provisions in the Rules requiring information to be supplied to the Registrar to assist him in deciding the place of trial.

Discretion statement.

The solicitor for the petitioner should, before drafting the petition and again before applying to the Registrar for his certificate, ask the petitioner whether, since the date of the marriage, he or she has committed adultery ; if so, the fact must be disclosed with full particulars in a statement known as a " discretion statement," which must be lodged in a sealed envelope with the application for the Registrar's certificate ; failure to do this at this stage would, if the facts were ultimately discovered, be very serious : the Court would probably dismiss the petition, and if a decree *nisi* had been made and it had not been made absolute, the Court would probably set it aside and order the petitioner to pay the costs.

Setting down for trial.

After the Registrar's certificate has been obtained the petitioner sets the cause down for trial or hearing which will be in London or at a Divorce Town in accordance with the directions issued by the Registrar with his certificate, and gives notice of having done so to each party who has appeared. If the petitioner fails to do this within fourteen days after the granting of the Registrar's certificate any party defending may set the cause down for trial or hearing. If an undefended cause is not set down within twenty-eight days after the granting of the Registrar's certificate, a renewal of the certificate is necessary.

Lists.

Where no answer is filed the case is put in the

undefended list. Other cases, including those in which
relief is sought on the ground of insanity, though in fact
undefended, and those in which a co-respondent claims
to be heard without filing an answer (p. 121, *ante*), are
entered in the defended list.

We have indicated that matrimonial causes may be
tried in London or at a Divorce Town (a list of these
towns is specified in Appendix III to the Rules). At each
Divorce Town the Registrar of the District Registry
prepares three numbered lists : the " undefended list,"
the " long defended list," and the " short defended list,"
and long defended causes can be tried only at certain
Divorce Towns.

The Hearing. Unless otherwise directed, all causes *The trial.*
come on for hearing before a judge or commissioner alone.
If it is discovered that adultery was committed prior to
the date of the presentation of the petition which has been
served, and that no charge was made in the petition in
respect of that adultery and it is desired to allege that
adultery at the hearing of the petition, then application
must be made to a Registrar on a summons for leave to
amend the petition by adding a paragraph dealing with
the additional evidence. If the further adultery was *Further*
committed after the filing of the petition which has been *evidence.*
served, the proper course is not to amend the petition,
but to bring the additional charges before the Court
by obtaining leave to file a supplemental petition which
must be served. A supplemental petition can only be
filed after the main petition has been served. The Court
of Appeal has held that if the original petition is dismissed, no relief can be given on the supplemental petition which is nothing more than a part of the original
petition and cannot be severed from it for the purpose of
giving relief.

In due course the case comes on for hearing and the *The hearing.*
petitioner and his or her witnesses give evidence. Owing
to the rule in *Russell* v. *Russell*, [1924] A. C. 687, neither
party to the marriage can give evidence of non-intercourse
after marriage, if the object or possible result would be
to bastardise a child born in wedlock, and so establish
that adultery must have been committed. There are

many qualifications to this so-called rule (see Vol. II, p. 503). Where there have been proceedings, either in the High Court for judicial separation, or in a Court of Summary Jurisdiction for an order under the Summary Jurisdiction (Separation and Maintenance) Acts, 1895–1925 (see p. 133, *post*), the Court may, on a subsequent petition for divorce, treat the decree of judicial separation or the order as sufficient proof of the adultery, desertion, or other ground on which it was granted, being, of course, a ground on which a decree of divorce may be granted, but the Court can not pronounce a decree of divorce unless the petitioner gives evidence in the subsequent proceedings (Matrimonial Causes Act, 1937, s. 6) Thus, whilst the Court may dispense with further proof of the matters already proved in the prior proceedings, it nevertheless does not automatically convert the prior order into a decree of dissolution. Apart from these exceptions the proceedings are similar to those of a witness action in the King's Bench Division (see Chapter 5, *ante*). If the judge grants a decree *nisi* he can also deal with questions of custody and maintenance of the children ; maintenance or secured provision, claimed in the petition. The judge can instead of deciding these matters in open Court sit in Chambers, thus excluding the public from being present ; or he can adjourn the matter into Chambers to come on at a later date.

It is now proposed to consider the liability of the co-respondent. He may set up in his answer a denial of the material facts alleged in the petition or any other defence available to the respondent, and (as a plea to any damages claimed) that he did not know that the respondent was a married woman. But the practice of not awarding damages or costs against a co-respondent who did not know the woman was married is discretionary only, and both may be awarded against him, when he, being ignorant, is also indifferent and did not " pause to consider." Where the husband is successful in establishing a charge of adultery against the co-respondent, the Court generally orders the co-respondent to pay the whole or part of the costs of the suit, if he knew at the time of the adultery that the respondent was a married woman.

The co-respondent is also liable to be condemned in damages to compensate the petitioner for the loss or injury he has suffered by the breaking up of the home. The Court has power to order the whole or any part of the damages awarded to be settled for the benefit of the children of the marriage or as a provision for the maintenance of the wife.

If the Court is satisfied that a matrimonial offence has taken place and that there is no absolute bar, it must, unless there is a discretionary bar, pronounce a decree *nisi*, and will make the appropriate order as to costs and custody. If there is a discretionary bar the Court will dismiss the petition, unless the Court exercises its discretion in favour of the petitioner. *Decree nisi.*

An appeal lies as of right to the Court of Appeal at any time between decree *nisi* and decree absolute, and thence by leave to the House of Lords. The party appealing to the Court of Appeal must, before the expiration of six weeks from the time the decree *nisi* was pronounced, serve notice of appeal upon the respondent to the appeal *and* after service of this notice leave with the proper officer of the Principal Probate Registry (or if the cause is proceeding in a district registry with the proper officer of that registry) two copies of the notice of appeal. After decree absolute there is no appeal, where there was opportunity for appeal against the decree *nisi*. *Appeal.*

In order to prevent the Court from being deceived, the King's Proctor if directed by the Attorney-General, or any other person wishing to show cause why the decree *nisi* should not be made absolute, may then do so on the ground that there has been collusion between the parties, or that material facts were, either intentionally or accidentally, not brought before the Court, or that the petitioner has committed adultery since the date of the marriage and has failed to disclose it to the Court on the hearing of the petition, or has committed adultery since the decree *nisi*; and the King's Proctor may pray that the Court will rescind the decree *nisi* and order the petition to be dismissed. With the leave of the Court the King's Proctor may intervene before a decree *nisi* usually but not necessarily for the purpose of showing collusion. *King's Proctor.*

Decree
absolute.

An application by a spouse to make absolute a decree *nisi* in his favour is made by lodging in the Registry, where the cause is proceeding, a Notice of Application on any day after the expiration of the period prescribed for making such decree absolute (usually six weeks after the decree *nisi* was pronounced). The Registrar makes the necessary searches and being satisfied, (*a*) that no appeal against the decree is pending, (*b*) that the time for appealing has not been enlarged by the Court of Appeal, or if enlarged has expired, (*c*) that no appearance has been entered or affidavits filed by any person wishing to show cause against the decree being made absolute, the Notice of Application will be filed and thereupon the decree *nisi* becomes absolute. If the application is made after the expiration of one year from the date of the decree *nisi*, an affidavit by the applicant accounting for the delay must be lodged with the Notice of Application and the notice will not be filed without the leave of the Registrar. If no Notice of Application is lodged within three months from the earliest date when the successful party could have applied, the guilty party is now entitled to apply by summons before the Registrar supported by affidavit to have the decree *nisi* made absolute.

Costs and
Taxation.

After the Registrar's certificate has been granted, or with leave at an earlier stage of the cause, a wife who is petitioner or has filed an answer may apply for an order that her husband gives security for her costs up to the hearing and of and incidental to such hearing. The Court has a discretion, and does not make an order as a matter of course. Evidence as to the means of the parties will be required. If the Court considers that the husband should provide security, he may be ordered to pay the sum ascertained into Court, or to give security therefor by bond to the Senior Registrar by the name of the Principal Probate Registrar. The bond is filed and cannot be sued upon without leave of the Registrar. If the wife succeeds she gets her actual taxed costs, even though these exceed the amount of the security ; if she fails, she will usually be allowed her costs up to the amount of the security.

After the decree *nisi* has been pronounced the wife then proceeds to tax her bill of costs giving credit for the amount in Court for the security. If the husband is the successful petitioner and the co-respondent is ordered to pay the costs, the husband then taxes his bill of costs against the co-respondent.

When the costs have been taxed by the Registrar or taxing officer an order of the Court for payment of the amount may issue.

Before serving a copy of the order on the party against whom payment has been ordered, it should be endorsed with a penal notice addressed to that party to the effect that if he fails to obey the order he may be liable to attachment for contempt of Court.

Ancillary relief. In addition to the principal relief claimed (*e.g.*, dissolution of the marriage), the petitioner may ask for other relief in the following ways.

The wife, whether a petitioner or respondent, may claim payment from her husband to support her, and if she has charge of the children of the marriage, some payment by way of an allowance for the children during the pendency of the suit, known as alimony pending suit (to be distinguished from the *permanent* alimony that may be granted after a judicial separation). The petitioning wife usually prays for alimony pending suit in her petition, although she may make a separate application to the Court. A respondent wife may apply to the Court for alimony pending suit at any time after entering an appearance. The husband may resist the claim on the ground that the wife has no need of alimony pending suit, *e.g.*, because she has adequate property, or is supported by the co-respondent, or on the ground that he has no income, or is bankrupt without earnings. Questions of this kind are decided by the Registrar, and he also settles the amount of alimony to be paid in cases where it is payable, and the parties cannot agree the amount. This will usually be an amount not exceeding one-fifth of the joint incomes of husband and wife, but the amount to be allotted is entirely in the discretion of the Court and may be less if the husband's income is very large, or more if the wife has to support the children. It will in cases of divorce be payable until petition is dismissed or the decree is made absolute, though if the unsuccessful petitioner be

Alimony pending suit.

the wife it may be continued by the judge pending an appeal. Alimony pending suit is not assignable by the wife. In proceedings for nullity, alimony pending suit is payable until the petition has been dismissed or the decree has been made absolute. If the proceedings are for restitution of conjugal rights, it is payable until the decree ordering the respondent to return has been served and disobeyed ; and in cases of judicial separation until the decree has been pronounced or the petition has been dismissed.

A respondent husband against whom a petition for divorce or judicial separation is presented on the ground of his insanity may make an application for alimony pending suit at any time after entering an appearance to the petition.

Maintenance.　　The Court may, if it thinks fit, on any decree for divorce or nullity of marriage, order the husband *to secure* to the wife, to the satisfaction of the Court, a gross or an annual sum of money for a period not exceeding her life, as having regard to her fortune, if any, to the ability of her husband and to the conduct of the parties, the Court may deem to be reasonable, and in any such case as aforesaid the Court may by order, either in addition to or instead of this, direct the husband *to pay* to the wife such monthly or weekly sum during their joint lives as the Court may think reasonable (Judicature Act, 1925, s. 190).

It will be noticed that under this provision secured maintenance may continue after the death of the husband, if it is awarded to the wife for her life and she survives him, but the direction to pay maintenance will cease on the death of either the husband or the wife.

The amount to be awarded by way of mainteance is not governed by any fixed rules or arithmetical calculations, but the Court in exercising the discretion conferred on it by s. 190 of the Judicature Act, 1925, to award maintenance and to decide the amount thereof, must take into consideration the matters which are specifically stated in that section and to which we have referred. The Court may, before the case is heard, go into the question of maintenance, but an order for maintenance cannot be made until after decree *nisi* and an order cannot take effect until decree absolute. An application for maintenance cannot be made later than two months after final decree except by leave which may be given by a Registrar.

It is not usual for the Court to decree maintenance in favour of a guilty wife ; but, in exceptional circumstances, the Court will compel a husband to make her a " compassionate allowance."

Permanent alimony is awarded to a wife who has obtained a decree of judicial separation, and in special circumstances even a guilty wife is entitled to apply for permanent alimony. An application for permanent alimony is dealt with on principles similar to those governing the allotment of alimony pending suit, except that the amount is usually about one-third of the husband's income. *Permanent alimony.*

A wife who petitions for divorce, or for judicial separation, on the ground of her husband's insanity may be ordered to provide maintenance or permanent alimony for her husband. An order for the payment of alimony pending suit, permanent alimony or maintenance (but *not* secured maintenance) may be discharged, varied, suspended or revived by the Court, having regard to all the circumstances of the case, including any increase or decrease in the means of either of the parties to the marriage (Administration of Justice (Miscellaneous Provisions) Act, 1938, s. 14). *Generally.*

Applications for alimony pending suit, maintenance or permanent alimony are dealt with by the Registrar, who may refer the application to the judge for his decision, but a claim for alimony pending suit or maintenance contained in the petition may be dealt with by the judge at the hearing (p. 115, *ante*).

After a final decree of nullity or dissolution of marriage, an order of the Court, which can be made on application to the Registrar (unless there are children of the marriage, in which case the application must be referred to the judge), may vary any ante-nuptial or post-nuptial settlements made on the parties whose marriage is the subject of the decree, the variation being for the benefit of the children or the parties to the marriage (Judicature Act, 1925, s. 192). This power is not exercised with *Variation of settlements.*

the object of punishing the guilty party, but to protect the interests of the innocent party and of the children of the marriage. The Court has power to vary ante- or post-nuptial settlements made by a guilty respondent wife in order to make provision for an innocent husband or the children of the marriage.

Other forms of ancillary relief. Maintenance of, or secured provision for, the children, when not claimed in the original petition (Judicature Act, 1925, s. 193) ; periodical payments, or secured periodical payments to a wife in suits for restitution of conjugal rights (*ibid.*, s. 187) ; modification of orders for such periodical payments, or for alimony pending suit, permanent alimony, maintenance, or maintenance of the children ; orders for the settlement of the wife's property in the case of a decree for divorce, or judicial separation by reason of her adultery, desertion or cruelty, or restitution of conjugal rights made against her (*ibid.*, s. 191), are other forms of ancillary relief which cannot be further discussed in a book of this scope.

(d) *Judicial Separation and Restitution of Conjugal Rights*

Jurisdiction. The Court has jurisdiction in these suits (apart from cases within the Matrimonial Causes Act, 1937, s. 13, p. 107, *ante*), if the parties are domiciled or resident within the jurisdiction, with the additional ground in restitution suits, if the matrimonial home was within the jurisdiction when cohabitation ceased.

Judicial separation. The petitioner has the right in all circumstances which would warrant the presentation of a petition for dissolution to ask in the prayer to the petition for the lesser remedy of judicial separation instead of dissolution. But this lesser remedy is also available in a case in which a decree of dissolution could not be granted. For a petitioner can ask for a decree of judicial separation where the respondent has failed to obey an order for restitution **Restitution of conjugal rights.** of conjugal rights. This is an order made by the Divorce Court when one party to the marriage has omitted to give to the other spouse the benefit of his or her society, when the " neglected " spouse has not committed a matri-

monial offence. Before instituting proceedings for restitution of conjugal rights it is usual for a letter couched in
friendly terms to be written by or on behalf of the petitioner to the respondent asking the respondent to return,
and if the petitioner is a male, offering to provide a home
for the respondent. The spouses are entitled to " *consortium,*" *i.e.*, companionship ; and if this is denied the
Court will make a decree of restitution of conjugal rights.
If this decree is not obeyed within the time specified in the
order, the wronged spouse can then apply to the Court for
a decree of judicial separation.

A decree for judicial separation does not bring the mar- *Effect of*
riage to an end, but it prevents the parties from claiming *judicial separation*
the right to *consortium*. On the decree being made a wife
may, as already explained (p. 129, *ante*) apply for permanent alimony.

(e) Nullity

If the parties are within the prohibited degrees or the *Nullity of marriage.*
so-called marriage is bigamous, or either party is under
the age of sixteen or an essential formality of the marriage
ceremony is not observed, the " marriage " is void *ab
initio*. On the other hand, if a party has not the capacity to
effect or permit consummation, the marriage is *voidable*.
The distinction between a void and a voidable marriage
has been stated in Vol. II, pp. 479–483.

A decree of the Court is sometimes sought to declare a
marriage to be void, in order that any doubts about the
matter may be set at rest, but a decree of the Court is
essential to declare void a marriage that was voidable only.

We have mentioned one ground which renders a marriage voidable. Other grounds are stated in the Matrimonial Causes Act, 1937, s. 7, and are : (*a*) that the
marriage has not been consummated owing to the wilful
refusal of the respondent to consummate the marriage ;
(*b*) that either party was at the time of the marriage of
unsound mind or a mental defective within the meaning
of the Mental Deficiency Acts, 1913 to 1927, or subject to
recurrent fits of insanity or epilepsy ; (*c*) that the
respondent was at the time of the marriage suffering from

venereal disease in a communicable form ; and (*d*) that
the respondent was at the time of the marriage pregnant
by some person other than the petitioner.

In the cases specified under (*b*), (*c*), and (*d*), the Court
cannot grant a decree of nullity unless it is satisfied :
(i) that the petitioner was at the time of the marriage
ignorant of the facts alleged, and (ii) the proceedings were
instituted within a year from the date of the marriage,
and (iii) that marital intercourse with the consent of the
petitioner has not taken place since the discovery by the
petitioner of the existence of the grounds for a decree.

Insistence by the respondent on the use of contracep-
tives against the wishes of the petitioner does not prevent
the consummation of the marriage (*Baxter* v. *Baxter*,
[1948] A. C. 274; [1947] 2 All E. R. 886) (see Vol. II, p. 483).

Jurisdiction.

The jurisdiction of the Court in nullity suits (apart
from cases within the provisions of the Matrimonial Causes
Act, 1937, s. 13, and the Matrimonial Causes (War
Marriages) Act, 1944, p. 107, *ante*), may be based on
domicil within the jurisdiction, whether the marriage is
alleged to be void or voidable. There is authority for
saying, that jurisdiction may be also based on residence
of the parties within the jurisdiction or on the marriage
being celebrated in England or Wales, but jurisdiction
on these grounds seems to apply only to marriages that
are alleged to be void and not to marriages alleged to be
voidable (*De Reneville* v. *De Reneville*, [1948] P. 100 ;
[1948] 1 All E. R. 56).

Medical
evidence.

The procedure is akin to what has already been
described in connection with dissolution. Where sexual
incapacity is alleged the Court usually requires evidence
from a medical inspector appointed by the Registrar as
to the condition of both parties, and if the respondent
refuses to attend to be medically examined the Court may
draw its own conclusion. The Rules also permit an
application to be made for the appointment of a medical
inspector on a petition for nullity on the ground of wilful
refusal to consummate the marriage. The Court must
be cleared while evidence of sexual capacity is given unless
the judge otherwise orders (Judicature Act, 1935, s. 4).

The Court, if satisfied as to the evidence, makes a decree

nisi, and it usually requires six weeks to elapse before making it absolute.

Similar considerations concerning alimony pending suit and variation of settlements apply as in cases of divorce (see pp. 127 and 129, *ante*). The Court also has a discretion with regard to giving a woman petitioner permanent maintenance (Judicature Act, 1925, s. 190). Ancillary relief.

(*f*) *Recognition of Foreign Divorce Decrees*

The English Courts recognise divorce decrees pronounced by a foreign Court of the country or state in which the parties are domiciled (*Harvey* v. *Farnie* (1882), 8 App. Cas. 43), or pronounced by a Court elsewhere and recognised by the law of the parties' domicil (*Armitage* v. *A.-G.*, [1906] P. 135). There must be a *bona fide* domicil in the foreign country or state, and the English Court will determine the domicil of the parties by applying the English conception of the term domicil. Recognition will not be refused solely on the ground that the decree was pronounced for a cause which would not support a petition for divorce in this country, *e.g.*, a sentence of imprisonment, but the respondent must have notice of the proceedings which will afford him or her an opportunity to participate in them. Foreign divorce decrees.

Section II. PROCEEDINGS IN COURTS OF SUMMARY JURISDICTION

Discussion on this subject would not be complete without giving some account of the proceedings in " Matrimonial Causes " before the justices. These proceedings are now more frequent in view of the lack of publicity attendant thereon, and the fact that they are conducted in as informal an atmosphere as possible, having regard to the rules of evidence that must be observed. The parties appear in many cases without solicitor or counsel. Summary proceedings.

Jurisdiction. A Court of Summary Jurisdiction may, by virtue of the Summary Jurisdiction (Separation and Maintenance) Acts, 1895 to 1925, grant relief on the application of a wife whose husband : Application by wife.

    (1) has deserted her (it is not necessary that the desertion should be for any specified period) ;

(2) has been convicted summarily of an aggravated assault upon her ;

(3) has been convicted on indictment of an assault upon her and sentenced to pay a fine of more than £5 or to a term of imprisonment exceeding two months ;

(4) has been guilty of persistent cruelty to her or of wilful neglect to provide reasonable maintenance for her or her infant children whom he is legally liable to maintain ;

(5) is an habitual drunkard or drug addict ;

(6) has been guilty of persistent cruelty to her children ;

(7) while suffering from a venereal disease and knowing that he was so suffering insisted on sexual intercourse with her ;

(8) has compelled her to submit to prostitution (where the husband has in the opinion of the Court been guilty of such conduct as was likely to result and has resulted in her submitting herself to prostitution he will be deemed to have compelled her so to submit herself) ; or

(9) (since the Matrimonial Causes Act, 1937) has been guilty of adultery.

The justices may issue a summons against the husband, and if they are satisfied that the case is proved they may make a separation, or a maintenance, order and order the husband to pay to his wife a weekly sum not exceeding £2 a week for herself and 10s. for each child until attaining the age of sixteen years. An order cannot be made if it be proved that the wife has committed adultery, unless the husband has condoned, or connived at, or by his wilful neglect or misconduct conduced to the adultery.

Application by husband.

A husband may apply for a separation order against his wife where she is an habitual drunkard, or has been guilty of persistent cruelty to his children, or has been guilty of adultery.

Effect.

Effect of Order. The effect of a separation order made by a Court of Summary Jurisdiction is similar to an order for judicial separation in the High Court, namely, the parties are now no longer bound to cohabit. The " non-cohabitation clause " before referred to should not be

inserted in an order unless there be a real need of it for
the wife's protection, as there may be when the order
is founded on persistent cruelty, but not when it is
founded on wilful neglect to provide reasonable maintenance or desertion, and if it is inserted in the latter
case, it will usually end the period of desertion and
adversely affect the success of a subsequent petition for
divorce on that ground. In considering the application
for a separation order the justices may have to determine
whether such matrimonial offences as adultery or cruelty
have been committed, which would be sufficient grounds
for a decree of divorce in the High Court, although they
themselves cannot grant such a decree.

Procedure. The proceedings are instituted by issuing
a summons upon a complaint being made to a justice or
justices and the application is made to a Court of Summary
Jurisdiction in the district where the complaint wholly or
in part arose, or in respect of (3) the Court before which the
husband was convicted. Applications must be made
within six months from the date of the offence complained
of, thus an application on the ground of adultery must be
made within six months of the commission of, not the
discovery of, the adultery. But this time limit does not
apply to continuing offences, such as, desertion or wilful
neglect to provide reasonable maintenance. The hearing
takes place before a Court of Summary Jurisdiction,
sitting to hear and determine " domestic proceedings,"
consisting of not more than three justices and including
as far as practicable a man and a woman. Only certain
specified persons may be present. The Court may, if it
makes an order, direct that the money be paid direct to
the wife or to the Court making the order. The Court
of Summary Jurisdiction has power, to vary or discharge
the order upon cause being shown upon fresh evidence,
i.e., evidence of something which happened after the
hearing, or evidence not in the possession of the applicant
at the hearing and of such importance that it would
affect the judgment of anyone if he had the opportunity
of hearing it at the trial.

If the wife commits adultery the order must be discharged, but the Court may refuse to do so, if the adultery

[margin note:] The procedure before justices.

was conduced to by the husband's failure to make payments under the order. The amounts payable under the order may be revoked, revived or varied upon cause being shown and either party may make an application for this purpose.

Appeal.

An appeal lies from any order, or the refusal of any order, to a Divisional Court of the Probate Division and a further appeal lies to the Court of Appeal with the leave of either tribunal.

CHAPTER 8

PROBATE PROCEEDINGS

When a person dies intestate all his real and personal estate, until adminstration is granted, vests in the President of the Probate, Divorce, and Admiralty Division (Administration of Estates Act, 1925, s. 9). If the deceased left a will which on the face of it was duly executed, the executor named in the will can obtain a grant of " probate " assuming that he is capable and willing to act as executor. In every other case a grant of " letters of administration " will be made to an administrator (see, Vol. I, Chapter 36). A sharp distinction is drawn between the authority of an executor and of an administrator to deal with the property of the deceased before obtaining a grant. As the executor derives his title from the will, he can deal with the property before obtaining a grant of probate which authenticates his title. On the other hand, an administrator derives his title from the grant of letters of administration and the property of the deceased does not vest in the administrator until the grant is made. He cannot therefore deal with the property before obtaining the grant, but when the grant is made, it is for some purposes—*e.g.*, suing a person who has in the meantime wrongfully interfered with the property—deemed to relate back to the time of death.

The grant of probate may be in two forms, either Probate. " common form " or " solemn form." Common form is where the matter is undisputed and the will has on the face of it been duly executed in accordance with the provisions of the Wills Act, 1837. The grant is made either by the Registrar at Somerset House or the District Probate Registrar in the country. In every other case the matter must be decided by the judge ; if he is satisfied as to the validity of the will in proceedings taken before him to prove the will, he pronounces in favour of it in " solemn form." The practical difference between a

grant in common form and a grant in solemn form is that
the former is always liable to be challenged and set aside,
but the latter can never be set aside, unless a later will is
afterwards discovered.

Letters of administration. Letters of administration are always in common form,
and grants of letters of administration are in practice not
infrequently set aside owing to a will being discovered at
a later date.

A purchaser dealing in good faith with a person to
whom probate or letters of administration has been
granted gets a good title to real or personal property
bought from him and a valid discharge for his money,
notwithstanding the grant may afterwards be set aside
(Administration of Estates Act, 1925, s. 37).

Grant in Common Form

Procedure for probate. The procedure to obtain a grant of probate in common
form is that the will, together with an affidavit by the
executor known as " the executor's oath," which provides
that he will administer the estate according to law and
will render a true account if called upon so to do, and
an Inland Revenue affidavit setting out the property of
the deceased are prepared.   The Inland Revenue affidavit
is first submitted to the Estate Duty Department of the
Inland Revenue for the estate duty to be assessed.
Estates where the gross value does not exceed £2000 are
exempt from duty.   Estates exceeding £2000 pay duty
at a rate which varies with the amount of the estate.
When the duty, if any, has been assessed and paid, the
Inland Revenue affidavit together with the other documents already mentioned in this paragraph are lodged at
the Registry ; and in due course if the papers are in order
the Court will issue a grant of probate.

Procedure for letters of administration. In order that letters of administration can be obtained,
instead of lodging the will and the executor's oath the
proposed administrator lodges " an administrator's oath,"
which also requires him to administer the estate according
to law and to render an account.   The Inland Revenue
affidavit showing that the estate duty, if any, has been
paid is also lodged with the other documents.   Unlike the

executor, an administrator must in nearly every case enter into bond together with sureties in order to implement his undertakings in his oath. The Court cannot make a grant of *administration* to an individual as a sole administrator in cases where there is a minority or life interest arising under a will or intestacy (Judicature Act, 1925, s. 160), unless the proposed administrator is the Public Trustee or a " trust corporation " which is the Public Trustee, or a corporation either appointed by the Court in any particular case, or authorised by rules made under the Public Trustee Act, 1906, to act as custodian trustee (this includes certain insurance companies). Administration would be granted though the deceased had made a will, if executors were not appointed, or executors were appointed but died before the testator, or renounced the executorship, the grant of administration in these cases being *cum testamento annexo*. In this respect a grant of letters of administration is distinguished from a grant of probate, as the Court has no power to insist on two executors proving for a grant of probate ; it frequently occurs that a deceased only appoints a sole executor, even in the cases mentioned above. But, probate or administration cannot be granted to more than four persons in respect of the same property (Judicature Act, 1925, s. 160).

Grant in Solemn Form

It is not uncommon in cases where someone wants to prevent a grant of representation being made to enter a caveat at the principal or at any district registry, and until this has been removed or otherwise disposed of, a grant of representation will not be issued. If the person who enters a caveat refuses to subduct it, *i.e.*, remove it, the person applying for a grant must obtain a warning from the principal registry. A warning is in the nature of a summons. It is served on the person entering the caveat, who, if he wishes to continue his opposition must enter an appearance to the warning. The caveat and the appearance to the warning do not amount to proceedings in an action. The procedure which is outlined hereafter

Contentious proceedings.

is adopted in order to prove a will in " solemn form."
The proceedings are commenced by writ of summons,
which is issued out of the Central Office, but, unlike writs
issued in the Chancery Division or the King's Bench
Division, the indorsement of the writ is verified by affidavit
filed in the principal registry before the issue of the writ
out of the Central Office. The pleadings and subsequent
proceedings are similar to proceedings in the King's Bench
Division, except that in probate proceedings both parties

Affidavit of scripts. have to file " affidavit of scripts." An affidavit of scripts
sets out all the testamentary documents and instruc-
tions for wills and former wills of the deceased, and
the affidavit must be filed with all these documents in the
registry within eight days of the entry of an appearance
by the defendant, unless otherwise ordered. When both
parties have filed their affidavits they can then inspect
the scripts of their opponents. If one party has no
" scripts " he must say so in his affidavit. In his defence
the defendant must state what is the substance of the case
on which he relies, and where he pleads that the testator
was not of sound mind, memory and understanding,
particulars must be delivered before the case is set down
for trial. With his defence a defendant may give notice
that he merely insists upon the will being proved in
solemn form and only intends to cross-examine the
witnesses produced in support of the will. If he serves
this notice he cannot afterwards dispute the capacity of
the testator or allege undue influence or fraud, but the
practical effect of serving this notice is, that he will not
be liable to pay the costs of the other side, unless the
judge is of opinion that there was no reasonable ground for
opposing the will. The proceedings come on for hearing
in due course before one of the judges of the Probate,
Divorce, and Admiralty Division, in London (occasionally
they are tried at the Assizes), and usually without a jury.

CHAPTER 9

ADMIRALTY PROCEEDINGS

Before the Judicature Act, 1873, the jurisdiction of the Admiralty Court rested mainly on the ancient jurisdiction of the Court (principally in cases of collision-damage, salvage, bottomry, and wages), and on the Admiralty Court Acts, 1840 and 1861, which extended the ancient maritime jurisdiction of the Court of the Lord High Admiral. From these main sources, and from others to be mentioned in due course, the Court derives jurisdiction to try the following causes relating to ships : (i) claims for damage done or received by any ship ; (ii) claims for salvage remuneration for salvage services rendered to a ship or her cargo (and this jurisdiction was extended by the Merchant Shipping Act, 1894, s. 544, re-enacting previous statutory provisions, to claims for saving life from a ship) ; (iii) claims by seamen for their wages (extended by the Merchant Shipping Act, 1894, s. 167 to include claims by the master of any ship for wages, or for disbursements made by him on account of the ship) ; (iv) claims to recover money lent on " bottomry bond," in respect of a ship, or money lent on a " respondentia bond " in respect of cargo ; (v) claims under towage contracts, for remuneration for towage services rendered to a ship ; (vi) claims to recover payment for necessaries supplied to a foreign ship, or to any ship, British or foreign, when in a port to which she does not belong, and when no owner is domiciled in England or Wales when the suit is begun ; (vii) by the Judicature Act, 1925, s. 22, claims (*a*) arising out of an agreement relating to the use or hire of a ship, (*b*) relating to the carriage of goods in any ship, or (*c*) in tort in respect of goods carried in any ship, provided that no owner or part owner of the ship is domiciled in England or Wales ; (viii) claims to recover possession of a ship, or to enforce other rights arising out

Origins of Admiralty jurisdiction.

Powers of the Court.

of the ownership of a ship or share thereof ; (ix) claims to enforce rights arising out of a registered mortgage of a British ship ; (x) claims to enforce rights arising out of an unregistered or equitable mortgage of a British ship, or any mortgage of a foreign ship ; and (xi) claims to recover payment for building, equipping, or repairing any ship ; provided, in each of the two last-mentioned cases, that the ship is already under the arrest of the Court, or has been sold in some other previously instituted suit (see generally, Judicature Act, 1925, s. 22).

Proceedings *in rem* and *in personam*.

The jurisdiction in all the cases above mentioned may be exercised under the Acts by proceedings *in rem* or *in personam* ; that is to say, instituted against the *res* (ship, or cargo, or both, as the case may be), or against the owner of the *res* personally. An action *in rem*, which is made effective against a ship by obtaining her arrest, after issue of a writ in an action *in rem*, is one in which the judgment may be enforced by selling the ship, or proceeding against the bail given to release her from arrest. It is a distinctive and peculiar feature of Admiralty jurisdiction.

Maritime lien.

In the first four of the cases above mentioned, the claimant has a *maritime lien* (see Vol. II, Book I, Chapter 11, and *The Ripon City*, [1897] P. 226), which is a privileged claim attaching to the *res* to which it relates from the moment of the happening of the cause giving rise to the claim, and continuing to attach to it, notwithstanding any subsequent change of ownership (*Harmer* v. *Bell ; The Bold Buccleugh* (1852), 7 Moo. P. C. 267), until the claim is satisfied ; and it is enforceable by the arrest of the *res* in an action *in rem*. But a maritime lien does not attach to a foreign state-owned ship at the time of a collision or other normal occasion of the accrual of a maritime lien, nor is such a ship liable to arrest in an action *in rem* if she is subsequently sold into private ownership (*The Tervaete*, [1922] P. 259).

Maritime Conventions Act— limitation of time.

The Maritime Conventions Act, 1911, s. 8, provides that collision and salvage actions must be brought within two years of the time of their accrual, or within such extended period as the Court may in any particular case

appoint ; unless, of course, some other and shorter period
of limitation is applicable ; as, for instance, where the
defendant is a commissioned officer in charge of one of
His Majesty's ships, so that under the Limitation Act,
1939, proceedings must be commenced against him for
damage by collision within twelve months (*The Danube II*,
[1921] P. 183). On the other hand, the Maritime Conventions Act, 1911, s. 8, binds the Crown, since the Crown
Proceedings Act, 1947, s. 30 (1), to the extent that
proceedings for damage to one of His Majesty's ships
by collision must be instituted within two years.

In the next three of the cases enumerated above, *Statutory right in rem.*
the claimant has not a maritime lien ; but, by reason
of the statutory provision above referred to, enabling
him to enforce his claim by proceedings *in rem*, he has
a statutory right *in rem*. Such a statutory right is
merely a right to enforce a personal claim against the
shipowner by arresting the ship to which the claim relates,
and gives no lien on the ship ; and the right to arrest is
lost, if, between the date of the accrual of the claim and
the date of the steps taken to arrest, the ship is sold, even
if the sale be to a purchaser who has notice of the claim
(*The Aneroid* (1877), 2 P. D. 189).

An action *in rem* may therefore be defined as a suit
instituted against a ship or her cargo to enforce a maritime lien on it or a statutory right *in rem* against it, or to
enforce rights arising out of the ownership or mortgage of
a ship.

By the Judicature Act, 1873, the jurisdiction of the *High Court Procedure under Judicature Act, 1873.*
High Court of Admiralty was vested in the High Court.
For the more convenient distribution of business in
the High Court, however, the maritime causes which
were previously within the exclusive jurisdiction of the
Admiralty Court, were assigned to the Probate, Divorce,
and Admiralty Division. The jurisdiction of the judge
sitting to hear Admiralty cases in the Probate, Divorce,
and Admiralty Division is, therefore, twofold. As a
judge of the High Court, he has all the powers and jurisdiction of any other judge of the High Court ; and, subject to the power of transferring any action commenced in
the Admiralty Division which ought under the Judicature

Acts or the Rules to have been brought in either of the other divisions, he has a concurrent jurisdiction to try any action. In practice, however, the actions *in personam* commenced in the Admiralty Division relate to ships. Second, he has, in practice, an exclusive jurisdiction to try actions *in rem*, which previously could only have been brought in the Admiralty Court. The jurisdiction *in rem* of the Probate, Divorce, and Admiralty Division is the same as that of the High Court of Admiralty before 1875 ; it rests principally upon the provisions contained in the Admiralty Courts Acts, 1840 and 1861, the Merchant Shipping Acts, and the Administration of Justice Act, 1920, s. 5, as amended and re-enacted by the Judicature Act, 1925, s. 22.

Most of the actions brought in Admiralty are either actions for damage by collision between ships, or actions for salvage ; and it may therefore be useful to explain and illustrate the peculiarities of Admiralty procedure by giving an outline of the various steps in an ordinary action *in rem* for damage by collision, and in an action for salvage.

Damage
by collision.

(*a*) *Action* in rem *for damage by collision.* The writ is issued out of the Central Office or a District Registry, after which it is taken to the Admiralty Registry, where an official number (called the " folio " number) is assigned to the cause, and wherein subsequent proceedings originate. The parties are usually not mentioned by name, but are described as " the owners " of the respective ships. Unless the solicitor for the defendant owners gives an undertaking to accept service and to put in bail, the writ is served on the ship proceeded against, if she be within the jurisdiction, that is, in a port in England or

Arrest of
vessel.

Wales, or within three miles from the shore. After issue of the writ, the plaintiff may procure the issue of a warrant of arrest ; whereupon the vessel will be arrested by the Marshal of the Admiralty Court or his substitute. From the time the ship is arrested, she is deemed to be in the custody of the Court ; and it is a contempt of Court, punishable by fine or imprisonment, to remove or interfere with her. She remains under arrest until her release, which may occur on bail being given for the amount of the claim and costs, or when the claim is satisfied, or is dismissed by the Court.

The defendants have frequently a cross-claim for their damage by the collision ; and they may procure the arrest of the plaintiff's ship by taking similar steps. But if they cannot do so, owing to her not being within the jurisdiction, or having been lost, the Court, in order to put them on an equal footing to the plaintiffs with regard to security, will stay the action until the plaintiffs give bail or other security for the counterclaim.

Bail in Admiralty actions is usually given in the form of a bond executed by two sureties, who undertake, in the event of the judgment not being satisfied, to pay the amount of it, not exceeding the sum fixed in the bond. **Bail.**

In every collision action, the plaintiff's solicitor is required to file in the Registry within seven days after the commencement of the action, and the defendant's solicitor within seven days after appearance, a most important document called a " Preliminary Act," containing a short statement of the material facts relating to the collision ; and this document is sealed up, and is not open to the inspection of the opposite party until after the pleadings are completed. The object of a preliminary act is, that each party should soon after the occurrence, and at an early stage in the proceedings, set out his version of the facts, before he knows his opponent's version. Each party is bound at the trial by his preliminary act ; and the Court will not usually allow any material amendment of it. **Preliminary Act.**

Pleadings are usually delivered in a collision action, and consist of a statement of claim, defence, and frequently a counterclaim, and a reply to the counterclaim. Summonses are generally heard by the Registrar, from whom an appeal lies to the Admiralty judge in Chambers. No summons for directions is required in an Admiralty action. **Pleadings.**

The action is tried by the judge, assisted by two of the Elder Brethren of the Trinity House as assessors. The functions of the Elder Brethren (or " Trinity **Assessors.**

Masters " as they are often called) are, however, solely
advisory, to assist the judge as experts on all matters
of nautical practice and skill ; so that witnesses as to
such matters are not allowable when the Elder Brethren
are present, as they are in actions for collision and salvage
as a matter of course. The case is opened without
speeches, by calling at once the witnesses for the respective parties ; and, after the evidence is closed, the
plaintiff's counsel addresses the Court, and is afterwards
entitled to reply to the speech of the defendant's counsel.
The judge, after consulting the Elder Brethren, delivers
judgment, in which he may pronounce one or both of the
ships to blame, or that the collision was the result of some
accident, for which neither is responsible.

Joint
negligence.

The former Admiralty rule as to joint negligence,
whereby, when each of two ships was held to blame
for damage by collision, the owner of each ship was
liable to bear half the total loss of both ships, has been
greatly modified by the Maritime Conventions Act, 1911,
ss. 1 and 9 (3) ; and the existing rule is, that where,
by the fault of two or more vessels, damage or loss
(whether by collision or not) is caused to one or more of
them, or to property on board, each vessel shall be liable
in proportion to the degree in which she was in fault (*Admiralty Comrs.* v. *S.S. Volute*, [1922] 1 A. C. 129). But
if it is impossible to establish different degrees of fault,
the liability is to be apportioned equally, as under the
old rule. Costs are in the discretion of the judge, with
the result that usually the successful party gets the
costs of the action ; when both ships are found to blame,
even though in different proportions of blame, the general
rule is that each party is made to bear his own costs, but
the discretion of the judge is paramount and in a recent
case the defendants were awarded one-third of their
taxed costs, though the extent of the blame attributable to
them was thirty per cent. (*The Salabangka*, [1943] P. 13).
Only the questions of liability are decided by the judge
at the hearing ; the damages being assessed in the
Admiralty Registry, by the Registrar and two merchants
drawn from a rota compiled by the President of the Probate, Divorce, and Admiralty Division.

An appeal from an Admiralty decision lies to the Appeal. Court of Appeal, and thence by leave either of the Court of Appeal or the House of Lords to the House of Lords, in both cases with the aid of the Elder Brethren when required. When an appellate tribunal takes the same view of the law and the facts as the Court below, only in very exceptional cases or circumstances, such as, where a number of reasons were given why one ship was to blame and the appellate tribunal finds that some of the reasons were not valid, or where the trial judge misapprehended a vital fact bearing on the distribution of blame, should there be any alteration or interference with the allocation of blame by the trial judge (*British Fame (Owners) v. Macgregor (Owners), The Macgregor*, [1943] A. C. 197 ; [1943] 1 All E. R. 33). Before 1875, an appeal lay from the Admiralty Court to the Judicial Committee of the Privy Council, and this is true to-day where the Court is exercising jurisdiction as a Prize Court.

(*b*) *Action* in rem *for salvage*. In this action, the Action for plaintiffs are usually the owners, master, and crew of salvage. the ship which has rendered the salvage services ; and the defendants are the owners of the ship to which the services have been rendered, and of her cargo and freight. And the parties are generally so described in the writ. The steps taken to arrest the salved property, or to get bail given for the amount of the claim and costs, are the same as those in a collision action *in rem*.

As the amount of salvage remuneration depends Ascertain-largely on the value of the salved property, the pro- value of ceedings to ascertain the value of the latter are im- salved portant. The usual practice is for the defendants to property. file an " affidavit of values " ; and the affidavit is, *prima facie*, conclusive. If, however, the plaintiffs consider that the values as sworn are too low, they may obtain an order for the *appraisement* of the property, by one or more valuers appointed by the marshal of the Court, whose valuation is final and conclusive. The plaintiffs are bound by the defendants' affidavit of values, if an appraisement was possible and they have not required it. If, on the other hand, they have required it, the question of the incidence of the costs of appraisement, which are often heavy, depends on whether the appraised values are substantially higher than those sworn to in the affidavit. Where there are two or more sets of salvors, and they have issued separate writs, the different actions are consolidated, and ordered to be tried together ; and the conduct of the consolidated action is usually given to the party who appears to have been the principal salvor.

In a salvage action, the statement of claim sets out particulars of the service rendered, and the nature of the danger or loss from which the defendants' property was thereby saved, and claims such an amount of salvage as may to the Court seem just. In the defence, it may be denied that any services of a salvage nature were rendered ; or, while admitting that the services were salvage, it may be contended that the description of them in the statement of claim is exaggerated or untrue. The defendants may also pay money into Court by way of tender, with a view to getting their costs of the action subsequent to the date of the tender, if it is upheld at the trial.

If the amount of salvage awarded by the Court is, together with the plaintiffs' costs of the action, considerably less than the amount of bail demanded by the plaintiffs, the judge will condemn them to pay the defendants' costs of providing bail beyond a reasonable amount. It is not the practice to claim a specific sum as salvage ; but if the amount awarded exceeds the amount for which bail has been given, the claim may, by leave of the judge, be amended, and, for the balance for which bail has not been given, execution may issue ; and the defendants' ship may, like other chattels of the defendants, be seized by the sheriff under a writ of *fieri facias*, notwithstanding its previous arrest and release.

Salvage of aircraft. The Admiralty jurisdiction of the High Court includes claims for salvage by or to aircraft, a subject that is governed by Statute and Orders in Council the details of which are outside the scope of this work.

The Crown and salvage. His Majesty may claim for salvage services rendered by any ship or aircraft belonging to His Majesty (Crown Proceedings Act, 1947, s. 8). Conversely, salvage claims may be made for assisting His Majesty's ships or aircraft, or in saving life therefrom, or cargo, or apparel (*ibid.*).

The High Court has permanent jurisdiction as a Prize Court, and no commission or proclamation of war is necessary to bring that jurisdiction into operation. Prize matters are assigned to the Probate, Divorce, and Admiralty Division, but care should be taken not to confuse either the jurisdiction or the functions of the Prize Court with those of the Admiralty Court.

CHAPTER 10

EVIDENCE AND ESTOPPEL

Value of
rules relating
to evidence.

Any person who tries to ascertain the truth about
anything is bound, consciously or unconsciously, to
follow in the process certain rules of evidence ; or else
he is unlikely to reach a valuable result. The English
Courts have in the course of centuries found it necessary
from time to time to decide points of evidence, and out
of their decisions has grown a body of case-law analogous
to the other branches of the Common Law. The result
is that there is much less that is unconscious and much
less that is indeterminate in the processes by which the
Courts come to a decision on a point of fact, than would
be the case where the investigator was a private individual.
No continental system of law has anything like the
English Law of Evidence, and it is generally acknowledged
that it has grown up as a result of the jury system in our
Courts. Where the investigator is an expert there can
be little objection to allowing him access to any material
whatever that might conceivably assist him in coming to
a right conclusion, and in those circumstances the Law of
Evidence can be little more than a few general warnings
to the judge not to pay too much attention to certain
types of testimony. But where, as was invariably the
case in the Common Law Courts until the second half of
the nineteenth century, the judges of fact are a jury of
laymen, it is perhaps advisable to keep from their notice
entirely those varieties of evidence which experience has
shown most likely to lead them astray. At any rate
English Law has chosen this course. It is obvious that
the absolute exclusion of varieties of evidence gives a real
distinctiveness to the English Law of Evidence, which continental systems cannot from the nature of things possess.

Rules of
evidence
based on
common
sense.

But except for this greater definiteness, the rules of
evidence observed in Courts of Law are not very different
from those which would commend themselves to any

150

person engaged in a problem of historical research. At the root of them is pure common sense. They are in general the products of experience, and where, as is sometimes the case, they appear to offend against reason, it will generally be found that they are the result of legislation. The main body of the Law of Evidence applies universally to all trials, whatever be the matter in issue, whether civil or criminal, but some rules apply only to certain kinds of case. In accordance with the plan which has been heretofore adopted, only the general principles will here be dealt with.

The first point to notice is that the facts relied upon by either party in support of his claim or defence must, if not admitted by his opponent, nor presumed by the Court in his favour, be proved by him in evidence. Some of the facts may be admitted in his opponent's pleading ; others may have been admitted as a result of a notice to admit facts ; in these cases there is no need to prove them at all, though it may conceivably be necessary to prove the admission itself, if not contained in a pleading, So, too, a litigant need not prove any fact which the law presumes in his favour ; unless his opponent adduces evidence to the contrary. Thus, for example, in an action for libel, the plaintiff need not prove that the words are untrue ; except to rebut evidence given by the defendant in support of a plea of justification. And most familiar of all is the rule, common to the great majority of, if not all, modern civilised systems, that a man is presumed to be innocent until he is proved guilty. A striking exception to this rule is the provision of the Matrimonial Causes Act, 1937, whereby the onus is placed upon the petitioner to satisfy the Court that the petitioner is not guilty of collusion, connivance, or condonation. Even in this case, however, the petitioner is entitled to rely in the first instance on the presumption of innocence : but the presumption is provisional, as opposed to compelling, only and is counterbalanced by circumstances which lead to suspicion, and thereupon the petitioner is left as he began, with the legal burden of negativing collusion or connivance (*Emanuel* v. *Emanuel*, [1946] P. 115 ; [1945] 2 All E. R. 494).

Facts must be proved unless admitted or presumed.

Certain facts
need not be
proved.

There are also certain facts of which the Court will take judicial notice, and of which evidence therefore is not required ; such as the public statutes, all local, personal and private Acts of Parliament passed since 1850 in the absence of provision therein to the contrary, customs settled by judicial decision, public matters connected with the government of the country, matters of common and certain knowledge, such as the meaning of common words and phrases, and events which must happen in the ordinary course of nature.

When it is said that judicial notice must be taken of a fact, it is not implied that the judge is expected to know it of his own knowledge, without being informed of it. That would in many cases be absurd and contrary to general experience ; for what judge knows by heart even the names of all the public statutes ? It means that his attention may be called to a fact, and that thereupon he is to accept it as true without requiring further proof.

Subject to these, and a few similar, exceptions, all facts relied on must be proved by the parties by oral or documentary or real evidence.

Relevant
facts only
can be
proved.

Relevancy. The only facts which can be relied on, and to which therefore the evidence must be confined, are the facts *in issue* on the pleadings, or, in a criminal prosecution, the facts which go to make up the charge, or other facts which are *relevant* to them ; that is to say, which tend to prove or disprove the facts in issue on which the claim or defence or charge is based. Any other fact is irrelevant to the issue ; and evidence tendered to prove it is inadmissible. Beyond this definition of relevancy it is impossible to go : every fact must be treated on its merits, and common sense is the only test. Many of our English rules of relevancy are designed to prevent the undue prolongation of trials and the waste of time in the Courts. The results in the dispatch of judicial business compare favourably with most foreign systems of procedure.

Evidence of
similar acts
and of
character
not generally
admissible.

But certain kinds of evidence which to the ordinary man might seem relevant are not relevant in the eyes of the law. For instance, in an action for damage by negligence. on a particular occasion, the fact that the defendant has been careless on other occasions would be irrelevant. Only in certain classes of cases is evidence of acts of a like nature admissible. If, for instance, it is clear that the defendant has done an act, but it is necessary to prove that he did it intentionally, then evidence of acts of a like nature is admissible to show that the act in question was not an accident and further that it was intentional. These exceptions, though applicable to both civil and criminal proceedings, are of particular importance in the law of Criminal Evidence.

So also evidence in chief, as opposed to cross-examination, to prove the character of either party is inadmissible, as being irrelevant : unless the character of the party is a fact directly in issue, as in an action by a servant for wrongful dismissal, or in an action for libel or slander, or is relevant to the question of damages, as in breach of promise of marriage or for seduction.

It might be thought that evidence of similar acts on other occasions and evidence as to character ought always to be admissible for what they are worth. It can hardly be said that they have no value in deciding whether an allegation is true or false. But it is felt that any claim they have to consideration on that account, and it would in any case be small, is far outweighed by the atmosphere of prejudice which would be introduced into a Court of law were they once admitted.

Estoppel. Not every relevant fact is allowed to be proved. Thus it frequently happens that a party is " estopped " from denying the truth of a statement which has previously been made. Estoppel, in general, is a rule of evidence which prevents a man, in the course of legal proceedings, from alleging, or indeed proving, the falseness of something which he has represented, either by words or by conduct, to be true. *{Even relevant facts sometimes inadmissible. Nature of estoppel.}*

The essence of an estoppel is that a party is not allowed to deny a state of facts which he has alleged to be true, either expressly in words or impliedly by conduct, on some previous occasion. It makes no difference that the state of facts is not true, for, in the words of Lord Coke, *{Estoppel in general.}*

> " a man's own act or acceptance stoppeth or closeth up his mouth to allege or plead the truth."

The statement must be clear and unambiguous, and it must purport to be of some fact which exists at the time, or which has already occurred. Thus a promise does not work an estoppel, though if a person says unequivocally that he has an intention to do a particular act, he may in a proper case be estopped from denying, for what it is worth, that he had the intention at the time when he made the statement.

Estoppel is not a cause of action and so it is not a weapon of attack, but only of defence, though it may of course be pleaded as a reply to a defence, and so materially help a plaintiff's case. For it may well be that an allegation which is an indispensable part of the statement of claim may not be disputed by the defendant although it is in fact untrue.

It may be asked, should a party ever be precluded from contesting a statement which is not incontestably true ? The answer to this question varies with the type of estoppel. There are three types of estoppel known respectively as estoppel by record, estoppel by deed, and estoppel by conduct, or " in pais."

1. *Estoppel by record.* It is clearly right that controversies should not be liable to be continually re-opened, and so parties to a legal proceeding in which final judgment has been given are estopped from denying the truth of the facts on which the judgment was based. The judgment is entered upon the *record* of the Court ; hence this variety of estoppel is known as *estoppel by record*.

Only the parties themselves and other persons who succeed to their claims are so estopped, for it would clearly be unfair that a person should be precluded from denying the truth of a statement which he has had no previous opportunity of contesting. This is true of judgments *in personam*, which are ordinary judgments between persons not affecting status. But, judgments *in rem* which operate to settle the status of any subject-matter, persons, or thing, are conclusive against all the world. Thus where a married woman has been divorced by a Court of competent jurisdiction, she is divorced for all purposes, and it is not open to any person who was not a party to the divorce proceedings to deny the validity of the decree.

Yet even a party to the action can impeach a former judgment on the ground of fraud or collusion, for in such a case he does not seek to show that the Court was mistaken but that it was misled, and obviously the opposite party ought not to be allowed to take advantage of his own fraud. It should be noted that an estoppel by record must be specially pleaded.

2. *Estoppel by deed.* A person who makes a statement in a deed or sealed document is estopped from denying its truth. In the majority of instances the statements contained in the deed will estop every party who has executed it, but if any statement is the statement of one party alone, he alone will be estopped by it. Here again proof of fraud will exclude the estoppel, and the estoppel must be specially pleaded.

Statements in a deed conclusive.

Estoppel by deed is restricted to statements contained in sealed documents. It may perhaps be thought curious that everything should depend on the presence or absence of a seal, but, as the student finds, when he studies the law of contract, the law of England often distinguishes transactions which are effected by means of sealed documents from all other legal acts, but it does not as a rule distinguish between things written and things spoken. The distinction is archaic, and dates from a time when the usual method of authenticating a document was by sealing it, and estoppel by deed, being of early origin, follows this old rule. In modern times greater weight is often attached by law to written than spoken words, even though they are unaccompanied by a seal ; but it is sometimes thought advisable even at the present day to insist that a document shall be subjected to the additional formality of sealing, for everybody knows when he executes a document under seal that he is doing something peculiarly solemn. Under these circumstances there is nothing irrational in conclusively presuming that a person intends to be peculiarly bound by a statement which he has made under seal.

Sealing essential.

3. *Estoppel by conduct* may occur in several ways. Only one of these, *estoppel by representation* (which though usually made by words may also be made by conduct), calls for special attention at this stage. If a person wilfully

Estoppel by representation.

causes another to believe in a certain state of affairs so that the person who is induced to believe it does some thing which he would not otherwise have done, the rule is that the person making the representation is not allowed at a later date to deny or repudiate the truth of the representation, notwithstanding that the statement may not in fact be true. The term " wilfully " is not limited to a representation known to be false, for a person will be acting wilfully, " if . . . he so conducts himself that a reasonable man would take the representation to be true, and believe that it was meant he should act upon it, and did act upon it as true."

The basis of estoppel by representation is that in business relations a man ought to be able to rely on statements made by other persons, at any rate, that his opponent ought not to be allowed to " blow hot and cold," if matters come to a controversy between them. This is a very useful and salutary principle, making as it does for honesty in business, and as it does not in any way depend on technicalities, the judges are always ready to extend its operation, whereas estoppels of record and estoppels by deed are said to be " odious," and are construed strictly.

" Without prejudice."   *Statements " without prejudice."* Proof is not allowed of statements made " without prejudice." These are statements made by parties in the course of negotiations for a compromise ; the law protects them in order that the parties may negotiate freely and without fear of making their position worse if a trial cannot eventually be avoided. If a letter is written " without prejudice " the reply to that letter, although not marked " without prejudice " is " without prejudice " if the letter in reply refers to the letter marked " without prejudice." In this connection we may pause to warn the student that it is not always wise to prefix the words " without prejudice" to letters to opponents. Very often a letter which shows a reasonable disposition towards the other side will create a favourable impression on the Court, and to prevent counsel from referring to it at the trial is clumsy strategy. Evidence is admissible of an offer made "without prejudice " and the acceptance of the offer to prove the new agreement.

Oral evidence is given by witnesses examined on oath or affirmation before the Court, or out of Court before an official examiner or on commission, if, owing to illness or absence abroad, the witness cannot attend the trial. In civil cases, every person is now competent to give evidence ; unless, owing to infancy, unsoundness of mind, or drunkenness, he is, in the opinion of the judge, unable to understand the nature of an oath, or the duty of speaking the truth, or to give rational testimony. Any oath is sufficient, so long as the witness believes in its binding character. It is not necessary that it should be accompanied by a belief in Christianity ; cases occur where witnesses swear according to the Chinese or Mohammedan forms, and Jewish witnesses frequently come before the Courts. The Court now has power to order that specified facts may be proved at the trial by affidavit with or without the attendance of the deponent for cross-examination, notwithstanding that a party desires his attendance for cross-examination and that he can be produced for that purpose.

Witnesses. The attendance at the trial of any witness who is within the jurisdiction can be secured by serving him with a writ of *subpœna ad testificandum,* or, where he is required to bring documents with him, by a *subpœna duces tecum* specifying the documents, and by paying or tendering him a sum to defray his reasonable expenses of attendance. The consequences of failing to answer the subpœna have already been noted.

Every witness who appears to give evidence is liable to undergo three examinations : (1) examination-in-chief ; (2) cross-examination, and (3) re-examination.

1. *Examination-in-chief.* He is examined in chief by counsel for the party on whose behalf he is called. Inasmuch as counsel is examining a witness who is presumably favourable to his client, no " leading " question, that is to say, no question which is put in such a form as to suggest to the witness the answer he is desired to give, is strictly, admissible in examination-in-chief. But leading questions may properly be asked with reference to facts which are merely introductory, or are not in dispute, *e.g.* the name, and (except in undefended divorce suits) the address, and occupation of the witness, or for the purpose

of contradicting a statement made by a witness on the other side, or occasionally identifying a person or thing.

If a witness turns hostile, the judge in his discretion may allow him to be cross-examined by counsel for the party on whose behalf he is called. The party producing a witness is not allowed to impeach the credit of the witness by general evidence of bad character, but he may contradict him by other evidence which shows that the witness is not telling the truth on any relevant point, or he may, if the witness in the opinion of the judge is adverse and if the judge gives leave, prove that the witness has previously made a statement inconsistent with his present testimony, the circumstances in which the statement was made being first put to the witness and he being asked whether or not he made such statement. The word " adverse " is used to mean " hostile " and the fact that his answers are not favourable does not by itself make him a hostile witness ; his demeanour is a matter of importance, and this factor must be considered by the Court before it allows the party calling the witness to treat him as a hostile witness.

Object of cross-examination.

2. *Cross-examination.* After examination-in-chief the witness is cross-examined by counsel for the opposite side, and evidence which has been given under such circumstances as to afford no opportunity for cross-examination is in general inadmissible. The purpose is primarily to test the evidence which has been given in chief. In cross-examination, more latitude is allowed than in examination-in-chief with regard to the kind of questions which may be put to the witness. The objects of the cross-examiner are, first, to weaken his opponent's case, by showing that the evidence of the latter's witnesses is untrustworthy ; and, secondly, to establish his own case by obtaining admissions from the witnesses called by his opponent. In pursuance of the second object it is his duty to indicate in his cross-examination what facts deposed to by each witness in examination-in-chief he disputes, and to put to each of them in turn so much of his own case as the particular witness is in a position to admit or deny. For instance, if counsel for defendant intends to prove a certain fact against the plaintiff he

must " put it to him in cross-examination," and so give him a chance of denial or explanation.

In cross-examination, therefore, questions may be put to elicit facts which, though not relevant to any fact in issue, tend to discredit the witness, by showing grounds for doubting his accuracy or his honesty. Thus, in cross-examination a witness may be asked any " leading " question, or any question to show his bias or interest in the action, or to show that he has, on a previous occasion, made statements inconsistent with the evidence he has given, or that he has been convicted of any crime.

Greater latitude in cross-examination.

But where a question is put to elicit a fact which is merely relevant to the credit of the witness, and not to any fact in issue in the action, the answer of the witness is final, and no evidence can afterwards be called to contradict it ; otherwise the case might branch out into all kinds of irrelevant inquiries. To this rule there is, however, the exception that, where a witness has in cross-examination denied bias, or that he has made a previous inconsistent statement, or that he has been convicted of a crime, evidence may afterwards be given to contradict his denial. Where the witness denies having made a previous inconsistent statement, then, if it was oral, the circumstances in which it was made must be mentioned to him, so as to give him an opportunity of remembering the occasion ; and, if it was made in writing, his attention must be called to the document, before it can be put in evidence to contradict him.

When answer of witness is final.

Counsel may also, in cross-examination, ask a witness quite irrelevant questions for the purpose of putting him off his guard. This is indeed often necessary where a witness has learnt up his story.

There are certain questions which, though allowed to be put, the witness is not bound to answer ; such as any question which tends to show that he has committed a crime (of which he has not been convicted), or which seeks to obtain the disclosure by a husband of any communication made to him by his wife during the marriage, or *vice versa* (Evidence Amendment Act, 1853, s. 3) (this privilege does not continue to exist after the marriage has come to an end : *Shenton* v. *Tyler*, [1939] Ch. 620 ;

Questions that need not be answered.

[1939] 1 All E. R. 827), or between legal adviser and client (where it is not made for the purpose of carrying out a fraud, or obtaining assistance in the commission of a crime and before the actual commission of the crime). But there is no similar privilege in the case of communications between a spiritual or medical adviser and his penitent or patient, though in practice a priest is not compelled to disclose a confession. In cases where the disclosure of a fact would be detrimental to the public interest, the witness will not be allowed to give evidence of it ; nor in the case of a Privy Councillor, who is bound by his oath of secrecy not to disclose the proceedings in the Privy Council or the Cabinet, unless he first obtains the Sovereign's permission. In practice permission is given by the King on the advice of the Prime Minister, by whom the request is transmitted to the Sovereign.

Limits to re-examination.

3. *Re-examination.* A witness, who has been cross-examined, may be re-examined by the party who called him ; but he cannot, except by the judge or with leave, be asked any question which does not arise out of his cross-examination. The object of re-examination is to explain more fully any matter referred to in cross-examination, or to give the witness an opportunity of explaining any inconsistency or mistake in the answers given by him in cross-examination. Re-examination is always regarded as being so vital that in cases where leading counsel are employed the responsibility is seldom left to the junior counsel, but the re-examination is conducted by the leader.

Mode of proving facts.

Proof of facts. Now, assuming that a fact is allowed to be proved, the question still remains, how may it be proved.

Hearsay evidence excluded.

A fact, generally speaking, can only be proved by the formal testimony of a witness who has personal knowledge of it, and not by any other person ; and it is by reason of this rule that hearsay evidence, as it is called, is not received by the Court : that is to say, the fact that someone not called as a witness has stated, either by word of mouth or in writing, that a certain fact does or does not exist, is not admissible as evidence of the existence or non-existence of that fact. That person must himself be called to testify to the matter in question. It will be understood, however, that what a person has said may be a relevant fact, and therefore may be proved by a witness who heard it stated. To take a simple example, suppose A has told B that C has stolen a book. It is clearly not permissible to ask B what A said in order to prove that C stole the book, but if C is suing A for damages for slander, it is obviously right that B should be allowed to give evidence of what A said, for the fact that A said that C stole the book is a fact in issue.

To the general rule that evidence is inadmissible of a statement made by a person not called as a witness, there are many exceptions. Some of these are peculiar to criminal proceedings. Of those which are of general application the following may be noticed here : Exceptions to general rule.

(*a*) A statement made by the opposite party, or by an agent with his express or implied authority, may be given in evidence *against* him as an admission.

(*b*) Statements in public documents are admissible, if made under a legal duty by the proper officer. This applies not only to British but also to foreign documents.

(*c*) Declarations by a deceased person are admissible in certain cases and for certain purposes. This exception is made by reason of the fact that otherwise there would probably be a failure of justice for want of sufficient evidence. Moreover, in every instance the facts create a strong presumption that the statement is likely to be true. These cases are :

(i) Declarations against interest. A statement, oral or written, made by a person since deceased, the whole or part of which was against his pecuniary or proprietary interest (*Higham* v. *Ridgway* (1808), 10 East, 109) as, for example, an entry in his cash-book showing that he received money in payment of a debt due to him.

(ii) Declarations in course of duty. A statement, oral or written, made by a person since deceased in the usual course of his business of a transaction done by him, his duty being to do the act recorded, and to record it at or about the time of doing it (*Price* v. *Torrington (Earl)* (1703), Holt, K. B. 300).

Declarations against interest establish the facts against such interest and all other facts in the same statement. Declarations in the course of duty establish only the fact which it was the declarant's duty to record. If these declarations are oral, they are not affected by the Evidence Act, 1938, but if they are in writing, this Act, as we shall try to explain later on, has extended their admissibility in *civil* proceedings.

(iii) Declarations by a deceased person upon questions of pedigree, or as to public rights or customs. These are generally admissible, but only when made before any controversy arose to the knowledge of the deceased.

(*d*) Evidence given in former proceedings is sometimes admissible. This exception is restricted in scope ; the proceedings must have been substantially similar and between the same parties and the person against whom the evidence is proposed to be admitted must have had an opportunity on the previous occasion of cross-examining the witness ; and, moreover, there must be some very good reason, such as death or insanity, preventing the witness from being brought before the Court.

Witness must
state facts
and not his
opinion. *Opinions of witness.* No question is admissible which is put to elicit the opinion of the witness on facts from which it is the function of a jury or other tribunal of fact to draw their own inferences. It is the duty of a witness to state facts and not opinions. But this is not to say that a witness ought to state categorically facts of which he is not quite certain ; he is always allowed in such cases to qualify his statement by some such words as,

" I believe to the best of my recollection that such and such is the case."

And the opinion of experts is always admissible for the assistance of the jury in matters requiring special skill or experience.

Admissibility
of docu-
mentary
evidence as
to facts in
issue. *Documentary evidence.* During recent years disputes between persons interested in commerce have been referred by the parties themselves to arbitration instead of having the matter decided in a Court of Law, and they have agreed, in order to save expense and to prevent delay, to admit as evidence facts stated in documents that have been brought into existence in the ordinary course of business. Much of the " Law Merchant," *i.e.*, the custom of merchants has become part of the Common Law, and this was very largely brought about by Lord Mansfield ; and what Lord Mansfield did with regard to substantive law the legislature is largely doing with regard to the law of evidence.

The Evidence Act, 1938, s. 1, provides that in any *civil proceedings* (except in an action tried by a jury when the Court has a discretion) where direct oral evidence of a fact would be admissible, any statement made by a person in a document tending to establish that fact, if either the statement was made by a person having personal know-ledge of the matter or, where the document in question is or forms part of a record purporting to be a continuous record, the statement was made by a person in perform-ance of a duty to record the information supplied to him by another person apparently having personal knowledge of the matter, shall, on production of the original docu-ment or, if the Court permits, a certified copy thereof, be admissible as evidence of that fact in all cases where the maker of the statement is called as a witness and in some cases where he is not, for example, if he is dead, or unfit to attend as a witness, or cannot be found.

For the purposes of s. 1 of the 1938 Act, a document is not deemed to be made by a person unless it, or the material part of it, was written, made or produced by him with his own hand, or signed or initialled by him, or otherwise recognised by him in writing as one for the accuracy of which he is responsible. In the Act the expression " document " includes books, maps, plans, drawings, and photographs. The provision as to recorded documents is applicable to private documents and resembles the case of public documents, such as statements in public registers, where an entry made by the proper officer is admissible though he has no personal knowledge of the matter dealt with by the statement.

In order to prevent the document being brought into existence for the purposes of being used as evidence after proceedings are " pending or anticipated," the Act provides that in these circumstances the document shall not be used. In any event it is provided that in estimating the weight, if any, to be attached to a statement rendered admissible as evidence by that Act, regard shall be had to all the circumstances from which any inference can reasonably be drawn as to the accuracy of the statement, and in particular to the question whether or not the statement was made contemporaneously with the occurrence or existence of the facts stated, and to the question whether or not the maker of the statement had any incentive to conceal or misrepresent the facts.

In order to save time and expense the document may be used for the purposes already indicated without calling the person who made it as a witness, if the Court in its discretion dispenses with his attendance.

Changes introduced by Evidence Act, 1938. An example may assist the student to grasp some of the changes in the law effected by the Evidence Act, 1938, in its treatment of statements contained in documents.

In *Price* v. *Torrington (Earl)* (1703), Holt, K. B. 300, a leading case on declarations in the course of duty, it was necessary in an action for the price of beer to prove delivery by A to B. An entry in A's books made by his drayman in the evening, whose duty it was to deliver the beer that day and afterwards to make the entry, was held to be admissible, the drayman having since died. These facts are within the exception (*c*), (ii) (p. 161). Now, let us consider some of the changes made by the Act, remembering that nothing in the Act prejudices the admissibility of any evidence which would, apart from the provisions of the Act, be admissible (s. 6 (2)). If the drayman is dead, his written statement is admissible as evidence of the fact of delivery without proving " the usual course of business " or his duty to do and to record the act, for the drayman had " personal knowledge of the matter " dealt with in his statement. Had the statement not been made contemporaneously, it would be admissible, though the weight to be attached to it might be affected. The written statement is admissible if the drayman is alive, but he must be called as a witness, though in certain circumstances this requirement may be excused. One other point may be mentioned. If the drayman had informed A's clerk of the delivery, and it is this clerk's duty to record the information in a book, being a continuous record, the delivery may be proved by producing the book and calling the clerk as a witness, whether the drayman is alive or dead.

Evidence of documents. No question is admissible which is put with the object of adding to, subtracting from, varying, or contradicting, the terms of a written document. But there are certain exceptions to and modifications of this rule (see Vol. II, pp. 81, 104).

Documentary evidence must, as a general rule, be proved by production of the original documents in Court at the trial. This is an application of the general principle that the best evidence must always be produced to the exclusion of all others ; for, if secondary evidence is produced where primary evidence exists, there is generally a suspicion that there is a discrepancy between the two, which favours the person who produces it. This is one of the objections to hearsay ; it is particularly strong in the case of documents because of the opportunities which they present for dishonest alteration of their contents. *Original documents.*

But the rule does not exclude secondary evidence entirely. As stated by an early writer on evidence (Gilbert), the rule is *Secondary evidence.*

"You shall not give evidence which shows that better is in existence."

If then it can be shown that there is no better evidence, or if the judge is satisfied that the party tendering secondary evidence of a document has made an honest attempt to find the original and to produce it in Court, and has been unable to do either, secondary evidence is admissible.

The Evidence Act, 1938, before referred to, has, in addition to making, in certain circumstances, the contents of a document evidence without calling the maker of the document as a witness, allowed with the leave of the Court, certified copies of documents to which the statute applies to be used in place of the originals, but apart from those documents that come within the scope of the Evidence Act, 1938, the law has not been altered. In the case of public documents, which, on account of the *Public documents.*

risk of loss or destruction, are not allowed to be produced in Court, the contents may usually be proved by a certified copy, signed by the official who has the custody of the original. Similarly, the contents of a judicial document may usually be proved by an office copy, made by the officer of the Court who has the custody of the original. And from motives of convenience, a concession has been made in the case of entries made in the ordinary books of business of a bank. These may be proved by an examined copy, produced by a clerk from the bank who has examined it with the original.

Secondary evidence of private documents.

The contents of a private document may be proved by a copy, or even by the oral testimony of a witness who can speak to its contents from memory, if the original has been lost or destroyed ; or if it is in the possession or control of the opposite party, and he does not produce it when called for at the trial (after having been duly served with a " notice to produce ") ; or if the original is in the possession of a stranger to the action and is a privileged document which he is not legally bound to produce (such as a title-deed), and he refuses to produce it after being duly served with a *subpœna duces tecum* ; or if the document is of such a nature that its production is physically impossible : for example, a placard stuck on a wall.

Proof of identity of documents.

So much for the contents of a document. But what is there to prevent a party from forging a document and putting it in evidence as genuine ? It is obvious that the identity of the document must itself be proved ; this is in the technical language of the law called, quite simply, proving the document.

So far as public documents and judicial documents are concerned, the copy operates as proof not only of the contents but also of the identity of the document. A private document, if required by law to be attested, must, unless it is twenty or more years old and it comes from a " proper " custody, that is, from a person in whose custody, and from a place where, one would naturally expect to find the document, or its due execution is admitted, be proved by calling some person to prove the signature of one or more of the attesting witnesses. A private document, which is not required by law to be attested, will be admitted as a result of a notice to admit being served unless notice to the contrary is given. If disputed by a cross notice the document may be proved by proof of the handwriting and signature of the person who executed the document ; and, if the document is a deed, the sealing and delivery must be proved.

Notice to admit.

Handwriting. Apart from the evidence of a witness who saw the actual document signed, a person's handwriting may be proved by the evidence of a person who has seen him write, or who is in the habit of corresponding with him.; or by comparison with any writing which has been proved to be his handwriting ; or by the evidence of an expert in handwriting. This last method is chiefly needed in cases where handwriting has been disguised or imitated.

Proof of handwriting.

Real evidence. Besides oral and documentary evidence, there is a third variety of evidence, namely, *real evidence.* This is evidence afforded by actual inspection of an object by the Court. Thus, if a question arises whether a dog is vicious, the dog may be produced in Court, to enable the jury to ascertain by personal observation whether he is in fact vicious or not. Or, in a trial for murder, the knife with which the murder is alleged to have been committed may be shown to the jury, who may draw their own conclusions whether, for instance, the wound could have been made with this particular knife in the particular manner alleged. But there is no need that the object should be actually produced in Court ; where, for instance, it is alleged that a consignment of coal was of inferior quality, it is not necessary to produce the coal or any part of it in Court.

Production of objects.

The " best evidence " rule in short does not apply to real evidence, and so oral evidence is admissible to describe an object which might have been produced for inspection. In any given case it is open to the jury to draw their own conclusions from the fact of non-production, and this they are not slow to do. (See article in the Law Quarterly Review, Vol. 65 (1949), p. 57.)

BOOK I
CIVIL PROCEDURE

PART III
OTHER PROCEEDINGS

SUMMARY

PAGE

CHAPTER 11. PROCEEDINGS IN THE COUNTY COURTS
AND OTHER COURTS 171

CHAPTER 12. PROCEEDINGS IN BANKRUPTCY ... 189

CHAPTER 13. ARBITRATION... 224

CHAPTER II

PROCEEDINGS IN THE COUNTY COURTS AND OTHER COURTS

SUMMARY   PAGE

Section I. Proceedings in the County Courts 171
   (a) Constitution   171
   (b) Jurisdiction   172
   (c) Procedure   175
Section II. Proceedings in Other Courts of Limited or Special
      Jurisdiction   182

Section I. PROCEEDINGS IN THE COUNTY COURTS

(a) Constitution

There are in England and Wales four hundred and thirteen county courts. These are grouped in fifty-four circuits, to each of which is normally assigned one judge, whose duty it is to visit each court in his circuit at least once a month. Despite their name, these tribunals have no connection with the mediæval Shire Courts, nor do the circuits correspond in any way to the division into counties. Their arrangement is subject to the control of the Lord Chancellor, who can alter it whenever he thinks fit. They vary greatly in area and in the number of court towns which they include. They are so constituted as to equalise, as far as possible, the amount of business transacted by the various judges. *(County Court circuits.)*

County court judges are appointed by the Lord Chancellor, and must be barristers of seven years' standing. They are also removable at the discretion of the Lord Chancellor. The correct procedure, therefore, to be adopted by any person who feels aggrieved by the acts of a county court judge is to petition the Lord Chancellor, who will then hold an inquiry for the purpose of ascertaining whether or not there is just cause for his removal. *(Judges.)*

Each court within a circuit has its own Registrar, who must be a solicitor of seven years' standing. He is *(Registrar.)*

appointed by the Lord Chancellor, and may also be
removed by him. As registrar he attends to the administrative work involved in the activities of the court, and
to a certain extent acts as a subordinate judge. On a
vacancy occurring in the office of high bailiff of the Court,
the Registrar becomes by virtue of his office the high bailiff
and in that capacity executes the judgments of the court.

(b) *Jurisdiction*

County courts are courts of record, but their jurisdiction is limited not only in respect of place, but also
as regards the nature and amount of the claim. The
former limitation is discussed in detail later on in this
chapter, where we deal with the court in which the action
must be brought. The ordinary jurisdiction is limited in
the second respect by the County Courts Act, 1934, and
this will now be described.

Common Law jurisdiction. A county court has jurisdiction in all actions founded
on contract or tort (except actions for breach of promise
of marriage, libel, slander, or seduction), provided that
the claim is not for more than £200. But the claimant
may bring his action in the county court by abandoning
the excess of his claim over £200 and stating the abandon-
ment in the particulars of his claim. Provided that if
the amount claimed exceeds £100 the defendant may
within such time as may be prescribed by the rules give
notice that he objects to the action being tried in the
county court, and where such notice is given the judge
shall order that the action be transferred to the High
Court. The plaintiff cannot, however, after judgment,
bring another action to recover the abandoned excess ;
nor can he divide his cause of action and bring two or
more actions for amounts within the limit. In actions
for the recovery of land, the jurisdiction of the county
court is limited to cases in which neither the annual value
nor the rent of the premises exceeds £100.

Where title in question. A county court has jurisdiction to entertain an action
where the title to any corporeal or incorporeal heredita-
ment comes in question where neither the yearly rent nor
the value of the hereditament exceeds £100. But it has
no jurisdiction, except by consent of the parties, to try

any action in which the title to any toll, fair, market, or franchise comes in question. Thus it has been held, that there is no jurisdiction in a county court to try an action for infringement of patent, in which the validity of the patent is disputed, since a patent is a " franchise."

In actions of Replevin to determine whether goods have been illegally seized the county court has jurisdiction up to any amount. But in certain cases the action may be removed to the High Court.

Actions of Replevin.

A county court has also a wide equitable jurisdiction, provided that the amount of the estate, property, or sum involved does not exceed £500. The proceedings must fall within certain wide categories laid down by the County Courts Act, 1934, such as the administration of estates, the execution of trusts, dissolution of partnerships, relief against fraud or mistake, and so on.

Equitable jurisdiction.

The judge of a county court has further a limited jurisdiction, concurrent with that of the Probate Division of the High Court, to decide any contentious issue as to the granting of probate or letters of administration where the personal estate of the deceased is under the value of £200, and the real estate under the value of £300.

Probate jurisdiction.

A limited jurisdiction to try certain Admiralty actions has been conferred upon most of those county courts which are held in the neighbourhood of the sea.

Admiralty jurisdiction.

In addition to the limited jurisdiction outlined above, a county court has a much wider jurisdiction by consent of the parties, where they so agree by a memorandum signed by them or their solicitors. The jurisdiction can thus be extended to cover any Common Law action ; but in the case of Equity and Admiralty the pecuniary limit may be removed but no additional types of case brought within the jurisdiction.

Jurisdiction by agreement.

There is nothing to prevent any person bringing in the High Court an action which could be brought in a county court ; but, having regard to the amount the plaintiff recovers, he runs the risk of being deprived of costs, or of being awarded costs as if the action had been brought in the county court. There are, however, specific provisions as to costs if the writ is specially indorsed. And where, in any *action founded on contract or on tort*,

Plaintiff may sue in High Court.

Where action
may be
transferred
from High
Court to
county court.

brought in the High Court, the amount claimed or
remaining in dispute in the action or on a counterclaim does not exceed £100, either party may apply
for an order that the claim and counterclaim be tried in
a county court. So also, if the plaintiff in any *action
founded on tort* in the High Court has no visible means of
paying the defendant's costs in the event of the plaintiff
failing in the action, the defendant may, whatever be the
amount claimed, apply for an order that, unless the
plaintiff give security for the defendant's costs, the action
be transferred to a county court for trial. In both cases
the Master or District Registrar has a judicial discretion
whether he will make the order, having regard to all the
circumstances of the case. In addition, actions in the
High Court for the recovery of land by a landlord against
a tenant or a person claiming through him, which could
have been commenced in a county court, may be transferred to a county court. Interpleader proceedings (see
Chap. 5, Section VII, *ante*) may also be transferred,
where the amount or value of the matter in dispute
does not exceed £500, and the questions at issue may be
more conveniently tried in a county court. And an order
may be made in the Chancery Division of the High Court
transferring any action therein, even though it would otherwise be outside the limits of the county court's jurisdiction.

Jurisdiction conferred by Statutes.—In addition to
the above-mentioned jurisdiction conferred by the County
Courts Act, numerous statutes have from time to time
been passed, which give further jurisdiction to county
courts in matters of the most varied kind. The jurisdiction so conferred is in some matters concurrent with
that of the High Court ; in others it is exclusive. It
comprises, amongst a large variety of matters, the following kinds of jurisdiction :

Many county courts have a wide bankruptcy jurisdiction, in virtue of which they have all the powers of the
High Court, and may decide any question of law or fact
arising in any bankruptcy case. In cases arising out of
the bankruptcy, there is no limit to such jurisdiction ;
but the judge may refuse to try cases in which large
amounts are involved, or, if a difficult question of law

arises, he may state a special case for the determination of the question by the High Court. In questions between the trustee in bankruptcy and strangers, the jurisdiction is limited to cases in which the amount in dispute does not exceed £200, unless all the parties consent. County courts exercising jurisdiction in bankruptcy have also certain powers in connection with deeds of arrangement.

Bankruptcy can take place only where the total indebtedness is £50 or more, but any county court, whether exercising bankruptcy jurisdiction or not, has power, where a defendant who has had judgment given against him to pay a certain sum of money is unable to pay, and his whole indebtedness does not exceed £50, to make an order for the administration of his estate, and for the payment of his debts—or such composition as appears practicable—by instalments.

A county court whose jurisdiction in this respect has not been excluded by the Lord Chancellor has power to make an order to wind-up a company, if the registered office is within the district of the court, and if the paid-up capital does not exceed £10,000. In such proceedings the county court has all the powers of the High Court. *Winding-up jurisdiction.*

Under the Landlord and Tenant Act, 1927, there is a jurisdiction to order the renewal of leases, and to award compensation. *Landlord and Tenant Act, 1927.*

(c) Procedure

Trial of actions. Actions in county courts are usually tried before the judge alone. But trial by jury is possible if an application is made to the court for that purpose and the court is satisfied— *When trial is by jury.*

(a) that a charge of fraud against the party making the application is in issue, or

(b) that a claim in respect of libel, slander, malicious prosecution, false imprisonment, seduction, or breach of promise of marriage is in issue (this provision relates to actions of those varieties which have been remitted from the High Court, or in cases where the parties have given the county court jurisdiction by consent).

In any other action, except Admiralty proceedings, or

proceedings arising under the Rent and Mortgage Restrictions Acts, or appeals under the Housing Act, 1936, which must be tried by a judge alone, the right to a jury is discretionary.

Where there is a jury, it consists of eight persons ; and it must be unanimous in its verdict.

Appeals lie on questions of law.

Appeals.—No appeal lies from the finding of any *fact* by a county court judge or jury ; but if either party to the action is dissatisfied with the decision of the judge in point of law or equity, or upon the admission or rejection of any evidence, the party dissatisfied may, if the particular point of law has been taken before the county court judge (but not otherwise), appeal to the Court of Appeal, though where the amount in dispute does not exceed £20 leave of the county court judge is necessary unless the action is for the recovery of land or the title to any hereditament has come in question. The appeal is brought, as a general rule, to the Court of Appeal, but bankruptcy appeals go before a Divisional Court of the Chancery Division. Admiralty appeals are governed by rules slightly different from those which govern other appeals. In all cases measures are taken to prevent the bringing of appeals where the amount in issue is very small.

In those cases where an appeal lies to a Divisional Court a further appeal lies to the Court of Appeal, provided that leave is given by the Divisional Court or by the Court of Appeal. An appeal lies from the Court of Appeal to the House of Lords either by leave of the Court of Appeal or of the Appeals Committee of the House of Lords, except in bankruptcy matters originating in the county court when no appeal beyond the Court of Appeal is permissible. The parties may agree in writing signed by themselves or their solicitors or agents not to appeal.

County court rules. Procedure in county courts is conducted in accordance with a special code, known as the County Court Rules ; and a rule committee exists analogous to the rule committee of the Supreme Court. It has power to frame and amend rules, but subject to the control of the rule committee of the Supreme Court.

Recovery of land.

In which court action to be brought. Actions for the

recovery of land must be brought in the court of the district in which the land is situate.

In other cases the plaintiff must bring his action either in the court for the district in which the defendant or one of the defendants resides or carries on business or in the court for the district in which the cause of action wholly or in part arose. Where the plaintiff sues as assignee of a debt, the action may be commenced in any court in which the assignor might have commenced the action but for the assignment, and not elsewhere. *General rule.*

Special considerations apply in cases where the purchase price of goods is to be made by instalments and hire-purchase. The Hire-Purchase Act, 1938, provides that where the action is to recover possession of goods from a hirer, under a contract for hire with an option to the hirer to return the goods at any time during the agreement, after one-third of the hire-purchase price has been paid or tendered, the action must be begun in the county court for the district in which the hirer resides or carries on business or resided or carried on business at the date on which he last made a payment under the hire-purchase agreement. Further, the county court rules provide that where the action is founded on a contract for the sale or hire of goods, and payment is to be made by instalments, unless the sum of money claimed exceeds £20 the plaintiff can only sue in the court of the district in which the defendant resides or carries on business or in the court of the district in which the contract was made by the defendant or by someone (not being a servant or agent of the plaintiff) authorised to make the contract on the defendant's behalf, and the defendant or the person so authorised was present when the contract was made. *Hire-purchase agreements.*

The last-named limitation on the plaintiff's right also applies where the defendant is, or is the wife of, a domestic or outdoor servant or a person engaged in manual labour, and in this instance no distinction is drawn between cases where the claim is for £20 or less and those in which it exceeds that sum. *Domestic servants.*

Actions of replevin, which lie in cases of illegal, as distinct from irregular or excessive distress, including distress for rent, must be brought in the court of the district *Replevin.*

in which the goods or cattle were illegally distrained. But it is possible to remove these proceedings into the High Court for trial by an order for *certiorari* if so directed by a Master of the King's Bench Division.

Security for costs. If the action is entered in the plaintiff's court and the defendant resides more than 20 miles from the plaintiff's court he may apply to the court for the plaintiff to give security for costs, and, if the Registrar is satisfied that the defendant has a defence, he may make an order for security, and, if it is not complied with, the action will be struck out.

Transfer of proceedings. If the action is entered in a court other than the court for the district in which the defendant resides or carries on business, the defendant may apply to the court either *ex parte* (and in that case he may make his application by writing a letter to the court asking for the action to be transferred), or, on having first given notice to the plaintiff, to have the action transferred for trial to the court of the district in which the defendant resides or carries on business.

Removal of proceedings. A judge or Master of the High Court has jurisdiction to order the removal of proceedings begun in the county court to the High Court for trial, upon such terms as to payment of costs, giving security, or otherwise as he thinks fit. This is done by an order for *certiorari*.

This must not be confused with the order of *certiorari* for the removal of the proceedings from an inferior court to the High Court, in order to quash the proceedings in the inferior court.

Præcipe. *Ordinary actions.* The plaintiff commences his action by filing a *præcipe*, containing the names and addresses of the parties, a short statement of the cause of action, and the amount of the debt or damages claimed ; at the same time a *plaint* is entered in a book kept by the Registrar for the purpose. At the time of entering the plaint, the **Plaint and particulars.** plaintiff must also file particulars of his claim ; unless, being for debt or damages only it does not exceed £2.

Ordinary summons. Thereupon an *ordinary summons* is issued by the Registrar, to be served on the defendant, and the plaintiff at the time of entering the plaint is given a *plaint note*, that is, a copy of the plaint entered by the Registrar ; but bearing the number and reference to the case. This plaint note must be produced by the plaintiff or his agent in all subsequent proceedings. These documents correspond to the three copies of the writ in the High Court, but it should be noted that a High Court writ is served by the plaintiff, whereas the county court summons is served usually by the bailiff as officer of the court.

On the day named in the summons, which is generally some three weeks or a month after the entry of the plaint, the plaintiff must appear to support his claim ; and, unless the defendant appears, the plaintiff, on proving his case in court, is entitled to judgment. Unlike the High Court, the county court has jurisdiction to order payment by instalments. A defendant in an ordinary action who disputes his liability should deliver his defence at the court office within eight days of the service of the summons upon him. Failure to do so, however, will not preclude him from delivering his defence at a later date, provided that it is before the return day, nor even from appearing on the return day and disputing the plaintiff's claim, though he may be ordered to pay the costs incurred in consequence of his delay or failure. But at any time after the lapse of eight days after the service of the summons, the court may order him to deliver a defence on pain of being debarred from defending altogether. *The hearing.* *Defence.*

The procedure at the trial closely follows that in the High Court, with the exception that counsel or solicitor for the defendant seldom " opens " the defence, though he often in a word or two just indicates its general nature. The county court judge is under an obligation to take a note of any evidence tendered or point of law submitted for the use of the Court of Appeal ; otherwise if there is an appeal and the appellant desires to raise the matter as a ground for his appeal and it is not on the judge's note he may be prejudiced by the omission.

Subpœnas for use in the county court are issued by the county court. *Subpœnas.*

Default action. The county court rules also give a plaintiff seeking to recover a debt or liquidated demand the opportunity, in most cases, of instituting a " default action." By means of a default action the plaintiff may, *Default action.*

unless the defendant delivers a notice of defence within
eight days of the service of the summons upon him, sign
judgment without further proof.

It has become a very common practice in recent years,
where the claim is really undisputed, for the defendant to
file a statement admitting the debt and offering to pay by
small monthly instalments. If the plaintiff accepts this
form of payment, with costs up to the time of filing the
admission, the matter is ended, subject to the plaintiff entering judgment in accordance with the defendant's offer. The
offer, however, is often of such small monthly payments
that the time required to liquidate the debt runs into
several years. In such cases the Registrar has power on
the parties attending before him to order a larger monthly
payment;   and   the   matter   is   thus   inexpensively
disposed of.

Enforcement of judgment. A county court judgment
for the payment of money may be enforced by execution
against the goods of the judgment debtor under a warrant
empowering the bailiff of the court to seize and sell
sufficient of them to satisfy the amount of the judgment
and costs. The judgment may be enforced within the district of another county court ; and may also be executed
in Scotland or Northern Ireland, by registering in the
corresponding court there a certificate of the judgment.
A judgment for the payment of money may also be enforced by a garnishee order of any debts due to the
judgment debtor or by any of the other modes of execution (adapted to the county court) that are applicable to
the enforcement of a High Court judgment.

Judgment
summons.

The usual procedure employed to enforce a judgment is
the issuing of a judgment summons. This is a summons
calling upon the debtor to be examined touching his means
to satisfy the judgment, and to show cause why he should
not be committed to prison for having made default. If
the judgment creditor can then prove that the debtor has
since the date of the judgment, had the means to pay, the
normal practice is for the judge to make an instalment
order for payment of the judgment debt by (monthly)
instalments, and on the debtor failing to pay the instalments to make a committal order (*Barefoot* v. *Clarke*,

[1949] 2 K. B. 97). The debtor is not committed to prison for owing money, but for wilfully disobeying the judgment. A married woman since the passing of the Law Reform (Married Women and Tortfeasors) Act, 1935, can now be committed on a judgment summons.

A judgment for the recovery of land or any tenement may be enforced by warrant of possession. The judge has power to appoint a receiver of an interest in land by way of equitable execution in cases within his jurisdiction. *Recovery of land.*

Appeals. The rules relating to the right to bring an appeal against the decision of a county court judge have been mentioned (p. 176, *ante*).

Here, it may be added, that the appeal is brought by notice in writing, which must be served upon the other side and the appeal entered in the Appeal and Cause Clerk's Department, High Court, within twenty-one days of the decision complained of. The appeal is usually heard by the Court of Appeal.

New trial. In every case the county court judge has jurisdiction to order a rehearing of the case in the county court—*i.e.*, a *new trial*. This is distinct from an appeal, as the case is not heard on legal objections in a higher court ; but retried from beginning to end in the same court. Some good ground for such new trial must be shown, such as the discovery of fresh evidence since the trial, the fact that one party was taken by surprise at the trial, the perjury of a witness, and like reasons. The judge must be satisfied there has been a substantial miscarriage of justice, and the granting or refusing of the new trial is in his discretion. Occasionally, upon the hearing of an appeal in the Court of Appeal, it becomes obvious that the only way to do justice is to have the case tried all over again in the county court. In such cases the new trial is often ordered to be had in another county court. *Power to order new trial.* *Grounds for new trial.*

Other proceedings in the county court. We have described in some detail the procedure in an ordinary or default action. The great majority of proceedings in the county court fall within these categories, and procedure by action is prescribed wherever it is sought to obtain relief against any person or to compel any person to do or abstain from doing any act. All proceedings do not, *When action applicable.* *Other proceedings.*

however, fall within this description, and the rule is itself subject to exceptions laid down by other rules and by Acts of Parliament, whereby other procedures are prescribed for particular occasions. Proceedings in the county court are, indeed, as varied as in the High Court, though they are much simpler. The student is warned of the existence of these other types of proceeding, since he may meet them in the course of his practice. But since they are comparatively seldom found they are not described in detail.

"Matters."

The three types of proceeding other than by action are grouped together as "matters," and are originating applications, petitions and appeals. The originating application is an extremely simple form of proceeding, to be used wherever no other form is applicable or prescribed. It is most often met with in those equity proceedings where the advice or leave of the court is required, parallel to those proceedings in the Chancery Division of the High Court. The petition is used only where specifically required. Special procedure is also available where an appeal to the county court from any tribunal or person is allowed by statute.

Special statutes.

In addition to these general forms special provisions are made by rule under certain of the statutes giving jurisdiction to county courts, such as the Landlord and Tenant Act, 1927.

Section II. PROCEEDINGS IN OTHER COURTS OF LIMITED OR SPECIAL JURISDICTION

In addition to the county court, there are, still existing, some tribunals whose powers are restricted either to a particular class of cases, or to cases involving a limited amount of money, or to cases arising within a particular area. We propose to deal very briefly with a few of the more important of these.

1. *Borough courts.* Although the establishment and rapid extension of the system of county courts largely superseded such of the ancient local courts as had not already ceased to act, yet a few of the latter have survived in the struggle for existence, and do useful work

at the present day. Conspicuous among them are the Lancaster Chancery Court, and the Palatine Court of Durham which are local courts of superior jurisdiction, and of which some account has been given (*ante*, p. 15); and the Liverpool Court of Passage, the Hundred Court of Salford, and the Bristol Tolzey Court. It is difficult, in a general work, to give any satisfactory account of the numerous borough and other local courts, owing to the fact that each is governed largely by its own special charters and statutes; but they are enumerated and briefly described in Halsbury's Laws of England (2nd Edn.), Vol. VIII, *Courts*, Part XVI.

2. *The Mayor's and City of London Court*, which is held in the City of London, was formed under the Mayor's and City of London Court Act, 1920, by amalgamating the City of London Court (which was made a county court in 1867) and the Mayor's Court, one of the most ancient courts in the kingdom. The judges are the Recorder of the City of London, the Common Serjeant, the assistant judge of the old Mayor's Court, and one or two additional judges appointed by the Lord Chancellor.

The new court thus formed has all the powers and jurisdiction of both the amalgamated courts. In the case of causes which are within the jurisdiction of a county court, the new court is deemed to be a county court; and, speaking generally, the statutes and rules applicable to county courts apply. In the case, however, of a cause or proceeding which could not have been brought in the City of London Court, but could have been brought in the Mayor's Court before the passing of the Act, called "an original Mayor's Court Action," the procedure consists of an adaptation of the rules of the Supreme Court in lieu of the somewhat antiquated procedure which prevailed in the Mayor's Court before the amalgamation (Mayor's and City of London Court Rules, 1944). The jurisdiction thus inherited by the new court from the Mayor's Court comprises both Common Law and Equity matters. It has a Common Law jurisdiction *concurrent* with that of the High Court, however large the amount in dispute may be, in all actions of contract, tort, or ejectment, where the cause of action arises *wholly* within the limits of the

Procedure and jurisdiction.

Jurisdiction within City of London.

City of London. It has also *exclusive* jurisdiction in claims arising out of indentures of apprenticeship in the City. If any part of the cause of action arises outside of the City, the court has no prescriptive jurisdiction; but by the Mayor's Court of London Procedure Act, 1857, it has jurisdiction in claims for debt or damages not exceeding £50, if the cause of action arose in part within the City, òr if the defendant dwelt or carried on business in the City at the time of the commencement of the action, or at some time within six months before action brought.

The new court also inherits a certain jurisdiction, conferred upon the Mayor's Court by Orders in Council, under the Arbitration Acts, 1889, and other statutes. The court has an equitable jurisdiction similar to that of the Court of Chancery before the Judicature Acts, in cases where the whole cause of action arises within the City. Independently, however, of its prescriptive equity jurisdiction, the court has the like power under the Judicature Act, 1873, to grant, in every action within its jurisdiction, the same equitable relief or remedy as a judge of the High Court or a county court. Thus, the court has power to grant injunctions and decree specific performance of contracts, and to give effect to any counterclaim.

Appeals lie (including any motion for a new trial, or to set aside a verdict, finding or judgment) to the Court of Appeal (Administration of Justice (Miscellaneous Provisions) Act, 1938, s. 15). In the case of " an original Mayor's Court Action " the appeal lies as if the cause or proceedings had been in the High Court, and in other cases as if the cause or proceedings had been in the county court (*ibid.*).

Appeals.

3. *The Sheriff's Court.* Although the old court of the Shire has lost all its jurisdiction, the sheriff still has power to determine certain matters with the aid of a jury, and it is therefore necessary to consider the sheriff's functions as a judicial officer. Except in the few cases where it is elective, the appointment of sheriff is made by the Crown at a curious old ceremony known as " pricking the sheriffs." On November 12 in each year (being the morrow of St. Martin's Day), three men or women of

Appointment of sheriffs.

each county are selected by the Chancellor of the Exchequer and certain judges and high officers of State as representing the old Barons of the Exchequer, sitting in the High Court of Justice. Subsequently the King, in the Privy Council, or some official delegated by him, pricks with a bodkin the name of one of the three so chosen ; and that person becomes the sheriff of the county, and acts as such until his successor is appointed. No one who has served the office of sheriff for one year can be compelled to serve the same again within three years after, if there be any other person within the county who is qualified for the office ; but otherwise service of the office of sheriff is compulsory upon the party chosen.

The sheriff is responsible for the holding of parliamentary elections and for summoning jurors for service at the Assizes and the Quarter Sessions, and for seeing to the carrying out of the capital sentence of a prisoner condemned in his county, and the execution of all writs addressed to him, and the holding of a court to assess damages in undefended actions. *Sheriff's duties.*

But the sheriff's court is in practice held, not by the sheriff himself, but by the under-sheriff, who is usually a solicitor, and is nominated to his office by the sheriff. *Under-sheriff.*

The sheriff must have a deputy in London for the purposes of receiving writs of execution in order that they can be transmitted to the under-sheriff for execution. The deputy sheriff is usually the under-sheriff's London agent, whose office must be within one mile from the Inner Temple Hall. *Deputy sheriff.*

The sheriff's court has jurisdiction to assess compensation for land acquired compulsorily under statutory powers, to assess damages—this is the most usual business of the court—in undefended actions, and to ascertain the value of an unsuccessful litigant's lands, as part of the process of executing judgment against those lands. *Sheriff's jurisdiction.*

4. *The coroner's court.* The coroner's office, though not so old as that of the sheriff, dates from mediæval times, for as early as the end of the 12th century a coroner was appointed to " keep the pleas of the Crown." He is only in a restricted sense a judicial officer, and the court which

he holds is, as its name " inquest " shows, a court of inquiry and not a court of trial.

Who appoints the coroner. Coroners ordinarily are appointed by county councils ; but boroughs which have Quarter Sessions of their own and which are either county boroughs or have a population of over 10,000, may appoint their own coroners. The appointment is for life, but a coroner is liable to be superannuated at any time after he reaches the age of sixty-five. The Lord Chancellor is empowered to remove a coroner for inability or misbehaviour and the coroner may also be removed by the court if it convicts him of extortion, corruption, misbehaviour, or neglect. Every coroner is required to appoint a deputy coroner, to be approved by the chairman or mayor, as the case may be, of the council or borough. He may also, subject to the same approval, appoint an assistant deputy coroner, if he desires to do so. The coroner to the Royal Household, who must not be confused with the King's Coroner and Attorney, is appointed by the Lord Steward to the King. His duties are to hold inquests on persons who lie dead in any of the Royal Palaces.

Qualifications. The coroner, deputy, or assistant deputy coroner must be either a barrister, or a solicitor, or a legally qualified medical practitioner, of five years' standing in his profession. And, as the coroner was originally appointed to keep a check on the sheriff, no person may hold the two offices at one and the same time. But the coroner acts as the sheriff's substitute and summons the jurors if the sheriff be interested in an action, or related to either plaintiff or defendant. He is also by virtue of his office a magistrate with power to cause offenders to be apprehended.

Inquests. But the principal duty of coroners is to hold inquests, and these, except in matters of infrequent occurrence, such as treasure-trove, *e.g.*, ancient coin found buried in the soil, which belongs to the Crown, take place only when any person is slain, or dies in circumstances which suggest death by some cause other than natural causes, or dies in prison or in a lunatic asylum. When a death in these circumstances happens, it is the duty of any person who becomes aware of it to give notice to the coroner.

The coroner then holds an inquiry into the manner of the death, and at or before the first sitting the body must be viewed by him. Where this is impossible, permission may be obtained from the Secretary of State to hold an inquest, if he deems it desirable.

The coroner's court is a court of record, and the coroner has power to order the appearance before him of the medical practitioner, if there be one, who attended the deceased at his death or during his last illness, or, where the deceased was not so attended, of any medical practitioner, being at the time in actual practice in or near the place where the death happened, or indeed of any person having knowledge of the facts, whom he may think it expedient to examine. He has power to examine on oath, and he may, if he thinks fit, direct a *post-mortem* examination to be held. *Court is court of record.*

The coroner is bound to summon a jury to assist him in certain circumstances ; for example where he has reason to suspect that the deceased came by his death by murder, manslaughter or infanticide ; or that the death was caused by an accident arising out of the use of a vehicle in a street or public highway ; or that the death occurred in circumstances the continuance or possible recurrence of which is prejudicial to the health or safety of the public or any section of the public. *Cases where jury necessary.*

In other circumstances he has a discretion whether he shall conduct the inquest with or without a jury. Where a jury is summoned, it may consist of not less than seven and not more than eleven persons. The jury need not now view the corpse unless the coroner directs or the majority of the jury so desire. If the jury fails to agree, and the minority consists of not more than two, the coroner must accept the verdict of the majority. Otherwise the coroner may discharge the jury and summon another.

If on an inquest touching a death the coroner is informed before the jury have given their verdict that some person has been charged before examining justices with the murder, manslaughter or infanticide of the deceased, he must, in the absence of reason to the contrary, adjourn the inquest until after the conclusion of the criminal *When inquest to be adjourned.*

proceedings. He may afterwards, if he thinks fit, resume the adjourned inquest. This provision has been introduced into the law in order to avoid any risk of prejudging the question of the prisoner's guilt before he is tried. At the adjourned hearing the coroner's jury is not permitted to return a verdict in conflict with the verdict given at the trial of the accused.

Where the coroner's inquisition charges a person with murder, manslaughter or infanticide, it becomes the coroner's duty to issue his warrant to arrest that person and to see that all the evidence he has heard be brought to the notice of the court which is to try him. The coroner can admit the accused to bail.

Inquests on executed prisoners.

It may here be noted that where judgment of death is executed by the prison authorities upon a prisoner the coroner of the district in which the prison is situated is expressly required to hold an inquest with a jury on the body within twenty-four hours after the execution, and to inquire thereat into, and to ascertain, the identity of the body, and whether the judgment was duly executed on the offender.

CHAPTER 12

PROCEEDINGS IN BANKRUPTCY

The beginning of the law of bankruptcy (which has no existence apart from statute) in this country is the statute 34 & 35 Hen. VIII. (1542), c. 4, which described bankrupts as those who, Bankruptcy legislation.

> " craftily obtaining into their hands great substance of other men's goods, do suddenly flee to parts unknown, or keep their houses, not minding to pay or restore to any their creditors their debts and duties, but at their own wills and pleasures, consume the substance obtained by credit of other men, for their own pleasure and delicate living, against all reason, equity and good conscience."

Since then our bankruptcy laws have undergone many changes of policy and of method.

The existing system was in the main introduced by the (now almost wholly repealed) Bankruptcy Act, 1883 ; and the principal statute on which it now rests is the consolidating Bankruptcy Act, 1914 (which it will be convenient to refer to as " the Act "), as amended by the Bankruptcy (Amendment) Act, 1926, together with a few unrepealed sections of earlier statutes. Rules have been made under statutory authority. Bankruptcy Act, 1914.

The bankruptcy system is in part administrative and in part judicial ; and the administrative functions involved are subject to the control of the Board of Trade. The tribunals having jurisdiction in bankruptcy are now the High Court of Justice, to which the jurisdiction of the London Court of Bankruptcy was transferred by the Bankruptcy Act, 1883, and such of the county courts as are not excluded from bankruptcy jurisdiction by order of the Lord Chancellor. The bankruptcy business of the High Court was dealt with by the King's Bench Division until 1921, when it was assigned to the Chancery Division. Courts having bankruptcy jurisdiction.

Upon every court having jurisdiction in bankruptcy

as now established, there has been conferred a general power of deciding all questions of priorities, and all questions whatsoever, whether of law or of fact, which may arise in any case of bankruptcy, and which it may be deemed by that court necessary or expedient to decide, for the purpose of doing complete justice, or of making a complete distribution of the property of the bankrupt.

Liability to be made bankrupt. In order that a person can be made bankrupt he must (*a*) have the requisite status, (*b*) be subject to the jurisdiction of the court, (*c*) commit an act of bankruptcy, (*d*) owe at least £50.

Any debtor may, *prima facie*, be made bankrupt ; but there are certain persons whose status either exempts them from the bankruptcy laws, or makes them only amenable *sub modo*.

Married women.

(i) Subject to a qualification of little and diminishing importance, a married woman, since August 2, 1935, is subject to the law of bankruptcy as if she were a *feme sole* (Law Reform (Married Women and Tortfeasors) Act, 1935, s. 1).

Infants

(ii) It appears that an infant cannot be made bankrupt ; inasmuch as he cannot bind himself by an ordinary trading contract. Whether he can be made bankrupt in respect of debts for necessaries or any other debt actually enforceable against him, or for liabilities in tort, seems never to have been decided. He cannot, however, be made bankrupt upon a judgment founded on a bill of exchange given in payment for necessaries (*Re Soltykoff*, [1891] 1 Q. B. 413). Nor can he be made bankrupt upon a debt contracted by a firm in which he is a partner (*Lovell and Christmas* v. *Beauchamp*, [1894] A. C. 607).

Lunatics.

(iii) Lunatics, in special circumstances, may be made bankrupt.

Corporations.

(iv) Corporations, and companies registered under the Companies Act are not amenable to the bankruptcy laws. The analogous procedure in the case of the latter is winding-up proceedings.

Partnerships.

(v) Partnerships, including limited partnerships, are not *as such* capable of being made bankrupt ; but the members of the partnership are liable as individuals to be made bankrupt, special provision being made for keeping distinct accounts of the partnership estate and the separate estates, and for the ranking of creditors against them respectively.

(vi) Aliens are subject to the bankruptcy laws, provided Aliens. that they satisfy the general provisions as to domicile or residence or carrying on business in England.

Jurisdiction in bankruptcy. Apart from these questions of status, the Act requires that the debtor should be subject to the jurisdiction of the court ; and this requirement is explained in two sections of the Act, of which the combined effect is not very clear. Section 4 (1) pro- Limitations vides, that a *creditor* shall not be allowed to present on presentation of a bankruptcy petition against a debtor, unless (amongst petition other matters) the debtor is domiciled in England, or by creditor. (within a year before the date of the presentation of the petition) has ordinarily resided or had a dwelling-house or place of business in England ; or, except in the case of a person domiciled in Scotland or Northern Ireland, or a firm or partnership having its principal place of business in Scotland or Northern Ireland, he has within the same period carried on business in England personally or by means of an agent or manager, or is or has been a member of a firm or partnership carrying on business in England, by means of a partner or partners or an agent or manager. But, in addition to that provision, section 1 (2) of the Act provides that a " debtor," *i.e.*, a person liable to be made bankrupt,

> " includes any person whether a British subject or not, who at the time when any act of bankruptcy was done or suffered by him (a) was personally present in England ; or (b) ordinarily resided or had a place of residence in England ; or (c) was carrying on business in England, personally, or by means of an agent or manager ; or (d) was a member of a firm or partnership which carried on business in England."

Acts of bankruptcy. Bankruptcy proceedings may be taken either by a creditor or creditors, or by the debtor himself ; the first step in each case being the filing of a petition praying for a receiving order. But, in the case of a creditor's petition, it is essential that the debtor shall have committed or suffered, within three months prior to the presentation of the petition, one or more of the following eight *acts of bankruptcy* (s. I (I) of the Act), and until a debtor has committed one of the eight acts of bankruptcy he does not come within the purview of the bankruptcy laws and consequently he cannot be made a bankrupt. For a person to be made a bankrupt, it must be proved that he has : (I) in England or elsewhere, made a conveyance or assignment of his property to a trustee or trustees for the benefit of his creditors generally ; (2) in England or elsewhere, made a fraudulent conveyance, gift, delivery, or transfer of his property, or any part thereof ; (3) in England or elsewhere, made any conveyance or transfer of his property, or any part thereof, or created any charge thereon, which would, under the Act or any other Act, be void as a fraudulent preference if he were adjudged bankrupt ; (4) with intent to defeat or delay his creditors, done any of the following things, viz., departed out of England, or, being out of England, remained out of England, or departed from his dwelling-house, or otherwise absented himself, or begun to keep house ; (5) suffered execution against himself to be levied by seizure of his goods, under process in an action in any court or in any civil proceeding in the High Court, and allowed the goods to be either sold or held by the sheriff for twenty-one days ; (6) filed in the court a declaration admitting his inability to pay his debts, or presented a bankruptcy petition against himself ; (7) after a creditor has obtained a final judgment or final order against him for any amount (not necessarily fifty pounds or more) on which execution has not been stayed, been served in England (or, by leave of the court, elsewhere) with a bankruptcy notice under the Act, requiring him to pay the debt in accordance with the terms of the judgment or order against him, or to secure or compound for it to the satisfaction of the creditor or of the court, and he has failed within (usually) seven days after service of the notice—either to comply with the requirements of the notice, or to satisfy the court that he has a counter-claim, set-off, or cross-demand which equals or exceeds the amount of the judgment debt, and which he could not set up in the action in which the judgment was obtained ;

Conveyance of property.

Fraudulent conveyance.

Fraudulent preference.

Concealment.

Allowing goods to be seized.

Admission of incapacity to pay debts.

Service of bankruptcy notice.

or (8) has given notice to any of his creditors that he has suspended, or is about to suspend, payment of his debts. In practice the most usual act of bankruptcy is non-compliance with a bankruptcy notice. The following is a bankruptcy notice issued in the High Court.

Notice to creditors suspend payments.

Precedent of Bankruptcy Notice on Judgment or Order of High Court.

No. 31 of 1948.

IN THE HIGH COURT OF JUSTICE.
IN BANKRUPTCY.

Precedent of bankruptcy notice on judgment or order of High Court.

Re Anne Object (spinster).

Ex parte Alfred Nobody.

To Anne Object of Misery Lodge, Golders Green, London, N.W.11, Spinster.

TAKE NOTICE, that within *seven* days after Service of this Notice on you, excluding the day of such Service, you must pay to Alfred Nobody of Rabbit Warren, London, N.W.11, the sum of £57 claimed by Alfred Nobody as being the amount due on a Final Judgment or Order obtained by him against you in the High Court of Justice, 1948, N. No. 8 dated April 1st, 1948 ; whereon execution has not been stayed, or you must secure or compound for the said sum to his satisfaction or to the satisfaction of this Court ; or you must satisfy this Court that you have a Counter-claim, Set-off or Cross-demand against him which equals or exceeds the sum claimed by him and which you could not set up in the Action or other proceedings in which the Judgment or Order was obtained.

DATED this 22nd day of April, 1948.

BY THE COURT.

A. GOODFELLOW.
. *Registrar.*

YOU ARE SPECIALLY TO NOTE.

That the consequences of not complying with the requisitions of this Notice are that you will have committed an Act of Bankruptcy, on which Bankruptcy proceedings may be taken against you.

If, however, you have a Counter-claim, Set-off or Cross-demand which equals or exceeds the amount claimed by Alfred Nobody in respect of the Judgment or Order, and which you could not set up in the Action or other proceedings in which the said Judgment or Order was obtained, you must within three days apply to this Court to set aside this Notice, by filing with the Registrar an Affidavit to the above effect.

This Notice issued out by

A. SLEEP.

1 Noisy Court, E.C.4.

Moreover, on an application under the Debtors Act, 1869, made by a judgment creditor for an order of committal against the judgment debtor, the court may, with the consent of the creditor, in lieu of committing, make a receiving order against the debtor ; in which event the debtor is deemed to have committed an act of bankruptcy at the time when such order is made (Bankruptcy Act, 1914, s. 107). This jurisdiction is seldom exercised.

Fraudulent alienations of property. The " fraudulent conveyance, gift, delivery, or transfer " of property which constitutes the second of the above-named acts of bankruptcy is also important for other purposes. Fraudulent alienations of property are either (i) fraudulent at Common Law or under s. 172 of the Law of Property Act, 1925, replacing and enlarging the provisions of the statute 13 Eliz. (1571), c. 5, which have been usually treated as being substantially identical with the Common Law, the old statute being avowedly declaratory (*Twyne's Case* (1601), 1 Smith's Leading Cases) ; or (ii) fraudulent under bankruptcy legislation.

Law of
Property
Act, 1925,
s. 172.

(i) The Law of Property Act, 1925, s. 172, provides that

> " every conveyance of property made, whether before or after the commencement of this Act, with intent to defraud creditors, shall be voidable at the instance of any person thereby prejudiced."

There is, however, a proviso (sub-s. (3)) which excludes from the operation of the section

> " any estate or interest in property conveyed for valuable consideration and in good faith or upon good consideration and in good faith to any person, not having at the time of the conveyance, notice of the intent to defraud creditors."

Badges of fraud.

The question of the necessary intent is one of fact in each case ; but, from time to time, and particularly in *Twyne's Case, supra,* the judges have indicated certain " badges of fraud " which *prima facie* amount to, or contribute to make up, adequate evidence of fraudulent intent. For instance, the fact that the alienor disposed of the whole of his property by the alienation, or that he " continued in possession and used them (his goods and chattels) as his own " ; the secrecy of the transaction ;

the imminence of proceedings against him ; the existence of a trust between alienor and alienee," for trust is the cover of fraud " ; or (on the principle that *qui s'excuse, s'accuse*) the existence in the deed or other document (if the transaction is in writing) of professions of good faith or other unusual and suspicious clauses—these are all " badges of fraud." There must have been (it seems) " actually existing, or in immediate contemplation, at the date of the (alienation), creditors capable of being injured by it " ; but, this condition being satisfied, any creditor, or the alienor's trustee in bankruptcy, may take steps to impeach the alienation and recover the property, and all the creditors will then participate in the fund thus recovered. These decisions, though given on the statute 13 Eliz. c. 5, will be of value in construing s. 172 of the Law of Property Act, 1925. It was held upon the old statute that a *bona fide* purchase for value without notice who buys from a donee with a defeasible title before the deed of gift is set aside, gets a good title (*Harrods* v. *Stanton*, [1923] 1 K. B. 516). *A fortiori*, this would seem to be the case under the new statute, which replaces the term " utterly void " of the old statute by the term " voidable."

(ii) An act of bankruptcy is also constituted by the making of an alienation, *i.e.*, parting with possession of property which, although not fraudulent within the Law of Property Act, 1925, s. 172, or conveniently capable of being dealt with under that statute, is fraudulent under the bankruptcy legislation ; as for instance an alienation which substantially conveys the debtor's whole property in consideration of a pre-existing debt, or (probably) one which conveys even a portion of his property in consideration of such a debt, if made voluntarily and in contemplation of bankruptcy, or if it otherwise has the effect of defeating or delaying the creditors. If the conveyance is fraudulent under the bankruptcy legislation a *bona fide* purchaser from the person taking as grantee under the conveyance is not protected (*Re Gunsbourg*, [1920] 2 K. B. 426 (contrast with *Harrods* v. *Stanton*, *supra*)).

Fraudulent alienation under bankruptcy legislation.

Presentation of creditor's petition. Any one act of bankruptcy having been committed by the debtor he is now liable to be made bankrupt. The next stage is the filing of a petition by a creditor.

This can only be done provided (i) that there must be a debt owing to the petitioning creditor amounting to £50 or upwards ; but any two or more creditors whose debts in the aggregate amount to £50 may join together to present a petition ; (ii) that the debt must be a liquidated sum, and payable either immediately or at some certain future time ; (iii) that it must be an actionable debt, *e.g.*, not statute-barred or founded upon an illegal consideration ; (iv) that the relevant act of bankruptcy on which the petition is grounded must have occurred within three months of its presentation ; an act of bankruptcy committed within this period of time is spoken of as " an available act of bankruptcy," *i.e.*, available for a petition in bankruptcy to be presented thereon ; (v) that the debtor must satisfy the requirement as to domicil or residence or carrying on business already set out.

If the debt of the petitioner should be a secured debt, then the creditor must, in his petition, state that he is willing to give up his security for the benefit of the creditors in the event of an adjudication of bankruptcy ; or else he must give an estimate of the value of the security, and then he is deemed to be a petitioning creditor in respect only of the balance of his debt above the value of the security.

The following is a creditor's petition :

No. 108 of 1948.

IN THE HIGH COURT OF JUSTICE.
IN BANKRUPTCY.

Re Alfred Dogsbody.
Ex parte George Muggins.

I George Muggins of the Rabbit Warren, Meadway, London, N.W.11, hereby petition the Court that a Receiving Order be made in respect of the Estate of Alfred Dogsbody of Kennel Cottage, Meadway, London, N.W.11, and lately carrying on business at (or residing at) Kennel Cottage, Meadway, London, N.W.11, and say :—

1. That the said Alfred Dogsbody has for the greater part of six months next preceding the presentation of this Petition resided at Kennel Cottage, Meadway, London, N.W.11, within the District of this Court.

2. That the said Alfred Dogsbody is justly and truly indebted to me in the sum of £51 due under a judgment of the High Court of Justice, King's Bench Division, 1946, M. No. 1, in respect of the price of goods sold and delivered whereby George Muggins was plaintiff and Alfred Dogsbody was defendant.

3. That I do not, nor does any person on my behalf, hold any security on the said Debtor's estate, or on any part thereof, for the payment of the said sum.

4. That Alfred Dogsbody within three months before the date of presentation of this Petition has committed the following act of bankruptcy, namely :—

On May 27, 1948, executed a Deed of Assignment for the benefit of his creditors generally, whereby he assigned all his property to Alan Nobody as trustee for the benefit of his creditors generally.

DATED this 11th day of June, 1948.

(Signed) GEORGE MUGGINS.

Signed by the Petitioner in my presence.

A. SLEEP.
Solicitor.

This is the Petition referred to in the Affidavit of George Muggins sworn before me this 11th day of June 1948.

Filed the 11th day of June 1948, and allotted to Mr. Registrar Pleasant.

INDORSEMENT

This Petition having been presented to the Court on the 11th day of June 1948, IT IS ORDERED that this Petition shall be heard at the Court sitting in Bankruptcy, Carey Street, Lincoln's Inn, W.C., on the 25th day of June 1948, at 11 o'clock in the forenoon.

And you, the said Alfred Dogsbody are to take Notice, that if you intend to dispute the truth of any of the statements contained in the Petition, you must file with the Registrar of this Court a Notice showing the grounds upon which you intend to dispute the same, and send by post a copy of the Notice to the Petitioner three days before the day fixed for the hearing.

VERY PLEASANT.
Registrar.

NOTE.—I hereby certify that all prior Petitions against the within-named Debtor have been dismissed.

The last Petition was dismissed on the 1st day of April 1947.

DATED this 11th day of June 1948.

(Signed) A. SLEEP.
Solicitor for the Petitioning Creditor.

The petition, which must be verified by affidavit, is to be filed either in a county court having bankruptcy jurisdiction (which in that case has, for this purpose, all the jurisdiction of the High Court) or in the High Court, according to the locality in which the debtor has been residing or carrying on business during the preceding six months.

A creditor's petition must be duly served on the debtor ; and, in order to prevent his avoiding such service, the debtor may, in a proper case, be arrested as an absconding debtor (s. 23 of the Act).

Debtor's petition. A debtor's petition must allege that the debtor is unable to pay his debts ; and the presentation thereof is to be deemed an act of bankruptcy without the previous filing by the debtor of any declaration of inability to pay his debts, and the court must thereupon make a receiving order. A debtor's petition cannot after presentation be withdrawn, without the leave of the court.

Precedent of debtor's petition. The following is a debtor's petition :

No. 2 of 1948.

IN THE HIGH COURT OF JUSTICE.
IN BANKRUPTCY.

Re Adolphus Marmaduke.

Ex parte Adolphus Marmaduke.

I, Adolphus Marmaduke of the Pigs Sty, London, N.W.11, President of the Black Market Association, having for the greater part of the past six months resided at the Pigs Sty, London, N.W.11, within the district of the Court, and being unable to pay my debts, hereby petition the Court that a Receiving Order be made in respect of my estate and that I may be adjudged Bankrupt.

DATED 11th June 1948.

(*Signature*) ADOLPHUS MARMADUKE.

Signed by the Debtor in my presence.

A. SLEEP.
1 Noisy Court, E.C.4.
Solicitor.

Filed the 11th day of June 1948, and allotted to Mr. Registrar Charm.

Receiving order. The next stage in the proceedings is the making of the receiving order upon the hearing of the petition (though at any time after the presentation of the Interim appointment. petition, the court may make an *interim* appointment of an official receiver as receiver of the debtor's property, and may stay any pending action or execution or other legal process). Upon the hearing of the petition, the creditor proves his debt, which is not necessarily a judgment debt, and of which, even when it is a judgment debt, underlying consideration is in a proper case examinable by the court. If not satisfied upon the proof of the debt and upon other essential points, the court may dismiss the petition ; but, unless it is dismissed, a receiving order will be made, and an official receiver will be thereby constituted *receiver* of the property of the debtor.

The following is a receiving order :

Receiving order on creditor's petition.

No. 108 of 1948.

IN THE HIGH COURT OF JUSTICE.
IN BANKRUPTCY.

Mr. Registrar Pleasant.

Re Alfred Dogsbody.

Ex parte George Muggins.

On the petition (dated the 11th day of June 1948, and numbered 108 of 1948) of George Muggins a creditor, filed the 11th day of June, 1948, and on reading the affidavit of George Muggins, and hearing Mr. A. Sleep, Solicitor for the said George Muggins, and it appearing to the Court that the following act of bankruptcy has been committed, viz. :—

That the said Alfred Dogsbody on May 27, 1948, executed a Deed of Assignment for the benefit of his creditors generally, whereby he assigned all his property to Alan Nobody as trustee for the benefit of his creditors generally, a receiving order is hereby made against Alfred Dogsbody of Kennel Cottage, Meadway, London, N.W.11, of no occupation, and John Alfred Spam, Esquire one of the Official Receivers of this Court is hereby constituted receiver of the estate of the said debtor.

DATED this 25th day of June 1948.

By the Court,
VERY PLEASANT,
Registrar.

NOTE.—The above-named debtor is required, immediately after the service of this order upon him, to attend the Official Receiver of the Court at his offices, Bankruptcy Buildings, Carey Street, Lincoln's Inn.

The Official Receiver's offices are open (except on Holidays) every week-day from 10 a.m. to 4 p.m., except Saturdays, when they close at 1 p.m.

The name and address of the solicitor to the petitioning creditor are—

A. Sleep,
1 Noisy Court,
London, E.C.4.

Position after receiving order made.

After such order, no creditor having a provable debt may commence an action or other proceeding against the debtor to recover such debt, unless with the leave of the court (s. 7 of the Act). The official receivers are officers of the Board of Trade, and also officers of the court to which they are attached. Their duties will sufficiently appear from the following pages.

It must be stressed that upon a receiving order being made the debtor is not at that moment a bankrupt and he only becomes one upon an order being made whereby he is adjudged a bankrupt. This order is known as an " adjudication order."

Procedure at hearing of petition.

It is open to the debtor at the hearing of the petition to be heard either in person or by solicitor or counsel. The debtor or his legal advisers can ask for the petition to be adjourned either to enable steps to be taken to pay off the petitioning creditor or to show by means of an affidavit that the debtor has no other debts which would be provable in his bankruptcy and accordingly the underlying object of bankruptcy namely to distribute the debtors property equally between his creditors would not apply. If the debtor desires an adjournment, notwithstanding he may be legally represented he ought to be present at the hearing to enable the Registrar to be satisfied from the debtor himself that there are no other petitions pending against him. Should the debtor fail to attend the Registrar may refuse to give an adjournment and may make a receiving order.

Debtor's statement of affairs. Within seven days from the date of the receiving order (if it is on a creditor's petition), and within three days from that date (if the petition is that of the debtor himself), the debtor makes out and submits to the official receiver a statement of his affairs, verified by affidavit, showing the particulars of his assets and liabilities.

Composition by debtor.

Within four days of submitting his statement of affairs, the debtor has an opportunity of lodging with the official receiver a written proposal for a *composition* or *scheme of arrangement* ; and thus perhaps he may be able to avert an adjudication of bankruptcy by inducing his creditors to accept his proposal as an alternative. The rules governing compositions and deeds of arrangement are dealt with later.

Public examination. As soon as conveniently may be after the expiration of the time for the submission of the debtor's statement of affairs, the court holds a public sitting (the date of which is duly advertised) for the examination of the debtor (s. 15 of the Act). This *public examination* of the debtor is based upon the statement of his affairs; and the official receiver, the trustee (if appointed), and the court, may put questions to the debtor, as likewise may any creditor who has tendered a proof of his debt. It is the duty of the debtor to answer all such questions. The debtor is of course bound, on the day appointed for his public examination, and on any adjournment of such examination, to attend the court; and, a note of his examination having been taken down in writing, such note is read over to or by, and signed by, the debtor, and is afterwards open to the inspection of any of his creditors, and may be used in evidence against him; except in any proceedings against him for certain offences under the Larceny Act, 1916, relating to larceny of wills, documents of title to land, or fraudulent conversion which relates to frauds by agents, bankers, and solicitors. When the court is satisfied that the affairs of the debtor have been sufficiently investigated, but not until after the day appointed for the first meeting of creditors, it makes an order declaring that the public examination is concluded. Until this order has been made, an application by a debtor, who has been adjudged bankrupt, for his discharge from bankruptcy will not be heard.

Debtor must appear at examination.

The debtor, besides submitting his statement of affairs, and besides attending on his public examination and on any adjournment thereof, is required to attend the meetings of his creditors; to wait on the official receiver or trustee; to execute necessary powers and instruments; to furnish an inventory of his property; and, generally, to do everything in relation to his property and the distribution of its proceeds amongst his creditors, which may reasonably be required by the trustee, or which may be ordered by the court (s. 22).

Debtor's attendance at creditors' meetings.

The court may, on the application of the official receiver or of the trustee, after the receiving order has

Apprehension of debtor by court.

been made, summon before it, and if necessary apprehend, the debtor, or his wife, or any other person known or suspected to have in his possession any of the estate or effects belonging to the debtor, or supposed to be indebted to him or thought capable of giving information as to him, his dealings or property, and examine such persons on oath (s. 25).

First meeting of creditors. As soon as conveniently possible after the receiving order has been made and advertised, the official receiver summons by advertisement a general meeting (usually called the " first meeting ") of the creditors, and sends to each of the creditors mentioned in the debtor's statement of affairs a summary of that statement. The meeting is summoned for a day not later than fourteen days after the date of the receiving order, unless the court otherwise orders.

Creditors to consider whether debtor to be made bankrupt.

At this meeting, usually presided over by the official receiver (or his nominee), the creditors consider whether the debtor shall be made a bankrupt or not, or whether, supposing any composition be offered by the debtor, it shall be accepted or not—a subject which will be dealt with later. If they, at such first meeting, or at any adjournment thereof, by ordinary resolution, resolve that the debtor be adjudged bankrupt—or if they pass no resolution, or do not even meet—the court adjudges

Debtor becoming bankrupt.

the debtor a bankrupt ; and thereupon the property of the bankrupt becomes divisible among his creditors, and for that purpose *vests* in a trustee. This is the first time it is proper to refer to the debtor as a bankrupt, namely when he has been adjudged one by order of the court. Until this has been done the debtor remains the owner of his property, although on the making of a receiving order the official receiver becomes the receiver of the debtor's property. On an adjudication order being made the debtor becomes a bankrupt, and it is only after the adjudication order that his property will vest in the Official Receiver until a trustee in bankruptcy is appointed (ss. 18 and 53 of the Act). Where the Official Receiver is appointed trustee as frequently happens he retains the property in his capacity as trustee in bankruptcy. A debtor may also be adjudicated a bankrupt, either (1) for

failing without reasonable excuse to submit to the official
receiver his statement of affairs hereinbefore mentioned ;
or (2) for default in the payment of any instalment due
in pursuance of any composition or scheme of arrangement arrived at as hereinafter mentioned ; or (3) for
absconding ; and in the other cases mentioned in the
Act. An adjudication order is advertised in the *London
Gazette* and in the local papers.

Appointment of trustee and committee of inspection.
Where a debtor is adjudged bankrupt, or the creditors
have resolved that he be adjudged bankrupt, they may
appoint some fit person (whether a creditor or not) to fill
the office of trustee of the bankrupt's property (s. 19) ;
and they may appoint from among the creditors fit
persons, not more than five nor less than three in number,
to form a " committee of inspection," for the purpose of
superintending the administration of the bankrupt's
property by the trustee.

Every creditor is required to prove his debt, as soon
as may be after the making of the receiving order, by
affidavit ; and no person is entitled to vote as a creditor,
either at the first or at any subsequent meeting, unless
he has first duly proved his debt in the prescribed
manner. *Proof of debt by creditors.*

The trustee has to give security to the satisfaction
of the Board of Trade unless the Official Receiver is
appointed trustee ; and his appointment only becomes
effective upon, and as from the date of, the certificate
of the Board of Trade, which is conclusive evidence of
his appointment. The property of the bankrupt thereupon passes from the Official Receiver and vests in the
trustee ; but the trustee remains subject to the control
of the Board, which is rendered effective by strict provisions requiring the trustee to furnish periodical accounts,
and statements of proceedings, and to pay all sums
received by him on account of the estate, and not required
for current purposes, immediately into the Bank of
England, or, in certain cases, a local bank, on pain of
removal by the Board of Trade. The trustee may also be
removed by the creditors by resolution, and, by the
Board of Trade, for misconduct or failure to perform his *Security by trustee.* *Removal of trustee.*

duties, or for incapacity due to lunacy, ill-health, or absence ; or on the ground that his connection with or relation to the bankrupt or a creditor might make it difficult for him to act with impartiality, or on the ground that in some other matter he has been removed from office for misconduct, or if the Board is of opinion that the trusteeship is being needlessly protracted without any probable advantage to the creditors.

Duty of trustee.

The duty of the creditors' trustee is, generally, to exercise his best discretion in the management of the estate until the bankruptcy is closed, and until he has obtained his release. Until that event, the trustee may from time to time summon general meetings of the creditors, for the purpose of ascertaining their wishes. He may also from time to time apply to the court for directions, in relation to any particular matter arising in the bankruptcy. And, as the bankruptcy proceeds, he consults with the committee of inspection as to his proceedings.

Powers of the trustee in bankruptcy. With a view to the full and due realisation by the trustee of the assets of the bankrupt, authority is specifically given to him by the Act to exercise certain powers ; either on his own authority or with the sanction of the committee of inspection. Thus, he is empowered, of his own authority

Trustee's power on personal responsibility.

(s. 55) : (1) to sell all or any part of the property of the bankrupt ; (2) to give effectual receipts for any money received by him ; (3) to prove, rank, claim, and draw a dividend in respect of, any debt due to the bankrupt ; (4) to exercise any powers vested in the trustee under the Act, and to execute any powers of attorney, deeds, and other instruments for the purpose of carrying into effect the provisions of the Act ; (5) to deal with any entailed interest to which the bankrupt is beneficially entitled, in the same manner as the bankrupt might have dealt with it, including the power to execute disentailing assurances under the Fines and Recoveries Act, 1833 (Vol. I., Book II, Chap. 6.).

Trustee's powers with sanction of committee.

Moreover, with the sanction of the committee of inspection, the trustee may (s. 56) : (1) carry on the business of the bankrupt, so far as may be necessary for the beneficial winding up of the same; (2) bring, institute, or defend any legal proceeding relating to the property of the bankrupt; (3) employ a solicitor or other agent; (4) accept as the consideration for the sale of any property of the bankrupt a sum of money payable at a future time; (5) mortgage or pledge any part of the property of the bankrupt for the purpose of raising money for the payment of his debts; (6) refer any dispute to arbitration, and compromise all debts and liabilities owed or incurred to the bankrupt; (7) make compromises or other arrangements with creditors of the bankrupt; (8) make compromises or other arrangements with respect to any claim arising out of or incidental to the property of the bankrupt; (9) divide in its existing form among the creditors, according to its estimated value, any property which, from its peculiar nature or other special circumstances, cannot be readily or advantageously sold; (10) employ the bankrupt himself to superintend the management of his property; and (11) make an allowance to him for his support, or in consideration of his services, if he is engaged in winding up his estate.

Although it is the duty of the trustee to do his best for the creditors in collecting the bankrupt's assets, yet he is an officer of the court and there are some things which, though he may have a legal right to do, he will be restrained from doing. This practice is frequently referred to as the doctrine in *Re Condon, Ex parte James* (1874), L. R. 9 Ch. 609, and was summarised by Lord Sterndale, M.R., in the case of *Scranton's Trustee* v. *Pearse*, [1922] 2 Ch. 87, at p. 119, as follows :

Trustee is officer of court.

> " A trustee in bankruptcy, being an officer of the court, ought not to be allowed to do anything which it would be dishonourable or unconscionable for an ordinary person to do ; and the court will restrain him from doing it."

(for instance, a refusal to restore money voluntarily paid to him by mistake and irrecoverable as the result of a technical rule). But the limitations upon this doctrine, as laid down by the Court of Appeal in the same case, should be noted.

What property vests in the trustee in bankruptcy. Upon the debtor being adjudicated bankrupt, the property of the bankrupt vests immediately, as we have said, in the Official Receiver, until a trustee is appointed and becomes divisible among the creditors. By force of his appointment, and subject to the exceptions which will presently be mentioned, the trustee takes, for the benefit of the creditors, all such property, real or personal, as may belong to or be vested in the bankrupt at the commencement of the bankruptcy, or which (with the exceptions about to be noticed) may be acquired by or devolve on him before his discharge ; and also all powers which he is entitled to exercise for his own benefit, except the right of nomination to any vacant ecclesiastical benefice (s. 38 of the Act). The debtor's property passing to the trustee includes even secret formulas known to the bankrupt and used in his business but never committed to writing ; and he must communicate these to the trustee in writing (*Re Keene*, [1922] 2 Ch. 475).

Reputed ownership clause. Moreover, in certain cases, the property even of strangers, if found in the bankrupt's possession, vests in the trustee. For, in order to protect creditors from fraud and fallacious appearances, it has been provided (s. 38) that where a bankrupt shall, at the commencement of the bankruptcy, have in his possession, order, or disposition, in his trade or business, by consent and permission of the true owner, any goods, under such circumstances that he (the bankrupt) is the reputed owner thereof, the goods shall be deemed to form part of the property of the bankrupt divisible amongst his creditors ; choses in action, other than trade or business debts, being, however, expressly excluded from this clause. The true owner must, however, have consented, not merely to the goods being in the possession, order, or disposition of the bankrupt, but also to their use in his trade or business (*Lamb* v. *Wright & Co.*, [1924] 1 K. B. 857). Goods included in a bill of sale by way of mortgage and registered under the Bills of Sale Act, 1882, are not protected from the reputed ownership clause, if they are in the bankrupt's possession by way of his trade or business, in such circumstances that the bankrupt is the reputed

Stranger's property may vest in trustee.

Reputed ownership clause.

owner of them (*Hollinshead* v. *Egan*, [1913] A. C. 564).
A well-established custom in a particular trade may
negative the reputation of ownership which naturally
arises from the possession of goods, *e.g.*, the custom of
hotel-keepers hiring furniture.

Other property of the bankrupt.   On the other hand, there
does not pass to the trustee any sums which the bankrupt
may earn purely by his personal labour or services, after
the bankruptcy has commenced (*Affleck* v. *Hammond*,
[1912] 3 K. B. 162) ; though the trustee may intervene
and claim such earnings except in so far as necessary for
the maintenance of the bankrupt and his family ; nor
any property held by the bankrupt in the capacity of
trustee for others (s. 38) ; nor the bankrupt's tools of his
trade, and the necessary wearing apparel and bedding of
himself and his family, up to a total value (inclusive of
tools, apparel, and bedding) of £20 (s. 38).   The bankrupt's right to sue for damages for breach of contract
passes to his trustee ; unless the breach is of a purely
personal contract which concerns the feelings of the bankrupt, such as a contract to cure or to marry.   Where a
contract for personal services is broken before bankruptcy, the right of action passes to the trustee ; but where
the breach occurs during the bankruptcy, the bankrupt
is entitled to sue in respect of it, even though the contract was made before his bankruptcy (*Bailey* v. *Thurston*
& Co., Ltd., [1903] 1 K. B. 137).   Where the bankrupt
has a right of action in tort, his right of action passes
to the trustee if, or so far as, the tort has caused damage
to the real or personal property of the bankrupt ; but it
remains in the bankrupt if, or so far as, the tort consists
of an injury to his person or his reputation, such as assault,
false imprisonment, libel, slander, or seduction (*Rose* v.
Buckett, [1901] 2 K. B. 449).

The right to receive military or other pay from the
Crown does not *ipso facto* pass to the trustee ; but
nevertheless the court may, with the sanction of the chief
officer of the department to which the bankrupt belongs
or belonged, order portions of such pay to be applied in
payment of his debts (s. 51).   Subject to due provision
for the carrying on of parochial duty, the benefice of a

*Personal
earnings of
bankrupt
protected.*

*Legal
rights of
bankrupt
passing to
trustee.*

*Trustee's
powers to
receive
earnings of
bankrupt.*

bankrupt clergyman may be sequestrated by his trustee for the payment of his debts (s. 50). And although the personal earnings of the bankrupt do not, generally, pass automatically to the trustee, the trustee, whenever the bankrupt is in receipt of any salary or income, may intervene, and obtain an order for payment of such salary or income to himself as trustee ; except so much thereof as is necessary for the support of the bankrupt and his family. But it seems that the income, if not a salary, must be in the nature of a salary or pension ; at any rate, the prospective earnings of a professional man dependent on his own skill or knowledge, and the wages of a miner, were held to be outside this provision and not liable to the intervention of the trustee (*Re Jones, Ex parte Lloyd*, [1891] 2 Q. B. 231).

Real and personal property obtained after bankruptcy. Both real and personal property acquired by the bankrupt after the adjudication and before he obtains his discharge vest in the trustee, but are liable to be divested unless the trustee intervenes and claims such property (*Re Pascoe*, [1944] Ch. 219).   Therefore, all transactions with regard to such after-acquired property between the bankrupt and a *bona fide* purchaser for value, if carried out before such intervention, are binding as against the trustee notwithstanding that the purchaser knows of the bankruptcy (s. 47 of the Act of 1914, which gives statutory effect to the rule in *Cohen* v. *Mitchell* (1890), 25 Q. B. D. 262).

Disclaimer within twelve months. *Disclaimer by trustee of onerous property.* When any property of the bankrupt consists of land of any tenure burdened with onerous covenants, of unmarketable shares in companies, of unprofitable contracts, or of any other property that is unsaleable or not readily saleable, the trustee may, by writing under his hand, *disclaim* such property at any time within twelve months from the date of his appointment as trustee, or within twelve months after he has become aware of it, if it does not come to his knowledge within one month of his appointment, and provided he shall not have omitted for twenty-eight days to reply to any due written inquiry made to him asking whether he intends to disclaim or not (s. 54) ; but usually in the case of **Effect of disclaimer.** leases, not without the leave of the court. And such disclaimer, as from the date thereof, operates to determine the rights, interests, and liabilities of the bankrupt and of his property, in or in respect of the property disclaimed, and also discharges the trustee of all personal liability in respect of the property disclaimed, as from the date when the property vested in him (s. 54 (2)).

It is sometimes very difficult to decide what effect a disclaimer of this kind has upon the rights of strangers ; but the Act provides, generally, that any person injured by the operation of this enactment, shall be deemed a creditor of the bankrupt to the extent of such injury, and may prove the same as a debt (s. 54 (8)). And, in particular, as regards disclaimers of the leases of the bankrupt, the court may make an order for the vesting of such leases in anyone appearing to the court to be interested therein—*e.g.*, an underlessee of the bankrupt, or his mortgagee, provided that such underlessee or mortgagee will assent to undertake the liabilities incident to the lease, that is to say, such of them as would have attached to any absolute assignee of the lease under an express assignment thereof (s. 54 (6)). *Effect of disclaimer on rights of strangers.*

Doctrine of relation back. The appointment of the trustee of a bankrupt has a retrospective relation which means that transactions by the bankrupt before he became a bankrupt are liable to be set aside. This, indeed, has been the principle of the bankruptcy law ever since the time of Queen Elizabeth ; and it prevailed, at that period, with an austerity which put wholly out of sight the consideration due to innocent parties, and the safety of commercial transactions. Under the Bankruptcy Act, 1869, however, its harshness was considerably mitigated ; protection having been extended by that Act to various *bona fide* transactions of the debtor, although they fell within the period covered by the relation back of the trustee's appointment. And now, by s. 37 of the Act of 1914, re-enacting earlier provisions, it has been provided, that the bankruptcy of any debtor shall be deemed to have relation back to, and to commence at, the time of the act of bankruptcy being committed on which the receiving order is made against him ; or, if the bankrupt is proved to have committed more acts of bankruptcy than one, to have relation back to, and to *Meaning of relation back.* *Bankruptcy relates back to time of committal of act of bankruptcy.*

commence at, the time of the first of the acts of bankruptcy proved to have been committed by the bankrupt within three months next preceding the date of the presentation of the bankruptcy petition. That is to say if a debtor fails to comply with a bankruptcy notice before the time expires and a petition is filed upon which a receiving order is made which is later followed by an adjudication order, the bankruptcy although it does not begin until the date of the adjudication order relates back for the purposes of the doctrine of " relation back " to the date when the act of bankruptcy was committed namely, the date when the debtor failed to comply with the bankruptcy notice.

Another example may help the student to grasp this important doctrine.

If a person committed an act of bankruptcy on February 1, another on March 1, another on April 1, and a petition, based on the last of these acts of bankruptcy, was presented on May 5, on which a receiving order was made on June 1, the bankruptcy would be said to commence on March 1.   Where the adjudication follows upon a receiving order made in lieu of a committal order under s. 107 of the Act, the bankruptcy relates back to, and commences at, the time of such order, or (if the debtor has committed any previous act of bankruptcy) the time of the first of such acts within three months next preceding the date of the receiving order.

Mitigation of doctrine of relation back. But this rule of " relation back " is mitigated by the following provisions :

(a) Payments by debtor. (*a*) Sect. 45 of the Act declares valid (1) any payment *by* the bankrupt to any of his creditors ; (2) any payment or delivery *to* the bankrupt ; (3) any conveyance or assignment by the bankrupt for valuable consideration ; (4) any contract, dealing, or transaction by or with the bankrupt for valuable consideration ; but these transactions are valid only upon the very important condition that they took place before the date of the receiving order, and the other party to them had no notice of *any* " available act of bankruptcy." The transaction must not be a fraudulent preference (p. 211, *post*).

(b) Sect. 46 of the Act provides, that a payment of money or delivery of property *to* a person subsequently adjudged bankrupt, or to a person claiming by assignment from him, shall, notwithstanding anything in the Act, be a good discharge to the person paying the money or delivering the property, if the payment or delivery is made before the actual date on which the receiving order is made, and (except in cases where the receiving order is made in lieu of a committal order, under s. 107 of the Act) without notice of the presentation of the bankruptcy petition, and is either pursuant to the ordinary course of business or otherwise *bona fide*.

(c) Sect. 40 of the Act provides, that executions against the bankrupt, whether by *fieri facias* against his goods, or by *elegit* against his lands, or by garnishee order, in general hold good, if completed before the date of the receiving order, and before notice of the presentation of any petition by or against the debtor, or of the commission of an available act of bankruptcy by him. For this purpose an execution against goods is completed by seizure and sale ; an attachment of a debt is completed by receipt of the debt ; and an execution against land is completed by seizure, or, in the case of an interest which cannot be seized by legal execution, by the appointment of a receiver. But this provision is subject, as regards execution against goods under a judgment for more than twenty pounds, to the provision hereinafter mentioned.

Avoidance of transactions. There are cases, however, in which transactions are void as against the trustee, even independently of the doctrine of relation back.

(1) As regards fraudulent conveyances, the trustee's title will prevail against all dispositions of property, under colour either of alienation or of legal execution, which are not *bona fide*, but of a merely feigned or collusive character (pp. 194–195) ; whether a prior act of bankruptcy has been committed or not.

(2) The trustee's title will prevail against all aliena- tions and payments voluntarily (that is to say, without pressure) made by the debtor shortly before his bankruptcy, with the intention of giving a preference to some particular creditor or creditors. For a transaction of this

kind evidently tends to defeat the main principle of the bankruptcy law ; and accordingly s. 44 of the Act provides that :

> " every conveyance or transfer of property, or charge thereon made, every payment made, every obligation incurred, and every judicial proceeding taken or suffered by a person unable to pay his debts as they become due from his own money, in favour of any creditor, or of any trustee for such creditor, with a view to giving such creditor, or any surety or guarantor for the debt due to such creditor, a preference over the other creditors "

shall, if the insolvent become bankrupt on a petition presented within three months afterwards, be deemed fraudulent and void as against the trustee. But this section is not to affect the rights of any person making title in good faith and for valuable consideration through or under a creditor of the bankrupt. To constitute a fraudulent preference, it is essential that the benefit should have been conferred upon the creditor by the debtor voluntarily, and with an intention to give him a preference, and not under genuine and spontaneous pressure from the creditor (*Sharp* v. *Jackson*, [1899] A. C. 419). A fraudulent preference is itself, as we have already seen, an act of bankruptcy.

Executions. (3) As regards executions, s. 41 of the Act provides (*a*) that where goods are taken in execution, and, before the sale thereof or completion of the execution (as therein defined), notice of the receiving order is served on the sheriff, he must on request deliver the goods, and any money seized or received in part satisfaction of the judgment, to the official receiver ; and (*b*) that where, under an execution in respect of a judgment for a sum above twenty pounds, the goods are sold, or money is paid in order to avoid a sale, the trustee, if notice of the bankruptcy petition has been served on the sheriff within fourteen days of such sale or payment, shall be entitled to the proceeds of sale or money paid, less the sheriff's expenses. But a purchaser in good faith from the sheriff acquiries a good title as against the trustee in bankruptcy.

Voluntary settlements. (4) As regards voluntary settlements, it is provided by s. 42 of the Act that every " settlement of property," including every such conveyance or transfer (written or

oral) as contemplates the retention of the property by the
donee either in its original form or in such form that it
can be traced—for instance, a gift of diamonds to a wife
(*Re Vansittart, Ex parte Brown*, [1893] 1 Q. B. 181)—
made by a debtor (not being an ordinary antenuptial
settlement or made in favour of a purchaser or incum-
brancer, *bona fide* and for valuable consideration, or a
postnuptial settlement on wife or children of property
accruing after marriage in right of the settlor's wife),
(i) shall, if the settlor become bankrupt within *two years*
after its date, be " void " as against his trustee ; and
(ii) shall, if he become bankrupt within *ten years*, be
" void " against the trustee, unless the parties claiming
under the settlement can prove that, at the time it was
made, the settlor was solvent without the aid of the
property settled, and that the interest of the settlor passed
to the trustees of the settlement, or the beneficiaries,
upon its execution. But it has been decided that " void "
in this section means " voidable," " liable to be avoided " ;
and so a *bona fide* purchaser for value of the property
settled, from the donee under the settlement, gets a good
title against the trustee in bankruptcy ; even if the purchase takes place after the commission by the bankrupt of
an act of bankruptcy, and therefore after the accrual
of the trustee's title, provided that the purchaser had
not notice of the commission of the act of bankruptcy
(*Re Hart, Ex parte Green*, [1912] 3 K. B. 6).

The same section (s. 42) also contains provisions for the
avoidance, in certain events, of covenants in marriage
settlements to settle after-acquired property wherein the
settlor had no interest at the time of the marriage, and
of payments of money and transfers of property in
pursuance of such covenants.

(5) General assignments of book debts, present or
future, made by any person engaged in any trade or
business who is subsequently adjudicated bankrupt, are,
by s. 43 of the Act, void against the trustee as regards any
book debts which have not been paid at the commencement of the bankruptcy ; unless the assignment has been
registered as if it were a bill of sale given otherwise than
by way of security under the Bills of Sale Act, 1878.

Assignments of book debts.

Distribution of bankrupt's property. One of the chief duties of a trustee in bankruptcy consists in declaring and distributing, from time to time and with all convenient speed, dividends amongst the creditors who have proved their debts. The first dividend ought to be declared and distributed within four months after the conclusion of the first meeting of creditors, unless the trustee satisfies the committee of inspection that there is sufficient reason for postponing the declaration to a later date ; while subsequent dividends ought, in the absence of sufficient reason to the contrary, to be declared and distributed at intervals of not more than six months (s. 62). When the trustee has realised all the property of the bankrupt, or so much thereof as can, in the joint opinion of himself and of the committee of inspection, be realised without needlessly protracting the trusteeship, it is his

duty to declare a final dividend ; but, before doing so, he must give notice, in the prescribed manner, to the persons whose claims to be creditors have been notified to him, but not established to his satisfaction, that if they do not establish their claims to the satisfaction of the court within a certain time, he will proceed to make a final dividend without regard to their claims (s. 67), Any surplus remaining after paying the creditors in full, with interest, and the cost of the proceedings, goes to the bankrupt.

Ranking of creditors. Dividends are, in the main, paid rateably among all the creditors, according to the *quantity* of their debts, no regard being in general had to the *quality* of them ; but by miscellaneous statutory enactments (some of which will be mentioned) there are some creditors who have a priority, and some whose claims are deferred. Judgments and recognisances, and other debts by record or specialty, are all put on a level with debts by mere simple contract ; voluntary covenants and bonds are not postponed to debts incurred for value ; and equitable debts are on the same footing as legal debts.

A creditor who has a specific security on the property of the bankrupt (such as a mortgage or pledge) is entitled, notwithstanding the bankruptcy, either (i) to give up his security and prove for his whole debt ; or (ii) to realise his security and prove for any balance, or (iii) to give credit for the value of the security, and to prove and receive a dividend *pari passu* with the other creditors in respect of any balance remaining unpaid. If a secured creditor proves for his debt without mentioning his security, the security must be surrendered for the benefit of the general body of creditors, unless the court is satisfied that the omission arose from inadvertence (Bankruptcy (Amendment) Act, 1926, s. 11).

A landlord may, either before or after the commencement of the bankruptcy, distrain for rent on the bankrupt's goods ; but if the distress is levied after the commencement of the bankruptcy, it will be only available for six months' rent accrued due prior to the date of the order of adjudication. For the remainder the landlord must come in *pari passu* with the rest of the creditors (s. 35 of the Act). Distraining landlord.

Priority is also given (and to some extent even as against the landlord's preferential right of distress) to, *inter alia*, contributions due from an employer under the National Insurance Act, 1946 ; to one year's rates and taxes ; to sums held by an employer under the P.A.Y.E. system ; to the wages or salaries of the debtor's clerks or servants, not exceeding fifty pounds each, due in respect of services rendered during the four months before the date of the receiving order ; and also to the wages of any labourer or workman, not exceeding twenty-five pounds, due in respect of services rendered during the two months immediately before the date of the receiving order. All these last-mentioned classes of debts are to be paid in full, if the property of the bankrupt is sufficient, in priority to all others, but are to abate *inter se* if the property of the bankrupt is insufficient for their payment (s. 33). Other preferred creditors.

There are certain claims which are only to be paid after all other debts for value have been satisfied in full, namely, that of the lender of money to a person engaged in business, the lender receiving a rate of interest varying with the profits or a share of the profits, or that of the vendor of the goodwill of his business who is paid by receiving a portion of the profits (Partnership Act, 1890, Deferred creditors.

s. 3) ; a claim for money lent by a wife to her husband or by a husband to his wife for the purpose of his or her trade or business (Bankruptcy Act, 1914, s. 36) ; but not if it is lent for any other purpose, and claims of persons entitled under certain covenants in a marriage settlement by the bankrupt to settle after-acquired property (s. 42 (2)). With these principal exceptions, all debts provable in the bankruptcy are payable *pari passu.*

Debts provable.

What debts and liabilities are provable. Demands in the nature of unliquidated damages, arising otherwise than by reason of a contract, promise, or breach of trust, are not provable in the bankruptcy ; and no person having notice of any act of bankruptcy " available " against the debtor can prove for any debt or liability contracted by the debtor subsequently to the date of such notice having been received. With these exceptions, however, all debts and liabilities (a term which is very extensively defined in s. 30 (8) of the Act), present or future, certain or contingent, to which the bankrupt is subject at the date of the receiving order, or to which he may become subject before his discharge by reason of any obligation incurred previously to such date, may be proved ; uncertain or contingent debts and liabilities being for this purpose estimated by the trustee, subject to an appeal to the court. But if in the opinion of the court the value is incapable of being fairly estimated, the debt or liability will be deemed to be one not provable in bankruptcy (s. 30). The position, therefore, of claims in tort against the bankrupt is as follows. Unless by the time of the receiving order the damages claimed have become liquidated, either by a judgment or under an award, or even (in certain circumstances) by agreement, they are not provable in the bankruptcy. On the other hand, the bankrupt is not released, upon obtaining his discharge, from unprovable claims in tort, because (s. 28 of the Act) his discharge only releases him from claims which are provable in the bankruptcy (with the exceptions specified in that section).

Claims in tort against bankrupt.

Application for discharge.

The bankrupt's discharge. In due course the bankrupt may hope to obtain his discharge ; and he may, at any time after being adjudged bankrupt, apply to the court for an order accordingly (s. 26). This application will not be heard until the public examination is concluded ; and, upon the hearing of the application, the court may grant the bankrupt an absolute order of discharge, the effect of which will be to release him from all debts provable in bankruptcy, with the following exceptions (s. 28) : *Effect of order of discharge.*

   (i) any debt on a recognisance ;

  (ii) certain kinds of debts to the Crown, or a sheriff or other public officer ;

 (iii) any debt or liability incurred by means of any fraud or fraudulent breach of trust to which the bankrupt was a party ;

 (iv) any debt or liability whereof he has obtained forbearance by any fraud to which he was a party ;

  (v) any liability under a judgment against him in an action for seduction, or under an affiliation order, or under a judgment against him as co-respondent in a matrimonial cause ; except to such an extent and under such conditions as the court expressly orders in respect of such liability.

A bankrupt, duly discharged, is moreover entitled, when the discharge is absolute and unconditional, to enjoy, free from the claims of his former creditors, other than those before mentioned as continuing, all future acquisitions of property. So that, in the language often applied to the case of a discharge under former statutes, " he becomes a clear man again," subject only to continuing to give to the trustee such assistance as may be required for the realisation and distribution of his former property ; failing which his discharge may be revoked. But, of course, the bankrupt's discharge does not free from liability any surety for, or co-surety or co-contractor of, the bankrupt, or any partner of the bankrupt ; though, on the other hand, the bankrupt cannot, by promise given, except for a new and valuable consideration, or (presumably) under seal, revive a debt from which he has been duly released by discharge. *Rights of discharged bankrupt.*

Suspension or refusal of discharge. But the bankrupt is not, as a matter of course, entitled to the absolute and unconditional order of discharge above referred to. For

the court takes into consideration the report of the official
receiver as to the bankrupt's conduct and affairs, including
a report as to his conduct during the bankruptcy proceedings. And the court *may* refuse the absolute order of discharge, or suspend the operation of such an order for
a specified time ; or grant the order subject to any
conditions with respect to any earnings or income which
may afterwards become due to the bankrupt, or with
respect to his after-acquired property. The court *must*,
either (i) refuse the discharge, or (ii) suspend the operation of it for a period of not less than two years, or
(iii) suspend it until a dividend of not less than ten shillings in the pound has been paid, or (iv) require the bankrupt, as a condition of his discharge, to consent to judgment being entered up against him for any unsatisfied
balance of the debts provable, under the bankruptcy,
where the bankrupt has committed any misdemeanour
under the Act, or any other misdemeanour or felony connected with his bankruptcy (s. 26 of the Act as amended
by the Bankruptcy (Amendment) Act, 1926).

One of the four orders mentioned must be made on
proof of any of these facts : (i) that the bankrupt's assets
are not of a value equal to ten shillings in the pound on
the amount of his unsecured liabilities, unless he satisfies
the court that this fact has arisen from circumstances
for which he cannot justly be held responsible ; (ii) omission to keep proper books of account within the three
years immediately preceding his bankruptcy ; (iii) continuing to trade after knowing himself to be insolvent ;
(iv) contracting any debt provable in the bankruptcy,
without having at the time of contracting it any reasonable or probable ground of expectation of being able to
pay it ; (v) failure to account satisfactorily for any loss or
deficiency of assets ; (vi) bankruptcy caused by rash
and hazardous speculation or unjustifiable extravagance
in living, or by gambling, or by culpable neglect of business affairs ; (vii) frivolous or vexatious defences to actions
properly brought against him by creditors ; (viii) incurring unjustifiable expense by bringing a frivolous or
vexatious action ; (ix) recently giving an undue preference
to any of his creditors ; (x) recently incurring liabilities

with a view of making his assets equal to ten shillings in the pound ; (xi) previous bankruptcy or composition or arrangement with creditors ; (xii) commission of any fraud or fraudulent breach of trust ; and (xiii) the execution of a fraudulent or unjustifiable marriage settlement. (Many of these acts and omissions only affect the discretion of the court upon an application for discharge when they take place within a certain period preceding the bankruptcy ; but for the details the student is referred to the Act (s. 26 (3))).

Disqualifications of bankrupt. An adjudication of bankruptcy has the effect of disqualifying the bankrupt from sitting or voting in the House of Lords, or being elected to, or sitting or voting in the House of Commons, and from holding various public offices, including membership of a county or borough council or being a Justice of the Peace. Such disqualification continues for five years after the bankrupt has received his discharge ; unless it is cancelled by the annulment of the bankruptcy, or he obtains from the court with the discharge a certificate to the effect that the bankruptcy was caused by misfortune, without misconduct on the part of the bankrupt (the principal authority is, the Bankruptcy Act, 1883, s. 32, amended by s. 9 of the 1890 Act and various other Acts). _{Duration of disqualification.}

Bankruptcy offences. Part VII of the Act (ss. 154–166 as amended by the Bankruptcy (Amendment) Act, 1926, s. 5), provides for the punishment of a bankrupt, or person in respect of whose estate a receiving order has been made, who is guilty of a *misdemeanour* as therein defined. The offences specified in these sections are numerous and so detailed that to set them out would not be consistent with the object of this work. _{Bankruptcy offences.}

It may be stated, however, that a person found guilty of any of these offences (some of which are only criminal if committed within a certain period before or after the presentation of a bankruptcy petition) is liable, in general, to imprisonment for any term not exceeding two years, if convicted on indictment, or six months on summary conviction.

Compositions and deeds of arrangement. It has always

been considered within the true spirit of our modern bankruptcy laws to enable a debtor and his creditors to carry into effect any amicable arrangements between them. Such arrangements are of three main types : a composition or scheme of arrangement sanctioned by the court either (i) before, and in lieu of adjudication, or (ii) after adjudication, and (iii) a deed of arrangement apart from bankruptcy proceedings.

(i) *Composition or scheme before adjudication.* In this case, which is governed by ss. 16–17 of the Bankruptcy Act, 1914, the debtor lodges his proposal with the official receiver within four days of submitting his statement of affairs. But the scheme is not binding on the creditors, unless it is carried by a resolution passed by a majority in number, representing three-fourths in value, of all the creditors who have proved, and is thereupon approved by the court ; the application for that purpose being made either by the official receiver or the trustee, or by the debtor. The application is not to be heard until after the public examination is concluded.

The court is required, before approving a composition or scheme, to hear a report of the official receiver or the trustee as to its terms, and as to the conduct of the debtor, and any objections which may be made by or on behalf of any creditor ; and no composition or scheme is to be approved which does not provide for the payment, in priority to other debts, of all debts entitled to priority in the case of bankruptcy. If the court is of opinion that the terms of the composition or scheme are not reasonable, or are not calculated to benefit the general body of creditors, the court *must* refuse to approve the composition or scheme. Also, if any such facts are proved as would under the Act justify the court in refusing, qualifying, or suspending the debtor's discharge in the event of bankruptcy, the court must, unless reasonable security is given for the payment of five shillings in the pound on the unsecured debts, refuse to approve the composition or scheme. And in all other cases, the court *may*, in its discretion, refuse to approve the composition or scheme. Speaking generally, the trustee under a composition or scheme has the same powers and performs

Approval of creditors required.

Condition for approval of scheme by court.

Grounds for refusal by court.

the same duties as a trustee in bankruptcy; the property of the debtor is distributed in the same manner; and, *mutatis mutandis*, the bankruptcy law, so far as the nature of the case admits, applies (s. 16 (17), (18)).

If duly accepted by the creditors and approved by the court, the composition or scheme is binding on all the creditors, so far as relates to any debts due to them from the debtor, and provable in bankruptcy. But (as in the case of bankruptcy) it does not release the debtor from any liability under a judgment against him in an action for seduction, or under an affiliation order, or under a judgment against him as a co-respondent in a matrimonial cause; except as may be ordered by the court. The aid of the court is available for enforcing the provisions of a composition; and, in the event of default under it by the debtor, or if, for any other reason, the composition is not working well, the court may annul it, and adjudicate the debtor bankrupt. *(margin: Approved scheme binding on creditors.)*

(ii) *Composition or scheme after adjudication.* By s. 21 of the Bankruptcy Act, 1914, the creditors may, after an adjudication, accept, and thereupon the court may approve, a composition or a scheme of arrangement of the debtor's affairs; in which event the court may in its discretion annul the bankruptcy. The proceedings are, speaking generally, the same as in the case of a composition before adjudication.

(iii) *Deed of arrangement.* The statutory composition or scheme accepted and approved under the provisions of the Bankruptcy Acts is to be distinguished from a debtor's deed of arrangement or composition permitted at the Common Law, but now regulated by statute, in respect that the latter arrangement or composition is not binding on the minority, even although accepted by a majority of the creditors, and in respect that, not being sealed with the seal of the court, or embodied in an order of the court, it is not summarily enforceable. Every such deed of arrangement or composition at the Common Law, is, however, now described as a " deed of arrangement," and is governed by the Deeds of Arrangement Act, 1914; which applies to any assignment of property, or agreement for a composition, or deed of inspectorship, or *(margin: Statutory composition distinguished from composition at Common Law.)* *(margin: Deeds of Arrangement Act, 1914.)*

letter of licence, made in respect of the affairs of a debtor for the benefit of his creditors generally or (in certain cases) for the benefit of any three or more of his creditors, otherwise than in pursuance of the bankruptcy laws. The

Registration with Board of Trade.

Deeds of Arrangement Act, 1914, provides, amongst other matters, that : (1) every such document is void, unless within seven clear days from the first execution thereof by the debtor it is registered with the Board of Trade ;

Assent of majority of creditors.

(2) it will be void, unless before or within twenty-one days after its registration, or within such extended time as the court may allow, it has received the assent of a majority in number and value of the creditors ; (3) the trustee under

Security by trustee.

such a deed is required to give security to the Registrar of the court having bankruptcy jurisdiction in the district of the debtor's residence or place of business, in a sum equal to the estimated assets for distribution among the unsecured creditors, unless a majority in number and value of the creditors dispense with his giving security ; (4) a trustee who acts under such deed after it has to his knowledge become void by reason of non-compliance with the statutory requirements, or after he has failed to give security, is subjected to pecuniary penalties ; (5) the

Effect of notice of deed to creditors.

trustee may serve on any creditor a notice in writing of such deed having been executed, and of the filing of the certificate of the creditors' assents, with an intimation that the creditor will not, after the expiration of one month after service of the notice, be entitled to present a bankruptcy petition founded on the execution of the deed, or on any other act committed by the debtor in the course of or for the purpose of proceedings preliminary to the execution of the deed, as an act of bankruptcy. The effect of serving such notice is that, after the expiration of that period, the creditor will not be entitled to present any such petition, unless the deed becomes

Audit of trustees accounts.

void ; (6) the accounts of a trustee of a deed of arrangement may be audited, if such audit is asked for by an application in writing to the Board of Trade, on the part of a majority in number and value of the creditors ; (7) a creditor assents by executing the deed, or by sending to the trustee his assent in writing attested by a witness.

In order that a deed of arrangement may bind a purchaser of any land comprised therein, it must be registered at the Land Registry in the name of the debtor, and re-registered every five years (Land Charges Act, 1925, ss. 8, 9).

CHAPTER 13

ARBITRATION

Voluntary arbitration is a means of settling disputes by referring them to an extra-judicial person or persons or tribunal (either agreed upon in advance, or *ad hoc* when a particular dispute arises), and agreeing to be bound by the decision of that person or body. It is largely resorted to in commercial matters, when the disputants wish to have the matter at issue between them disposed of by some person who is familiar with the usages and intricacies of their trade ; it is also useful in partnership disputes, where the common interests of the partners make the privacy of an arbitrator's room preferable to the publicity of a court of law. Another important class of question constantly being referred to arbitration is that of claims upon life or fire insurance policies. These are, however, merely illustrations ; and any dispute in any matter affecting the civil rights of the parties to it may be referred by them to the decision of an arbitrator or umpire. An agreement by which persons refer existing or future differences to arbitration is called a " submission " ; and the decision of the arbitrator or umpire is called an " award." Every person capable of making a contract may enter into a binding submission to arbitration. The submission may be by word of mouth, but is usually made in writing. When the submission is in writing, the provisions of the Arbitration Acts, 1889 and 1934, apply ; unless a contrary intention is expressed in the agreement. We shall therefore consider briefly the effects of a written submission to which the Acts apply.

Appointment of arbitrators. The arbitrator may be named in the submission, or may be left to be appointed at a future time. Many forms of contract in general use contain a clause providing that if any dispute between the parties should arise out of the contract, it shall be referred to arbitration ; and the contract frequently names one or more alternative arbitrators, or prescribes a method for their selection, for instance, by the nomination of the Lord Chief Justice of England or the President of some professional or commercial association. If no other mode of reference is provided in the submission, the reference is to a single arbitrator. When the parties disagree as to the person to be appointed, or if the person appointed refuses or is unable to act, the court may, on the application of either party, appoint an arbitrator. Arbitration may be, and usually is, an entirely extrajudicial proceeding ; but, under the Arbitration Acts, 1889 and 1934, means of access to the High Court are provided in the event of its assistance being required in the course of the proceedings. Applications to the court under the Act are made, if in the King's Bench Division, by summons before a Master in Chambers (except in a few cases, such as an application to remove an arbitrator for misconduct or to set aside an award, where they must be made on motion) ; and if in the Chancery Division, on motion to the Judge in Chambers or in court. When an arbitrator is appointed, his authority cannot be revoked by either party, except by leave of the court.

Single arbitrator.

Assistance of court in arbitration.

If the submission provides that the reference is to be to two arbitrators, one to be appointed by each party, and one of the parties refuses to appoint his arbitrator, he may be served with a notice requiring him to appoint his arbitrator. If he fails to appoint for seven clear days after this notice then (and not before) the party who has already nominated his arbitrator may appoint his arbitrator to act as sole arbitrator ; and that arbitrator's award will be binding on both parties, as if he had been appointed by consent (Act of 1889, s. 6). Where two arbitrators are appointed, they must appoint an umpire, immediately after they themselves are appointed (Act of 1934, s. 5 (1)), or, if they do not appoint an umpire, or he refuses to act, the court may appoint one. The practice of appointing two arbitrators, with power to appoint an umpire, cannot be regarded as entirely satisfactory. Too frequently each arbitrator regards himself as the representative of the party appointing him, rather than as sitting in a judicial capacity ;

Two arbitrators.

Appointment of umpire in case of two arbitrators.

an attitude of mind which is encouraged by the knowledge that, if they disagree (as arbitrators taking this view of their functions probably will), there is a third and impartial person, the umpire, who will do justice between the parties. On grounds of economy both of time and money many persons regard the system of appointing a sole arbitrator in the first instance as preferable to the appointment of two arbitrators with powers to appoint an umpire. This inconvenience has been mitigated by s. 5 (2) of the 1934 Act, which empowers the court to order that the umpire shall enter on the reference in lieu of the arbitrators as if he were a sole arbitrator.

Three
arbitrators.

Sometimes the submission provides that the reference is to be to three arbitrators, as distinguished from two arbitrators and an umpire. By the Act of 1934, s. 4 (1) the third arbitrator is to be an umpire.

Effect of a submission. A submission has this important effect on the right to bring an action : viz., if a party to a submission brings an action against the other party to it, in respect of any matter which they have agreed to refer to arbitration, the defendant may apply to the

Stay of
proceedings.

court for an order to *stay the proceedings*. The application *may* be made after the defendant has entered an appearance ; and it *must* be made before he takes any other step in the action, as, for example, by applying to the court for an order that the plaintiff give security for costs, or for discovery, or for leave to deliver a defence or to administer interrogatories, or by acquiescing without objection in an order made on the plaintiff's summons for directions, or by delivering a defence. But negotiations or correspondence between the parties or their solicitors with reference to the action, or the defendant's request by letter to the plaintiff for further time to deliver his defence, do not constitute steps in the proceedings ; so

Affidavit in
support.

as to bar an application to stay. In support of the application, the defendant must show by affidavit that the action relates to a dispute which falls within the terms of the submission, and that he was, and is still, willing to do all things necessary to the proper conduct of the arbitration. The defendant is *prima facie* entitled to have the action stayed, unless the plaintiff can satisfy the master or the judge that the matters in dispute ought not to be decided by arbitration. But, the court has a discretionary power to refuse to grant a stay ; and has refused a stay where the only question in the case was one of law, or was more suitable for decision by the court than by an arbitrator, and by s. 14 of the 1934 Act, the court may refuse a stay on the ground that the arbitrator is not, or may not be, impartial, or that the dispute involves the question whether a party has been guilty of fraud.

Ground for refusal of stay by court.

The court, in granting a stay of proceedings, is, in effect, acquiescing in the agreement of the parties to suspend its jurisdiction ; as Viscount Haldane said in *Jureidini* v. *National British, etc. Insurance Co.*, [1915] A. C. 499, at p. 505 (a case of a claim on a fire insurance policy) :

> " by the law of this country you can make most contracts which you desire, and, among others, a contract that you will not come under a liability under a contract unless that liability is defined in a particular way, it may be by arbitration."

A clause in a contract which has the effect of making arbitration a condition precedent to action, is known as the " *Scott and Avery* clause." The Act of 1934, s. 3 (4) has curtailed the operation of this clause by providing that, where under an arbitration agreement an award under the agreement is a condition precedent to the bringing of an action, the court, if it orders that the agreement shall cease to have effect as regards any particular dispute, may further order that the condition precedent shall also cease to have effect as regards that dispute.

Scott and Avery clause.

However, delicate problems may arise when a dispute involves the existence of a contract containing an arbitration clause. If the dispute is, whether a contract was ever entered into, or whether a contract was void *ab initio*—for example—on the ground of illegality, an action, in general, will not be stayed, for the arbitration clause may perish with the contract. On the other hand, if the dispute involves the assertion that circumstances have arisen which discharge one or both parties from all subsequent liability under the contract—for example—that there has been an accepted repudiation, or a frustration,

Position where existence of contract disputed.

of the contract, the arbitration clause may survive, and the court may order an action to be stayed (*Heyman* v. *Darwins, Ltd.*, [1942] A. C. 356). But, it is important to bear in mind, that an arbitration clause must be construed according to its language and the circumstances in which it was made.

Powers of the arbitrator or umpire. The arbitrator or umpire may examine the parties to the reference, and witnesses, on oath or affirmation, and compel the production of documents in their possession relating to the matters in dispute. Witnesses may be summoned by *subpœna* to give evidence or produce documents. To

Subpœna.

obtain a subpœna an *ex parte* application supported by an affidavit is made to a Master of the King's Bench Division.

Special case. Sect. 9 (1) of the Arbitration Act, 1934, provides that :

Arbitration Act, 1934, s. 9 (1).

" An arbitrator or umpire may, and shall if so directed by the court, state :—

    (*a*) any question of law arising in the course of the reference : or

    (*b*) an award or any part of an award, in the form of a special case for the decision of the court."

Sect. 9 (1) (*a*) relates to the stating of *any question of law*, in the form of a special case (sometimes called a " consultative case ") ; and we shall proceed to deal with that now. Sect. 9 (1) (*b*) relates to the stating of *an award* ; and we shall deal with that on p. 230.

Special case stated by arbitrator.

Returning to s. 9 (1) (*a*), if any question of law arises in the course of the reference, the arbitrator or umpire may, on his own initiative or at the request of either party, state such question of law in the form of a *special case* for the opinion of the court, and delay making his award until the court has decided the question of law submitted. If the arbitrator or umpire refuses, at the reasonable request of either party, to state a case, he may be com-

Court's power to insist on case stated.

pelled to do so by order of the court. The application to the court must be made before the arbitrator makes his award ; and it may be made before he has indicated his opinion on the point of law raised. If the arbitrator or umpire after refusing without reasonable grounds to state a case, or to adjourn the reference pending an application to the court, makes his award before such application can be made, the court may set the award aside on the ground of the arbitrator's misconduct. A special case stated under s. 9 (1) (a) of the Arbitration Act, 1934, for the opinion of the court is, in the King's Bench Division, argued before a Divisional Court ; and no appeal lies from the decision of the court without the leave of the court or of the Court of Appeal (s. 9 (3), *ibid.*).

Any attempt to exclude by previous agreement the right to apply to an arbitrator for the statement of a " consultative case " for the opinion of the court under s. 9 (1) (a) of the 1934 Act, is contrary to public policy, and void (*Czarnikow* v. *Roth, Schmidt & Co.*, [1922] 2 K. B. 478). Exclusion of special case by agreement forbidden.

The award. In the absence of any term in the submission to the contrary, an arbitrator or umpire has power to make his award at any time, but on the application of any party to a reference the court may remove an arbitrator or umpire who fails to use all reasonable dispatch in entering on and proceeding with the reference and making the award, and an arbitrator or umpire removed by the court for this reason is not entitled to receive any remuneration for his services (s. 6, Act of 1934). Time for making award.

The arbitrator may, by his award, deal with the question of the costs of the reference and the award, according to his discretion (s. 12, Act of 1934). He may direct to and by whom, and in what proportion, the costs are to be paid, and may tax or settle the amount to be paid, and may even award costs to be paid as between solicitor and client ; but he has no power to order a party (*e.g.*, a foreign corporation) to give security for costs. An arbitrator is usually entitled to be remunerated for his services, even if there is no express agreement to pay his fees ; and he can maintain an action for them. He has also a lien on the award for the amount of his fees ; and, in practice, usually retains possession of the award until they are paid (s. 13, Act of 1934). Costs of award.

An arbitrator, after making his award, has power to correct any clerical error arising from any accidental Correction of award.

slip or omission ; but he cannot make any material alteration in his finding or proceed to expound his award, unless the award is remitted by the court to him for reconsideration. If the rights of the parties depend on questions of law, the arbitrator has power to *state his award* in the form of a *special case* for the opinion of the court (s. 9 (I) (*b*), Act of 1934), and frequently embodies in it alternative directions in the event of the court finding his award to be erroneous in point of law. If he adopts this course, he ought to set out in the award all the material facts found by him, and leave the court to determine on those facts the respective rights of the parties.

Arbitrator's position on stating special case. On stating his award in the form of a special case, the arbitrator exhausts his powers, and becomes *functus officio* ; unless his powers are revived by the court sending back the award to him for reconsideration. In the King's Bench Division, an award stated in the form of a special case is argued before a single judge ; and an appeal lies from his decision to the Court of Appeal without leave.

Setting aside or remitting an award. By s. 7 of the Act of 1934 arbitrators or umpire have the same power as the court to order specific performance of any contract other than a contract relating to land or any interest in land. The court may set an award aside where the arbitrator or umpire has been guilty of misconduct (for instance, by hearing each party in the absence of the other), or the award has been improperly procured, or is bad in point of law on the face of it. But, instead of setting it aside, the court has a discretionary power to remit it to the arbitrator for reconsideration and amendment. An application to set aside an award is made in the King's Bench Division by notice of motion to the Divisional Court, and must be made within six weeks from the date of the publication of the award (R. S. C., Order LXIV, r. 14).

Enforcing an award. An award is *prima facie* final and binding on the parties to the submission and the persons claiming under them. It may, by leave of the court, be enforced in the same manner as a judgment or order to the same effect. The application (which is usually made in the King's Bench

Division) is by *originating summons*, and is generally granted, unless there is a doubt as to the validity of the award. If it is granted, the award can be enforced by any of the modes of execution appropriate to a judgment to the same effect, and judgment may be entered in terms of the award (s. 10, Act of 1934) ; thus the award is turned into a final judgment. In some cases, leave to enforce the award may be refused on the ground of doubt as to the validity of the agreement under which the arbitration took place ; thereupon the party in whose favour the award is made may bring an action on it, and thus obtain a decision upon the validity of the award.

Conclusion. In these pages we have been describing the procedure which is popularly known as " arbitration," more technically described in the words of the Arbitration Act, 1889, as " references by consent out of court." It must, however, be remembered, that the Supreme Court of Judicature Act, 1925, ss. 88, 89, and the Rules of the Supreme Court make provision for " references under order of court," which are either " references for inquiry and report " by an official or special referee, or " references for trial," before a special referee or arbitrator agreed upon by the parties, or before an official referee or other officer of the court, of questions such as those involving long and detailed investigation of accounts and documents. There are also a number of Acts of Parliament which provide for the compulsory arbitration of claims and disputes.

Other kinds of arbitration.

BOOK I
CIVIL PROCEDURE

PART IV
THE LEGAL PROFESSION

SUMMARY

PAGE

CHAPTER 14. SOLICITORS 235

CHAPTER 15. BARRISTERS (" COUNSEL ")... ... 259

CHAPTER 14

SOLICITORS

SUMMARY   PAGE
Section I. How to become a Practising Solicitor 237
Section II. Offences by Solicitors aud Unqualified Persons ... 243
Section III. A Solicitor's Work, Privileges, and Disabilities 248
Section IV. Solicitors' Remuneration 252

The main distinction between a professional man (or woman) and one in any other occupation is that the former is subject to controls and restrictions designed, first, to secure that none but properly qualified candidates shall be admitted to the profession ; secondly, to maintain a proper standard of efficiency and character in its members; and, thirdly, to protect the public and the members of the profession from the activities of unqualified persons. Some professions, such as those of chartered or incorporated accountant or chartered surveyor are regulated on a non-statutory basis : others are regulated by Acts of Parliament and Regulations made thereunder. The medical profession, mainly governed by the Medical Acts, and the solicitors' branch of the legal profession, are the best known examples of the latter. Indeed solicitors are perhaps more closely bound by Statute than any other professional men. This is doubtless due to the highly confidential relationship existing between solicitors and their clients and to the fact that solicitors as a body receive and deal with such a large amount of other people's money. It is, therefore, of fundamental importance that solicitors should be absolutely trustworthy.

Solicitors are officers of the Court and as such amenable to the inherent jurisdiction of the High Court. They are also governed by the Solicitors Acts, 1932 to 1941. The Solicitors Act, 1932 (which is the principal Act) was a consolidating measure which repealed and re-enacted the provisions of some twenty-eight Statutes affecting solicitors passed between the years 1839 and 1928. The 1932 Act has itself been amended and extended by eight subsequent Acts. In this chapter of this book the Solicitors Act, 1932, is, for the sake of brevity, referred to as " the 1932 Act," the Solicitors Act, 1933, as " the 1933 Act," and so on.

Under the Solicitors Acts various powers are vested in the Master of the Rolls, The Law Society, and the Disciplinary Committee.

The Law Society, the governing body of the profession, was first incorporated by Royal Charter in 1831. It is governed by a Council consisting of solicitors representing the whole of England and Wales. Every solicitor is eligible for membership of the Society and, as such is entitled to its protection when he properly requires it and obtains Club and Library facilities and the right to expect from the Society help and guidance on his professional problems, in return for his support for the work which the Society does in a wide variety of ways towards maintaining and advancing the interests of the profession as a whole. In addition to these domestic and non-statutory functions The Law Society, through the Council, acts as Registrar of Solicitors under the Solicitors Acts (1932 Act, ss. 1 and 74) and to it are entrusted the registration, education and (subject to what is said below as to the Master of the Rolls and the Disciplinary Committee) the discipline of solicitors.

The jurisdiction of the Master of the Rolls relates to the admission and restoration to the Roll of solicitors, and the hearing of appeals from the exercise of various discretions vested in The Law Society as Registrar of Solicitors.

The Disciplinary Committee is a body entirely distinct from the Council of The Law Society. It is a Court of Law whose nine members are appointed by the Master of the Rolls from among members and former members of the Council of The Law Society. An appeal lies to the High Court from its decision.

With this brief introduction to the *dramatis personæ* let us consider briefly how to become a solicitor.

Section I. How to Become a Practising Solicitor

The first essential is to apply to The Law Society (on six weeks' previous notice) for consent to the applicant's entry into articles of clerkship (1936 Act, s. 2). To obtain consent the applicant must satisfy the Council as to his character, fitness, and suitability for service under articles. The consent, once granted, is valid for six months. A foreigner may be allowed to enter into articles, but only British subjects may be admitted as solicitors.

Consent to entry into articles.

Corresponding to this control by the Society over the intending articled clerk there are also restrictions on principals. Thus, a solicitor cannot take, or retain an articled clerk if he has ceased to practise as a solicitor or while employed as a clerk by another solicitor (1932 Act, s. 18) ; a solicitor who has not at some time been in continuous practice for five years requires the Society's leave before he may take an articled clerk (1936 Act, s. 1) ; where there is a discretion to refuse a solicitor's application for a practising certificate (as to which, see below) the Society may prohibit him from taking an articled clerk (1941 Act, s. 14) ; and no solicitor may have more than two articled clerks at the same time (1932 Act, s. 17).

Restrictions on solicitors taking articled clerks.

Before the applicant may enter into articles he must pass or have obtained exemption from The Law Society's Preliminary Examination. This is an examination in general knowledge (1932 Act, s. 14) : the exempting examinations, which are specified in the Solicitors Acts and Regulations made thereunder, are, broadly speaking, of University entrance standard, Latin being a compulsory subject (1936 Act, s. 6).

The Preliminary Examination.

The articles of clerkship are a deed binding the solicitor (the principal) to teach the clerk, and the clerk to serve the principal as his clerk for the required term. The object of them is to ensure that the clerk obtains practical experience of work in a solicitor's office. The normal term of service under articles is five years, but this is reduced to three years if, before entering into articles, the clerk has obtained an approved University Degree or can prove ten years' *bona fide* service as a solicitor's clerk : it may be

Service under articles.

reduced to four or four and a half years if the clerk has passed certain other specified examinations. At various stages the clerk and his principal are required to satisfy the Council that the clerk's service has been good. Good service normally means actual employment of the articled clerk in the proper business, practice, and employment of a solicitor by the solicitor to whom he is articled or, for not more than one year, his London agent (1932 Act, ss. 19 and 20). If the articles are for four years or longer, one year may be spent as a *bona fide* pupil to a practising barrister (*ibid.*, s. 20). Special permission must be obtained from The Law Society if the clerk is to hold any office or engage in any other employment during his articles (1932 Act, s. 21 ; 1941 Act, s. 26).

Further articles. If the principal dies or ceases to practise during the term of the articles, or the articles are cancelled or discharged (as may be done by consent of both parties or by the Society under s. 5 of the 1936 Act, or s. 14 of the 1941 Act), the clerk must, if he wishes to qualify, enter into further articles for the unexpired residue of the original term. Any interval between the ending of the original contract and the start of the new one does not count as good service.

The articles of clerkship must be registered with The Law Society within six months after their execution (1932 Act, s. 16) : failing this the service may be reckoned as beginning only upon the date of the production of the articles for registration.

Cases where service under articles not required. Barristers of five years' standing and certain Dominion and Colonial solicitors are not required to serve under articles before admission in England. Apart from this, no-one may be admitted without serving under articles. By certain Statutes, however, a person may, without admission, act as solicitor to the City of London, the Treasury, Customs, Post Office, or any other branch of His Majesty's Revenue, or as assistant solicitor to the Admiralty: these offices are in practice held either by solicitors admitted in the normal way or by barristers.

Attendance at a Law School. Unless he holds a recognised Law Degree or has proved ten years' service as a solicitor's clerk before entry into articles or is specially exempted by the Council for " geographical or other reasons," no articled clerk can be admitted to the Final Examination without having satisfied the Society as to his attendance for a year at a Law School provided or approved by the Society (1932 Act, s. 32 ; 1936 Act, s. 7). The provided School is the Society's School of Law in London, and the approved Schools function under arrangements made with most of the Universities and University Colleges in England and Wales. The courses at the approved Law Schools, which are largely financed by grants made by the Council out of moneys raised from the profession for purposes of legal education, are normally part-time for a year of three academic terms : those at the Society's School are different, as they are divided into a whole-time Intermediate course of about five and a half months and a whole-time Final course of about six months. The clerk must begin his Law School attendance not later than fifteen months (and, where he attends the Society's School, not earlier than six months) after the execution of his articles. Many of the Schools offer a year's course before Articles, on satisfactory completion of which the clerk may be articled for four years instead of five.

At the Society's School, and at most of the approved Law Schools, it is possible for an articled clerk to read for a Law Degree concurrently with his service under articles.

We must not forget the Society's Intermediate, Final, and Honours Examinations.

The Intermediate Examination is in two parts—the Law portion and the Trust Accounts and Bookkeeping portion : the holding of a Degree in Law of an approved University confers exemption from the former portion, and barristers of five years' standing and certain Dominion and Colonial solicitors are also exempt from both portions. Students at the Society's School of Law may not take the Intermediate Examination until they have completed their Intermediate course : other students articled for more than four years may not take it until one year after their entry into articles, unless the Examination Committee in special circumstances otherwise determine. A candidate who is not exempt and who has not passed the Law portion of the Intermediate Examination within twelve

The Intermediate Examination.

months after the expiration of half of his term of service under articles may not sit for the Final Examination until six months after the earliest Final Examination that he could otherwise have taken. The Council have power to dispense with these requirements in suitable cases.

The Final Examination.
The Final Examination is an Examination of candidates as to articles and service thereunder, and their fitness and capacity to act as solicitors in all business and matters usually transacted by solicitors, and also, if any allegation is made by the Registrar as to the moral unfitness of any candidate to be an Officer of the Supreme Court, an inquiry into the truth of the allegation (1932 Act, s. 14). The essential purpose of the Examination is to test the applicant's practical knowledge. The earliest Final Examination which an articled clerk may take is that held next before the expiration of his articles (1932 Act, s. 31) ; but he may if he wishes take any subsequent Examination.

The Honours Examination (entry for which is optional) is designed to test both academic and practical knowledge.

Admission.
Subject to disposing of the questions of service under articles, Law School attendance, and Examinations, the articled clerk may apply for admission. This must be done on at least six weeks' notice to the Society, and it may be advisable to give the notice even before the result of the Final Examination is known, in order to avoid delay in admission. Only those of full age can be admitted.

What is said above is merely a brief outline of the law governing qualification as a solicitor, and every intending solicitor would be well advised to seek the advice of The Law Society at the earliest moment on the various steps which he should take, since each case may present special features with which it is beyond the scope of this book to deal.

Practising certificates.
After admission the name of the newly admitted solicitor is placed on the Roll of Solicitors, but no solicitor can call himself a solicitor or practise as such unless he holds an annual practising certificate. Without such a certificate a solicitor is, like the layman, an unqualified person, and he can only do work or take employment for which a

practising certificate is not required. The holding of a practising certificate is, therefore, a matter of much importance and serious offences may be committed by those who disregard that fact.

Practising certificates are issued by The Law Society as Registrar of Solicitors. Normally the solicitor applies for a practising certificate under s. 37 of the 1932 Act (as amended by ss. 5 (1), 7, 8, and 9 of the 1941 Act and Sched. II to the Solicitors, Public Notaries, &c. Act, 1949). This involves the applicant's personally completing a declaration stating whether s. 38 of the 1932 Act (with which we shall deal in a moment applies to him and whether he has complied with the Solicitors' Accounts Rules (to which we refer later). Ordinarily the application is made at the beginning of the practice year which runs from November 16, to November 15 following, and where the certificate is issued before December 16, it is deemed to have had effect from the beginning of the practice year. *Declarations as to issue of practising certificates.*

We have said that in his declaration the solicitor must state whether or not s. 38 of the 1932 Act applies to him. That section (as amended and re-enacted by s. 10 of the 1941 Act and further amended by Sched. II to the 1949 Act) provides that in certain cases an application for a practising certificate must be made on six weeks' notice and that the Registrar may, in his discretion, grant or refuse the application or decide to grant it subject to conditions : there is a right of appeal to the Master of the Rolls against the Registrar's decision. The cases to which s. 38 applies are where a solicitor applies for a practising certificate :

(a) when for twelve months or more he has ceased to hold a practising certificate in force ; or

(b) whilst he is an undischarged bankrupt or a receiving order in bankruptcy is in force against him ; or

(c) when, having been suspended from practice or having had his name struck off the roll, the period of his suspension has expired, or his name has been restored to the roll, as the case may be ; or

(d) not having held a practising certificate in force

within the twelve months next following the date of his admission to the roll ; or

(e) whilst he is a person to whom the powers and provisions of Part IV of the Lunacy Act, 1890, relating to management and administration apply ; or

(f) without having paid a penalty or costs ordered by the Disciplinary Committee to be paid by him ; or

(g) after he has been invited by the Council to give an explanation in respect of any matter affecting his conduct and has failed to give to the Council an explanation in respect of that matter which the Council regard as sufficient and satisfactory, and has been notified in writing by the Council that he has so failed ; or

(h) after having had an order made against him for the issue of a writ of attachment ; or

(i) after having been adjudicated a bankrupt and obtained his discharge or after having entered into a composition with his creditors or a deed of arrangement for the benefit of his creditors ; or

(j) after having had given against him any judgment which involves the payment of moneys other than costs and is not a judgment as to the whole effect of which upon him he is entitled to indemnity or relief from any other person, and without having produced to the Registrar evidence of the satisfaction of such judgment.

Once a solicitor falls within any of the cases (a), (c), (d), (g), (h), (i), and (j) above, similar discretionary powers are exercisable on his subsequent applications for a practising certificate until such time as he obtains a certificate free from conditions.

A practising certificate becomes suspended if the holder is adjudicated bankrupt (1941 Act, ss. 11 and 12).

Prohibition from taking articled clerk.

At any time when the Registrar has power to refuse a solicitor's application for a practising certificate under s. 38, the Society may, by notice in writing to the solicitor, prohibit him from taking any articled clerk, and may discharge the articles of any clerk then articled to him.

Such prohibition will remain in force unless and until withdrawn (1941 Act, s. 14).

Section II. OFFENCES BY SOLICITORS AND UNQUALIFIED PERSONS

Let us now consider some of the provisions creating criminal offences (punishable by the Criminal Courts) and professional offences (normally dealt with by the Disciplinary Committee, although the High Court also has, but rarely exercises, concurrent jurisdiction) by or in respect of unqualified persons. The Law Society is the body primarily concerned with the enforcement of them, and they illustrate the importance of a practising certificate when it is remembered that a solicitor without such a certificate is an unqualified person for the purpose of them.

By s. 45 of the 1932 Act no unqualified person may act as a solicitor, or as such sue out any writ or process, or commence, carry on or defend any action, suit or other proceeding, in the name of any other person or in his own name in any Court of civil or criminal jurisdiction in England and Wales, or act as a solicitor in any cause or matter, civil or criminal, to be heard or determined before any Court of Assize, any general or Quarter Sessions, any justice or justices, or any Revenue Commissioners. A person guilty of an offence against this Section is guilty of a misdemeanour and of contempt of Court, and is punishable accordingly ; he is incapable of maintaining any action for any costs and may be liable for each offence to a penalty of £50 (to be applied to the use of His Majesty) and costs on action brought by The Law Society with the sanction of the Attorney-General. *[marginal: Unqualified person acting as solicitor in actions, etc.]*

By s. 46 of the 1932 Act (as amended by s. 22 of the 1941 Act) any person not having in force a practising certificate who wilfully pretends to be or takes or uses any name, title, addition or description implying that he is qualified or recognised by law as qualified to act as a solicitor, is liable, on summary conviction, to a penalty not exceeding £50 for each such offence. *[marginal: Unqualified person describing himself as a solicitor.]*

By s. 47 of the same Act (as amended by s. 23 of the *[marginal: Unqualified persons.]*

preparing
documents.

1941 Act and Sched. I to the 1949 Act) any person not being a duly certificated solicitor nor having the other professional qualifications specified in the section, who, unless he proves that the act was not done for or in expectation of any fee, gain or reward, either directly or indirectly, draws or prepares any instrument relating to real or personal estate or any legal proceeding, is liable, on summary conviction, to a fine not exceeding £50. This section does not extend to any public officer drawing or preparing instruments in the course of his duty, or to any person employed merely to engross any instrument or proceeding. For the purposes of the section the expression "instrument" does not apply to wills, agreements under hand only, powers of attorney or transfers of stock containing no trust or limitation. S. 48 (as amended by s. 23 of the 1941 Act and Sched I to the 1949 Act) contains similar provisions as to instruments for use under the Land Registration Act, 1925. S. 49 of the 1932 Act (as similarly amended) likewise prevents legally unqualified persons from taking instructions for or drawing or preparing any papers on which to found or oppose a grant of probate or letters of administration on pain of being liable to a penalty of £10 for each offence.

Costs irre-
coverable
where no
practising
certificate is
held.

S. 50 of the 1932 Act prevents the recovery of costs in any action in respect of anything done by a person who acts as a solicitor without a practising certificate.

Aiding un-
qualified
person to
practise.

S. 51 of the 1932 Act prohibits a solicitor from wilfully and knowingly acting as agent in any action or in any matter in bankruptcy for any unqualified person, or permitting his name to be made use of in such action or matter upon the account or for the profit of any unqualified person or sending any process to any unqualified person, or from doing any other act enabling any unqualified person to appear, act or practise in any respect as a solicitor in any such action or matter. If a solicitor commits a breach of this section his name must be struck off the Roll and the High Court may sentence the unqualified person to imprisonment for not more than one year. It should be noted that this is the only professional offence where on conviction striking off the Roll must inevitably follow: lesser penalties are, as we shall see, available in other cases.

S. 52 of the 1932 Act provides that no solicitor shall, in connection with his practice, without the written permission of The Law Society, employ or remunerate any person whose name to his knowledge has been struck off the Roll otherwise than at his own request, or who is suspended from practising as a solicitor. There is a right of appeal to the Master of the Rolls against the refusal of the Society's permission in such cases. Any solicitor who contravenes this section must be struck off the Roll or suspended from practice.

S. 55 of the 1932 Act makes it a criminal offence punishable by a fine not exceeding £10 for a person who has been struck off the Roll or is under suspension from practice, to seek or accept employment by a solicitor in connection with that solicitor's practice without previously informing him that he is disqualified from practising.

S. 16 of the 1941 Act provides that where a solicitor's clerk has been convicted of certain criminal offences in respect of money or property belonging to or held by his employer or his employer's client, or where it appears to The Law Society that a solicitor's clerk has been party to some act or default of a solicitor in respect of which disciplinary proceedings might be taken against the solicitor, the Disciplinary Committee may, on the application of the Society, order that no solicitor shall, in connection with his practice, take or retain such clerk into or in his employment or remunerate him without the written permission of the Society.

We have spoken above of the constitution of the Disciplinary Committee and referred to certain statutory professional offences in respect of which proceedings may be taken before them. These offences, however, by no means exhaust the Committee's jurisdiction. Under s. 5 of the 1932 Act (as amended by s. 19 of the 1941 Act) any person may apply to the Committee to strike the name of a solicitor off the Roll or to require him to answer allegations contained in an affidavit. On the hearing of any such application the Committee have power to make any such order as to removing from or striking off the Roll the name of the solicitor, as to suspending him from practice, as to payment by him of a

Solicitors not to employ certain persons.

General jurisdiction of Disciplinary Committee.

penalty not exceeding £500 (which shall be forfeit to His Majesty), as to payment by any party of costs or of a contribution towards costs and otherwise in relation to the case as they may think fit. It will be noted that there are no statutory restrictions as to the grounds on which the Disciplinary Committee may make these orders, and accordingly any conduct which is unbecoming to a solicitor as an Officer of the Court may cause the Committee to exercise their powers.

We have referred to professional offences prescribed by Statute and to the general statutory powers of the Disciplinary Committee. Yet a further body of law remains for consideration, viz., offences against Rules made by The Law Society under statutory powers.

Solicitors' accounts. Under s. 1 of the Solicitors Act, 1933, the Council of The Law Society are required to make Rules as to solicitors' accounts and may, if they see fit, make Rules for regulating in respect of any other matter the professional practice, conduct and discipline of solicitors.

The Rules which the Council have made as to accounts are the Solicitors' Accounts Rules : a copy of these is printed on the back of every application for a practising certificate and it will be recalled that every applicant for a practising certificate has to declare whether he has complied with these Rules. The main requirements of them are that the solicitor must keep his clients' monies in a bank account separate from that containing his own monies, that he must keep proper books of account to distinguish his clients' monies from his own and those of other clients. The Society has power to inspect his books, papers, and accounts to make sure that the Rules are being observed. Proceedings may be taken before the Disciplinary Committee if the Rules are broken.

As an additional means of ensuring that the Solicitors' Accounts Rules are observed, s. 1 of the 1941 Act requires the Council to make Rules as to the annual delivery to the Registrar by solicitors of accountants' certificates. By this section and the Accountant's Certificate Rules, 1946, made thereunder every solicitor must (unless he satisfies the Council that in the circumstances of his case it is unnecessary) deliver to the Registrar once during each practice year a certificate by a qualified accountant stating whether or not the solicitor has complied with the Solicitors' Accounts Rules, 1945, and, if not, what breaches have been committed.

Another statutory provision with regard to solicitors' accounts is s. 18 of the 1941 Act under which the Council have made the Solicitors' Trust Accounts Rules, 1945, which require solicitors to keep separate from their own monies, monies of certain trusts of which they are trustees.

Under the permissive power to make Rules contained in s. 1 of the 1933 Act the Council have made the Solicitors' Practice Rules, 1936. These prohibit solicitors from advertising, " touting " for business or doing anything calculated to attract business unfairly ; agreeing to share costs with unqualified persons ; holding themselves out, or allowing themselves to be held out, as prepared to do business for less than certain remuneration ; or acting for any person introduced to them by any organisation or person (commonly known as ambulance chasers) whose business is to make claims for damages for personal injuries. Solicitors' Practice Rules, 1936.

There is, inevitably, a very small minority of cases where a solicitor or solicitor's clerk abuses his position and clients or third parties suffer loss. In order to relieve such losses and preserve the honour of the profession as a whole, s. 2 of the 1941 Act establishes a Fund called the Compensation Fund which is administered by the Society. Solicitors who take out practising certificates are required to contribute to this Fund, the normal amount of the contribution being at present £5. No contribution is payable in respect of the first three practising certificates which a solicitor takes out and the contribution is only £2 10s. 0d. in respect of each of the next three. Out of the Fund the Council may make grants at their discretion in respect of losses sustained by any person in consequence of dishonesty on the part of any solicitor or any clerk or servant of any solicitor in connection with any such solicitor's practice as a solicitor or any trust of which such solicitor was a trustee, and whether or not he had a practising certificate in force when the act of dishonesty was committed, and notwithstanding that subsequently The Compensation Fund.

to the commission of that act he may have died or had his name removed from or struck off the Roll or may have ceased to practise or been suspended from practice. Rules known as the Solicitors Compensation Fund Rules, 1942, have been made by the Council governing applications under this section.

Additional provisions in connection with the Compensation Fund are contained in the First Schedule to the 1941 Act. Among other things these empower the Council, where they have reasonable cause to believe that a solicitor or his clerk or servant has been guilty of dishonesty, to take possession of all deeds, wills, securities, papers, books of accounts, records, vouchers, and other documents in the possession or control of the solicitor or his firm, or relating to certain categories of trusts of which he is a trustee. Furthermore, if the Council are satisfied that a solicitor or his clerk or servant has been guilty of such dishonesty the High Court may on their application order that no payment shall be made without the leave of the Court out of any bank account in the name of the solicitor or his firm.

Section III. A Solicitor's Work, Privileges and Disabilities

General scope of solicitors' work.

If one were to ask the man in the street his idea of a solicitor's work he would probably say that it was to act for parties in litigation. While it is an important function of solicitors to act in litigation, this is by no means their only or even their most important work. Conveyancing, administration of estates, and trust and family work must use up far more " man hours " of solicitors than does litigation. The private practitioner may specialise to some extent in a particular field—insurance work, " running down cases," Magistrates' Court work, advocacy in the county court or the like—but in general it may be said that the successful solicitor in private practice is the adviser and confidant to whom members of the general public come with problems of all kinds, and that to deal with these he requires not merely an academic knowledge of the law but practical experience of affairs and knowledge and understanding of human beings. His training—the mixture of academic learning and practical experience—makes him specially fitted for holding posts where legal knowledge or administrative ability or both are required. Thus solicitors will be found acting as Chief Officers of Local Authorities, or holding appointments such as Clerks to Justices and important posts in the world of industry and commerce. The popular way of referring to one's solicitor was once "my man of business." That phrase has dropped out of general use, but the qualities which it denoted are as important now as ever they were to the successful practitioner.

The special position of solicitors is recognised by the fact that they are exempted from serving on juries or as churchwardens, constables and the like, and generally from all public services of a personal character which might interfere with the due discharge of their professional duties.

Exemption from jury service, etc.

Solicitors are entitled to practise as such before the House of Lords and the Privy Council, in the Court of Appeal and in the High Court, in the Ecclesiastical Courts and generally in the inferior courts. This right to practise does not, however, necessarily carry with it the right of audience, *i.e.*, the right to act as advocates. Broadly speaking, solicitors have a right of audience in the county courts, petty sessional courts, and inferior courts generally, but before the House of Lords, the Privy Council, the Court of Appeal and the High Court they have only a right of audience in certain interlocutory matters not dealt with in open Court.

Courts in which solicitor may practise.

A solicitor who is managing clerk to another solicitor now has the right to appear for and represent his principal in the conduct of a case in Court, but one solicitor may not as such employ another as an advocate.

The relation between a solicitor and his client is constituted by a retainer, that is to say, the acceptance by the solicitor of the client's instructions to him to act. In litigation a solicitor should, as a general rule, obtain a written retainer, but an oral retainer is sufficient except where the litigant is a corporation (where the retainer should be under seal) or where the retainer amounts to an agreement not to be performed within the year (when it must be in writing). As regards non-contentious business

Retainer and authorities.

the retainer is, in general, implied from the circumstances. The retainer may be a general one or it may be an authority limited to some particular matter or to some particular proceeding in an action, but in either case it must not be exceeded.

Ordinarily a solicitor will refer important questions to his client for instructions, but, under his general retainer, he has power to agree to a matter in dispute being referred to an arbitrator and may even, after an action has been begun, agree to a compromise of it unless the client has expressly forbidden this : before the commencement of an action the solicitor cannot compromise his client's claim without the client's express consent.

In litigation the authority of the solicitor continues until the conclusion of the whole cause or matter or until his name has been removed from the Record of the Court after notice of change of solicitors has been given. A solicitor is deemed to warrant the authority of his client throughout every step in an action ; so that if his client should be an infant or die or become insane, with or without the knowledge of the solicitor, and the solicitor continues to act, although in ignorance, he is personally liable to the other side for their costs (*Yonge* v. *Toynbee*, [1910] 1 K. B. 215).

"Privilege."   The peculiarly close relation between a client and his solicitor is recognised in law in a way that applies to no other professional man—not even a doctor or Minister of religion : this is that a solicitor cannot be compelled to disclose the communications and documents of his client. A solicitor who objects to such disclosure is said to " claim privilege." It must be understood, however, that the privilege is the privilege of the client and not of the solicitor, and it is only on the client's instructions that the solicitor can make disclosure of the client's affairs.

There are limits to the doctrine of privilege : thus while communications made by a client to his solicitor for the purpose of his defence in a criminal prosecution are privileged, no communication made by a client to his solicitor is privileged if it is made in furtherance of a criminal purpose ; information which is not derived through professional confidence is not privileged and accordingly a solicitor cannot refuse to disclose the name of his client nor, unless secret and confidentially communicated, his client's address ; the solicitor's privilege can be no greater than the client's right, so that where the client cannot refuse disclosure the solicitor cannot claim privilege.

There is another way in which the confidential relation between a client and his solicitor is recognised. This is that the Court, assuming that the client may be overswayed by his solicitor's advice, regards as suspect and out of the common a transaction whereby a solicitor purchases from his client property, whether real or personal. The solicitor is not incapable of making such a purchase (unless it be of property which is the subject of an action in which the client is concerned) ; but the onus is thrown upon him of showing that the purchase price was not inadequate, that he took no advantage and that there was no concealment of any kind. In other words, quite apart from any question of undue influence, the contract is one *uberrimæ fidei*, that is to say, voidable by the client for mere non-disclosure on the part of the solicitor. For his own protection, therefore, the solicitor should see that in such a case the client has separate and independent advice. Dealings
between
solicitor
and client.

While there is no objection to a solicitor's accepting the offices of executor or trustee of a client's will (and indeed it is very common for a solicitor to do this), he cannot charge and be paid for either professional or non-professional work (*i.e.*, which an executor or trustee who is not a solicitor would do without payment) unless the will contains a clause (known as a " charging clause,") expressly entitling him to do so. Such a clause should not be inserted without the client's express authority.

Furthermore a solicitor cannot validly accept a gift *inter vivos* from a client unless it is of a trifling character, nor is a client bound by his acknowledgment of a statute-barred debt owed to his solicitor. The principle is that such gifts and acknowledgments are presumed to have been made through the undue influence of the solicitor. A solicitor may, however, accept a legacy from a client.

A solicitor represents himself as possessing the requisite ability and skill to undertake any usual legal work that Negligence.

may be entrusted to him. Accordingly if by negligence or ignorance he does not perform such work properly, the client has a right of action for damages against him. A solicitor is also liable for the want of care, knowledge or honesty of his partner, clerk or London agent. These rules apply even though the solicitor is paid no remuneration.

Section IV. SOLICITORS' REMUNERATION

Solicitors, unlike barristers, have a legal right to their remuneration. A solicitor cannot, however, make what charges he likes : he is bound by somewhat strict rules. These differ for non-contentious business on the one hand and contentious business on the other.

Non-contentious business—the Solicitors' Remuneration Orders.

As regards non-contentious business, s. 56 of the 1932 Act sets up a Committee consisting of the Lord Chancellor, the Lord Chief Justice, the Master of the Rolls, the President of The Law Society, a President of a Provincial Law Society, and (so far as work under the Land Registration Act, 1925, is concerned) the Chief Land Registrar. This Committee have power to make general orders prescribing and regulating, in such manner as they think fit, the remuneration of solicitors in respect of non-contentious business. Under that section (which reproduces a corresponding provision of the Solicitors' Remuneration Act, 1881) there are in force the Solicitors' Remuneration Order, 1883, and a number of amending Orders.

The 1883 Order contains two Schedules. Sched. I fixes certain scales of charges which are applicable to sales, purchases, mortgages, and leases of freehold or leasehold property. The remuneration payable under these scales varies according to the amount of the consideration money, *i.e.*, the money passing on the transaction.

Sched. II prescribes certain "item charges" such as fees for the solicitor's attendance on clients and others, and for drawing, engrossing, fair copying, and perusing documents. These item charges are applicable to various conveyancing transactions, such as the preparation of a settlement, which are not covered by Sched. I, and to other non-contentious matters, such as giving legal advice.

The charges prescribed in Sched. II are not a complete

list because the Order itself prescribes that where item charges are applicable the solicitor shall charge " according to the present system " as altered by Sched. II. This means that in order to make out an itemised bill one must go back to the system in force before 1883 : the origins of that system can be traced back for some hundreds of years to the time when lawyers were among the few literate members of the community. Viewed in this light the items in a solicitor's bill such as " Writing you . . .," " Perusing draft . . . " may seem less remarkable than they so often do to the layman.

The charges laid down in Sched. I do not include disbursements, such as stamp duties, counsel's fees, auctioneer's charges, travelling or hotel expenses, search fees, and the like, and the solicitor may be allowed additional remuneration for any business which is by special exertion carried through in an exceptionally short space of time.

A solicitor may charge under Sched. II instead of under Sched. I if he so elects and informs his client before entering upon the business, and must so charge for Sched. I business which is not completed. The charges under Sched. II may be increased or diminished for special reasons. If the solicitor's remuneration falls to be charged under the old system as altered by Sched. II he may, if he chooses, deliver a bill in one gross sum without specifying the various items : the client may, however, demand details of the bill within twelve months of its delivery or one month after payment (Solicitors' Remuneration (Gross Sum) Order, 1934).

Having regard to altered financial conditions resulting from the two World Wars, the remuneration chargeable under the 1883 Order has been increased by subsequent Orders to 50 per cent. above that authorised in 1883.

As regards contentious business, solicitors' charges are normally made out on an item basis, but the items are governed by the Rules of the Supreme Court (Order LXV and Appendix N), the County Court Rules or as the case may be. In contentious business too the charges are now 50 per cent. above what they were before the 1914–1918 War. *Contentious business— item charges.*

A discussion of the detailed items in a bill of costs in a contentious matter is beyond the scope of this book, but there is one general principle that should be grasped ; this is that a solicitor's bill in a contentious matter may be one of three kinds, viz., on a party and party basis, on a solicitor and client basis, or on a solicitor and own client basis (*Giles* v. *Randall*, [1915] 1 K. B. 290). The first is what is normally payable by an unsuccessful litigant who is ordered to pay costs to his opponent and covers the bare minimum of work necessarily done by the successful party's solicitor to contest the proceedings : it does not cover any costs which appear to the Taxing Master to have been incurred or increased through over-caution, negligence or mistake or by payment of special fees to Counsel or special charges or expenses to witnesses or other persons or other unusual expenses (Order LXV, Rule 27 of the Rules of the Supreme Court). The second, which is slightly more generous, is applicable in certain cases where the Court so orders and the costs are payable by some person other than the party who incurred them. The third is the full charges which are incurred by the client to his own solicitor and, unlike a party and party or solicitor and client bill, covers items which the client required or needed but were not vital to the successful conduct of the proceedings—for example, work done before action brought, briefing one counsel at a fancy fee of, say, 1,000 guineas (instead of another at a normal fee of, say, 50 guineas, letters to the client reporting developments, and copies of the writ, statement of claim, and the like which the client wishes to have for his own use. The unsuccessful party does not have to pay his opponent's costs of such items and accordingly an order for costs in an action is, indeed, never a complete indemnity against the successful party's liability to his own solicitor.

Taxation of costs. Both in contentious and non-contentious matters a solicitor may, under certain conditions, make an agreement with his client as to costs instead of charging in accordance with the scales or items. Before discussing these conditions, however, we must refer to the machinery for securing that solicitors do not overcharge. This machinery is known as taxation.

Attached to the Supreme Court is a department known as the Supreme Court Taxing Office. It is staffed by a number of Taxing Masters (all solicitors themselves) and their clerks whose duty it is to consider, when questions arise, bills of costs in the High Court, and Court of Appeal and all other bills except those in respect of proceedings in some inferior court which fall to be taxed by officers of that inferior court. The Taxing Master's authority to act is an order for taxation made by the Court in the particular matter and his decisions are open to review by the Court. He considers the bill item by item—both charges and disbursements—and " taxes off " entirely or reduces any that seem to him excessive.

A solicitor who presents a petition for the taxation of his own costs against his client has to pay the costs of taxation in any event unless the client attends at the taxation. On the other hand if the client presents the petition and less than one-sixth is taxed off the amount of the bill, the costs of taxation are payable by the client.

We can now return to the subject of agreements as to remuneration. Here, too, there is a distinction between contentious and non-contentious matters. *Agreed fees— non-con- tentious business.*

In non-contentious business such an agreement must be in writing and signed by the person to be bound by it or his agent (1932 Act, s. 57). It may provide for the remuneration (inclusive or exclusive of disbursements) to be on a percentage basis or by gross sum or by way of salary or otherwise. The agreement may be enforced like any other, except that it is subject to review by the Court on any taxation where it is relied on by the solicitor and objected to by the client as unfair or unreasonable.

Agreements for costs in contentious business are hedged about by stringent provisions (1932 Act, ss. 59 to 63) designed to protect the interests of the person liable for or chargeable with the costs in question. The agreement may be in respect of either past or future service ; it must be signed by the client ; the amount payable cannot be recovered until the agreement has been allowed by the Taxing Master ; it may be set aside by the Court if the Court considers it unfair or unreasonable ; no action can be brought upon it and only the Court can enforce *Agreed fees— contentious business.*

it after inquiry into its fairness. Moreover, any provision in the agreement whereby the solicitor shall be expressed to be rendered not liable for negligence or to be relieved from any responsibility to which he would otherwise be subject, is wholly void. Also, no validity is given by the statute to any purchase by a solicitor of his client's interest in the property involved in the action, or to an arrangement whereby he is to be paid only in the event of the success of the action : both of these transactions are against the policy of the law. There is, however, no impropriety in a solicitor's conducting a speculative action, if he honestly takes pains to inform himself that there is a *bona fide* cause of action. An agreement as to costs in contentious matters is not prejudicially to affect the interests of persons not parties to it.

A solicitor may validly agree, either in non-contentious or contentious matters, to make no charge or to charge disbursements only. Such an agreement precludes him from recovering profit costs either from his own client or any other party. It should be noted that while such an agreement is valid, it would be professionally improper for the solicitor to make it, if by doing so he committed a breach of the Solicitors' Practice Rules, 1936 (mentioned above), prohibiting undercutting.

Recovery
of costs
by action.

A solicitor who seeks to recover his costs by action must comply with certain formalities which do not apply to other people who seek to recover what is due to them. S. 65 of the 1932 Act provides that no action shall be brought to recover any costs due to a solicitor until one month after a bill has been delivered in accordance with the requirements of the section. The requirements are that the bill must be signed by the solicitor (or a partner in the case of a firm of solicitors) or accompanied by a letter so signed and referring to the bill, and that the bill must be delivered to the party to be charged either personally or by post. By s. 66 the party chargeable with the bill may, within one month after its delivery, require it to be taxed and in certain circumstances may even obtain an order for taxation after the expiry of that month. S. 67 contains provisions enabling third parties ultimately liable for the costs (such as beneficiaries under trusts) also to obtain orders for taxation. It is also possible for a client or party chargeable with a solicitor's costs to obtain an order directing the solicitor to deliver his bill, where the solicitor has not already done so, and, on payment, to deliver up all deeds, papers, and other documents, in his possession touching the matters comprised in the bill. Even after payment a taxation may be ordered on the ground of special circumstances, such as a manifest overcharge, provided the application is made within twelve months after payment.

In suitable cases a solicitor should deliver with his bill of costs a cash account containing particulars of payments made during the progress of the matter which ordinarily a solicitor does not make out of his own pocket *e.g.*, purchase monies, estate duty and stamp duties paid on the registration of a company. *Cash account.*

It remains to consider the steps, other than bringing an action, which a solicitor can take to obtain payment of his costs.

First, a solicitor may accept from his client security for the amount to become due and for interest on such amount, but so that interest is not to commence until the amount due is ascertained either by agreement or taxation. He may charge interest at 4 per cent. per annum on his charges and disbursements from the expiration of one month from demand made upon the client. *Security for costs.*

Secondly, the solicitor may obtain a " charging order " under s. 69 of the 1932 Act upon any property that may have been recovered or preserved as the result of any proceeding in any Court in which he has been employed : this remedy is limited to the costs incurred in respect of the particular property recovered or preserved. *Charging order.*

Thirdly, the solicitor may enforce the submission to pay which is contained in orders for taxation made in the Chancery Division. *Enforcement of submission.*

Fourthly, the solicitor may enforce his general lien against all deeds and other documents (except his client's will) belonging to the client which may be in the solicitor's possession. This type of lien, known as the solicitor's " retaining lien " is the only *general* lien which he can *Liens.*

exercise. By virtue of it he is entitled to retain any documents in his possession whether they relate to the business in which the costs were incurred or to some entirely different business.

A solicitor may also exercise a *particular* lien (often called his common law lien—although the retaining lien is also valid at common law) over personal property preserved or recovered by his efforts ; but this lien only extends to the costs incurred by him in such preservation or recovery.

A solicitor's lien, whether statutory or common law, only secures his " taxable costs, charges, and expenses," *i.e.*, such charges as should be properly allowed on taxation by a Taxing Master. It does not cover advances to the client.

CHAPTER 15

BARRISTERS ("COUNSEL")

The term "barrister" (which is more correct than the usual expression "barrister-at-law") is applied to persons who have been "called to the bar" by one of the four Inns of Court. No person can practise as a barrister unless he is a member of one of these Inns. Membership of an Inn.

The Inns of Court, known as the Inner Temple, the Middle Temple, Lincoln's Inn, and Gray's Inn, are unincorporated Societies independent of any State control, though subject to visitation by the judges. They are governed by the senior members of the Society, called "Masters of the Bench," or "Benchers," who are responsible for the education and discipline of persons intending to become barristers, for their admission as barristers when they have sufficient educational qualifications, and for the discipline over barristers after they have been called. This discipline they can enforce, in the last resort, by expelling the barrister from his Inn, or by disbarring him, that is to say, depriving him of the privilege of acting as a barrister. But a barrister may also be disbarred on his own petition, if he desires to adopt some profession for which barristers are disqualified ; and this not uncommonly happens when a barrister wishes to become a solicitor, which he may do on getting himself disbarred and passing the solicitors' Final Examination, although, if he is of less than five years' standing at the bar, he will (as we have seen) have to serve as a clerk in a solicitor's office for three years before he can be admitted as a solicitor. The Inns of Court. Powers of the Benchers.

The four Inns of Court have agreed upon a series of Regulations relating to the admission of students, and their call to the bar, and similar matters. Under these Regulations, students must, before they are eligible for call, have kept twelve terms (equivalent to three years) Regulations relating to admission and call.

by dining on a specified number of occasions in the hall of their Inn in each term, must be of the age of twenty-one years, and must have passed the prescribed examinations. The Benchers of each Inn have power to dispense with some of these requirements ; and there are special rules governing the call to the bar of solicitors, and of barristers from other parts of the British Commonwealth.

General Council of the Bar. In addition to the Masters of the Bench of each Inn, there is another body which controls matters of professional etiquette and generally represents the Bar. This is the General Council of the Bar, which is composed of forty-eight members elected by members of the Bar as a whole, six additional members elected by the forty-eight members to represent barristers in special classes of practice, and the Attorney-General and Solicitor-General as official members. A Joint Standing Committee consisting of members of the Bar Council and of members of the Council of the Law Society meets at regular intervals to consider matters of common concern to both branches of the profession. The Chairman of the Bar Council and the President of the Law Society are prepared to appoint, when required, a joint tribunal to settle any difference between a solicitor and a barrister who agree to be bound by the tribunal's decision.

Exclusive right of audience. Barristers have the right of audience in practically all judicial proceedings. In some cases, this right is shared with solicitors ; in other cases it is an exclusive right. In the House of Lords, before the Judicial Committee of the Privy Council, in the Court of Appeal, and (generally speaking) in the High Court of Justice, they have an exclusive right of audience as advocates. A party may appear in person in these Courts, as elsewhere ; but, if he wishes to be represented, he must be represented by a barrister.

Concurrent right with solicitors. In bankruptcy matters in the High Court and Divisional Court, in chambers of the High Court and the Palatine Courts, in all county courts, and in many other Courts, solicitors as well as barristers are allowed to appear for their clients. In other cases, barristers are allowed to appear at the discretion of the tribunal, although

No right of audience. they have no right of audience. The general rule is, that, where a tribunal is set up without any enactment or precedent governing its procedure, the tribunal itself has the power to decide whether audience shall be given to counsel; it is part of the inherent jurisdiction of every judicial or quasi-judicial tribunal to settle its own rules of procedure.

Barristers in modern times are divided into two classes, viz., King's Counsel, who wear silk gowns and sit within the bar in the Law Courts (being called "silks" or "leaders"), and Juniors. It is the usual practice for a King's Counsel not to appear in Court unless a junior is briefed to appear with him; and no junior can accept a brief under another junior whose call to the bar was subsequent to his own. There are many other professional rules governing the rights and privileges of barristers *inter se*; but we cannot set them out here. The enforcement of them rests, as a rule, with the General Council of the Bar, or, in some cases, with "circuit men," *i.e.*, the body of barristers going a particular circuit.

Two classes of barristers.

As regards the relationship between barristers and solicitors, it is the general practice that no barrister gives his services to a lay client except upon the instructions of a solicitor. The retainer of a solicitor carries with it an authority to employ counsel and to pay his fees, which should be marked on the brief before delivery and may not be subsequently altered. A barrister has no right to sue for his fees; and, if he fails to secure payment upon delivery of the papers to him, he has no legal remedy either against his professional client (the solicitor) or against his lay client. So his fees, even if paid by the lay client to the solicitor, cannot be recovered while in the solicitor's hands. The solicitor, however, who has received from his client fees specifically for counsel and fails to pay them over is liable to disciplinary proceedings for misappropriation: even if he has not received the fees from his client the solicitor should, as a matter of professional etiquette, pay the proper fees due to counsel. A barrister is bound, in the absence of special circumstances, to accept any brief in the Courts in which he professes to practise, at a proper professional fee, according to the length and difficulty of the case. He cannot, however,

Employed through solicitor

Cannot sue for fees.

Incurs no liability. be sued for failure to attend the Court. Nor can he be sued for negligence in the performance of his duty ; and, moreover, when a solicitor acts upon the advice of a barrister, he also is, as a general rule, immune from an action for negligence. This immunity does not, however, extend to every case in which a solicitor is charged with negligence ; for it is well recognised that a solicitor remains, even when counsel is employed, liable for the mismanagement of so much of the conduct of an action as is usually allotted to his branch of the profession, for instance, for want of care in the preparation of the cause for trial, or for the consequences of his non-attendance thereon with his witnesses.

It is illegal for a barrister to agree with a solicitor that the amount of his fees shall depend upon the event of a suit ; and, if the agreement were to take the form of giving the barrister a share in the proceeds of litigation, it would amount to the offence of " champerty."

It is the practice of barristers, on the common law side, to charge special fees over and above the ordinary brief fees for appearing on a circuit or at Quarter Sessions to which they do not belong.

Retainer. Barristers may be " retained " : that is to say, their services may be engaged by a particular client upon payment of a retaining fee. The effect of a retainer is, that the barrister who is thus retained is bound, subject to certain exceptions, not to accept a brief from the opposing side without giving the party who retained him the opportunity of briefing him. Retainers may be general or special. A *general* retainer is an engagement applying to all proceedings to which the client may be a party. A *special* retainer is one given for a particular case ; and it entitles the barrister to a brief on every occasion on which counsel is briefed in a proceeding to which the retainer applies, provided that it does not entitle leading counsel to a brief on an occasion where it is usual to instruct a junior only.

Clerk's fees. Barristers' clerks invariably charge certain fees, which are usually paid to the barrister together with his own fees ; and the clerk may maintain an action for his fees against the barrister if the latter has received them. But

neither the barrister nor the clerk has a legal right to sue
the solicitor or lay client if the clerk's fees are not paid.

Barristers are not officers of the Court, and are not sub- Discipline.
ject to the discipline which the Court exercises over
solicitors. But any serious misconduct on the part of a
barrister would be reported by the judge to the benchers
of the barrister's Inn, who would take the necessary disciplinary steps. An appeal lies from the decision of the
benchers to a panel of judges nominated by the Lord
Chancellor. Further, the Court can punish a barrister for
contempt of Court, by fining and even imprisoning him.

The education and examination of candidates for entry Council of
to the barrister's branch of the legal profession are en- Legal
Education.
trusted to a body known as the Council of Legal Education, constituted by representatives of the four Inns of
Court appointed by such Inns, and' drawing its revenue
from subsidies granted by the Inns and from certain
funds under the control of the High Court. The Council
has a staff of Readers and Assistant Readers, who. deliver
lectures to, and otherwise assist with their advice, students
preparing for call to the bar.

BOOK II

CONSTITUTIONAL AND ADMINISTRATIVE LAW

PART I

GENERAL INTRODUCTION

SUMMARY

PAGE

CHAPTER 1. THE SCOPE AND SOURCES OF CONSTITU-
TIONAL AND ADMINISTRATIVE LAW 267

CHAPTER 2. THE THEORY OF GOVERNMENTAL
POWERS AND DUTIES 271

CHAPTER 3. THE KING'S PLEASURE 284

CHAPTER 4. THE SOVEREIGNTY OF PARLIAMENT ... 288

CHAPTER 5. THE ROYAL PREROGATIVE 294

CHAPTER 6. THE DOCTRINE OF STATE NECESSITY
AND ACT OF STATE 309

CHAPTER 7. THE DEVELOPMENT OF CABINET
GOVERNMENT AND THE CONVENTIONS
OF THE CONSTITUTION 315

CHAPTER 8. SUBORDINATE LEGISLATION AND
ADMINISTRATIVE JURISDICTION ... 321

CHAPTER 9. THE SEPARATION OF POWERS AND
THE RULE OF LAW 333

CHAPTER I

THE SCOPE AND SOURCES OF CONSTITUTIONAL AND ADMINISTRATIVE LAW

Scope and definition of the subject.   The subject of this Book is the law relating to the government of the country. It is customarily divided by jurists into constitutional law and administrative law, but no clear and precise line can possibly be drawn between them, and there is bound to be a difference of opinion as to the way in which the division ought to be made.   For our purpose it is unnecessary to make any such attempt.   Our intention is to give a reasonably complete account of the government of the country in its legal aspects, omitting all unnecessary detail and confining ourselves as far as possible to statements of general principle.

But, even though we are not concerned to draw the line between constitutional law and administrative law, we are still faced with the difficulty of defining the field covered by *both* these branches of law *together*.   English Law is not susceptible of neat division, and it is not possible to give an accurate and exhaustive definition of the scope of our subject.   But there is no serious difficulty in giving some indication of it ; and for our purpose it will include the principles which regulate the exercise of central and local government ;   the organisation and functions of government authorities ;   and the relation of government authorities to the general public and the individual citizen.

Sources.   The difficulty of delimiting the sphere of constitutional and administrative law in England is to a great extent due to the character of their sources.

The English Constitution is often spoken of as an " unwritten " Constitution.   This does not mean that we have no statutes and no reported judicial decisions that deal with matters of government.   The meaning is that there is no single document or statute, or series of

Scope of subject can be indicated but not precisely defined.

An unwritten constitution.

documents or statutes, that has as its purpose the inclusion of certain matters, definitely and expressly, within the law of the Constitution. The word "unwritten" is used merely to indicate the difference between Constitutional Law as it is understood in England and the same term as it is understood in many other countries, which have followed the example set by the United States at the close of the eighteenth century. In the United States (which in *other* respects are in legal matters so similar to England) the fundamental principles of the Constitution are stated in a written document, called "The Constitution," which is looked upon as so peculiarly sacrosanct that its terms can be amended only by a legislative process quite different from the ordinary law-making system of the community. But in England we make no distinction between fundamental and non-fundamental laws. The only fundamental law affecting the people of this country is that all our laws can be altered by Parliament.

Comparison with the U.S.A.

The fact that *all* our laws, whatever their subject-matter, are susceptible of alteration by one and the same method, namely, by the passing of an Act of Parliament, renders our Constitution a "flexible" one, as it is called, in contrast with "rigid" Constitutions, which can be altered only by means of some *special* formality. In the United States, when some years ago Congress wished to enact a law prohibiting the consumption of alcoholic liquors, it was found that such "prohibition" would be at variance with the written Constitution, which had first to be altered by an amendment, proposed by two-thirds majorities in both Houses of Congress and ratified by the legislatures of three-quarters of the States. In England even such a law could be made in accordance with the ordinary legislative procedure of Parliament.

Flexible nature of our Constitution.

This description may seem at variance with the facts. What, one may ask, will be said of Magna Carta, of the Petition of Right, of the Bill of Rights, and of the Act of Settlement? Are not these quasi-statutes, as they have been called, these compromises between the King and the people, to be treated as peculiarly sacred and exempt from change by ordinary Act of Parliament; and are we not to say the same of quasi-treaties, such as the Act of Union

Magna Carta, Petition of Right, etc.

with Scotland ? There is indeed no doubt that these quasi-statutes and quasi-treaties are felt to possess a peculiar sanctity and that they ought not to be altered or repealed without some very good cause. Yet they are in fact no more than statutes, and their provisions can be changed in exactly the same way as those of an ordinary statute. Their peculiar character arises rather from political than from purely legal causes.

Case law, statutes—including delegated legislation— and quasi-statutes and quasi-treaties are the sources of constitutional law *in the strict sense of that term.*

But there are rules or usages to which the constitutional lawyer must pay attention which are not rules of *law, i.e.,* they are not rules which a court of law would recognise. These rules or usages have come to be known as " Conventions of the Constitution." Blackstone, writing in the eighteenth century, hardly saw the importance which conventional rules had attained even in his day ; and, in reading his original work, one is struck constantly by some statement of the law which is universally known to have been inconsistent with the facts of the working Constitution. It is possible to argue in his favour that as a lawyer he was only concerned with, and could not disregard, laws which the Courts would regard as laws, even though they might never be applied in actual practice. But a description of the Constitution which omits any consideration of the conventions which have grown around, and indeed have often overgrown, the strict legal conceptions can only be misleading to any person who is not forewarned of the enormous part which conventional usage plays in the ordinary course of the government of the country.

Conventions of the Constitution.

We shall have opportunity presently of illustrating the distinction between law and convention. Here we may content ourselves with one well-known instance. If the Government are defeated in the House of Commons upon an issue which they have recognised as vital to their policy, it is a convention of the Constitution that they should either resign or appeal to the electorate. But the *law* does not call upon them to do so ; and every act legally performed by them after the defeat would be treated by

Law and convention distinguished.

the Courts as valid, just as if they had never been defeated. In practice, however, so strong is the traditional force of this convention that it is invariably adopted ; and it only falls short of being a *law* because it would not be recognised as such by the Courts.

"The law and custom of Parliament."   There is another part of our subject, of the utmost interest and importance, which nevertheless cannot (except for the smallest fraction) be described as constitutional law *in the strict sense above explained.* We refer to " the law and custom of Parliament." Some of the rules governing Parliamentary procedure (*e.g.*, the Parliament Act, 1911, as recently amended, and the Statutory Orders (Special Procedure) Act, 1945) are *law* in the strictest sense, but by far the greater proportion, including the Standing Orders of the Houses of Parliament, would not be recognised as law by the Courts. (See, further, *post*, pp. 381 *et seq.*).

CHAPTER 2

THE THEORY OF GOVERNMENTAL POWERS
AND DUTIES

The government of the country is conducted in virtue The law
confers
powers.
of powers conferred and duties imposed by law on the
various agents of government. All power and authority
are derived from the law, and must be exercised in accordance with the law. A person who is invested with a power
is not thereby exempted from the law, but is authorised by
the law to exercise that power in the manner and for the
objects contemplated by the law. If he acts outside that
authority, he acts illegally, and the Courts of law will,
unless Parliament has deprived them of the necessary
jurisdiction, treat his act as they would any other illegal
act ; to this end they can control the acts of government
agents no less than those of private persons. Indeed,
questions arising out of the exercise of governmental
powers come before the Courts from day to day.

It will be found that these questions can always be
brought within one of three forms :

1. Has the person in question power to do a certain
act at all ?

2. Has he power to do it in this particular way ?

3. Is he under a duty to exercise his power ?

1. *Has the person in question power to do the particular* Sources of
power.
act ? The power, as has been explained, can be conferred
only by law. Its source, therefore, may be either Common Law or Statute, but nothing else.

(*a*) *Common Law powers.* These are of various kinds. Common Law.
Thus a constable has a Common Law power to arrest a
person whom he suspects of having committed a felony ;
and a sheriff has a Common Law power of executing a writ
of *fi. fa.* upon the goods of a judgment debtor. But
such powers, though important, are of little relevance
in the work of modern government. The only Common
Law powers which still play a considerable part in the
government of the country are those exceptional powers

271

which the Crown possesses in virtue of its Prerogative. These will be described in a subsequent chapter (*post*, p. 294).

Statute.

(*b*) *Statutory powers.* The powers conferred by Common Law do not suffice for the complex work of modern government. Every year it is found that some public authority requires new powers to enable it to perform functions which are necessary in the interests of the community. These powers can only be created by or under the authority of an Act of Parliament ; for their creation involves an alteration in the law of the land. They may be conferred either *immediately* by Act of Parliament or *mediately* through some act of subordinate legislation (see *post*, pp. 322 *et seq.*).

A further distinction must be drawn between the different kinds of Acts of Parliament which confer powers of government :

Public General Acts.

Some are intended to impose a uniform system upon all authorities of a given class. Such, for instance, are the Local Government Acts, 1933 and 1948, and the Public Health Acts, 1936 to 1939, which constitute a considerable portion of our code of local government. These are Public General Acts (see *post*, p. 390).

Adoptive Acts.

Or the statute may take the form, now uncommon, of an " adoptive Act," which is in force in any given locality only if the local authority, in its discretion, resolves to adopt it, *e.g.*, the Lighting and Watching Act, 1833.

Local Acts and Provisional Orders.

Finally, it may be a Local (or Personal) Act or Provisional Order Confirmation Act (see *post*, pp. 397–398). Such legislation must be expressly applied for by the local or other authority or the public utility undertaking which requires it. Parliament will normally confer powers only on conditions, and it becomes the duty of the promoters of the legislation to fulfil those conditions if they decide to exercise their powers. Many

Clauses Acts.

of the " common form " clauses conferring powers and discretions, and requiring the performance of duties as conditions precedent to their exercise, have been enacted once and for all in several so-called Clauses Acts, such as the Railways Clauses Acts and the Lands Clauses Acts, which may be expressly or impliedly incorporated (usually with variations) in the Local Act or Provisional Order (see, further, *post*, pp. 540–1). The number of these Local Acts and Provisional Orders is far too immense for general study, but every lawyer should know something of the local legislation in force in his particular locality.

It may be observed that statutory powers are the only powers that the majority of our Local Government authorities possess. Such authorities are generally statutory corporations, and as such are subject to the doctrine of *ultra vires*. Even those which were originally created by royal charter are now for the most part governed by statutory provisions (see *post*, pp. 460–1). According to the doctrine of *ultra vires*, a statutory corporation possesses only such powers as are expressly or impliedly conferred upon it by statute.

> Doctrine of *ultra vires*.

2. *Has the person in question power to do the act in this particular way?* The answer to this question will in every case depend on the construction of the empowering enactment. But it is always presumed that private rights are not to be interfered with. Lord Blackburn said in *Metropolitan Asylum District* v. *Hill* (1881), 6 App. Cas. 193, at p. 208 :

> Interference with private rights.

> " . . . the burden is on those who seek to establish that the legislature intended to take away the private rights of individuals to show that by express words or by necessary implication such an intention appears."

Therefore, where the particular mode of exercising a power involves an interference with private rights, a person must show, not only that he was authorised to do the act, but also that he was expressly or impliedly authorised to do it even though the result may be to injure private individuals.

3. *Is the person upon whom a power has been conferred under a duty to exercise it?* The distinction must here be drawn between permissive and imperative powers. Where the legislature confers a power but leaves it to the discretion of the person on whom it is conferred to decide whether he will use it or not, the power is said to be permissive ; but if the legislature, while granting the power, also imposes on the grantee an obligation to exercise it, the power is no longer permissive but imperative

> Permissive and imperative powers.

In the case of a permissive power, there can be no question of enforcement ; the grantee of an imperative power is, however, under a duty to exercise it and can therefore be compelled to do so ; for, unless the legislature has definitely provided to the contrary, the performance of an imperative duty can always be enforced at the suit of a person injured by non-performance, although difficult questions frequently arise as to the precise remedy available in a given case. We shall see later (see *post*, p. 572) that this distinction between permissive and imperative powers must be kept in mind in any answer to the question whether the exercise of a power properly conferred can be unlawful.

We must now investigate the different varieties of powers and duties which will most frequently be encountered in practice.

Examples of
ministerial
duties.

(*a*) *Ministerial duties*. The common examples of ministerial duties are those which are associated with the execution of judicial decisions. The constable who arrests an offender by virtue of a magistrate's warrant, or a sheriff whose officers levy execution upon the property of a defaulting judgment debtor by virtue of a writ of *fi. fa.*, are both of them acting

(i) without any discretion and in obedience to the instructions of the Court ;

(ii) without any inquiry of their own into the facts relating to the charge or the debt.

In other words, the inquiry already undertaken by the Court into the facts of the case is enough, and the ministerial officer must rely upon it. Not all ministerial duties, however, are thus associated with judicial functions. The ministerial officer may be set in motion, not by any Court, but by some high officer of State, or even by some private person. Familiar examples are the bailiff employed by a landlord to levy a distress, and the constable who takes an offender into custody on information laid by a private citizen. Ministerial officers, however, are by no means the only persons upon whom ministerial duties are laid. An interesting example of this may surprise the reader : if a man of full age and sound mind is indicted for high treason, it is the duty of the judge both to preside over the trial and on a conviction to sentence him to death. The duty in both these respects, though laid upon a judicial officer, is nevertheless of a ministerial kind, because it allows the judge no alternative course of action that he can take.

These examples reveal a ministerial duty as " one in respect of which nothing is left to discretion," as the Supreme Court of the United States pronounced in *State of Mississippi* v. *Johnson* (1866), 4 Wall., at p. 498. This does not mean that the carrying out of a ministerial duty is a kind of mechanical process by a human machine. A constable or bailiff's obedience to orders is compatible with his own good sense in carrying them out. All that is meant, therefore, by saying that the absence of discretion is the mark of a ministerial duty is that the person upon whom it is cast is not free to decide for or against carrying it out—though he may perhaps be free to choose between different ways or methods of carrying it out.

Speaking generally, the ministerial officer acts at his peril, even when his only fault is to have done his duty in obedience to a false or mistaken order, and he must run the risk of the facts afterwards turning out to be otherwise than as he had supposed them to be. But it will be found that certain ministerial officers (*e.g.*, sheriffs, constables, customs officers) are on public grounds relieved from the full measure of liability for failure to perform their duty exactly. But these cases are statutory exceptions, and will be dealt with later on (see *post*, p. 567). We postpone also for the present the consideration of the methods, in particular the order of *mandamus*, by which the Courts enforce the performance of a ministerial duty. (See Chap. 26, p. 574, *post*.)

Liability of ministerial officer.

(*b*) *Discretions*. What measure of control will the Courts exert over the exercise of a discretion ? The answer is very far from being straightforward, and we can best approach it after some examination of the nature of a discretion and of the difference between a discretion and a decision. Now, when we speak of decisions, we must remember that they may be reached in various ways. The rough division is into two main classes : (i) decisions to be reached only by applying some pre-determined

Discretions and decisions.

standard ; these can be called *objective* decisions ; and
(ii) decisions involving a freedom of choice, because
there is no fixed standard to be applied, or because the
only standard is that of policy and expediency ; these
can be called *subjective* decisions.

Objective decisions. (i) It is in the making of decisions of the first or objective kind that the Courts are normally engaged, that is to
say, in ascertaining the facts of a case and then applying
the law to them.   There are, however, many occasions
when even decisions of the Courts can be of the second
or subjective kind, and the tendency of statute is to add
Discretions exercised by Courts. to the opportunities for them.   Thus a Divorce Court has
discretion to grant a divorce to a petitioner notwithstand-
ing his (or her) adultery, and a Bankruptcy Court can in
its discretion refuse a discharge to a bankrupt.   Again,
under s. 448 of the Companies Act, 1948, the Court
may, if it thinks fit, relieve defaulting directors from
having to make good their default.   If we revert from the
present to the past, we shall find an example of judicial
discretion in the issue from the Court of Chancery of
injunctions and decrees of specific performance ;   even
to-day these equitable remedies are still spoken of as
discretionary.   In all these cases the Courts, as we have
said, depart from their normal activity, and the discretion which they exercise is referred to as judicial.

Subjective decisions. (ii) We must now turn to those bodies—and their
number is rapidly increasing—whose normal activity
involves the exercise of a discretion.   What is exceptional
in the functions of the Courts is the normal feature of the
work of these bodies.   The decisions of the Courts are, in
the majority of cases, *objective*, in the sense that they have
been reached by the application of fixed standards, *i.e.*,
the pre-determined standards of the law.   On the other
hand, the decisions of these other bodies are usually
subjective, in the sense that there is either no standard at
all to be applied in reaching them or merely the standard
set by what is expedient and politic in all the circum-
Administrative functions. stances.   For lack of a better name, the functions of these
bodies are usually termed " administrative."   Common
examples are the tribunals or authorities that consider
applications for the various kinds of licences—e.g. to keep

public-house, or put up a factory. Nowadays both Government Departments and Local Authorities have an abundance of discretionary powers which may affect the rights of the citizen. It is not very helpful to say that these bodies are administrative ; but the use of that vague and ambiguous term has at least the merit of emphasising the essential difference between the functions of the Courts and those of Rent Tribunals or Justices in Licensing Sessions. Just as the absence of discretion is the mark of the ministerial duty, so it is the presence of discretion which distinguishes the administrative function, from the ministerial on the one hand, and from the judicial on the other ; and indeed the effect of exercising a discretion is, not to pronounce upon existing rights or liabilities, but rather to create or take away rights or liabilities. Even if the deciding body is itself labelled " administrative," it by no means follows that all its functions—which may well be vast and heterogeneous, as in the case of say the Ministry of Health—conform to the same general label. Hence, as the course of recent litigation has shown, the initial task which a court must perform in passing judgment upon the exercise of those functions must be to classify them correctly according to their essential nature; in other words to decide whether an administrative body's decision is of a " purely " administrative kind, having nothing in common with those of the Courts, or whether on the contrary it bears some sort of resemblance to them. It may well be entirely " judicial," in character, though pronounced not by a judge but by an administrator, and therefore to be arrived at only after observing the essential requirements of all judicial proceedings, which will be described shortly (see *post*, pp. 278–281). It may, though not completely judicial in all its stages, yet properly be termed "quasi-judicial", and therefore made partially subject to those requirements. On the other hand, it may be so completely lacking in judicial characteristics that its alien character should be made doubly manifest, as the House of Lords have lately taught, by pre-fixing " purely " to the surname " administrative."

Thus, from time to time, there are judicial functions even for an administrative body to fulfil. It may be necessary, as the next example shows, to arrive at some decision in the objective sense before exercising the discretion ; to apply first of all the fixed standard in the manner of a Court of law, and then to pass on to the discretion. Thus licensing justices may have to exercise their power of deciding whether an applicant is legally qualified to hold a licence before they can see fit to grant him a licence (*R.* v. *Woodhouse*, [1906] 2 K. B. 501 ; on appeal, *sub nom. Leeds Corporation* v. *Ryder*, [1907] A. C. 420). This co-existence of both judicial and administrative functions in one and the same body is so frequent that, as we have already seen, difficulties of classification and terminology become inevitable. Thus

Quasi-judicial functions.

the graceless term " quasi-judicial " has come into current use, and a few years ago the Committee on Ministers' Powers used it in a vague sense to signify administrative bodies whose functions are " not exactly " judicial. But the term is probably easier to understand in a more literal sense ; and we may say that the functions of a tribunal or other deciding body are quasi-judicial if it is under a duty to act *as if it were a judge* at some point or at some stage in reaching its decision. Such bodies need to be distinguished from those other so-called administrative tribunals whose functions are so purely judicial that they are Courts in all but name (see *post*, pp. 328–331).

Judicial control over exercise of discretions.

We are now in a position to examine the extent of the control exerted by the Courts over those who exercise judicial or quasi-judicial discretions. The control is not confined to " administrative " bodies ; it may extend to the judges themselves, both in respect of their usual " objective " decisions and also of their occasional exercise of a discretion. Indeed, an outstanding and extreme example of the control involved the Lord Chancellor himself, whose decision in favour of a company was set aside because he happened as a shareholder to have a personal interest in the company (*Dimes* v. *Grand Junction Canal Proprietors* (1852), 3 H. L. Cas. 759). The appeal succeeded, *not* because the decision " on the merits " would have been better the other way, but rather because the Lord Chancellor, in making any decision at all, had broken one of the fundamental principles of natural justice. This breach sufficed to vitiate his decision, and a review of it on the merits would have been superfluous.

No review *on the merits* would have been even permissible if the Lord Chancellor's decision, instead of being of the normal " objective " kind, had been of the abnormal kind that calls for an exercise of judicial discretion. In that event, complaint against his decision—just like complaint against a decision of an administrative body exercising a judicial or quasi-judicial discretion—would have to be directed *exclusively* to the breach of a fundamental principle of natural justice. The demands of natural justice are paramount, and if a judicial or quasi-judicial discretion is exercised in defiance of them, the Courts are willing to intervene on the ground that there has been an abuse of jurisdiction. They do not substitute their own discretion for that of the officer or body in question ; for the standard by which the exercise of the discretion must be judged is a standard not of law but of policy ; and this means in effect that a decision so arrived at cannot be reviewed on the merits. If these restrictions on the exercise of judicial or quasi-judicial discretion by policy-making bodies went further than they do, the judges would in effect be carrying out their own ideas of policy instead of impartially administering the law. Indeed, even the strictness with which the Courts have insisted upon the observance of the demands of natural justice has been regarded by some critics as an undue fetter upon administrative bodies.

What, then, are the broad principles, commonly spoken of as the requirements, of natural justice ? In the first place, we have the rule that no man may be a judge in his own cause—a rule which precludes not only a judge from deciding a case to which he is a party but also a member of a local authority from taking part in the determination of a matter in which he has an interest. For example, in *Frome United Breweries Co.* v. *Bath Justices*, [1926] A. C. 586, justices resolved to refer a certain licensing application to the compensation authority and to instruct a solicitor to appear on their behalf before the authority in opposition to the application. Three of the justices who had been parties to this resolution afterwards

No review on the merits.

Requirements for natural justice:—

Bias.

sat and voted as members of the compensation tribunal
when the application was heard. It was held that they
were disqualified on the ground of bias. But "the use
of the word 'bias' should be confined to its proper
sphere." This is "to denote a departure from the
standard of even-handed justice which the law requires
from those who occupy judicial office, or those who are
commonly regarded as holding a quasi-judicial office, such
as an arbitrator. The reason for this clearly is that, having to adjudicate as between two or more parties, he must
come to his adjudication with an independent mind, without any inclination or bias towards one side or other in the
dispute." So if—as in the recent case from which these
words come—some duty of a purely administrative kind,
being neither judicial nor even quasi-judicial, is laid by
statute upon a Minister of the Crown, it is irrelevant to
consider whether he was without bias in the carrying
out of such a duty (*Franklin* v. *Minister of Town and
Country Planning*, [1948] A. C. 87).

Audi alteram partem.

Again, no decision must be taken which will affect the
rights of any person without first giving him an
opportunity of putting forward his case, the maxim being
audi alteram partem. So in *R.* v. *Huntingdon Confirming
Authority*, [1929] 1 K. B. 698, a confirming authority
heard the case for and against an application for a new
licence and confirmed the licence subject to certain conditions. At a later meeting of the authority it was decided
to vary the conditions, but no notice of this meeting was
given to the parties concerned, though they were entitled
to be present, and they had no opportunity of arguing their
case in respect of the variation in the conditions. It was
held by the Court of Appeal that the *audi alteram partem*
rule applied.

Procedure need not be judicial.

An administrative tribunal may, however,
come to its decision in any way consonant with this
requirement of natural justice; its procedure need not be
that of a Court of law. Thus it may sit and decide in
secret, and, so long as it gives any person likely to be
affected an opportunity of putting forward his case, it is
not bound to allow him to meet his judges face to face,
though it must, of course, conform to all provisions binding
upon it, whether derived from statute or by agreement.

Thus, in the well-known case of *L. G. B.* v. *Arlidge*, [1915] A. C. 120, the Local Government Board (the predecessor of the present Ministry of Health) sent an inspector to hold a public inquiry in the locality where property would be affected by the making of closing orders under statutory authority relating to housing. The owner had his case argued, and he was heard in evidence, before the inspector. He did not, however, have any opportunity of appearing in person before the Board, who acted on the report of the inspector, though the Board invited him to make any further representations in writing. It was held by the House of Lords that the owner had had an adequate opportunity of presenting his case, and that the Board were free to follow a procedure entirely different from that of a Court of law.

Finally, natural justice requires judicial or quasi-judicial discretions to be exercised in good faith, and the Court will quash a decision which has clearly been arrived at maliciously, *i.e.*, for some unworthy or improper motive or for some purpose other than that for which the discretion was conferred (see *Marshall* v. *Blackpool Corporation*, [1935] A. C. 16). *Malice.*

Statute or contract may allow a tribunal to decide capriciously and in disregard of these requirements of natural justice. The language, however, must be clear, and the Court will construe it strictly. Thus the person affected may have agreed in advance to forgo the right of defending himself (*Hayman* v. *Governors of Rugby School* (1874), L. R. 18 Eq. 28), or to endure a decision that is biased or even malicious (*Russell* v. *Russell* (1880), 14 Ch. D. 471). *Derogations by statute or contract.*

We have said that the control of the Courts takes the form of checks upon the excess of jurisdiction that is involved in any disregard of the requirements of natural justice. It is hardly necessary to add that the Courts (if no statute speaks to the contrary) will restrain any wrongful assumption of jurisdiction by the general doctrine of *ultra vires*, and, as has already been said, they will compel a body to exercise a discretion when it has neglected to fulfil a ministerial duty to do so. *Ultra vires.*

Dereliction of duty.

We must again point out that in certain special cases the *Absolute discretion.*

Courts are powerless to control the *intra vires* use of discretion, even though the requirements of natural justice have been flouted. Thus, if the Home Secretary expels an alien from this country without giving him any opportunity to plead his case, the deportation cannot be questioned in the Courts even on the ground that he has neglected to obey the rules of natural justice. The Home Secretary is entrusted by Parliament with a discretionary power that is absolute in the matter, and the only control is political or diplomatic (*R.* v. *Leman Street Police Station Inspector, Ex parte Venicoff*, [1920] 3 K. B. 72). So, too, the decision of the Home Secretary as to the exercise of the prerogative of mercy is completely free from any legal control.

Judicial immunity. We shall see elsewhere (see *post*, pp. 566–7) that, in compensation for the greater procedural strictness required of a Court, its members are protected in the carrying out of their duties by judicial immunity which includes *absolute* freedom from the law of defamation. On the other hand, it was held in *Royal Aquarium and Summer and Winter Garden Society* v. *Parkinson*, [1892] 1 Q. B. 431, that bodies other than Courts do not share this immunity but enjoy at best only *qualified* privilege.

(*c*) *Legislative powers.* As has been already remarked (p. 272), and as will be further elaborated later (pp. 322 *et seq.*), there are many bodies besides Parliament which exercise legislative powers. **Judicial control of subordinate legislation.** The legislative acts of such bodies will be treated by the Courts (unless their jurisdiction is ousted by Parliament) as null and void if found to be *ultra vires*, and if they are by-laws they will not be enforced by the Courts if they are " unreasonable " (see *post*, p. 325). Otherwise the exercise of legislative powers is wholly free from judicial control.

(*d*) *Consensual powers.* Powers may be conferred on a person by the consent of another. Thus a person who joins a club is held to agree to abide by the rules of the club. Those rules may well contain a provision for the exclusion of any member who acts contrary to the rules or otherwise in such a way as to render him an unfit person to remain a member. **Domestic tribunals.** Such a provision constitutes the club, or it may be a committee of the club, a " domestic tribunal." Such a domestic tribunal, exercising a consensual jurisdiction, is just as bound by the " rules of natural justice " as a public authority exercising a quasi-judicial discretion ; and its members will likewise be liable only for such acts as they have done in excess or abuse of their jurisdiction.

CHAPTER 3

THE KING'S PLEASURE

The omnipo-
tence of the
King and the
supremacy of
the law.

The history of our Constitutional Law was for long dominated by two apparently irreconcilable ideas, namely, the " omnipotence " of the King and the supremacy of the law. A reconciliation between these two doctrines was ultimately effected by two means ; first, by recourse to the principle that the King can do no wrong, and secondly, by insisting on the observance of certain modes in the expression of the royal pleasure. Thus a pardon may be issued only by means of a document under the Royal Sign Manual, *i.e.*, under the signature of the King himself, countersigned by a Secretary of State, and the Courts

Special
modes of
expressing the
Royal Will.

would disregard it if couched in any other form. On the other hand, were the King by Royal Sign Manual to impose a tax, no Court of justice would consider it legal, for the only appropriate mode of taxation is by Act of Parliament ; and were the King by Royal Sign Manual to order an arrest, instead of by warrant from one of his justices, the command would be void. The law, therefore, in insisting on these special modes of expressing the royal will, may be said to exert its supremacy.

At the same time the law contrived to preserve the doctrine that the King can do no wrong ; for, until the recent overthrow of that doctrine (see *post*, p. 568), if anything was done in a manner other than that specified by law, it was not accounted a royal act. What was done was either disregarded altogether, or, if that was impossible because the act had caused some injury to a subject, the King's part in it was disregarded. In such cases some other person had almost inevitably co-operated with the King, and it was upon that other person that the penalties provided by the law would fall. It is, indeed, a recognised convention of the constitution that the Sovereign never carries out any function of government except in the presence of some Minister of the Crown, who takes responsibility for it.

Thus we have at any rate the *formal* reconciliation of royal " omnipotence " with the supremacy of the law. But how much substance lay, and still lies, behind the shadow ; in other words, how far has the royal will become subjected to external control ?

Here only a brief answer can be given by way of introduction.

1. *The Royal Pleasure in Parliament.* The plenitude of royal power can be exercised only by Acts of Parliament. It is one of the most striking peculiarities of our Constitution that the authority which alone is entitled in law to absolute obedience is a body which can do nothing but legislate. The House of Commons may ask questions of Ministers or criticise the policy of the Government ; so may the House of Lords ; and the King may receive an ambassador or inspect the Fleet. But for Parliament— or, as we should more properly speak, the King in Parliament—there is only *one* function ; the trinity of King, Lords, and Commons may *only* legislate. Thus obedience to the commands of the King in Parliament is obedience to the law ; for the royal pleasure can be expressed in Parliament only in the form of law ; and the sovereignty of Parliament is synonymous with the supremacy of the law. (The topic of Parliamentary sovereignty will form the subject of Chap. 4.)

[margin: King absolute only in Parliament.]

2. *The Royal Pleasure in Justice.* All justice throughout the nation is administered in the King's name, and the superior judges act under commissions from the King. But the King himself cannot judge at all ; he must act through his delegates. Moreover, though he appoints them in his executive capacity, he cannot dismiss them unless he receives an address from both Houses of Parliament ; and he cannot, except by Act of Parliament, give them orders which they are bound to obey. They exist for the purpose of ensuring the supremacy of the law, which gives them their authority. (These points will be further discussed in Chap. 5.)

[margin: King must act through delegates.]

3. *Executive acts,* as they are conventionally called, are done only with the co-operation and consent of Ministers of the Crown. We have indicated already that

[margin: Ministers of the Crown must co-operate.]

no expression of the royal pleasure is here operative except with the consent of a Minister, who by his signature renders himself liable for any illegality involved.

4. *Personal acts of the King.* There remain certain acts which *in law* the King may do without the co-operation of any other person. Such, for instance, are the opening and dissolving of Parliament and the appointing and dismissing of his Ministers. Nevertheless, owing to the development of the Cabinet system of government during the past two centuries, these powers have gradually become limited by convention ; so that some of them, such as the power of withholding the royal assent to a statute, are now obsolete, while others, such as the power of dissolution, may be exercised only on the advice and with the consent of the Prime Minister. The King would, if he were to disobey these conventions, be acting " unconstitutionally." In fact there now remains practically no department of public business in which the King is free to act at his own discretion. He has ceased to possess the substance of power, and has become a confidential adviser to successive administrations. Indeed, unless we desire to speak of some particular holder of the royal office, we prefer to speak of the Crown instead of the King; and then we usually mean the Government of the day. Nevertheless, many of the powers exercised by the Central Government still belong *in law* to the King.

Conventional limitations.

It is important that the student of the Constitution should be acquainted with the traditional modes in which the orders of the Crown are conveyed and made known to the people. The best known of these modes is the Order in Council, which is used for executive as well as for legislative purposes (see *post*, pp. 322 *et seq.*).

Orders in Council.

The second recognised mode in which the executive commands are promulgated is by means of various documents—orders, warrants, and commissions—under the Sign Manual, that is, signed by the King himself, with the counter-signature of a Secretary of State. These are principally used for the appointment of certain high officials. We have said already (p. 284) that the prerogative of pardon is also exercised in this manner and

Royal Sign Manual.

authenticated by the counter-signature of the Home
Secretary.

Thirdly, there are various executive acts which have to Great Seal.
be expressed in documents to which the Great Seal has to
be affixed. The sealing has to be authorised by some prior
act, such as a warrant under the sign manual or an Order
in Council or, in the case of writs for a by-election of
members of the House of Commons, the Speaker's
warrant. The documents which require the Great Seal
are the following :—

Proclamations, which are usually either formal Documents
requiring the
Great Seal.
announcements of executive acts or mere declarations
by the Crown for the information of the nation at large
of the provisions of existing laws ; though *in certain
cases* the Crown has *statutory* authority to put into force,
by means of a Proclamation, an Act or part of an Act of
Parliament which would otherwise not be operative.

Writs, or written commands to a particular person to
do or abstain from doing some particular act. The
familiar " writ of summons " by which an action in a
Court of justice is commenced does not require the
Great Seal ; it passes under the seal of the Court and is
said to be " tested " (*i.e.*, witnessed) by the Lord Chancellor. But, amongst writs which pass under the Great
Seal, are writs dissolving Parliament ; writs summoning
peers to Parliament ; and writs calling upon returning
officers (under the Representation of the People Act,
1949) to conduct an election for Parliament.

Letters patent (*i.e.*, *litteræ patentes*—an open document)
under the Great Seal. They are used for a variety of
purposes, such as to constitute a corporation by charter,
to confer a judgeship in the High Court, to grant licences
for the election of a bishop. Letters patent for an inven-
tion, however, are sealed with the seal of the Patent
Office, not with the Great Seal.

CHAPTER 4

THE SOVEREIGNTY OF PARLIAMENT

Sovereignty of Parliament involves: Independent State.

The statement that Parliament is "sovereign" involves two propositions :

The first is that Parliament legislates for a sovereign state, that is to say, a state which is " independent " of all other states and acknowledges the supremacy of no other state.   No legislature of a dependent state can itself be sovereign.

Freedom from judicial control.

The second proposition is that there is *in law* nothing which Parliament may not do if it chooses to do it by the full formality of a legislative act.   It is not open to any Court within the realm to question the validity of an Act of Parliament.   This absolutely binding character is not an essential feature of all legislation everywhere.   For example, the validity of Acts of Congress of the United States may be questioned in the Courts, and any Act of Congress which transgresses the Constitution of the United States is treated as *pro tanto* invalid.   Most countries in their Constitutions set limits to the legislative authority even of their Parliaments.   The Parliament of the United Kingdom is almost unique in its independence *in law* of all " external " control.   But it must be noted that the proposition is one of law and not of politics.   *In practice*, the censure of public opinion, here and abroad, is an all-powerful external control.   Parliament is especially sensitive as a rule to the reactions of such representative associations as the Churches, Chambers of Commerce, Trade Unions, professional bodies like the Law Society, and so on.

No direct authority for sovereignty of Parliament.

It is a curious fact that no direct authority in the shape of decided cases can be adduced in support of the legislative omnipotence of Parliament.   For almost three centuries it has been universally acknowledged ; and no doubt the only reason why during all that period it has never been directly called in question in a Court of law is that no one has ever thought it worth while to dispute it.

Yet, although the doctrine of parliamentary sovereignty is so firmly established at the present day, it is a modern conception, and as late as the seventeenth century judges and legal writers, such as Coke, still maintained that no statute would be valid if it was against the " reason " of the Common Law.

No more striking example could be given of the exercise of sovereignty by Parliament than the power, which it has more than once exercised, of prolonging its own existence. The Triennial Act of 1694 had provided that a new Parliament should be summoned at least as often as once in three years ; yet the Parliament which was sitting in 1716, fearing the result of an election held in a time of national disturbance, enacted in the Septennial Act that henceforth the maximum duration of a Parliament should be seven years and itself took advantage of the prolongation of its term.   A still more startling example is to be found in the Parliament of 1911 to 1918.   It had itself by the Parliament Act, 1911, curtailed the possible duration of a Parliament to five years, and yet, in view of the inconvenience which would have attached to the holding of a general election in time of war, prolonged its own existence successively for a year at a time until eventually it lasted for a longer period than any previous Parliament since the seventeenth century.   Even greater longevity was achieved, in the same way, by the Parliament that came to an end in 1945, after having existed long before and all through the recent war.   A peculiar interest attaches to these precedents, since a Parliament might in reliance on them prolong its own existence indefinitely, as indeed the celebrated Long Parliament succeeded in doing.   But no one suggests that a modern Parliament would be so foolish as to follow the example of that Parliament, though the possibility is indeed envisaged by the Parliament Act, 1911 (see *post*, p. 377).

Most writers seem to agree that, to the rule that no Act of Parliament can in law be inoperative, one apparent exception must be made.   It is thought to be impossible for any Parliament by statute to fetter the legislative freedom of any *subsequent* Parliament.   As Blackstone says :

Marginal notes:
Former doubts.

Power of Parliament to prolong its own life.

Parliament cannot fetter subsequent Parliaments.

" Acts of parliament derogatory from the power of subsequent parliaments bind not. . . . And upon the same
principle Cicero, in his letters to Atticus, treats with a
proper contempt these restraining clauses, which endeavour
to tie up the hands of succeeding legislatures. ' When
you repeal the law itself,' says he, ' you at the same time
repeal the prohibitory clause, which guards against such
repeal.' "

This is the traditional view, and our parliamentary
history is not without some striking examples of the futile
effort to ensure for some piece of legislation an eternal
life. Yet the contrary opinion is not without supporters;
and it would seem to be more in harmony not only with
the Regency Act, 1937, but also with the Statute of
Westminster, 1931, which provides that no Act of the
Parliament of the United Kingdom shall extend to a
Dominion unless it is expressly declared that that
Dominion has requested and consented to the enactment
thereof. But it is worth noting that the draftsman
apparently thought this provision by itself too weak to
withstand repeal by the Imperial Parliament, and
sought to fortify it by a statement in the preamble
of the " convention " to the same effect, which was
already in full force. It is a curious notion that convention should be more sacrosanct than law; but it only
brings out an important truth, already indicated (p. 288),
regarding parliamentary sovereignty; for nothing is
clearer than that the *legal* omnipotence of Parliament is
very extensively curtailed by *practical* considerations of
politics. But is it equally clear that Parliament would
still be legally omnipotent if there were a Regency?
Here is an entertaining problem for discourse with Blackstone in the Elysian Fields. It is provoked by those
prohibitions of the Regency Act, 1937, to be mentioned
later (p. 302), and—if we rightly suppose that while the
King is in his cradle there can be no legislation of the
prohibited sort and no repeal of the Regency Act itself—
then in humility let us pose our problem for an unsophis-
ticated answer in Elysium.

In the preceding chapter we concluded that the
sovereignty of Parliament is synonymous with the
supremacy of the law; and we gave as our reason that

Parliament can only give orders by passing a law, so that obedience to the orders of Parliament must be obedience to the law. But, on the other hand, the sovereignty of Parliament is an ever present danger to the supremacy of the law. For the supremacy of the law rests *in practice* on the power of the Courts to investigate all questions where a party alleges that the law has been broken. Once their jurisdiction is gone, the supremacy of the law would be all shadow and no substance. Nevertheless, there can be no doubt of the capacity of Parliament to legislate so as to destroy the jurisdiction of the Courts ; it follows that the *practical* supremacy of the law is at the mercy of Parliamentary sovereignty.

Danger to Supremacy of the Law.

A short explanation of Statute Law was given in the Introduction to the Laws of England and their Sources in Vol. I. To avoid repetition, we propose to add here only a few observations on the important subject of the interpretation of statutes.

Statute law.

Interpretation of statutes. Statute law is differently interpreted by the judges from the Common Law, which is, as we have seen, mainly to be sought in judgments of the Courts. In interpreting the latter, the Court has to find the *ratio decidendi* (*i.e.*, the principle which led the judge in the precedent case to arrive at the conclusion at which he did), and then to apply that principle to the case before the Court ; in interpreting a statute, or indeed any document, the Court is not allowed to inquire what the draftsman had in mind, but is confined to the task of applying the *litera legis* (*i.e.*, the express words of the enactment).

Distinction between ratio decidendi and litera legis.

This is the great canon of interpretation for statutes, but the student must be prepared to find that it sometimes appears to contradict plain English or common sense. For instance, when he finds the expression " term of years absolute " in the Law of Property Act, 1925, he would assume that it could not possibly refer to a weekly or a monthly tenancy. Yet the Act expressly says that the expression " term of years " includes a tenancy for less than a year. That settles the point, and despite all other reasoning a tenancy from week to week is, for the purposes of *this* Act, a term of years.

This principle of " strict " or " literal " interpretation is all too likely to compel deplorable decisions in the Courts. Nevertheless,

> " It is clearly beyond the province of the courts either to correct hardship or afford justice by an implication which is not based on the language of the statute." (*Per* Lord Thankerton in *Canadian Eagle Oil Co., Ltd.* v. *R.*, [1946] A. C. 119, at p. 142.)

The same point was put as follows by Lord Greene, M.R. in *Re Leicester Temperance, etc., Society's Application*, [1942] Ch. 340, at p. 344 :

> " . . . we are not here to legislate, but to interpret and administer the Act as we find it, and, however much we think that this is a case which ought to have been given the protection of the Act, we cannot extend that protection to it unless the language justifies it."

Ambiguity.   It is true, unfortunately, that the words of a statute are often not free from ambiguity (otherwise there would be no cases on the meaning of statutes) ; and therefore the Court is entitled, *if there is ambiguity*, to seek the meaning of the words, not only from the internal evidence of the statute itself, but even, with caution, from its knowledge of the state of affairs which existed when the statute was passed and of any particular defects in the law which it was intended to remedy. This is called " liberal " or " benevolent " as opposed to " literal " or " strict " interpretation, and it enables the Court to choose between the two or more possible meanings that ambiguous language can bear. But it does *not* enable the Court, where there is *no* ambiguity, to substitute, even for the sake of avoiding hardship or injustice, some other meaning for the clear meaning of the enactment. The broad principle is that the mistakes of Parliament should be undone by Parliament, or not at all.

Palpable absurdity.   Unduly restricted as the Courts probably are in this respect, they are not so impotent that they cannot put things right where a literal enforcement of the words of a statute would lead to a palpable absurdity. But this may only be done when the Court feels quite convinced that the words used did not really express the intention of the legislature, *e.g.*, when s. 105 of the Law of Property Act, 1925, says that, after a mortgagee has sold the mortgaged property and paid himself what is due, the residue of the money " shall be paid to the person entitled to the mortgaged property." Such a person, in most cases, would be the purchaser, and so the Court assumes that what the section meant to say was : " shall be paid to the person who was entitled to the property immediately before the sale took place." But, however absurd the Court may think the provisions of an Act of Parliament, yet, unless it is quite sure that such provisions do not express the intention of the legislature, it is bound to give effect to them. In other words, what the Court has to seek for in interpreting and applying a statute is, not the *ratio decidendi*, but the *litera legis*.

CHAPTER 5

THE ROYAL PREROGATIVE

In dealing with the Royal Prerogative, and especially in examining any attempt to define the term, two propositions must be kept constantly in mind : In the first place, the Prerogative comprises only such powers as the King can exercise in his " executive " and " personal " capacities, and in conjunction with his Ministers. Secondly, only such powers of the Crown as are derived from the Common Law are comprised in the Prerogative, and not such powers as are conferred upon it by statute.

History of the Prerogative. For a complete understanding of the theory of the Prerogative it is necessary to pay some attention to its history.

Residuary authority of the King.

Although in the Middle Ages the making of law had become a matter for Parliament, and the administration of justice for the judges, there remained in the King an unexhausted residue of authority. It was his task to ensure that justice should prevail, and this might entail the adjustment of the law to unusual conditions by ordinance or proclamation, the granting of dispensations from statutes when their rigorous enforcement would cause undue hardship, and the exercise of extraordinary jurisdiction in his Council in cases which were inadequately provided for by the Common Law or even by the new system of Equity which the Chancellor was beginning to enforce. It was generally admitted that the King must possess some reserve of power for use in an emergency, and in the Middle Ages it was but rarely that Parliament had to complain that the royal power was being used in an improper manner or under circumstances which did not justify its exercise.

The Tudors and Stuarts.

Under the Tudors all was changed, and extraordinary powers, intended for use only in an emergency, were used very freely and without any appreciable opposition. The

294

result was an enormous increase in the royal power. The King was, in the language of the time, set above the law, so far at least as matters of government were concerned. His supremacy was said to be due to his Prerogative, and when the men of the seventeenth century spoke of Prerogative they regularly meant this extraordinary " absolute " power which they ascribed to the King in matters of government, as distinct from the *ordinary* transactions of life, such as the holding of property or the making of bargains.

Now the existence of this residue of " discretionary " power was not *in itself* a bad thing ; for it is very necessary that a Government should have a reserve of power for use in an emergency, as the events of recent years have so abundantly shown ; and so long as the " absolute " power of the King was habitually exercised only in time of emergency, his subjects might have been willing to tolerate it. But when its exercise became a matter of everyday occurrence, men began to realise that it was a most dangerous instrument of " arbitrary " government. The dangerous possibilities inherent in the doctrine of the Prerogative, as put forward by the Crown lawyers, were demonstrated to the full in famous cases which were decided in the seventeenth century.

Dangers inherent in King's discretionary power.

Was the King to be allowed to commit his subjects to prison without trial, or to tax them without sanction from Parliament ; was his royal hand to " suspend " a law, so that none should come within it, or by special " dispensation " to set some favourite free ?

But, although the Stuart Kings obtained many decisions in their favour, in the end they were defeated ; and the effect of their foolishness in straining their emergency prerogatives was that those prerogatives were destroyed altogether. Thus the power of " arbitrary " commitment was abolished by the Petition of Right in 1628 ; the levying of taxation by pretence of Prerogative and without the consent of Parliament was finally declared to be illegal in 1689 by the Bill of Rights ; and that enactment also abolished entirely the *suspending* power, and left the effect of exercising the *dispensing* power so uncertain that it has never since been found practicable to use it.

Abolition of : arbitrary commitment; unparliamentary taxation ; suspending and dispensing powers.

Coke.

But the victory of Parliament in the great constitutional struggle of the seventeenth century had other results which went far beyond those which we have just indicated ; for ultimately it gave full effect to certain doctrines of the Common Law which are associated with the name of Chief Justice Coke. Thus : (*a*) although the King may by his Proclamation call attention to the existing law and warn his subjects not to transgress it, yet he cannot create any new offence or in any way change that law without the consent of Parliament ; (*b*) the King in his own person cannot adjudge any case ; and (*c*) the King cannot by his Prerogative establish any new Court to administer any but the Common Law.

The Privy Council and Star Chamber.

Whether or not these doctrines were accepted by the Courts of Common Law in the time of Coke, they were certainly not followed in the Privy Council and the Court of Star Chamber. These tribunals were quite prepared to enforce Royal Proclamations and to accept the decisions of the King. They were also the regular tribunals for dealing with servants of the Crown, and were in a position to withdraw cases involving matters of State from the cognizance of the Courts of Common Law. Under these circumstances it was not of much importance what the latter thought of the limits of the King's Prerogative. But in 1641 the Long Parliament, which realised the dangerous character of the power of the Privy Council and Star Chamber, abolished the latter altogether, and took away the jurisdiction of the former, *except* in disputes from what were then the meagre possessions of the Crown *outside the realm.* Henceforth, there was no rival to the Common Law Courts except the Chancery, and the Chancery, after toying with the idea of erecting itself into a Court for the determination of matters of State, finally refused to enter into competition in such matters with the Courts of Common Law. In these changed circumstances the doctrines enunciated by Coke became of decisive authority.

The King and the judges.

All the more reason why the King should no longer have influence over the judiciary. The appointment of the judges lay with him, and they held office *durante bene placito nostro*, so that they could be dismissed by the King at his pleasure. The events of the latter half of the seventeenth century showed that, though the Courts of Common Law were not so easily controlled as the extraordinary tribunals which the Long Parliament had abolished, they might still too easily be turned into instruments of " arbitrary " government. This danger was finally removed by the Act of Settlement of 1700, which provided that the judges should from the accession of the House of Hanover hold their offices *quamdiu se bene gesserint* (during good behaviour), but should be liable to removal upon Addresses presented by both Houses of Parliament. They were thus rendered absolutely independent of the Crown. The Supreme Court of Judicature (Consolidation) Act, 1925, s. 12, in effect continues the protection of the Act of Settlement for the benefit of their descendants now in the High Court and the Court of Appeal. We must add that the efficacy of this protection, and indeed of anything like it that might have been put on the statute book, is wholly dependent on the survival of moral standards in public affairs ; and it would become worthless upon a degeneration of government into political corruption or tyranny. It should be noticed, however, that the judges of the County Courts (the statutory creation of which a century ago was long years after the Act of Settlement) are liable to be removed for inability as well as misbehaviour ; the discretion is vested by statute in the Lord Chancellor—or, for Lancashire, in the Chancellor of the Duchy—and in him is also a power to remove Justices of the Peace for good cause.

Act of Settlement.

RESULTS OF STRUGGLE AS TO PREROGATIVE. Now let us consider the results of this long struggle. It must not be supposed that the Prerogative had been abolished. The King still possessed wide powers of government which he could exercise independently of Parliament and the Common Law Courts. Many of these powers have survived and form the greater part of what we now know as the " Prerogative." Though some may still be exercised by the King in person, such as the formality of opening and dissolving Parliament and of appointing Ministers, they must all be exercised with the co-operation of

Ministers, so that these powers may be said to belong rather to the Central Government than to the King.

In what then lies the difference between the legal attitude of the Stuart period and that which we now hold ? It may be, perhaps, best expressed in these terms. To the Crown lawyers of the beginning of the seventeenth century, the King's Prerogative meant a general power in the King to act at his discretion in all cases where the public interest demanded such action ; and, in their view, if the King was of opinion that the public interest required a particular exercise of his discretionary power, his opinion was conclusive. It was also an essential part of the royal doctrine of the Prerogative that the King's discretionary powers could not be taken away by statute. It was also necessary for a royalist of the day to hold that, even where these conflicted with the rights of the subject, they must prevail.

Now, if this royal view of the Prerogative had ultimately prevailed, the King would have become " above the law," for he could have justified any breach of the law as an exercise of his general prerogative to protect and further the public interest. But the result of war and strife was to make it clear that the King was " below the law," and, since the jurisdiction of the Privy Council and Star Chamber had been abolished, below the law as interpreted by the *ordinary* Courts. It followed that *the limits of the Prerogative* (though not the way it happens to be exercised *within* its proper limits) are a matter of Common Law ; and it is the duty of the Courts to investigate, if called upon for that purpose, any claim of the Crown to exercise a discretion by virtue of its Prerogative, and, if they find that there is no warrant for the claim at Common Law, to disallow it. It followed also that an Act of Parliament, which can alter the Common Law, can also take away, and it has indeed often taken away, any portion of the Prerogative ; so that the Crown has no longer any "inseparable" prerogatives. The King's Prerogative is therefore no longer a general discretion to override the law in the public interest, but an aggregate of specific powers, conferred by the Common Law, and consequently limited by the provisions of the Common Law itself and by the great statutes, such as the Bill of Rights, which have been passed to provide general principles governing the relations between Crown and subject.

There has been no change in the general theory of the Prerogative since the end of the seventeenth century, but the scope of the various prerogatives has been subject to constant limitation, and certain points which were left undecided in that century have later come up for discussion. Thus it was long established that, whereas a prerogative could be taken away by express words in an Act of Parliament or by necessary implication, in the absence of these there was a presumption that the Prerogative remained intact ; though the rule was subject to certain exceptions. But it was still possible to argue that, where the Crown originally had a Prerogative, and was afterwards given statutory powers by an Act of Parliament which dealt with the whole sphere formerly covered by the Prerogative, the Crown might act under either its prerogative or its statutory powers at its option. The effect of such an option might be that the Crown could, if it were prepared to forgo any additional powers conferred on it by the statute, disregard any of the statutory conditions or safeguards. The point was raised in the *Case of Requisitions* (*A.-G.* v. *De Keyser's Royal Hotel*, [1920] A. C. 508), where the facts were as follows. The Army Council, wishing to take over at a rent for war purposes the hotel belonging to the respondent company, negotiated with the receiver for the debenture-holders, who was carrying on the business. Negotiations broke down, and the Army Council then took possession, against the will of the receiver but without resistance on his part, under the Defence of the Realm Act and Regulations. After the war the company brought a petition of right (see *post*, p. 568) against the Crown to claim compensation *as of right* for the use of the hotel.

The Attorney-General, on behalf of the Crown, denied that they were entitled to compensation as of right, and contended that the proper course for them to take was to apply for an *ex gratia* payment of compensation, the amount to be determined by the Defence of the Realm (Losses) Commission. He alleged that the Crown had

Prerogatives subject to constant limitation.

A.-G. v. *De Keyser's Royal Hotel.*

a prerogative to take the land of a subject in case of emergency in time of war.

The company did not admit that this prerogative in fact existed, but they argued that, even if it had ever existed, the Crown was not at liberty to act under it, by reason of the fact that the compulsory acquisition of land for war purposes had been regulated by the Defence Act, 1840, which had been incorporated into the Defence of the Realm Act, 1914. The Defence Act imposed conditions upon the exercise of the power of compulsory acquisition by the Crown, and provided for the payment of compensation *as of right* to persons who had been forced to surrender their land for the public good. Where the Crown, said the company, has prerogative powers, and also statutory powers which cover the whole field formerly occupied by those prerogatives, it can act *only* under its statutory powers. As a matter of fact, they said, the Crown had taken possession under the Defence of the Realm Act and Regulations and, having done so, could not fall back on the Prerogative.

The Court of Appeal and House of Lords adopted the reasoning of the company. They held that possession had actually been taken under the Act, but that in any case, so long as a statute giving powers of the same nature as the Prerogative remains in force, it supersedes the Prerogative for the time being, and the Crown is not entitled to act under the Prerogative. They would also have been prepared to hold, had it been necessary, that no prerogative to requisition the land of a subject for war purposes, without paying compensation, had been sufficiently proved.

CLASSES OF THE PREROGATIVE.   Many of the surviving prerogatives of the Crown will be noticed incidentally in the course of the following pages, but it is convenient to enumerate at once some of the more important heads.

Three main classes.   Prerogatives are divided into three main classes : (1) those which relate to the royal dignity ; (2) those which relate to the royal authority ; and (3) those which relate to the royal income.

The last named are concerned with the collection and

expenditure of the public revenue, and will be dealt with in a later chapter (see pp. 423 *et seq*.).

(1) The prerogatives which relate to the royal dignity are mentioned here only because from these somewhat exaggerated attributes have been derived certain rules of practical importance. *(1) The royal dignity.*

The King is said by Blackstone to be possessed of the three attributes of sovereignty, absolute perfection, and perpetuity.

Sovereignty. Even in the days of Blackstone this did not imply any division of sovereignty between King and Parliament. The struggle for supremacy had been won, as we have seen, in the previous century, and the victory was with Parliament. In theory some mark of sovereignty can still be seen in the formality of the royal assent that every Act of Parliament must bear ; but in practice (after 1947) a reference to the royal sovereignty can merely mean that no Court has jurisdiction over the King *in his purely private capacity, e.g.*, if the King, carelessly driving his motor-car, injures a subject (see *post*, pp. 568 *et seq*.).

Perfection. As from January 1, 1948, when the Crown Proceedings Act, 1947, came into operation, though the traditional doctrine that the King can do no wrong will no longer frustrate litigation against the King *in his public capacity*, it will still be the general principle that the Crown cannot be guilty of *laches, i.e.*, losing the right to sue by sleeping upon it too long. This principle, combined with the omission in the past to include the Crown by express words within the purview of the Statutes of Limitation, operated to preserve rights of action to the Crown long after they would have been barred to a subject. The maxim is *nullum tempus occurrit regi*. *Nullum tempus occurrit regi.*

But this Common Law rule has been radically qualified by statute, and the Limitation Act, 1939, now brings the Crown within the normal time-limits, unless anything different is prescribed by statute. Even this recent Act, however, does itself permit the Crown a period of thirty years, instead of the normal twelve, to enforce its rights in relation to landed property. *Civil actions.*

Moreover, there are certain statutes which necessitate a *Criminal prosecutions.*

prosecution being commenced in a certain limited time in the case of particular offences. Subject, however, to any such statute, a criminal prosecution may be commenced at any time, however long after the commission of the offence.

Infant monarch. It would be right, until recently, to say that the King cannot be a minor, and that his royal grants and assents to Acts of Parliament are good, though he has not in fact attained the age of twenty-one. But the point will now hardly arise, for by the Regency Act, 1937, if " the Sovereign is, at His Accession, under the age of eighteen years, then, until He attains that age, the royal functions **Regency.** shall be performed in the name and on behalf of the Sovereign by a Regent." The Regent, however, has no power to assent to any Bill for changing the order of succession to the Crown or for repealing or altering an Act of the fifth year of the reign of Queen Anne made in Scotland entitled " An Act for Securing the Protestant Religion and Presbyterian Church Government." Here lurks a fascinating problem for constitutional theorists (see *ante*, p. 290).

Perpetuity. Blackstone says :

The King never dies.
> " The law ascribes to him, in his political capacity, an absolute immortality. The King never dies. Henry, Edward, or George may die ; but the King survives them all."

In law one should not speak of the death of the King, but only of his *demise*, an expression which signifies merely a transfer of property. Hence the language used of Edward VIII, the present Duke of Windsor, in His Majesty's Declaration of Abdication Act, 1936—" His Majesty shall cease to be King and there shall be a demise of the Crown."

Former inconveniences. But this " absolute immortality " did not, for instance, prevent the determination of all engagements of service with the Crown on the death of the reigning monarch ; Parliament became dissolved, without any formality of dissolution, until summoned afresh by the new King ; judges had to be reappointed by the new King. These, and other inconveniences, have had to be removed by statute.

(2) We must now consider those prerogatives which The Royal relate to the royal authority. The King is the supreme authority. " executive " authority in the State. It is often said that he possesses this executive authority by virtue of the Prerogative, but this is misleading because it implies that all the executive powers exercised by the Crown are derived from the Prerogative ; on the contrary, many of them have originated in Acts of Parliament. Nor must it be imagined that all the governmental powers so conferred have been conferred on the Crown itself, for many statutes expressly empower this or that Minister to do a given act.

The prerogatives which are now to be discussed belong principally to the King as supreme executive authority. They concern either this nation's intercourse with foreign nations or its own domestic government. Those prerogatives which belong to the former class will be described in the chapter which deals with Foreign Affairs. The latter class of prerogatives may be grouped as follows :

1. *The King as a constituent part of Parliament.* This subject will be fully dealt with in the chapter on the legislature. The prerogatives comprise the right to give the royal assent to Bills, and the right to summon, prorogue, and dissolve Parliament.

2. *The King as Generalissimo.* At Common Law the King is Commander-in-Chief of the Royal Forces, and in this capacity he once had the sole power of raising and regulating fleets and armies. But by the Bill of Rights, 1689, it is provided that the King cannot raise or keep a standing army within the kingdom in time of peace without the consent of Parliament ; hence in every year the Army and Air Force (Annual) Act is passed which, reciting this provision of the Bill of Rights in the preamble, authorises the maintenance of the requisite forces. The Navy, however, is still manned and maintained under the Prerogative ; though even this is exercised in accordance with the Naval Enlistment Acts and—temporarily—the National Service Acts, 1948. As regards the actual command, this has been delegated by the King to the Lords of the Admiralty, the Army Council and the Air Council. But in great part the

internal government of the forces, including the appointment and promotion of officers, is still carried out in the
name of the King by virtue of the Prerogative. It is
hardly necessary to say that there is no immunity from
Parliamentary control ; indeed, the opportunity of the
Annual Act, already referred to, is usually taken in order
to introduce some statutory innovation or reform. We
defer discussion of these matters to the subsequent
Chapter on the Royal Forces (Chap. 19).

The adminis-
tration of
justice.

3. *The King as Fountain of Justice.* The King is said
to be the fountain of justice. All the superior judges
are appointed in his name. It should, however, be noted
that the appointment and control of the county court
judges has been entrusted by Parliament to the Lord
Chancellor—or, in certain cases, the Chancellor of the
Duchy of Lancaster (see the County Courts Act, 1934,
s. 4). But, as we have seen already (p. 296), the superior
judges are, once appointed, no longer subject to the
royal pleasure ; and although the ordinary writ of
summons, with which an action in the High Court commences, is in form a command by the King to the
defendant to enter an appearance at the suit of the

Civil
justice.

plaintiff, the Crown no longer possesses a prerogative
right to interfere with the administration of civil justice.
Indeed, the exercise of civil jurisdiction no longer has any
real connection with the Prerogative.

Criminal
justice.

It is otherwise where criminal justice is concerned.
There the prosecution is in the name of the King ; for
all criminal offences are against his peace or against
his crown and dignity, and were formerly so laid in
every indictment. It is true that he is prosecutor only
in name, and the true prosecutor some other person or
authority ; but the Crown retains a very real control over
every prosecution. Thus the Attorney-General, as representing the Crown in the exercise of this Prerogative, can

*Nolle
prosequi.*

at his absolute discretion enter a *nolle prosequi,* and by so
doing effectually stop all further proceedings ; whereas
the " true " prosecutor *may* be allowed by the judge to
withdraw a charge, but has no absolute right to do so.
So also the King, against whom all crimes are in theory

Pardon.

committed, has a *prerogative of mercy,* which empowers him

to pardon the offender or to commute the penalty into some less severe one. The exercise of this prerogative is entrusted to the Home Secretary (see *ante*, pp. 282 and 286).

The conservation of the peace is an even older pre- Conservation of the Peace.
rogative of the Crown than the administration of justice. In fact, the administration of justice has largely developed out of the conservation of the peace, as the words " against the peace of our Sovereign Lord the King " (which, as we have just said, used to form a part of every indictment for a criminal offence) clearly show. In early times, the conservation of the peace was held to consist simply in the repression of violence and disorder. But, with the complexity of modern social life, the mere prevention of violence and disorder is not sufficient to preserve the life of the community. It is essential that services on which Maintenance of Public Services.
the very existence of social life depends shall be continued, even though the action (or inaction) which threatens them may be perfectly legal This need was satisfied even in the pre-war years by the Emergency Powers Act, 1920 (see *post*, p. 554), and the difficulties and dangers of these later years of transition from war to peace have caused Parliament also to permit much of the governmental power of the recent war to remain in force for yet a while. (See the Supplies and Services (Transitional Powers) Act, 1945, and the Supplies and Services (Extended Purposes) Act, 1947.)

4. *The King as Fountain of Honour.* The King has Honours and titles.
a prerogative to confer titles of nobility and knighthood, and it is in virtue of this prerogative that the Government can in his name control the composition of the House of Lords. He can also create new offices ; but with this restriction, that he can neither create new offices with new fees annexed to them, nor annex new fees to old offices; for this would be a tax upon the subject, which cannot be imposed without an Act of Parliament. These prerogatives will be discussed at length in connection with the Legislature, the Ministry, and the Civil Service.

5. *The King as Head of the Church.* The King is The Church.
considered by the laws of England as the Head and

Supreme Governor of the Established Church. It is by virtue of this supremacy that the King convenes and dissolves all ecclesiastical synods or convocations. He also has the right of nomination to all bishoprics, and to certain other ecclesiastical preferments. And he is the ultimate Court of Appeal in ecclesiastical causes ; his functions in this respect being delegated to the Judicial Committee of the Privy Council. These matters will be dealt with hereafter in the Chapter on the Church of England (Chap. 23).

Incorporation by Charter. 6. *Corporations.* The last prerogative right of importance that we shall mention is that of creating corporations by charter. In recent times the vast majority of corporations derive their incorporation, directly or indirectly, from Parliament. Incorporation by Royal Charter is, however, still sometimes sought (by petition to the King in Council), but such incorporation is no longer granted for association in trade.

7. *Miscellaneous prerogatives.* There are also certain other prerogatives of minor importance, but many of these have fallen into disuse or been superseded by statute.

Shores and harbours. The King has certain prerogative rights relating to the shores and harbours along the coasts of the realm. He is lord of the whole shore ; and the space between high-water and low-water mark is vested in him.

Ports and havens. He has the prerogative of appointing ports and havens, and of taking dues from ships using them ; and he may grant his rights to a subject. When a port has been appointed, it must remain open to the public, upon payment of the proper dues, and cannot be closed by virtue of the Prerogative. But since 1876 the King's rights in regard to ports have been delegated by statute, first to the Treasury and later to other Departments, who may appoint ports and declare their limits and order that certain quays and warehouses shall be used for the loading and unloading of goods.

Beacons, lighthouses, etc. The erection of beacons, lighthouses, and sea-marks is also incident to this branch of the Prerogative ; but by the Merchant Shipping Act, 1894, a similar power is vested in, and in practice is always exercised by, the Trinity

House, a corporation who act as the general lighthouse authority for England and Wales, and as controllers of pilotage, and also as nautical advisors in Admiralty cases.

The King is also, as *parens patriæ*, invested with a kind of guardianship over various classes or persons who, from their legal disability, stand in need of protection, such as infants, mental defectives, and persons of unsound mind ; but this royal function is so much overlaid with the elaborate statutory duties of modern authorities that its prerogative character has long ceased to be of any practical significance. *[Guardianship.]*

The student will understand that the foregoing is by no means a complete list of the prerogatives of the Crown. The Crown still has, for instance, certain incidental advantages in litigation, though these have been drastically reduced by legislation in recent years, especially in 1947 (see *post*, pp. 568 *et seq.*). Crown grants are generally construed as is most favourable to the Crown, whereas a grant by a private individual is always construed against the grantor. The King can legislate by right of his Prerogative for a conquered (or ceded) colony, and this forms, or used to form, part of the work of the Colonial Office (see pp. 588 *et seq.*). And, with certain exceptions, appeals lie to the Judical Committee of the Privy Council from conquered and settled colonies alike (see pp. 602–3 But our enumeration of the several prerogatives must suffice for the purposes of this work. *[Other prerogatives.]*

It must be added that, since all prerogatives are vested in the Crown, it follows that, although the King in most cases *delegates* their exercise to his Ministers and other agents, the general rule is that he cannot without statutory authority grant them away to another. Thus he cannot grant away the right to give the assent to Parliamentary Bills, or to appoint a judge or a bishop, or the right to hold a Court of justice. But, where the Crown has the right, under its Prerogative, of taking possession of certain articles or of collecting tolls or other fees, there is an exception to the general rule. Such rights are grantable, and are called " franchises." But few of these rights have not perished in old age by the hand of time or *[Franchises.]*

statute. They include—or they used to include—the
Crown's right to take possession of wrecks and treasure
trove, and to take toll at markets and fairs, ferries and
fisheries.   Moreover, even where the subject is unable to
prove his title to a franchise by royal grant, he may after
long enjoyment establish it by prescription.

CHAPTER 6

THE DOCTRINE OF STATE NECESSITY AND ACT OF STATE

The triumph of the Long Parliament in 1640 rendered impossible any complete separation between public and private law. The Privy Council and the Court of Star Chamber, which had existed for the purpose of exercising a judicial control in " matters of policy and government," lost, the one its jurisdiction *within the realm*, the other its very existence. No separation of Public and Private Law.

Though the Courts had to acknowledge the existence of the Prerogative, they took care to limit its extent, and for this purpose applied in particular the rule that the Crown could not by its Prerogative interfere with the person or property of the subject.   The Crown could not tax by Prerogative, nor could it by Proclamation legislate so as to increase the scope of its prerogative powers. *Prerogative powers limited.*

Secondly, the Courts did not dispute the soundness of the maxim " The King can do no wrong."   On the other hand, the House of Commons made it perfectly clear that they at least would not consent to treat Ministers of the Crown as irresponsible for the acts of the Crown. They impeached Danby in 1678 for his share in the conclusion of the Treaty of Dover, by which Charles II virtually sold himself to Louis XIV, and when the King took responsibility for Danby's acts and acknowledged that they had been done by the royal command, the House refused to listen to the plea and went on with the impeachment.   The King dissolved Parliament to save his Minister, but the Commons went on with the impeachment in the next Parliament, and, when Danby produced a pardon under the Great Seal, refused to allow the plea. The proceedings were eventually allowed to drop, though Danby remained several years in the Tower ; but the principle that a Minister is personally responsible for his acts, and cannot be shielded by the Crown, had been firmly *Personal responsibility of Ministers of the Crown.*

Danby's Case.

established.   Henceforth, no Minister could plead against a subject that he had acted in a matter of State in obedience to the orders of the Crown (*Earl Danby's Case* (1678–85), 11 State Tr. 600).

Plea of State
necessity no
shield for
accused
person.

Thirdly, it became recognised in the long run that even the plea of State necessity would not avail a person accused of committing an unlawful act.   For a long time indeed the notion prevailed that the Government was entitled to exceptional treatment at the hands of the Courts, and libels against the Government were punished with great ferocity.   But in his famous judgment in *Entick* v. *Carrington* (1765), 19 State Tr. 1029, Lord Camden roundly condemned the doctrine.   His words have become famous :

Entick v.
Carrington.

> " With respect to the argument of state necessity or a distinction which has been aimed at between state offences and others, the Common Law does not understand that kind of reasoning, nor do our books take notice of any such distinction."

In spite of this decision, the doctrine died hard, and faint echoes of it were still heard in the nineteenth century.

The Crown
and aliens
outside the
realm.

But when Parliament and the Common Law Courts between them cut down the Prerogative and ensured that it should not transgress its proper limits, they were concerned with the Crown's own subjects rather than those of other states.   *Within the realm* the power of the Crown was to be limited ; there was no need to curtail the Crown's " absolute " authority to act at its discretion against aliens *outside the realm.*

ACTS OF STATE.   Such acts are of many kinds ; they include the recognition of conquest and the suppression of piracy.   As Fletcher Moulton, L.J., said in *Salaman* v. *Secretary of State for India,* [1906] 1 K. B. 613, at p. 639 : " Acts of State are not all of one kind ; their nature and consequence may differ in an infinite variety of ways, and these differences may profoundly affect the position of . . . Courts with regard to them."   We are here concerned chiefly with the limits within which the defence of Act of State may be successfully pleaded by a servant of the Crown in an English Court.   In other words, we want to

know if and when an English Court will suffer an officer
of the Armed Forces or an official of the Civil Service, for
example, to escape from liability for his act by pleading—
" Granted that I acted without warrant from statute and
in defiance of common law ; but I was only doing my duty,
and I did it in the name and with the sanction of my
Department in Whitehall." The general answer (to be
readily guessed from the historical note that introduces
this Chapter) is that it would be quite contrary to the hard-
won heritage of liberty in accordance with law for any
English Court to tolerate any such plea in defence of
arbitrary conduct against any one who, owing allegiance
to the Crown, is entitled to its protection.

Who, then, are they who come within the allegiance and No Act of
protection of the Crown ? British subjects, of course, State against
persons
whether by birth or by naturalisation, and wherever they owing
allegiance.
may happen to be, as the language of their passport
proudly proclaims when they travel abroad. Against
them, no arbitrary conduct by Crown officers or officials,
here *or abroad*, can be tolerated by an English Court.
Aliens, too, are safeguarded by the English Courts against
such arbitrary conduct—but upon two conditions : they
must be *both* friendly *and* within the realm, for they then
owe *local* allegiance to the Crown. Alien enemies, however,
and even friendly aliens *outside the realm*, can get no relief
in the English Courts for their sufferings by the arbitrary
hand of Crown officers or officials if the latter can explain
away their otherwise unlawful behaviour as an Act of
State. Relief in such cases has to be sought, not in the
precincts of the law, but along the corridors of diplomacy.

The rule that there can be no Act of State between the
Crown and one of its own subjects was finally established
by the case of *Walker* v. *Baird*, [1892] A. C. 491, where *Walker* v.
Baird.
the facts were as follows. The plaintiff, a British subject
sued the defendant, a naval officer, in trespass for entering upon his lobster factory on the coast of Newfoundland. The defendant pleaded that what he had done
was an Act of State, done by authority of the Crown
for the purpose of enforcing an arrangement which
had been arrived at with the Government of France.
The Supreme Court of Newfoundland rejected the plea,

and the Judicial Committee of the Privy Council affirmed the decision, on the ground that there can be no Act of State between the Crown and any of its own subjects.

Johnstone v. Pedlar.

The rule concerning a *friendly* alien residing *within* the realm is illustrated by *Johnstone* v. *Pedlar*, [1921] 2 A. C. 262. An American citizen was arrested in Ireland (then still an undoubted part of the King's realm) for illegal drilling. The police illegally took and detained a sum of money found upon him, and refused to return it to him. Their action was, however, ratified by a Minister of the Crown. The American thereupon brought an action against the Chief Commissioner of Police ; and it was held by the House of Lords that it was no defence to allege that the plaintiff was an alien and that the wrongful confiscation of his property was an Act of State. It is of interest to note that the decision seems to take for granted the continuance of the Crown's protection of the plaintiff, notwithstanding his hostile conduct within the realm.

The rule concerning an alien residing *outside* the realm was vividly vindicated a century ago in the celebrated case of *Buron* v. *Denman* (1848), 2 Exch. 167, the facts of which we give below.

Act of State must be an act of sovereign power.

Again, an Act of State must be an act of " sovereign power." This excludes, for instance, mere commercial contracts between the Crown and a foreign company, hitherto enforceable against the Crown by petition of right and now under the Crown Proceedings Act, 1947.

Act of State must be that of the State itself.

Moreover, the act must be the act of the State itself, and not of a private individual. But the Crown must in the nature of things act by means of agents, and so in every case the question may be raised whether authority has been given to the person who commits the act. The authority may be conferred by prior authorisation, or even by subsequent ratification, as was decided in the

Buron v. Denman.

above-mentioned case of *Buron* v. *Denman* (1848), 2 Exch. 167. In this case the defendant, a British naval officer, was sued by a Spaniard for £100,000 damages for trespass and for loss of slaves and other property, in respect of acts done in the course of suppressing the slave-trade on the West Coast of Africa. His high-handed, though high-minded, initiative was taken against a foreigner who dwelt abroad. It was not disputed that his plea of Act of State must succeed if he could prove that his acts were authorised by the Crown. He had in fact acted without sufficient prior authorisation, but his acts had been subsequently ratified. Was such a subsequent ratification equivalent to a prior authorisation? The Court, not without hesitation by a great judge, decided that it was.

Now the question may be raised whether the authority given to the servant by the Crown is wide enough to justify the plea. This question is of great importance where Colonial Governors are concerned, and the leading case on the subject is *Musgrave* v. *Pulido* (1879), 5 App. Cas. 102, where the defendant, who was Governor of Jamaica, had seized and detained the defendant's schooner. He pleaded that his acts were done by him as Governor, and were Acts of State. The plea was rejected, on the ground that a Colonial Governor does not possess " general sovereign power." His authority is conferred by his commission and is limited by its terms, express or implied. Therefore, for the defence of Act of State to succeed, it is not sufficient for him to allege that he has acted as Governor. He must go on to show that he had authority from the Crown to do the particular acts in question. *[margin: Musgrave v. Pulido.]*

The efficacy of an Act of State is not limited to its operation as an occasional defence to an action in tort. It may also, for example, have the effect of conferring a title on the Crown, *e.g.*, the title to newly-acquired territory, with succession to the rights of the previous sovereign. It has thus a positive as well as a negative side. *[margin: Positive side.]*

It remains to be said that our law accords a *reciprocal* recognition to Acts of State committed by foreign sovereigns whom the Crown has recognised. Thus, on the *negative* side, no action will lie in an English Court for a tort committed outside the realm and for which a foreign sovereign takes responsibility, even though the agent by whom the tort has actually been committed is a British subject, and even though the act complained of is a crime according to English law (*Dobree* v. *Napier* (1836), 3 Scott, 201). Similarly, on the *positive* side, an English Court is bound to accept an Act of State by a foreign *[margin: Reciprocal recognition to other States.]*

sovereign, recognised as a sovereign *de facto* by the
Crown, as constituting a good root of title. Thus, in
Aksionairnoye Obschestvo A. M. Luther v. *James Sagor &
Co.*, [1921] 3 K. B. 532, the defendant was held to have
acquired a good title to certain timber by purchase from
the Russian Government, who had confiscated it ; and the
plaintiffs, who had been its former owners, were left without redress.

Facts of
. State.

It rests with the Crown to give information of the truth
of certain facts to the Courts. In all such cases the Courts
must accept the information as conclusive. These facts
have been termed " Facts of State." They include the
answers to such questions as :

Is such and such a State a sovereign State ?

Has it been recognised as such by the Crown ?

Is X its monarch and Y its ambassador ?

Is it at peace or at war with this country ?

In these cases the answer of the Crown is conclusive
because it rests with the Crown whether it will recognise
the foreign State as a sovereign State, or X and Y as its
representatives, and whether it will make war or peace
with it. In practice the information would usually be
supplied to the Court by letter from the Foreign Office.

CHAPTER 7

THE DEVELOPMENT OF CABINET GOVERN-
MENT AND THE CONVENTIONS OF THE
CONSTITUTION

The most difficult constitutional problem which arose
between the years 1660 and 1832 was that of devising some
method of controlling the exercise of the King's Prerogative. It was eventually solved by the development of the
Cabinet system. That system has grown almost imper- Imper-
ceptibly out of the conditions created by certain legal growth of
doctrines ; but it is not itself governed by rules of law. Cabinet system.

By the year 1660 it was clear that the King could neither
legislate nor levy any taxation beyond his hereditary
revenue without the consent of Parliament, and although
the King could control the composition of the House of
Lords by nominating his supporters as bishops or by
conferring peerages upon them, his power over the King could
House of Commons was quite insufficient to ensure the House of
approval by that body of any course of policy on which he Commons.
chose to embark ; and even the extensive exercise of
corruption at elections, and the scattering of preferments
and pensions among the members of Parliament, were
insufficient to secure a permanent majority in favour of
the King.

It became, therefore, necessary in the interests of steady Ministers of
government that the King should choose such Ministers State.
as could guarantee the granting of monies by the House of
Commons ; and this dependence of Ministers upon the
confidence of the House of Commons became more and
more essential. For a long time the King still chose his Party
Ministers for himself, and William III was the first to system.
form a Government composed exclusively of members
of the party for the time being dominant in the House of
Commons ; but thereafter the practice begun by him was
followed with but few exceptions, and the Ministry of the
day became a committee of the more important leaders
of one of the two parties in the State.

Genesis of Cabinet.

Within the Ministry there grew up a body called the Cabinet. It was no more than a small number of the King's confidential advisers, who met together at irregular intervals in order to concert a common policy. Its members were invariably Privy Councillors, yet the Cabinet could not *and cannot* correctly be described as a committee of the Privy Council. Its composition and its meetings were quite informal, and if anything formal required to be done in order to clothe a Cabinet decision with legal validity, it was done at a subsequent meeting of the Privy Council or perhaps in Parliament itself.

The Prime Minister.

Originally the King himself presided at Cabinet meetings, but George I was so ignorant of English that he soon ceased to attend, and the chairmanship and general direction of the Cabinet gradually devolved on the Prime Minister. By the accession of Queen Victoria, the Ministry, so far from carrying out the will of the Sovereign, had become accustomed to impose its own will on him,

Establishment of certain conventions.

and certain "conventions" for the proper conduct of Cabinet government had already been established ; these have changed but little since that date. Thus it is a recognised convention that a Cabinet which has lost the confidence of the House of Commons must either advise the King to dissolve Parliament or resign. It is a convention that the members of the Cabinet are *collectively* responsible to the House of Commons for the acts of each of them ; for it is assumed that the major questions of policy and administration will have been discussed by the Cabinet as a whole. But, just as the Cabinet is politically responsible to the House of Commons, and is ultimately bound to carry out its wishes, so also the King is bound to choose as Prime Minister one who will have the confidence of the House of Commons, and to accept the advice tendered by him and his Cabinet. These are, however, not the only constitutional conventions ; it is also a convention, which has nothing directly to do with the Cabinet itself, that Parliament must sit at least once a year ; and the King is by convention forbidden to refuse his assent to a Bill which has passed both Houses of Parliament—or even the House of Commons alone, under the Parliament Act, 1911.

These conventions have been so called—first by Dicey— in an attempt to distinguish them from rules of law ; for, though their non-observance would endanger the very basis of constitutional government in its present form, nevertheless no Court of law could enforce them by legal process. This distinction between law and convention may not always be easy to draw with precision, but it is nevertheless a distinction upon which Dicey and his followers rightly lay much stress. They go on to mislead us, however, by an argument that is more attractive than true ; the *ultimate* sanction of these conventions, according to Dicey, is a matter of law. If, so runs the argument, the Government were not to summon Parliament in any one year, they would be unable to obtain a supply of money sufficient for the current needs of administration ; for, ever since the Revolution of 1689, the House of Commons has taken care to make so many of its grants annual ones that, without the help of Parliament, the Ministry would start every new financial year with too little money for the work of government. So, the argument proceeds, if a Cabinet which had lost the confidence of the House of Commons did not resign or appeal to the electors, or if they clung to office despite their defeat at the polls, the House of Commons might refuse monies to the Ministers. Now, if they attempted to carry on the government without sufficient funds, they would find themselves in a dilemma : *either* they would be compelled to levy taxation without the consent of Parliament, and so break the law, and for such a breach of the law neither the royal commands nor the plea of State necessity would afford them any defence, *or* the government would stop working altogether for lack of funds. Even the legislation which must be passed every year in respect of the Army and Air Force is also used to support this argument of Dicey. As such legislation cannot be passed if Parliament is not in session, and may not be passed if Parliament is defied, Ministers would be in a similar dilemma if they attempted to govern after the keeping of a standing Army and Air Force had become illegal. Perhaps the greatest objection to Dicey's reasoning is that it cannot extend beyond a few of the con-

Conventions are not Rules of Law.

Dicey's theory of sanctions.

Criticism of Dicey.

ventions ; there are others—including those all-important
conventions that have united this country and its self-
governing Dominions overseas—in respect of which no
ultimate legal sanction could arise. In any case, the
argument belongs to an unreal world, and it deserves
attention only because of the frequency with which it
has been repeated in the books.

The conventions of the Constitution are those rules for
the conduct of public business which, though not themselves rules of law, are essential to the smooth and
efficient conduct of public business according to law.
Even though, in respect of a limited number, the ultimate
legal sanction may haunt the background, it is well known
that the conventions of the Constitution are not really
observed from any fear of the possibility of a breach of
law ; they are really observed because they exist to ensure
the smooth running of government business, and because
defiance of them must sooner or later bring the administration into unpopularity and contempt.

Legal posi-
tion of the
Cabinet. Political writers are in the habit of speaking of the
Prime Minister and the Cabinet as the true Government of
the country, and of regarding the powers of the Crown as
obsolete. This may be good politics, but it is not good
law. The Crown may no longer be able to use its powers
without the restraint of Ministers, but they are no more
obsolete than, to take an example from the Law of
Property, the legal estate in the hands of a trustee. The
trustee is bound to use the property, in which he has a legal
estate, for the benefit of his *cestui que trust* ; but he could
not use it at all if he had not got it to use. It is far from
the truth to say at the present day that *all* the powers
wielded by the Central Government belong to the Crown ;
for, as we have already seen (p. 303), many powers are given
by Parliament to individual Ministers ; but much of the
government of the country is still carried on by means of
the powers allowed to the Crown as part of the Prerogative
and also of those other powers which have been conferred upon it by Acts of Parliament. All these powers
belong to the Crown *at law*, and just as a trustee is bound
to use the property in which he has a legal estate as the
rules of equity direct, so the Crown is bound to use its

legal powers in the way prescribed by the conventions of the Constitution.

In the eighteenth century the Cabinet had succeeded in imposing its will upon the Crown ; in the nineteenth it went far to dominate Parliament. The King and Parliament are no longer rivals, but component parts of a single system of Cabinet government.

Until the year 1832 the House of Commons was controlled by the great territorial magnates, who owned the notorious pocket and rotten boroughs. It was not in any true sense of the term a popular body or one responsible to the people as a whole. During the nineteenth century it was by successive stages reformed and made increasingly representative of the people. This development of democratic government brought with it a stricter party discipline, and the modern elector tends to vote rather for the party than for the individual candidate. It follows that, if a two-party system is in force, the Prime Minister is in practice designated by the electorate rather than by the House of Commons, where his own party is expected to support him faithfully once he has been appointed. Our present system of government has thus become in a very real sense a system of Cabinet government ; for the Cabinet, and the Prime Minister in a peculiar degree, is responsible for the determination of policy, and can, by the use of the " Whips " and other expedients of party discipline, to a very great extent ensure the passing of such legislative measures as are necessary for its prosecution. *Party discipline.*

Yet we should be careful to guard against an exaggeration of this dependence of the House of Commons upon the Cabinet. There are, in practice, certain checks upon the powers of the Cabinet in respect of legislation. The first of these is time. *Un*contested legislation may be passed without difficulty, but any measure which is seriously opposed by the Opposition may take a very long time to pass into law, and the amount of *contested* legislation which can be accomplished within the full five years' life of a House of Commons is thus severely limited, however hard the Government may drive. It is this lack of time that explains, in part at least, the persistent demand in *Checks on Cabinet power.*

many quarters, not only for even more delegation of legislative power, but also for a radical and ruthless overhaul of the whole machinery of parliamentary procedure. In the second place, although the Prime Minister may at any time threaten refractory members of his own party with the pains and penalties of party discipline, and so on most occasions force them to assist in carrying out his policy, there are occasions on which he finds himself compelled to subordinate his own will to that of his party. Indeed, if the Government enjoys a very large majority, the danger from the Opposition may well be less potent than the outcry and rebellion of its own supporters.

CHAPTER 8

SUBORDINATE LEGISLATION AND ADMINISTRATIVE JURISDICTION

SUMMARY					PAGE
Section I. Introduction	...	...	...	...	... 321
Section II. Subordinate Legislation	...	...	...	... 322
Section III. Administrative Jurisdiction	...	...	... 328

Section I. INTRODUCTION

The classification of governmental powers that is most often met with in books on constitutional law is the three-fold division of such powers into the legislative, the executive and the judicial. All these three terms are difficult enough to define : most of all the term " executive."

Executive government does not, as might be supposed, involve merely putting the laws into execution. If that were so, the most appropriate use of the term would be in connection with the work of sheriffs and their officers, who levy execution upon the property of defaulting debtors, or of prison authorities, who inflict the punishments awarded by the Courts. Indeed, in works of repute the term executive has even been used to indicate the work of the judges ; for it may well be said that it is they who put the laws into execution. Nevertheless, in spite of the objections to it, the term executive is in most common use as indicating the functions of *central* as distinct from *local* government. Tradition and authority lie behind it, and a more suitable term has yet to be found. *Executive government.*

" Executive " government has extended the sphere of its activity as the passing years have added to the complexity of our social and economic life. It still includes the management of State property, the prosecution of foreign policy, and the conduct of military operations, but at the present day it includes also the provision of educational facilities, the furtherance of public health, and even the control of economic organisation. The executive government of the country is now much more miscellaneous, much less homogeneous in character, than either legislation or the administration of justice.

Executive government has always implied the exercise of discretionary powers, the nature of which has been described above (pp. 275 *et seq.*), and within the present century there has been a tendency to widen their operation to an ever increasing extent, even where they impinge on the rights of the citizen. In many countries, notably in France, a regular and highly developed system of administrative law (*droit administratif*) has grown up to regulate all such matters. In this country, the law is still in an empirical and formative stage, and even its main outlines are not always easy to detect ; but it is clear that executive government now includes much that is of a legislative and at least quasi-judicial character. Moreover, it is now the practice to commit to bodies other than the ordinary Courts, and closely connected with the executive government, the decision of purely judicial questions arising out of the operation of schemes of social reform. Thus a very large part of the government of the country is now occupied by the closely related topics of subordinate legislation and administrative jurisdiction.

Section II. Subordinate Legislation

Orders in Council. The most dignified act of subordinate legislation is the Order in Council, that is, an Order issued by His Majesty's Most Honourable Privy Council. The Privy Council was *in its origin* a sort of Royal Cabinet, composed of those whom the King himself selected to advise him personally upon the conduct of national business. It consists nowadays of a fluctuating number of persons, about three hundred in all, who are formally nominated by the King from amongst his natural-born or naturalised subjects, and who, on their appointment as members, become entitled to the prefix of " Right Honourable." The choice has ceased long ago to be a personal one for the King, and the members are mostly those who hold, or have held, high office in the State, *e.g.*, Cabinet Ministers, the Lords Justices of the Court of Appeal, and certain officials of the Royal Household. Unless His Majesty is present in

Composition of Privy Council.

person, the Council is presided over by the Lord President of the Council, who is usually a Cabinet Minister. The Council *as a whole* only meets upon a few State occasions, such as the demise of the Crown ; its *ordinary* meetings are attended only by those who are specially summoned. But even the business at these ordinary meetings can only be of a purely formal kind, and anything involving discussion rather than ceremony can only be taken in committees of the Privy Council, which are either *standing* committees, such as the Judicial Committee (see *post*, pp. 602–3), or committees *specially appointed* from time to time to advise the Crown upon any particular subject.

Where an Act of Parliament confers upon " His Majesty in Council " (this phrase being the statutory term for the Privy Council) the power to issue any Order, the actual passing of the Order is done at a meeting of the Council consisting of a few councillors summoned for the purpose. But their proceedings are purely formal ; for the exercise of the power has already been deliberated and determined upon by the Department responsible for the administration of the Act. That Department, with or without the advice of the Parliamentary Counsel, draws up the Order ; and it is invariably passed by the Council in the form approved by the Department. In this type of delegated legislation (which is becoming more and more frequent as the demands upon the time of Parliament increase), the body which legislates is *in form* the Privy Council but *in reality* the Government Department concerned. Further, a single statute may confer the power to legislate by Order in Council upon several different Departments ; for the wording of the enabling section is simply to the effect that " His Majesty in Council may by Order in Council provide . . ." This leaves the Cabinet free to decide, if the matter is in doubt, which particular Department or Departments is or are to exercise the powers in question. An illustration of such a statute is the Defence of the Realm Act, 1914, which merely provided that : *Procedure as to Orders in Council.*

D.O.R.A.

> " His Majesty in Council has power during the continuance of the present war to issue regulations for securing the public safety and the defence of the realm."

Under this authority practically every Government Department, at one time or another during the first Great War, framed and issued regulations, by the process above described, in the form of Orders in Council ; and, indeed, the section was so widely drawn that in effect it amounted to a delegation by Parliament of its own sovereignty to the Executive, for all purposes connected with the conduct of the war. Even so, any assumption of authority by a Department in excess of its powers under the delegated legislation was liable to be checked by the Courts, as was shown in *A.-G.* v. *Wilts United Dairies* (1922), 91 L. J. K. B. 897, where the Food Controller was restrained from making an unlawful charge for a licence.

A similar large-scale delegation of its legislative power by Parliament was necessary for the prosecution of the second Great War, and it was effected by the Emergency Powers (Defence) Acts, 1939 and 1940. The Act of 1939 introduced a general power to legislate by Orders in Council " for securing the public safety, the defence of the realm, the maintenance of public order and the efficient prosecution of [the war], and for maintaining supplies and services essential to the life of the community." In the following year this general power was thought to have been enlarged by an Act, passed in the expectation of imminent invasion, which empowered Orders in Council to be made " for requiring persons to place themselves, their services, and their property at the disposal of His Majesty." Much of this legislative power has been temporarily preserved and made available, not merely for " the orderly transition from war to peace," but also for " increasing production and redressing the balance of trade " (Supplies and Services (Transitional Powers) Act, 1945, and Supplies and Services (Extended Purposes) Act, 1947).

Other forms of subordinate legislation. However, not all subordinate legislation is done by Orders in Council, for not only is power to make regulations, rules, orders or by-laws conferred directly by Parliament on Government Departments, Local Authorities and other bodies, but Orders in Council may themselves empower Departments to legislate by order, and a Department may by its own order reserve to itself power to issue directions. Thus, upon the foundation of a Parliamentary delegation of legislative power, there may well be a tier of sub-delegation and even of sub-sub-delegation.

By far the greater part of these powers of subordinate legislation are derived mediately or immediately from a parliamentary grant. As will be seen later, the constitutions of all Local Government authorities nowadays rest upon statute, and it is from these constitutions that the authorities in question derive their legislative powers ; so also the King in Council and the Central Government Departments legislate for the most part under authority granted by Parliament. But, so far as the internal arrangements of a Department are concerned, the power to make regulations comes mainly from the Royal Prerogative. *Powers derived from a Parliamentary grant.*

Unless Parliament has otherwise provided (see *post*, p. 326) the validity of acts of subordinate legislation, whether regulations, rules, orders or by-laws, can be questioned in a Court of law on the ground that they are made without authority, being *ultra vires* of the statute which is alleged to authorise them, or beyond the powers recognised at Common Law to belong to the King in virtue of his Prerogative. By-laws run the further risk of being adjudged void because they are unreasonable. Whether a by-law is unreasonable is a matter of law for the Court ; but the case of *Kruse* v. *Johnson*, [1898] 2 Q. B. 91, is authority for the proposition that, whereas a Court requires to be satisfied that a by-law made by a public utility company, or indeed any body other than a Local Government authority, is reasonable, any by-law made by a Local Government authority is *prima facie* reasonable, and will be enforced as such, unless it is established to the satisfaction of the Court that it is unreasonable, on the ground that it differentiates unfairly between different classes of persons or that it is grossly oppressive. For such by-laws are the work of representative bodies, and are subject to disallowance by the Crown or, in certain cases, require the approval of some Government Department before they can come into force. The presence of these safeguards, while it does not relieve the Courts of the *Doctrine of ultra vires.* *By-laws.* *Kruse v. Johnson.*

responsibility of inquiring into the validity of local government by-laws when they are brought in question, renders it much less likely that they will be found to be unreasonable.

But though the general rule is that all acts of subordinate legislation are subject to the control of the Courts, within recent years there has appeared a tendency for Parliament to oust that jurisdiction more and more. An illustration of this tendency is a provision that rules, orders, and regulations made by some Government Department for the better carrying out of some Act " should have effect as though they were included in the Act itself." This was formerly thought to operate so as to exclude entirely the doctrine of *ultra vires* ; the argument being that the Courts have no more authority to question the validity of a piece of legislation which is thus included in an Act of Parliament than they have of passing judgment upon the validity of the Act itself. But it was

held in *Minister of Health* v. *R., Ex parte Yaffe*, [1931] A. C. 494, that this applied only to *intra vires* departmental legislation. Following this decision, the present tendency in statutes seems to be to allow a party aggrieved to attack a departmental regulation or order, but only within a very short period. Thus, if an order for compulsory purchase is made, *e.g.*, under the Housing Act, 1936, or the New Towns Act, 1946, a complainant may need to be warned that Parliament has fixed a brief time-limit (sometimes only six weeks or even less) after which no relief can be got from the Courts, even on

the ground of *ultra vires*. Again, there are statutes, of which the Rating and Valuation Act, 1925, is an example, that even give the Crown power, for the removal of difficulties, to amend the Act itself by Order in Council. This extreme power, sometimes nick-named as the " Henry VIII clause," is not often given, the purpose being to enable the Department concerned in the initial administration of the Act to have, for a limited time and subject maybe to severe conditions, the power of dealing with unforeseen troubles that prevent the Act from becoming a workable scheme.

Publication. Some further and recent attempt has

been made to ensure more adequate publicity for acts of subordinate legislation. Both in and out of Parliament the complaint has been : lack of actual knowledge is bad enough, and hard indeed to put right (see *infra*) ; but lack of the very means of knowledge is something worse, for it not only mocks the vigilant but also makes nonsense of the precept *ignorantia juris non excusat.* Much of this complaint is now silenced by the general requirements of the Statutory Instruments Act, 1946, but its scope was thought by Scott, L.J. to be so limited that there remains " the crying need of immediate publication of all matter that is truly legislative " (*Blackpool Corporation* v. *Locker*, [1948] 1 K. B. 349). Though the detailed provisions of this Act of 1946, and their amplification by Treasury regulations made with the concurrence of the Lord Chancellor and the Speaker of the House of Commons, are thought to lie beyond the purpose of this treatise and to be of little direct concern except to those charged with their day-to-day observance, nevertheless it is of general interest to note the convenient provision for the publication of official *lists*, any entry wherein— {.margin-note Publicity for subordinate legislation.}

> " shall be conclusive evidence of the date on which any statutory instrument was first issued by His Majesty's Stationery Office."

Such lists should be especially useful as a ready means of finding out if an Act of Parliament, the operation of which is postponed to some indefinite future date, has or has not been brought into operation by governmental action.

Parliamentary control. The Houses of Parliament often reserve to themselves an express control over subordinate legislation. Not infrequently the Act conferring legislative power provides that the regulation or other enactment shall " lie on the table of each House " for a specified period, and that it shall *either* not come into force until it has been approved by an " affirmative " resolution of each House *or* shall cease to have effect if disapproved within that period by a " negative " resolution of either House. Regulations made under the Emergency Powers (Defence) Acts, 1939–40, and regulations and orders made under the Supplies and Services {.margin-note Parliamentary approval necessary sometimes.}

Acts, 1945 and 1947, are subject to this control. There
has in the past been much complaint that members of
either House have had insufficient means of informing
themselves of the contents of such subordinate legislation,
and that this control has in consequence been nugatory.

Select Committee for subordinate legislation.
Since 1944, however, there has existed a Select Committee of the House of Commons which has the duty
of deciding whether the special attention of the House
should be drawn to such subordinate legislation on any of
the following grounds :

   (i) that it imposes a charge on the public revenues,
or contains provisions requiring payments to be
made to the Exchequer or any Government
Department or to any local or public authority
in consideration of any licence or consent or of
any services to be rendered, or prescribes the
amount of any such charge or payments ;

   (ii) that it is made in pursuance of an enactment containing specific provisions excluding it from
challenge in the Courts, either at all times or
after the expiration of a specified period ;

   (iii) that it appears to make some unusual or unexpected
use of the powers conferred by the Statute under
which it is made ;

   (iv) that there appears to have been unjustifiable delay
in the publication of it ;

   (v) that, for any special reason, its form or purport
calls for elucidation.

Of this—let us say—watch from Westminster upon
Whitehall, a learned writer has very recently said that
" it remains to be seen whether the Select Committee as
at present constituted can continue to carry what may be
an ever-increasing burden " (Modern Law Review (1949),
Vol. 12, p. 297).

Section III. ADMINISTRATIVE JURISDICTION

Special tribunals.

For many centuries tribunals have existed for special
purposes outside the ordinary judicial hierarchy. Such,
for instance, are Courts Martial and Ecclesiastical Courts,
which enforce discipline in the armed forces and over

clergymen of the Church of England. But within the present century such tribunals have multiplied exceedingly, and it has become common to concentrate the working of a particular service, including the decision of questions arising out of it, into the hands of the central and local authorities who administer it.

It is believed that the trial of criminal offences is never withdrawn from the ordinary Courts, so that even if an enactment imposes a penalty upon persons who offend against it, they will always be tried by a judge and jury or at petty or quarter sessions ; though certain Marketing Boards, which to some extent derive their powers from the consent of the industries concerned, can fine offenders against the marketing schemes without appeal to the ordinary Courts. But it is often the case that the decision of other questions arising in connection with a service, whether they involve findings of fact or law or the exercise of a discretion, is committed to the appropriate administrative authorities or to special tribunals closely connected with them.

The general considerations which underlie this modern administrative justice seem to be the following : — Reasons for special tribunals.

In the first place, the ordinary Courts, especially the ordinary local Courts, are already over-burdened with work.

Secondly, the cost of proceedings in the ordinary Courts would be prohibitive.

Thirdly, it is felt that questions arising out of a service are better decided by persons who have an intimate knowledge of the working of the service.

Further, where questions of policy are material to a decision, it can obviously be made more appropriately by an administrative authority than by an ordinary Court.

This administrative jurisdiction is of the most varied character and defies classification. We shall encounter many instances in the later course of this work, and all that need be done here by way of introduction is to call attention to some of the main types.

From the point of view of form and procedure, we may note a gradation from (*a*) permanently established bodies following a procedure hardly, if at all, distinguishable from Main types of administrative jurisdiction.

that of a Court of law, through (*b*) tribunals following a more rough and ready procedure, yet one that is prescribed by regulations, and (*c*) persons or bodies appointed *ad hoc* to hold a particular inquiry, the procedure being quite informal, to (*d*) a Ministry or local authority following its ordinary administrative procedure in coming to a decision. Some of those included in (*a*), such as the recently created Transport Tribunal, are actually Courts. Others, such as the Disciplinary Committee of the Law Society (see *ante*, Book I, Part IV) and the Commissioners for the Special Purposes of the Income Tax (see *post*, p. 440) are not Courts in the strict sense of the term ; though these two bodies in particular and some others decide subject to an appeal to the ordinary Courts. Under (*b*) come the various tribunals employed in determining questions arising out of such enactments as the Pensions Appeal Tribunal Act, 1943, or the National Insurance Act, 1946. Under the latter Act, questions as to the right to benefit are decided in the first instance by an officer appointed by the Minister. Appeals lie from him to a local tribunal composed of an employers' representative, a representative of insured contributors and an independent chairman (usually a lawyer) appointed by the Minister, and from them to the National Insurance Commissioner or his deputy, who must be barristers of at least ten years' standing. Under (*c*) come the various public local inquiries which are required by statute before a Minister can exercise his discretion, *e.g.*, the purely administrative one whether or not to confirm, in face of objections, his order that a particular area shall be the site of a " new town."

" Objective " and " subjective " decisions.

From the point of view of function, a rough distinction may be made between persons or bodies entrusted merely with the finding of facts and, it may be, the application of the law to those facts, in other words, with the making of " objective " decisions (*ante*, p. 276), and persons or bodies who are entitled and expected to exercise their discretion in accordance with standards or policy of their own making, in other words, to come to " subjective " decisions (*ante*, p. 276). *To the first class* belong, for instance, various fact-finding tribunals of inquiry, *e.g.*, into local allegations of abuse of his office by a clerk to magistrates, or inadequate supervision of foster-parents by a Local Authority, or incompetence of the Fire Service in fighting a serious fire ; the Commissioners for the Special Purposes of the Income Tax ; and the officers and tribunals already mentioned in connection with the National Insurance Act. *To the second class* belong, for instance, Local Authorities concerned with the closing or demolition of unfit houses or with slum clearance (*post*, pp. 494 *et seq.*), for they have to apply their own standards of fitness. Most familiar examples of bodies exercising a discretion based almost purely on policy are now the various authorities concerned with Town and Country Planning. Commonly, perhaps generally, local authorities exercise their discretion subject to an appeal to the appropriate Minister, but very rarely is there an appeal to the ordinary Courts (see *e.g., post*, p. 478). It must be noted that even persons or bodies belonging to this second class may have to decide incidentally questions of fact or law.

We have already noticed (pp. 278 *et seq.*) that anyone whose decision, though it be called administrative, is made judicially or quasi-judicially must not only keep within his powers but also observe certain " requirements of natural justice." The technique by which the Courts control the activities of administrative authorities will be discussed later (pp. 573 *et seq.*). Here it must be noted that the general rule of English law is that all inferior Courts or other tribunals are subject to the control of the High Court, and where there is no provision to the contrary in the Act establishing an administrative tribunal, it is necessarily subject to this same judicial control as any inferior Court. But here also we find this same modern tendency at work which has withdrawn so many acts of subordinate legislation from the jurisdiction of the Courts, for it is sometimes provided that the decision of an administrative tribunal shall not be reviewed in any way whatever. The effect of such a provision seems to be that the ordinary Courts cannot even consider whether the tribunal has exceeded its powers or failed to observe the requirements of natural justice. There is, however, *in another direction*, a tendency to extend

[margin note:] Power of control by High Court.

[margin note:] Modern tendency to withdraw power of control from High Court.

Appeal on
points of
law.
the jurisdiction of the ordinary Courts. Although certain administrative tribunals, such as the Commissioners for the Special Purposes of the Income Tax, decide subject to appeal on points of law, the general rule is that no appeal lies from an inferior Court either on fact or law, unless specially given by statute, so that in principle administrative tribunals decide questions of law without appeal to the ordinary Courts. Of recent years, however, provision has occasionally been made, *e.g.*, by the Pensions Appeal Tribunal Act, 1943, and the National Insurance Act, 1946, for an appeal from an administrative tribunal *on a point of law* to a judge of the High Court.

Relation
between
subordinate
legislation
and adminis-
trative
jurisdiction.
It is customary to speak of subordinate legislation and administrative jurisdiction as two separate, though perhaps related, topics. But the separation is really fallacious. As has already been remarked (p. 277), administrative bodies exercise the discretions committed to them, not usually for the purpose of determining the rights and liabilities of parties, but for the purpose of creating or destroying such rights and liabilities. In so doing they are really making new law, that is to say, enacting a sort of private legislation. In relation to one particular kind of administrative activity, that of framing schemes in such matters as slum clearance or the supply of electricity, it is very evident that there is a blending of the quasi-judicial and the legislative. The scheme that ultimately appears is clearly an act of legislation, but the inquiry that precedes it has such obvious affinities with judicial proceedings that it was held in the leading case of *R.* v. *Electricity Commissioners* (see *post,* p. 577), to be subject to control by *prohibition,* which is not an appropriate order for restraining *legislative* functions. A parallel example of this blending of the judicial or quasi-judicial and the legislative is the Local or Personal Act of Parliament, which is legislation passed after a judicial form of procedure (see *post,* pp. 397 *et seq.*).

CHAPTER 9

THE SEPARATION OF POWERS AND THE RULE OF LAW

The development of subordinate legislation and administrative jurisdiction is in apparent conflict with two famous doctrines, known as " the separation of powers " and " the rule of law." The former doctrine has played a most important part in the history of modern Constitutions, and in the form in which it has become popular it dates from the celebrated French jurist Montesquieu, who acknowledged that it represented a generalisation from the facts of the English Constitution of the first half of the eighteenth century, as they appeared to him. *The doctrine of the separation of powers.*

The doctrine is best stated in his own words (*Esprit des Lois*, Book XI, Chap. VI) : *Montesquieu.*

> " When the legislative and executive powers are united in the same person, or in the same body . . ., there can be no liberty ; because apprehensions may arise, lest the same monarch or senate should enact tyrannical laws, to execute them in a tyrannical manner.
>
> Again, there is no liberty, if the judicial power be not separated from the legislative and executive. Were it joined with the legislative, the life and liberty of the subject would be exposed to arbitrary control ; for the judge would then be the legislator. Were it joined to the executive power, the judge might behave with violence and oppression.
>
> There would be an end of everything were the same man, or the same body, whether of the nobles or of the people, to exercise those three powers, that of enacting laws, that of executing the public resolutions, or that of trying the causes of individuals."

Now it is a truism that the full effect of gradual change is not easily appreciated in the generation in which it takes place, least of all by a foreign observer ; and Montesquieu was not able to predict the development of the monarchical executive of the preceding century into the parliamentary executive of later times. Nevertheless, he did qualify his doctrine to make it fit the facts of the English Constitution which he professed to observe.

333

Development
since
Montesquieu.

The doctrine has since suffered from the blind enthusiasm bestowed upon it by the followers of Montesquieu, who saw in it, not merely the broad view taken by a foreign observer of the English constitutional scene, but rather a fundamental precept of political faith. The doctrine had a decisive influence in the framing of the American Constitution, and a very considerable influence elsewhere, particularly in France. Perhaps no better example of this enthusiasm can be found than the following declaration by the framers of the Constitution of Massachusetts : " In the Government of this Commonwealth the legislative department shall never exercise the executive and judicial powers or either of them ; the executive shall never exercise the legislative and judicial powers or either of them ; the judicial shall never exercise the executive and legislative powers or either of them : to the end that it may be a government of laws and not of men."

Application
to England.

At no period, however, does the doctrine really fit the facts of English constitutional history. In our organs of government there has always been an overlapping of functions. Thus the House of Lords is both the Second Chamber of our Legislature and our final Court of Appeal : the Privy Council has extensive legislative power over, as well as judicial power in respect of appeals from, the Empire beyond the seas. This dual capacity of the House of Lords and of the Privy Council is, of course, only a legacy from the past, and it cannot be pressed in argument against the theory of separation ; nor, indeed, can the combination of all three governmental functions in the person of the Lord Chancellor, who is Speaker of the House of Lords, a member of the Cabinet, and the highest judicial officer.

Law making
by judges.

Theoretically more serious, though in practice not at all disturbing, is the fact that our judges now enjoy a large measure of law-making power that has been delegated to them by Parliament in matters of procedure and practice. This is in addition to the indirect power of legislation that is inherent in our system of case-law.

Administrative functions
of judges.

Further, the functions of the Courts are in many cases judicial in name but administrative in substance, *e.g.*, the guardianship of infants, the management of trust property, the supervision of bankruptcy and liquidation. Indeed, if we turn from the judges to the justices of the peace, we shall find in their combination of administrative and judicial functions an exception to the doctrine of separation that was of greater weight in the days of Montesquieu than it has since become ; for few of the *administrative* functions of the past now remain in the justices.

What has always been recognised as a true breach in the separation of powers is to be found in the relations between legislature and executive. So far from excluding all Ministers of the Crown from membership of the House of Commons—as our Constitution would have to do if it followed Montesquieu's doctrine in the strict, and politically inconvenient, fashion of the American Constitution— the rule with us is that no one shall cling to ministerial office without a seat in Parliament, either in the Commons or in the Lords. The rule guarantees—though as a matter of constitutional *convention* and not of *law*—that the executive shall be parliamentary. The result is a partnership in government and a balance of power between the partners ; in contrast with the deadlock that occurs from time to time in the United States, where a rigid system of separation discourages the liaison and mutual co-operation that would result from common membership of executive and legislature.

Relations between legislature and executive.

However, so long as Parliament reserved to itself the function of legislating, and to the ordinary Courts that of judging, it might reasonably be contended that the substance of the separation of powers still remained. But what if, unduly influenced by its partnership with the executive in a single system of party government, Parliament were to use its sovereign power to confer both legislative and judicial powers on the executive ? Surely there would then be a real infringement of the separation of powers, which might, if the process were carried far enough, disappear altogether. We have seen that subordinate legislation and administrative jurisdiction are now normal and important features of English government ; in times of emergency the former is all-important, and neither is likely to become insignificant even in times of profound peace.

Now it must be noted that both are regular features of government in the United States, where the separation of powers is taken much more seriously than here, and is indeed regarded as a fundamental principle of the Constitution. It has there been held that :

> " the Constitution has never been regarded as denying to Congress the necessary resources of flexibility and practicality, which will enable it to perform its function in laying down policies and establishing standards, while leaving to selected instruments the making of subordinate rules within prescribed limits and the determination of facts to which the policy as declared by the legislature is to apply."

But it has been held that Congress cannot delegate the power to lay down the broad outlines of legislative policy. In this, of course, it differs from Parliament, which has full power to do so. But has Parliament yet done so ? The answer must be that, except under the exceptional regimes established by the Defence of the Realm Act, the Emergency Powers (Defence) Acts, the Supplies and Services Acts, and apart from the permanent provisions of the Emergency Powers Act, 1920 (see *post*, p. 554), Parliament has almost invariably laid down policies in sufficiently narrow terms to acquit it of the
charge of over-delegation. It is true that our system of Cabinet Government places the initiative in legislation almost entirely in the hands of the executive, and the latter can usually insist on having its proposals passed into law ; and so it might appear that there is little to differentiate parliamentary from subordinate legislation. But this is not so, for any controversial Bill is likely to be thrown into the forefront of party politics, and so must run the gauntlet of full and public criticism. It is, therefore, proper that the main outlines of policy should be laid down by Acts of Parliament. On the other hand, it must always be remembered that, even when legislative power is delegated to a Minister of the Crown, it is delegated, not to an independent body, as the President is independent of Congress, but to one whose acts are open to constant criticism in the House of Commons. Moreover, the practice of subordinate legislation by no means precludes consultation or even discussion ; though the audience is narrower than Parliament.

There would seem to be fair ground for the Lord Chancellor's recent commendation to Parliament of the ways of modern Whitehall : " We go to the trade or interest concerned and deal with it by getting them round the table, hearing what they have to say, and then drafting the rules after obtaining their views." Indeed much of the criticism to which subordinate legislation is constantly subjected comes from those who, on political or economic grounds, dislike the intensity of modern legislation and the " controls " which it is used to enforce.

The problem of administrative jurisdiction is undoubtedly more difficult. It is at this point that " the rule of law " becomes important. For it is clear that the doctrine of the separation of powers is designed to secure the citizen against any interference with his rights otherwise than by law. Granted that there is nothing to prevent a conspiracy between legislature, executive and judiciary to treat him unjustly ; yet so long as the three powers remain true to their several characters, it is probable that the legislature will try to lay down general principles of action upon a basis of reason, and that the Courts will protect the citizen against any interference by the executive except in accordance with those principles. Any other action on the part of the executive will be " arbitrary " in the true sense of that word, namely, not in accordance with principle. Now the great constitutional lawyer Dicey, writing in 1885, was so deeply impressed by the absence of arbitrary government in England, in contrast to several other governments present and past, that he coined the phrase " the rule of law " to express the regime under which Englishmen lived ; and he tried to give precision to it in the following words, which have exercised a profound influence on all subsequent thought and conduct :

The " rule of law."

> " That ' rule of law,' which forms a fundamental principle of the Constitution, has three meanings, or may be regarded from three different points of view.
>
> It means, in the first place, the absolute supremacy or predominance of regular law as opposed to the influence of arbitrary power, and excludes the existence of arbitrariness, . . . or even of wide discretionary authority on the part of the Government. Englishmen are ruled by the law, and by

Dicey's enunciation.

the law alone ; a man may, with us, be punished for breach of the law, but he can be punished for nothing else.

It means, again, equality before the law, or the equal subjection of all classes to the ordinary law of the land administered by the ordinary Courts ; the ' rule of law ' in this sense excludes the idea of any exemption of officials or others from the duty of obedience to the law which governs other citizens or from the jurisdiction of the ordinary tribunals. . . .

The ' rule of law,' lastly, may be used as a formula for expressing the fact that with us the law of the Constitution, the rules which in foreign countries naturally form part of the constitutional code, are not the sources, but the consequence of the rights of individuals, as defined and enforced by the Courts ; that, in short, the principles of private law have, with us, been by the action of the Courts and Parliament so extended as to determine the position of the Crown and of its servants ; thus the Constitution is the result of the ordinary law of the land.''

Dicey's
first pro-
position.

Dicey's third proposition, which is not very important, is criticised elsewhere in this book (see *post*, pp. 550–1) ; but his first two propositions contain aspirations which have been and still are common to most Englishmen. It is, however, difficult to say how far they represent the present state of affairs.

So far as personal rights such as personal liberty, freedom of speech and freedom of conscience are concerned, Dicey's first proposition is substantially true. This is not merely in the sense that anyone can seek the protection of the Courts against interference by the executive, but in the further sense that the law relating to them is hardly ever modified by subordinate legislation, and but little by Parliament itself. It is true that the famous Regulation 18B, made under the Emergency Powers (Defence) Act, 1939, empowered the Home Secretary to intern certain suspected persons, and that in *Liversidge* v. *Anderson*, [1942] A. C. 206, the House of Lords held that in so doing he was free from judicial control ; but it is also noteworthy that the Regulation was revoked as soon as hostilities in Europe were over. Nor need we attach much importance to the fact that disputes concerning such topics as unemployment benefit or workmen's compensation are decided by administrative tribunals outside the control of the ordinary Courts, for those tribunals follow a procedure which, though

simplified, is judicial in character, and act in a truly
judicial spirit. But the application of Dicey's proposition Difficulty of
application in
cases of
property and
business.
to rights of property, or freedom to do business according
to one's own ideas, gives rise to serious difficulties. For, as
will be explained in greater detail later (see pp. 539 *et seq.*),
administrative authorities now have very wide powers to
take property compulsorily, and many hitherto privately
run services have been or are about to be nationalised.
No doubt compensation is always paid, but great difficulty
is often encountered in finding a basis of assessment which
does not appear arbitrary to the person whose property
is being taken, without being unduly generous to him.
Moreover, many administrative acts relating to property
involve the exercise of a discretion ; and the granting of
licences, always necessary for the conduct of certain
kinds of business and of immense importance in times of
stringency, is always a matter of discretion.

To say that all this is done by virtue of Acts of Parliament, and therefore by the law, is merely to effect a
formal reconciliation with the rule of law, which Dicey
would certainly not have accepted. For, on these terms,
there is nothing, apart from the democratic character of
Parliament, to differentiate it from the acts of a dictator
such as Mussolini or Hitler, whose power likewise had a
legal foundation ; and clearly we are not speaking of
democracy here. If the regularity and impartiality of
administrative jurisdiction and its freedom from caprice
are emphasised, we are nearer the mark, for these are some
of the essential characteristics of law. The regular
administrative tribunals, such as the Commissioners for
the Special Purposes of the Income Tax and those which
decide questions relating to insurance benefit, certainly
possess those qualities. It is, moreover, the habit of
Government Departments to base their policy and
exercise their discretion upon well-considered principles
and to follow their own precedents almost as consistently
as Courts of law. Indeed, apart altogether from their
own traditions and the obvious convenience of the
practice, they recognise that any unreasonable variations
of policy or apparent injustices will give rise to criticism
in the House of Commons, from which any good civil

servant will try to guard his Minister.   There is, therefore,
much to be said for the view—though many of Dicey's
followers would not agree—that even the discretionary
aspect of government conforms to the rule of law, in the
sense that it is infused with the spirit of justice.   For, so
long as there are genuine differences of opinion as to the
policy to be followed where the claims of private property
and enterprise and of state planning are in conflict,
justice cannot dictate the actual lines of policy.   The
Courts recognise this when they refuse to review upon the
merits the decisions of administrative bodies.   But they
show a clear understanding of the ordinary Englishman's
point of view when they insist on conformity to what they
call the " requirements of natural justice " (see *ante,*
pp. 279–281) ; and it would seem that the chief objection to
much of our administrative jurisdiction is that it does not
always provide sufficiently obvious guarantees against
bias, or failure to give full consideration to opposing points
of view, or the use of powers for purposes not intended by
Parliament.   Above all, administrative authorities are
often less willing than they might be to " show their
hand," to give sufficiently full reasons for their decisions
where they affect the person or property of the subject.
Doubtless they are usually just ; it may well be that they
are sometimes juster than they appear to be ; but the
ordinary Englishman expects justice " not only to be done
but to be seen to be done."

Dicey's
second pro-
position.
As will be seen later (p. 342), there are certain exceptions to the operation of Dicey's second proposition,
but for the most part it stands.   Certainly all administrative authorities and officials work under the eye of the
ordinary Courts, and always have in mind the possibility
that they may be made responsible for anything they do
beyond their powers.   But what Dicey more particularly
had in mind was the absence in England of any true
distinction between public and private law ; and this
requires closer examination.

Distinction
abroad
between
public and
private law.
Most countries which have not derived their law from
England, that is to say, most countries outside the British
Empire and the United States, make a fundamental distinction between public and private law, between the law

relating to government and the law governing the relations
between private persons, whether individuals or corporations ; and they usually commit the decision of disputes
arising out of government to a special system of Courts,
separate from the ordinary Courts and more closely connected with the executive. It is felt that problems of
government are so essentially different from those of
private and commercial intercourse that the law relating
to them should breathe a different atmosphere, and that
specialist judges are required to deal with them. In
particular, there is a feeling that that equality before the
law, which is the ideal to be aimed at, though not always
the reality, in the relations between private persons, is
wholly out of place in public law, where it is to be expected, and even desired, that public authorities should
exercise authority over the private citizen, who is bound to
obey unless he can show that authority is being exercised
over him contrary to law.

Now in England also public authorities enjoy certain
powers, often of a wide nature, which private persons do
not ; but Englishmen, and English lawyers in particular,
have never since the middle of the seventeenth century
seen any reason to segregate public authorities from
private persons, or, what they suspect to be a better way
of stating the matter, an individual when he is acting
on behalf of a public authority from an individual acting
in his own interest. Each may in certain circumstances
exercise authority over other persons, but there is no
essential difference between such authority exercised in
public matters and authority exercised in private matters
in virtue of, say, parental status or the contract of master
and servant. The actual wielders of power are in principle
equal, and their equality is only disturbed for certain
purposes laid down by law ; and we do not detect any
differences between the problems of public and private life
fundamental enough to necessitate the establishment of
different systems of Courts. Moreover, there is a subtle
but unmistakable difference between obedience which
Englishmen and that which most continental Europeans
accord to those in authority. The latter tend to obey
the official himself, though in countries with a liberal

(margin note:) Distinction between public and private law not recognised in England.

Constitution he is allowed to command only within limits set by law; whereas Englishmen think of themselves as obeying the law, which the official merely sets in action, and they instinctively resent having to obey if they think the law unjust or unreasonable. There is much history behind this difference; for in England the exercise of discretionary powers over persons and property has come late, after a long period during which the rule of law, in Dicey's sense, was almost complete, whereas on the Continent the rule of law, to the extent that it exists, has followed a long period of absolute monarchy. The doctrine of state necessity, which was finally outlawed in England in 1765 (see p. 310), was formerly a commonplace on the Continent, and was easily revived by the recent dictatorships.

Only in two respects do we accord special treatment to public authorities as such : (1) legal proceedings must be brought against them within a much shorter period (*one* year after the cause of action accrued) than against other persons, and a person who sues them unsuccessfully is mulcted more heavily in costs (*post*, pp. 581–2) ; and (2) by-laws made by public authorities are less likely to be treated as unreasonable by the Courts than those made by public utility undertakings (*ante*, p. 325).

Crown proceedings. The popular instinct towards equality before the law has recently been shown by the enacting of legislation to assimilate proceedings against the Crown to proceedings against ordinary persons ; and although a few reservations have had to be made in the public interest, the result has been to reduce even the Crown itself to a fundamental equality with the subject. From now on, the only serious breach in equality before the law will be in the interest, not of public authorities, but of trade unions, which cannot be sued at all *in tort*. There are, too, a few instances where a public officer may successfully plead that he overstepped his powers not unreasonably and in good faith.

This failure to differentiate between public and private law is undoubtedly connected with our reference of all justiciable disputes to the same set of Courts, which have a strong bias in favour of equality ; and there is some danger that, if it becomes an established practice to exclude their supervisory jurisdiction over administrative tribunals, the latter may habitually prefer the claims of the public to those of private persons and so work in an entirely different atmosphere. But the more recent development of *Droit administratif* in France seems to show that this is by no means inevitable, for there the separate administrative Courts have become a bulwark of individual liberty against the Government, and have frequently anticipated the ordinary civil Courts in the provision of new remedies for wrongs. Indeed, it may be doubted whether much difference now survives there between the spirit of public law and that of private law. *Recent comparison with France.*

It cannot be too strongly emphasised that no institutions will give just or good results unless those who work them have the necessary ability and sense of justice. Although the Constitution of Massachusetts (quoted at p. 334 above) suggests that a strict application of the separation of powers will produce a government of laws and not of men, all governments are, as President Wilson once said, governments of men. Good institutions are a useful safeguard against injustice, and they tend to educate men in the habit of justice; but they cannot ensure good or just government. *Conclusion.*

BOOK II
CONSTITUTIONAL AND ADMINISTRATIVE LAW

PART II
PARLIAMENT

SUMMARY

		PAGE
CHAPTER 10.	THE CONSTITUENT PARTS OF PARLIAMENT	347
CHAPTER 11.	DISQUALIFICATIONS FOR MEMBERSHIP OF PARLIAMENT	354
CHAPTER 12.	THE ELECTION OF MEMBERS OF THE HOUSE OF COMMONS	359
CHAPTER 13.	THE ASSEMBLING, ADJOURNMENT, PROROGATION AND DISSOLUTION OF PARLIAMENT	372
CHAPTER 14.	THE POWERS OF THE CONSTITUENT PARTS OF PARLIAMENT	375
CHAPTER 15.	THE PROCEDURE OF PARLIAMENT	389

THE CONSTITUENT PARTS OF PARLIAMENT

SUMMARY   PAGE

Section I. The Title to the Crown 347
Section II. The House of Lords 350
Section III. The House of Commons 352

Section I. THE TITLE TO THE CROWN

" The grand fundamental maxim," says Blackstone, " upon which the *jus coronæ*, or right of succession to the throne of these kingdoms, depends, I take to be this : ' that the crown is, by common law and constitutional custom, hereditary ; and this in a manner peculiar to itself : but that the right of inheritance may from time to time be changed or limited by act of parliament ; under which limitations the crown still continues hereditary.' "

Blackstone on the Title to the Crown.

Let us take these points in order.

1. The Crown is hereditary, and not elective. It descends to the next heir on the demise of each sovereign. The significance of the word " demise " is explained elsewhere (see *ante*, p. 302).

2. The rules of descent are, with very few exceptions, the same as those which, *before the property legislation of 1925*, regulated the descent of freehold estates. As Blackstone says :

" Like estates, the crown will descend lineally to the issue of the reigning monarch. . . . As in common descents, the preference of males to females, and the right of primogeniture among the males, are strictly adhered to. . . . Like lands or tenements, the crown, on failure of the male line, descends to the issue female. . . . But, among the females, the crown descends by right of primogeniture to the eldest daughter only and her issue ; and not, as in common inheritances, to all the daughters at once ; the evident necessity of a *sole* succession to the throne having occasioned the royal law of descents to depart from the common law in this respect. . . . Again, the doctrine of representation prevails in the descent of the crown, as it does in other inheritances ; whereby the lineal descendants of any person deceased stand in the same place as their ancestor, if living, would have

347

done. . . . . Lastly, on failure of lineal descendants, the crown goes to the next collateral relations of the late king ; provided they are lineally descended from the blood royal, that is, from that royal stock which originally acquired the crown. . . . But herein there is no objection (as in the case of common descents) to the succession of a brother, an uncle, or other collateral relation, of the *half* blood ; that is, where the relationship proceeds not from the same *couple* of ancestors (which constitutes a kinsman of the *whole* blood) but from a *single* ancestor only ; as when two persons are derived from the same father, and not from the same mother, or *vice versa* : provided only, that the one ancestor, from whom both are descended, be that from whose veins the blood royal is communicated to each. . . ."

It is interesting to notice that Blackstone raised no doubt as to the succession of an eldest daughter to the exclusion of younger daughters. He would have agreed that the Princess Elizabeth is now the *sole* heir presumptive to the Throne.

3. But these feudal rules may at any time be changed by Parliament. As Blackstone says :

" . . . . It is unquestionably in the breast of the supreme legislative authority of this kingdom, the king and both houses of parliament, to defeat this hereditary right ; and . . . to exclude the immediate heir, and vest the inheritance in any one else."

We shall notice elsewhere in this chapter that the succession was changed by statute as recently as 1936.

4. But, although Parliament has often intervened to change the succession to the Crown, it has never abolished its *hereditary* character ; so that, subject to the restrictions imposed by statute, the Crown remains hereditary. Yet there is nothing (apart from the need for the assent of the Dominions that is recited in the preamble to the Statute of Westminster, 1931) to prevent Parliament, if it so desired, from substituting an elective kingship for our present system. But to do so in defiance of the wishes of the Dominions would, even before 1931, have been a gross breach of constitutional convention ; and some think it would now be a breach of the law itself The preamble to the Statute of Westminster, 1931, recites that :

Statute of Westminster, 1931.

" . . . it would be in accord with the established constitutional position . . . that any alteration in the law touching the Succession to the Throne or the Royal Style and Titles should hereafter require the assent as well of the Parliaments of all the Dominions as of the Parliament of the United Kingdom."

(See *post*, p. 598.)

The fact that the agreement of four of the Dominions was secured before the passing of the Abdication Act of 1936 is recited in a preamble to that Act (see *post*, p. 599).

THE TITLE TO THE CROWN. The present title to the Crown is derived from the Act of Settlement of 1700, which provides that :

<small>Derivation of present title.</small>

" the Crown and Regal Government . . . shall be, remain and continue to the said most Excellent Princess Sophia [the then Electress and Duchess Dowager of Hanover, who was grand-daughter to James I] and the Heirs of her Body being Protestants."

This provision has received qualification from His Majesty's Declaration of Abdication Act, 1936, which, after enacting that " His Majesty shall cease to be King and there shall be a demise of the Crown," excludes from the Throne any issue and descendants of King Edward VIII (now the Duke of Windsor).

It is by this statutory title of 1700 and 1936, and as Protestant heir of the Electress Sophia, that His present Majesty is King.

The Act of Settlement further confirmed the provisions enacted in 1689 in the Bill of Rights, that is to say :

<small>The Protestant Succession.</small>

" That all and every person and persons that is are or shall be reconciled to or shall hold Communion with the See or Church of Rome or shall professe the Popish Religion or shall marry a Papist shall be excluded and be forever uncapable to inherit possesse or enjoy the Crowne and Government of this Realme. . . . And the said Crowne and Government shall from time to time descend to and be enjoyed by such Person or Persons being Protestants as should have inherited and enjoyed the same in case the said person or persons soe reconciled holding Communion or Professing or Marrying as aforesaid were naturally dead."

By the same Acts a further safeguard against the Crown falling into the hands of a Roman Catholic was provided by the Declaration against Transubstantiation, which the King was bound to make on his accession. But, in view of the offence given by the antiquated terms of the

declaration to the many and loyal Roman Catholic subjects of the Crown, it was abolished by the Accession
Declaration Act, 1910, and replaced by a simple declaration by the King that he is a faithful Protestant, and
that he will uphold and maintain the enactments which
secure the Protestant succession to the throne.

Regency
Act, 1937.

The succession to the throne is not itself affected by the
Regency Act, 1937, but the royal functions are to be entrusted to a Regent if (1) the King is under the age of
eighteen at his accession, or (2) " by reason of infirmity
of mind or body " he is incapable of performing the royal
functions, or (3) for some definite cause he is " not available for the performance of those functions." The Regent
is to be—with some qualification—that person who is
next in line of succession to the Crown. The Act also

Counsellors
of State.

provides—following to some extent the precedents set
during the later years of King George V—that if the King
is suffering from illness that is not serious enough to warrant a Regency, or in a case of his absence from the
United Kingdom, he may appoint Counsellors of State to
discharge *most* of the royal functions ; but *some* of those
functions he may *not* so delegate. Thus, during the visit
to South Africa in 1947 of the King with the Queen and
both Princesses, the Counsellors of State were His
Majesty's brother (the Duke of Gloucester), his sister
(the Princess Royal), and his nephew (now Earl of Hare-
wood). They were next to Princess Margaret in the line of
succession—excluding all royal children not then of full
age—and their appointment was governed by the principal
Act of 1937, after the correction of some unforeseen faults
by the Regency Act, 1943.

Royal
marriages.

Certain restrictions are placed by the Royal Marriages
Act, 1772, upon the right of any descendant of George II
to contract a marriage, and the Act therefore established
some sort of control over the future succession to the
Crown.

Section II. THE HOUSE OF LORDS

The House of Lords is composed of persons called Lords
of Parliament, being either Lords Spiritual or Lords
Temporal. In theory, the King may sit with the Lords

in the House of Lords; but, except on ceremonial occasions, such as the opening and dissolution of Parliament, he has not been present personally during the business of the House for centuries.

The Lords Spiritual consist of the Archbishops of Canterbury and York, the Bishops of London, Durham, and Winchester, and the twenty-one seniors *in office* among the other English bishops. The Lords Spiritual and the Lords Temporal are *in theory* two distinct " estates of the realm," and are generally described as such; but *in practice* both estates are blended together under the one name of " the Lords." They vote together; and the majority of votes bind both estates. _{Lords Spiritual.}

The Lords Temporal consist : first, of all the peers of the United Kingdom, whether they be dukes, marquesses, earls, viscounts, or barons; second, of a certain number of Scottish and Irish peers who sit in a representative capacity; and third, of the Lords of Appeal in Ordinary, who are Lords of Parliament during their lives only, and, like the bishops, are not technically " peers," as their rank is not hereditary. _{Lords Temporal.}

The representative peers are those who, under the Acts of Union with Scotland and Ireland, are elected to represent the Scottish and Irish nobility—the Scottish representative peers being sixteen in number, elected for one parliament only, and the Irish twenty-eight, elected for life. With regard to the latter, it may be better to say " were elected " instead of " are elected "; for, in the legislation of 1922 relating to Ireland, there is no reference to the position of the Irish representative peers; and there seems to be no longer any authority or procedure to fill vacancies as they arise through death or resignation. _{Representative Peers.}

The aggregate number of the Lords Temporal for the time being is indefinite, and may be increased at will by the power of the Crown. But it was decided, perhaps unfortunately, in the *Wensleydale Peerage Case* (1856), 5 H. L. Cas. 958, that the power of the Crown does not extend to the creation of *life* members of the House of Lords; except under the provisions of an Act of Parliament specifically authorising such creation. It is in virtue of such a Statute, namely, the Appellate Juris- _{Life Peerages.}

diction Act, 1876 (as amended by subsequent legislation), that the Lords of Appeal in Ordinary sit in the House of Lords.

Section III. THE HOUSE OF COMMONS

The House of Commons consists of the representatives of the nation at large, exclusive of the peerage and the prelates. A member of Parliament is a representative, not a delegate. As Blackstone says :

Representatives, not delegates.

" Every member, though chosen by one particular district, when elected and returned, serves for the whole realm."

This was emphasised by Burke when he said :

" You choose a member indeed, but when you have chosen him, he is not Member for Bristol, but he is Member of Parliament."

It is his duty as a member of Parliament, in which capacity there are confided to his care the interests of the whole community as opposed to those of any sect or locality, to cast his vote in the House in favour of the proposal which he considers right and most conducive to the welfare of the nation as a whole. This principle of legislative independence, though perhaps still of full effect in theory, has without doubt been weakened in practice by the Trade Union Act, 1913, as restored by the Trade Disputes and Trade Unions Act, 1946, under which trade unions exercise their power to levy a political fund, which may be used for the purpose of paying members of Parliament. But there is nothing even in this legislation to destroy Lord Shaw's well-known argument in the celebrated case of *Amalgamated Society of Railway Servants* v. *Osborne*, [1910] A. C. 87, namely, that any undertaking by a member of Parliament to vote in obedience to the instructions of those who pay him would be void in law on the ground of public policy. But this argument would seem to go too far if, as its critics protest, it condemns even an honourable undertaking that is in effect no more than a reaffirmation of allegiance to the member's own party organisation.

Principle of legislative independence.

Members' salaries.

It should be noted that ordinary members of the House of Commons are now entitled to a salary of £1,000 a year (less income tax), irrespective of their attendance during the session. They have also certain limited rights, recently extended somewhat, to free travel ; but secretarial expenses and postage (except to Government Departments) have to be paid for by the members themselves.

The salaries of Ministers, which are now mostly fixed by the Ministers of the Crown Act, 1937, hardly concern us here, but under that Act the Leader of the Opposition —and the Speaker is to certify who *is* the Leader of the Opposition—receives a salary in addition to his salary as an ordinary member. Recent legislation goes further, and Junior Ministers, whose ministerial salary is less than £5,000 a year, are now entitled to a part of their salary as members of the House of Commons ; and a former Prime Minister is similarly entitled in spite of his statutory pension (see the Ministerial Salaries Act, 1946).

CHAPTER II

DISQUALIFICATIONS FOR MEMBERSHIP OF PARLIAMENT

There are certain disqualifications which render a person unable to sit as a member of either House of Parliament. But most of them concern only the House of Commons. We can do little more than give the chief headings, under some of which the law is " archaic, confused, and unsatisfactory," as a Select Committee reported in 1941.

1. *Infancy.* No infant can sit in either House.

2. *Conviction* on a charge of treason or felony disqualifies for either House, provided the sentence awarded exceeds twelve months' imprisonment. Upon a pardon or the completion of the punishment, the disqualification is removed. There is no disqualification in a case of misdemeanour, but the convicted member may be expelled from the House.

3. *Alienage.* No alien can sit in either House.

4. *Bankruptcy.* A bankrupt is disqualified from acting as a member of either House. If the adjudication is annulled, or if the bankrupt obtains his discharge with a certificate that the bankruptcy was caused by misfortune without misconduct on his part, the disqualification at once ceases. But if neither of those contingencies occurs within six months, his seat becomes vacant ; and if he is afterwards discharged without such a certificate, the disqualification lasts for five years from the date of the discharge.

5. *Peerage.* With the exception of those Irish peers who are not representatives of the Irish peerage in the House of Lords, no peer may be elected to the House of Commons. But the eldest sons of peers, if they hold no peerage but only a " courtesy title," are allowed to seek election ; as are also the wives of peers and, it would seem, peeresses in their own right.

Disqualifications.

354

6. *Election offences.* Under enactments dating back to the last century and now consolidated by the Representation of the People Act, 1949, there are severe disqualifications upon candidates for the House of Commons and their agents and supporters who are either indicted and convicted of certain " corrupt practices " or condemned for such offences in the report of an election court (*post.* pp. 368–371). Though these statutory disqualifications have recently become less severe than hitherto, even so they will enable such offenders to be disqualified for ten years from serving for the constituency in question, and for five years from serving for any *other* constituency. Similar but less drastic results follow in cases of " illegal," as distinct from corrupt, practices.

7. *Office.*

    (a) Some disabilities are ecclesiastical. Thus clergy of the Established Church of England, ministers of the Established Church of Scotland, and clergy of the Roman Catholic Church are disabled from sitting in the House of Commons. But these are the only ecclesiastical disabilities which have survived, and consequently all Nonconformist ministers and also clergy of the Disestablished Church in Wales may now sit. *Ecclesiastical.*

    (b) Some disabilities are judicial. It may be stated with reasonable accuracy that all paid judges of superior and inferior courts are disqualified from sitting in the House of Commons. But Recorders, being only part-time judges, are able to sit for any constituency other than the borough for which they are appointed. Coroners seem not to be disqualified. Nor are the unpaid Justices of the Peace as such under disability. But many officials whose duties are connected with the administration of justice, or with local government, are excluded from the House of Commons. *Judicial.*

    (c) Holders of royal pensions, either during pleasure or for a term of years, are similarly disqualified. This disability does not attach to the holding of Civil Service or diplomatic pensions. *Royal pensions.*

Government
contractors.

(*d*) Persons concerned in contracts with the Government or on account of the public service are likewise disqualified by legislation of George III ; but whatever the scope of these old Statutes in all their surviving vagueness may be, they do not at any rate disqualify those who merely subscribe to Government loans (the House of Commons Disqualification (Declaration of Law) Act, 1931).

Civil Servants.

(*e*) Of outstanding importance is the disability of the great mass of the " permanent " officials of the Civil Service. If they happen to be peers, they may attend debates in the House of Lords provided they refrain from speaking or voting. But, before becoming even candidates for election to the House of Commons, they must have ended their careers as civil servants. This disability, however, does not affect the " Ministerial " heads of the more important Government Departments or those of their subordinates who share their " political " character, recent Statutes having removed the necessity for re-election to which they were formerly subject on accepting an office of profit under the Crown. Upon the rules disabling civil servants (the easing of which seems probable) there rests one of the distinguishing characteristics of modern English government, namely, the co-operation between each transient Ministerial head of a Department, who is a prominent party leader charged with the determination of policy and as such responsible to the House of Commons, and the permanent Civil Service, which exists to furnish technical advice to, and carry out the lawful orders of, successive party Governments.

It should be observed that, though the general rule is that the holding of a *political* office, paid or unpaid, in the Government no longer constitutes a disability or even the need for re-election, there are complicated statutory provisions limiting the number of Ministers who may at one and the same time sit in the House of Commons. These provisions are intended to secure an adequate Government representation in the House of Lords. They have been somewhat simplified by the Ministers of the Crown Act, 1937, and various statutory amendments to it, but the whole complex subject of disqualification by the holding of office under the Crown should receive reforming and consolidating legislation that is long overdue, as a Select Committee recommended in 1941. The shadows of the seventeenth and eighteenth centuries linger upon the surviving law, too much of which defies the precept *cessante ratione legis cessat lex*. The complicated and obscure state of the law is too often made manifest in the need for Acts of Indemnity to spare unwitting offenders who would otherwise suffer crushing penalties. Such need has extended from certain past Presidents of the Board of Trade to those back-bench members of the present House who endangered themselves by membership of a rent control tribunal.

(*f*) Though, in the case of serving members of the regular armed forces, the question of legal disability is far from straightforward, the practice of the House of Commons in recent years would seem to exclude only those on the active list or those on active service in peace time. There was, of course, appropriate relaxation during and after the recent war. *The forces.*

(*g*) Salaried membership of the many modern administrative bodies, though they are not emanations from the Crown, is usually made a disqualification by the creating Statute, *e.g.*, membership of the National and Regional Coal Boards, the British Electricity Authority and its Area Boards, the Gas Council and its Area Boards, or the Transport and the Boundary Commissions; to take but a few examples at random. *New statutory authorities.*

8. *Sex.* Until 1918 no woman could sit in either House of Parliament. Now, as a result of legislation first passed in that year, membership of the House of Commons is open equally to both sexes ; but (unless reform unexpectedly follows a recent resolution of the House of Lords) a peeress in her own right (commonly called a woman peer) is still not entitled to sit in that House ; it seems she may be elected to the House of Commons in spite of her peerage, though it is not certain whether she would be permitted to sit.

Cessation of membership. A peer remains a peer until his death ; but membership of the House of Commons is determined, not only by death, but upon the dissolution of Parliament (*post,* p. 373), or by disqualification in any one of the ways mentioned above. Straightforward resignation of a seat is impossible, and it is therefore customary for a member who wishes to resign to apply for the post of Steward of the Chiltern Hundreds or of the Manors of Northstead, East Hendred, or Hempholme, *i.e.* sinecure offices of nominal value under the Crown, which are expressly excepted from the purview of the Statutes enabling Ministers of the Crown to sit in the House without re-election, and the acceptance of which accordingly vacates the seat.

CHAPTER 12

THE ELECTION OF MEMBERS OF THE HOUSE OF COMMONS

SUMMARY   PAGE

Section I. *The Parliamentary Franchise*   359
Section II. *The Process of Election*   366

Section I. THE PARLIAMENTARY FRANCHISE

The legal qualification of a Parliamentary elector is now both simple and democratic. It betokens adult citizenship. No longer is there discrimination on the ground of status or wealth or sex. Any person will be entitled to be registered as a voter provided that he or she is of full age and is not subject to any legal incapacity—is not, for instance, an alien or a peer or a lunatic or a felon—or in any other way disqualified from voting. *Legal qualification of electors.*

But electoral rights, though simple and democratic, would lack the substance of true political democracy if representation in Parliament were not fairly and evenly shared out among the electorate. So, in dividing the whole country into constituencies, the modern purpose has been to ensure that each representative shall sit in Parliament for more or less the same number of electors. Hitherto this purpose has not been achieved without capricious anomalies and serious inequalities, the root of the trouble being that constituencies kept their rigid shape while the density of population within them was ever changing. As a remedy for this rigidity, there have now been set up four Boundary Commissions—one each for England, Wales, Scotland, and Northern Ireland—who shall keep periodic watch and initiate change (House of Commons (Redistribution of Seats) Act, 1949). *Constituencies.*

In every constituency is kept a register of those entitled to vote. Any one whose name is on it may vote; but (except for those who come of age between one register and the next) no one whose name is not there may vote, *Register conclusive.*

359

no matter whether he is qualified to be registered or not. The register is conclusive on the matter. But if the voter ought not to have been registered, his vote will be disallowed on a scrutiny or petition, and he will be liable to any penalty for voting.

Annual compilation. The register, after two decades of economy, was again to have become a twice-yearly affair, compiled as a " spring register " for use at elections held between March and October and as an " autumn register " for use at elections held between October and March. But this change from an annual compilation, though among the many recent reforms enacted first by the amending Representation of the People Act, 1948, and then re-enacted by the consolidating Representation of the People Act, 1949, has been unexpectedly frustrated by an " economy " enactment of 1949 that returns the register to an annual basis and suppresses the intended "autumn" register (Electoral Registers Act, 1949).

Responsibility for the Register of Electors. The official responsible for the preparation of the register is the " registration officer," who is the clerk to the local county or borough or urban district council, as the case may be ; and, as the duties of the "returning officer " (*post*, p. 367) will also normally fall upon him, it will be seen that his responsibility is considerable.

Legislation from 1918. THE REPRESENTATION OF THE PEOPLE ACTS. In the thirty years since the Representation of the People Act, 1918, which was the principal Act until largely replaced by the Act of 1948, there has been a long procession of amending provisions, many of them only temporary enactments of the war and post-war years. Of those whose force is spent, some were cancelled in a process of trial and error, while others met only some transient need, *e.g.*, for a " supplementary register " in 1946. On the other hand, many of these earlier amendments survived as provisions of the Act of 1948, which not only implemented practically all the procedural recommendations of the post-war Committee on Electoral Registration, *e.g.*, for a revival of the pre-war system of compiling the register, and for the permanent abolition of any qualifying period of residence, but also introduced some drastic

changes of an acutely controversial sort, *e.g.*, the sweeping
away of the " one man one vote " principle of both the
University and the Business Premises franchise. Moreover, the legislation relating to corrupt and illegal
practices received many detailed amendments, the
most interesting being the reduction in the periods of
incapacity and the extension of summary jurisdiction to
cover corrupt as well as illegal practices. The amended
Act of 1948 has been followed by consolidation in the
Representation of the People Act, 1949, which we shall
hereafter speak of as the new or recent Act.

Residence qualification. Hitherto, in order to be
registered as resident in a constituency, a person had
roughly speaking to live in or near the constituency during
a short qualifying period of residence After being made
shorter and shorter by successive enactments, this
qualifying period has now vanished altogether The wartime experiment of doing without it has been made
permanent by the recent Act, and residence in the
constituency on a prescribed date, called " the qualifying
date," now suffices for registration there without any need
for residence during the previous so many weeks or
months. The qualifying date in England and Wales is
the 20th November (Electoral Registers Act, 1949).

Residence qualification.

Evidence of residence for the compilation of the electoral
register would be most simply and surely obtainable, so
one would imagine, by the wartime expedient of relying on
the National Registration machinery and treating the
address on a person's identity card on the qualifying date
as proof that he was or was not then resident in the constituency. But this expedient is apparently too unreliable
to deserve preservation, and the new Act implements the
Electoral Registration Committee's recommendation for
a return to the older and surer practice of compiling
electoral registers only from information specially collected for the purpose, *e.g.*, by house-to-house canvas
or the distribution of forms on which householders must
reveal those who will be living with them on the qualifying date.

Service qualification. We should think of this innovation, not as a really distinct qualification conferring a

" Service voters."

second vote on minorities like the two now defunct qualifications mentioned hereafter, but only as a modified version of the residence qualification that seeks to prevent " one man one vote " from degenerating into " one man no vote " in the case of that substantial minority of adult citizens who would otherwise find their names nowhere upon electoral rolls because in the service of the Crown they are " here to-day and gone to-morrow " or " over the seas and far away." Wider and better electoral facilities have been enacted for such citizens in recent years, and the culmination is the *service qualification*, which any of the following shall have—

(a) any one serving on full pay in the regular armed forces of the Crown raised in the United Kingdom ;

(b) any one employed in the service of the Crown in a prescribed kind of post outside the United Kingdom ;

(c) the wife of any one having a service qualification and residing with her husband outside the United Kingdom.

But though such persons " shall have " this qualification by virtue of their service, they will find themselves unable to vote on the strength of it unless they have seen fit beforehand to make a " service declaration," which states *inter alia* " that on the date of the declaration the declarant was, or but for the circumstances entitling him to make the declaration would have been, residing at an address specified in the declaration." The probability that the majority of them will *not* see fit to do so is recognised, maybe with dry humour, in the statutory command to such bodies as the War Office to arrange, though only so far as circumstances permit, that every person having a service qualification by virtue of his (or her) service shall not only have an effective opportunity of exercising from time to time as occasion may require the electoral rights conferred upon him by the recent Act but also receive such instructions as to the effect of this Act and any regulations made under it, and such other assistance, as may be reasonably sufficient in connection with the exercise by him and, in the case of a man, by his wife of any rights conferred on them as aforesaid. But the

" Service declaration."

burden of Parliament's command is eased by a proviso that the arrangements need not extend to members of the forces who are for the time being under the age of twenty-one and will in the ordinary course cease to be members of the forces before attaining that age. It would be unfair not to add that the true aim of this easing proviso is not so much the saving of executive effort as the saving of futile effort; for, though conscribed youths in uniform are free to make a service declaration if they so fancy, they cannot thereby entitle themselves to vote while still infants.

On the one hand, adult failure to make a service declaration wastes, so to speak, the service qualification; for a person who on the qualifying date has a service qualification is not entitled to be registered except in pursuance of a service declaration properly made and in force on that date. On the other hand, such a service declaration entitles the person who has made it to be treated for the purposes of registration as resident at the address specified in the declaration and entitles him to cast his vote as a " service voter " in that constituency.

Of the ways and means that enable him to do this by proxy or even by post, instead of having to comply with the normal requirement of personal attendance at the polling station, we shall speak later.

Business premises qualification, now abolished. Passing **Business premises qualification.** mention must be made of this minority right, long criticised as undemocratic because it gave a second vote to the few and not to all. In recent years the second vote no longer extended to the wife (or husband) of the person entitled, and now even the business occupier's own right has ceased and become a thing of the past.

University qualification, now abolished. Mention must **University qualification.** also be made of another right that has recently perished. No longer will graduates of universities be registered as voters in their own university constituencies, seven in all, returning twelve representatives to Parliament, those sitting in the House of 1945–1950 being the last of their kind. It is thought that few of them would have sought election in the ordinary way and that the character and contribution of such members, especially in recent years,

has justified the survival hitherto of a form of franchise
that put university graduates in the privileged position
of being able to vote twice over, first in the constituency
of their residence like other citizens, and again in their
university constituency by virtue of their degree. But
tempora mutantur and we bid farewell to a venerable
anomaly by remarking upon one of its characteristic
features, namely, voting by post, which is still the
exception and not the rule of electoral procedure, as we
shall later observe.

One Man, one vote. *Plural voting.* It is clear from the account we have
just given that, even after the recent overthrow of both
the university and the business premises qualifications, a
person might still—by virtue of residence in more than
one constituency on the qualifying date—be in a position
at a general election to cast his vote more than once and in
different constituencies. In days of old he would be free
to do so, and indeed it was all the easier for him to exploit
his advantage before it was first enacted that as far as
possible polling should take place throughout the whole
country on the same day. But the new Act, as we might
well guess, makes it an offence at a general election " to
vote as an elector in more than one constituency," and
even before " one man one vote " had become so sacrosanct it could at any rate be said " one man not more than
two votes," and the second vote had to be a choice between
either a business premises vote or a university vote ; in
other words, even before recent legislation made the
residence (or the service) qualification the only qualification, it was already prohibited to cast a residence vote in
more than one constituency at the same general election.

Procedure. *Registration.* If we may speak of the " office work "
that the preparation of the register necessitates, this is
provided for in the recent Act, which not only enables a
local authority to " assign officers to assist the clerk of the
council in carrying out any of his duties in relation to the
registration of electors and the conduct of parliamentary
elections upon such terms as may be agreed between the
council and the clerk " but also divides the " registration expenses " equally between the national and local
purses.

One of the statutory duties that the registration officer is thus assisted to fulfil is the preparation and publication of " electors lists showing the persons appearing to him to be entitled to be registered together with their qualifying addresses." Unless the elector happens to be a service voter, there seems to be no need for him to claim his vote ; for his name should be entered on the list, and he is invited and encouraged to examine the list as soon as it is published and to ensure that he gets registered. If his name should be omitted, and he should consider himself entitled to vote, he must send a claim to the registration officer. Objection may be made to his name being registered, or, if it has already been entered, application to have it removed may be made by any person whose name appears on the electors lists ; and, further, the registration officer himself must be satisfied that there is due ground for entering the name on the register. If there is a claim, or if objection is taken either by the registration officer or by another elector, the registration officer has to decide whether the claim or objection is valid or not ; and from his decision there is an appeal to the County Court, and thence, on a point of law only, to the Court of Appeal, whose decision is final. The registration officer is now empowered (as was recommended by the Committee on Electoral Registration) to dispose of claims and objections " without formal hearings."

A novelty when introduced by the Act of 1918 was the provision authorising *absent* voters to cast their votes at elections. The categories of such absentees have been so much extended by later legislation that their enumeration here would be out of place. Instead, let us be content to say that those registered as service voters now head the long list of those allowed to vote *in absentia* because unable or likely to be unable to go in person to the polling station for a prescribed reason such as the general nature of their occupation, service or employment, *e.g.*, merchant seamen. There is similar permission for those unable or likely to be unable, by reason of blindness or any other physical incapacity, to go in person to the polling station or, if able to go, to vote unaided.

Any such absentee may as a rule vote by post after

Absent voters.

Voting by post.

making a satisfactory application to the registration officer to be treated as an absent voter and after furnishing an address in the United Kingdom to which a postal ballot paper is to be sent. And, in the event of an election, the registration officer must prepare " the absent voters list " giving the name and number on the register of every person entitled to vote at the election as an absent voter.

Voting by proxy.

For all service voters, and sometimes for some of the other categories of absent voters, there is a choice between voting in absence by post and doing so by proxy. Moreover, if the latter course is preferred and the absent voter appoints some person as proxy to vote for him, the person so appointed may himself apply to be treated as an absent voter in order to be able to vote by post on behalf of the absentee instead of having to do so in person. In all this

Safeguards.

freedom of choice there must be safeguarding provisions against abuse, especially by those wishing so to speak to blow hot and cold ; but these somewhat long and elaborate safeguards of the recent Act are of no general interest, and they may well be left to confound, for example, the wanderer, home at election time, who seeks to vote in person, though his name is already upon " the absent voters list " and maybe also upon " the list of proxies."

Section II. THE PROCESS OF ELECTION

Dissolution and summoning of Parliament.

Parliament is not a permanent body. It *may* be dissolved at any time by the King on the advice of his Ministers ; it *must* be dissolved after it has existed for five years, unless it prolongs its own existence by Act of Parliament. Upon its dissolution, it merely ceases to exist ; and there is no Parliament until the King summons a new one. It is interesting to note that under the Regency Act, 1937, the power to dissolve Parliament cannot be exercised by the Counsellors of State " otherwise than on the express instructions of the Sovereign (which may be conveyed by telegraph)." The summoning of a Parliament is carried out by royal writ ; and, in theory, there is no obligation on the King to summon a Parliament more often than once in three years, as provided by the Triennial Act, 1694. But, without a Parliament, government in England would break down ; hence, in practice, the invariable rule is that the same Proclamation which dissolves one Parliament makes known " Our Royal will and pleasure to call a new Parliament," and directs the issue of writs to that end. The result is that, except for the short interval while the General Election is taking place (and Statute prescribes how long must elapse between the issue of the Proclamation and the date of the first meeting), there is continuously a Parliament in existence.

Different writs are employed for the summoning of the Lords and of the Commons. Each Peer is entitled to a *separate* writ of summons ; it is obvious that no such writ can be issued to a member of the House of Commons, for he is yet to be elected. We must therefore consider the mode of electing members of Parliament. *Election writs.*

An election of a member takes place *either* upon the summoning of a new Parliament to replace one which has been dissolved *or* when a particular member ceases to be a member of the existing House of Commons through death or any other cause. Such elections are known respectively as General Elections and By-elections. In each case, a writ has to be issued by the Clerk of the Crown in Chancery, addressed to a person in each constituency, called the " returning officer," who is either the sheriff, or the mayor, or the chairman of the urban council, calling upon him to " cause election to be made," in the words of the writ, " according to law of a member to serve in Parliament " for the particular constituency. After the writ is received, the returning officer is relieved by statute of all responsibility by the registration officer (*ante*, p. 360) who, as " acting returning officer," takes over all duties save in so far as the returning officer retains them in his own hands. Statute also enables " deputy acting returning officers " to be appointed. *General and By-Elections.* *Returning Officer.*

The election proceedings must follow a statutory timetable (now enacted afresh) which ensures that at a General Election the polling throughout the country shall take place on the same day ; and the returning officer must give public notice of the election. *Time-table*

The next step is the nomination of candidates, which is effected by the delivery to the returning officer of one or more " nomination papers " for every candidate, each of which must be subscribed by a proposer and seconder and eight other persons, all of whom must themselves be registered electors for the constituency.   Every candidate

Deposit.

must deposit with the returning officer the sum of £150. This sum is returned to him " as soon as practicable " after the election, unless he fails to obtain one-eighth of the total number of votes polled ; in which case it is forfeited to the Crown.   This risk of losing the deposit is intended to discourage a " freak " candidature—that of persons with no reasonable chance of election.

Election.

If only one candidate stands nominated for a constituency, the returning officer at once declares the candidate to be elected ; and the election is said to be " unopposed."   But if, as is more usual, it is a contested election, the returning officer proceeds to adjourn the election, and to " take a poll," *i.e.* to take the votes of the electors. Voting is mostly by ballot ; very detailed provisions are contained in the 1949 Act (re-enacting the Ballot Act, 1872, as later amended), to ensure the secrecy of the ballot.

Return of
result of
Election.

The votes are then counted, lots having now to be cast in the rare event of a tie ; and the returning officer declares the successful candidate to be elected, and returns his name to the Clerk of the Crown in Chancery, who enters it in the Return Book, which is an official record of the election.   The Return Book is then sent to the Clerk of the House of Commons, who retains it for reference.

Bribery and
corruption.

FREEDOM OF ELECTIONS.   Apart from direct violence and intimidation, which might require an election to be adjourned or even set aside in accordance with provisions now in a Schedule to the recent Act, it has been the policy of the legislature to make stringent provisions against the more secret forms of influence upon voters, such as the " infamous practices of bribery and corruption."   Even at Common Law, bribery at elections is an offence ; but the law against these practices is now contained in Acts passed chiefly during the last century, which as later amended are for the most part consolidated in the Act of 1949.

A very important distinction is drawn between *corrupt* practices, which are *mala in se* and necessarily imply guilty knowledge or intention, and merely *illegal* practices, which are *mala prohibita* and may be done through inadvertence or ignorance, without any intention to violate the law. Amongst corrupt practices, the following may be mentioned : Corrupt and illegal practices distinguished.

Corrupt practices.

Bribery, whether before, at, or after the election. The briber and the bribed are equally guilty.

Treating, a species of bribery in which the reward offered takes the form of food, drink, or other entertainment.

Personation, which includes the assumption of a false identity at the polls. This offence, now widely defined, may be committed by a proxy.

Undue influence, which consists in the application of force, physical or moral, or threats or intimidation, with a view to influencing the casting or withholding of a vote.

Corrupt practices are now to be made punishable summarily as well as on indictment. And a corrupt practice, if proved, has the effect of excluding the guilty party from all electoral rights, and all capacity for public office, for five years, as the new period is to be. Penalties.

Illegal practices are such election offences as do not necessarily involve any corrupt design on the part of those who are guilty of them. They include such offences as the following, the penalties for which are less severe than those with which corrupt practices are visited. Illegal practices.

Hiring conveyances to take electors to the polls.

Hiring spaces for advertisements other than from an elector whose ordinary business it is to post advertisements.

Setting up an excessive number of committee rooms.

Excessive expenditure on the part of a candidate or his election agent. The legislature has laid down a maximum limit, excluding the personal expenditure of the candidate, and every candidate is bound to make a return, in a specified form, of his election expenses, within a short while after the election.

False statements of fact relating to candidates, even though these do not amount to defamation.

Acting in a disorderly manner at a political meeting for the purpose of preventing the transaction of the business for which the meeting was called together.

These are only a small number of the numerous illegal practices defined by statute, and Parliament has just added such modern novelties as the use of foreign wireless stations, or the too close copying of official poll cards, for election propaganda.

Old procedure.

Election petitions. Besides the penal provisions, a further safeguard of the purity of elections is to be found in the power, which the House of Commons itself possesses, to exclude any member whom it considers unfit to take his place in Parliament. Formerly this power was used both where the member was considered unsatisfactory on personal grounds and also where the disqualification arose from the mode in which his election had been conducted ; but this latter jurisdiction was

Transference to the Courts.

transferred by the Parliamentary Elections Act, 1868, to the Courts, and now under the consolidating Act of 1949 all questions relating to controverted elections—that is to say, where it is alleged that the election has been vitiated by some informality, or that the successful candidate has won the seat with the aid of voters who were not entitled to vote or whose votes were procured through improper inducements, such as the corrupt and illegal practices above mentioned—are tried and decided by a proceeding known as an " election petition." The procedure upon such petitions is too complicated to be set out in any detail in this work ; but its chief features may be summarised as follows.

Petition.

A petition setting forth his complaint must be served by the petitioner on the candidate whose name has been returned, and the petitioner must give security, to the amount of one thousand pounds, for the payment of all costs, charges, and expenses. The petition is then heard

Hearing of petition.

and discussed, as though it were an ordinary civil case, before two judges of the High Court, sitting in open court without a jury, and with witnesses examined on oath, and, as a general rule, in the borough or county where the election has been impugned.

At the conclusion of the trial, the judges certify their findings in writing to the Speaker. The determination of the judges is final to all intents and purposes ; but, on receiving the judges' certificate, the House itself gives directions as to confirming or altering the candidate's return, or issuing a writ for a new election, as circumstances may require. *Determination of petition.*

Where it is represented to His Majesty, by a joint Address of both Houses of Parliament, that there is reason to believe, or that an election court has reported to the Speaker, that corrupt or illegal practices have extensively prevailed in any county, borough, or other place sending a member to Parliament, His Majesty may appoint Commissioners to make inquiry into these alleged practices. And it has been customary for the Legislature, where the report of such Commissioners has been unfavourable, to deprive the constituency in question, either permanently or for a time, of its right to send members to Parliament. In modern days, however, this procedure is intended rather as a safeguard than for actual use. *Widespread corruption, etc.*

CHAPTER 13

THE ASSEMBLING, ADJOURNMENT, PROROGATION AND DISSOLUTION OF PARLIAMENT

Assembling of Parliament.

Upon the day fixed in the writ for the meeting of Parliament, the Commons are summoned to the House of Lords ; and the King " opens " the Parliament, either in person or—in accordance with modern practice—by commission. The Commons then retire to elect their Speaker (whose position will be explained hereafter), and, at a later day, they again proceed to the House of Lords, where the Speech from the Throne, indicating the general policy of the Government, is read, by the King in person if he is present, otherwise by the Lord Chancellor. The monarch plays no part in the preparation of the speech ; it is entirely the work of the Government—the labour of many hands—and the reading of it in the House of Lords is later followed by discussion and criticism of its policy by the Commons.

Adjournment of Parliament.

An adjournment, as the word itself signifies, is no more than a continuance of the session from one day to another. This is done by the authority of each House separately every day ; and sometimes the adjournment is for a fortnight or a month, as at Christmas or Easter or upon other particular occasions. But the adjournment of one House is no adjournment of the other. At the end of the adjournment each House resumes business where it left off, without further formality.

Prorogation effected by King's authority only.

Prorogation is more formal than adjournment. The King's authority is a necessary formality, given either by him in person or—as is more usual—by commission ; it applies to both Houses of Parliament, for a prorogation can only be of a Parliament, not of the individual Houses ; and its result is to bring the session of Parliament to an end. Thus a session of Parliament is the period between an assembling or reassembling and a prorogation (or dissolution). But prorogation is distinct from dissolution in that Parliament still remains in existence ; and the date of its reassembling is fixed in the royal command ordering the prorogation. The Crown further has power to accelerate or postpone the meeting of Parliament so fixed. Nevertheless, prorogation puts an end to all pending business ; and, if a measure thus extinguished is taken up again, it must begin afresh just as if it were a new bill. This is one of the least intelligible rules of Parliamentary practice.

Dissolution. The right to dissolve Parliament at any time may be exercised by the King either in person or by commission, or, if, as is usually the case, the dissolution is preceded by prorogation, by Royal Proclamation. This power of dissolving Parliament is one of the most important of the royal prerogatives; for, by virtue of it, the King in theory, and the Prime Minister in practice, can bring into being a new Legislature. Though for over a century no monarch has refused a dissolution at the request of his Ministry, there is said to be no " convention " that prevents a refusal in exceptional circumstances ; indeed, the absence of a convention seems to be confirmed by the reference to a dissolution in the Regency Act, 1937 ; see *Regency.* *ante,* p. 366. By sect. 6 the Counsellors of State have no power to dissolve Parliament otherwise than on the express instructions of the Sovereign—in spite of the latter's illness or infirmity. Parliament is also dissolved by the lapse of time. But this has never been common, and it is unlikely that any Government (unless very sure of its own return) will allow a Parliament to run to its full length of life instead of seeking some earlier and more favourable moment for an election. By the Parliament *Parliament Act, 1911.* Act, 1911, the duration of Parliament is five years at most, reckoning from the time of its first summons. But Parliament, in the exercise of its sovereignty, may, as we saw in Chap. 4, extend its life for any length of time.

At Common Law, the demise of the Crown (see *ante,* *Demise of the Crown.* p. 302) effected a dissolution of Parliament ; but this rule was altered by Statute ; and the law at the present day is as follows. If the King dies while Parliament is in session, the same Parliament continues under his successor. If his death occurs during a prorogation or adjournment, the existing Parliament is to meet at once, without summons. If his death occurs after one Parliament has been dissolved and before the day appointed for the meeting of the new one, the old Parliament is reconvened, and sits for six months, unless it is sooner prorogued or dissolved by the new King. If the death occurs on or after the day appointed for the meeting of the new Parliament, the new Parliament meets as directed by the writs. There appears to be no provision for the case of a King dying between the dissolution of one Parliament and the actual issue of writs for a new one. But the need for any such provision has in practice been made most improbable, though perhaps not quite impossible, by the invariable rule of practice already mentioned (p. 367) whereby the same Royal Proclamation which dissolves one Parliament directs the issue of writs summoning a new one.

CHAPTER 14

THE POWERS OF THE CONSTITUENT PARTS OF PARLIAMENT

SUMMARY   PAGE

Section I. *Conditions for the Validity of an Act of Parliament*   375
Section II. *The Parliament Act, 1911*   377
Section III. *King, Lords, or Commons, acting separately*   ...   380
Section IV. *The Law and Custom of Parliament*   381

Section I. CONDITIONS FOR THE VALIDITY OF AN ACT OF PARLIAMENT

All legislation is initiated in one or other House of Parliament in the form of a Bill ; after passing through various stages in that House, it is sent on to the other House, and is finally presented to the King for his assent, upon the granting of which it becomes an Act of Parliament, which the Courts will administer as part of the law of the land.   This tripartite division of legislative function is emphasised in one or other of the " enacting clauses " with which every Act of Parliament so passed begins, which run as follows :

Process of legislation.

> " Be it enacted by the King's most Excellent Majesty, by and with the advice and consent of the Lords Spiritual and Temporal, and Commons, in this present Parliament assembled, and by the authority of the same, as follows."

or

> " Most Gracious Sovereign,
> We, Your Majesty's most dutiful and loyal subjects the Commons of the United Kingdom in Parliament assembled, towards making good the supply which we have cheerfully granted to Your Majesty in this session of Parliament, have resolved to grant unto Your Majesty the sums hereinafter mentioned ; and do therefore most humbly beseech Your Majesty that it may be enacted, and be it enacted by the King's most Excellent Majesty, by and with the advice and consent of the Lords Spiritual and Temporal, and Commons, in this present Parliament assembled, and by the authority of the same, as follows : "

Consents
necessary to
Acts of
Parliament.

Until 1911, the above account would have been true
of every Act of Parliament. Before the passing in that
year of the Parliament Act, *three* consents were necessary
in law to the enactment of a Statute : that of the Commons, that of the Lords, and that of the King. But *in
practice* only the House of Commons had retained intact
its power of withholding its consent. For over two
centuries the King had never refused his assent, and
that for the following reason. In all such matters the
King is bound to follow the advice of his responsible
Ministers (see *ante*, p. 318). The royal veto would therefore be the veto of the Cabinet, and so indirectly of the
dominant party in the House of Commons, and would in
consequence be superfluous. (Moreover, few measures
disliked by the Cabinet can nowadays be even considered
by the Commons, so very little parliamentary time being
allowed for private members to initiate legislation.)

Disuse of
royal veto.

Principles
governing
veto of the
Lords.

The House of Lords had preserved a very large measure
of independence, and often withheld its consent from Bills
which had passed the House of Commons. But it had
for several centuries been a recognised convention of the
Constitution that the Commons should have the *exclusive*
right of initiating *financial* legislation—a fact that the
longer " enacting clause " proclaims (see *supra*)—and,
moreover, that the House of Lords should not amend
any financial proposal submitted to it by the House of
Commons, though it might reject the proposal altogether.
Thus, subject to the Lords' right of rejection, which was
practically never exercised, the Commons already exercised *sole* control over *financial* legislation. And, in respect of *other* measures, it was well understood that the
Lords were not to use their veto in such a way as to
stultify the will of the people at large. They were expected to reserve it for occasions when they were convinced that the will of the Commons was not truly in
accord with the will of the people. If the Government
of the day was determined to have its way, the Prime
Minister advised the King to dissolve Parliament, and
appealed to the electorate against the decision of the
House of Lords. Moreover, there was a means of coercing
the Lords. The King might be asked by his Ministers

Coercion of
the Lords.

to create new peers to a number sufficient to ensure the passing of a given measure. This request has been made only on three occasions, and then in extreme circumstances; and the threat of creating new peers has in every case but one sufficed to break down the opposition of the Lords. It was by means of this threat that the veto of the House of Lords was legally curtailed by the passing of the Parliament Act, 1911.

Section II. THE PARLIAMENT ACT, 1911

The normal course of legislation is explained later in Chapter 15, and we are here concerned only with an exceptional procedure for enacting laws in defiance of the Lords. By this very means the amending Parliament Act, 1949, has now become law: It shortens the time-limits of the principal Act to those we give below in italics.

Summary of its provisions.

The principal Act specifies two classes of Bills : Money Bills, and Public Bills other than Money Bills. A Money Bill is defined as a Public Bill which is certified by the Speaker of the House of Commons to be a Money Bill. The opinion of the Speaker is final and cannot be questioned ; but the intention is that all Bills dealing with the raising and spending of public money are to be considered as Money Bills. In practice, however, there have been Bills which would at first sight appear to be " financial," but which have not been certified by the Speaker as Money Bills ; the converse is equally true, and Bills which do not appear to be financial have been certified as Money Bills. The Speaker's discretion, as so exercised, is a protection against the danger of " tacking " ; it would be an abuse of the Act if the Commons were allowed to treat ordinary Bills as Money Bills by the simple expedient of adding to them some financial clause. If a Money Bill, after passing through the House of Commons, is sent up to the House of Lords at least one month before the end of the session, and is not passed (without amendment) by the Lords within one month after it is sent up, it will (unless the House of Commons otherwise directs) be presented to the King, and, upon his assent being signified, will become an Act of Parliament.

Money Bills.

The effect of this enactment is that, while a Money Bill

is still sent up to the House of Lords, the functions of that House have ceased to be of any importance with regard to it. The Lords cannot prevent the Bill becoming law by merely throwing it out ; they cannot even amend it ; they can only criticise its provisions. And if, for any reason, they have not passed it within a month after it reaches them, it automatically becomes law upon receiving (as in practice it always will receive) the royal assent.

Non-money Bills. With regard to Public Bills other than Money Bills, the restriction on the powers of the Lords is far less stringent. A period of not less than *one* year must elapse from the first occasion on which the Bill was first considered (*i.e.* was first given a second reading) in the House of Commons. During this period, the Bill must be passed by the House of Commons (though not necessarily the same House of Commons) in *two* successive sessions, in substantially the same form, and, in each session, must be sent up to the Lords one month before the end of that session. The Lords may amend the Bill ; but their amendments will be of no effect unless the House of Commons agrees to them ; and such agreed amendments will not make the Bill a different Bill for the purposes of the Act. If the Lords do not pass the Bill (or refuse to pass it without amendments which the Commons refuse to accept) before the end of the session in question, and if they do not pass it in the next session, then, on the *second* occasion, the Bill will (unless otherwise directed by the Commons) be presented to the King for his assent, on the giving of which the Bill will, as in the case of a Money Bill, become an Act of Parliament. The only Public Bill to which these rules are not applicable is one extending the maximum duration of Parliament beyond five years, which can never become law without the consent of the Upper House.

Bills for extending duration of Parliament.

The enacting clause of an Act passed under the provisions of the Parliament Act, 1911, runs as follows :

> " Be it enacted by the King's most Excellent Majesty, by and with the advice and consent of the Commons, in this present Parliament assembled, in accordance with the provisions of the Parliament Acts, 1911 and 1949, and by authority of the same, as follows".

The constitutional importance of the Parliament Act is clearly very great. But its effect, even after the recent reduction of the " veto " from a minimum of two years to only *one*, is less drastic than at first sight appears.

Constitutional importance of Act.

So far as Money Bills are concerned, the Act merely deprives the House of Lords of a veto which it had scarcely ever exercised until the crisis which occasioned the passing of the Act. Its effect on other Public Bills is no doubt more serious, for it enables the House of Commons to enforce its will in certain cases against that of the House of Lords without having recourse to a dissolution and a general election. When the procedure under the Act is adopted, the utmost that the House of Lords can do is to suspend the proposal for a minimum of *one* year and for a maximum of *two* Parliamentary sessions, assuming that the House of Commons passes the Bill in *two* successive sessions. But this suspensive veto may well prove to be of great value ; indeed, the exercise of such a veto may well mean the death of the Bill. It often happens that a Bill, if it is to be of any use, must be passed at once, and in such cases a suspensive veto is equivalent to an absolute veto. And even when these conditions do not apply, the action of the Lords in rejecting a Bill will at once focus public attention upon its provisions ; and for many months it will be exposed to criticism outside Parliament, with the result that public opinion may prove hostile to the proposal and the Government be forced by the pressure of such opinion, and the hostility of the Press, to abandon the measure. On the other hand, the House of Commons may seek to strengthen its position by an appeal to the country at a General Election. If the Government retains its majority at the election, it will obviously resume the disputed measure with renewed energy ; for, as has been observed, the *two* successive sessions in which the Bill must be passed by the Commons need not be sessions of the same Parliament. In this connection, too, the provision of the Act restricting the duration of a Parliament to five years has an indirect result that may not be at once apparent ; any Bills not started in the Commons until after the first *four* years of a Parliament cannot be passed into law

Veto of Lords now suspensive.

Practical limits to efficacy of Act.

against the opposition of the House of Lords, except after a general election has intervened, and the electors have had an opportunity of giving their opinion upon the proposed legislation. The period will indeed usually be less than *four* years, for it is the general rule that a Parliament does not run out its full course. Thus the position of a House of Commons towards the end of its career—having perhaps grown out of sympathy with the country—is hardly better than it was before the passing of the Parliament Act.

Save for the measures which were the subject of contention between the two Houses when the Act was passed, there had until recently been no occasion on which the question of adopting its provisions had to be considered ; indeed, during most of the years between the passing of the Act and the present time, the chance of conflict was unlikely because majority opinion in both Houses had, so to speak, the same political colour. But with the recent ending of this harmony, use has been made of these provisions, so long in disuse, to enact fresh legislation for their own amendment in the manner already explained.

Section III. KING, LORDS, OR COMMONS, ACTING SEPARATELY

From the general rule requiring the co-operation of King, Lords, and Commons in the work of legislation, it follows that neither the King alone, nor the House of Lords alone, nor the House of Commons alone, by their own authority can work a change in the law. This is not to say that Parliament as a whole may not delegate to any of its parts legislative power to be exercised within the limits specified by the delegating Statute, *e.g.* the Parliamentary Papers Act, 1840, which followed *Stockdale* v. *Hansard* (see *post*, p. 383) ; and indeed it has of recent years become increasingly common, as we have already seen, to delegate legislative power to the King in Council. Again, the general rule of which we have spoken does not exclude certain spheres within which the King or either of the Houses may legislate alone.

It was decided in the great *Proclamations' Case* (1611), 12 Co. Rep. 74,

> " that the King cannot by his Proclamation create any offence which was not an offence before, for then he might alter the law of the land in a high point ; also that the law of England is divided into three parts, common law, statute law, and custom, but the King's Proclamation is none of them."

But although the King cannot, of his own motion, or even with the advice of the Cabinet but without the consent of the Lords and Commons in Parliament assembled, alter the law, nevertheless the Prerogative (by which the Crown still in great part conducts the central administration) gives it a wide power to lay down general rules for the conduct of business, which its servants are bound to obey. So also, although nothing can be more certain than that neither the House of Lords nor the House of Commons can, of its own authority, alter the law, yet there is a wide territory of parliamentary practice and procedure, *i.e.* territory governed by the so-called Law and Custom of Parliament, within which either House is recognised to possess " absolute " power.

The King's Prerogative.

The law and custom of Parliament.

Section IV. THE LAW AND CUSTOM OF PARLIAMENT

We have already seen (p. 270) that the Law and Custom of Parliament must be considered a part of our Constitution. Why is it so called ? The answer can perhaps be best given by examples. The power of the Speaker to certify a Bill as a Money Bill, or to designate the Leader of the Opposition for the receipt of a salary, is a power that must be regarded as within the *law* of the Constitution ; for the one comes from the Parliament Act, 1911, and the other from the Ministers of the Crown Act, 1937. The Courts can neither question the manner in which the power has been exercised nor compel the Speaker to exercise it ; they can only inquire whether the power has in fact been exercised. Nevertheless, such powers are as much a part of the *law* of the Constitution as, say, the right of succession to the Throne. Take, on the

Introductory.

other hand, the rule that a Bill must be read a third time before it is considered to have passed the House. We hesitate to say that the rule is within the *law* of the Constitution, not so much because the Courts would be powerless to interfere if this rule were broken, but rather because the rule is not established either by statute or by judicial decision. The sources of such rules are the standing orders and the precedents of the House itself. Its precedents are to be found, not in the Law Reports, but in the Journals, *i.e.* Minutes of the House. These examples are an indication of the difficulties of terminology and definition that have been evaded in the use of the phrase Law *and* Custom of Parliament.

The *Lex et consuetudo Parliamenti.*

It includes, not only such powers and rules as we have just mentioned, but also the so-called *privileges* of Parliament. It has been recognised by the Crown and by the Courts that the Houses of Parliament and their members possess certain privileges, and that, within the limits marked out by those privileges, the Houses themselves are the sole judges of right and wrong. The significance of this principle of non-interference is shown by the famous case of *Bradlaugh* v. *Gossett* (1884), 12 Q. B. D. 271, where the House of Commons resolved that Mr.

Bradlaugh v. *Gossett.*

Bradlaugh, who had been elected Member of Parliament for Northampton, should not be allowed to take the oath required by the Parliamentary Oaths Act, 1866, and that the Serjeant-at-Arms, the executive officer of the House, should exclude him from the House "until he shall engage no further to disturb the proceedings of the House." Mr. Bradlaugh sued for a declaration that the resolution of the House of Commons was void, and for an injunction restraining the defendant, the Serjeant-at-Arms, from carrying it into effect.

The main ground on which he based his claim was that by the Parliamentary Oaths Act he had a legal right to enter the House and take the oath, and that the resolution of the House constituted an infringement of the Act, but the Court decided against him on the ground that what is said or done within the walls of Parliament cannot be inquired into in a Court of law. They recognised as one of the privileges of the House of Commons the exclusive right to regulate its own internal affairs. Stephen, J., said :

> " It seems to follow, that the House of Commons has the exclusive power of interpreting the statute, so far as the regulation of its own proceedings within its own walls is concerned ; and that, even if that interpretation should be erroneous, this Court has no power to interfere with it directly or indirectly."

But the Courts have insisted that it is for them, and for them alone, to determine as a matter of law whether a privilege claimed by either of the Houses actually exists or not, and what its limits are, and in deciding that question they will have no regard to any resolution which may have been passed by the House concerned in support of its privilege. The Courts have reasoned that, though the *contents* of the Law and Custom of Parliament are not part of the Common Law, its *limits* are to be decided in accordance with Common Law and are as such within the cognisance of the ordinary Courts. Neither House of Parliament can by its own resolution (*i.e.* by something which is *not* an Act of Parliament) alter the law, and by parity of reasoning, neither House can make a declaration as to the limits of its privileges which will preclude the Courts from exercising their own independent judgment if a case arises concerning those limits. This was, *so far at least as the Courts are concerned*, settled once and for all in the great case of *Stockdale* v. *Hansard* (1839), 9 Ad. & El. 1. In this case the House of Commons ordered the publication by Hansard, its printer, of certain matters which were defamatory of the plaintiff, who thereupon sued the printer for libel. The defence was that the order of the House of Commons gave the defendant privilege from any action in the ordinary Courts of law ; and, in order to support this defence, the House passed resolutions to the effect that no Court of justice could deal with any question of Parliamentary privilege, that the declaration by the House of any privilege was binding upon all Courts, and that it was a privilege of the House to order the publication of papers without involving those concerned in the publication in any liability.

The Court gave full consideration to the claims made by

Determination by Courts as to existence of privilege.

Stockdale v. *Hansard.*

the House, and decided against them. In Lord Denman's words,

> "The supremacy of Parliament, the foundation upon which the claim is made to rest, appears to me to completely overturn it, because the House of Commons is not the Parliament, but only a co-ordinate and component part of the Parliament. That sovereign power can make or unmake the laws ; but the concurrence of the three legislative estates is necessary : the resolution of any one of them cannot alter the law or place any one beyond its control."

After due inquiry the Court came to the conclusion that the House had no privilege to authorise the publication of a libel outside the House.

Middlesex Sheriff's Case. The deplorable sequel throws considerable light on some of the difficulties of this most obscure subject. The House of Commons refused to acquiesce in the judgment of the Court, and, on the Sheriff of Middlesex attempting to levy execution on the goods of Hansard, the House committed the Sheriff to prison. The Sheriff applied to the Court for a writ of Habeas Corpus, whereupon the Serjeant-at-Arms was directed by the House to make a return to the writ that he held the Sheriff "by virtue of a warrant under the hand of Mr. Speaker for a contempt and a breach of the privilege of the House." The Court, although they knew full well what the contempt was for which the Sheriff was imprisoned, accepted this as a good return, on the ground that there was no need for it to specify the contempt for which he had been committed, and that they had no jurisdiction to go behind the return. If the return had specified the particular contempt, the Court held that they would have been at liberty to adjudge it bad, and accordingly to release the prisoner. As the matter stood, they had no option but to remand him to prison (*Middlesex Sheriff's Case* (1840), 11 Ad. & El. 273).

Thus the House of Commons had their own way. But after this somewhat unscrupulous protest, they thought it better to regularise their position by legislation, and in *Parliamentary Papers Act, 1840.* the same year the Parliamentary Papers Act, 1840, was passed, declaring that, where defamatory matter is published by order of *either* House of Parliament, it shall be a complete defence to any proceedings for defamation that it was published in pursuance of such order. This was tantamount to a recognition by the House that the Court's decision was right ; for it had to procure the passing of an Act of Parliament to get over it. The actual decision in *Stockdale* v. *Hansard* was thus reversed, but the case remains—in the eyes, at least, of the Courts— an authority for the proposition that the *limits* of Parliamentary privilege are a matter of Common Law, and as such within the cognisance of the Courts of law.

PRIVILEGES OF PARLIAMENT. The privileges of Parliament were originally established for the protection of its members from being oppressed by the Crown or molested by their fellow-subjects. Their object, generally speaking, is to secure the independence of members of Parliament and their freedom from outside interference with the discharge of their duties. Thus it would be a breach of privilege to assault a member within the precincts of the House, and the matter would be inquired into and punished by the House itself. *Object of.*

It is beyond the scope of this work to attempt to give an exhaustive list of the privileges that have been or might be claimed ; and in fact, save where light has been thrown on the question by some decision of the Courts, the whole matter of Parliamentary privilege is obscure.

Certain privileges are, however, formally claimed by the Speaker of the House of Commons at the beginning of every Parliament. Two of these are only formal : that the best construction may be put upon its proceedings by the Crown, and that the members of the House, *collectively*, may have access to the King for the purpose of tendering advice. (This obsolete privilege would have to be exercised through the Speaker.) Two are substantial, namely, freedom from arrest and freedom of speech. They are common to both Houses, though the Lords do not go through the formality of claiming them. *Formal privileges.* *Substantial privileges.*

Freedom from arrest does not mean freedom from arrest for a criminal offence or for contempt of Court, to which a peer or member of Parliament is as liable as any other subject. Further, the privilege can only be claimed by a member of the House of Commons during *Freedom from arrest.*

the actual session of Parliament and for forty days before and after. For the Lords, the period seems to be somewhat different. It was imprisonment for debt that gave value to this privilege in the past ; but after 1869, when the law relating to this kind of imprisonment was radically reformed, the privilege has been of little importance.

If a person having privilege of Parliament commits an act of bankruptcy, he may be dealt with as if he had no such privilege.

Freedom of speech. As regards freedom of speech, it is declared in the Bill of Rights of 1689 that the freedom of speech and debates or proceedings in Parliament " ought not to be impeached or questioned in any Court or place out of Parliament." Thus any defamatory statement made by a member of either House *in the House* enjoys " absolute " privilege ; so that no action for slander can be founded upon it in a Court of law, no matter what the motive of the speaker may have been. But this privilege does not extend to the repetition by a member outside the House of a defamatory statement which he has previously made within the House. As ancillary to this right of freedom of speech, the House of Commons has from time to time exercised, and the Lords would no doubt exercise if occasion arose, the right to exclude strangers from their debates, as was done during the so-called " secret sessions " of the recent war, and also the right to prohibit the publication of their proceedings.

Right to provide for proper constitution. There are certain important privileges, common to both Houses, which the Speaker does *not* formally claim. Thus both Houses have, as it is said, the right to provide for their proper constitution. Now that the House of Commons has transferred the trial of disputed elections to the High Court of Justice (see *ante*, pp. 370–1), the only effect of the privilege is to give the Houses the right to expel members for good cause and to declare whether a member is disqualified from sitting.

If there is a vacancy in the House of Commons, it is the Speaker who issues a warrant to the Clerk of the Crown in Chancery for the issue of a writ for the necessary by-election. The House of Lords has the exclusive right of determining whether a person is entitled to sit as a

Lord of Parliament (see the *Wensleydale (Peerage) Case* (1856), 5 H. L. Cas. 958) ; but, in trying peerage claims, it acts only in virtue of a reference from the Crown. If, for example, X claims to be an Irish peer, his claim is only a peerage claim, and not a claim to a seat in the House.

Again, as we have seen, the two Houses have full control of all that passes within the walls of Parliament, with the possible exception that the Courts may assert their right to try cases of crime which arise even within Parliament. It is in virtue of this privilege that each House has full power to make such rules for its internal procedure as it may think fit. No better illustration of this privilege could be found than the proceedings brought into the High Court for the express purpose of challenging the authority of the House of Commons, through its Kitchen Committee, to supply alcoholic refreshment within the House—even to non-members—without compliance or any pretence of compliance with the restrictions of the Licensing Laws. The Court agreed—in spite of strong persuasive authority to the contrary—that

> " in the matters complained of the House of Commons was acting collectively in a matter which fell within the area of the internal affairs of the House, and, that being so, any tribunal might well feel, on the authorities, an invincible reluctance to interfere " (*R.* v. *Graham-Campbell, Ex parte Herbert*, [1935] 1 K. B. 594).

Exclusive control of what passes in Parliament.

We have also found (p. 384) that, in any case in which the privileges of either House of Parliament have been violated, whether by a member of the House or by any other person, the House concerned has power to commit to prison the person guilty of contempt. But, if the commitment is by the House of Commons, it can only be for the remainder of the session ; whereas the House of Lords can commit for a definite term, which may last over a prorogation.

Power to commit for contempt.

There are two minor privileges, enjoyed by the Upper House alone, which require mention : first, the right of every peer, when a vote passes contrary to his opinion, to enter his dissent, called his " protest," on the Journals of the House ; and second, the right of every peer (unlike a member of the Commons) to have *individual* access to the person of the Sovereign.

Minor privileges of Lords.

Judicial
functions of
House of
Lords.

Trial of peers
by peers, now
abolished.

We must also notice that the House of Lords exercises very important judicial functions, but for these reference should be made to Book I, Part I, of this Volume. All that need here be said is that the privilege, only recently abolished, of trial by peers *for treason or felony* was a privilege of peerage, which members of the House of Lords shared with peeresses and with peers not entitled to a seat in the Upper House. It was not therefore a privilege of the House of Lords. Indeed, on the last occasion of this rare and troublesome mode of trial, the accused (on a charge of manslaughter) was a non-representative Irish peer and so not a member of the House (*De Clifford's (Lord) Trial*, [1936] W. N. 4, a full account of which was published by H.M. Stationery Office). The privilege could not be waived in favour of an ordinary trial, a fact which made it all the more desirable to abolish the anachronism, as the Criminal Justice Act, 1948, has at last done.

CHAPTER 15

THE PROCEDURE OF PARLIAMENT

Each House is presided over by a Speaker. The The Lord Chancellor Speaker of the House of Lords is, in practice, the Lord and the Chancellor; although the King may appoint another Speaker. person (not necessarily a peer) or, in default of such appointment, the Lords may elect their own Speaker. On the other hand, the Speaker of the House of Commons (always spoken of as " the Speaker ") is a member of the House, and is elected by the House, though the choice has to be approved by the King. The Lord Chancellor may, and constantly does, take part in debates in the Lords ; but the Speaker never takes such part in the Commons, apparently not even when the House has resolved itself into Committee in the manner explained below. Again, the Speaker never votes unless the votes of the House are equal, in which case he has a casting vote, which he must exercise in accordance with the precedents of former Speakers ; whereas the Lord Chancellor is entitled to vote in all divisions, but has no casting vote, the rule in the Lords being that, upon an equality of votes, the negative opinion prevails. In the absence of the Lord Chancellor, his place is taken by one of several Deputy-Speakers appointed by the Crown, whereas in the House of Commons the Chairman (or in his absence the Deputy-Chairman) of Ways and Means (*post*, p. 395) acts as Speaker in the absence of the Speaker himself. The Speaker occupies a much more important position in the House of Commons in relation to the business of the House than does the Lord Chancellor in the other House. Thus the Speaker is the formal channel of communication between the House and the Crown ; he has certain powers, for instance, the power of certifying that a Bill is a Money Bill for the purposes of the Parliament Act, 1911, or that a certain member is the Leader of the Opposition for the purposes of the Ministers of the Crown Act, 1937 ; and, finally, his powers with regard to the control of debate and maintenance of order in the House are far greater than those of the Lord Chancellor, who has no disciplinary powers over the peers.

Classification.

Public.

BILLS. All Acts of Parliament begin their life as Bills. Bills are divided into two classes : (1) Public Bills, subdivided into (a) those which are, and (b) those which are not, Money Bills ; and (2) Local and Personal Bills, which may be either (a) Bills dealing with matters of purely

Local and Personal.

individual interest, such as the alteration of the terms of a trust, or (b) Bills which form far the greater part of private legislation, and are concerned with all kinds of matters of local interest, and especially with the powers of municipal corporations and large " public utility " concerns, where the nature of the undertakings is bound to interfere with private rights, so that statutory authority is necessary to enable them to be carried on with immunity from endless litigation (see *ante*, p. 272, and *post*, p. 397).

Standing and Sessional Orders.

The procedure relating to the passing of Bills is laid down in Standing (or permanent) and Sessional (or temporary) Orders, made by each House. These Orders, which are exceedingly detailed and are liable to alteration at any time to suit the requirements of Government legislation, prescribe, amongst other things, the nature of the business to be taken at each sitting of the House ; and one naturally finds that Government Bills obtain precedence over the small minority of Public Bills introduced by private members.

Indeed, until only recently, the private member's chance to introduce legislation was still in war-time abeyance and its revival is little more than a gesture ; but, even before the war, so short was the time allowed for the Bills of private members that there was a ballot to decide who should have the meagre opportunity.

Introduction.

1. *Ordinary Public Bills.* The first step is the introduction of the Bill, which has sometimes to be in the form of a motion for leave to bring in the Bill. But usually the Bill is presented without leave by the Minister (or private member) who is introducing it ; and the question is put and carried, usually without debate, that the Bill

be read a first time and printed. This is called the
" first reading " of the Bill ; and, as may be seen, it is
really a purely formal process.

The next stage is the " second reading." Owing to Second
the congestion of Government business, it is very difficult Reading.
for a private member to get his Bill put down for second
reading in the crowded time-table ; and the effect is that
no legislation can be passed through the House of Commons without the support of the Government. The
debate on the second reading is the occasion on which the
general principle involved in the Bill is discussed, and
amendments are not allowed to be moved ; the sole
question being whether the alteration proposed to be
made in the law, or the proposed tax, or whatever it may
be, is desirable. The question is put : " that the Bill be
read a second time " ; and, on this being carried, the Bill
is said to have passed its second reading.

The detailed consideration of the provisions of the Bill Committee.
then begins ; and it is " committed," that is to say,
referred to a committee, which is usually *either* a standing committee consisting of about thirty to fifty members
of all the major parties, *or* a select committee of about
fifteen members, *or*, if the occasion should warrant it, a
committee of the whole House, composed of every
member. In order to form a committee of the whole
House, the Speaker quits his Chair ; and the Chair at the
table of the House is taken by. the Chairman, or one of
the Deputy Chairmen, of Committees. In these committees, the Bill is debated clause by clause, alterations
are made, and gaps are filled in ; sometimes the Bill is
entirely remodelled.

After it has gone through committee, the Chairman The Report
" reports " the Bill to the House, with such amendments Stage.
as the committee may have made. The House, either
forthwith or on some later date, with the Speaker in the
chair, reconsiders the whole Bill once more ; first dealing
with any new proposed clauses, and then considering any
amendments made in committee. But it must be
observed that a Bill is not required to pass through this
particular stage, technically known as the " report stage,"
unless it has been amended in committee.

Third
Reading.

When the House has dealt with all the new clauses and amendments proposed, the Bill is read a third time and passed.   Only alterations of language—not affecting the substance of the Bill—are as a rule undertaken on the third reading, the usual purpose being to eliminate ambiguities and contradictions in the wording of the Bill.   Finally, it is carried by the Clerk of the Commons to the House of Lords.

It will be seen that there are three stages at which the subject-matter of the Bill can be criticised—upon the motion for second reading, in committee, and at the report stage.   There is also the preliminary stage of the " money resolution " (see *post*, p. 395) in the case of Bills, not necessarily Money Bills, which in some way do—so to speak—come upon the public purse.

Formerly there was no limitation upon the right of every member to address the House (or the committee) at any length, provided that he was not irrelevant or disorderly ; but it became the adopted policy of certain sections of the House to utilise this freedom as a means of obstruction.   Partly to overcome this obstruction, and partly to enable the Government to cope with the ever-increasing demands upon the time of the House, three devices have been invented, which are of sufficient importance to be mentioned here.

The
" Closure."

The first is called the " closure."   At any stage in the debate, any member may move that the question be now put ; and if the Speaker (or Chairman) accepts the motion and it is carried, the question is at once put and decided without further amendment or debate.

The
" Guillotine."

The second is the " guillotine," which consists of a resolution passed by the House, allotting a certain definite time to each portion of the Bill.   Upon the expiration of that time, whether all the clauses in that portion of the Bill have been discussed or not, the guillotine falls ; and no discussion is allowed of the clauses which have not been reached.

The
" Kangaroo."

The third device is called " the kangaroo."   By means of it, the Speaker on the report stage or the Chairman of a committee—which may or may not be a committee of the whole House—may select, from amendments proposed to a Bill, those which he deems to be most important as representing all sides of criticism, and withhold the others from discussion.

The effect of these three devices is, of course, that the Government can ensure that any given Bill shall pass the House of Commons by a given date.

When the Bill reaches the House of Lords, it passes through more or less the same stages as in the House of Commons. If it is rejected, the matter passes *sub silentio*, but in the next session the Lords may hear of it afresh under the Parliament Act (see *ante*, p. 377). If it is passed, the Lords send a message to the Commons that they have agreed to the Bill. But if any amendments are made, such amendments are sent down with the Bill, to receive the concurrence of the Commons. If the Commons disagree with the amendments, there are certain formal and informal ways (which cannot here be explained) whereby the disagreement between the two Houses can be dealt with in the hope of avoiding deadlock. But if both Houses remain inflexible, the Bill may, if passed afresh by the Commons in the next session, be sent up again under the Parliament Act, 1911, previously described. _{Procedure in House of Lords.}

When the Houses are agreed on a measure other than a Money Bill, it is lodged at the House of Lords until a convenient opportunity occurs of presenting it for the Royal Assent. But a Money Bill, and presumably any other Bill passed under the provisions of the Parliament Act, 1911, remain in the custody of the House of Commons until presented for the Royal Assent. _{Royal Assent.}

It will, of course, be understood that legislation (other than Money Bills) may, and frequently does, originate in the House of Lords ; in which case similar forms are observed *mutatis mutandis* as in the case of measures which begin in the House of Commons. But in the details of the progress of a measure, there are many minor differences in the procedure of the two Houses.

The Royal Assent to a Bill may be given either in person or by commission. But by virtue of the Statute 33 Hen. VIII (1542), c. 21, it is in practice always given by three Commissioners named by the King for that purpose. The Commons are summoned to appear at the bar of the House of Lords, their attendance there being _{Procedure on Royal Assent.}

desired, not *commanded,* in the absence of the Sovereign ; the titles of all the Bills to receive the Royal Assent are then read, and the King's answer is declared by the Clerk of the Parliaments in Norman-French. If the Sovereign consents to a Public Bill, the Clerk declares " *le roy* (or *la reyne*) *le veult.*" If the Sovereign refuses his assent—which in fact never happens—it is in the gentle language of " *le roy* (or *la reyne*) *s'avisera.*"

Procedure after Royal Assent. When the Bill has received the Royal Assent, it is then, and not before, a Statute or Act of Parliament—two terms that mean in practice the same thing ; and, by the Acts of Parliament (Commencement) Act, 1793, the Clerk of the Parliaments is directed to endorse on every Act, immediately after the title thereof, the day, month, and year when the same received the Royal Assent. Such endorsement is part of the Act, and is the date of the taking effect of the Act, *where no other time for its commencement is prescribed by the Act itself.* But it is a common practice in recent years for an Act to give power to some government authority to bring the Act into force at some convenient future time, and even to specify different times for different parts of the Act. It must not be too readily assumed, therefore, that an Act is in operation merely because it has already received the Royal Assent. It may well be necessary to find out if some Minister has " brought the Act into force."

Having received the Royal Assent, the Act is then placed among the records of the kingdom, and the King's Printer is bound, by virtue of his office, to print each Act for the information of the whole land.

Procedural peculiarities. 2. *Money Bills.* There are certain peculiarities in the procedure relating to Money Bills. We have seen that they must originate in the Lower House, and that the functions of the House of Lords in relation to them have been reduced to a nullity. There is a definition of Money Bills in the Parliament Act, 1911, and we have already seen (p. 377) that it is for the Speaker to certify that a Bill is within the definition.

Only Minister may propose. The first point to notice is that only Ministers make proposals for the raising or spending of public money ; the reason is that, *in theory,* the public revenue is asked for and spent by the Crown, so that it must be a representative of the Crown, one of the Ministers of State, who declares the purposes for which the money is required. *In practice* this rule served (until the private members' procedure went into decline) as a very necessary restraint upon private members, who might be all too ready to sponsor some luxury at the public expense. The result of the rule is that if a private member wishes to introduce a measure that imposes some charge upon the public funds, he has to get a Minister to undertake the passing in Committee of a financial resolution relating to the Bill.

Secondly, resolutions preparatory to the usual financial legislation of the year are invariably dealt with in a committee of the whole House, sitting either as a Committee of Supply for the purpose of allocating public money to particular State purposes, or as a Committee of Ways and Means to consider the sources whence the necessary money is to be raised. *Committees of Supply and of Ways and Means.*

The estimates of the various Government Departments for the next year are published after their detailed examination by the Treasury (see *post*, p. 427). Later, they come before the Committee of Supply, and the necessary resolutions are passed to authorise the proposed expenditure, after an examination of the estimates that is— for various reasons—somewhat formal and perfunctory. The effective control of expenditure is thus with the Treasury rather than the Commons. On the other hand, the control of the Committee of Ways and Means is real and effective, and the Chancellor of the Exchequer's proposals to the Committee (the so-called Budget) are often modified and sometimes even abandoned. *Control of expenditure.*

The resolutions passed in these latter committees finally become embodied in two Acts in each session, the Appropriation Act, which " appropriates " money from the Consolidated Fund for " supply " services (*i.e.* the monies that must be authorised year by year), and the Finance Act, which fixes the taxes to be levied during the year. *Appropriation Act.* *Finance Act.*

But, as the Finance Act is usually a complicated measure, which is not passed until towards the close of the session, it has long been the practice of the House to resolve at once that certain new duties, when imposed, *New duties to be operative at once.*

Bowles v.
Bank of
England.

Provisional
Collection of
Taxes Act,
1913.

should be retrospective in their operation, in order that
they might be collected at once ; and, on the strength
of a resolution thus passed, the practice of the Customs
and Inland Revenue officials has been to act as though
they had legal authority to collect accordingly. But, until
1913, no taxes, though resolved by the Commons, could
be legally enforced until they had been embodied in an
Act of Parliament passed through all the proper stages ;
and, in *Bowles* v. *Bank of England*, [1913] 1 Ch. 57, Mr.
Gibson Bowles, from whose dividends the Bank had
deducted " at source " the income tax voted but not
formally enacted, sued the Bank for the recovery thereof.
The Court upheld Mr. Bowles' contention in a case which
is a modern echo of *Stockdale* v. *Hansard* (see *ante*,
p. 383) ; and it therefore became necessary to provide
by law for the continuance of a practice which was deemed
necessary for the proper collection of the revenue.
Accordingly, by the Provisional Collection of Taxes Act,
1913, it was enacted that when the Committee of Ways
and Means has resolved to vary an existing tax or to
continue a tax, and the resolution contains a declaration
that it is expedient in the public interest that the variation or continuation should have statutory effect under
the provisions of the Act, the resolution shall have statutory effect accordingly as from its passing. But, though
this delegation of legislative authority was to no less a
body than a Committee of the whole House, it was made
subject to severe restrictions and conditions. Thus the
limit of such statutory effect is four months ; and it
ceases altogether if the resolution of the Committee is
not agreed to by the House within ten sitting days after
it is passed, and if a Bill embodying it is not initiated
within the next twenty sitting days and ultimately passed
by the House. Moreover, the Act only applies to resolutions relating to customs and excise duties and income
tax and sur-tax ; and, of course, any money collected
under it must be returned on a demand by the person
paying such money if the statutory effect of the resolution comes to an end before it is confirmed by the passage
of an Act of Parliament embodying it.

It must be noted that, whereas law-making by authorities outside Parliament has long become an accepted necessity, such authorities have rarely been empowered, even in time of war, to enact any form of taxation. But, as was shown by the powers delegated to the Treasury in the Import Duties Act, 1932, and in the Emergency Powers (Defence) Act, 1939, there may well be occasions when Parliament is willing, for some quite exceptional reason, to permit its traditional monopoly of revenue-raising power to be shared by its delegates. *Subordinate legislation exceptional.*

A peculiarity relating to Money Bills is that the words in which the Royal Assent is given differ from those used in the case of other Public Bills. They are : " *le roy* (or *la reyne*) *remercie ses bons sujets, accepte leur benevolence, et ainsi le veult.*" *Royal Assent.*

3. *Local Bills.* A Local or Personal Bill originates by petition, which must be deposited in the appropriate Office of the House of Commons or of the House of Lords. It is necessary to give certain notices and otherwise to ensure that the project contained in the Bill has been sufficiently advertised, so as to give to every person interested an opportunity of opposing the Bill. The procedure laid down in the Standing Orders of the House of Commons—or the slightly different procedure of the House of Lords, if the Bill is to be introduced there—must be followed ; and, subject to this, the Bill is read a first and second time in the House, and is then " committed." Even the second reading is more or less a formality, and the merits of the Bill are not discussed until the Committee stage. The procedure in committee is judicial. Witnesses are examined ; and the parties promoting and opposing the Bill are entitled to appear by counsel and argue their case. If the Bill is not rejected by the committee, it is, like a Public Bill, " reported," with any amendments that may have been made, to the House. Afterwards it is read a third time, sent to the other House, and finally presented for the Royal Assent, which, in the case of a Local Bill, is given in the form : " *soit fait comme il est désiré.*" The interesting point to notice about Local Bill legislation is the way in which Parliament takes care to hear every side of the case before passing an Act which may gravely infringe *Procedure.*

Committee stage.

Royal Assent.

the existing rights of individuals. The result in practice is that the procedure involved is elaborate and dilatory, and therefore expensive.

The promotion of, and opposition to, Local Bill legislation is usually conducted by special classes of solicitors and barristers, known as " Parliamentary Agents " and " Parliamentary Counsel " respectively.

Provisional Order Confirmation Bill. One particular type of Local Bill—a Provisional Order Confirmation Bill—requires an explanation. Its use is largely the result of the difficulties involved in the procedure above described. Certain Government Departments, principally the Ministry of Health, have statutory powers to make (after holding public local inquiries) Provisional Orders authorising the execution of useful public undertakings by local bodies or companies, *subject to the approval of Parliament*. From time to time these orders are grouped together in a schedule to a Provisional Order Confirmation Bill, which is treated as a Local Bill and usually passed without opposition. But, should there be opposition, it gets an opportunity twice over of being heard : first, there is the departmental inquiry on the spot ; and later on, after the Ministry has already made the Order, a Select Committee of one or other House hears any surviving opposition before the Bill to confirm the Order finally reaches the Statute Book. Thus, to take a recent example, we have the Ministry of Health Provisional Order Confirmation (Shrewsbury) Act, 1948, but Shrewsbury is only one of the nine towns contemporaneously concerned. But, though intended as a suitable method for authorising local schemes that bear departmental patronage, nevertheless this Provisional Order procedure is all too liable to share the evils—delay and high cost—that characterise the older procedure by Local Bill, of which it is only a variant.

Little wonder, then, that a radically different procedure has come into fashionable preference (especially for local schemes of a " now or never " kind), the essential difference being that departmental confirmation suffices without the need for confirmation in Parliament. Thus, by virtue of some Statute, the local authority proposes a scheme, which is confirmed, after inquiry, by a Government Department. The confirmation gives the Order, in most cases, the same effect as if it were part of the Statute empowering the Department.

But a special category of orders—the "Special Procedure Orders"—has been evolved ; and if any order is put into this limited category by any future empowering enactment, then the whole procedure to be followed, in and out of Parliament, has been mapped out in advance by the Statutory Orders (Special Procedure) Act, 1945, a belated enactment seeking to ensure uniformity in the steps leading to the ratification of a "special" order by Parliament. Whether any particular order is of this limited kind— whether, in the statutory language, it is "to be subject to special parliamentary procedure "—is a question that is answerable only on examination of the empowering enactment (*e.g.* the Water Act, 1945) that happens to govern the case.

Special Procedure Orders.

The actual drafting of most Government Bills is performed by certain officials, highly trained in this important and difficult work, called the Parliamentary Counsel to the Treasury. It is their duty to draft a Bill in such a form that it expresses the wishes of the Government Department promoting it, that it is clear and unambiguous, and that no unintended interference with the existing law creeps into it. But it not infrequently happens that they are thwarted in their endeavours by circumstances which are beyond their control, and in most cases it would be unfair to hold them responsible for the unfortunate obscurities and inconsistencies which are so marked a feature of our legislation.

Drafting of Bills.

They are usually called in at a comparatively early stage. As soon as the Department concerned has made up its mind what it wants to have included in the Bill— perhaps after consultation with the "vested interests" that would be affected by the passing of the Bill—it draws up a list of its proposals and communicates them to the Parliamentary Counsel to the Treasury. The latter mould them into the correct terminology and send them back to the Department in the form of a Bill. But, even before it is introduced into Parliament, the Bill runs a

risk of deleterious amendment. The Minister in charge
of the Department may feel himself compelled to introduce changes in deference to the opinions of interested
parties, whether friendly or hostile. Such amendments,
which are often unalterable compromises, are a great
source of ambiguity and inconsistency.

After its introduction into Parliament, anything may
happen to the Bill. The Minister in charge of it may
wish to conciliate opponents of the Bill by making some
concession, which to his mind is quite harmless, but
which turns out afterwards to jeopardise seriously the
operation of the Act. The Parliamentary Counsel, who
are in continuous attendance during the debate, have to
make the alteration as best they can at short notice, and
there have been rare occasions when they were even
compelled to insert some amendment in the exact form,
good or bad, agreed upon in Committee.

BOOK II

CONSTITUTIONAL AND ADMINISTRATIVE LAW

PART III

CENTRAL AND LOCAL GOVERNMENT

SUMMARY

PAGE

CHAPTER 16. THE ORGANS OF CENTRAL GOVERN-
MENT   403

CHAPTER 17. THE NATIONAL BUDGET   423

CHAPTER 18. FOREIGN AFFAIRS   443

CHAPTER 19. THE ROYAL FORCES   446

CHAPTER 20. THE ORGANS OF LOCAL AUTHORITIES   455

CHAPTER 21. THE FUNCTIONS OF LOCAL AUTHORI-
TIES   477

CHAPTER 22. CENTRAL CONTROL OF LOCAL GOVERN-
MENT   503

CHAPTER 16

THE ORGANS OF CENTRAL GOVERNMENT

SUMMARY   PAGE
Section I. The Prime Minister, the Ministry, and the Cabinet   403
Section II. The Civil Service 408
Section III. The Central Government Departments 410

Section I. THE PRIME MINISTER, THE MINISTRY AND THE CABINET

The Prime Minister, or Premier, is a member of Parliament, selected by the King (as the person most likely to command a working majority in the House of Commons) to be the head of the Government. It is thought now to be a convention of the Constitution that the Premier should *not* be a member of the House of Lords. Until recently, at any rate, his office was quite unknown to the law; indeed, almost the earliest reference in any official document to the position of Prime Minister occurs in a Royal Warrant, issued in 1905, conferring upon him place and precedence next to the Archbishop of York. Yet, for all practical purposes, the government of the country has, ever since the death of George I, been directed by this holder of an office known only to convention. Not until 1917 did statute speak of the office, and even then the reference is only an incidental one to an official " now popularly known as " Prime Minister. There is still no statutory attempt to define the office or to prescribe its duties, but we can now at least say that the Ministers of the Crown Act, 1937, made express provision for the salary and pension of Prime Ministers.

His selection is entirely in the hands of the King, who in practice is always guided by his knowledge of the conditions existing in Parliament; and his task is facilitated by the traditional division of the House of Commons into parties, which we call the " party system." Each

Appointment.

Party system.

403

party has a recognised " leader " ; in practice, too, nearly every person who seeks election as a member of the House of Commons undertakes to his constituents that he will support one particular party. If a party secures a clear majority in the House of Commons, it is upon the leader of that party, as a matter of course, that the King's choice will fall for the office of Prime Minister. But where three or more parties are represented in such proportions that no one of them has a clear majority (as happened in recent years), the King's task becomes more delicate, and in selecting the Prime Minister he will not necessarily call upon the leader of the largest party ; for it may be that a more stable government will be secured by placing in power a party which can on most subjects command the support of one or other of the remaining parties.

Dismissal.

Resignations.

Just as the King has a discretionary power of appointing his Prime Minister, so in theory he may dismiss him at any time. In practice, however, a Prime Minister is never dismissed ; for, when he loses the support of the House of Commons, he either resigns, with all his colleagues, or advises the King to dissolve Parliament. If he adopts this latter alternative and his party is defeated at the polls, the Ministry resigns. But Prime Ministers have resigned, without being defeated either in the House or at a general election, when it was clear from the trend of public opinion, as revealed at by-elections or otherwise, that the Government had lost the confidence of the country. When the party in power is unable to form a majority from its own ranks, as in the case of the Labour Government of 1924, so that the Prime Minister is able to govern only by means of a compromise with the other parties, if at any time they determine to turn the Government out, it will become incumbent on the Prime Minister to resign or go to the polls. Formerly, indeed, any adverse vote in the House of Commons was thought to make it obligatory on the Prime Minister to resign ; but it has long been recognised that a mere "snap" vote against a Government project will not have this result. And, where the party in power is without its own majority, it may frequently be outvoted in quite important divisions without entailing upon the Prime Minister the duty of resigning his office.

It should be observed that the existence of the Government is not affected by an adverse vote in the House of Lords. For many years, both before and since the Parliament Act, 1911, Governments have held office in spite of the presence of a hostile majority in the Upper House ; and it was not until 1909 that an issue was first raised which brought the Government and the House of Lords into an irreconcilable conflict, with the result we have already seen (pp. 376-7). *No responsibility to House of Lords.*

Hitherto, in order that a salary should be payable to him, a Prime Minister has had to take one of the recognised executive offices, usually that of First Lord of the Treasury, which has merely nominal duties but is an office known to the law, and to which a salary is attached. But since 1937, as we have already said, the office of Prime Minister—or, rather, the combined office of Prime Minister and First Lord of the Treasury—has itself become a salaried (and pensionable) office known to the law.

The Ministry. The Prime Minister's first task on his appointment is to form a Ministry, that is to say, to choose persons from amongst his followers to fill the great executive offices of State. Each of the Departments of State, except a few of minor importance, has a political head : that is to say, a member of one or other of the Houses of Parliament, who is appointed to the position by the Crown upon the advice of the Prime Minister. Unlike the permanent Civil Servants, who constitute the personnel of each Department, the political heads of Departments, or Ministers, resign their offices upon change of Government ; or they may be asked to resign at any time by the Prime Minister, who can rely upon the Crown to dismiss any office-holder who has refused to resign at his request. Besides the actual heads of Departments, there are various minor political officials, called Parliamentary Secretaries or Under-Secretaries, attached to the more important Departments, who are appointed by, or at any rate subject to the approval of, the Prime Minister, and hold their positions on the same political terms as their departmental chiefs. *Personnel of the Ministry.*

Offices are
legal, not
conventional.

These high offices, to which Ministers are appointed, were first created *either* under the prerogative powers of the Crown *or* by statute ; hence they are *legal* offices, not merely dependent on usage.

Ministers need not *in law* be members of Parliament ; but, in practice, as soon as a Minister is appointed—or, at any rate, within a short while after—he must secure a seat in one or the other House, if he has not one already.

Individual
responsi-
bility.

As a servant of the Crown, according to the doctrine of Ministerial responsibility, every Minister is accountable to Parliament for all executive acts done by him or by his subordinates. But, although the theory is that Ministers are individually responsible, in fact a vote of censure passed by the House of Commons on a Minister would be regarded usually as a vote of censure on the Government, and the Ministry would resign ; for the Ministers settle all major questions of policy in consultation with one another, and accordingly are by constitutional usage regarded as a

Collective
responsibility.

collective whole, which must stand or fall together. But there have been certain events in recent years which tend perhaps to show that this principle of collective responsibility is not being quite so strongly adhered to now as in the past. Thus, at the time of Italy's dispute with Abyssinia, the Foreign Secretary alone resigned office after his negotiations with France had provoked popular outcry.

No legal
status.

The Cabinet. By a further convention of the Constitution, the Prime Minister invariably forms, out of the persons composing the Ministry, a smaller group called the Cabinet, whom he consults upon all important questions of policy. The Cabinet is, like the Prime Minister himself, the product of convention. Members of the Cabinet, *as such*, have no *legal* status whatsoever. Statutes made no mention of the Cabinet until an incidental reference in the Ministers of the Crown Act, 1937. Yet the part which it has played in ruling the country has led to the term " Cabinet Government " being applied to our system of government in its modern form.

Constitution
of the
Cabinet.

Cabinet Ministers must be Privy Councillors, and the oath sworn by a Privy Councillor is a safeguard for the secrecy of Cabinet debate ; but, apart from this, the functions, size, and membership of the Cabinet depend upon the will of the Prime Minister, whose decisions will be governed by what is politically expedient. For some years it has consisted of about twenty members, but during the latter part of the first Great War, and throughout the second, a small War Cabinet was more practicable ; and it may well be that, even for government in time of peace, the Cabinet, as at present constituted, is too unwieldy. Indeed, as testimony that in size the Cabinet is, if not too large, then as large as it can practicably be, we have the present practice whereby many Ministers are given " Cabinet Rank " but without actual membership.

The Cabinet is not an executive but a deliberative body, whose decisions are put into force by the Government Departments concerned, they having definite legal status and powers, or—if legislation is needed—by Parliament itself.

Not an executive but a deliberative body.

The Cabinet cannot rightly be described as a committee of the Privy Council, although, as we have seen, all its members must be Privy Councillors, and as such take the Privy Councillor's oath of secrecy. It is a purely informal body, and has, until recently at any rate, prized its informality very highly. But the growing complexity of modern government has made some sort of permanent organisation necessary, and the present practice is for agenda to be prepared by the Cabinet Secretary, and for Cabinet decisions to be recorded by him and promulgated to all Ministers whose departmental work may be concerned.

Informal and secret.

Cabinet Secretariat.

The control by the Cabinet of the Executive Government of the country, which it exercises by the tender of advice which in practice cannot be rejected, is complete. Its control over legislation is not so effective as is commonly supposed. Even a Government with a large working majority may have to make concessions to the Opposition, to dissentient members of its own party, or, perhaps, even to the House of Lords. Few Bills pass through both Houses entirely unamended ; many undergo very serious changes. In other words, parliamentary procedure has not yet been reduced to the farce which

Control of Cabinet over legislation.

it would be if the Opposition or hostile Government supporters had no chance of influencing the course of legislation.

Section II. THE CIVIL SERVICE

Tenure of Civil Servants. Each Government Department is staffed by permanent officials, who constitute the Civil Service. Holding office, *in theory*, at the pleasure of the Crown, they can be dismissed at a moment's notice, any express provision in their appointment notwithstanding; for the broad rule, already mentioned, is that the Crown cannot fetter its future executive action (see *Rederiaktiebolaget Amphitrite* v. *R.*, [1921] 3 K. B. 500; *Reilly* v. *R.*, [1934] A. C. 176). Indeed, the House of Lords has affirmed that civil servants have no enforceable right even to the pensions conferred by the Superannuation Acts (*Nixon* v. *A.-G.*, [1931] A. C. 184). Yet, although *in law* a Civil Servant's tenure is precarious, it is well known that *in practice* he is perfectly sure of being retained unless he is guilty of inefficiency or misconduct or disloyalty.

Regulated by Prerogative. The rules which regulate the examination and appointment of candidates, determine the pay, and prescribe a code of conduct for all Civil Servants are made by Prerogative Orders in Council and not by statute; for the Crown is, by its Prerogative, head of the Executive Government, and has power to direct its working. On the other hand, provision for payment of salaries (though not the fixing of their amount) and superannuation must be made by Act of Parliament; for Parliament alone has power to impose a charge on the taxpayer. This is emphasised in a useful definition quoted by a Royal Commission on the Civil Service : " Civil Servants are those servants of the Crown, other than holders of political or judicial offices, who are employed in a civil capacity, and whose remuneration is paid wholly and directly out of monies voted by Parliament."

Treasury supervision. By its control of expenditure, and in accordance with the terms of the Orders in Council which regulate the Civil Service, the Treasury exercises a general supervision over the Service, and the Secretary to the Treasury is styled " Head of H.M. Civil Service." So it is not uncommon to find Treasury Minutes laying down new regulations, and calling the attention of Departments to, and giving rulings upon, the peculiar obligations of Civil Servants.

But although the Crown may by its Prerogative lay down rules for the government of the Civil Service, our failure to develop a logical system of administrative jurisdiction (on the Continental model) has left the Crown without any Courts (analogous to Courts Martial) for the enforcement of discipline in the Service. Discipline is actually enforced by dismissal or threats of dismissal or by stoppages of pay, but these measures are taken by the Crown according to its absolute discretion. *Civil Service discipline.*

In recent years, however, something has been done to remedy this state of affairs, and now claims affecting the emoluments, weekly hours of work, and leave of the lower classes of Civil Servants may be submitted for arbitration to the Industrial Court, which was established under the Industrial Courts Act, 1919. There is also a system of " Whitley " Councils which aims at removing difficulties in connection with the terms of service.

The conduct of examinations—practically all Civil Service posts have since 1870 been filled by competitive examination—is in the hands of the Civil Service Commissioners, who are directly responsible to the Treasury and through it to Parliament. *Civil Service examinations.*

By reason of the requirement that a Civil Servant shall be ready to obey and co-operate loyally with Governments of any party, participation in party politics, at any rate active participation, is strictly forbidden to members of the Service, and, if a permanent official wishes to become a candidate for Parliament, he must resign from the Service. On the other hand, the Civil Servant is not disfranchised, and no attempt is made to investigate his private opinions on political matters, unless they make him a disloyal citizen. It must be remembered, too, that Civil Servants are not permitted to defend themselves in public against criticism except through the *political* head of their Department, who may do so in Parliament. That is why parliamentary questions concerning the administration of a Department are addressed to the *The Civil Service and politics.*

Minister in charge, however detailed or trivial the matter may be.

Section III. THE CENTRAL GOVERNMENT DEPARTMENTS

The executive government of the country is carried out by the Departments, together with one or two high officials, such as the Lord Chancellor, who perform functions similar to those of a Department. At the head of all the more important Departments there is a Minister, who is probably, though not necessarily, a member of the Cabinet or a non-member of Cabinet rank, and who holds office only for such time as the party to which he belongs remains in power. Under him are usually one or more subordinate members of the Ministry who do not hold Cabinet rank, and are known as Parliamentary Secretaries or sometimes Parliamentary Under-Secretaries of State. There is also in every such Department a Permanent Secretary or Permanent Under-Secretary of State, who is the head of the permanent staff of the Department, which often includes a legal adviser to the Department, who is either a barrister or a solicitor but is in any event known as its Solicitor. Some of the minor Departments are non-political Departments ; that is to say, their chief is not a Minister but an official of the Civil Service, who cannot be in either House, so that the Department is put, so to speak, under the wing of some Minister, who shall answer for it to Parliament.

His position in the Constitution.

THE LORD CHANCELLOR. Owing to the antiquity and dignity of the office, which confers upon the holder rank and precedence next to the Archbishop of Canterbury and above all other subjects except princes of the blood royal, it is fitting to begin our list with the Lord Chancellor, or, to give him his full title, the Lord High Chancellor of Great Britain. This great officer occupies a unique position in the Constitution. He combines in himself the Speakership of the House of Lords in its legislative capacity ; the presidency of that House and of the Judicial Committee of the Privy Council when sitting as Courts of Law ; the patronage of certain ecclesiastical preferments of the Crown ; the custodianship of the Great Seal ; and the

direct or indirect control of the whole judicial machinery
of the State. He is the head of the judiciary in two
senses ; he is himself a judge, and the chief judge, of the
country and is able to sit in any Court ; and he has wide
powers of supervision over the working of our legal
system. He advises the Crown as to the appointment of
the *puisne* judges of the High Court and of county and
borough Justices of the Peace ; and he himself appoints,
directs, and may dismiss the county court judges without
reference to the Crown. So also may he dismiss a Justice
of the Peace. Recent statute has empowered him to
transfer a High Court judge, with the judge's consent,
from one Division to another. He is *ex officio* a member
of all Rule-making Committees ; and in this capacity has
a voice in the internal procedure of the Courts. And all
writs of summons in the High Court are "tested" (or
witnessed) in his name.

These executive functions are such as, in many Not a
countries, are entrusted to a Ministry of Justice ; but the Department.
Lord Chancellor does not constitute a Department,
though he has certain permanent officials attached to him.

The Lord Chancellor is almost invariably a Cabinet
Minister, and acts as spokesman for the Government upon
all manner of topics in the House of Lords. When a
Commoner is made Lord Chancellor, he is invariably
raised to the peerage, though this is not legally necessary.

THE TREASURY. The Treasury is the great Finance The Board.
Department. In theory it consists of a Board of Lords
Commissioners of His Majesty's Treasury, composed of the
First Lord of the Treasury, the Chancellor of the
Exchequer, and (at present) five Junior Lords of the
Treasury ; and the Department is characterised as "their
Lordships" in correspondence. But this Board has been
obsolete for many years. The office of First Lord, as we
have seen, is that held by the Prime Minister ; while the
Junior Lords act, *with others*, as Government "whips,"
responsible for organising the party affairs of the Government, and for ensuring that an adequate majority is
present in the Commons to pass its measures and support
its policy.

It is the Chancellor of the Exchequer who is the really responsible head of the Treasury. Finance enters directly or indirectly into all affairs of State ; and this fact renders the Department the most influential of all Government Departments, while its chief must be a member of the House of Commons, where all financial legislation is initiated. There are also three subordinate political officers, the Financial Secretary to the Treasury, who deputises for the Chancellor in the House of Commons, a Parliamentary Secretary, who acts as Chief Government Whip, and an Economic Secretary, whose office is very recent. The Permanent Secretary (see *ante*, p. 410) advises the Prime Minister, *inter alia*, as to the choice of permanent heads for the other Departments.

The part which the Treasury plays in revenue matters will be discussed hereafter in Chap. 17, where we shall be brought into touch with some of the following subordinate Departments or public corporations, which work in close connection with the Treasury.

1. *The Board of Customs and Excise and the Board of Inland Revenue*, each consisting of permanent Civil Servants, who carry out the administrative work in collecting their respective sources of revenue.

2. *The Comptroller and Auditor-General*, who fulfils two functions of very great importance : first, in authorising the Bank of England to give credit to the Treasury for all payments out of the Exchequer Account at the Bank, which he will only do when he is satisfied that the demands of the Treasury have been sanctioned by Parliament ; second, to audit the State accounts. He is a permanent official, but, in order to mark the importance of his office and his independence of political influence, his salary is paid out of the Consolidated Fund, instead of being voted annually by Parliament ; and, like the judges, he holds his office during good behaviour, though he can be dismissed by the King upon Addresses presented by both Houses of Parliament.

3. *The Paymaster-General*, a *political* officer, who pays out to the Departments, or other recipients authorised by the Treasury, the sums which he receives from the Bank of England. As these duties have long been dele-

gated to the Civil Service, the office is among the sinecures (*post*, p. 419) which a Government can assign to its followers in Parliament for the carrying out of special duties.

4. *The Bank of England*, no longer a private corporation, but now a " nationalised " corporation, whose close association with the Treasury has been hardened into a matter of law by recent legislation.

5. *The Commissioners of Crown Lands*, who manage the Crown Lands (see *post* pp. 424 and 431–2).

6. Of special interest to lawyers is the work of the *Procurator-General and Treasury Solicitor*, who, in addition to his duties as legal adviser to the Treasury in the discharge of its manifold duties, acts as solicitor for the Crown in all civil cases, save where the Department concerned has a " solicitor " of its own (see *ante*, p. 410). He is also King's Proctor in matrimonial causes.

THE SECRETARIAT. The secretariat derives its origin Origin. from the King's Secretary, who was, as the name implies, the person in the secrets of the King. He became a great executive officer, and obtained the title of Secretary of State. As time went on, the duties became too onerous for a single officer to discharge ; and they became divided between a number of Secretaries of State, of whom there are now seven, each at the head of a Department. But in legal theory there is but one office ; and powers conferred Theoretically
one office. by statute upon any one of the Secretaries of State are generally expressed to be conferred upon " a " Secretary of State, without specifying which particular Secretary of State is to discharge the functions in question. This anachronism, which makes it *formally* proper for one Secretary of State to act *in lieu* of another, has upon occasion been of departmental convenience in an emergency.

1. *The Home Secretary*, or Secretary of State for the Home Department, has been described as a " residuary legatee," on the ground that all national affairs that are not specially allotted to other Departments fall, or used to fall, into his province ; but his sphere now makes him a Minister of the Interior (as a foreign observer might not unfairly say) for the affairs of England and Wales, the

Channel Islands, and the Isle of Man.   He also stands in much the same relation to Northern Ireland as the Secretary of State for Commonwealth Relations does to the self-governing Dominions.

It is usual to classify the functions of the Home Secretary into three divisions.

Channel of communication between Crown and subject.

(*a*) He is the recognised channel of communication between the Crown and the subject in all cases where no other procedure is laid down.   Thus he receives all petitions addressed to the Crown, in particular petitions for the reprieve of condemned prisoners.

Maintenance of internal order.

(*b*) He is responsible for the maintenance of internal order.   Thus he controls the Metropolitan Police directly, and all other police forces indirectly, as will be seen in a later Chapter (*post*, p. 480). He (and not the Lord Chancellor) appoints stipendiary and metropolitan police magistrates and Recorders of Quarter Sessions.   He is charged with the duty of naturalising aliens and of deporting undesirable aliens, whether under an extradition treaty or otherwise.   He controls all prisons, Borstal institutions, remand and detention centres, probation homes and hostels.

Other Statutory Powers.

(*c*) He administers a mass of statute law relating to the welfare of the community, ranging from the control of burial and cremation to the issue of certificates for carrying firearms and the operation of " summer time."

2. *The Secretary of State for Foreign Affairs* is in charge of the relations between this country and foreign States. (See further, Chap. 18.)

3. *The Secretary of State for War* is the head of the War Department or War Office, which controls the land forces of the Crown.   (See further, Chap. 19.)

4. *The Secretary of State for Commonwealth Relations* holds a modern office, recently renamed, that was called into being by the emergence of the Dominions as virtually independent nations within the British Commonwealth. The new name avoids the outmoded word Dominion. (See further, Chap. 27.)

5. *The Secretary of State for the Colonies*, whose office is much older, is in charge—broadly speaking—of Colonial as distinct from Dominion relations. (See further, Chap. 27.)

6. *The Secretary of State for Air*, who is in charge of the Air Ministry, stands in very much the same relation to it as the Secretary of State for War to the War Office. (See further, Chap. 19.)

7. *The Secretary of State for Scotland* is the head of the Scottish Office, which, with the subordinate Departments for Scotland (Health ; Education ; Agriculture), controls in these and in various other matters the greater part of the internal government of Scotland. The Office is now divided between London and Edinburgh.

THE BOARDS. Three Departments are still administered, as a fiction if not as a fact, by Boards, consisting of a number of Commissioners, with a Ministerial head. The Treasury is one of these Boards ; but, as we have already seen, the Board never meets. Only two others still survive :

1. *The Board of Admiralty*, which does really meet. The members are called Lords of the Admiralty, and their president, the First Lord, ranks as a member of the Cabinet. (See further, Chap. 19.)

2. *The Board of Trade* itself never meets ; it has long been only a shadow, and the work of this Department is superintended by the President of the Board, who is a Minister in all but name.

It is the function of the Board of Trade to supervise the national " industries and manufactures," both in internal and foreign relations. Though many of its former activities have been taken over by other Ministries, the Board's function is spread over the enormous and increasing complications of production and distribution for the home and export markets. Apart from all this, it carries out, through officials called Official Receivers, the administrative (as opposed to the judicial) side of bankruptcy and winding-up proceedings ; it superintends the administration of the law relating to patents, designs and trademarks, the Comptroller-General of the Patent Office being

Its activities.

a permanent official of the Department ; and the regulation of the standard weights and measures also falls within its sphere.   In recent years it was given powers in matters like the rationing of clothing and furniture, which brought the Board closely into touch with the domestic as well as the commercial life of the country.

THE MINISTRIES.   Most of the Departments constituted or reconstituted in recent years are under the control of a political head who is frankly called a Minister.

The number of Ministries has about doubled in less than a decade, and further additions may be in contemplation. The account of them in an elementary treatise like this cannot be much more than a list.

Further, by the Ministers of the Crown (Transfer of Functions) Act, 1946, there is no longer the need for legislation to redistribute Ministerial functions ; and Orders in Council now suffice " for the transfer to any Minister of the Crown of any functions (hitherto) exercisable by another Minister of the Crown."   This means that changes may be both sudden and frequent, and they may concern any Department of State, though like the Treasury or the Board of Trade it may not be a Ministry in actual name.

Its functions.   1. *The Ministry of Health* was established in 1919 in order to centralise into one Department the control of all matters affecting the public health.   The Ministry's parental relation to all local authorities in respect of matters like housing would, however, be better indicated if it had taken over the name as well as the work of the Local Government Board.   (See further, Chap. 22.)

But in recent years the " health " activities of the Ministry have become more and more prominent, and " the establishment of a comprehensive health service " as envisaged by the National Health Service Act, 1946, is indeed a major duty for the Ministry to carry out.

2. *The Ministry of Agriculture and Fisheries* was also constituted in 1919, and its functions cover practically the whole sphere of agricultural interests and the administration of a number of statutes relating to fisheries.   The Ordnance Survey, which is responsible for the issue of

maps and plans of the country, is under the authority of this Department.

The Forestry Commission, which was set up as an inde- The Forestry
Commission. pendent body charged with the general duty of developing afforestation and the supply of timber, is also now under the Ministry of Agriculture and Fisheries.

3. *The Ministry of Labour and National Service*, as it is now called, was set up in 1916, and is charged with the administration (now under the Act of 1948) of the Employment (Labour) Exchanges, and of much legislation relating to wages and industrial disputes, *e.g.*, the Wages Councils Acts, 1945–48, and the Catering Wages Act, 1943.

The Ministry's operation of the National Service Acts, and its control and " direction " of labour, are set deep in the daily life.

4. *The Ministry of Transport* was created by an Act of 1919 " for the purpose of improving the means of and the facilities for locomotion and transport," and to it were transferred all executive powers and duties relating to railways, canals, roads and harbours. Additional functions were conferred by successive enactments, in particular by the Road Traffic Acts, 1930–34, and by the Trunk Roads Acts, 1936 and 1946. (See further, Chap. 21.)

During and since the war it has taken over the supervision of shipping and the mercantile marine, and of the " nationalised " inland transport, but none of these industries is managed by the Ministry.

5. *The Ministry of Pensions.* This Department controls the payment of pensions in respect of the casualties of the two Great Wars.

6. *The Ministry of Education*, long in existence as the substance behind the shadow of a Board that never met, was allowed its present name to mark the passing of the Education Act, 1944. The permanent staff is organised into separate branches for English and Welsh education, and includes a large outdoor staff of inspectors distributed throughout the country. It administers the national system of education in " partnership " with the " local education authorities," whose responsibilities have been drastically revised under the new legislation.

7. *The Ministry of Works*, originally only a small organisation for the supervision of the royal parks and palaces and of government buildings, has now become a Ministry in recognition of its enormously increased activities during and since the recent war.

The Ministries that follow are all of recent creation :

8. *The Ministry of Supply*, which was set up on the eve of the Second World War to revive and extend the work of its predecessor, the Ministry of Munitions ; but its activities unlike those of its predecessor have not ceased with the ending of the war. On the contrary, not only do they include those of the former Ministry of Aircraft Production, but they now range over a wide field of peacetime industry, more particularly of the " basic " kind such as steel. It must be left to those with intimate knowledge to indicate the borderlines between the Ministry's functions and those of its departmental neighbours, in particular the Board of Trade, but it needs little knowledge to foretell that periodic and perhaps frequent changes will be made by Orders in Council under the Ministers of the Crown (Transfer of Functions) Act, 1946, to which we have already called attention.

9. *The Ministry of Food*, in peace as in war *parens patriæ*. Created a decade ago to ensure that war-time conservation and fair distribution of our food supplies which national experience in an earlier conflict had proved to be essential, the Ministry continues to flourish as a vast organisation with offices throughout the land whose complicated machinery for the allocation and rationing of food in these times of stringency has brought the Ministry and its work close indeed to the daily life of every citizen.

10. *The Ministry of Fuel and Power*, which has grown out of the Board of Trade into the separate Ministry that now supervises the various undertakings—Coal, Electricity, Gas—now in public ownership as the result of recent " nationalisation " legislation. But such supervision—which is not to be confused with the day-to-day " running " of these quasi-commercial undertakings—does not by a long way exhaust the Ministry's activities, as citizens in need of petrol or of coal are very well aware.

11. *The Ministry of Town and Country Planning*, whose functions inherited from other Departments have been magnified by the New Towns Act, 1946, and the Town and Country Planning Act, 1947. (See further, Vol. I, pp. 372 *et seq.*)

12. *The Ministry of National Insurance*, which administers the social services now integrated and enlarged under the National Insurance Act, 1946, and the National Insurance (Industrial Injuries) Act, 1946.

13. *The Ministry of Civil Aviation*, which relieves other Ministries of duties that needed concentration and post-war stimulation.

14. *The Ministry of Defence*, to whose long overdue emergence as the instrument of co-ordination between the Fighting Services, we shall refer later.

SINECURE AND OTHER OFFICES. We must now mention certain salaried offices, with only nominal or formal duties, which nevertheless are of considerable importance in modern government. They are, on the one hand, the ancient offices of Lord President of the Council, Lord Privy Seal, and Chancellor of the Duchy of Lancaster, and, on the other hand, the Ministries of State, of which three may be filled under the Re-election of Ministers Act, 1919. The salaried holders of these sinecures, being free from departmental duties, are entrusted with special duties, *e.g.*, the Leadership of the House of Commons, or the Chairmanship of Cabinet Committees, or diplomatic missions and international negotiations.

Of special interest, in conclusion, are two offices, both political, but below Cabinet rank : the Post Office, and the Law Officers' Department.

The Postmaster-General has a monopoly over the postal and telegraph arrangements of the country ; that is to say, with certain exceptions, no letter may be conveyed and no telegram may be despatched by any person other than a servant of the Post Office, under a penalty of a fine. The Telegraph Acts apply to telephones and wireless telegraphy, which are likewise subject to the monopoly ; but licences may be granted by the Postmaster-General to private individuals or companies ; and, as is well known,

Postal and telegraph services.

the licensed undertakings of Cable and Wireless Limited have recently passed by statute into public ownership.

Other business transacted by the Post Office.

The Department has an office in almost every village throughout the country ; and its services have, therefore, been utilised in many directions for the discharge of various executive functions, unconnected with postal business, which require to be dealt with locally while remaining under the control of a Central Department. It acts as a channel for investment in various Government stocks ; it conducts a Savings Bank, deposits in which are secured on the Consolidated Fund ; it collects many duties and taxes for the Inland Revenue Department ; it issues licences of one kind or another. Thus, through its agency, the ordinary person is brought into touch at many points with the Executive ; and there are few Government Departments which have not, at one time or another, employed the personnel of the Post Office as an efficient and economical means of performing their functions locally.

The *Law Officers' Department* consists of the two Law Officers, the Attorney-General and his deputy, the Solicitor-General (see the Law Officers Act, 1944), of whom both are invariably members of the House of Commons. They are selected from the ranks of the most successful barristers who have rendered political services to the party in power ; and, owing to the large (though recently much limited) remuneration attached to the positions, and to the certain prospects which they offer of promotion to high judicial or political office, they are the coveted goal of practising barristers.

The functions of the Law Officers.

The primary function of the Law Officers is to represent the Crown in the courts of justice, and to act as legal advisers to the Government Departments whenever their services are required. No less important is their political duty to speak in debate in the House on legal matters. Further, the Crown is deemed to be interested whenever questions of public rights are raised in the Courts ; and it is therefore open to the Attorney-General to take part or be represented in proceedings relating to the national revenue, charities, mental deficiency patents, and other matters, as the representative of the public interests.

Until recently, at any rate, it was not uncommon for the Law Officers to appear in person for the prosecution of important criminal cases. They also performed judicial functions in connection with the grant of patents, but this jurisdiction is now vested in a more appropriate tribunal.

This account of the great executive Departments of State is by no means exhaustive. There are also a large number of minor non-political Departments, such as the Charity Commission, the Royal Mint, the Public Works Loan Board, the Stationery Office, the Government Chemist, and the Public Record Office, to name only a few at random, which would require some treatment in a full statement of the working of the Constitution.

Minor Departments.

But though " non-political " seems appropriate to describe these minor Departments—both the few named and the many unnamed—it must not be supposed that no Minister is made answerable to Parliament for their activities. Nor must their status as emanations from the Crown be confused with the status—far too novel as yet for constitutional theory to define—of the powerful public bodies recently created, of which some mention is made elsewhere in this treatise, which are already of such tremendous importance in the social and economic life of our post-war community that it might well be thought fitting to speak of them in some detail even in this work of elementary character. But on balance it seems prudent to say little concerning their constitutions and powers until the judgment of experts has had time to mature. Some general propositions must, however, be attempted ; for otherwise this chapter would omit an aspect of contemporary government that seems likely to become of ever increasing importance. So, first and foremost, let us notice that, although a public corporation of this recent sort—typified on the one hand by the National Coal Board or the Transport Commission and on the other hand by the Central Land Board or one of the Regional Hospital Boards—is, as Dr. Friedmann explains, " politically and, to some extent, economically, a Government responsibility, it should not be legally identified with the Government " ; indeed, " the very purpose of the

The recent Public Corporations.

conduct of nationalised industries by public corporations is their separation from Government Departments." On the other hand, it would be even more fallacious to classify these " instruments of public policy under the direction of the Government which is responsible to Parliament " with ordinary commercial companies or even with those of the class to which railway companies belonged ; for, as the same learned writer goes on to explain, " even the formal similarity is limited, because of the absence of private shareholders and the appointment of the managing board by the Minister." Nor can we even comprehend these recent bodies as " public authorities," broad though the embrace of that term may be, unless we observe, not only that they are excluded from the advantages of the Public Authorities Protection Act (see *post*, p. 581) by the legislation creating them, though that legislation does itself curtail in their favour the years of grace normally allowed for litigation, but also that their similarity with local authorities is by no means close. The local authorities, if we may quote Dr. Friedmann's contrast in conclusion, " are not under the immediate direction of the Minister, although the Government exercises control, through grants, inspections, the right of sanctioning plans and schemes, and other supervisory functions. The public corporations, on the other hand, are a direct instrument of national policy although they are given far-reaching legal and functional autonomy " (Modern Law Review (1947), Vol. 10, pp. 233 and 377).

CHAPTER 17

THE NATIONAL BUDGET

It is difficult to give an adequate and intelligible account of public finance without straying into the realms of politics and economics. Law is important here, as in other branches of national activity, but, apart from a very few general principles, which are easily grasped, the law which regulates the British financial system is apt to appear as a mass of disconnected and often exceedingly obscure rules. There is practically no Common Law of taxation or expenditure ; some of the Statute Law is to be found in consolidated form ; but fragments of revenue law still remain scattered up and down the Statute Book. Many of the rules which are of the greatest practical importance are in either Standing Orders of the House of Commons or Prerogative Orders in Council or even in mere circular letters from the Treasury to the other Government Departments. Some of these rules are legal rules, but not in the sense that they are binding upon the ordinary citizen ; others are mere announcements of the policy and procedure which one Department will pursue when another asks it to forward demands for public money to Parliament. We shall try in the following pages to indicate what are, from the lawyer's point of view, the most important features of the system of national finance, avoiding as far as possible, on the one hand political and economic considerations, and on the other the profusion of apparently unconnected detail which is such a feature of our revenue law.

British national finance is notable for its unity and concentration. These characteristics manifest themselves in four different ways : *constitutionally* in the two principles that (i) the whole national revenue is the King's Revenue, and that (ii) Parliament has full control over the levying of taxation, and over the spending of public money, in whatever way collected ; *administratively* (i) in the establish-

Revenue Law a profusion of disconnected rules.

Financial unity and concentration.

423

ment of one common Government account, the Consolidated Fund, into which, with very few and unimportant exceptions, all revenue is paid, and out of which, with the same exceptions, all expenditure is met, and (ii) in the unified technical control of estimates which is exercised by the Treasury.

Let us elaborate these points.

1. *The King's Revenue.* The whole national revenue is the King's Revenue. This principle has been constantly borne in mind by the House of Commons, and the rule is long fixed that only a Minister of the Crown can ask the House of Commons either to raise money by taxation or to give authority for its expenditure. A private member may move to reduce a particular tax or appropriation, but not to increase it. Thus the doctrine that the revenue is the King's is no mere theory, but has had important results in practice, making the Government of the day responsible to the Commons for all taxation and expenditure, and operating as a salutary check on governmental extravagance (see *ante*, pp. 394–5).

Charge or Tax can be proposed only by a Minister.

2. *Control of Parliament.* Though the revenue is the King's, its raising and spending is completely subject to the control of the House of Commons. This result has only come about after severe struggles between Parliament and the Crown. It involves two propositions.

Act of Parliament necessary for taxation.

(*a*) Apart from certain revenues which belong to the Crown by virtue of the Prerogative, and are as such limited by the Common Law and subject to further limitation by Act of Parliament, for example, the revenue from Crown lands and certain property which falls to the Crown as *bona vacantia* (see *post*, pp. 432–3), the Crown cannot levy any money except by the Act of Parliament. The Bill of Rights says :

> " That levying Money for or to the Use of the Croune by Pretence of Prerogative without Consent of Parlyament for longer time or in other Manner than the same is or shall be granted is Illegal."

Moreover, it is a firm article of the policy of the House of Commons that it will grant to the Crown only enough money to satisfy the claims of government for the next financial year. That is not to say that there are no permanent taxes, but as so many of the most important taxes, such as the Income Tax, are in force only from year to year, the Government would find it impossible to carry on the government of the country without submitting to the procedure whereby the House of Commons exerts its control.

(*b*) No public money may be expended without the consent of the House of Commons. It is the practice of the House to appropriate every penny of the national revenue to some specific purpose, and any unauthorised expenditure—if it should take place—is likely to be a matter for comment in the House, and, if it is serious, may be made a question of confidence involving the fate of the Minister responsible, and possibly of the Government as a whole. *Consent of Commons necessary for expenditure of money.*

Complete appropriation has been secured only by slow degrees. Formerly the King had full control of his so-called " hereditary revenues," including the prerogative revenues which have been mentioned above and certain permanent revenues granted to him by Parliament in return for the renunciation of other prerogative revenues. He was indeed bound to pay out of them a large part of the expenses of the civil government, including the salaries of the Civil Servants and the Judges, but his hereditary revenues were only appropriated to these purposes in the sense that, unless he could convince Parliament that he had properly applied them and that they were insufficient, Parliament would not give him any more money for these purposes. In other words, Parliament took into account when appropriating money that the greater part of the ordinary expenses of government were already provided for ; but, apart from this, the King was at liberty to allocate the proceeds of his hereditary revenues as he thought fit. For a long time past, however, it has been the custom for a new Sovereign, on his accession, to surrender his hereditary revenues, and with them the obligation to pay for the ordinary expenses of government, and in return to receive a Civil List, or annual income to be spent on the personal expenses of the monarch. Thus, by the Civil List Act, 1937 (which replaced the Civil List Act, 1936, after the abdication of King Edward VIII), a Civil *Slow acquisition of control by Commons.*

Civil List.

List was granted to, and settled on, His present Majesty during his reign, and for six months afterwards, to the amount of £410,000 per annum. Of this sum £110,000 is assigned to His Majesty's privy purse, and the remainder is applicable chiefly to the salaries and expenses connected with his Household. The Act (as amended on the marriage of the Princess Elizabeth) also makes provision for other members of the Royal Family, and in particular for the Queen in the event of her surviving His Majesty.

3. *The Consolidated Fund.* All moneys accruing to the National Exchequer, from whatever source, are paid into an account at the Bank of England, and there form a fund which is known as the Consolidated Fund. The Consolidated Fund is thus the nation's account at the Bank of England. Formerly it was the habit to earmark certain items of taxation for certain purposes, and to that end to keep separate accounts, a practice which was the source of inelasticity and confusion. Only since 1787 have all Government accounts been consolidated. Even now there is *one* exceptional case where moneys are *not* paid into the Consolidated Fund ; that is to say, where a Department has received money, for instance, from trading operations, and uses it to defray departmental expenses.

Appropriations in aid.

This is called an " appropriation in aid," and there is no need for Parliamentary authorisation of such an appropriation. Thus the Post Office might use its profits from the sale of stamps to pay the wages of its postmen, without going to the trouble of paying the money into the Consolidated Fund and then obtaining Parliamentary authorisation for its subsequent withdrawal. But even such appropriations are always dealt with in the departmental estimates presented to Parliament ; and if an estimate should be exceeded, it would be a matter for criticism.

4. *Treasury control.* It would take an entire chapter to explain adequately how the Treasury controls the national finances. Here we can only hope to draw attention to a few salient points in the system of Treasury control.

The Chancellor of the Exchequer and his staff.

As we have seen, the Chancellor of the Exchequer is the *political* head of the Department ; and it is an important part of his responsibility to introduce in the House of Commons those financial proposals (the "Budget" speech) which take final shape in the Finance Bill for the year, as well as the other financial measures which we have previously described (see *ante*, p. 395).

It is the business of the Treasury to see that the government of the country is run as economically as possible. It is the guardian of the taxpayers' interests, and it must attempt to check the extravagance of the "spending" Departments. All Departments are bound to submit to it their Estimates for the forthcoming financial year, and it is only when the Treasury has approved them that they can be included in the Budget and put before the House of Commons. Of course, the personal influence of the Chancellor of the Exchequer counts for much. He ought to be able to restrain his colleagues in the Cabinet, being himself restrained by the prospect of having to face the House of Commons on "Budget day." But everything in the long run depends on policy, and if the Cabinet deems a certain policy necessary which inevitably involves an increase in taxation, the Chancellor's duty is limited to ensuring that it shall be carried out as economically as possible.

Submission of estimates to the Treasury.

The Treasury's function is confined to the *examination* of the Estimates presented to it by the other Departments, and to discussing them with the Departments concerned and endeavouring to persuade the latter to reduce them to the lowest limits. But even this has sometimes been rendered very difficult in the past, for a Department might obtain a Cabinet decision in favour of its proposals before the Treasury had had an opportunity of criticising them. This danger has now been to a great extent obviated by Cabinet circulars which have laid it down that no proposal involving the taxpayers' money can be brought before the Cabinet for decision until, not only the Treasury, but also every other Department which may be concerned, has examined it completely, and then only after a few days have elapsed since the papers, including all the criticisms of the proposal, have been circulated to the various members of the Cabinet. There is therefore some guarantee that a policy shall not be entered upon

The Treasury and the Estimates.

without a full examination of its financial implications. No Government Department is exempt from this control.

Now let us consider what expenses the Chancellor of the Exchequer has to provide for and what sources of revenue he has at his disposal. This we can best do by taking the Budget of 1947, as shown on the following page, and considering the more important items, first of the expenditure and then of the revenue accounts.

EXPENDITURE. In the Expenditure column the student will observe that the items are grouped together under two heads, namely, Consolidated Fund Services and Supply Services. The distinction between these two groups must first be explained.

Consolidated Fund Services and Supply Services distinguished.

No payment can be made out of the Consolidated Fund except upon the authority of Parliament, in the form of a statute granting certain moneys to the Crown as the head of the Executive. This authority may be given either once and for all, so as to hold good for a number of years or without limitation of time ; or it may be given in each year for that year alone. Payments of the former class, made by authority of a permanent grant under an Act of Parliament, are called " Consolidated Fund Services " ; those of the latter kind, which are voted each year by the House of Commons, are called " Supply Services." The distinction is of some importance, because, if a particular payment is charged permanently on the Consolidated Fund, the recipient of it knows that he is bound to obtain his money unless Parliament were to take the active step of passing an Act depriving him of the right already belonging to him under the previous Act ; whereas a Supply Service only exists by virtue of the exercise each year of a renewed Parliamentary authority. Thus the recipient of a Consolidated Fund payment is much more independent of Parliamentary control than a person who, or Department which, has to rely on the passing of an *annual* Act for his or its supply. Where therefore it is desired to increase the independence of the recipient, as in the case of the Judges, the Speaker of the House of Commons, the Leader of the Opposition, and the Comptroller

BUDGET ESTIMATES, 1947–8

A.—ORDINARY REVENUE AND EXPENDITURE

ESTIMATED REVENUE	£	ESTIMATED EXPENDITURE	£	£
Inland Revenue—		Interest and Management of National Debt ...		525,000,000[1]
Income Tax ...	1,073,000,000	Payments to Northern Ireland Exchequer ...		23,000,000[2]
Sur-tax ...	80,000,000	Miscellaneous Consolidated Fund Services ...		8,000,000
Death Duties ...	155,000,000	Total ...		556,000,000
Stamps ...	57,000,000	Supply Services—		
Profits Tax and Excess Profits Tax ...	202,000,000	*Defence—*		
Other Inland Revenue Duties ...	1,000,000	*Excluding Pensions* { Army Votes ... 372,972,000		
Total Inland Revenue ... 1,568,000,000		Navy Votes ... 182,935,000		
		Air Votes ... 211,482,000		
		Ministry of Supply ... 100,300,000 }		867,689,000
		Pensions { Army Votes ... 15,028,000		
		Navy Votes ... 13,765,000		
		Air Votes ... 2,518,000 }		31,311,000
Customs and Excise—		*Civil—*		
Customs ...	736,960,000	I. Central Government and Finance ...	13,150,000	
Excise ...	643,040,000	II. Foreign and Imperial ...	61,832,000	
Total Customs and Excise ...	1,380,000,000	III. Home Department, Law and Justice ...	34,386,000	
		IV. Education and Broadcasting ...	183,976,000	
		V. Health, Housing, Town Planning, Labour and National Insurance ...	387,647,000	
		VI. Trade, Industry and Transport ...	188,784,000	
		VII. Common Services (Works, Stationery, &c.) ...	79,211,000	
Motor Vehicle Duties ...	50,000,000	VIII. Non-Effective Charges (Pensions) ...	100,609,000	
TOTAL RECEIPTS FROM TAXES ...	2,998,000,000	IX. Exchequer Contributions to Local Revenues ...	66,412,000	
		X. Supply, Food and Miscellaneous Services...	582,019,000	1,698,026,000
		Post Office Vote (Excess over Revenue) ...		2,688,000
Sale of surplus war stores ...	95,000,000	*Tax Collection—*		
Surplus receipts from certain trading services ...	55,000,000	Customs and Excise and Inland Revenue Votes (including Pensions, £1,988,000) ...		25,653,000
Wireless Licences ...	11,000,000			
Crown Lands ...	1,000,000	TOTAL EXPENDITURE ...		3,181,367,000
Receipts from Sundry Loans ...	21,000,000	SURPLUS ...		269,633,000
Miscellaneous ...	270,000,000			
TOTAL REVENUE ...	3451,000,000			3,451,000,000

[1] In addition £6,500,000 for Interest on the National Debt will be met from receipts under the following Acts:—Bank of England Act, 1946, Coal Nationalisation Act, 1946, New Towns Act, 1946, Local Authorities Loans Act, 1945, Building Materials and Housing Act, 1945, Housing (Temporary Accommodation) Act, 1944, Housing (Scotland) Act, 1944, and Overseas Trade Guarantees Act, 1939.

[2] This item consists of:
(a) £20,000,000, being proceeds of reserved taxes in Northern Ireland after deduction of Imperial Contribution and the cost of reserved services in Northern Ireland, and
(b) £3,000,000, issues under the Unemployment and Family Allowances (Northern Ireland Agreement) Act, 1946.

B.—SELF-BALANCING REVENUE AND EXPENDITURE

			£
... 193,230,000	Post Office expenditure corresponding to Revenue (including Pensions £10,976,000) ...		144,230,000
	Excess Profits Tax, Post-war refunds (Part deducted for tax) ...		49,000,000
	Total ...		193,230,000

and Auditor-General, the salary will be charged permanently on the Consolidated Fund. Where, on the other hand, the object is to give to Parliament the opportunity of criticising each year the work of the official or Department, the payment will be made a Supply Service.

Consolidated Fund Services.   The following are some of the chief Consolidated Fund Services.

1. *The National Debt.* The interest and management expenses of the National Debt are a charge on the Consolidated Fund, and are paid under permanent statutory authority. Provision is also made for the gradual reduction of the debt by the annual payment of a sum of money *Sinking funds.* known as the " New Sinking Fund." The sinking fund is no longer included in the Consolidated Fund services, and the annual payment is liable to suspension or reduction by Parliament, as Finance Acts in recent years have shown. Moreover, it is open to Parliament to vote that any surplus, on the year, of income over expenditure shall be applied to the same object ; any sums so allocated being called the " Old Sinking Fund." Further, the Treasury is authorised to purchase (through the Government broker) any Government securities, with a view to their cancellation ; and this procedure is frequently adopted.

2. *Grant to the Exchequer of Northern Ireland.* This represents in the main a return to the Government of Northern Ireland of revenues collected within Northern Ireland by the Imperial Government. Some of those revenues are retained for Imperial purposes, with which the local Parliament is incompetent to deal ; the rest, after deduction has been made to cover the cost of collection, are returned to the Exchequer of Northern Ireland.

3. *Local Taxation Accounts.* This represents payments to local authorities throughout the country, being in the nature of contributions towards the cost of the local administration of certain national services.

4. *The King's Civil List* (see *ante*, pp. 425–6).

5. *Annuities and pensions.* These include payments to ex-Judges and ex-Speakers and other distinguished persons.

6. *Salaries and Allowances,* including those paid to the Judges, the Speaker, the Leader of the Opposition, and the Comptroller and Auditor-General.

7. *Courts of Justice.* The payments under this head are almost confined to those made to the Lords of Appeal in Ordinary, the Judges of the Supreme Court and of the County Courts, Metropolitan Magistrates, and the corresponding judicial officers in Scotland and Northern Ireland. £6,000 of the Lord Chancellor's salary is paid out of the Consolidated Fund, the remaining £4,000 being charged as a Supply Service on the House of Lords vote. The remaining costs of the administration of justice are likewise a Supply Service.

Apart from a few miscellaneous items, all other national expenditure is comprised in the Supply Services. These are usually divided into three classes, namely, the Fighting Services, the Civil Services, and the Revenue Services. The first comprises the Navy, Army, and Air Force. They are subject to Treasury control to a smaller degree than the other Services, and the Admiralty and War Office, at least, have their own sub-departments of finance, charged with the more detailed supervision of the departmental estimates. The second class comprises all the other spending Departments. The third comprises the Boards of Customs and Excise and of Inland Revenue. *The Supply Services.*

REVENUE. At one time, as we have already seen (p. 425), the King possessed certain hereditary revenues, which he could collect and spend independently of parliamentary authority. He was expected to defray all the charges of government out of these hereditary revenues, which were in consequence styled the Ordinary Revenue of the Crown, whilst all moneys granted by Parliament, being regarded as exceptional in character, were known as the Extraordinary Revenue. At the present day the so-called " extraordinary " revenue forms by far the greater proportion of the national income ; but, before dealing with it, we shall give a short account of the " ordinary " revenue. *Ordinary Revenue.*

It is derived mainly from two sources :

1. *The Income of Crown Lands.* The Crown is the owner of considerable landed estates. The rents and profits of these, so far as they have been surrendered to the

public, are received and paid into the Consolidated Fund
by the Commissioners of Crown Lands.

The foreshore, that is to say, the space between high-
and low-water mark, is also vested in the Crown, which
enjoys a limit of sixty years for bringing action for its
recovery, even under the Limitation Act, 1939.   Income
arising from it is collected by some Department of State.

2. *Bona vacantia.*   Strictly, *bona vacantia* include only
things found without any apparent owner ;   and the
general rule regarding them is that they are vested in the
finder (subject, of course, to the claims of the real owner,
if he is discovered) and not in the Crown.   But there are
certain classes of *bona vacantia* which may be claimed
under the Royal Prerogative ;   and the phrase is used
loosely to cover a number of *other* things, which are
either incapable of being owned by a private individual *or*
the right to which has been relinquished by the conduct or
circumstances of the owner.   It is usual to class under this
head :

(*a*) *Wreck*, that is, things washed up on to the shore
as distinct from things " jetsam, flotsam, and ligan," that
is, roughly speaking, things which stay at sea.   But the
true owner may claim his property within one year, and
in that case it must be returned to him, after payment of
salvage, that is to say, the cost of recovery.

(*b*) *Treasure-trove, i.e.,* money (but *not* paper-money),
coin, gold, silver, plate, or bullion, found hidden in the
earth or other secret place, the owner being unknown.
But if the owner is afterwards found, he and not the Crown
is entitled to it.   (See further, Vol. I, Chap. 26.)   This
right of the Crown is a means of securing things of value
and interest for safe custody in public museums—compensation being usually paid *ex gratia* to the finder.

(*c*) *Royal mines, i.e.,* silver and gold mines.   Apparently
there are no such mines in this country at the present
day ;   but if gold or silver is discovered in any *other* mine,
the Crown may purchase the ore on paying a price fixed by
statute.

(*d*) *Property of an intestate dying without a spouse or
near blood relatives.*   The Administration of Estates Act,

1925, now prevents any intestate acquisition by relatives beyond a certain degree of affinity.

The " extraordinary " revenue is derived mainly from taxation, whether direct or indirect. *Direct* taxation (*e.g.*, income tax and death duties) is intended to fall as a burden on the actual person who pays the tax, whereas *indirect* taxation (*e.g.*, the duties on petrol, tobacco, beer) is intended to be passed on—in part at least—by the actual taxpayer to the consumer.

Extraordinary Revenue.

TAXATION. All taxation must, as we saw, be based on statutory authority. Taxes are levied either under the Finance Act of each year, or under specific Acts, such as the Income Tax Act, 1918, which contain a code of regulations governing the particular tax in question, and either fix the rate of tax or leave this to be fixed by subsequent Finance Acts.

The most important items of taxation are :

1. *The Customs Duties,* which consist of certain duties imposed by Parliament—or exceptionally by delegated legislation—upon commodities imported into this country from foreign nations. As soon as it is enacted that any goods are to be liable to a customs duty, those goods can only be imported into the United Kingdom by such quay, wharf, etc., and subject to such regulations, as the Commissioners of Customs and Excise may prescribe. In default, the goods are liable to forfeiture ; and the Customs Consolidation Act, 1876, as later amended, contains a series of provisions imposing penalties upon those who attempt to import dutiable articles without paying the duties. But the goods may be taken free of duty into a *bonded* warehouse ; that is to say, a warehouse the owner of which has entered into a bond with the Crown that, upon the goods being released for the home market, the proper duties will be paid. Bonded warehouses are used, *inter alia*, for the storage of dutiable articles which are manufactured into saleable commodities (*e.g.*, tobacco into cigarettes) for re-exportation to other countries ; and so these articles escape payment of the duty which would be charged if they were brought into the country in the ordinary way.

Customs procedure.

Some customs duties are imposed by the Finance Act of each year ; others are collected under the authority of permanent Acts, such as the Import Duties Act, 1932, now much amended.

Excise procedure.

2. *Excise duties*, which are also controlled by the Commissioners of Customs and Excise, are those duties which are imposed by Parliament upon commodities produced and consumed in this country. They are directly opposite in their nature to the customs duties ; for they are an *inland* imposition, paid sometimes on the consumption of the commodity, frequently upon the retail sale. Inasmuch as this type of duty is peculiarly liable to evasion, the officers of the revenue have a statutory power to enter and search the places of business of such as deal in exciseable commodities. Excise offences are summarily dealt with, either before the Commissioners of Inland Revenue or before Justices of the Peace ; subject, in either case, to an appeal.

Meaning of " Excise duty."

The term " excise duty," which, in its proper sense, means an impost upon *commodities*, has been extended to cover a large number of *other* duties—ranging from the stern levy on pool betting to the less novel payments for licences of various sorts.

(*a*) Licences to manufacture certain articles, such as beer, spirits, tobacco, patent-medicines, saccharin, methylated spirit.

(*b*) Licences to carry on certain trades and professions : *e.g.*, some forms of bookmaking or as a pawnbroker, moneylender, hawker, or as a retailer (as opposed to manufacturer) of beer, spirits, wine, tobacco.

(*c*) Licences in respect of certain activities, for instance, to have ones own motor car on the roads, to keep a dog, to kill game, to carry a gun, to *drive* a motor car. These licences are called " local taxation licences," because they are levied by county councils and county borough councils throughout the kingdom, instead of by the Commissioners. " Wireless " licences do not fall into this category.

Taxation of liquor.

Until the very recent heavy duty on tobacco, by far the largest proportion of the contribution from the excise to the Exchequer came from the duties on alcoholic liquor. The brewer, for instance, is taxed twice : he has to pay for a licence to brew beer, and he has to pay a duty—far larger than the cost of the beer—on every barrel which he produces.

The other excise duties are eclipsed by the taxation of liquor and tobacco. Even the ubiquitous " purchase tax " of recent years is only a next best revenue producer, while the less recent but equally familiar " entertainments duty " compares still more unfavourably. Other well-known excise duties are those upon patent-medicine labels, matches, and playing cards. *Purchase tax and entertainments duty.*

It should be added, before we leave the subject of Customs and Excise, that these duties are subject to " drawbacks," *i.e.*, to the repayment, upon the exportation of the goods in question to a foreign country, of duties paid upon them. Thus, if tobacco in the raw state is imported into this country, manufactured into cigarettes here, and re-exported in the form of cigarettes to a foreign country, the manufacturer is entitled to claim repayment of the customs duty paid on the importation of the tobacco. So, in the case of beer, the exporter is allowed to claim a drawback of the excise duties paid on the manufacture. The object of these drawbacks is to assist British manufacturers to sell their goods in foreign countries in fair competition with merchants of other nations who have not had to pay duties on the same commodities. *Drawbacks.*

3. *Motor vehicle duties.* These duties are, or used to be, imposed primarily for the purpose of maintaining the main roads of the country. By s. 13 of the Finance Act, 1920, as altered and extended by subsequent Finance Acts and by Regulations issued by the Minister of Transport, trade vehicles and motor-cycles are still to bear tax in proportion to their size ; private motor cars, however, by a recent innovation, are now as a rule to be taxed at an annual " flat rate " of £10 per car, regardless of its size.

4. *Death duties.* The law relating to these duties, to which important modifications are made by the Finance Act, 1949, is dealt with in Vol. I, Chap. 43.

5. *Stamp duties.* The use of an adhesive or impressed stamp is clearly a convenient mode of collecting revenue upon a varied host of legal transactions. The normal effect of failure to stamp a document which by statute

requires to be stamped is to render it inadmissible as evidence in civil proceedings and unavailable for any purpose whatever ; in certain cases, however, the statute goes further and imposes penalties for omitting to stamp an instrument. But the document can usually be made available if it is stamped subsequently, and the appropriate penalty paid.

Stamp duties are infinitely various, and (apart from death duties, and several of the excise duties) most of them are levied by virtue of the Stamp Act, 1891, as amended by Finance Acts of subsequent date.

Redemption of Land Tax.
6. *Land Tax.* This tax, though of small importance and soon to disappear, has been interesting for two reasons. In the first place, it is redeemable. That is to say, the landowner can, by arrangement with the Commissioners of Inland Revenue, and upon payment of a capital sum, commute for all future payments, so that the land is freed for all time from the tax   A large part of the land throughout the country has been thus redeemed, with the result that the yield has become very small. (It may be of interest to notice, in passing, that land may be freed from a tithe redemption annuity, under the Tithe Act, 1936, by a similar kind of arrangement with the Tithe Redemption Commissioners.) In the second place, it is administered by the Land Tax Commissioners, who are, like the Justices of the Peace, a body of laymen, having no connection with the Executive. Their importance is due to the fact that they elect from their number the General Commissioners for the Income Tax (see *post*, pp. 439-4o).

Land Tax Commissioners.

Income Tax Act, 1918.
7. *Income Tax.* The law relating to Income Tax was consolidated in 1918 by the Income Tax Act of that year, but further consolidation is now long overdue, and the patchwork of amendments over three decades is indeed of bewildering complexity.

The yearly Finance Act.
Each year the rate of Income Tax and Sur-tax for the year is fixed by the Finance Act ; this annual Act also contains such amendments of the earlier legislation as may be thought necessary. The student who wishes to acquire a detailed knowledge of Income Tax law must be prepared to consult the principal Act and its amendments,

and the leading text-books on the subject. Here we can only give the most summary account.

It is a peculiar feature of English Income Tax law that a man's income is not treated *as an indivisible whole* for the imposition of the tax. The sources of income are divided somewhat artificially into five different kinds, each of which is struck at by a separate Schedule to the Act.

Schedule A imposes the tax on the *owner* of land and buildings, at the rate of so many shillings (as laid down in the current Finance Act) for every pound of the annual " rack-rent " value, subject to various deductions for repairs. Tax under this Schedule can hardly be spoken of as a tax upon income. It is a property tax ; and indeed in daily usage it is most frequently spoken of as the " property tax," or the " landlord's property tax." In the case of a landlord, however, what we have just said is now not quite so true as in the case of an owner-occupier; for the landlord has in recent years been taxed on any " excess rent," *i.e.*, the difference, roughly speaking, between the actual rent and the lower figure on which tax under Schedule A is being paid. Property tax.

Schedule B imposes the tax on the *occupier* of land ; the basis of the charge being the " assessable value," recently fixed at one-third of the annual value as assessed under Schedule A. The tax is chargeable in addition to tax under Schedule A ; the owner-occupier of land has thus to pay tax under *both* Schedules. But the incidence of Schedule B is now so restricted that the tax imposed by it falls as a rule only on " amenity " land exceeding one acre and certain woodlands. It used to be pre-eminently the farmer's income tax. But assessment under Schedule D, with the inevitable need for keeping books, was in recent years imposed on all who farm except in a small way. And now Parliament has brought *all* farmers, even the very humblest, within the scope of Schedule D instead of Schedule B, which will mean great numbers having for the first time to keep accounts. Tax on occupier of land.

Schedule C imposes the tax on income received from any public revenue, *i.e.*, from British, dominion, colonial, and foreign government securities, provided it is payable Tax on income from public revenue.

within the United Kingdom.   The tax, as in the case of ordinary dividends under Schedule D, is deducted " at the source " by those who pay the income ; and the certificate which they must give the recipient will enable him to recover the tax, or some of it, from the Inland Revenue if his financial circumstances do not warrant full liability for the amount deducted.

Tax on annual profits, dividends, etc.

Schedule D is the great " sweeping Schedule." It imposes the tax on the annual profits and gains that accrue to the taxpayer from any kind of property, from any trade or profession, or from any other source not specifically charged under any one of the other Schedules.

Tax on salaries, etc.

Schedule E imposes the tax on all salaries, wages, perquisities and profits of every kind, arising from any office or employment of profit.

Allowances and deductions.

Individuals (but, as a rule, *not* corporations or societies) are entitled to various allowances and deductions in accordance with personal and family circumstances ; the object of the Acts being to provide a graduated tax, so that only the richer members of the community shall be charged tax at the full rate.   Prominent among these are the deduction in respect of *earned* income and that allowed to a married man in respect of the maintenance of his wife and children.

P.A.Y.E.

Hitherto there has had to be lapse of time between the taxpayer getting paid his salary and having himself to pay tax upon it under Schedule E.   The interval, for all except the minority of prudent taxpayers, was all too likely to be one of thoughtless overspending.   It had always been an inherent fault of the system of tax collection that it took no account of the human weakness above-mentioned, but this fault became magnified enormously during the earlier years of the recent war, when liability to tax under Schedule E had to be borne for the first time by the wage-earning population in general, large numbers of whom were moving and being moved from place to place as the needs of wartime industry might demand.   It became imperative, therefore, to hasten into force an entirely new system whereby tax deductions should be made " at the source," *i.e.*, by the employer, in respect of any remuneration falling under Schedule E.   Such deductions at the source could

not, however, be in the straightforward way long familiar
in the case of dividends or annuities, because account
would have to be taken there and then of the various
allowances to which each individual wage-earner might be
entitled, instead of leaving these to be dealt with long
afterwards by way of an overpayment claim by the taxpayer. Hence the now familiar P.A.Y.E. (pay-as-you-
earn) system, with its wealth of code symbols and voluminous tabulations. No longer is it enough for an
employer merely to make a return to the Inland Revenue
of what he has been paying to those employed by him ;
he has become the very agent, so to speak, upon whom
the duty of tax collection primarily rests.

Certain classes of property are totally exempt from **Exemptions.**
income tax. Thus the Crown is not taxable in respect of
its revenues, or of its property which is occupied by
Crown servants for public purposes ; but the King's
private estates are rendered liable by a special Act.
Charities (*e.g.*, a University or College) as a rule can claim
exemption in so far as their lands are occupied, and their
income from investments or land applied, solely for charitable purposes. Friendly Societies, Trade Unions, Savings
Banks, and Industrial and Provident Societies also enjoy
certain exemptions.

Besides the ordinary income tax, there is an additional **Sur-tax.**
graduated duty, formerly called *super tax*, and now *sur-tax*,
upon all individuals whose total income exceeds £2,000.
Sur-tax is only a species of income tax and, generally
speaking, is governed by all the appropriate provisions of
the Income Tax Acts.

The administration of the income tax is conducted on **Adminis-**
the following lines. The Commissioners of Inland **tration of the**
Revenue, a Government Department acting under the **income tax.**
control of the Treasury, are charged with the general
management of the tax ; and it is their function to
represent the interests of the Crown. Under them are **Inspectors.**
appointed various officials, known as Inspectors, who carry
out the duties of the Commissioners in each locality.
But, besides these Commissioners, there is a body of
persons in each district or " division " known as the Commissioners for the General Purposes of the Income Tax,

General Commissioners.

more shortly called the General Commissioners, who are similar in character to the Justices of the Peace and are chosen, as we have seen, from out of their own number by the Land Tax Commissioners. They hold office quite independently of the Executive, and are interposed as a quasi-judicial tribunal between the Crown and the taxpayer. It is upon the General Commissioners, as a rule, and not upon the Commissioners of Inland Revenue, that is imposed the duty of formally assessing and—until recently—also of collecting the tax ; and their existence is intended to be a most valuable protection to the taxpayer. In practice, however, the actual routine work of assessment is done by the office staff of the Inspector, subject to the formality of confirmation by the General Commissioners. The latter no longer appoint the Collectors, who have now become officials holding office " during the will and pleasure of the Commissioners of Inland Revenue." It is they who are responsible for getting in the tax from the taxpayer, and their *summary* powers include distress of goods, or even the imprisonment of the defaulter, if payment cannot be obtained by any other means. The scope of their responsibility has, however, been substantially reduced by the recent innovation of P.A.Y.E.

Special Commissioners.

The Commissioners of Inland Revenue themselves (with whom may be joined experts appointed by the Treasury) act as assessors in certain cases, the most important of which are the assessments of income of all persons liable to sur-tax. When exercising this jurisdiction, they are called the Special Commissioners. No appeal lies from their assessment to the General Commissioners. The Special Commissioners also have sole jurisdiction over claims by charities to exemption from tax ; and they exercise certain appellate functions.

Duty of citizen as to income tax.

The whole scheme of our income tax law is to throw upon the citizen the right and the duty (recently sharpened by statute) of declaring his own income. Accordingly, the assessment of income for income tax is carried out on the basis of annual returns made by the tax-payer. (It is no longer necessary, as a rule, for a return to be made in more than one district.) But the Inspector may increase or surcharge the assessment, if dissatisfied with the return. The assessment, when complete to the satisfaction of the Inspector, is signed and allowed by the General Commissioners. The taxpayer may then, if he so desires, appeal to the General Commissioners, or even to the Special Commissioners, against the asessment ; and from their decision, if the necessary steps are *immediately* taken, an appeal lies by way of " case stated " to the High court *on a point of law*, on the demand of either the taxpayer or the Inspector. The appeal is heard by a judge of the King's Bench Division, from whom a further appeal lies to the Court of Appeal and (with the necessary leave) to the House of Lords.

We have now to consider how payments are made out of the Consolidated Fund. Even though a payment out of the Consolidated Fund has been authorised by Parliament, whether as a Consolidated Fund Service or as a Supply Service, a further step is necessary before the money is actually credited to the spending Department. This step is the obtaining of the sanction of the Comptroller and Auditor-General, an official who, as we have seen (p. 412), is quite independent of the Government. An order, for payment on account of a Supply Service, is made out under the Royal Sign Manual, and presented to him ; and it is thereupon his duty to ensure that the payment has been properly authorised by Parliament, and, if it has not been so authorised, to refuse to allow the payment to be made. For the Bank of England is forbidden to make advances even to the Treasury (unless, as during the recent war, special statutory power is given it to do so) without the authority of the Comptroller and Auditor-General. For a payment on account of a Consolidated Fund Service, however, a royal order is not needed, but nevertheless the Comptroller and Auditor-General's sanction must be sought.

Upon his giving the Treasury a credit upon the Exchequer account at the Bank of England, the power to draw upon this fund is delegated to the actual officials charged with making the payments to the Departments concerned. The chief of these officials is the Paymaster-

(margin note) Method of payments out of Consolidated Fund.

General, whom we have already spoken of as a sinecure Minister nominally at the head of a body of Treasury officials (see *ante*, pp. 412–3).

The object of this complicated system of checks is to put it practically beyond the bounds of possibility that money shall be spent by the Executive without the authority of the Legislature.

Audit of public accounts.

The audit of the public accounts is the second function performed by the Comptroller and Auditor-General. He examines the accounts of all the spending Departments, and reports thereon to the Public Accounts Committee— a standing Committee of the House of Commons—calling attention to any case in which a grant made by Parliament has been exceeded, and to any other instance of unconstitutional practice in the expenditure of public money. The Public Accounts Committee, in turn, makes a report to the House of Commons ; so that once again the Legislature is given an opportunity of ensuring that nothing has been done by any Department in conflict with the fundamental rules of revenue law.

CHAPTER 18

FOREIGN AFFAIRS

The conduct of foreign affairs is the one great department of governmental activity in which the Prerogative is still of supreme importance. Blackstone says : *Prerogative decisive.*

> " With regard to foreign concerns, the king is the delegate or representative of his people. . . . What is done by the royal authority, with regard to foreign powers, is the act of the whole nation ; what is done without the king's concurrence is the act only of private men."

But here, as elsewhere, the King has in practice delegated the exercise of his prerogative powers to a Department of State, the Foreign Office, which is specially competent to deal with the business with which it is entrusted. But it would be altogether wide of the mark to suggest that the conduct of foreign affairs is in any way removed from the ordinary control which the House of Commons exercises over all branches of government, though the necessary secrecy attaching to it tends to make that control rather less effective in practice. There is also to be remembered the allegiance to party, which makes debate in the Commons an ineffective check upon governmental conduct, especially in foreign affairs ; it has publicity value, but it can rarely have any appreciable influence upon the main course of foreign policy, so long as the Government is firmly in office. *The Foreign Office.*

The Foreign Secretary, who is the *political* head of the Foreign Office, is the principal agent of the Crown in dealing with foreign powers. He also advises the Crown in appointing British diplomatic agents and in deciding whether or not to receive those of foreign powers. *The Foreign Secretary.*

The doctrine that the Crown is the sole representative of the nation in international dealings gives rise to several specific prerogatives, the most important of which is that of making treaties. *Specific prerogatives.*

So far as the foreign sovereign is concerned, the act of the Crown in making a treaty is an act of State. But

443

if it is sought to bind the subject by a treaty, the question at once arises whether the Crown has a *prerogative* to do so, for between the Crown and its subject no wrongful acts shall be counted as acts of State (see *ante*, p. 311). And in this connection, it must be remembered that the King cannot by his Prerogative alter the substantive rights of any of his subjects. The treaty may be made ; but, so far as it conflicts with the rights of any private individual under the Crown's protection, it cannot be enforced. The

utmost that a treaty by itself can do is to bind the King, in his executive capacity, according to the obligations of International Law, to observe its terms in transactions in which the Government of this country can act *without infringing private rights*. Hence it is the invariable practice, where a treaty has been concluded, the terms of which may or will be inconsistent with the ordinary law of this country, to pass an Act of Parliament giving statutory effect to the treaty ; and the treaty itself is

usually expressed to be dependent upon Parliamentary sanction being obtained. International agreements relating to such matters as copyright, carriage of goods by sea and by air, currency stabilisation, and air navigation have thus been made the subject-matter of Acts of Parliament. And the terms of the Peace of Versailles, after the 1914–18 War, were made binding on British subjects in this country by the Treaty of Peace Act, 1919. As an illustration of the principle that treaties cannot *per se* affect private rights, reference may be made to the case

of *The Parlement Belge*, decided in 1880 (5 P. D. 197, C.A.), where a Belgian packet boat collided with an English vessel, and the owner of the latter sought to sue the Belgian owners for damages. One of the defences was that the Belgian ship was a public ship (which would render it immune from the action) ; and the defendants gave evidence that England had entered into a treaty with Belgium conferring upon Belgian packet boats the status of ships of war, *i.e.*, of public ships. But this treaty had not been embodied in an Act of Parliament ; and the Court held that the royal prerogative of making treaties would *not* extend to depriving a subject of the right which he would otherwise have possessed of recovering damages in an action. It is true that this decision was reversed on appeal (5 P. D. 197), but only on the ground that the particular kind of procedure adopted by the claimant was the wrong way to take action.

Again, the Crown has the very important prerogatives of making war and peace. A declaration of war by authority of the King binds all his subjects, with the possible exception for those in the self-governing Dominions, whereas any act of war committed by a subject against a foreign power, not only does not operate to create a state of war between this country and that power, but even renders him liable to be dealt with as a pirate or robber. So also the King may by his Prerogative end the war by a treaty of peace.

The making of War and Peace.

But although no parliamentary sanction is necessary *in law* to the *declaration* of a war, *to carry on* a war without the consent of Parliament would be legally impossible on account of the control which is exercised over finance by the House of Commons.

As it lies with the Crown to declare war on, or make peace with, foreign states, so it is to the Foreign Secretary, as representing the Crown, that application is made on behalf of the Courts for the purpose of ascertaining whether a state of war or peace subsists between us and a foreign power. And similarly the declaration of the Foreign Office that a state is a *sovereign* state, recognised as such by the Crown, is conclusive upon the Courts; for it rests with the Crown to decide whether it will recognise a claim to sovereignty. This power on occasion brings the Foreign Office into contact even with the ordinary individual, for sometimes it hangs upon the word of the Foreign Office whether some foreign defendant to an action is or is not a sovereign, and so immune from being sued in an English Court, or whether some act of State on which a defendant relies was the act of a duly recognised foreign sovereign (see also Chap. 6).

Statement of certain facts by Foreign Office.

The granting of passports, facilitating the travel of British subjects in foreign countries, is another prerogative of the Crown, exercised on its behalf for the United Kingdom by the Secretary of State for Foreign Affairs.

Passports.

CHAPTER 19

THE ROYAL FORCES

SUMMARY   PAGE

Section I. The Army   446
Section II. The Royal Navy   449
Section III. The Royal Air Force   450
Section IV. The Central Departments   450
Section V. The Status of Members of the Armed Forces   ...   451

Section I. THE ARMY

In this country, the existence of a military force has from a very early period been looked upon with suspicion. The fear that some person—be he the King or a subject—might make himself master of the Army and attempt, by the use of force, to subvert the legal rights and liberties of the people culminated in our experiences of military absolutism during the Commonwealth ; and the danger of a repetition of military government under James II led to the Revolution of 1688 and to the Bill of Rights, 1689, which enacted, in very famous words, that " the raising or keeping of a standing army within the kingdom in time of peace, unless it be with the consent of Parliament, is contrary to law." The Act does not prevent the King in the event of an invasion of this country, or of a domestic rebellion, from calling upon all able-bodied citizens to take up arms in the national defence. It does not prohibit the maintenance of a military force *outside* the kingdom, nor does it limit the right of the Crown to conduct a foreign war without reference to Parliament. But in reality it would be impossible for the Crown to do either of these things without Parliamentary authority ; for Parliament alone can supply the money necessary for the upkeep of such a force.

The Bill of Rights, 1689.

But so far does the traditional fear of militarism penetrate our institutions that we are not content merely to have this statement of law inscribed on the statute-book. Under the Bill of Rights, Parliament could, without

The Army and Air Force (Annual) Act.

affecting the terms of that statute, pass a single Act authorising the maintenance of an Army for several years, for a century, or indeed as a permanency. But it is a recognised convention that the existence of the Army is never prolonged beyond one single year, so that the passing of an annual Act has long been necessary. Originally this was called the Mutiny Act, since, in addition to stipulations regarding enlistment, payment and billeting of troops, etc., it contained provisions for their punishment in the event of mutiny or desertion. The contents of this Act were ultimately consolidated into the Army Act, 1881, which is a codification of " military law," that is to say, of the statutes relating to the raising, regulation and discipline of the military forces. It is brought into force annually, frequently with amendments, by the Army and Air Force (Annual) Act, which also permits the raising and keeping of a definite number of troops for the following year. The preamble to the Act (which every year takes the same form) invariably recites the clause of the Bill of Rights mentioned above. At the expiration of the year, the Act ceases to be law ; and, were it not that a new Act is always passed before the old one has ceased to be in force, the maintenance of the Army (or the Air Force) would, unless the country were engaged in actual war, become illegal; for it would lack the authority of Parliament.

" *Military law*," as codified in the Army Act, is, of course, quite distinct from what is called " Martial Law," the nature of which will be explained later (see pp. 558 *et seq*.) ; though in some old books and statutes the terms are interchangeable ; and indeed to this day " martial law " is used in the preamble to the Army and Air Force (Annual) Act in the sense of military law. *Military law.*

" Military law " is that system of law, other than the Common Law of the realm, under which the soldier is placed on enlisting or being conscripted or on accepting his commission. The relationship between soldier and officer, and between officer and superior officer, is solely derived from military law : for disobedience to military superiors is no offence at Common Law. Nor, speaking very generally, will it be more than a breach *Distinguished from the Common Law.*

of contract if a servant leaves his master's service during the term for which he has agreed to serve him. By military law, however, a soldier who leaves the Army is guilty of the offence of desertion, which is punishable with severe penalties in time of peace, and sometimes even with death in time of war. By military law, again, an officer may be punished for " conduct unbecoming to an officer and a gentleman," though his act be no crime known to the general law of the land.

All the rules necessary for the upkeep of discipline thus form part of military law, as it is codified in the Army Act and the regulations (known as the King's Regulations) issued thereunder. And, by that Act, offences against military law are triable by special military Courts, called Courts Martial, established by the Act.

Courts Martial and the ordinary Courts. Courts Martial have also jurisdiction to try persons subject to military law for offences against the ordinary criminal law wherever committed ; but this jurisdiction does not extend to very serious crimes, such as murder and treason, and it is in general expedient even in other cases to hand over the offenders to the ordinary Courts. The latter can always insist on their right to try offences known to the ordinary law, and the military authorities are bound to surrender offenders if called upon to do so. In such cases, a prior conviction or acquittal by a Court Martial is no bar to further proceedings in an ordinary Court, though the latter is under a statutory duty to take into account any sentence passed by the former and actually served by the offender. On the other hand, no person can be tried again by a Court Martial after conviction or acquittal by an ordinary Court.

Courts Martial are " inferior " courts. Courts Martial cannot exercise any powers that are not conferred upon them by the Army Act. They are " inferior " courts, and, as such, subject to the control normally exercised over inferior courts by the King's Bench Division of the High Court (see pp. 573 *et seq.*).

Army not entirely governed by Army Act. *The Royal Prerogative and the Army.* So far we have dealt mainly with the Army Act. But the Army is not governed merely by the Army Act and by the King's Regulations issued under its authority. For, although the King may not maintain an Army in his Kingdom in time of peace except by authority of Parliament, and although he cannot, apart from statutory provisions, enforce discipline within it by any rules which would be invalid at Common Law, yet the Prerogative of the Crown as head of the armed forces of the realm is by no means extinct. It is in virtue of this Prerogative that the Crown, through the War Office, administers the Army, controls the movements of troops, and gives all necessary orders for those purposes. The employment of officers, too, is still largely a matter of prerogative and not of statute. In fact the Crown may, in respect of its control of the Armed Forces, do anything under its Prerogative which is not actually contrary to the general law of the land.

Section II. THE ROYAL NAVY

The Navy is still, as it always has been, maintained by the Crown by virtue of the Prerogative, without any need for annual permission by Parliament—though it is, of course, true that Parliament alone can sanction the expenditure of public money for the service, so that it exercises a complete though indirect control over naval policy. The Navy is a standing force ; and the Acts which govern it, as the Army Act governs the Army, viz., the Naval Enlistment Acts and the Naval Discipline Acts, are really permanent Acts, and do not require to be re-enacted annually, although they are not infrequently amended. *[Maintenance by virtue of the Prerogative.]*

Naval officers and seamen are subject to naval law (to be found not only in the above-mentioned Acts but also in the King's Regulations) in precisely the same way as officers and soldiers in the Army are subject to military law. *[Application of Naval Law.]*

Offences under the Naval Discipline Acts are tried by naval Courts Martial. The persons subject to their jurisdiction are principally confined to such as belong to the King's Navy. Necessary exceptions include civilian passengers aboard men-of-war. *[Naval Courts Martial.]*

In addition to naval Courts Martial, there are *naval inquiry courts*, which are Courts held out of the United Kingdom, and are confined to inquiring into matters *[Naval inquiry Courts.]*

connected with British ships, whether men-of-war or merchantmen.

The Royal Marines are a force of infantry and artillery, capable of fighting both on sea and on land. They are enrolled and maintained by the Admiralty, and, when on board ship, are regarded as part of the naval forces ; but when quartered, as they often are, on shore, or sent to do duty on board transports or merchant ships, or in other circumstances in which they are not subject to the Naval Discipline Acts, their discipline and regulation are provided for by the Army Act, the provisions of which, with certain modifications, apply to the Royal Marine forces. Moreover, their maintenance must be sanctioned by the Army and Air Force (Annual) Act, though the Act does not set any limit to their numbers.

Section III. The Royal Air Force

The Royal Air Force was constituted by the Air Force (Constitution) Act, 1917, and is governed by the Air Force Act, which, in the same way as the Army Act, is only in force for a year at a time. In each year since 1917, the Army (Annual) Act has been used to bring both these Acts into force ; and the title of that Act is now always the Army and Air Force (Annual) Act. Save that the Air Force is controlled by the Air Ministry and not by the War Office, it is regulated constitutionally in the same manner as the Army, and its regulation does not call for further notice here.

Section IV. The Central Departments

Of the Central Departments which control the fighting services, the Admiralty is the oldest, and the others correspond very closely in their internal organisation to the model which it set. Each Department has a Ministerial head, namely, the First Lord of the Admiralty, the Secretary of State for War, or the Secretary of State for Air, who presides over a Board or Council which consists partly of professional members of the forces, and partly of politicians, together with a permanent Civil Servant who is secretary to the Department. Every member of the

Board or Council is responsible for a definite branch of activity to the Ministerial head, who is himself responsible to the Crown and to the House of Commons for the general policy of his Department. Each Department has the usual permanent staff of Civil Servants.

The problem of co-ordinating the activities of the three Fighting Services—which was left to desultory experimentation before the war, and was solved during the war by the Prime Minister being himself Minister of Defence —has at last found permanent solution in the statutory emergence of a Ministry of Defence, now in charge of one of the leading members of the Cabinet. (See *ante*, p. 419.)

Ministry of Defence.

Section V. THE STATUS OF MEMBERS OF THE ARMED FORCES

The relationship between an officer or soldier and the Crown is not strictly a contractual one : thus, even where the man has joined the Army in consideration of the promise of a certain rate of pay, the Crown may at its discretion reduce that rate, and there is no litigious means to recover the balance (*Leaman* v. *R.*, [1920] 3 K. B. 663). In other words, all military pay is in the nature of an *ex gratia* allowance. The same principle applies in regard to the term of service ; for, both by the Prerogative and under the Army Act, a soldier may be discharged from the Service at any time, even though the period for which he enlisted has not expired. But upon its expiration he becomes entitled to his discharge. All this is equally true of the sailor or airman.

Relationship to Crown not strictly contractual.

An officer receives his appointment through a document called a " commission." Once he is commissioned as an officer, he is liable to serve for as long as the Crown requires his services ; and so he cannot resign without the permission of the Crown. But the Crown may terminate his service at pleasure.

The Officer's Commission.

When a person joins the armed forces, he subjects himself to military law and undertakes all the obligations imposed by it. But he does not thereby cease to be subject to the ordinary law ; his military obligations are

Dual subjection to Military and Civil Law.

binding on him in addition to, and not in substitution for, his civil obligations. Likewise, except so far as the statutes creating military law provide, he retains all the rights possessed by the ordinary citizen.

This dual capacity of the soldier or sailor or airman may on occasion place him in a very awkward situation, where the fulfilment at one and the same time of both his military and his civil obligations seems impossible. *In theory*, there is never any incompatibility between the demands of military law and those of civil law. Military law rests upon statute, and is part of the law of the land ; accordingly, obedience to it cannot ever be unlawful. But it cannot be denied that very serious difficulties have arisen in respect of the soldier's duty to obey the orders of his superior officers. Even here there is *in theory* no discrepancy, for the soldier is bound to obey only the *lawful* orders of his superiors. So it would appear that a soldier who obeys an order does so at his peril, and is liable for the civil consequences of his act, for clearly he cannot plead in his defence the *un*lawful order of his superior. On the other hand, if he disobeys an order, he likewise does so at his peril, and may be punished by his military superiors for disobedience, should it turn out that the order was in fact lawful. But this would put far too great a strain on the ordinary soldier or sailor or airman, who cannot be expected to know in every case whether an order given by his superior officer is legal or not. In extreme cases, if, for example, his captain were to order him to shoot his colonel, or to fire upon a procession moving peacefully down the street, the soldier ought clearly to disobey ; but it is equally clear that there would be an end to all military discipline if the soldier were allowed to investigate before obeying whether the order given him were legal or illegal. Obedience, if it is to be of any use, must be prompt. It is reasonable, therefore, that the soldier should only be allowed to disobey at his peril. But there would seem to be no very serious danger to civil liberty if the soldier obeyed orders which, though in fact illegal, were not *manifestly* illegal, and it would be unreasonable to make him liable in the ordinary Courts under such circumstances. There is on this point no authority which is absolutely

Difficulties arising therefrom.

binding on an English Court, but a great judge, Willes, J., in *Keighly* v. *Bell* (1866), 4 F. & F. 763, uttered a dictum in accordance with the view just stated ; and in *R.* v. *Smith* (1900), 17 Cape of Good Hope Reports, 561, where the question was definitely raised, a special tribunal adopted his opinion and acquitted the prisoner.

Apart from this somewhat unsettled concession, members of the armed forces have without doubt the benefit of certain privileges and exemptions from the ordinary *civil*, as distinct from the ordinary criminal law. Some of these, such as the limited right to disregard the usual requirements of will-making, or to make a will though under age, or not to have estate duty payable after death in action, are established in the interest of the soldier or sailor or airman himself ; others are intended to prevent the possibility of his services being lost to the Crown if he is involved in civil proceedings of trifling importance. Thus, for example, a soldier may not be taken out of His Majesty's service by being arrested, or by having to attend in person before a Court of law, unless he is charged with a crime or there is a civil claim against him exceeding £30. This long-standing immunity, or something like it, applies also to members of the Air Force. Those in the Navy are entitled to similar exemptions of a still wider extent. *(margin: Exemptions from certain requirements of Civil Law.)*

As has already been indicated, members of the armed forces have also the civil rights of the ordinary subject, except in so far as they have been taken away by the statutes creating military law. In respect of these rights they are entitled to the protection of the ordinary Courts. It is true that the opinion once prevailed that no soldier could bring an action in an ordinary Court for a tort committed against him by his superior officer, not indeed on the ground that such a wrong ought not to count as a tort, but because it was right that such questions should be decided by military tribunals alone. But this doctrine is now to be accepted as true only in a modified sense. McCardie, J., in *Heddon* v. *Evans* (1919), O'Sullivan's Military Law and Supremacy of Civil Courts, at p. 87, held that : *(margin: Civil rights.)*

> " a military tribunal or officer will be liable to an action for damages if, when acting *in excess of or without jurisdiction,*

they or he do or direct that to be done to another military
man, whether officer or private, which amounts to assault,
false imprisonment, or other common law wrong, even
though the injury inflicted purport to be done in the course
of actual military discipline."

But that, on the other hand :

" if the act causing the injury to person or liberty *be within
jurisdiction* and in the course of military discipline, no action
will lie upon the ground only that the act has been done
maliciously and without reasonable and probable cause."

Remedies
when mili-
tary status
alone is
concerned.
In this latter respect, the soldier—or the sailor or the
airman—is in a definitely worse position than the ordinary
citizen. It must not, however, be supposed that he is
entirely at the mercy of his superiors, for he has a special
mode of redress, under military law, by way of complaint
to still higher authority.

It must further be understood that the soldier's remedy
by action in an ordinary Court is limited to such rights as
he possesses by the *ordinary* law, and does not extend to
rights which belong to him only in his military character ;
such rights being conferred on him by special legislation
protection for them must be sought according to the
special legislation itself, and the ordinary Courts cannot
interfere.

CHAPTER 20

THE ORGANS OF LOCAL GOVERNMENT

SUMMARY   PAGE

Section I. Introduction 455
Section II. Local Authorities (outside London)   459
Section III. London   467
Section IV. Local Government Elections   469
Section V. Other Bodies   472

Section I. INTRODUCTION

The work of internal government within the country involves in many cases local administration. There is in England no clear-cut theory as to how this work of local administration should be organised, but, as convenience dictates, a choice in each case has been made between three agencies. In some cases the Central Government itself carries out local administration through its own servants, as, for instance, in the Post Office or the Inland Revenue Department. In other cases semi-independent statutory corporations have been created to administer particular services through their own servants, more or less free from control by the political Central Government. An instance of such an offshoot from the Central Government is afforded by the National Assistance Board. Lastly, in other cases what are called local authorities are employed for the administration of services in their own areas. The work of these local authorities is called local government, but, so much has convenience and historical accident affected its content, that it is hard to find any definition of local government other than that it is carried on by local authorities. Local authorities, however, in contrast to the local agencies of the Central Government or of such bodies as the National Assistance Board, have certain characteristics which serve to distinguish them and which they all, to a greater or less degree, possess. These are :

(1) Local authorities are not servants of the Crown, from which it follows that they are not subject to the

[margin notes: Administrative organisation. Central Government. Public corporations. Local authorities. Characteristics of local authorities : Legal independence.]

455

peculiarities of judicial proceedings against Government
Departments, and that the officers and servants they
employ are in law their servants and not servants of the
Crown.

Election .

(2) In modern conditions local authorities consist of
councils elected by the local government electors of the
areas which they control, and are not mere nominees of
the Central Government.

Rates.

(3) Local authorities again have independent powers
of financing their activities by imposing local taxes, called
rates, on the occupiers of property in their areas, though,
as we shall see, the whole of their expenses is not in fact
met in this way.

Partial
autonomy.

(4) Lastly, though local authorities are not truly autonomous bodies, free to do as they wish, since they can
only act within the powers which have been conferred
upon them by statute, yet within the limits of these
powers they are free to decide questions of policy for the
administration of their own areas.   The extent to which
this is possible obviously depends upon the terms of the
statute in question, and in this matter there is great
variety.   Further, as we shall see below, a certain degree
of control is exercised over the activities of local authorities, even within their statutory powers, by the Central
Departments of State ; but, when this is admitted, there
is still scope for decision on questions often of some
importance.

The Committee System.   The exercise of their powers
by local authorities is largely performed through a " committee system," which is as marked a feature of local
government as the cabinet system is of the Central
Government.   The size of councils prevents all the work
of local government being dealt with efficiently at their
meetings, and it is therefore largely carried on through
committees to which the details of local administration are entrusted by the councils for consideration or
control.   Local authorities have powers to appoint committees, and in some cases they are even required to do
so.   Normally the acts of a committee require the
approval of the local authority which appointed it, but
in most cases the local authority may expressly delegate

powers to a committee, so that, within the limits of such delegation the committee may directly exercise the powers of the local authority.

Officers. It may be said as a general principle that the supervision exercised over the details of administration by the elected members of local authorities is closer than that which Ministers of the Crown can exercise over the work of their Departments. The actual work of carrying into effect the decisions of councils and committees is, of course, performed by the paid officers and servants which each local authority may, or, in some cases, must appoint. The officers are in law the servants of the local authorities which employ them, though in some cases the law directly casts upon them, when appointed, independent duties. Broadly speaking the elected members must decide and take responsibility for questions of policy, while the paid officers, who are not directly responsible to the electors, must carry out that policy. But in fact considerable influence over policy is exercised by the paid officers through their expert knowledge.

Administrative Areas. The scheme of administrative areas for local government as well as the constitutions of the various classes of local authorities are now contained mainly in the Local Government Act, 1933, and the London Government Act, 1939. England and Wales are, in the first place, divided into administrative counties and county boroughs. The organisation of local government in the administrative county of London is, however, London. peculiar, and must be dealt with separately hereafter. The other administrative counties are not entirely co-incident with the geographical counties, for, in the first counties. place, the county boroughs are excluded from the administrative counties, and, secondly, for historical reasons the residue of the geographical county is in some cases divided into two or more administrative counties. Thus each of the three Ridings of Yorkshire forms a separate administrative county, and the total number of administrative counties, excluding London, is sixty-one.

The County System. The administrative county is governed as a whole for certain purposes by a county council. But for other purposes it is divided into smaller

County
districts.

areas called county districts. County districts are classified as urban or rural, the former being composed of
towns, the latter of groups of villages. The urban districts are governed either by borough councils (in which
case they are called municipal, or non-county boroughs
to distinguish them from the county boroughs) or by
urban district councils, and they are not further sub-

Rural
parishes.

divided for local government purposes. Rural districts
are governed by rural district councils, but they are
composed of groups of rural parishes each governed for
certain minor matters by parish meetings and parish
councils.

The County Borough System. The local government of
county boroughs forms a marked contrast to the system
in force in the administrative county. County boroughs
are the largest towns, and each is exclusively administered
for all the purposes of local government by its own
borough council, which in contrast to the non-county
borough council is spoken of as a county borough council.
There is no sub-division of the county borough.

County and
county
borough.

Two characteristics of the organisation of local government outside London will be apparent. First, the contrast between the system in the county borough and the
system in the administrative county. The former is uni-
tary, all the powers of local government being concentrated in one local authority ; the latter is divided, the
powers being spread among a hierarchy of authorities,
as the diagram on page 459 shows. Secondly, boroughs
appear in both systems. This is the result of
historical development, and the borough serves to
disturb to some extent the symmetry of English local
government.

Alteration of Areas. The Local Government (Boundary
Commission) Act, 1945, established a Boundary Commission to review and, if expedient, to alter local govern-
areas in England and Wales. This Act was repealed by
the Local Government Boundary Commission (Dissolution)
Act, 1949, which revived with amendments ss. 139–146
of the Local Government Act, 1933, giving powers, exercisable subject to certain conditions, for the alterations
to be made by order of the Minister of Health, and in

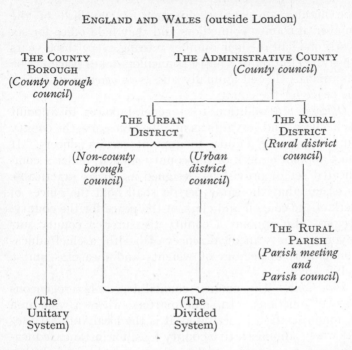

some cases by order of the County Council confirmed by the Minister.

We must now turn to the examination of these local authorities themselves, and it will be convenient first to consider the administrative county.

Section II. LOCAL AUTHORITIES (OUTSIDE LONDON)

THE COUNTY COUNCIL. County councils were created Composition by the Local Government Act of 1888 to take over from the justices in quarter sessions the bulk of the administrative duties which they formerly performed. The county council is a body corporate with perpetual succession, a common seal and power to hold land for the purposes of its constitution without licence in mortmain. It is composed of a chairman, county aldermen and county councillors. The county councillors are elected, one for Councillors. each electoral division of the county, by the local government electors : they hold office for three years and then retire together, their places being filled by a new election.

Aldermen.

The number of county aldermen is one-third of the number of county councillors and they hold office for six years, one-half of their number retiring every three years when the election of county councillors takes place. The

Chairman.

chairman is elected annually and is *ex officio* a justice of the peace for the county.

Officers. In addition to a general power to appoint such officers and servants as may be necessary, the county council is under a duty to appoint certain officers. It must appoint a clerk of the county council, under a complicated set of provisions designed as far as practicable to ensure that the same person shall hold the offices of clerk of the council and clerk of the peace for the county. It must also appoint a county treasurer, a county surveyor, a county medical officer of health, a chief education officer, inspectors of weights and measures and a public analyst.

Functions. The county council has a heterogeneous

Exclusive.

mass of functions. In some matters, where a wide area of administration is desirable, it is the local authority for the whole administrative county ; as, for instance, education and town and country planning. Again in other

Concurrent.

matters, such as highways, it is the local authority for the whole of its area with, however, certain exceptions in favour of some lesser authorities. The administration of the police is also, with exceptions in favour of a few of the largest non-county boroughs which maintain their own forces, on a county basis, but the county police authority is the Standing Joint Committee of the county council and quarter sessions, though the county council must finance the expenses of this body. Lastly, the

Supervisory.

county council exercises some degree of supervision over the smaller authorities within its area, such as the alteration of parish boundaries.

Municipal
Corporations.

THE NON-COUNTY BOROUGH COUNCIL. Boroughs frequently represent the survival of ancient self-governing communities with special powers and privileges conferred by Royal Charter. The ancient boroughs were reformed and their constitutions unified by the Municipal Corporations Act of 1835, and the tendency of modern legislation has been to assimilate the position of non-county boroughs to that of other urban districts ; but traces of their historical antiquity still remain to distinguish them both in their constitutions and, to a lesser degree, in their functions. A new borough is still created by Royal Charter ; but the grant of such a Charter of incorporation is now regulated by legislation which prevents any departure from the uniform type. Boroughs are, therefore, common law corporations, whereas all other local authorities are created by statute. Though this distinction does give the boroughs some freedom which other local authorities do not possess, it does not in practice relieve them from the necessity of relying on statutory powers to the extent which might be expected. Again, in the case of any other local authority the body corporate is the council ; but in boroughs it is the mayor, aldermen and burgesses who form the municipal corporation. As the burgesses are the local government electors of the borough, the Charter in effect incorporates the inhabitants. But once more this is a distinction with little difference, because the municipal corporation can only act by the council of the borough, which is thus the executive body of the wider municipal corporation. {.marginnote Charter.}

Composition of the Council. The council of the borough is composed of the mayor, aldermen and councillors. The councillors are elected by the local government electors and hold office for three years, one-third of their number retiring annually. Frequently, except in the smallest boroughs, the borough is divided into wards for the purposes of election ; otherwise the annual election is held for the whole borough. As in the case of county councils, the number of aldermen is one-third of the number of councillors and they hold office for six years, one-half of their number retiring every third year. The mayor is elected annually. He presides at council meetings and has precedence in the borough. He is *ex officio* a justice of the peace for the borough and remains so for one year after ceasing to be mayor. The mayor of a non-county borough is also a justice of the peace for the county, but only during his year of office. {.marginnote Councillors. Aldermen. Mayor.}

Officers. A non-county borough council must appoint a town clerk, a treasurer, a surveyor, a medical officer of health, a sanitary inspector and inspectors of weights and measures. It has also a general power to appoint other necessary officers.

Functions. Non-county borough councils are, like urban district councils, primarily public health authorities, and also have powers in connection with rating, housing and minor highways. Unlike urban district councils a few of the larger borough councils may be police authorities maintaining their own forces controlled by their watch committees.

DISTRICT COUNCILS. Urban and rural district councils were first established under those names by the Local Government Act of 1894 to take the place of a variety of authorities which formerly exercised what were primarily sanitary powers. In both cases the council is a body corporate with perpetual succession, a common seal and power to hold land for the purposes of its constitution without licence in mortmain. In both cases again the council consists of a chairman and councillors, there being

Councillors.
no aldermen. The councillors are elected by the local government electors and hold office for three years. Normally one-third of the councillors retires each year, but the county council may on the application of the district council provide by order for the simultaneous retirement every third year of the whole body of councillors. Elections in urban districts are either by wards or for the whole district : in rural districts they are normally by parishes, but the county council may by order combine two or more small parishes or divide a large parish into wards for the purpose. The chairman

Chairman.
of a district council is elected annually. He is *ex officio* a justice of the peace for the county.

Officers. An urban as well as a rural district council, in addition to a general power to appoint necessary officers, must appoint a clerk, a treasurer, a medical officer of health and a sanitary inspector. But an urban district council is also bound to appoint a surveyor.

Urban and rural.
Functions. Though urban and rural district councils

are alike in constitution, yet, as the areas they administer are apt to be dissimilar in character, their functions are somewhat different. Both are primarily public health authorities, though even here the powers of urban district councils are wider than those of the councils of rural districts. Both again are local authorities for rating and housing. But urban district councils alone are authorities for minor highways.

RURAL PARISHES. The law as to the organs of local government in rural parishes is of such complexity that its statement requires an amount of space disproportionate to the importance of its subject-matter. The present organs were set up by the Local Government Act, 1894, which took their civil functions from the inhabitants in vestry assembled and from the churchwardens. For civil purposes the Act provided for parish meetings and in some cases parish councils as well. These parish councils must not be confused with the parochial church councils first set up for purely ecclesiastical purposes under the Church of England Assembly (Powers) Act, 1919. The parish council is a civil authority with no ecclesiastical functions. Indeed, the parish for civil purposes has no longer any connection with the ecclesiastical parish, and their boundaries do not necessarily coincide. Again, the organisation set up by the Local Government Act, 1894, is found only in rural parishes, that is, parishes in rural districts. Urban districts have no parochial organisation for local government purposes, but their borough or urban district councils can have conferred upon them the powers of a parish council by order of the Minister of Health.

Organisation. In every rural parish there is a parish meeting composed of all the local government electors of the parish. In some rural parishes there is also a parish council constituted by order of the county council. The county must establish a parish council (i) if the population of the parish is three hundred or more, or (ii) if, though under three hundred, the population is two hundred or more *and* the parish meeting requests it. Finally, the county council may at its discretion establish

Parish meeting.

Parish council.

a parish council at the request of the parish meeting in a parish with a population under two hundred. Conversely, where the population falls below two hundred, the county council may on the petition of the parish meeting dissolve the parish council.

Parish Council. The parish council is a body corporate with perpetual succession and power to hold land for the purposes of its constitution without licence in mortmain. But it has no common seal, documents being executed by the signature or under the seal of two of its members.

Councillors. The parish council is composed of a chairman and councillors. The councillors are elected by the local government electors and hold office for three years, at the end of which period they retire simultaneously. The chairman of the parish council is elected annually.

Chairman.

Relations between Parish Meeting and Parish Council. It will be seen that in every rural parish there is a parish meeting, while in some there is both a parish meeting and a parish council as well. If there is only a parish meeting, it must meet at least twice a year, and it annually elects its chairman. The parish meeting, though in such cases it is the administrative organ of the parish, is not incorporated, but the " representative body " of the parish, consisting of the chairman of the parish meeting and the representative of the parish on the rural district council, is a body corporate with perpetual succession and power to hold land for the purposes of the parish without licence in mortmain.

Representative body.

In a parish which has both a parish meeting and a parish council, the powers of the former are curtailed, while the parish council has somewhat wider powers than a parish meeting can alone exercise. The parish meeting need assemble only once in each year, and the chairman of the parish council is *ex officio* chairman of the parish meeting. But though the parish council is the executive organ of the parish, the parish meeting still retains a certain control. It alone can bring into force in the parish any of the " Parochial Adoptive Acts," the most frequently adopted being the Lighting and Watching Act, 1833, which authorises the provision of street lighting.

Powers of parish meeting.

Officers. Like their functions, the powers of parish councils to appoint officers are restricted. They may appoint a clerk, who may be one of their number, but Clerk. may only pay for his services if he is not a member of the council. They may also appoint a treasurer, but in no Treasurer. case may they remunerate him.

Functions. The powers of rural parishes relate to Powers minor matters. Mainly they are concerned with foot- of rural paths, parish property, such as village greens, certain nuisances, the provision of allotments and recreational facilities, and, if there is a parish council, the provision of baths and bathing places. Perhaps the most important function of the local government organisation in rural parishes is that it provides a means of ascertaining parochial grievances and of making them heard by the rural district or county council.

THE COUNTY BOROUGH COUNCIL. As we have seen, English local government draws a sharp distinction between the system of administration in the county and in the county borough. But in contrast to the non-county borough, which falls within the system in force in the administrative county, the county borough, which stands outside that system, differs practically speaking only in its functions and not in its constitution. The county borough is administered by its own borough council, which is identical in its composition and election Composition. with the council of a non-county borough, consisting of a mayor, aldermen and councillors elected in precisely the same manner. Again a county borough is a borough, and its municipal corporation is created by Royal Charter which incorporates the mayor, aldermen and burgesses, but this municipal corporation can only act through the council of the borough.

Functions. In its functions, however, the county Powers of borough council is unique. It exercises in the county county boroughs. borough all the powers which are split up among two or more authorities in the administrative county. In effect the county borough council is at once the borough council and also the county council of the county borough. There are concentrated in the county borough council powers relating to education, highways, public health, rating, planning, housing and police.   Promotion to this peculiar position, which is only possible if the population is at least one hundred thousand, is obtained by local Act of Parliament.

Other forms of Borough.   The county borough is not subject to the jurisdiction of the county council, since for local government purposes it does not lie in the administrative county.   For other purposes, however, these large towns are not excluded from the geographical county.   They do not, simply as being county boroughs, constitute separate counties for the holding of assizes or for the service of jurors.   But in earlier days, when local government was often carried on under judicial forms by judicial officers, some of the larger boroughs sought exemption from the control of the county by obtaining for themselves the grant of a certain judicial organisation of their own.   In more modern times also, some measure of honour has been conferred on certain boroughs by the grant of special titles to their chief magistrate or to themselves.   These factors, which at the most only slightly affect modern local government, make necessary a further classification of boroughs, cutting across the distinction between county and non-county boroughs.

Judicial arrangements.

(i) *Counties of Cities and Towns.*   Charters made some boroughs counties in themselves.   Since this secured to them a completely separate judicial organisation, it formerly served to secure for them exemption from the control of the county.   To-day the distinction is important only in connection with the judicial organisation of the country.   Such counties of cities and towns appoint their own sheriffs and have their own quarter sessions and commissions of the peace, and often still have their own assizes.

(ii) *Quarter Sessions' Boroughs.*   Some boroughs have their own quarter sessions and commissions of the peace. Separate quarter sessions may still be granted by the Crown to a borough, but borough quarter sessions are held before the recorder appointed by the Crown and not, as in counties, before the whole body of justices.

(iii) *Boroughs with separate Commissions of the Peace.*

Some boroughs have their own commissions of the peace, which may still be granted by the Crown. This gives them a body of borough justices who can hold petty sessions for the borough, but they must rely on the county for the use of the county quarter sessions.

(iv) *Boroughs with no Judicial Organisation.* Such boroughs must rely on the county for all their judicial organisation, but it must be remembered that the mayor and last ex-mayor are *ex officio* justices for the borough and may as such hold petty sessions.

(v) *Cities.* Cities were originally the seat of a bishop, but the title, which may be conferred by letters patent by the Crown, has become a title of honour for some large boroughs. It only affects the name of the municipal corporation, which in the case of a city is called " the mayor, aldermen and citizens " instead of " burgesses." Cities.

(vi) *Boroughs with Lord Mayors.* The honorary title of lord mayor has been conferred by letters patent on the mayors of certain boroughs. Lord Mayors.

Section III. LONDON

Partly for historical reasons and partly for reasons of practical convenience the local government of the Metropolis is different from that of the rest of the country both in its organs and its functions. Indeed, special legislation exists for London, such as the Public Health (London) Act, 1936, and the London Building Acts, and the sections in most other local government statutes which fit their general provisions to the peculiar circumstances of the Metropolis.

Local Authorities. The law governing the structure of metropolitan local authorities (other than the City of London) is now contained in the London Government Act, 1939. The Local Government Act, 1888, created an administrative County of London and set up the London County Council. This is a body corporate composed of a chairman, aldermen and councillors comparable in constitution to other county councils, except that the aldermen are only one-sixth of the number of councillors. London County Council.

Within the County of London the London Government

Metropolitan borough councils.

Act, 1899, set up twenty-eight metropolitan borough councils. Unlike ordinary boroughs these are purely statutory bodies, the councils, and not the inhabitants, being incorporated. Each is composed of a mayor, aldermen and councillors. The councillors are elected by the local government electors, and hold office for three years, but all retire simultaneously. The number of aldermen is only one-sixth of the number of councillors. They are elected for six years, one-half of their number retiring every third year.

City of London.

Apart from these modern statutory authorities stands the Corporation of the City of London, unreformed by the Municipal Corporations Act, 1835, or later legislation, and still governed largely under its Charters. The main body by which the Corporation acts is the Court of Common Council, consisting of the Lord Mayor, twenty-five other aldermen, elected for life by the local government electors in each ward, and two hundred and six common councilmen. For some purposes the aldermen form a separate Court.

Relation of L.C.C. to:
(i) City.

Interrelation of Metropolitan Authorities. The relations between these three types of local authority are exceptional. In the first place, the City of London stands apart. It is both a city and a county of itself with its own sheriffs and with many privileges derived from its Charters. But it lies within the administrative County of London, and in respect of certain services administered by the County Council it is in a position of subordination to that body similar to that occupied by the metropolitan borough councils : such matters include education, main drainage, and planning. In other matters the City is independent of the London County Council and much in the position of a county borough, for instance in sanitary matters.

(ii) Metropolitan boroughs.

The relations between the London County Council and the metropolitan borough councils are also peculiar. Because of the urban character of the whole County of London, the powers of the London County Council are peculiar. Thus it has primary functions in public health and housing, the metropolitan borough councils having subsidiary powers. On the other hand the London

County Council has no highway powers ; these are vested in the metropolitan borough councils.

A number of special authorities exist in the Metropolis as elsewhere, and because London, in the popular sense, has far outgrown even the boundaries of the administrative County, the areas within which some of these special metropolitan authorities administer their services overlap the areas of other non-metropolitan local authorities surrounding the administrative County of London. *Other authorities.*

(i) *The Metropolitan Police.* Except in the City of London, which maintains its own police force, the administration of the police in the Metropolis is not a local government service at all. The Metropolitan Police Force, covering an area roughly fifteen miles in radius from Charing Cross, is directly controlled by the Home Secretary, through the Commissioner of the Metropolitan Police. *Metropolitan Police.*

(ii) *The Metropolitan Water Board* supplies water throughout the administrative County of London and a wide area adjoining. *Metropolitan Water Board.*

(iii) *The London and Home Counties Traffic Advisory Committee* acts within an area composed of a rough circle twenty-five miles in radius. Its function is to advise the Minister of Transport who may in this area make regulations for the relief of traffic congestion. *Traffic Advisory Committee.*

(iv) *The Thames.* The Port of London, which stretches up the Thames as far as Teddington Lock, and the docks and wharfs on its banks are controlled by the Port of London Authority ; but for sanitary purposes the Common Council of the City acts as port health authority. Above Teddington, the Thames is regulated by the Thames Conservancy. *Port of London Authority.* *Thames Conservancy.*

Section IV. LOCAL GOVERNMENT ELECTIONS

As will have been seen above, membership of a local authority is dependent on election : councillors, aldermen and the chairman or mayor are all elected members. But the elections of these three classes differ, and require separate treatment.

(1) *Election of Councillors.* The importance in the English system of local government of the electors will have become apparent : the local government electors elect the councillors in all forms of local authority and themselves directly compose the parish meetings in rural parishes. We must now inquire who are local government electors.

The Representation of the People Act, 1949, now defines the local government franchise, which is somewhat wider than the Parliamentary franchise. All persons who are registered as Parliamentary electors for an area, that is, all persons who have the necessary residence qualification (see p. 361), are also local government electors for that area. In addition, however, for local government, as opposed to Parliamentary electors, there is also a non-resident qualification. This latter qualification applies to persons who on the " qualifying date "—the 20th November for the succeeding spring register and the 15th June for the autumn register—are occupying, as owners or tenants, any land or premises in the area. For this purpose neither a tenant of a furnished house for a period less than nine weeks nor a lodger of a furnished room is regarded as being an occupier.

As in the case of the Parliamentary franchise the right to be registered as a local government elector is limited to persons who are British subjects of full age and not subject to legal incapacity. The legal incapacities are similar to those which affect the Parliamentary franchise, save that a peer is not incapacitated from being a local government elector.

The actual right to vote at a local government election is dependent upon being registered in the register of local government electors for the area, and at an ordinary election a person who is registered in two or more electoral areas for the same local authority—perhaps as residing in one and occupying property in another—may only vote in one of those areas.

The procedure for preparing the register of local government electors is identical with that applying to the registration of Parliamentary electors and the law relating to corrupt and illegal practices in local government elections is similar, but not identical with that relating to Parliamentary elections (see p. 369).

The qualifications for membership of a local authority are, with slight variations in the case of a parish council, uniform. To be qualified for election a person must be a British subject ; *and* of full age ; *and either* (*a*) registered as a local government elector for the area, *or* (*b*) the owner of freehold or leasehold property in the area, *or* (*c*) resident in the area during the preceding twelve months. In the case of a parish council the last qualification is extended to cover residence within the parish or within three miles of its boundaries since the preceding March 25.

Qualification of councillors.

A number of disqualifications exist, preventing membership of local authorities and continuing for various periods. Among the more important causes of such disqualification are the holding of an office of profit under the council, bankruptcy, conviction for a serious offence, certain election offences, and surcharge by a district auditor in a sum over £500.

Disqualification.

Disabilities, falling short of disqualification for membership, apply to a member of a local authority who, or whose spouse, has a direct or indirect pecuniary interest in any contract or other matter being considered by the local authority or any of its committees. Such a member must disclose his interest, either by a general notice to the clerk, or at the meeting when the matter arises, and, except where his interest amounts to no more than the ownership of a small fraction of the share capital of a company, he is also prohibited from taking part in the discussion or from voting thereon. Moreover the council may provide for the exclusion of an interested member while the contract or other matter is under discussion.

Disabilities

(2) *Election of Aldermen*. In the case of borough and county councils, of which aldermen form a part, the aldermen are elected by the councillors. The election is held at a meeting of the council and takes place by each councillor delivering a written voting paper to the mayor or chairman who is required to read it aloud. To be qualified for election as an alderman a person must either already be a councillor or must be qualified for election as a councillor.

Aldermen.

Mayor or
chairman.

(3) *Election of Mayor or Chairman.* The mayor or
chairman is elected by show of hands by the whole
council. To be qualified for election a person must either
already be a member of the council or must be qualified
for election as a councillor.

Section V. OTHER BODIES

SPECIAL AUTHORITIES. There is some danger lest the
student should think that all the work of local government is transacted by the bodies we have just described.
This is not the case. There are in addition a large
number of special authorities which exercise powers of
various kinds. Among these we may direct particular
attention to the following :

Lord
Lieutenant.

1. *Lord Lieutenants.* Each county has a Lieutenant,
called by courtesy a "Lord Lieutenant." The position is
now mainly honorary ; but the Lord Lieutenant is the
President of the County Association which administers
the Territorial Army, he appoints Deputy-Lieutenants,
and recommends persons for appointment as Justices of
the Peace, and he is *custos rotulorum,* or keeper of the
county records, in which capacity he is himself the principal Justice of the Peace for the county. The Lord
Lieutenant is appointed by the King, acting on the advice
of his responsible Ministers ; and the office is, like most
official appointments under the Crown, held at the King's
pleasure. In practice, however, the Lord Lieutenant
holds his office till he dies or resigns.

Sheriff.

2. *Sheriffs.* We have already dealt with the judicial
functions of the Sheriff, and with his duties in connection
with the execution of judgments. But the sheriff was
originally the chief administrative officer of the county,
and, although his importance has greatly declined, he
has still administrative functions to perform. Thus he
is charged with the duties already specified (p. 367) in
regard to parliamentary elections. He returns the jury
in criminal trials. He is a keeper of the King's peace,
and as such he may command all the people of his county,
the *posse comitatus,* as they are called, to assist him under
pain of fine and imprisonment if they fail to obey his

summons (see, further, p. 531, *post*). He is also the proper officer to levy all fines and forfeitures, wrecks and the like, to which the Crown is entitled as part of its hereditary revenues.

3. *The Justice of the Peace.* Although the justices were deprived in 1888 of the greater part of their administrative functions, they still transact important business which is of an administrative rather than a judicial nature. Of those functions which they exercise alone the most important are connected with the granting of licences for the sale of intoxicating liquor by retail (see *post*, p. 499). In a number of cases statutes confer upon persons aggrieved by decisions of local authorities a right to appeal therefrom ; sometimes this appeal lies to a Central Department of State, sometimes to the county court, but in many cases the appeal lies to the local justices. Justices of the Peace.

4. *Joint Committees and Joint Boards.* The areas of the regular local authorities may not be the most suitable for efficient administration of different services. To meet this difficulty local authorities have powers of concurring in appointing joint committees for matters of mutual interest and of delegating their functions to them. Such joint committees are not, however, independent of the authorities appointing them : they are not separate bodies corporate and they depend, both for the powers they can exercise and for their finance, upon the will of their constituent authorities. On the other hand, in some cases joint boards have been created to control some service in which more than one local authority is interested. A joint board is created either by a local Act of Parliament specially procured for its creation, or under special powers contained in some general legislation, as for instance, a joint board for public health purposes constituted by order of the Minister of Health. Unlike joint committees, joint boards are in effect independent authorities : they are themselves incorporated, with special powers expressly conferred upon themselves, and independent financial powers. Joint committees. Joint boards.

A statutory joint committee, partaking, however, of some of the characteristics of a joint board, is the Standing Standing joint committee.

Joint Committee of the county council and quarter sessions, which is the county police authority.

5. *Port Health Authorities* are charged with the enforcement of public health legislation in a port. They are created by order of the Minister of Health and are either ordinary local authorities or joint boards.

6. *River Boards.* Land drainage requires special areas for its administration, and these areas are also convenient for protection of freshwater fisheries and the prevention of river pollution. The River Boards Act, 1948, provides

for the creation of river board areas, each drained by a particular river or group of rivers. These areas are controlled by river boards, composed of nominees of the Minister of Agriculture and Fisheries, of the Minister of Health and of the county councils and county borough councils in the area. The Thames and Lee areas are controlled by their respective Conservancy Boards.

Some river board areas are divided into internal drainage districts administered by internal drainage boards.

7. *Miscellaneous.* There are a number of local com-

mittees set up to assist, mainly in an advisory capacity, in the administration of services which are centrally controlled. Instances of such bodies are the local advisory committees under the National Insurance Act, 1946, and the area advisory committees set up by the National Assistance Board.

PRIVATE ORGANISATIONS. Much of the work that might well be done by public authorities is in fact done by private organisations. Indeed, some services which are now publicly administered, such as education, were in origin privately organised, and at the present day the policy of nationalisation of the basic industries is still further transferring to public ownership services which hitherto have been provided by public utility companies or by local authorities or by charitable trusts. Nevertheless it is important to understand the legal principles which have governed these services, some of which will continue to be supplied through means other than the Central Government or special statutory corporations administering them on a national scale.

1. *Statutory Undertakers.* To this class belong companies carrying on some public utility undertaking, such as water companies. These companies carry on business for profit, but, as the services they provide are of public utility, they are regulated by statute. Such companies need special statutory powers to enable them to interfere with the streets or to acquire land compulsorily, and these are obtained either by private Acts of Parliament or by statutory orders granted by a Central Department of State in pursuance of general legislation. To give uniformity both to these statutory powers and to the conditions to be imposed on public utility companies as a *quid pro quo* for these special privileges, Parliament has passed a number of " Clauses Acts," such as the Waterworks Clauses Acts (now re-enacted in the Water Act, 1945), which are incorporated in the company's special Act or statutory order. These Clauses Acts give the necessary statutory powers, and indeed, often give a monopoly to the company in its area, but also rigidly control in the public interest such matters as the rate of profit to be earned, the scale of charges and the standard of service provided. *[Clauses Acts.]*

In many places public utility undertakings are conducted by the local authorities. Indeed, in some cases the statutes governing a public utility company give the local authority or authorities of the neighbourhood an option to purchase the undertaking after a given number of years. Local authority undertakers are similarly controlled by the appropriate Clauses Acts incorporated in their special Acts or statutory orders. Their undertakings are not, of course, conducted with a view to private profit, but any profits earned are used for reducing the charges made for the service, or are applied in relief of the local rates. In such cases the areas of supply of local authority undertakers frequently differ from their own administrative areas, a county borough council, for instance, often being the authorised water undertaker for a large area surrounding its own boundaries. *[Local authority undertakers.]*

Nationalisation has already taken from public utility companies and local authorities the service of electricity and gas supply. These services are provided through the

Area Boards of the British Electricity Authority and the Gas Area Boards, while the powers conferred by the Transport Act, 1947, on the British Transport Commission to co-ordinate transport are leading to similar transfers of road transport undertakings.

Schools.

2. *Charitable Trusts.* To this latter class belong, *inter alia*, most of the " public " and " endowed " schools, which are such an important feature of our educational system. They are, of course, subject in varying degrees to the control of the Ministry of Education, while all are, in their capacity of charities, supervised by the Charity Commissioners. The Colleges of Oxford and Cambridge are eleemosynary corporations.

CHAPTER 21

THE FUNCTIONS OF LOCAL AUTHORITIES

SUMMARY   PAGE

Section I. *Rating and Valuation* 477
Section II. *Police* 479
Section III. *Highways* 483
Section IV. *Public Health* 490
Section V. *Housing* 494
Section VI. *Town and Country Planning* 497
Section VII. *The Licensing Laws* 498

The functions of local authorities are too many and varied for complete discussion here. Some, however, such as education, are primarily of an administrative nature, and we can confine our attention to the more important parts of those services which the practising lawyer may be expected to meet with.

Section I. RATING AND VALUATION

Apart from the fees and tolls charged by it in certain cases, and the income derived from its property, the finances of a local authority are mainly derived from two sources : Government grants and rates.

Grants in aid are paid by the Central Government to *Grants in aid.* local authorities in recognition of the fact that some of the services administered by them are in reality national in character. Specific grants are thus paid in aid of the services of police, housing, education and highways. In addition Exchequer Equalisation Grants, unallocated to any particular service, are also paid in general aid of local authorities' finances.

The main source of the finances of local authorities is *Rates.* the rates. Rates are taxes on the occupation of certain types of immovable property called " hereditaments," imposed and collected by " rating authorities," that is the councils of county boroughs, non-county boroughs and urban and rural districts, acting under statutory

powers. The incidence of this tax is determined by a
valuation list, in which the net annual value of each rateable hereditament is shown ; and the total sum required
to be raised is divided among the occupiers of these
hereditaments *pro rata*. Hence a valuation list must be
made before rates can be levied.

The Rating and Valuation Act, 1925, and the Local
Government Act, 1948, provide that quinquennial re-
valuations of each rating area shall be carried out by the
Valuation Office of the Inland Revenue. The general
basis of valuation for each hereditament is the rent that
a tenant from year to year might reasonably be expected
to pay, if the landlord did repairs and paid for insurance ;
but in the case of dwelling-houses special rules apply
which require valuations to be based on a percentage of
capital cost at 1938 figures or on 1939 rents. Certain

types of property are, however, de-rated, or exempted
in whole or in part from liability for rates. This result
is achieved by providing that agricultural hereditaments
are to be shown as having no rateable value, while industrial and freight-transport hereditaments are shown
as having rateable values only one-quarter of what they
otherwise would be. The valuation officer prepares a
draft valuation list in accordance with these principles
and gives public notice of its completion.

An owner or occupier aggrieved by anything in the
draft valuation list may " object " and, unless his objection is accepted by the valuation officer and the draft list
amended accordingly, he may appeal to the local valuation court and thence to the county court. After the
valuation list has come into force, the valuation officer or
the owner or occupier of any hereditament may make a

" proposal " to amend it, when the matter is dealt with
as in the case of an " objection " to the draft list.

When the valuation list has been settled and signed by
the valuation officer it becomes the substantive valuation list, on which rates may be made and levied. Each

rating authority receives precepts from other authorities, such as the county council and joint boards, stating
the amounts they require to be raised for their use, and
the rating authority then comes under a duty to make a

sufficient rate to cover, not only its own requirements, but those also of the precepting authorities. The rate is expressed as a figure in the pound of rateable value, which enables the amount due from each occupier to be simply calculated from the valuation list. The rating authority sends demand notes to the ratepayers, and, if necessary, can enforce its claim by distress warrant obtained from the justices.

Section II. POLICE

Although it is the duty of every subject to assist where necessary in the preservation of the King's Peace, the maintenance of order has long been the special task of the constable. The office of constable has existed since the fourteenth century, and the Common Law attaches to it special powers, privileges and duties, which have been considerably extended by statute. He is bound on his own initiative to apprehend persons breaking the King's Peace, and for this purpose is armed with powers of arrest wider than those conferred on the ordinary citizen. Moreover he is bound to obey the lawful orders of a magistrate, and to arrest in all circumstances on a magistrate's warrant. On the other hand a constable is subject to the jurisdiction of the ordinary courts, and an action can be brought against him if he exceeds his powers to the damage of a private citizen. But though in modern times employed by police authorities, a constable yet remains a servant of the law and does not impose a vicarious liability on his employers when engaged in the preservation of the peace or the arrest of malefactors (*Fisher* v. *Oldham Corporation*, [1930] 2 K. B. 364). When acting in obedience to a warrant of a justice of the peace, a constable is protected against illegality due to want of jurisdiction, if he produces the warrant when called upon to do so, and furnishes a copy to the complainant within six days of demand (Constables Protection Act, 1750).

Until less than a century ago constables were regularly appointed for each parish by the justices of the peace. The office was compulsory and unpaid; but the old

Constables.

parish constable has now been replaced by the professional police force.   However, the older idea still lingers on in the provisions relating to special constables.

Special constables.

The Special Constables Acts, 1831 and 1835, permit the appointment and swearing in by any two justices of special constables to supplement the ordinary force in times of tumult, or riot, or felony, actual or apprehended. The office is, in the absence of volunteers, compulsory, and the special constables so appointed have during the period of their appointment in general all the powers of an ordinary constable.   So too, the Lord Lieutenant may, by direction of the Home Secretary, cause special constables to be appointed to act for the whole county, or any portion of it.   These powers have been extended by the Special Constables Act, 1923, which permits the appointment of special constables although tumult, riot, or felony are not immediately apprehended.

Police forces.

Special constables are, however, at the present day only intended to act as supplementary to the professional police forces of which there are five main types.

Metropolitan Police.

1. *The Metropolitan Police* are directly controlled by the Home Secretary through the agency of a Commissioner and five Assistant Commissioners appointed by the Crown.   The Metropolitan Police District includes the whole of London and its vicinity within a radius of approximately fifteen miles from Charing Cross, with the important exception of the City of London.   The Commissioner has wide powers, under various Acts affecting the Metropolis, of ensuring the good government of London.   The cost of the Force is borne partly by a Government grant and partly by a police rate, fixed by the Home Secretary, and raised by precept on the rating authorities in the District.   The headquarters of the Force are at Scotland Yard, where, besides the ordinary constabulary, there is an expert body of detectives, known as the Criminal Investigation Department, whose services can be employed for the assistance of any local police force in the detection of crime.

City of London.

2. *The City of London Police* are independent of the Metropolitan Police.   The Commissioner is appointed by the Common Council of the City, subject to the approval

of the Home Secretary. The expenses of the City Police are paid for in part by a Government grant.

3. *County Police.* The county police authority is the Standing Joint Committee of the county council and quarter sessions. This body is responsible for administration, but the actual control of the force is in the hands of a chief constable appointed by the Standing Joint Committee with the approval of the Home Secretary. The chief constable, with the approval of the Standing Joint Committee, appoints the superintendents and constables, and may dismiss any of them, subject to the Police Regulations. The cost of the force is in part paid out of a Government grant and in part out of the rates. County police force.

4. *Borough Police.* Only county boroughs and such non-county boroughs as in 1939 had a population exceeding one-half of the population of the administrative county in which they lie may maintain separate police forces. Borough forces are organised on a different principle to that obtaining in county forces. The police authority in a borough is the Watch Committee of the borough council, which has independent functions. It appoints and dismisses the constables and generally controls the force, while the justices of the peace may suspend, but cannot dismiss, constables. The Watch Committee appoints a chief constable with the approval of the Home Secretary, but the chief constable of a borough force is merely the chief officer, and has not the same independent powers of the county chief constable. The expenses of a borough force are paid partly out of Government grants and partly out of the rates. Borough police force.

5. *Combined Police Forces.* Two or more county or borough police authorities may, with the approval of the Home Secretary, agree to amalgamate their forces into a combined police force governed by a joint board composed of representatives of the combining authorities. Powers compulsorily to amalgamate police forces and to place them under the control of combined police authorities are also vested in the Home Secretary.

The Home Secretary is the police authority for the Metropolitan Police and is directly responsible for its The Home Secretary.

administration. In relation to county and borough forces and combined forces he is the central authority, the local authorities with direct responsibility being the Standing Joint Committees and the Watch Committees and the Combined Police Authorities respectively. Nevertheless the Home Secretary has wide powers of control. A Government grant of one-half the net expenditure of local police forces is paid if the Home Secretary is satisfied that the force is efficient. Hence, such forces are required to submit to inspection by H.M. Inspectors of Constabulary, who report to the Home Secretary. Moreover under the Police Act, 1919, the Home Secretary is empowered to make regulations as to the government, mutual aid, pay, allowances, pensions, clothing, expenses and conditions of service of the members of all police forces.

Police regulations.

Policemen are prohibited from being members of any trade union, but the Police Act, 1919, set up a Police Federation for the purpose of enabling members of forces to bring to the notice of the authorities all matters affecting their welfare and efficiency. The Police Council, which must be consulted concerning any police regulations which the Home Secretary desires to make, is composed of representatives of the Police Federation, of chief constables and superintendents and of police authorities. By the Police (Appeals) Acts, 1927 and 1943, any member of a police force may appeal to the Home Secretary against dismissal or reduction in rank or pay. Lastly, the Police Pensions Acts, 1921 to 1948, have introduced a uniform system of pensions throughout the country.

Police Federation.

Police Council.

Police authorities are under a duty to provide sufficient protection to life and property, and they are not entitled to any payment for services necessary to this end. But, if on request they provide some special form of protection outside the scope of their ordinary duty, they may receive payment for it (*Glasbrook Brothers, Ltd.* v. *Glamorgan County Council*, [1925] A. C. 270).

Duty to provide protection.

Further, police authorities have, by the Riot (Damages) Act, 1886, taken over the liability, which at Common Law rested on every hundred, to preserve the peace, and to make compensation for any damage to property occasioned by riot. An injured party must make a claim

Riot.

Damage by riot.

in due form and within a prescribed time to the police authority of the district (in London, the Receiver of the Metropolitan Police or the Common Council). If the claim is disallowed, he may sue the police authority, in the county court if the claim does not exceed £100, otherwise in the High Court. In order to succeed, he must prove that all the essential constituents of a Common Law riot were present.

Section III. HIGHWAYS

A highway may be defined as a right of passage open to all the King's subjects. Such public rights of way must be carefully distinguished from private rights of way, which are easements vested in the owner of one piece of land entitling him to pass over another's property. Highways take various forms, from carriage ways and bridle ways to mere footpaths, and the repair of footpaths not along public roads may be undertaken by parish councils. The public right of way over a highway is simply a right of passage and re-passage, for the ownership of the soil is not changed by the existence of a highway. Thus the owner may successfully sue for trespass a person using a highway otherwise than in pursuance of the public right of passage. (See also Vol. I, Chap. 22.) Rights of way.

It is not essential that a highway should also be a thoroughfare : it may be a *cul de sac* ; though dedication from mere user is difficult to presume if a way leads nowhere. On the other hand, the passage must be a more or less defined way, leading from somewhere to somewhere ; a right to roam at large is a right unknown to the law, except under the express provisions of a statute or trust.

A highway may be created under an Act of Parliament, as, for instance, an Inclosure Act. In default of such creation, a highway can only be created by dedication and acceptance. Creation of highways.

Land is said to be dedicated when it is given by the owner to the public for the purposes of passage, and, if such dedication is followed by acceptance by the public, the land becomes a highway. Such dedication may be Dedication and acceptance.

express or implied. Express dedication arises when the owner of land does an act which unequivocally indicates an intention to give the public a right of passage—for instance, throws open a path or a newly formed street joining one road to another.

Inferred from user.

Dedication and acceptance may be, and in fact generally are, inferred from the fact that the way has been used by the public openly and as of right for so long a time that it must have come to the knowledge of the owner. The length of time, the intention and position of the owner are all matters for consideration in determining whether from the facts dedication and acceptance are to be inferred. With a view to giving some certainty to this branch of the law the Rights of Way Act, 1932, has laid down certain fixed rules for presuming dedication, as well as for enabling landowners to avoid the risks of finding that complacency on their part may lead to the creation of public rights of way over their property. But the Act does not abolish the Common Law principles, and dedication may in a proper case be inferred from public user for periods shorter than it lays down. The Act provides that if a way is used by the public as of right and without interruption for a full period of twenty years before the right is brought into question, then it is to be deemed to have been duly dedicated, unless it can be shown that during that period there was no intention to dedicate or no person in possession of the land capable of dedicating. If the way is similarly used for forty years, it is to be deemed to have been dedicated, unless there was no intention to dedicate ; but incapacity of the possessor of the land is no defence. The Act also provides various methods by which a landowner may show that there was no intention to dedicate, so as to protect himself from the effects of user for either period. This he may do by affixing a notice visible to those using the way, or depositing with the county council and borough or district council a map, together with a statement of the public rights of way which he admits to exist over his land, and at intervals of not more than six years lodging with these councils statutory declarations to the effect that no further ways have been dedicated.

Rights of Way Act, 1932.

Restrictions may be placed on the dedication by the owner. Apart from dedication as, for instance, a footpath only, he may dedicate subject to a right to maintain existing obstructions in it, or to plough it up at certain times of the year, or to carry on a market thereon. Or he may dedicate to the public a right of footway over a road, over which he has already granted private rights of carriage-way to the owners of neighbouring property. *Limited dedication.*

Once, however, a highway has been dedicated to the public, the dedication cannot be revoked, nor can action on the part of private individuals curtail the public rights. The maxim is, " Once a highway, always a highway." Hence powers to stop or divert a highway must rest on statute. *Once a highway, always a highway.*

Powers to stop or divert highways may be conferred on particular local authorities or undertakers by private Act. Also certain general Acts confer such powers, as, for instance, the Housing Acts. But a general procedure for diversion and stopping up of highways is laid down in the Highways Acts. If the justices in quarter sessions are satisfied, upon the certificate of two justices who have viewed it, that a highway is unnecessary, or that it will be replaced by a new highway which is nearer or more commodious to the public, they may make an order for stopping it up or diverting it, as the case may be. If a private individual makes the application, the consent of the highway authority and of the parish council or parish meeting must be obtained before the order can be made. *Stopping and diversion of highways.* *Highways Acts, 1835 and 1862.*

Repair of Highways. At Common Law the liability to repair all highways was *prima facie* on the inhabitants at large, or in other words the parish, and this liability was enforced by indictment. Modern statutes have cast the duty to repair on local authorities. No standard of repair is fixed by the law. The road must be kept reasonably passable for the ordinary traffic of the neighbourhood ; whether it is so or not is a question for the jury on the trial of the indictment. *Liability of the parish.*

Liability ratione tenuræ or clausuræ. The liability of the parish, or in modern times of the highway authority, is rebutted if it can be shown either that by an Act of

Parliament some other body or person is expressly made liable in substitution, or that some other person is liable *ratione tenuræ* or *ratione clausuræ*. Liability *ratione tenuræ* may attach to occupiers of land by reason of their tenure of such land ; and it is an obligation running with the land and every part of it. This obligation is generally proved by evidence that the occupiers have, for a great length of time, in fact repaired the highway, such conduct, unexplained, being almost conclusive. Liability *ratione clausuræ* arises in cases of inclosure by the owner of land adjoining a highway which formerly ran over open country. In such case, if the public had acquired an immemorial right of deviation over the adjoining land when the road was impassable, the owner, by enclosing the adjoining land, renders himself liable *ratione clausuræ* to repair the highway. But this liability does not arise in the case of a modern highway, where the extent of the land dedicated is known, and the circumstances of the case exclude the right of deviation.

Many highways, which were formerly repairable *ratione tenuræ*, or *ratione clausuræ*, have now become repairable by the highway authorities in perpetuity, either under an order of justices made under s. 62 of the Highway Act, 1835, or under agreements made between these authorities and the persons formerly liable to repair.

Limitation on Liability to Repair. By s. 23 of the Highway Act, 1835, a great limitation was put upon the number of roads repairable by the inhabitants at large, that is, in modern times, by the highway authorities. By that statute, no road made after 1835 by any private person or corporation is to become repairable by the inhabitants at large, unless the same has been made in a manner satisfactory to the highway authority, and been formally adopted by that authority. Thus a highway made since 1835 may not be repairable by the inhabitants at large, though the public have the right to use it as a highway ; and, in fact, there are many highways for the repair of which no one is responsible. However, under several statutory provisions roads made after 1835, so as not to comply with the requirements of the Act of 1835, may become repairable by the inhabi-

Ratione tenuræ.

Ratione clausuræ.

Adoption of highways.

tants at large. The most important of these provisions are those relating to private streets.

Adoption of Private Streets. The term " street " means, in ordinary speech, a road with houses aligned upon it ; but it is defined in the Public Health Act, 1875, in a wider sense as including " Street."

> " any highway and any bridge (not being a county bridge) and any road, lane, footway, square, court, alley, or passage, whether a thoroughfare or not."

Highway authorities have powers of " making up," that is to say, sewering, levelling, paving, channelling, and lighting, such streets as are not repairable by the inhabitants at large. Such streets are of two kinds ; those which have never been dedicated to the public use, and those which have been dedicated to the public use as highways since 1835, but have never become repairable by the highway authority by reason of non-compliance with the Highway Act, 1835.

Under the Public Health Act, 1875, notice has to be given to the persons, whose property abuts on the street, to do the necessary works ; in their default the highway authority executes the work and recovers the expenses from the owners in proportion to their respective frontages. The owners may appeal against the requirements of the highway authority to the Minister of Health. When the work is completed the highway authority may, unless the majority of owners object, adopt the street as a highway repairable by the inhabitants at large. An alternative procedure is provided by the Private Street Works Act, 1892. In this case the owners have no option of themselves doing the work, but they may appeal against the highway authority's requirements to the justices. When the work is completed the highway authority may adopt the street as a highway repairable by the inhabitants at large, and the owners have no power of vetoing this. But, on the other hand, the majority of the owners can require the highway authority to adopt the street. Public Health Act, 1875. Private Street Works Act, 1892.

Highway Authorities. There are four cases to be considered.

(1) *Trunk Roads.* Under the Trunk Roads Acts, 1936 and 1946, the Minister of Transport is the highway Classes of highway authority.

authority for certain roads forming the national system
of routes for through traffic.

(2) The county borough council is the highway authority for all other highways in the county borough.

(3) *County Roads.* The county council is the highway
authority for county roads, that is, all other highways in
rural districts and all classified roads in non-county
boroughs and urban districts.

(4) The councils of non-county boroughs and urban
districts are the highway authorities for unclassified roads
in their areas.

But the councils of the larger non-county boroughs and
urban districts may claim to retain the maintenance of
their county roads, and the county council may by agreement delegate the maintenance of county roads to district
councils.

Vesting of highways. At Common Law, the soil of a highway remained
vested in the person who dedicated it to the public,
which acquired only a right of using the highway, and
not any title to the soil. But now streets and highways
repairable by the inhabitants at large vest in the highway
authority. This vesting gives the authority a proprietary
right in the soil of the highway, but only in so far as this
is necessary for the user and maintenance of the highway.

Access to highways. At Common Law the owner of lands adjoining a highway has a private right of access from his land to the
highway at any point. This right was, however, limited
Ribbon development. in the interests of traffic by the Restriction of Ribbon
Development Act, 1935, which required the consent of
the highway authority to building near, or the making
of a new access to certain main traffic roads. These
powers were, however, closely related to the functions of
town and country planning and, under the Town and
Country Planning Act, 1947, have been replaced by similar
powers exercisable by planning authorities.

Liability of highway authorities. Highway authorities are not liable to be sued civilly
by a person who has suffered damage by reason of neglect
of their duty to repair. Highway authorities are under
Nonfeasance. no civil liability for a mere *nonfeasance* such as by allowing the highway to fall into disrepair. But an action for
damages will lie against a highway authority, as much

as against any other person, for particular damage resulting from *misfeasance* on a highway, such as by placing a heap of stones upon the highway without lighting or guarding it. Moreover an interference with the public right of passage over a highway is an indictable nuisance.

Bridges. The original liability for the maintenance of bridges carrying a public highway over water was on the inhabitants of the county at large. But this *prima facie* liability could be displaced by showing that by custom the inhabitants of some other area were liable, or that some person was liable *ratione tenuræ*. However, a limitation was placed on the liability of the county by the Bridges Act, 1803, which provided that no bridge erected after 1803 should be repairable by the inhabitants at large unless it was built under the supervision of the county surveyor and was adopted by the county. The liability of the inhabitants at large was transferred to county councils and county borough councils by the Local Government Act, 1888, and as a result of the Local Government Act, 1929, and the Trunk Roads Acts, 1936 and 1946, the position now is that public bridges are repairable by the Minister of Transport in respect of bridges in trunk roads ; county borough councils in respect of all other bridges in county boroughs ; county councils so far as county roads are carried by bridges ; non-county borough and urban district councils so far as bridges in their districts do not carry county roads.

Bridges erected under statutory powers by public utility undertakers are repairable by the undertakers, since at Common Law there is an obligation upon all persons cutting through a highway, even though empowered by statute so to do, to maintain a bridge for all time for the passage of the King's subjects. This obligation is reinforced by the provisions of the Railway Clauses Consolidation Act, 1845, which cast the obligation of erecting and maintaining necessary bridges and their approaches on the railways.

The Bridges Act, 1929, which applies to all types of bridges which are not repairable by the highway authority, makes provision for the reconstruction and maintenance of such bridges on terms to be agreed between

Repair of bridges.

Bridges Act, 1803.

Railway and canal bridges.

Bridges Act, 1929.

the owner and the highway authority or to be fixed by the Minister of Transport. These provisions are designed to permit private bridges to be made suitable for modern traffic requirements.

Section IV. Public Health

The Public Health Acts began in the nineteenth century as purely sanitary legislation, now mainly contained in the consolidating Public Health Act, 1936, but with the passage of time they have been widely extended to cover the modern science of preventive medicine, though the National Health Service Act, 1946, restricts the former powers of local authorities in this latter field. We must confine our attention to certain selected topics which the legal practitioner may be expected to meet with.

Public health authorities.

The public health authorities are the councils of county and non-county boroughs, and of urban and rural districts, though the latter have slightly less wide powers. County councils have, however, important health functions, and must appoint county medical officers of health. Even parish councils have minor functions relating to such matters as offensive ponds and ditches and water supply. It must be noticed, however, that certain parts

Adoptive Acts.

of the public health code are adoptive ; that is, they only apply in areas where special formalities have been observed to bring them into force ; and it is important in any given case to ascertain whether particular provisions have been so adopted.

1. *Nuisances.* The procedure by action or by indictment is apt to be cumbersome and unsatisfactory for dealing with many common nuisances, and the Public Health Act, 1936, provides a summary procedure. It imposes on local authorities the duty to inspect their districts and to deal with certain specified types of

Statutory nuisances.

nuisances, termed " statutory nuisances," such as premises, or accumulations, or deposits of matter likely to be prejudicial to health or amounting to a nuisance, and in certain cases with smoke nuisances. When such statutory nuisances are found to exist, it is the duty of the local authority to serve an abatement notice requiring the nuisance to be abated. If this is not obeyed, the person in default is summoned before a court of summary jurisdiction, which may make an order directing the nuisance to be abated and its recurrence prevented. Failure to observe this order makes the defaulter liable to penalties, and the local authority may abate the nuisance and recover the cost from the person in default.

2. *Food and Drugs.* The Food and Drugs Act, 1938, empowers an authorised officer of a local authority to enter any premises and examine any food intended for human consumption which has been sold, or is exposed for sale, or deposited for the purpose of sale or preparation for sale. If the article appears to be unfit for human consumption, he may seize it and convey it before a justice to be condemned, and the person to whom it belonged, or on whose premises it was found, is liable to a fine and, in some cases, to imprisonment. *Unsound food.*

The Act carries the protection of the public a stage further. No person may add anything to any food, or drink, or to any drug so as to render it injurious to health, or so as injuriously to affect its quality or potency, with intent that it may be sold, or when so adulterated sell it. Moreover, no person may sell to the prejudice of the purchaser any article of food or drink or any drug which is not of the nature or substance or quality of the article demanded by the purchaser. A breach of either of these provisions renders the offender liable to penalties, and the Act provides machinery for authorised officers of local authorities to sample such articles and to prosecute. *Adulteration.*

3. *Building By-Laws.* The Public Health Act, 1936, provides that every local authority may, and, if required by the Minister of Health, must, make by-laws for regulating the construction and materials of new buildings and such matters as lighting, ventilation, the dimensions of rooms for human habitation, sanitary conveniences, drainage and water supply. Building by-laws may provide for the giving of notices and the deposit of plans with the local authority for approval, the inspection of work and the testing of drains. To keep such by-laws

in touch with developments in building technique, it is further provided that they shall remain in force only for periods of ten years, after which they must be reconsidered by the local authority.   When plans are deposited under the by-laws the local authority must, in general within one month, give notice to the applicant of their passing or rejection.   It is the duty of the local authority to pass the plans unless one or more of certain specified objections exists, such as that the plans are defective, or show that the by-laws would be contravened, or show no satisfactory provision for drainage, closet accommodation, or water supply.   A dispute as to the application of the by-laws, or as to whether plans satisfy their requirements, may be submitted by consent of the parties to the Minister of Health for a final decision. If work is executed, which is not in compliance with approved plans, the local authority has three courses open to it.   It may prosecute the offender summarily for a penalty, or it may serve on the offender a notice requiring the work to be pulled down or altered, and, in default, it may itself do the necessary work and recover the cost, or it may take proceedings in the High Court in the name of the Attorney-General for an injunction.

Passing of plans.

Contraventions.

4. *Sewers and Drains.*   The Public Health Act, 1936, makes it the duty of local authorities to provide sufficient sewers for the drainage of their district, but this duty does not impose on them a liability to provide sewers in advance of building development.   In discharging their duty local authorities may lay sewers in streets and, subject to paying compensation, in private land.   Local authorities must moreover, dispose of the sewage collected in their sewers, and must not pollute any river, stream or lake.   In practice sewers are usually provided by the private developer of land, and questions then arise as to the liability to maintain them in repair and to prevent nuisances therefrom.

Sewers and drains.

Prior to the coming into force of the Public Health Act, 1936, the liability to maintain a pipe for the removal of sewage depended upon whether it was a " sewer " or a " drain." " Drains " were defined as drains used for the drainage of one building only, and they, together with the liability of maintenance, remained in private ownership. " Sewers " were all other drainage pipes, that is, pipes draining more than one building ; and sewers vested in the local authority, which was thus liable for their maintenance even though they lay in private property. To relieve local authorities of what was felt to be an unfair burden, the Public Health Acts Amendment Act, 1890, authorised local authorities to recover from the owners the expenses of maintenance where two or more houses belonging to different owners connected with a public sewer by a " single private drain." This inelegant piece of legislation therefore permitted local authorities to recover the cost of maintaining certain lengths of sewer vested in them, but it led to great difficulties of legal interpretation.

The Public Health Act, 1936, accordingly re-cast the law, by drawing a distinction between private and public sewers. Where after that Act a developer constructs a sewer, it remains a private sewer, which does not automatically vest in the local authority, and the expense of maintaining which remains, as in the case of a drain, with the owner. Public sewers include all sewers vested in the local authority at the commencement of the Act, including any " single private drains " within the Act of 1890 ; all sewers constructed by the local authority at its own expense ; and private sewers which have been adopted by the local authority. Thus local authorities may take over by adoption what were previously private sewers, and the owner may apply to them to adopt such sewers, in either case the owner having a right of appeal. Public sewers must be maintained by the local authority, but in two cases they may recover the costs of such maintenance : (1) where immediately before the Act a private individual was liable to maintain a length of public sewer, and (2) where a length of public sewer was not constructed by the local authority and lies in a garden or other private property or in a road, not being a highway repairable by the inhabitants at large, and used solely or mainly as access to the premises served by the sewer. These provisions are designed to meet the difficulties which previously gave

Public and private sewers.

Adoption of sewers.

rise to the attempted solution contained in the Public Health Acts Amendment Act, 1890.

Section V. HOUSING

Housing legislation.
The scope of housing legislation is wide, and the emphasis which has been laid on particular topics has shifted from time to time. At the moment it lies upon the provision of houses to meet the unprecedented housing shortage resulting from the war. Nevertheless the Housing Acts deal with (1) the sanitary condition of individual houses; (2) slum clearance; (3) overcrowding; and (4) the provision of new houses.

Housing authorities.
In general the local administration of the Housing Acts is in the charge of the councils of county and non-county boroughs and of urban and rural districts, though in some matters duties are also cast on county councils.

Implied warranty.
1. *Individual Houses.* The basis of modern housing law may be said to lie in the provision of the Housing Act, 1936, which implies in the letting for human habitation of any small house, whose annual rental does not exceed £40 in London and £26 elsewhere, a condition that at the commencement of the tenancy the house is in all
Reasonably fit for habitation.
respects reasonably fit for human habitation, and an undertaking that it will be so kept by the landlord (see Vol. I, Book II, Chap. 13). This general principle is reinforced by a duty cast on local authorities to inspect, and a power to make by-laws with regard to the state of working-class houses.

Individual unfit houses.
If a local authority is satisfied that a house is in any respect unfit for human habitation then, if it can be rendered fit at reasonable expense, the local authority must serve a notice requiring specified repairs, and in default may itself execute the repairs and recover
Demolition or closing order.
the cost from the person receiving the rent. If, on the other hand, the house cannot be rendered fit at reasonable expense, the local authority must serve a notice on the owner stating the time and place when the matter will be considered. The owner may attend and make any offer as to repairs or user which he feels advisable, and this may, if satisfactory, be accepted. If no satis-

factory offer is made, the local authority must make either a demolition order, requiring the demolition of the house if it is wholly unfit, or a closing order, prohibiting the use of part of it, if a part only is unfit. In any of these cases the owner is permitted to appeal within twenty-one days to the county court. If no successful appeal is made, the owner must obey the demolition or closing order and is entitled to no compensation for so doing.

Appeal.

2. *Slum Clearance.* Where groups of unfit houses exist the local authority has a variety of powers it may exercise.

Clearance areas.

If the local authority is satisfied that an area is unfit or dangerous or injurious to health and that the best way of dealing with it is by demolition, it must declare it to be a clearance area. The local authority then has a choice of procedure. It may on the one hand make a clearance order, which ultimately requires the owner to demolish the houses in the area, but leaves him in possession of the site. On the other hand, the local authority may make a compulsory purchase order, under which it buys the area and itself demolishes the houses, becoming owner of the site. In either event the order is advertised and must, before becoming operative, be confirmed by the Minister of Health, who must first hold a local inquiry at which objectors may appear and be heard. When the order is confirmed, a person aggrieved may, within six weeks, apply to the High Court, who may quash the order, only however, if satisfied either that it is not within the powers of the Act, or that the applicant has been substantially prejudiced by a failure to comply with any of the requirements of the Act. Thus the appeal to the Courts against the validity of the order is limited both as to time and as to the grounds of objection.

Clearance order.

Compulsory purchase order.

Application to High Court.

When a clearance order becomes operative the owner must clear the area of houses, or in default the local authority may do the work and recover the cost. In general the owner is not entitled to compensation, except that the Minister of Health may, in the case of a well-maintained house, order the payment by the local authority of a sum representing the cost of recent maintenance.

Compensation.

When a compulsory purchase order becomes operative

the local authority buys the area and itself demolishes the houses. The owner receives, as the price for his property so acquired, only its value as a cleared site ; that is, he receives nothing for the unfit houses, except, again, in the case of any well-maintained houses in the area, or in respect of any houses included in the area not because of sanitary defects, but merely because of their bad arrangement.

Re-development areas.

Where the group of unfit houses is large, wider powers exist. If an area includes at least fifty working-class houses, of which at least one-third are unfit, and the area is required for re-housing purposes, the local authority may declare it to be a re-development area. The local authority then prepares a re-development plan, showing the re-development of the whole area. This must go through the same procedure of advertisement, local inquiry, confirmation by the Minister and opportunity for appeal to the High Court, as a clearance order. When the re-development plan finally becomes operative, the local authority makes compulsory purchase orders and acquires the area on the same terms as to limited compensation as in the case of a compulsory purchase order applying to a clearance area. It must then demolish the property in the area and re-develop it according to the approved plan.

Re-development plan.

Re-development by owners.

Owners of house property, with the possibility of these stringent powers being exercised against them, will naturally be loth to expend money on their property, unless they have some guarantee that their expenditure will not be wasted by action taken by the local authority for demolition or clearance. Accordingly the Housing Act, 1936, permits owners, proposing to re-develop or to effect improvements to their property, to submit their proposals to the local authority for approval. If this is given, it prevents action being taken by the local authority under its demolition, clearance or re-development powers for specified periods.

Standard of accommodation.

3. *Overcrowding.* Houses sanitary in themselves may be a source of danger to health if they are overcrowded. The Housing Act, 1936, accordingly fixes a standard according to the accommodation in each house, and if

this is exceeded the house is overcrowded. It is an offence for a landlord or an occupier to cause or permit a house to be overcrowded. It is the duty of local authorities from time to time to inspect their districts for overcrowding, and to take appropriate measures by providing new houses or prosecuting.

4. *Provision of Houses.* Local authorities have wide powers of providing and managing new houses, which in the present conditions of housing shortage are of great importance. Government grants are paid towards the cost of providing new houses, the local authority also making a contribution from the rates, and the balance of the annual cost of the houses being raised from the rents for which they are let. New houses.

Section VI. Town and Country Planning

The importance of securing the orderly use of land has led to planning legislation, which has gradually extended its scope from small beginnings in 1909 to the comprehensive powers of the Town and Country Planning Act of 1947. Purpose of planning.

Under the Act of 1947, the local planning authorities are the county councils and county borough councils, or joint planning boards composed of representatives of two or more such councils, though much of the detailed administration of planning control in county areas will rest upon district councils, to whom county councils or joint planning boards may delegate these functions. Planning authorities.

These local planning authorities have three principal duties : Functions.

(1) To prepare development plans, indicating the manner in which they propose that the land in their areas shall be used. Before becoming effective development plans must be approved by the Minister of Town and Country Planning, and at five-yearly intervals the local planning authorities must reconsider their development plans and submit to the Minister their proposals for modifications.

(2) To deal with applications for permission to carry

out " development." Subject to specified exceptions, all development now requires planning
permission.   There is an appeal to the Minister
from a refusal of permission by a local planning
authority.

(3) To serve "enforcement notices" where unauthorised
development takes place.

These functions of local planning authorities are discussed more fully in the treatment of " Land Law," in
Vol. I, Book II, Chap. 22, where the meaning of " development " is discussed.

Financial provisions. The present town planning system involves certain
financial adjustments, namely, the levying of " develop-
ment charges " and the payment initially of compensation for loss of " development value " ; these matters are
not within the province of the local planning authorities
but are dealt with by the specially constituted Central
Land Board.   This subject also is dealt with in Vol. I,
Book II, Chap. 22.

Section VII. THE LICENSING LAWS

At the Common Law there was no restriction on the
manufacture or sale of intoxicating liquors ; but the
Legislature has intervened with a view to repressing
drunkenness and increasing the revenue, and, in the law
as it exists to-day, it will be found that there are two
quite distinct types of licences which have to be obtained
before intoxicating liquor can be sold by retail, namely
an excise licence, issued by the revenue authorities both
to manufacturers and to retailers of intoxicating liquors,
and a justices' licence, issued by the local magistrates
authorising—not the sale of liquors—but the issue of the
excise licence to retailers.

Excise licence. The excise licence is a licence which is paid for, but
which cannot be issued to retailers without the prior issue
of a justices' licence, for which no payment is made, but
which the justices may refuse, if in their discretion they
determine to do so.

Justices' licence. The justices' licence is thus an authority to the revenue
authorities to issue an excise licence to retailers ; and,

once it has been issued, the revenue authorities are bound to issue the excise licence upon payment of the necessary duty.

The excise licence alone is sufficient to enable the manufacture and wholesale trade in intoxicating liquors to be carried on. Thus the excise licence is designed to secure revenue, and the justices' licence to prevent drunkenness. This authority of the justices over intoxicating liquors is a relic of their formerly extensive administrative powers. It is of great practical importance, for it makes the justices generally responsible for the good conduct of their district.

The Licensing Act. The law on this subject is now contained in the Licensing (Consolidation) Act, 1910, as amended by the Licensing Acts, 1921 and 1949.

In the first place, intoxicating liquors are defined by the Act of 1910 as including spirits, wine, beer, porter, cider, perry, and " sweets "—this latter term comprising liquors made from fruit and sugar which have undergone a process of fermentation. But liquors which have less than a certain alcoholic content are not regarded as intoxicating liquors for the purposes of the Acts. Definition of intoxicating liquors.

Justices' licences are of two principal classes : on-licences, which are required for retailing intoxicating liquor for consumption *both on and off* the premises where it is sold, and the off-licences, under which liquor can only be sold for consumption *off* the premises where it is sold. Justices' licences.

On-licences, again, are of many kinds. The first and best known is the " publican's on-licence," which entitles the holder to take out an excise licence for sale of any intoxicating liquor for consumption on or off the premises. This is the licence held by the ordinary inn or fully licensed house. It is only granted in respect of premises of a certain annual value. On-licences.

Next in importance comes the " beer-house licence," under which spirits cannot be sold, but under which the holder can obtain an excise licence for the sale of beer, cider, and perry, for consumption on or off the premises. Besides these, there are, " cider licences," " wine licences," and " sweet licences," the nature of which will be gathered from their names. An applicant for an on-licence may apply for an *early closing licence,* which requires him to close his premises an hour earlier than would otherwise be required, or for a *six-day licence,* under which his premises must be closed on the whole of Sundays.

Off-licences. Off-licences, which enable the holder to obtain an excise licence for sale for consumption off the premises *only,* may be for (i) spirits, (ii) beer, (iii) cider, (iv) wine, or (v) sweets.

New Licences. A *new* justices' licence is granted by the licensing justices, but is not valid until it is confirmed **Licensing justices.** by the confirming authority. The licensing justices are the licensing committee of the justices of the licensing district. Licensing districts are county boroughs, non-county boroughs with separate commissions of the peace and, elsewhere, the petty sessional divisions of the county. **Confirming authority.** The confirming authority is, in counties, a committee of the quarter sessions and, in boroughs, whether county boroughs or non-county boroughs, a committee of the borough justices. In the first fourteen days of February **General annual licensing meeting.** in every year, there is held a general annual licensing meeting of the licensing justices, at which applications for the grant of new licences and for the renewal of old licences are heard.

If the licensing authority grants a new licence, the applicant must, after an interval of not less than twenty-one days, apply to the confirming authority for confirmation of the licence ; and, on that application, any person who has opposed the grant before the licensing authority, and no other person, may oppose the confirmation.

Off-licences can be granted for one year only ; and, at the end of that period, expire unless they are renewed. But the justices may, if they think fit, grant a new on-licence for a term not exceeding seven years ; and such a licence does not require renewal during the term. Subject to the qualification that justices cannot refuse to renew a licence without hearing evidence on oath in support of an objection duly preferred to such renewal, the justices have an absolute discretion to refuse the renewal of any licence.

Old Licences. But in the case of certain licences which were originally granted before a certain date, the justices may refuse a renewal only on certain specified grounds. Both the date and the grounds of refusal vary with the character of the licence. If they are of opinion that the renewal of the licence requires consideration on other grounds, they must refer the matter to the " compensation authority." This is the same body as the confirming authority, save that in a county the justices of each non-county borough are entitled to appoint one of their number to act as an additional member of the county confirming and compensation committee when acting as compensation authority. This body may, after giving the persons interested an opportunity of being heard, refuse the renewal of any licence so referred to them, subject to the payment of compensation. The compensation so payable to those interested in the licence is paid from a fund raised by a charge on all persons holding any of the licences to which the Act applies, in the county or county borough in which the premises in respect of which the renewal of the licence was refused are situate.

Compensation authority.

Besides the annual licensing meeting, the justices hold from time to time " transfer sessions," at which they may authorise the transfer of a licence from one person to another, and removals from one premises to other premises. They are also empowered (subject to confirmation by the confirming authority) to grant provisional licences to persons interested in new premises about to be constructed, or in course of construction.

Transfer sessions.

Provisional licences.

Subject to overriding provisions contained in the Licensing Acts, it is left to the discretion of the licensing justices of each district to fix which actual hours within the statutory limits are to be the " permitted hours." Thus it is open to the justices, if they wish to do so, to close all licensed premises in their area at an earlier hour than the latest hour fixed by the statute. But the justices must allow the opening of licensed premises for a full eight hours in the day in extra-metropolitan areas, and for nine in London.

Hours of sale.

On Sundays all licensed premises are closed in Wales and Monmouthshire ; but in England intoxicating liquors

Sundays, etc.

may be sold or supplied on Sundays, Christmas Day, and Good Friday, during a maximum of five hours ; the actual hours being selected by the justices for the district.

Any person resident on the licensed premises may be supplied with intoxicating liquor at any time. Intoxicants may be ordered and despatched from the premises during prohibited hours. Private friends of the licensee may be supplied with liquor at any time. Any person who has ordered liquor with a meal may continue to drink the liquor for a further half-hour after closing time. And, finally, military, naval, and air force messes and canteens are exempt from the rules.

The Acts also impose penalties on unauthorised sales of liquor and ill-conducted public-houses, and further, subject to certain exceptions, make any contract for the supply of liquor on credit on licensed premises or in clubs illegal and the making of it a criminal offence.

Clubs. The enactments as to the sale of intoxicating liquors are now applied to clubs in which intoxicating liquors are sold. Every such club must be registered with the clerk to the justices ; and its rules must include a statement of the " permitted hours " applicable to the club. But such registration does not constitute the club licensed premises, or render legal any sale of intoxicating liquor which would otherwise be illegal. In an unregistered club, intoxicating liquor may not be sold, under heavy penalties. A club may, on certain specified grounds, be struck off the register by a court of summary jurisdiction, on complaint in writing made by any person. And if a Justice of the Peace is satisfied, by information on oath, that there is reasonable ground for thinking that a registered club should be struck off the register, he may grant a search warrant to a constable to enter the club.

Registration.

CHAPTER 22

CENTRAL CONTROL OF LOCAL GOVERNMENT

Local authorities cannot in modern conditions be permitted absolute autonomy. For instance, a serious breakdown of the health services of one area might result in a national calamity. Hence the central authorities in the national interest exercise varying degrees of control over the activities of local authorities. This central control is exercised in three forms : through Parliament ; through the law courts ; and through the administrative Departments of State. Central control :

Parliament exercises a general control over local government. In passing general legislation, when it decides on the powers and duties of all local authorities, and in dealing with local legislation, when it decides what powers it will confer by private Act on a particular local authority, Parliament settles the scope of local government, and so controls local authorities in the national interest. (1) Parliamentary.

The general control of Parliament is supplemented and enforced by the Courts. Local authorities are not servants of the Crown, and, subject to the litigious privileges conferred upon them by the Public Authorities Protection Act, 1893, and the Limitation Act, 1939, they are not immune from the jurisdiction of the Courts, as was the Crown prior to the Crown Proceedings Act, 1947. If local authorities act outside their powers, they act illegally, and may be restrained by the Courts, or may be sued for damages by individuals injured in consequence. Moreover, the Courts have effective machinery for compelling local authorities to perform their statutory duties. (2) Judicial.

Even within the limits of their statutory powers local authorities are subject to an administrative control over their actions, which is exercised by the central Departments of State, mainly the Ministry of Health, the Ministry of Education, the Ministry of Transport, the (3) Administrative.

Home Office, the Ministry of Agriculture and Fisheries, and the Ministry of Town and Country Planning. This administrative control is nowadays so wide that some people deny that there is any true local government, but maintain that at most there is a system of dual control. In reality, however, the powers of administrative control do not form anything which can be called a system. These powers have grown up piecemeal with the growth of each particular service, so that the administrative control over different services varies widely, though there is a tendency for recent statutes to recognise that the Central Department is responsible for ensuring that local authorities conform to the national policy. The matter is still further complicated by the fact that law and practice do not always agree : some services are legally subject to rigid powers of control which are loosely applied ; while other services, which appear legally to be comparatively free from administrative control, are in fact most carefully supervised by the Central Department. In these circumstances we can merely give illustrations of the legal powers of administrative control, remembering that no uniform system is applicable to all local government services.

Subordinate legislation, issued under statutory powers by the Departments, obviously gives scope for a general control over the duties and powers of local authorities. In many cases express Departmental consent is needed before a local authority can do a particular act. Again, inspection by the Central Department, as in police and public health, and the modern practice in legislation of giving an aggrieved person a right of appeal from a local authority to a Central Department, both afford room for the exercise of administrative control. Again, some local government officers are in a peculiar position as regards the tenure of their offices. For instance, certain medical officers of health and sanitary inspectors cannot be dismissed by the local authority employing them without the consent of the Minister of Health. These powers are, however, far from uniform. The nearest approach to a systematic administrative control is through finance.

Marginal notes:

"Dual control."

Rules and orders.

Inspection.

Appeals.

Control over officers.

The accounts of all local authorities, with the exception Audit. of certain of the accounts of certain borough councils, are subject to audit by the district auditor. The district auditor is an officer of the Minister of Health, and has, moreover, the exceptional power of disallowing illegal expenditure and surcharging the sums involved on the persons responsible for allowing it. An appeal lies from him to the High Court or to the Minister of Health. Strictly the district auditor is concerned only with the legality of payments, but the line between an illegal and an impolitic payment is often fine. Thus local authorities, who decide as a matter of policy to pay their servants wages at rates far higher than those current for similar work among private employers, may find that the excess is properly treated as an illegal payment (*Roberts* v. *Hopwood*, [1925] A. C. 578). Borough councils may Borough adopt the district audit for all their accounts ; but, in so audit. far as they have not done so, certain of their accounts are audited either by borough auditors, consisting of a member of the council appointed by the mayor and two elected auditors, or, at their option, by professional auditors. Professional Borough auditors and professional auditors have not, audit. however, the district auditor's power of disallowance and surcharge.

Local authorities frequently borrow for capital expen- Loans. diture, so that the cost may be gradually repaid over a number of years, rather than cast upon the ratepayers in one year. To borrow, local authorities must have statutory powers, but these powers require in general for their exercise the sanction of the Minister of Health. In Loan deciding whether to sanction a loan the Ministry does sanctions. not confine itself purely to the financial aspects of the proposal, and so is able to exercise a wide administrative control over projects involving capital works.

We have seen that Government grants are paid in aid Grants of certain local services and that Exchequer Equalisation in aid. Grants assist the general finances of local authorities. Grants are, however, only payable in respect of approved expenditure, or subject to the power of the Central Department to withhold them. In this way a wide measure of control is exercised over such services as police, education and roads, where the service is expensive and the grant relatively high. Exchequer Equalisation Grants are also subject to reduction for lack of efficiency and progress in discharge of local authorities' functions, or for excessive and unreasonable expenditure.

Default powers.

In many cases in the event of a local authority failing to perform its duties, the Central Department has special default powers, enabling it to see that the service is properly maintained. These powers vary greatly, but often in modern legislation they take the form of permitting the Central Department to transfer to the county council the functions of a defaulting non-county borough or district council, and in other cases itself to undertake the duties, in the performance of which the local authority has defaulted.

BOOK II

CONSTITUTIONAL AND ADMINISTRATIVE LAW

PART IV

CHURCH AND STATE

SUMMARY

PAGE

CHAPTER 23. THE CHURCH OF ENGLAND ... 509

CHAPTER 24. OTHER RELIGIOUS BODIES ... 523

CHAPTER 23

THE CHURCH OF ENGLAND

SUMMARY   PAGE

Section I. *The Establishment* 509
Section II. *Holy Orders*   512
Section III. *Officers of the Church*   512
Section IV. *Representative Assemblies of the Church*   ... 516
Section V. *Ecclesiastical Courts*   519
Section VI. *Meaning of Ecclesiastical Law* 522

Section I. THE ESTABLISHMENT

Like so many English institutions, the Church of England cannot be completely understood without some inquiry into its history. Its present constitution dates in great part from the 16th century, but those who made the Elizabethan Settlement did not start everything afresh, but maintained many of the characteristics that the Church of England had possessed as part of the Western Mediæval Church. *(History of the Church.)*

In the Middle Ages the Church of England had been very largely independent of the State, and there had been many serious conflicts between them. The clergy had been forced, very much against their will, to admit that, in civil matters and to some extent in criminal matters, they were subject to the law of the land. Even in matters ecclesiastical they had on occasion felt the royal power, but it was recognised in theory that such matters must be regulated according to the Canon Law of the Western Church, interpreted by the Ecclesiastical Courts of England, and, in the last resort, by the Pope. All questions of doctrine and ritual came within this category, in practice as well as in theory. In theory, the appointment to benefices and the election of bishops were also governed by Canon Law, but in practice appointments and elections were often arranged by bargains between the King and the Pope. *(Mediæval conceptions of Church and State.)*

The Reformation. This system could not survive the rupture with the Papal See which took place under

Henry VIII. From the legal point of view, the main
interest of the Reformation lies in the reversal of mediæval
conceptions of Church and State, and the substitution for
them of a new theory of the absolute sovereignty of the
State. The change was carried through by the King in
Parliament, and the Church ever since has been compelled
to accept the legislative supremacy of Parliament in
ecclesiastical matters. But the immediate effect of the
change was rather to enhance the prerogative power of
the King. This was finally established in 1559 by the
Act of Supremacy, which forbade the exercise of ecclesiastical jurisdiction by any foreign power within the realm,
and transferred any jurisdiction which formerly had been
so exercised to the King. Thus, in many respects, the
King stepped into the position long occupied in *Anglicana
Ecclesia* by the Pope, but in some ways he was still more
powerful, for he added to the Papal prerogatives others
which he already possessed as King. Thus he retained
the right to summon Convocations, or provincial
assemblies of the clergy, and henceforth his consent was
necessary for the enactment of canons by them. His
former *de facto* share in the appointment of bishops was
now enlarged to an exclusive right. He acquired the
appellate jurisdiction which the Pope had hitherto possessed, and so obtained complete control over the
Ecclesiastical Courts. Much later, with the development
of cabinet government, the powers of the King in ecclesiastical matters have come to be exercised on the advice of
responsible Ministers, and in particular the Prime Minister.

Royal supremacy.

But the English Reformation, besides working a revolution in the relations of Church and State, developed somewhat tardily into a reformation of doctrine and worship.
In both these departments it was found necessary to
establish a new standard by Act of Parliament. The
standard of doctrine, the " Thirty-Nine Articles," was
finally adopted in 1571. The standard of worship, the
Book of Common Prayer, was finally confirmed in its
present form by the Act of Uniformity, 1662.

Doctrine and worship.

The new regulations thus introduced by Parliament,
taken in connection with other legislative enactments of
the same era, and with the Canon Law, which still gives

the rule where the statutes are silent, constitute the standard of faith, worship, and discipline in the Church of England ; but within the last century many factors have contributed to make it very difficult to enforce obedience to them, even on the part of beneficed clergy, and only in very clear, and therefore exceptional, cases of irregular conduct is any attempt made to subject the latter to legal control in matters of doctrine and worship.

The Establishment. The sum total of the relations between Church and State, as they now exist and have existed since the Elizabethan Settlement, are known as the Establishment, and the Church as " the Church of England as by law established." In the words of Phillimore, J., in *Marshall* v. *Graham*, [1907] 2 K. B. 112, at p. 126 : What is Establishment?

> " A Church which is established is not thereby made a department of the State. The process of establishment means that the State has accepted the Church as the religious body in its opinion truly teaching the Christian faith, and given to it a certain legal position, and to its decrees, if rendered under certain legal conditions, certain civil sanctions."

Establishment in former days implied exclusion of all other forms of worship : a refusal to conform to the doctrines and observances of the Established Church entailed civil consequences and disabilities. As a result of modern legislation, these consequences and disabilities have vanished—leaving only a few remnants of no great importance : the State now recognises liberty of conscience, and gives its protection to the property and observances of other religious bodies, as will be outlined in the next Chapter.

It is curious that establishment does not confer on the Church any separate personality in law. The Church is not a corporate body and has, strictly speaking, no property. What is commonly and for convenience called " Church property " is the property of the various ecclesiastical corporations. They are corporations aggregate, such as a dean and chapter, and corporations sole, such as a bishop or a parson. But special mention should be made of the Ecclesiastical Commissioners and the corporation known as Queen Anne's Bounty, in one or Church property.

other of which was vested practically all ecclesiastical property except what is held locally. The separate existence of these two corporations has come to an end, and they are united under the title of the Church Commissioners for England, a body corporate having perpetual succession and a common seal and power to acquire and hold land without a licence in mortmain.

Section II. Holy Orders

The clergy. The clergy of the Church of England consist of such, and such only, as have been admitted into *Holy Orders :* that is to say, bishops (including archbishops), priests and deacons.

Privileges, exemptions and disabilities. A clergyman of the Established Church has certain privileges, exemptions and disabilities. For example, he cannot be compelled to serve in the armed forces or on a jury ; and he is incapable of being elected as a member of the House of Commons, though he may now become a municipal councillor.

Section III. Officers of the Church

The *clerical* officers of the Church are : archbishops and bishops ; deans and provosts ; canons and prebendaries ; archdeacons and rural deans ; rectors, vicars, and curates.

A few remarks will be made here concerning only some of these officers.

Archbishops and Bishops are nominated by the Crown, on the advice of the Prime Minister, and elected by the Chapter of the Cathedral Church by virtue of a licence—*Congé d'élire.* known as the *congé d'élire*—from the Crown. Since the sixteenth century it has been an example of an election which is not really an election at all ; for the nominated person *must* be elected.

There are two archbishops in England—the Archbishop of Canterbury, and the Archbishop of York—but the former no longer has jurisdiction in Wales, which is now a separate province, with its own Archbishop, whose election (like that of its Bishops) is independent of the Crown.

An Archbishop is the chief of all the clergy in his province ; he formally confirms the election of the bishops of that province, and afterwards consecrates them. By virtue of the King's writ only, he calls upon the bishops and clergy of his province to meet him in Convocation ; and he has a Court with original and appellate jurisdiction of a rare and limited kind. For his own *diocese* of Canterbury or York—not to be confused with the *province* of the same name—an Archbishop is of course the Bishop, with all the usual episcopal duties.

It is the privilege of the Archbishop of Canterbury to crown the Kings and Queens of the kingdom ; he has power (which he exercises only in exceptional circumstances) to grant special licences to marry at any place or time.

A bishop is the chief of the clergy within his diocese, being subordinate only to the Archbishop of the province. Among the principal powers which he exercises are those of ordaining priests and deacons, consecrating churches, and confirming those to be admitted to Holy Communion. In addition, the bishop is still to some extent an ecclesiastical judge, and as such is spoken of as the " Ordinary."

There is another class of bishops, of modern creation, known as *suffragans*, whose duties are to assist the diocesan bishops. They are appointed in a straightforward way by the Crown, without any fictitious capitular election, and they are not entitled to sit in the House of Lords or in the Upper House of either Convocation.

A Dean and Chapter are a corporation aggregate and stand to a cathedral in the same position as the incumbent to an ordinary parish church. The Chapter, as distinct from the Dean, consists of certain dignitaries called canons (or, sometimes, prebendaries).

Rectors, Vicars and Perpetual Curates. The three kinds of parochial preferments, rectories, vicarages and *perpetual* curacies, are usually comprehended under the term " benefice." No person is capable of being admitted to any benefice unless he has been first ordained priest. The right of presentation is exercised by the patron of the advowson, see, Vol. I, Book II, Chap. 17. (Advowsons are real property and the law concerning them is under review by the Church Assembly.) Before exercising his right, the patron must consult the parochial church council, which can, if it takes the proper steps under a Measure of 1931, exercise a suspensive veto pending a decision by the bishop, or in turn the Archbishop, as to the suitability of the presentation for the needs and traditions of the particular parish. If the patron neglects for six months to present to the vacant benefice, the right of presentation lapses to the bishop of the diocese; if the bishop is guilty of a similar neglect, to the Archbishop of the province; and, if he in turn fails to present, to the Crown itself. Temporary legislation, however, enables the bishop to postpone presentation in the case of war-destroyed churches.

Bishop's power as to presentation. Any priest may be presented to a benefice; but when presented, the bishop may refuse, on certain statutory grounds, to institute him, upon giving notice both to him and to the patron, and subject to an elaborate right of appeal. These statutory grounds, now a half-century old, are too narrow and rigid to enable a bishop to intervene in order to avoid—in popular language—a square peg getting into a round hole; and it is thought that their practical effect has gone with the coming of the much more recent procedure above-mentioned whereby a parochial church council can make its voice heard whenever, and whatever the reason, it resents a patron's choice. As Lord Greene, M.R., recently said in *R.* v. *Canterbury (Archbishop)*, *Ex parte Morant*, [1944] K. B. 282, at p. 288; [1944] 1 All E. R. 179, at p. 180:

> " parishes have very often strong views as to what their needs and traditions require in the matter of a pastor,"

and if patron and parish reach deadlock, it then becomes the duty of the bishop—and of the Archbishop, on appeal by the patron—to exercise his discretion for or against the presentee.

Institution. If the bishop allows the presentation, in the majority of cases he next " institutes " the presentee; where the bishop is also the patron and confers the living, the presentation and institution are one and the same act, and are called a " collation " to the benefice. Institution invests the presentee with the cure of souls of the parish committed to his charge ; and he may forthwith enter upon the parsonage house and property. But he may not grant or let them, nor bring an action for them, till induction.

"Induction" to the temporalities (*i.e.*, the property annexed to the benefice) is performed by a mandate from the bishop to the archdeacon, and the ceremony usually follows immediately after the institution and may form part of the same occasion. It is done by giving the parson corporal possession of the church, as by holding the ring of the door, tolling a bell, or the like. The ceremony is almost the sole survival of the ancient solemn "livery of seisin," once the universal method of conferring title to freehold land. *Induction.*

Finally, the title of any parson, though already inducted to a benefice with cure of souls, will be afterwards divested unless, on the first Lord's Day on which he officiates in the church of the benefice, or such other Lord's Day as the bishop may appoint, he publicly reads in the church, in the presence of the congregation, the Thirty-Nine Articles, and immediately afterwards repeats the declaration of assent which he made both before his ordination and previous to his institution and induction. This formality is called "reading in." *Reading in.*

The distinction between rectors and vicars depends upon what is known as the doctrine of *impropriation* or *appropriation*. The doctrine deals with the sharing of the emoluments of a benefice, and its explanation is to be found in many works on the Law of Property. (See also, Vol. I, Book II, Chap. 17). *The doctrine of impropriation or appropriation.*

> "After the dissolution of the monasteries . . . a sharp distinction grew up between two words, ' impropriations,' which was the term properly applied where the temporalities of a benefice were held in lay hands, and ' appropriations,' which was the term used in cases where the benefice was annexed to a spiritual corporation, sole or aggregate,"

(*per* Lord Wright in *Representative Body of the Church in Wales* v. *Tithe Redemption Commission*, [1944] A. C. 228 ; [1944] 1 All E. R. 710).

In a non-appropriated or non-impropriated living there is no vicar, but a rector only, who must be a priest, and who has the cure of souls in the parish, with the

Vicars.

exclusive title to all the emoluments of the benefice. In an appropriated or impropriated parish there is generally a vicar, who has only a part of the emoluments of the living, the rest going to the appropriator or impropriator, *i.e.*, to the rector, an outsider, spiritual or lay ; but in such cases the rector, though spiritual, never has the cure of souls within the parish, that being committed exclusively to the vicar. Sometimes, instead of a vicar, there is a permanent minister in Holy Orders, called a Perpetual Curate, who is entitled to emoluments for his services, and is in most respects like a vicar. This traditional terminology does not apply to many of the urban parishes of modern creation, the incumbents of which are permitted by statute to use the title of vicar.

Perpetual Curates.

We must mention that an incumbent's lifelong security of tenure—popularly spoken of as the " parson's free-hold "—has been much disturbed in recent years by successive Measures of the Church Assembly. Special procedure, newly enacted with elaborate safeguards against unfairness or hardship, is already or soon will be available in cases, not only of unbecoming conduct or neglect of duty, but also of physical or mental infirmity.

Dereliction of duty, etc.

The lowest rank among the parochial clergy is that of the Assistant Curate, appointed to assist the incumbent.

Assistant Curates.

Churchwardens. There are ordinarily two *lay* officers known as Churchwardens in each parish, one nominated by the incumbent and the other (the " people's warden ") elected by the Vestry (see *post*, p. 517) and the Parochial Church Meeting sitting together. Most of the powers and duties of the wardens have been transferred to the Parochial Church Council (see *post*, p. 518).

Section IV. REPRESENTATIVE ASSEMBLIES OF THE CHURCH

Convocations are representative assemblies of the clergy of a Province, summoned by a mandate of the Archbishop, issued in pursuance of the King's writ. There are two Convocations, one for the Province of Canterbury, the other for that of York. In each Convocation there are two Houses, the Upper consisting of the Archbishop and the diocesan bishops of the Province ; the Lower, of deans of cathedrals, archdeacons, the proctors (*i.e.*, elected representatives) for the Chapters, and the proctors for the parochial clergy. It is the function of these Convocations to pass " canons," *i.e.*, enactments affecting ecclesiastical matters, which are, when assented to by the King, binding on the clergy ; and to transact such other ecclesiastical business as may be committed to them by the King. They cannot legislate, without parliamentary approval, so as to bind the laity. _{Canons.}

Though of the greatest historical interest, and though somewhat revived from their moribund state throughout the eighteenth and early nineteenth centuries, these assemblies *as such* are anachronisms whose survival value lies mainly in the new integration in the National Assembly (see *infra*) of all the Convocation clerics with representatives of the laity.

Vestry meetings. Before 1919, apart from a few tentative experiments, the only Church assembly at which the laity were officially represented was the *vestry meeting*, which was the council of the parish for ecclesiastical purposes. It includes the incumbent and all persons of both sexes who are ratepayers of the parish, without distinction as to religious belief. Its powers are now practically limited to its share in the election of the people's warden (see *ante*, p. 516).

The National Assembly. But, since 1919, a great measure of self-government has been secured to the Church. The Church of England Assembly (Powers) Act, 1919—commonly known as the Enabling Act—gave Parliamentary approval to a Measure which was presented in the form of a petition by the Convocations of Canterbury and York. Under the constitution granted by that Act, the National Assembly of the Church of England consists of three Houses : the House of Bishops (which includes all the members for the time being of the Upper Houses of the Convocations) ; the House of Clergy (consisting of the members for the time being of the Lower Houses of the Convocations) ; and the House of Laity (consisting of indirectly elected representatives of the laity of the Provinces of Canterbury and York). The Enabling Act of 1919.

The electorate consists of those lay members of the Electorate.

Church of England, of both sexes, who have sought and secured enrolment upon the Church Electoral Roll, which must now be kept in every parish in accordance with the Representation of the Laity Measure, 1929. These electors may attend the Parochial Church Meeting, which must be held annually, usually under the chairmanship of the minister, for the purpose of electing parochial lay representatives to the Parochial Church Council, the Ruri-decanal Conference (if any), and (unless otherwise appointed) the Diocesan Conference, which the Bishop must summon at least once a year. The Diocesan Conference, in its turn, sends representatives to the House of Laity in the Church Assembly.

The Parochial Church Council.
As before stated, the Parochial Church Council has taken over most of the duties of the Churchwardens, and it is now the executive council of the minister. It is a body corporate, having power *inter alia* to acquire property, to frame an annual parochial budget, to levy a voluntary church rate, and to make representations to the bishop with regard to any matter affecting the welfare of the Church in the parish.

Church Assembly and Parliament.
Into the internal arrangements of the Church Assembly we cannot go, but something must be said of its powers, and of its relation to Parliament. It is bound to appoint a Legislative Committee to work in conjunction with an Ecclesiastical Committee of Parliament. When a Measure has been duly passed by the Assembly, it must be presented by the Legislative Committee to the Ecclesiastical Committee, which may invite the Legislative Committee to a joint conference to discuss the Measure. The Ecclesiastical Committee must then draft a report " stating the nature and legal effect of the Measure and its views as to the expediency thereof, especially with relation to the constitutional rights of all His Majesty's subjects." The draft must be communicated to the Legislative Committee, and, upon that body signifying its desire that it be presented to Parliament, it is so presented, together with the Measure itself. If both Houses of Parliament by resolution so direct, the Measure is presented for the Royal Assent ; upon receiving such Assent it has the force and effect of an Act of Parliament.

The Assembly's legislation may relate to any matter concerning the Church of England, and its Measures may amend or repeal any Act of Parliament, except so far as concerns the composition, powers or duties of the Ecclesiastical Committee and the procedure in Parliament under the Enabling Act.

Thus the Church Assembly, unlike the Convocations, has received ample powers of governing the affairs of the Church ; but it is clear from the action of the House of Commons in rejecting the proposed alternative Prayer-Book of 1928, and in vigorously debating certain radical and recent Measures of the Assembly, that the assent of the two Houses of Parliament is no mere formality. It is interesting to note that a Measure, though it has the force and effect of an Act of Parliament, and though it appears in the same printed volume as Public General Acts, is not in the strict sense an Act of Parliament, and lacks the enacting words (see p. 375, *ante*) which are characteristic of an Act.

Section V. ECCLESIASTICAL COURTS

The lowest ecclesiastical court is that of the archdeacon ; but this is now practically obsolete.

The Consistory Courts. Every diocesan bishop has a Court, called the *Consistory Court*, in which he is always represented by his *chancellor*, who is usually a member of the Bar in active practice. The chief function of the Consistory Court is, or has hitherto been, to deal with offences of the clergy against morality, as distinguished from questions of doctrine or ritual.

The proceedings are taken under the Clergy Discipline Act, 1892, and subject to restrictions (see *post*, p. 521), appeal lies *either* to the provincial court of the Archbishop *or* to the King in Council. This statutory jurisdiction has escaped repeal by the Incumbents (Discipline) Measure, 1947, and there may be good, though not very obvious, reason for its preservation notwithstanding the overlap of the new jurisdiction (see *ante*, p. 516). ^{The Clergy Discipline Act, 1892.}

The consistory court also has jurisdiction in certain cases to grant " faculties," *i.e.*, permission to make specific alterations in a consecrated building or churchyard. But this jurisdiction, which does not touch matters of ceremonial or ritual, can now be delegated to some extent to archdeacons.

The very word " faculty " indicates the non-coercive character of ecclesiastical jurisdiction. No sanction lies behind the " monition " of the Court that, for example, an illegal altar be removed.

Appeals from Consistory Courts.

The Provincial Courts. From the consistory court of the bishop, an appeal may lie to the *Provincial Court* of the Archbishop, and in certain cases the latter Court may act as a Court of first instance. The Provincial Court of Canterbury is known as the *Court of Arches* ; that of York as the *Chancery Court of York.* (The former became so called only because its venue was St. Mary-le-Bow, the famous London Church built on arches.) The judge of the Provincial Courts is usually styled the Dean of the Arches, the same person being appointed by the Archbishops for both provinces.

Other matters dealt with by Provincial Courts.

The Provincial Courts also have power to deal with offences against ceremonial, ritual, and the like, under the Public Worship Regulation Act, 1874. This Act requires the Provincial Courts to entertain and determine complaints in regard to alterations in the fabric or ornaments or furniture of any church, or in respect of the burial ground, or of the manner in which the ritual prescribed by the Book of Common Prayer is observed. There is also concurrent jurisdiction to try offences as to doctrine, ritual, and the like, under the Church Discipline Act, 1840. But, as we have already indicated, the cross-currents of opinion during the past century have made it very difficult to enforce discipline in these matters, so that all such statutory jurisdiction is sterile except in the most flagrant and exceptional cases of disobedience.

A special provincial court for the trial of a bishop for an ecclesiastical offence, or *in theory* for the trial of any person dwelling in the province for heresy, may be held by the Archbishop sitting either alone or with assessors. But this somewhat remote and unreal jurisdiction over the bishops is to be reinforced by a new statutory procedure, recently ratified by Parliament, for the compulsory retirement of those no longer worthy or capable of epis-

copal office. The general policy of the new Measure is to
extend recent reforms (see *ante,* p. 516) from the ordinary
clergy to their bishops.

Apart from the provincial courts, the Archbishop of
Canterbury has jurisdiction over *both* provinces for the
granting of faculties and licences. This jurisdiction,
which we have already mentioned, is delegated to an
official called the Master of the Faculties, who is in fact the
same person as the Dean of Arches. *Other jurisdiction of Archbishop of Canterbury.*

Appeals. Appeals from the provincial courts and from
the Archbishops are heard by the *Judicial Committee of the
Privy Council* sitting with ecclesiastical assessors (see
post, p. 602). In cases under the Clergy Discipline Act,
1892, there is an alternative appeal from the Consistory
Court *either* to the Judicial Committee *or* to the Provincial
Court ; but, if the latter is chosen, there is no further
appeal to the Judicial Committee. Whether to the
Provincial Court or to the Privy Council, an appeal lies
of right upon questions of law ; while, upon questions of
fact, if the appellant satisfies the appellate court that he
has a *prima facie* case for a rehearing, he may be granted
leave to appeal. *To the Judicial Committee.*

Neglect or excess of ecclesiastical jurisdiction can be
corrected in the High Court by way of *mandamus* or
prohibition (see *post,* pp. 573 *et seq.*), and a recent case
reveals the interesting fact that, though the recognition of
the ecclesiastical courts as in no way inferior to the lay
courts has meant no immunity from *mandamus* or *prohibition,* it has sufficed at all times to make *certiorari* completely unavailable. "We are not prepared to make a
precedent after 600 years," said Lord Goddard, C.J., in
recently dismissing an application to have the decision of
a Consistory Court reviewed in the High Court by way of
certiorari (*R.* v. *St. Edmundsbury and Ipswich Diocese
(Chancellor), Ex parte White,* [1947] K. B. 263 ; [1946]
2 All E. R. 604 ; affirmed by the Court of Appeal, [1948]
1 K. B. 195 ; [1947] 2 All E. R. 170). *Mandamus, prohibition, certiorari.*

Mention must again be made of the peculiar sanctions
that characterise ecclesiastical jurisdiction. There is : *Sanctions.*

" no power to give damages or grant injunctions or, subject
to certain minor exceptions, inflict any of the punishments

open to the temporal Courts.   The remedies open to it are monition, suspension *ab ingressu ecclesiae*, penance and excommunication, and against clerks in Holy Orders further remedies such as suspension from office or benefice, deprivation of benefice, inhibition from exercising the cure of souls, deposition or degradation " (*per* Uthwatt, J., in *A.-G.* v. *Ripon Cathedral (Dean and Chapter)*, [1945] Ch. 239 ; [1945] 1 All E. R. 479).

Section VI. MEANING OF ECCLESIASTICAL LAW

" Ecclesiastical law is part of the law of the land. . . . The law is one, but jurisdiction as to its enforcement is divided between the ecclesiastical Courts and the temporal Courts. . . . The unity and coherence of the law is not affected by the division of jurisdiction as to its enforcement " (*per* Uthwatt, J., in *A.-G.* v. *Ripon Cathedral (Dean and Chapter)*, [1945] Ch. 239 ; [1945] 1 All E. R. 479).

" ' Ecclesiastical law ' is used in a general sense and also in a technical sense.   In its general sense it means the law relating to any matter concerning the Church of England. . . . The matters concerning the Church of England fall into three categories :   (1) those where the law is exclusively declared and enforced by the ecclesiastical Courts.   That is clearly ' ecclesiastical law ' ;   (2) those where the law is exclusively declared and enforced by the temporal Courts, even though dealing with ecclesiastical affairs.   That is not ' ecclesiastical law ' in its technical sense ;   (3) those where the law is enforced by both the ecclesiastical and the temporal Courts.   That is a borderland which is as difficult to chart as the borderland between contract and tort . . ." (*per* Denning, L.J., in 60 Law Quarterly Review, 235).

Should the student think all this to be unlikely ground for practical disputes, let him read for himself the recent cases cited in this Chapter, especially the House of Lords decision in *Representative Body of the Church in Wales* v. *Tithe Redemption Commission,* [1944] A. C. 228 ; [1944] 1 All E. R. 710.

OTHER RELIGIOUS BODIES

The disabilities attaching to persons unwilling to conform to the Established Church, formerly very serious, have now been reduced to so small a compass that there is no need to do more than recall attention to the necessity for the King to be a member of the Church of England, and to the incapacity of Roman Catholics and Jews to hold the office of Lord Chancellor. To all intents and purposes the civil and political disabilities of non-conformists have long disappeared. *Removal of disabilities.*

It is much more important and more interesting to consider the position *in law* of religious bodies other than the Church of England. They are purely voluntary bodies, of the type that is often called Unincorporated Associations. Except where their rules have obtained legislative sanction, their government is based on consent, the jurisdiction of their domestic tribunals is consensual, and they cannot legislate to bind their members, except in so far as those members have previously consented to be so bound. In all these respects they are not *legally* different from clubs. This is true even of Churches, formerly established, for which Parliament has provided that ecclesiastical law " shall cease to exist as law." Thus : *Legal position of other religious bodies.* *Disestablished Churches.*

> " by the abolition of ecclesiastical law in Ireland and in Wales it would seem that the legal effect of consecration there is gone. . . . All that the members of the Church can say is that ' we have agreed between ourselves to treat the place as holy ground ' "

(*per* Denning, L.J., in 60 Law Quarterly Review, at p. 240). Indeed, even the continuance of the episcopate and the traditional hierarchy of clergy is made consensual by the disestablishing legislation.

Again, from a legal point of view, the Roman Catholic Church in this country, although part of a monarchically *Roman Catholic Church.*

governed international society, is no different from the
Methodist Church, which is a purely national body under
the centralised government of a Conference, or from a
single Congregational Chapel.   The members of all of
them may complain to the ordinary Courts, when their
rights are infringed, but, generally speaking, religious
bodies take care that their constitutions shall as far as
possible exclude the interference of the Courts.   For this
and for other reasons, questions arising out of the internal
affairs of religious bodies rarely come before the Courts,
and the law in respect of them is open to considerable
doubt.

Property.   But on one topic we are well informed.
Where a permanent unincorporated association desires to
hold property, it is practically necessary that there should
be a trust ; and, in order that the rule against perpetuities
should not interfere with the permanence of the endow-
ments, it is essential that the trust should be a charitable
trust ; charitable trusts include those created for the
advancement of religion.

The Chari-
table Trust.

Now a charitable trust must have a definite purpose,
and so long as that purpose can be followed, the trust
property must be applied to it, in the manner specified in
the trust deed.   If the purpose becomes impossible of
fulfilment, the Court may, in accordance with the doctrine
of *cy près*, apply the property to some similar purpose
which is still possible of fulfilment ; but if the original purpose is still a possible one, the mere fact that all the
trustees or a majority of the persons interested in the trust
wish to abandon the original object of the trust will be of
no effect.   Now let us apply this reasoning to religious
bodies.   Suppose that property has been given in trust
for a specified religious body, and that such a body has an
ascertainable doctrine ;   then, unless the trust deed
explicitly recognises that body's power to change its
doctrine, or unless it is a well-known part of its Constitution that it has such a power, the property is only at the
disposal of the body so long as it continues to hold that
doctrine ; and if a majority do not continue to hold that
doctrine, the trust property is at the disposal of the
minority who do.   Otherwise the trust property would be

in danger of being applied in a manner foreign to that contemplated by the original donor. This is the point of the famous Scottish case of *Free Church of Scotland (General Assembly)* v. *Overtoun (Lord)*, [1904] A. C. 515— the report of which takes nearly 250 pages—where a majority of the Free Church decided to unite with another Scottish Church called the "United Presbyterians," and for that purpose to make certain alterations in what were alleged by the minority to be essential portions of the doctrine which the Free Church had been established to maintain. The minority were overruled, and thereupon claimed in the Courts that the whole proceedings were *ultra vires*, and that they themselves, who alone preserved intact the original doctrine of the denomination, were the true Free Church of Scotland.

Free Church of Scotland v. *Lord Overtoun.*

The House of Lords ultimately found in favour of the claim of the minority, who had only 27 votes in the Free Church Assembly to their opponents' 643, and adjudged to them the whole of the property of the Free Church, thus almost causing a revolution in Scotland. The legislature was indeed forced to intervene and by statute to divide the property between the majority and the minority on an equitable basis.

Thus, where the title to property is in dispute, the Courts may have to decide incidentally points of doctrine. But in the majority of cases such questions do not arise, for the more powerful denominations have Model Trust Deeds for use by persons who give property to the denomination, and these deeds make the gift subject to the denomination's constitutional powers of modifying its doctrine from time to time. The Model Trust Deed of the Wesleyan Methodists was drawn up at great length over a century ago. Where such a deed is employed there can, of course, be little occasion for interference by the Courts. In some cases, however, trust deeds have been so vague in this respect that it was found necessary to pass the Nonconformist Chapels Act, 1844— commonly known as Lord Lyndhurst's Act—which provides that, where the deed of trust does not expressly state the religious doctrines or opinions or mode of regulating worship, for the preaching or promotion of

Model Trust Deeds.

which a meeting house has been founded, twenty-five years' usage (immediately preceding any suit relating to such meeting house) of the congregation frequenting it shall be taken as conclusive evidence.

Other matters.

Thus the law recognises the existence of religious bodies as holders of property. But it goes further. For instance, Roman Catholic priests, recognised ministers of Protestant Nonconformist Chapels, and rabbis are exempted from certain civil and political obligations ; and where a place of religious worship has been duly registered, marriages may take place in it, and it is no longer rateable. Moreover, the law punishes severely any disturbance in a place of religious worship, though not belonging to the Established Church.

BOOK II

CONSTITUTIONAL AND ADMINISTRATIVE LAW

PART V

THE SUBJECT

SUMMARY

PAGE

CHAPTER 25. THE CONSTITUTIONAL POSITION OF
THE SUBJECT 529

CHAPTER 25

THE CONSTITUTIONAL POSITION OF THE SUBJECT

SUMMARY   PAGE

Section I. *The Duties of the Subject* 529
Section II. *The Rights of the Subject* 534
Section III. *Interferences with the Fundamental Liberties* ... 552

Section I. THE DUTIES OF THE SUBJECT

Allegiance is the tie which binds the subject to the ruler, in return for the protection which the ruler affords to the subject. This relationship is coloured by the ideas of feudalism, a system under which it was the custom for the vassal to admit his obligation to his lord by swearing an oath of fealty. There exists at this day a similar oath of allegiance, but this oath is only exacted from certain persons on acceptance of office, from members of Parliament, and from a few other subjects. Aliens, however, who seek naturalisation are required to take the oath of allegiance. Any of these persons may, however, substitute an affirmation for the actual oath. *The meaning of allegiance. Oath of allegiance.*

But, apart from any express oath or affirmation, there is an *implied* allegiance owing from every subject to the sovereign. Thus in Coke's words, *Implied allegiance.*

> " all subjects are equally bounden to their allegiance as if they had taken the oath ; and the taking of the corporal oath is but an outward declaration of the same."

This duty of allegiance is not confined to the King's subjects ; corresponding to the " natural " allegiance, which subsists between them and the Crown, is the so-called " local " allegiance which every resident alien friend owes to the King whose protection he enjoys. But no oath of allegiance is ever exacted of him, unless he should seek naturalisation. Otherwise his local allegiance has almost the same effect on his relations towards the Crown as natural allegiance has upon those between the subject and his sovereign (see *ante*, pp. 311–2). *Local allegiance.*

Effect of allegiance.

We have this conception of allegiance still lying behind the rule that only a person who owes allegiance can be guilty of treason or analogous crimes; and resident friendly aliens are in this respect in the same position as the subjects. But the local allegiance of the former, generally speaking, lasts only as long as they continue to reside within the realm. It continues, however, in spite of absence abroad, if the friendly alien allows " his family and effects " to remain under the protection of the Crown, or if—as a notorious prosecution for treason recently showed—he himself continues while abroad to be under such protection, *e.g.*, by holding a British passport, though improperly obtained. (See *Joyce* v. *Director of Public Prosecutions*, [1946] A. C. 347; [1946] 1 All E. R. 186.)

Active duties of the subject.

Let us now consider the active duties of the subject. Most of these duties have been already mentioned incidentally. It is, nevertheless, convenient to collect together a few of the more important active duties of the citizen in order that we may present a coherent account of his constitutional status. For our purpose they may be classified as follows :

Liability to serve if called upon.

1. Certain duties, once of vital importance to the government of the country, but now practically obsolete; for instance, it is a doctrine of the Common Law that a person is bound to serve the Crown when called upon for that purpose. So a person chosen as sheriff cannot as a general rule refuse to accept office; so also most persons could be made to serve as parish constables or as special constables if occasion required; and it is interesting to note that, even under quite modern statutes, persons qualified to serve as members of municipal corporations are liable to penalties if they refuse to accept office.

Military service.

2. In many continental states the citizen has for long been under a general duty to serve for a period in the army, but up to comparatively recent years it would have been correct enough to say that there was no corresponding duty in England. Compulsory military service seemed a thing of long ago. But experience during the two World Wars has shown that the State still claims the right to exact compulsory service in case of necessity. It

should be noted, however, that the obligation to serve
was imposed by statute, in 1939 as in 1916, and that no
attempt was made to rely on any Common Law right, had
such right in fact existed. Likewise the present continuance of the obligation is entirely dependent upon
statute, *viz.*, two National Service Acts, 1948, the temporary character of which may not be without constitutional significance.

3. What are the duties of the subject in relation to the
maintenance of order? We are accustomed to think
of the maintenance of order as being exclusively the
function of the police, but the basis of the power of the
police to maintain order is the right and duty of every
citizen to assist in the quelling of disturbances and the
maintenance of the King's peace. Statutes no doubt
have made additions, and the additional powers are not
as a general rule shared by the ordinary individual. For
example, the Public Order Act, 1936, gives power to a
constable, on the request of the chairman of a meeting, to
demand the name and address of any one whom he suspects of an offence under the Act, and to arrest without
warrant in the event of a refusal or false compliance.
It is true also that the existence of the police force has in
practice relieved the general public from its primary duty
of maintaining order; but any man may in case of
necessity be called upon by a magistrate or a sheriff or,
for that matter, by any constable to assist in preserving
the peace, and cases have not been wanting where members
of the general public have been punished for refusing to
accede to the request of a constable for assistance in case
of emergency (*R*. v. *Brown* (1841), Car. & M. 314).

4. Now in all these cases it may be said that, though the
subject has been and still is under a Common Law duty of
service or assistance, that duty is enforced, generally
speaking, only in an emergency. The old amateur
government contemplated by the Common Law has given
way to a professional government under statutory powers.
But not all the active duties of citizens are obsolete. As
regards the administration of justice, they are still fully
operative. Thus any person can be compelled to give
evidence in a criminal trial and, though the duty in respect

Duties as to maintenance of order.

Obligation to give evidence.

of civil proceedings is not so stringent, even there a person can be forced to appear in the witness box on payment of reasonable expenses. This does not apply to the " expert " witness, who is entitled to be paid by the party in need of the evidence, *e.g.*, a foreign lawyer giving his opinion as to the effect of a foreign system.

Jury service. Still more striking is the obligation to serve on a jury. But of this little can be said that may not be out-of-date by the time this treatise reaches the student ; for the whole subject of jury service and its exemptions—now a chaotic compound of modern commonsense and surviving anomalies—is being inquired into with a view to radical reformation by Parliament. The main fault, broadly speaking, is the undemocratic character of an obligation from which large sections of the community are exempt—*either* because of their status or profession, *e.g.*, peers, the clergy, lawyers, doctors, dentists, officers and men of the fighting services, including the Territorial Army, *or* because they do not own enough land or pay enough rates. If, when we spoke of the wholly democratic character of the modern parliamentary franchise, the student wondered why the clerical work of preparing the lists of electors is still generally put upon the rating authorities, he will now know that one reason at any rate is the still surviving need for them to indicate those electors who have the necessary property qualification for service as jurors. Reforming legislation may be expected sooner or later to abolish the property qualification altogether—the distinction between common and special jurors being already a thing of the past—and also to rationalise the grounds of exemption.

Many of these are already sensible enough, particularly the exclusion of people under twenty-one or over sixty. Women, too, who have become liable to service since 1919 —whether married or unmarried—may be excused by the Court " by reason of the nature of the evidence or of the issue to be tried," or " for medical reasons " ; they are not liable, even though their name remains on the register, if vowed members of a religious order living in a convent or other religious community. Further, there is a general right to be excused " on the ground of illness," and a convenient provision empowers the Sheriff—without affecting the power of the Court to excuse any person from attendance—to receive from any person *in writing* some good reason why he should be excused and to excuse such person from attendance ; the Sheriff is required, however, to produce all such applications to the Court in question, and to give his reasons for complying with any of them. Aliens, though long domiciled here, are to be excluded " in any judicial or other proceedings if challenged by any party to such proceedings " (Aliens Restriction (Amendment) Act, 1919). In the case of Coroners' Courts there are some modifications of the usual rules relating to juries.

Jury service is still, so far as criminal trials are concerned, as great a burden as ever. The tendency in civil justice is for the number of jury cases to decrease. During the recent war, juries of seven instead of twelve sufficed—except in treason or murder trials ; and hearings by judge alone in practically all civil cases. Until just recently, with the solitary exception of the special jury (now, with one exception, abolished), the old Common Law principle was of personal unpaid compulsory service ; but the Juries Act, 1949, now provides for payment of travelling and subsistence allowances and a moderate compensation for loss of earnings.

5. Within the last hundred years many statutes have imposed active duties which, if more definite in their operation than those imposed by the Common Law, are of just as burdensome a character.

Let us look first at taxation. Not only has the citizen to pay rates and taxes, but, as we have already seen (pp. 440–1), a great deal of the preliminary work of assessment to income tax is performed by the taxpayer himself or his employer. In other words, the duty of the citizen is not limited to paying the tax imposed upon him, but includes also the duty of making returns of one kind or another in accordance with which the amount of taxation is eventually determined. The duty of making returns is, however, by no means limited to the field of taxation. Employers of labour have to make returns, *e.g.*, under the Factory Acts, the Road Traffic Acts, and the National

Duties as to taxation.

Duty to make various returns.

Insurance Acts. To all this must now be added the novel tax-gathering responsibility of employers under the P.A.Y.E. procedure already mentioned (pp. 438–9).

Duty of registration. Analogous to the duty of making returns is that of registration. The duty of registering births and deaths falls, in the first instance, not upon officials, but upon parents or other relatives ; nor should we forget the duty under which every householder is placed in respect of the decennial census. Indeed, the wartime emergence of the " identity card " has brought home the duty of registration to the whole community. But the active duties of citizens extend far beyond the making of returns and registration.

Duty to give children education, etc. Thus a duty is imposed by the Education Acts, and the by-laws made under them, on the parent or guardian of every child in the country to cause that child to attend school. So, until just recently, a parent or guardian of a child was bound to have the child vaccinated, unless statutory exemption was claimed ; so, also, a householder is under a statutory obligation to notify the existence of any infectious disease within the household.

These are only a few of the more important active duties which have been imposed by comparatively recent statutes on the private individual. Whether their origin is Statute or Common Law, almost all these duties, with the exception of those relating to the acceptance of office under the Crown, military service, and to some extent jury service, are incumbent upon the resident alien friend no less than upon the subject.

Section II. THE RIGHTS OF THE SUBJECT

Right of protection. Now let us consider the rights and liberties of citizens. In return for allegiance, it is said that the Crown must afford protection to its subjects ; but, whatever this may have meant in time past, the duty of protection seems at the present day to mean no more than that no servant of the Crown can set up the defence of Act of State to an action in tort brought by a subject. This benefit, being correlative to allegiance, belongs also to the resident alien friend (*ante* p. 312). In a fairly recent case, concerned with the armed protection by the Crown of British subjects against piracy in Chinese waters, the Court refused a declaration that the Crown was under an obligation to provide such defence without payment (*China Navigation Co., Ltd.* v. *A.-G.*, [1932] 2 K. B. 197).

Even the right to the protection of the law must not be exaggerated. The subject is entitled to have the law impartially administered ; but he has no right that the law shall not be altered to his detriment. In other words, he has no " absolute " rights which are guaranteed against change by Act of Parliament. This is of course a consequence of the general principle that Parliament is a sovereign legislature. Thus Parliament can—and sometimes does—legislate so that the Act shall have retrospective operation. Further, it has been held that, even if the holder of an office has been appointed for a definite period under express statutory authority, he has no right to compensation if—without special provision in his favour—the office is by statute abolished (*Reilly* v. *R.*, [1934] A. C. 176). Yet, though the subject has no rights which may be properly considered as absolute or guaranteed rights, some common law rights of the subject are regarded as peculiarly sacred. Parliament can abridge them just as it can abridge any other rights, but it is not likely that it will do so, at least under ordinary circumstances ; and it may fairly be said that, in the case of some of them, a definite presumption exists which precludes the interpretation of an Act of Parliament so as to interfere with them, except where it is absolutely clear that Parliament has had that express intention. {No rights guaranteed against statutory interference.} {Presumption against abridgment.}

Let us consider then, first, the varieties of these so-called absolute rights, and secondly, the occasions upon which the subject can be interfered with in his enjoyment of them.

1. *The right of personal freedom.* Every subject or resident alien friend has a right to his personal liberty. This is, generally speaking, protected by an action in tort for false imprisonment ; but personal liberty would not be absolutely secure unless a person who is kept in confinement without legal justification had some means of being set free. The means are provided by

the writ of *habeas corpus*, which Blackstone has called :
" The great and efficacious writ, in all manner of illegal
confinements."

The writ is most commonly granted by a Divisional
Court of the King's Bench Division, or by any judge of the
High Court during vacation, and it may be applied for
either by the person detained *or* by any one on his behalf.
The usual practice nowadays is to make application for a
rule *nisi* directed to the respondent, that is to say, the
person who detains the prisoner, bidding him appear and
show cause why a rule *absolute* for the issue of the writ
against him should not be made.   The respondent appears
on the day named in the rule *nisi* ; and the case is then
argued on its merits. If the Court decides against the
respondent, a rule *absolute* issues against him, ordering
him to produce the prisoner on an appointed day, and
upon the appointed day the prisoner is released without
more ado.   This procedure has been invented to avoid the
inconvenience of unnecessarily bringing up the body of
the prisoner, possibly from a distance ; under the old
procedure, the main argument took place on the return
to the writ.   A good instance of the modern procedure is
to be found in the documents cited in the report of *Secretary of State for Home Affairs* v. *O'Brien*, [1923] A. C. 603,
at p. 614 :

There is a *right* to apply for the writ to any tribunal of
the High Court, and a modern case has again affirmed the
surprising rule that refusal by one tribunal will not prevent another of equal rank from granting it (*Eshugbayi
Eleko* v. *Nigeria Government* (*Administering Officer*),
[1928] A. C. 459).   From a decision against the prisoner,
an appeal may be made to the Court of Appeal and, with
leave, to the House of Lords.   In other words, application may be made on behalf of the prisoner to one Court
after another until he has been successful, or until he has
exhausted all the available Courts or judges.   But the
other side has no such right ; for, when once any Court has
decided after hearing a discussion on the merits of the case
that the prisoner ought to be released, there is no appeal
from its decision.   This was decided finally in the above-
mentioned case of *O'Brien*.

Disobedience to the writ is punishable by fine or imprisonment for contempt of Court ; and in many cases the offender is exposed to heavy penalties recoverable by the person injured. It is useful as a method of testing the legality both of official and public imprisonments, and also of private and even domestic detention. Thus, on the one hand, it may be granted against the governor of a prison who has in his custody a prisoner detained without trial, or against the commanding officer of a camp who is detaining a man, alleging that he is liable to military service. On the other hand, it may be used to try the legality of a husband's detention of his wife, or the detention of a child in an institution contrary (as the parents allege) to their wishes.

Punishments for disobedience to writ.

The Habeas Corpus Acts require further consideration ; for it is a general belief that the right to the writ of *habeas corpus* was originally conferred by these Acts. This is incorrect. The writ itself, and the right of the subject to obtain it under ordinary circumstances, are as old as the Common Law itself. The Habeas Corpus Acts only made more effective the Common Law writ, and improved the procedure by which writs could be obtained, and checked the devices by which their effects could be evaded. Thus, before the passing of the great Habeas Corpus Act in 1679, it was a not uncommon practice to transfer a prisoner from one prison to another in order to render uncertain the person to whom the writ would effectually issue, or to remove the prisoner to some such place as the Channel Islands to which the writ would not run ; and only a short time before, in *Jenkes's Case* (1676), 6 State Tr. 1190, it was decided that there was no power to issue the writ in vacation. The Act remedied the greater number of the defects which attached to the writ ; it rendered the writ more peremptory than it had been, thus making it more difficult or impossible to transfer the prisoner from one prison to another ; it made the writ issuable in vacation as well as in term, and by a very unusual provision subjected any judge who refused the writ in vacation to a penalty of £500 recoverable by the party injured ; it enacted that the writ should run into the Channel Islands and privileged places within England,

The Habeas Corpus Acts.

into which it had not formerly run ; and it forbade under most severe penalties the sending of any prisoner to places outside the realm of England.

Defects remaining.

Certain defects still remained after the passing of the Act.   In the first place, it was still open to a judge or other magistrate to refuse to release a prisoner except on payment of excessive bail.   This defect was removed by the Bill of Rights in 1689, which declared " that excessive bail ought not to be required."   Secondly, it only applied to imprisonment on criminal or supposed criminal charges ; civil imprisonment was entirely outside the purview of the Act.   Thirdly, it was still possible for the respondent to assign a false cause of detention, and the Court was unable to go behind the return.

Acts of 1816 and 1862.

These last two defects were remedied by the Habeas Corpus Act, 1816.   The latest of the Habeas Corpus Acts, that of 1862, provided that no writ of *habeas corpus* shall issue out of England into any colony or foreign dominion of the Crown in which there is a lawfully established Court with authority to grant and issue the writ, and with power to ensure its due execution throughout such colony or dominion ; but, except for the very considerable limitation of this Act, the writ may be enforced out of England in any part of the dominions of the Crown.

Parliament and the right of property.

2. *The right of property*.   Every person, it is said, has a property in his lands and goods, and this property can only be taken away by his consent.   But every subject is deemed to be present in Parliament and to consent to everything that is done there ; that is to say, the collective assent of the whole nation, expressed through its constitutional organ, Parliament, is equivalent to the particular assent of any private individual.   It follows from this reasoning, which is not without some force, that the taking of the subject's property under Parliamentary authority is no true infringement of his fundamental rights.

There are two ways in which Parliament, even in time of peace, may authorise the taking of the subject's property.

Taxation.

The first is by way of taxation.   We have seen how jealously the Courts insist upon the necessity for Parliamentary consent in this regard.

The second is not so familiar to the ordinary man, though it occurs every day. It is clear that there must be some means of interfering with private rights in the public interest. It may be that the proper development of a town requires the widening of a particular street, and that this can be done only if the Corporation can force the owners of houses on one or both sides of the street to convey them to it ; or it may be that the War Office is in need of more land for purposes of military training ; or the Ministry of Health for its national water scheme ; or it may be that a gas authority ought to be allowed to lay pipes under a certain field ; or an education authority to build a school upon it. *Compulsory purchase of land.*

Since powers of interfering with private rights are needed, they must come from Parliament ; and in the past such powers have been regarded, both by Parliament and by the Courts, as reluctant concessions or necessary evils that work alteration of the law in favour of a promoter, *i.e.*, some person who approaches Parliament to obtain the powers necessary for his undertaking. It was for the local authority, the railway or gas company, or whoever the promoter might be, to take the initiative in securing such powers as Parliament might be willing to concede ; and any concessions had to be effected in statutory words of a definite and inescapable kind, for in their absence Parliament was presumed never to intend any interference with vested rights. Even if it was clear that Parliament had so intended, there was a further presumption that the permitted interference was only to be on payment of compensation.

It seems right to speak of these presumptions as belonging to the past, when liability to compulsory purchase was much more the exception than the rule. But, now that the necessary powers have been conferred by general legislation on so vast a scale that liability to compulsory purchase extends far and wide, it seems no longer good sense to regard these powers as an encroachment, conceded here and there, upon the common law liberty of a private owner to please himself whether to sell or not to sell. Acquisition of these powers has ceased to be merely a matter for local or private initiative, and Parliament has *Comparison of past and present.*

taken it upon itself in recent years to pass more and more general legislation that confers these powers, with bewildering variations of detail, upon all the different kinds of authorities—central, local, public utility, and so forth.   Thus, in creating the modern law of housing, town and country planning and new towns, trunk roads, electricity and water supply, forestry, air navigation, or whatever it may be, Parliament as a matter of course includes any inevitable powers of compulsory purchase— sometimes confined to some particular Department or one kind of authority, sometimes overlapping or interlocking.

Even if the magnitude and intense complexity of the relevant legislation were not enough reason for our attempting no summary of it here, there is the further reason that the law is at present in a fluid and transitional state.   On the one hand, there is *temporary* machinery in force under the Acquisition of Land (Authorisation Procedure) Act, 1946, for the more " speedy " exercise of compulsory powers in " urgent " cases ; on the other hand, fundamental and far-reaching changes, comprehending compulsory purchase and much else, are taking effect under the Town and Country Planning Act, 1947.

" Better-
ment."

One of its novel purposes is to ensure that the community shall get all " betterment," *i.e.*, all

> " increase in the value of land . . . arising from central or local Government action, whether positive, *e.g.*, by the execution of public works or improvements, or negative, *e.g.*, by the imposition of restrictions on other land " (Cmd. 6386).

Because legislation conferring powers of compulsory acquisition makes such frequent reference to the " Lands Clauses Acts," it may be useful to give a brief explanation. Down to 1845, provisions for compensation were inserted in each and every public or local Act which conferred powers of taking.   This was found to be inconvenient, wasteful of time and paper, and not infrequently productive of hardship to the persons affected by the powers conferred.   Accordingly a comprehensive code was passed to regulate the giving of compensation whenever powers

Various
Clauses Acts.

of compulsory acquisition are conferred.   This code, the Lands Clauses Consolidation Act, 1845, was followed by several other codes of the same kind, such as the Railways Clauses Consolidation Act, 1845, the Waterworks Clauses Act, 1847, and the Towns Improvement Clauses Act, 1847. These Acts have been amended from time to time, and the principal code is now known as the Lands Clauses Acts, 1845–1895. They are divided for convenience into parts, any one or more of which may be made applicable to the particular case. The general rule is that the whole code is automatically incorporated into any Act, whether public or local, which confers powers of taking a person's land ; but in practice the special Act expressly incorporates the code, or parts of it, usually with certain exceptions which have themselves reached a high degree of standardisation, *e.g.*, in such legislation as the Housing Acts, 1936–49, the Water Acts, 1945 and 48, and the New Towns Act, 1946.

Hitherto one has been accustomed to think of compulsory purchase as a liability to which only land and buildings are subjected—whether in regard to the compensation of the owner or in regard to conflicting public interests, *e.g.*, when land of high fertility or natural beauty is taken for military training or for water or electricity supply. But examples abound, not all of them recent, where property *in general* is bought under statutory compulsion. Prewar examples include the elimination of mining royalties and tithe, the grouping of the railways, and the formation of London Transport ; during the war British investments abroad passed to the State ; and it is common knowledge that the subsequent " nationalisation " schemes have so far included the statutory transfer from private to public ownership of the Bank of England, the Coal Industry, and the Transport and Electricity and Gas undertakings. Compensation has invariably been paid, though its scale and mode of assessment have been most variable. Moreover, it may be generally assumed that the various newly-created public corporations now operating these nationalised concerns (of whose ambiguous constitutional status we spoke briefly at the close of Chapter 16) are themselves able directly or indirectly to acquire by compulsion, applied in accordance with whatever variety of procedure the creating legislation may have prescribed. But here, though bewildered by the absence

Compulsory purchase of property in general.

of uniformity and the complex variations of detail, we may perhaps see not an opening of novel avenues of power but rather an extension of those previously open, on the one hand to Local Authorities, and on the other hand to all public-utility concerns long years before their recent nationalisation.

3. *The right of freedom of discussion and the freedom of the Press.* They are no more than particular instances of the rule that any person may act as he pleases so long as he does not break the law. So the right of freedom of discussion, and in particular the freedom of the Press, extends no further than is allowed by the general law of libel and slander, of blasphemy, obscenity and sedition, and does not operate to relieve the citizen from the consequences of an illegal act. Recent years have seen the passing of Statutes imposing further restrictions ; thus the Press is no longer free to publish the evidence in divorce and separation cases, wherever decided, or to reveal the identity of delinquents in the Juvenile Courts ; the law of sedition has been intensified by the Police Act, 1919, and the Incitement to Disaffection Act, 1934 ; and words spoken at public meetings may now be dealt with under the Public Order Act, 1936 (see *post*, p. 549).

Absence of censorship.

This state of the law involves the absence of any censorship as such, and it is a fact that since the House of Commons refused in the years 1695 to continue the Licensing Act, there has, with the exception of periods of emergency, been no permanent censorship of the Press. Even during the recent war, though the Government had power (and used it) to ban a newspaper, the Press was able to take pride in the fact that the censorship was a matter of voluntary submission rather than compulsion.

The law of libel is indeed strict and needs reform, but its chief defect is that it facilitates blackmail ; it does not appear to restrain the most outspoken criticism of political action. And if we except the power of the Courts—a power very rarely exercised before trial—to restrain by injunction the publication of a libel, there is no judicial power to prevent beforehand the commission of an offence (see, further, *post*, p. 552).

Historically, the freedom of the Press is associated with

the career of John Wilkes in the middle of the eighteenth century. In three famous cases, *Leach* v. *Money* (1765) 19 State Tr. 1001 ; *General Warrants Case* ; *Wilkes* v. *Wood* (1763), 19 State Tr. 1153 ; and *Entick* v. *Carrington* (1765), 19 State Tr. 1029, it was decided that a "general warrant" may not be issued to arrest the unnamed author or printer of a publication, or to search the papers of an unnamed or even of a named person. Search warrants for various purposes, *e.g.*, for the recovery of stolen goods, are of course well known to the law, but they were until recently of little use in controlling the formulation or expression of opinion. The powers of the police have now been increased by the Official Secrets Acts and the Incitement to Disaffection Act, 1934, and, even at Common Law, by the decision in *Elias* v. *Pasmore*, [1934] 2 K. B. 164.

4. *The right of association.* Associations for an illegal purpose are, of course, themselves illegal, but with very few exceptions it is not illegal to associate for a legal object. One of the chief objects of association has always been the protection of the trade interests of the members of the association. This has often involved what the Common Law knew as restraint of trade ; difficulty has been introduced into the law of conspiracy by this concept, and much of the modern law of trade unions can only be understood in relation to it. At the present day it plays a much smaller part than formerly. But, though the law does not as a rule prohibit associations which are established for a lawful purpose, it has been at pains to control them, and to specify rules for their government. Thus, at various times charitable trusts, friendly societies, trade unions, and large partnerships have been subjected to statutory regulation ; while, if a group of persons wishes to obtain the advantages of incorporation, it must promote the passing of a special Act of Parliament *or* obtain a charter from the Crown *or* go through such statutory formalities as those of the Companies Act, 1948. *Restraint of Trade.*

5. *The right of public meeting.* Our law knows no explicit right of public meeting. The holding of lawful meetings is protected from disturbance by the Public Meetings Act, 1908, but this protection only implies the *No explicit right.*

right to meet, which arises (in the same way as the right of free speech) from the general principle that any person is at liberty to do as he likes, so long as he commits no breach of the law. We have therefore to consider the particular torts and crimes which those who organise or take part in a public meeting are in danger of committing.

In the first place, entry upon private land in order to hold a meeting is restrained by the law of trespass. Only in exceptional cases is a criminal penalty available, but an action in tort can succeed without proof of any damage.

No trespass or nuisance must be committed. Again, no nuisance must be committed, and in particular it is to be noticed that in the words of Charles, J., in *R.* v. *Cunninghame Graham and Burns* (1888), 16 Cox, C. C. 420:

> " The law recognises no right of public meeting in a public thoroughfare—a public thoroughfare being dedicated to the public for no other purpose than that of providing a means for the public passing and repassing along it. A place of public resort is analogous to a public thoroughfare ; and although the public may often have held meetings in places of public resort without interruption by those having control of such places, yet the public have no right to hold meetings there. . . ."

It follows that if such persons are indicted for public nuisance or sued for a private nuisance, they cannot set up any right of public meeting by way of defence. Similarly, criminal proceedings may be brought, under the legislation relating to the highways, to enforce the prescribed penalties for *obstruction* ; it is said to be unnecessary for the prosecution to prove that the holding of the meeting was in fact an obstruction ; the mere holding of the meeting is, apparently, enough. In practice, however, this legislation is not likely to be used as a means of suppressing a public meeting, unless the highway is in fact obstructed by the meeting.

Illegal meetings. Apart from all questions of nuisance, certain assemblies are of themselves illegal. The law of unlawful assembly is a part of the Criminal Law, and only a brief indication of its main principles is necessary in a treatise on the Constitution. There are three classes of meetings, participation in which may render a person guilty of a crime. These, in increasing order of gravity, are unlawful assemblies, routs and riots.

An " assembly " is constituted by the congregation of Unlawful
assemblies. three or more persons for the accomplishment of some common design. The design, however, need not be put into execution, or any further step taken towards it other than that of assembling. In order that the assembly may be " unlawful " it is not necessary that the object of the meeting should itself be illegal. The test is, not the illegality of the purpose for which the persons are met, but the danger to the peace which their meeting involves. The mere fact, therefore, that the purpose is unlawful is not enough ; it must be shown that it involves reasonable apprehension of a breach of the peace. Thus, if a number of persons meet to plan a fraud, they may be guilty of a conspiracy, but their meeting is not an unlawful assembly. On the other hand, although the object of the meeting is perfectly lawful, nevertheless, if the manner of the meeting is such as to cause fear in the mind of a reasonable man that a breach of the peace will occur, it is an unlawful assembly. Thus, in *Wise* v. *Dunning*, [1902] 1 K. B. 167, *Wise* v.
Dunning. a Protestant " crusader " held meetings in public places in Liverpool, and in the course of his addresses he used words and gestures highly insulting to the Roman Catholic inhabitants, of whom there were a large number present. The natural consequence was actual or apprehended breach of the peace. It was held that he could be bound over to keep the peace.

If the meeting is not only convened for lawful objects but also conducted in a quiet and peaceable manner, will it become unlawful merely because its promoters know that it will be opposed and that the *opposers* may be guilty of a breach of the peace ? *Beatty* v. *Gillbanks* (1882), *Beatty* v.
Gillbanks 9 Q. B. D. 308, a case on which Dicey laid great stress, is at any rate an authority for saying that the promoters ought not to be charged with being unlawfully assembled. In that case, members of the Salvation Army held a meeting which they intended to conduct lawfully and peaceably. They knew, however, that their meeting was likely to be opposed by a so-called Skeleton Army. This opposition took place, and a free fight resulted in the public streets. It was held that the members of the Salvation Army were *not* guilty of an unlawful assembly.

No act on their part, save the perfectly lawful act of holding the meeting, provoked the disturbance.

Quite apart from statutory restrictions—in particular those of the Public Order Act, 1936—there are serious limitations, revealed in other cases, that reduce the principle of *Beatty* v. *Gillbanks* to unimportance in modern law. If the charge is framed, *not* as one of unlawful assembly, but as one of obstructing the police in the execution of their duty, then *Beatty* v. *Gillbanks* will afford no defence. This may be seen in *Duncan* v. *Jones*, [1936] 1 K. B. 218, where the facts were briefly as follows : The speaker was about to address a public meeting near the entrance to a training centre for unemployed workers. There was no material obstruction of the highway ; the purpose of the meeting was lawful, and its conduct was orderly and peaceable. The speaker was, however, ordered by the police not to proceed with the meeting, and on her attempting to do so, she was arrested and later convicted of the statutory offence of obstructing the police in the execution of their duty. (The relevant Acts were the Prevention of Crimes Act, 1871, and the Prevention of Crimes Amendment Act, 1885.) The police were able to show, in justification of their order, that on the previous occasion of a meeting at the same place there had in fact been disturbance in the training centre, and that since they *reasonably* believed that the present meeting, if it were allowed to be held, would result in a breach of the peace, it was their duty to stop it.

We can see that the principle of *Beatty* v. *Gillbanks* becomes irrelevant if, as is likely, the charge is framed as in *Duncan* v. *Jones*, and not as one of unlawful assembly. It is in this technical sense that we must understand these words of Lord Hewart, C.J., in *Duncan* v. *Jones*, at p. 222 :

> " If I thought that the present case raised a question which has been held in suspense by more than one writer on Constitutional Law—namely, whether an assembly can properly be held to be unlawful merely because the holding of it is expected to give rise to a breach of the peace on the part of persons opposed to those who are holding the meeting— I should wish to hear much more argument before I expressed an opinion. This case, however, does not even touch that important question."

Duncan v. *Jones*.

To reduce the offence to its lowest terms, we may say that an unlawful assembly is a meeting of three or more persons which is designed to effect a common purpose and of which the natural consequence is a breach of the peace or the reasonable apprehension that it will be broken. It is, moreover, the duty of magistrates and of the police to disperse the assembly, and a refusal by those assembled to disperse may be opposed with a reasonable degree of force. Such a refusal is itself illegal and may—as we shall see—constitute a riot. The extent of the powers of the police to enter upon *private* premises in execution of this duty has given rise to recent controversy. It would seem that, without any previous request from those assembled, the police may enter if the meeting is a public one ; and perhaps even if the meeting is a private one. This is thought to be the uncertain state of the law as left by the much criticised case of *Thomas* v. *Sawkins*, [1935] 2 K. B. 249, where the facts were briefly as follows : The police were refused admission to a public meeting, but insisted upon entering the hall and being present throughout the proceedings. No objection could be taken to the conduct of any of those attending the meeting, but the police maintained that they had reasonable grounds for believing that sedition and disorder might occur if they were not present at the meeting. The Court, apparently approving the police contention, held it to be no assault for a police officer to resist an attempt to eject him from the hall. *Thomas v. Sawkins.*

To constitute a rout, the members of the unlawful assembly must take some step towards the achievement of their object. A crowd assembled for the purpose of destroying machinery is an unlawful assembly. As soon as its members start on their way to attack a particular factory, it becomes a rout. But indictments for the offence are rarely drawn, as the jury can convict of a rout on an indictment for a riot, if the latter is not proved. *Routs.*

The rout becomes a riot when the purpose of the unlawful assembly is actually put into execution. Completion of the purpose is not essential, but there must be a further degree of accomplishment than that found in a rout. Further, those assembled must have the intent to help *Riots.*

one another by force, if necessary, against any person who may oppose them in the execution of their common purpose ; and there must be force or violence displayed in such a manner as to alarm at least one person of reasonable firmness and courage. These are the requirements of a riot, as specified in *Field* v. *Metropolitan Police Receiver*, [1907] 2 K. B. 853, and an illustration of their application is afforded by the case of *Ford* v. *Metropolitan Police District Receiver*, [1921] 2 K. B. 344. On Peace Night, 1919, a crowd assembled to make a bonfire. Armed with crowbars and pickaxes, but in good humour, they stripped an empty house of woodwork to provide fuel. A next-door neighbour gave evidence that he dared not interfere, because he was afraid of injury had he done so. It was held that the assembly amounted to a riot.

A riot, like an unlawful assembly or a rout, is at Common Law a misdemeanour, punishable with fine and imprisonment, but in certain circumstances it may become a felony. This is the effect of what is popularly known as " reading the Riot Act." By the provisions of the Riot Act, 1714, a magistrate, on receiving information that twelve or more persons are engaged in an assembly which threatens the peace, must proceed to the place of disturbance and make a proclamation, in the form presented in the Act, ordering them to disperse. The effect of the proclamation is twofold. In the first place, if the assembly fails to disperse within an hour, its members are guilty of felony and may be most severely punished. In the second place, the magistrate and those acting with him are protected from any liability for any hurt inflicted or death caused in dispersing the meeting after the lapse of the hour.

The Riot Act.

It must be remembered, however, that, independently of the Riot Act, there is a Common Law right and indeed a duty, not only on a magistrate, but also on every citizen, to use such force as may be necessary to disperse an unlawful assembly. Any one who refuses to help in the dispersal, when called upon by a constable for assistance, is— generally speaking—liable to be indicted for misdemeanour at Common Law. It is in the case of *R.* v. *Pinney* (1832), 5 C. & P. 254, that the Common Law is to be found stated

Suppression of riots.

as to this right and duty that lies upon ordinary citizens as well as those in authority.

Finally, it should be noted that any individual whose property is damaged by a riot may be paid compensation out of the " police rate " of the district in which the riot took place—Riot (Damages) Act, 1886. This provision was intended as a spur to the police in the suppression of disturbances, but it may be presumed that this stimulus has lost some of its sharpness since the abolition of all the smaller police areas by the amalgamating Police Act, 1946. *Compensation.*

There does seem to be emerging in recent years a form of preventive justice, administered by the police with the encouragement of the Courts. *Duncan* v. *Jones, supra,* and *Thomas* v. *Sawkins, supra,* may be regarded as examples of this tendency. *Preventive justice.*

It is in the law of riots, routs and unlawful assemblies that the limits of the so-called right of public meeting must be sought ; but certain meetings which were perfectly legal at Common Law have been rendered illegal by statute. It is unnecessary to give a list of the relevant statutory provisions. They relate to revolutionary and seditious meetings, unlawful drilling, and to disorderly conduct at lawful public meetings ; and local authorities, too, by their by-laws have rendered certain meetings illegal. An important Act has, however, been fairly recently passed, and something must be said about it even in these pages. The Public Order Act, 1936, was designed to safeguard the peace by suppressing the wearing of quasi-military uniform and the keeping of " private armies " for political purposes ; also to give extensive powers to the police and local authorities to enable them to regulate and even to prohibit public processions and meetings in public places. Section 5 of the Act contains a wide provision modelled on what had hitherto been found in the by-laws of certain municipalities : any person " who in any public place or at any public meeting uses threatening, abusive or insulting words or behaviour with intent to provoke a breach of the peace or whereby a breach of the peace is likely to be occasioned " is guilty of an offence under the Act. The section increases the jurisdiction of the Justices on a *Meetings illegal by statute.* *Public Order Act, 1936.*

charge of disturbing the peace by such words or behaviour ; they can now inflict imprisonment or a fine.
Hitherto, in such cases, they had only a jurisdiction to
bind over—an old jurisdiction of rather uncertain limits
and obscure origin.

It is interesting to notice the Seditious Meetings Act,
1817, which prohibits the convention of any meeting of
more than fifty persons within one mile of Westminster
Hall, during the sitting of either House of Parliament,
for the purpose of petitioning the King or either House of
Parliament. This statutory prohibition, which also
applied to the Courts of Justice, did not avail after their
removal from Westminster Hall, and later legislation gave
their sittings similar protection within one mile of the
present buildings in the Strand.

Mention is made elsewhere of the Emergency Powers
Act, 1920 (see *post*, p. 554), under which a Government, in
time of emergency, has power to interfere with the ordinary
course of the law—including the law of public meeting.

Nature and
basis of so-
called
absolute
rights.

The basis of all these so-called absolute rights is the
fundamental principle of English law that every Englishman is entitled to do what he pleases so long as it is not
prohibited by law. On the other hand, the Government
has not any corresponding general right to do whatever
it considers necessary for the good of the country. Therefore we start from the principle that the ordinary individual
is *prima facie* entitled to do anything, whereas the Government must point to some specific authorisation at Common
Law or by statute before it may interfere with the person
or property of the subject. Under these circumstances
it is natural that English law should specify, not what the
individual may do, but what he may not do ; and his
so-called absolute rights are merely a name for his immunity from interference except within the limits at
any moment of specially conferred power in the Government. They cannot, of course, be absolute in any real
sense, because they are subject to the sovereignty of
Parliament, but Englishmen have been prepared to trust
Parliament not to curtail them unnecessarily.

On the other hand, Continental states have usually

started from the opposite position, that the Government has full power of interference whenever it considers it expedient in the public interest. Where government has remained, or has again become, authoritarian, this power is irreconcilable with any true rights in the citizen. But even in liberal countries, such as France, the Government has retained in principle this general power, and so the fundamental liberties of the citizen are, as it were, carved out of it. The result is that it is those liberties, and not the powers of the Government, that required definition, and it is that very need for definition that explains their prominence in the Constitution. Thus this distinguishing characteristic of English as opposed to foreign constitutional law, which Dicey thought significant enough to be considered one of the bulwarks of the Rule of Law, turns out to be little more than an historical accident and not necessarily a sign of superiority ; and in fact the final result in England and France seems to be very much the same, allowing for national differences of temperament and tradition.

The Americans have refused to acknowledge any un- limited power either in the Executive or in the Legislature, and, whilst retaining the notion that the citizen may do anything he is not forbidden to do, have *also* guaranteed against *legislative* interference certain defined rights corresponding to the " rights " already inherent in the Common Law. While this certainly has all the appearance of a triumph of law over arbitrary power, there is perhaps something to be said for the view, indistinctly suggested by Dicey, that a better guarantee is to be found in popular vigilance, which may be stimulated by the lack of any defined constitutional safeguards.

There is also a certain danger of over-emphasising the im- portance of these absolute rights, and so of suggesting that governmental activity is necessarily, or at least normally, detrimental to the citizen. In fact, of course, it may confer a plenitude of benefits upon him, such as free education and protection against disorder and disease, all the various insurances, the health and cultural amenities, and so forth, though these involve a corresponding interference with property in the shape of taxation.

Section III. INTERFERENCES WITH THE FUNDAMENTAL LIBERTIES

(a) By Judicial Process

Interference by the Courts.

It is clear that a person's liberty or property may be interfered with by the Courts. This right of interference is so universally accepted that it is usually overlooked. We have already noticed all the ways in which the Courts interfere with the rights of the subject. It will be sufficient here to notice that imprisonment by order of a Court is an infringement of the right of personal freedom ; that every time a jury awards damages against an unsuccessful defendant, or a sheriff executes judgment, an infringement of the subject's right of property inevitably takes place. So, too, by an injunction the Court restricts the full freedom of action of the individual. This effect is also produced by an order of the Justices binding over a defendant or forcing him to find security for his future good conduct. Still more interesting, because more drastic, is the power of any Court of Record to commit any person for contempt of Court ; for the power of the Court in this instance is discretionary, and is exercised summarily and without the intervention of a jury. This power is thought by some to deter unduly the freedom, especially of the Press, to make criticism of the Judiciary. Be that as it may, the ambit of the power is clearly defined in the following statement of the Judicial Committee :

Contempt of Court.

" . . . whether the authority and position of an individual judge, or the due administration of justice, is concerned, no wrong is committed by any member of the public who exercises the ordinary right of criticising, in good faith, in private or public, the public act done in the seat of justice . . . provided that members of the public abstain from imputing improper motives to those taking part in the administration of justice, and are genuinely exercising a right of criticism, and not acting in malice or attempting to impair the administration of justice, they are immune. Justice is not a cloistered virtue ; she must be allowed to suffer the scrutiny and respectful, though outspoken, comments of ordinary men " (*Ambard* v. *A.-G. for Trinidad and Tobago*, [1936] A. C. 322, at p. 335.)

(b) *In Case of Emergency*

BY STATUTE. The necessity for the exercise of extended powers to interfere with the liberties of the subject in case of emergency is recognised both at Common Law and by statute. Let us consider the statutory provisions first. The attitude of the Common Law is much more difficult to define.

1. *Habeas Corpus Suspension Acts*. It was at one period not infrequent in times of emergency for Parliament to deprive those imprisoned on suspicion of treason of their right to speedy trial or release on bail. These were popularly known as Habeas Corpus Suspension Acts. It is to be observed that they were usually passed only for a year at a time, and so had to be renewed annually. They did not necessarily render the imprisonment legal, and they did not indiscriminately affect all persons suspected of crime. They merely deprived the citizen, within the limits of their operation, of his right to seek a release from prison by means of the writ of *habeas corpus*. On any eventual release, he would be at liberty to sue the persons who had detained him (or authorised his detention) for the tort of false imprisonment, and the Suspension Act itself would not have provided them with any defence to his action. It was customary, therefore, on the expiration of a Suspension Act to pass an Indemnity Act, relieving those who had acted under the Suspension Act from liability to answer for what they had done. The terms of an Act of Indemnity, *e.g.*, the Act passed after the first Great War, might be wide or narrow. It might even provide a complete bar to all judicial proceedings. On the other hand, it was more usual not to relieve an officer of the consequences of his acts unless they had been done *bona fide* in the public interest. (See, further, *post*, pp. 561–2.)

Acts of Indemnity.

2. *Coercion Acts, etc.* It might, however, be the case that Parliament gave to the Executive definite powers of discretionary imprisonment. Legislation of this kind, under the names of Coercion Acts or Prevention of Crime Acts, was not uncommon during the difficulties which arose in Ireland in the third quarter of the nineteenth century. It is a feature of the constitution of Northern

Ireland at the present time. As these Acts gave extended powers to the Executive, they rendered imprisonment under their provisions, not merely indeterminable, but lawful, and accordingly there was no necessity for subsequent legislation in the form of an Indemnity Act.

3. *Defence Acts*, 1914–15, *and* 1939–40. During the two Great Wars, Parliament gave to the Government extremely wide powers of subordinate legislation, and under these powers (see *ante*, pp. 323–4) the Executive assumed control over the lives and liberties of the whole community. A world war can no more be fought in accordance with Magna Carta than on the principles of the Sermon on the Mount, as a distinguished judge remarked in a leading wartime case (*R*. v. *Halliday*, [1917] A. C. 260). So, though the *habeas corpus* procedure was by no means in suspense, its use was made futile in cases of governmental detention by the very fact that the wartime law permitted such detention to be a matter for the discretion of the appropriate Minister. The Executive also greatly extended its right to acquire compulsorily the property of the subject for purposes of national defence ; but it was decided in the case of *A.-G*. v. *De Keyser's Royal Hotel* (see *ante*, pp. 299–300), that the Crown was under a liability to make proper compensation.

4. *Emergency Powers Act*, 1920. After the first Great War it was felt that it would be an advantage to give to the Government permanent powers similar to those exercisable under the Defence of the Realm Act, but of a narrower extent, to be used in any case of emergency.

Proclamation.

Accordingly the Emergency Powers Act, 1920, was passed, giving the Crown power to proclaim a state of emergency whenever it appears that the supply and distribution of food, water, fuel or light, or the means of locomotion, or generally the essentials of life of the community or any substantial portion of it, are in danger of being interfered with. So long as the proclamation is in force, the

Emergency regulations.

Crown has power to make emergency regulations by Order in Council for the purpose of safeguarding the public safety and the life of the community, and such regulations are to have the force of statute. Effective safeguards are, however, established against arbitrary executive action. In the first place, no proclamation may be enforced for more than one month unless renewed. Secondly, Parliament if not sitting must be convened within five days, and the proclamation of emergency must be communicated to Parliament without delay ; emergency regulations must be laid forthwith before Parliament, but lose their force after seven days unless approved by a resolution of both Houses. Parliament may also by resolution add to, alter, or make any regulation. Thirdly, as the recent use of the Act made manifest, it preserves the right of workers to strike. But above all, though regulations may provide for the trial by Courts of summary jurisdiction of persons guilty of offences against the regulations, no alteration may be made in the existing procedure in criminal cases, or any right conferred to punish by fine or imprisonment without trial. *No alteration in criminal procedure.*

5. *Supplies and Services Acts*, 1945 *and* 1947. After the recent war, too, there have been Acts (*ante*, pp. 305, 324, 336) to confer or continue many emergency powers.

AT COMMON LAW. The effect of an emergency at Common Law is very uncertain, and it is for this very reason that special statutory powers have from time to time been given to the Executive ; but one general principle may be laid down : *Quod necessitas cogit defendit.* How far, it may be asked, may a person plead in defence to a charge of crime or action of tort that what he did was absolutely necessary ? *Public* necessity may often justify the commission of what would otherwise be a crime. Thus the preservation of the peace and the advancement of justice may sanction the employment of force in arrest of a rioter or a criminal. *Private* necessity, however, is a matter of excuse only within strict limits. Self-defence, as we shall see, may indeed justify the use of violence against the assailant. But beyond this, the criminal law recognises few, if any, exceptions to the ordinary principles of liability. So, except in the case of defence against violent assault, a person can never justify the homicide of another by the plea that it was required for his own preservation. In the words of Chief Justice Holt, " he ought rather to die himself than kill an innocent." In *General principle— quod necessitas cogit defendit.* *Public necessity.* *Private necessity.*

R. v. *Dudley and Stephens* (1884), 14 Q. B. D. 273—the
strange case of the shipwrecked sailors who killed one
of their number for the purpose of eating his flesh—Lord
Coleridge said that there was no " absolute or unqualified necessity to preserve one's own life." Even a man in
extreme want of food or clothing is not justified in stealing
to relieve his own immediate needs. There may, however,
be cases in which the preservation, not of a man's own life,
but of another's life at the expense of a third, may be
justified ; for example, the case of a doctor who has to
choose at child-birth between the life of the mother and
that of the child. In the law of tort, too, the defence of
necessity is available : certainly in cases of injury to
property (*e.g.*, pulling down a building after a fire to
prevent its falling in the highway), and most probably,
also, in cases of injury to the person. (See, further,
Vol. II, Book II.)

These observations show that the defence of necessity
is very wide in its operation. Where it applies it protects,
not merely the private individual, but any government
authority. The necessity must be absolute, and the steps
taken must not exceed the requirements of the emergency.
Let us consider in greater detail the chief occasions on
which these extended powers sanctioned by necessity are
called into operation.

When force may be used.

1. *Self-defence, etc.* Any person has a right to use
all necessary force for the purpose of protecting his own
person and the persons of those dependent upon him. He
has a right to use force to resist force. The right includes
the defence of a master by his servant, and of a servant by
his master. Indeed, it may well be that the defence of
any one by any one is allowed. The term " self-defence "
is accordingly too narrow : and it is sometimes replaced by
the term " private defence." We have said that the
amount of force used must be reasonable ; in other words,
it is for the defender to maintain a sense of proportion.
It is a popular fallacy that all burglars are " fair game "
who may be shot at sight.

This right to the use of necessary force extends to the
protection of property, but " there is a difference between
protecting yourself from any injury which is not yet

suffered by you, and getting rid of the consequences of an injury which has occurred to you " (*per* Lindley, L.J., in *Hurdman* v. *N. E. Rly. Co.* (1878), 3 C. P. D. 168). This principle was applied by an early statute which makes it an indictable misdemeanour for even the person lawfully entitled to the possession of land to seek its recovery by force ; once his possession has been lost, no matter how wrongful the dispossession may have been, he must re-enter only " in peaceable and easy manner " (5 Rich. II, st. 1, c. 8). In other words, force may be used to keep out or turn out a trespasser, but not to recover possession itself. Thus, again, it is lawful to defend one's land against a flood, even though the result may be damage to one's neighbour ; but the law does not allow water already gathered upon the land to be released to the hurt of a neighbour.

What amount of force may lawfully be applied in a defence against trespass ? It is indicated in the language of the pleaders : *molliter manus imposuit* ; the force must be no more than is reasonably required in the circumstances to effect the removal of the trespasser, and there should be no beating or other punitive assault of the trespasser. If the trespasser himself commits an assault, he may be assaulted in defence of the person ; and if his entry is felonious, he may be repelled with all the force that is necessary to prevent the commission of the felony. The right to use all necessary force is extended for the prevention of a felony or the capture or detention of a felon. It is further extended so as to cover the use of all necessary force, not only to resist force, but also to put down force. It is on this right that the power to suppress riots and insurrections is based. Every citizen not only has the right but is bound to do all that in him lies, usually by the command of magistrates or other lawfully constituted authorities, but if occasion arises on his own initiative, to suppress disorder and restore the King's peace. And if, in so doing, he interferes with the life or liberty or property of a fellow-subject, he will be protected to the extent to which his act was necessary for the purpose.

Use of force to resist or put down force.

2. *Taking measures for the public safety.* It was said

in the case of the *King's Prerogative in Saltpetre* (1606), 12 Co. Rep. 12 :

> " when enemies come against the realm to the sea coast, it is lawful to come upon my land adjoining to the same coast, to make trenches or bulwarks for the defence of the realm, for every subject hath benefit by it. And therefore by the Common Law every man may come upon my land for the defence of the realm."

Does the Common Law ensure compensation in such a case of emergency ? The answer is obscure, though the judgment in the *Saltpetre* case states that " after the danger is over, the trenches and bulwarks ought to be removed, so that the owner shall not have prejudice in his inheritance." The question will call for solution only in the unlikely event of acquisition by the Crown in exercise of the Prerogative and *not* in reliance upon the provisions of any enabling emergency statute (see the *De Keyser's Hotel* case, *supra*, pp. 299–300). Experience during both the World Wars goes to show that all-sufficing statute law, superseding the Prerogative, is made available in abundance.

3. *Martial law.* In most continental countries the Government has power, in case of serious disorder, to declare what is known as a " state of siege," and to transfer the task of maintaining order and executing justice from the civil to the military authorities. What we have now to consider is whether such a power exists in England.

Since 1628, the year of the Petition of Right, no case has ever arisen in the English Courts out of an attempt by the military authorities to exercise any " extraordinary " jurisdiction within England itself ; but it has not infrequently happened in Ireland, in South Africa, and in British territories overseas, that the Commander-in-Chief, having been entrusted by the Government with the task of restoring order, has proclaimed " martial law," has issued regulations prescribing the conduct to be followed by the inhabitants of the area covered by the proclamation, and has set up " military Courts " to deal with offences against the regulations. Out of these " exercises of martial law " cases have arisen, and the decisions in these cases, though with one possible exception not binding on English Courts,

Irish and Colonial precedents.

are high persuasive authority as to the view of " martial
law " taken by the Common Law. In the light of these
decisions, certain propositions may be laid down concerning the legal position of the military authorities and of the
general public during the purported exercise of martial law.

(i) The true effect of a proclamation of martial law is
thus stated by the Law Officers of the Crown in an opinion
written by them to the Secretary of State for the Colonies
in 1838 :

Proclamation has no legislative force.

> " The Governor of Lower Canada has the power of pro-
> claiming, in any district in which large bodies of the in-
> habitants are in open rebellion, that the Executive Govern-
> ment will proceed to enforce martial law. We must, how-
> ever, add that in our opinion such proclamation confers no
> power on the Governor which he would not have possessed
> without it. The object of it can only be to give notice to the
> inhabitants of the course which the Government is obliged
> to adopt for the purpose of restoring tranquillity " (Forsyth,
> *Cases and Opinions on Constitutional Law*, p. 198).

(ii) Two questions arise which cannot be considered
apart. They are : what is the true criterion of a " state
of war " ? and what effect, if any, has the existence of a
" state of war " upon the powers of the military authorities
and their relations to the ordinary law and the ordinary
Courts of law ?

Until quite recent times the answer to both questions
was simple. The maxim of the Common Law was *Inter
arma silent leges*. If the Courts of law were open, so as to
exercise their regular jurisdiction, it was a time of peace ;
if they were closed, it was a time of war. Therefore, in
time of peace, there were Courts, but there could be no
military government ; in time of war, a system of military
government might exist, but there could be no Courts of
law to control it. So, under the old system, there could
never be even the chance of the Courts " sanctioning "
the exercise of martial law.

State of war—old criterion.

But the Judicial Committee of the Privy Council
decided in *Ex parte Marais*, [1902] A. C. 109, that the old
criterion of a state of war is not applicable to modern
conditions of warfare, and that the question whether a
state of war exists is purely a question of fact. Therefore, in the changed conditions, a state of war may exist
although the ordinary Courts of law are still open. The

State of war now a question of fact.

question accordingly arises, which could never have arisen in the days of old, what is a Court of law to do if a person imprisoned by order of the military authorities applies for a writ of *habeas corpus* and no return sufficient in law is made ? That was the exact point raised in *Ex parte Marais*, and it was decided that, *while war is actually raging*, the Courts have no power to interfere with the acts of the military authorities.

The question whether a state of war exists is, as we have said above, a question of fact. But two other questions still remain to be decided, namely, who is to judge whether a state of war exists, and what really constitutes a state of war ?

Court shall decide whether state of war exists.

The former point was definitely raised in *R. (Garde) v. Strickland*, [1921] 2 I. R. 317, at p. 329. Counsel for the military authorities had contended that the Court was bound to accept the allegation of the Commander-in-Chief that a state of war existed ; he was silenced by the Court with the words :

> " We desire to state, in the clearest possible language, that this Court has the power and duty to decide whether a state of war exists which justifies the application of martial law."

Must be a condition in which military should have free hand.

The second question is also answered by implication in the same passage, for no Court will rule that a state of war exists unless it is satisfied that affairs are in such a condition as to require the unimpeded action of the military in restoring tranquillity. Thus the Courts will renounce jurisdiction over the military authorities, if there is a state of war ; they will hold that there is a state of war only if they come to the conclusion that they ought not to interfere with the military authorities. This really means that the Courts will not interfere with the military authorities when they think they ought not to interfere with them.

The attitude of the Courts to martial law.

(iii) But we must be careful not to mistake the attitude of the Courts to martial law. A state of war justifies the Courts in refusing to restrain the fighting men while the fight is still on. It does not justify the Courts in absolving them from being answerable for their excesses when the fight is over. Thus the decision in *Marais's* case does not by any means imply that the Courts will not be able *after*

Military act at their peril.

the cessation of a state of war to call in question the acts of military authorities done in the purported exercise of martial law. There is little definite authority on the point, but it is clear from the tenor of all the judgments that the Courts reserve to themselves perfect freedom of action on this head.

(iv) The lack of case-law on this question—whether the Courts can sit in judgment over the military authorities *after a state of war has come to an end*—is due to the invariable practice of Parliament in passing Acts of Indemnity relieving all persons from liability for acts done by them for the purpose of restoring order. Such Acts of Indemnity are not intended merely to legalise illegal acts which the military authorities may have committed in performing what they have conceived to be their political and moral duty. They are passed just as much for the purpose of relieving them from the necessity of defending vexatious and ill-founded actions, and in order to provide compensation from the national Exchequer for damage done in the course of military operations. An Act of Indemnity may, of course, cover *all* acts done for the purpose of restoring order, even those done maliciously. But protection so abundant has been held to need explicit adoption by the Act itself, and it is in fact more usual for the Act to go the other way and to make *bona fides* a necessary condition of protection under the Act. Thus the Indemnity Act, 1920, which followed the first Great War, enacts (subject to certain provisos) that : [margin: Acts of Indemnity.]

> " No action or other legal proceedings whatsoever, whether civil or criminal, shall be instituted in any Court of law for or on account of or in respect of any act, matter or thing done, whether within or without His Majesty's dominions, during the war before the passing of this Act, if done in good faith, and done or purported to be done in the execution of his duty or for the defence of the realm or the public safety, or for the enforcement of discipline, or otherwise in the public interest, by a person holding office under or employed in the service of the Crown in any capacity, whether naval, military, air-force, or civil, or by any other person acting under the authority of a person so holding office or so employed."

But it has been common for an Act of Indemnity to provide some special remedy against the State, *in lieu* of that which is rendered unavailable against the officer, and so its effect is rarely to deprive the injured subject of all opportunity of redress.

What is martial law? We now come to a question which is more academic than practical. What *is* martial law? At the outset the warning must be given that martial law does *not* mean military law, *i.e.*, the code that is sanctioned by Parliament each year for the regulation of the Army, and enforced in some cases by Courts Martial set up under the Army Act. We have said that the proclamation of martial law is not conclusive evidence of the existence of a state of war, and that it does not increase the powers of the military authorities to suppress disorder. We may now go further and say that martial law is, in the eyes of the Common Law, no law at all. A proclamation of the Commander-in-Chief, which lays down regulations for the conduct of those subordinate to him and also of the inhabitants of the proclaimed area, is not a source of law, but a mere arbitrary claim for obedience which may or may not be justified by the necessity of the case. So, also, any military Courts established by the Commander-in-Chief to deal with offences against his own regulations are not Courts at all, but merely committees of officers sitting for the purpose of informing the mind and carrying out the orders of the Commander-in-Chief.

We conclude with a quotation from the judgment of Lord Halsbury in *Tilonko* v. *A.-G. of Natal*, [1907] A. C. 93, at p. 94 :

> " It is by this time a very familiar observation that what is called ' martial law ' is no law at all. The notion that ' martial law ' exists by reason of the proclamation . . . is an entire delusion. The right to administer force against force in actual war does not depend upon the proclamation of martial law at all. It depends upon the question whether there is war or not. If there is war, there is the right to repel force by force, but it is found convenient and decorous, from time to time, to authorise what are called ' Courts ' to administer punishments, and to restrain by acts of repression the violence that is committed in time of war, instead of leaving such punishment and repression to . . . casual action. . . . But to attempt to make these proceedings of so-called ' courts martial,' administering summary justice under the supervision of a military commander, analogous to the regular proceedings of Courts of Justice is quite illusory."

Martial law no law at all.

Military Courts not Courts.

BOOK II

CONSTITUTIONAL AND ADMINISTRATIVE LAW

PART VI

THE JUDICIARY

SUMMARY

PAGE

CHAPTER 26.   THE CONSTITUTIONAL FUNCTIONS OF
             THE JUDGES   565

CHAPTER 26

THE CONSTITUTIONAL FUNCTIONS OF THE JUDGES

SUMMARY   PAGE

Section I. Introduction 565
Section II. Remedies against the Crown   568
Section III. Remedies against other Public Authorities   ... 571
Section IV. Orders in Lieu of Prerogative Writs   573
Section V. Limitation of Actions against Public Authorities   581

Section I. INTRODUCTION

The importance of the judicial element in our Constitution can hardly be exaggerated, for it rests with the Courts to ensure the conformity of government with law. On the other hand, it is easy to exaggerate the extent of this activity of the judges. The " Rule of Law " (discussed on pp. 337 *et seq.*, *ante*), which Dicey held to be a leading principle of our Constitution, does not involve the decision of every dispute by Courts of law. But it does imply *Judicial control.* that all authorities in the State act under the eye of the Courts, and are liable to have the legality of their conduct inquired into. So far as Parliament is concerned, this means nothing at all, for whatever Parliament *as a whole* does is not only legal but has the force of law. To all *Of legislation.* other legislative bodies—including, as we have seen, even the Commons or Lords acting alone—it means a great deal, for if they attempt to legislate beyond the powers conferred on them by law, then there is the general safeguarding rule that their acts are liable to be treated by the Courts as *ultra vires* and therefore void. " By-laws " run the further risk of being declared void for unreasonableness (see *ante*, p. 325). But even this traditional safeguard is, of course, subject to the supremacy of Parliament, and in recent years Statutes have frequently included language designed to exclude the legislation of subordinate bodies from any review by the Courts. Such language has not always succeeded in its purpose owing to the strictness with which the Courts have presumed against the intention of the legislature to exclude judicial control (see *ante*, p. 326).

Of executive agents.

Likewise all executive agents are subject to judicial control, unless they have been expressly exempted from it by the legislature, and if they act outside their powers or neglect to do their duty, they are liable to any penalties which the law provides. We have already seen that if they have a discretion committed to them, the Courts will not interfere with them in their exercise of the discretion, unless they overstep it or exercise it in a manner not consonant with the principles of natural justice. But if they are under a duty to exercise it, and neglect to perform that duty, they are liable to be called to account before the Courts of law (see Chap. 2, *ante*, pp. 275 *et seq.*).

Of administrative tribunals.

We have also seen that a system, already begun in the last century, has become of enormous importance as part of the present governmental control of the social and economic life of our people ; it is the system of administrative tribunals, to which is committed the decision of matters which affect the rights of the citizen but are unsuitable for decision by the ordinary Courts. We have met with many such tribunals in the course of this work. Some decide subject to appeal to the ordinary Courts, though this is exceptional. However, all these administrative tribunals are regarded as " inferior " courts and, in the absence of statutory provisions to the contrary, are subject to the control of the High Court if they exceed or fail to exercise their jurisdiction or exercise it in a manner not consonant with the principles of natural justice.

The two Houses of Parliament, when they decide questions within their own privilege, are, as we have already seen, not subject to the control of the Courts (pp. 382 *et seq.*).

Relation of Courts to citizen and Government.

The Courts then, although they do not decide every question, either of fact or law, which arises in the course of government, do in a real sense stand between the citizen and the Government, and ensure that government shall be carried on according to law. But, if they are to do this effectively, they must clearly be independent of both the Government and the citizen. It is for this reason that (as we have already seen) the superior judges, though appointed by the Crown, are made to hold office

Judges' security of tenure.

during good behaviour and not at the pleasure of the Crown, but may be removed on an Address to the Crown by both Houses of Parliament (p. 297). It is for this reason also that they are made absolutely immune from all legal proceedings in respect of acts done by them within their jurisdiction (see *ante*, p. 282). Judges' immunity from legal proceedings.

A Court of justice requires subordinate officers, *e.g.* sheriffs, bailiffs, constables, etc., for the purpose of carrying out its orders ; and it would be unreasonable to expect these persons to examine the validity of every order before they executed it, or to act at their peril. Accordingly they are in large measure protected from liability to be sued or prosecuted in respect of acts committed by them in the execution of an order of the Court. If the order emanates from a *superior* Court, the executive officer who carries it out has complete protection, provided he acts in conformity with it. For instance, a sheriff who is commanded to seize the goods of A is protected, even though the order should be proved afterwards to be irregular ; but he is not protected if he wrongfully seizes the goods of B. Protection of subordinate Officers of Courts.

But, in the case of the orders of an *inferior* Court, the executive officer is usually protected only when the matter is within the jurisdiction of the Court ; though there are several important statutory exceptions to this rule. Thus a county court bailiff is protected " notwithstanding any defect of jurisdiction or other irregularity in the warrant " (County Courts Act, 1934, s. 147) ; and constables and others executing magistrates' warrants are protected against the consequences of defects in the magistrates' jurisdiction (Constables Protection Act, 1750).

Similar to this statutory protection for the subordinate officers of the Courts is the protection for administrative officers, *e.g.* the Customs Consolidation Act, 1876, and the Inland Revenue Act, 1890, introduced provisions for the protection of Customs and Excise Officers.

We must now consider the procedure which the Courts employ in their dealings with public authorities. It is in the main the same as that which they employ towards private persons, but several topics call for special treat- Procedure in dealing with public authorities.

ment.   One preliminary remark must be made.   When
we say that the Courts control the acts of public authorities, we do not mean that they do so of their own
motion.   It is characteristic of judicial bodies that they
have no initiative.   They must be set in motion by some
one else.   They can therefore only control public authorities if they are asked to do so ; and accordingly we shall
have to deal with the remedies which are open to the
citizen against public authorities who have caused him
injury.

It is necessary to deal separately with the special rules
which apply to the Crown.

Section II. REMEDIES AGAINST THE CROWN

Position of
Crown until
1948.

Until quite recently it was the traditional rule of English law that no action could be brought against the
King, either in his private or in his public capacity.   For
tort there was no remedy whatever by which the victim
could touch the public funds : his only recourse was
against the actual servant of the Crown who had committed or authorised the tort, though usually the latter
would, if found guilty, be placed in funds by the Crown
so that he could satisfy judgment.   For everything else,
e.g., claims to property or compensation or claims arising
out of contract, there was a remedy known as *petition of
right*, the proceedings in which were closely akin to those
in an ordinary action ; but before the claim was brought
into Court the consent of the Crown had to be communicated through the Home Secretary by the *fiat* " Let
right be done."   It was the Home Secretary's constitutional duty to advise the granting of the *fiat* if the sup-
pliant had the shadow of a claim.   It would seem that
what is above stated is still the law if a subject wishes
to make good a claim against the King in his *private*
capacity ; but for claims against the King in his *public*
capacity, or, as we commonly say, the Crown, *i.e.*, for
anything done in the course of government, it has been
completely superseded after January 1, 1948, by the
Crown Proceedings Act, 1947, and the Supreme Court
Rules and County Court Rules made under it.

That Act in effect assimilates proceedings against the

Crown to ordinary litigation between citizens. Actions will in fact be brought against the particular Government Department concerned or, if it is not included in the appropriate list published by the Treasury or if the plaintiff is in doubt which the appropriate Department is, against the Attorney-General. Even in tort, for breach either of common law or of statutory duty, there is now a general liability upon the Crown, and the ordinary principles of vicarious responsibility now extend to the Crown in respect of torts committed by its servants within the scope of their employment or otherwise in the discharge of their functions, provided these are not of a judicial nature. Payment of salary out of funds provided by Parliament is made the general test for deciding whether a wrongdoer is among the servants of the Crown. The Crown still remains generally immune from liability in respect of postal services, but has accepted a limited liability for loss of or damage to *registered* inland postal packets, unless it can be shown that the loss or damage was not due to the neglect or default of the Post Office. If whilst on duty one member of the armed forces of the Crown causes death or personal injury to another such member, he does not thereby subject either himself or the Crown to a civil action at the suit of the latter ; and the Crown enjoys the same immunity where the death or injury results from the defective nature of supplies, equipment, etc. But the victim is not without a remedy, for the immunity of the Crown or its servants exists only in cases where the Minister of Pensions certifies that the victim or his estate is entitled to an award for disablement or death.

Although the Crown may now be ordered to make discovery of documents or to answer interrogatories, it retains its power to withhold any document or refuse to answer any question on the ground that the disclosure or answer would be injurious to the public interest. Nor can the Crown be in any way coerced into satisfying an award of damages or costs, though it may itself as plaintiff make use of all the usual means for reaping the fruits of successful litigation ; moreover, no relief may be granted against it by way of injunction or specific performance

Crown Proceedings Act, 1947.

Liability of Crown in tort.

Peculiarities of Crown proceedings.

or specific restitution, though a *declaration* may be made *in lieu* thereof.

The Crown's liability in contract carries with it certain exemptions : thus there can be no liability if Parliament fails to vote the necessary funds (*Churchward* v. *R.* (1865), L. R. 1 Q. B. 173). This means that any contract involving the expenditure of public money is subject to the assumed consent of the House of Commons. Again, all those in the service of the Crown may be dismissed at will, for the venerable rule—broad but not boundless, as a recent decision reveals—is that the Crown cannot fetter its own future executive action (see *ante*, p. 408).

Now that effective remedies have been provided against the Crown, litigants will seldom be tempted to sue Crown servants for anything done by them in the performance of their functions. It is, however, worth mentioning that agents and servants of the Crown are not as regards third parties in any different position from agents of any other principal or servants of any other master. So, when a Minister or other servant of the Crown contracts as agent for the Crown, he cannot be made personally liable on the contract (*Macbeath* v. *Haldimand* (1786), 1 Term Rep. 172). In such a case the remedy is against the Crown itself. It has indeed been laid down that " an agent of the Crown is not personally liable on any contract entered into by him on behalf of the Crown," and from this principle it was concluded in *Dunn* v. *Macdonald*, [1897] 1 Q. B. 555, that even the action against an agent for breach of warranty of his authority does not lie against an agent of the Crown. But the decision is unsatisfactory, and can perhaps be explained away as a decision that turned on the peculiar facts of the case.

When, on the other hand, the injury for which redress is sought is not a breach of contract but a tort, the actual tortfeasor *is* liable. He is not protected by his official position, nor does the newly established vicarious liability of the Crown exclude his own personal responsibility. Moreover, it must not be assumed that every tort committed by a servant of the Crown will be committed in the course of his employment : where that is not so, an action against *him* will be the *only* remedy.

Section III. REMEDIES AGAINST OTHER PUBLIC AUTHORITIES

So far we have dealt only with the Crown and such organs of government as are regarded as emanations from the Crown. Local government authorities, however, and indeed most public authorities, are not emanations from the Crown, and did not partake of the immunity hitherto inherent in the maxim : " The King can do no wrong." How and where is the line to be drawn ? No concise and general answer has hitherto been possible, but the Crown Proceedings Act, 1947, after defining a Crown servant, leaves it to the Treasury, so to speak, to beat the bounds of Whitehall.

We must now consider the procedure by which the Courts control all the various public bodies.

If a public authority has committed an act which is at Common Law a crime or a tort or a breach of contract, it may have to answer for it in the Courts. If, as is likely, the public authority is a corporate body, then in litigation with it the doctrine of *ultra vires* may still sometimes apply. So it may be asked whether a given contract is of a kind that the corporation was empowered by its " constitution " to enter into. A further question may arise : whether the use of the corporate seal was necessary for the execution of the contract. Likewise there may be some difficulty in deciding whether a crime imputed to it is such as, having regard to the peculiar status of a corporation, it could be guilty of. But such topics are essentially matters of contract, tort and crime, and they fall to be discussed under those heads. *[Common Law liability.]*

The questions concerning public authorities which come before the Courts usually arise out of their statutory duties. These must be considered in somewhat greater detail.

The question often arises whether a person damaged by non-compliance with a statutory duty has a remedy in tort against the offender. No straightforward answer is possible, and the question is likely to be at its hardest in those cases where the statute, not only creates the duty, but also prescribes some special penalty or provides some special remedy for non-compliance. The *[Breach of statutory duty.]*

answer entirely depends in most cases on the construction
of the statute, and it is a cause for regret that the intention of Parliament should not in each case be made
manifest by the use of statutory language that is clear
and explicit. Silence and ambiguity in this matter is an
unnecessary cause of uncertainty and expense to an injured party. Each statute must accordingly be studied
on its own merits, and there is little of value in the
attempts to draw general precepts from the mass of
judicial decisions as to the effect of particular statutes.
The decided cases form part of the Law of Torts.

Further questions often arise in the construction of
statutes that lay down duties : If the duty is carried out
and damage results, can the defendant escape liability
by proving the absence of all negligence in carrying out
the duty ? Again, is the duty " imperative," in the
sense that it *must* be carried out, nuisance or no nuisance ?
If it is only " permissive," can the duty be carried out
even if nuisance is likely to result ?   In the leading case
a local authority had power by statute to build a hospital
for smallpox, but their power was held to be permissive
only, and they were not allowed to build where there
.would be a danger to the neighbourhood (*Metropolitan
Asylum District* v. *Hill* (1881), 6 App. Cas. 193).   Finally,
does the carrying out of the duty fall under the rule of
strict liability founded in *Rylands* v. *Fletcher* (1868),
L. R. 3 H. L. 330 ?   The answers to these questions must
be found by examining, in each and every case, what
the relevant statute has laid down and also what it has
not laid down. It is the statutory origin of the duty
that must be considered, and the nature and limits of
the duty follow therefrom.

Highway authorities.   Attention must, however, be drawn to the rule, already
mentioned in Chap. 21, Sect. III, *ante*, that a highway
authority is not answerable in damages for *non*-feasance
as distinct from *mis*-feasance. The rule does not, however, cover a failure to keep a *bridge* in repair ; nor does
it cover even highway non-feasance unless the authority
in fault is none other than the *highway* authority.

Remedy by injunction.   If an action for damages would lie for failure to perform a duty imposed at common law or by statute, the

injured party may seek an injunction to restrain the public authority in question from doing or continuing to do the damage complained of. But the remedy by injunction is not limited to cases in which an action for damages would lie. For example, an injunction is an available remedy to restrain a statutory corporation from acting *ultra vires*, or a chartered corporation from doing something that may forfeit the charter ; and it is probable that it would also be granted to restrain certain breaches of *statutory* duties even where no action for damages would lie at the suit of any party damaged by the breach.

It seems clear also that the Courts have jurisdiction to make *declarations* as to the legality of acts contemplated by a public authority, and as to the conflicting rights of public authorities and private persons. *Also by declaration.*

This description of a notoriously difficult subject must suffice for our present purpose ; but the student must be warned that so much depends on the construction of particular Acts of Parliament that general principles are of comparatively little value.

Section IV. ORDERS IN LIEU OF PREROGATIVE WRITS

One of the most interesting of constitutional developments has been the gradual extension of their scope which has enabled the Prerogative Writs to become a most important way of bringing up the decisions of public authorities for review in the Courts. Of these writs, the most famous, *habeas corpus* (see *ante*, pp. 535–8), is rarely encountered in practice ; its operation is so certain that unlawful imprisonments are now rare. Of far more frequent use in practice are *Mandamus, Prohibition,* and *Certiorari,* which afford means of challenging the defaults as well as the activities of public authorities. *Extension of scope.*

These remedies take the form of commands from the High Court—in exercise of the jurisdiction previously vested in the Court of King's Bench—and they were called " prerogative " because they were originally issued only at the suit of the Crown. They were in fact the *Originally Crown remedies.*

regular process by which the Crown compelled sub-ordinate authorities to carry out their duties properly, but from the early years of the eighteenth century they have been available to the citizen also, as supplementary remedies against the wrongdoing of public authorities, and, as a rule, of public authorities alone.

Simplification of procedure.

The procedure connected with these remedies was highly technical and complicated—varying considerably according to the particular writ that was required—but legislation in recent years has done a good deal to implement a recommendation of the Committee on Ministers' Powers that these " archaic and in some ways cumbrous and in-elastic " remedies should be replaced by " a simpler, cheaper and more expeditious procedure." After 1938 the writs themselves have ceased to exist, and their place has been taken by *orders* of *mandamus, prohibition,* and *certiorari.*

1. *Mandamus.* The word itself means "we command," and its continued use indicates the great age of a remedy which, like *prohibition* and *certiorari*, takes the

Demands activity.

form of a peremptory order from the High Court. It differs, however, from these other orders in the *positive* character of the demand made upon the body or person to whom it is addressed. Thus a clerk to justices may be called upon to register a club, on receipt of the proper form and fee, in accordance with sect. 92 of the Licensing (Consolidation) Act, 1910 (*Ashton* v. *Wainwright,* [1936] 1 All E. R. 805). His duty is purely ministerial, involving no exercise of discretion, and the compulsion of the Court may be sought on behalf of those aggrieved by his refusal to carry out that duty. So, again, the Registrar of Companies may be ordered by *mandamus* to incorporate a new company if the Court is of the opinion that the Companies Act, 1948, allows him no discretion to refuse registration (*R.* v. *Registrar of Companies, Ex parte Bowen,* [1914] 3 K. B. 1161). Not infrequently the remedy is sought against some inferior Court that has refused to deal with a complaint on the ground that it has no jurisdiction to do so. The application for *mandamus* gives an opportunity for the High Court to decide, after hearing argument, whether the tribunal in question was right or wrong in denying its own competence.

In the past, the usual cases for the use of this remedy would be those brought against the lower Courts, but the legislation of the past century relating to local government has added enormously to its scope. Thus, to cite fairly recent cases, its machinery has been used to secure a necessary election of aldermen (*Re Barnes Corporation, Ex parte Hutter*, [1933] 1 K. B. 668) and the production of municipal accounts (*R.* v. *Bedwellty U. D. C., Ex parte Price*, [1934] 1 K. B. 333). Moreover, the multiplication of statutory tribunals administering the modern social services has hitherto been responsible for much increase in the scope of *mandamus*, but this will cease if Parliament persists in the recent practice, already referred to more than once, of excluding judicial review by prerogative orders in favour of an alternative procedure carrying a short time-limit for appeal to the Courts. It must not, however, be thought that the use of *mandamus* is confined to matters of local government and social services. Statutes conferring special powers upon public utility undertakings have frequently provided corresponding duties, in respect of which the remedy of *mandamus* may be available. Thus, a railway authority may have been under a statutory duty to build a bridge over land which it acquired by compulsory purchase, and the absence of any other effective remedy might result in the enforcement of such duty by *mandamus*.

We must now deal briefly with the limitations upon the use of the order. In the first place, as we have already indicated, and in conformity with the principles laid down in Chapter 2 (*ante*, pp. 273 *et seq*.), *mandamus* will not be available to compel an authority to exercise a discretion unless it is under a duty to exercise it ; even so, the authority is only commanded to face up to its duty, and the order will leave the authority as free as before to decide for itself without any interfering direction from the Court. Even if, by the omission of one of the requirements of natural justice, the authority has failed in the eye of the law to exercise a discretion, the *mandamus* will only command the authority to exercise it fairly and properly.

Control of local and other authorities.

Public utility undertakings.

Limitations of mandamus.

The same will be true if it has exercised its discretion *mala fide* or for a purpose other than that for which it was entrusted with the discretion.

Position of Crown servants.

Mandamus will not issue to a servant of the Crown if the result would be to enforce the performance of a duty imposed on the Crown itself, for it is clear that the Courts cannot *command* the Crown either directly or indirectly ; and perhaps the most interesting limitation of the remedy is that which renders it unavailable for the purpose of enforcing a duty owed *only to the Crown* by one of the Departments of State (*R. v. Treasury Lords Commissioners* (1872), L. R. 7 Q. B. 387). This is really an application of the general principle that no third party can force an agent to do his duty to his own principal. On the other hand, a *statutory* duty owed *to a subject* by a Department of State *can* be enforced by *mandamus*, though the line may be difficult to draw between such a case and one in which the duty is owed by the Crown (*R. v. Income Tax Special Purposes Commissioners* (1888), 21 Q. B. D. 313). In the latter case, though the new facilities of 1947 would permit ordinary action against the Crown, *mandamus* would not be available, for the reason already given.

Duty must be of legal kind.

Mandamus will be refused if the authority in question owes to the applicant merely an informal duty, the result perhaps of some " gentleman's agreement," but not a duty known to the law (*R. v. Barnstaple Justices, Ex parte Carder*, [1938] 1 K. B. 385 ; [1937] 4 All E. R. 263).

Remedy within the discretion of the Court.

Finally, the issue of the writ is a matter for the discretion of the Court, and it will not be granted if the Court is satisfied that there is an alternative remedy which is sufficient and convenient (*Stepney Borough Council v. John Walker & Sons, Ltd.*, [1934] A. C. 365).

Jurisdiction of Chancery Division.

It is often stated that *mandamus*—the " flower " of the old Court of King's Bench—is now within the exclusive jurisdiction of the King's Bench Division. The competence of the Chancery Division to issue the writ was, however, clearly asserted in *Re Paris Skating Rink Co.* (1877), 6 Ch. D. 731, and though there seems to be no decision on the point, there is text-book authority for the view that the Chancery Division can by *mandamus* compel the officers of companies to carry out such statutory duties as the holding of meetings.

2. *Prohibition.* This remedy differs from *mandamus*, not only in commanding inactivity instead of activity, but also in being traditionally available only against Courts. The development of the writ, however, is constantly displaying the elasticity of the term Court. Borough Courts and other local Courts and the sessions of the Justices of the Peace have always been considered Courts; so also Ecclesiastical Courts; and it was decided as long ago as 1792 in *Grant* v. *Gould* (1792), 2 Hy. Bl. 69, that a Court Martial assembled under the Mutiny Act was included in the term. In speaking of the ecclesiastical courts (*ante*, p. 521) we said that a recent case, while asserting them not to be inferior courts, affirmed the right of the High Court to confine them by *prohibition* to their spiritual jurisdiction, though *not* to correct their errors by *certiorari*.

But during the past hundred years *prohibition* has been awarded to restrain the acts of bodies which are not Courts in the ordinary sense. Thus it has issued to Enclosure Commissioners, to Local Boards, and to Licensing Justices (*R.* v. *Woodhouse*, [1906] 2 K. B. 501), and in more recent cases to Traffic Area Licensing Authorities, and to County Valuation Committees. Its issue is not, however, confined to such bodies, and even the Departments of State can be reached—unless, of course, they enjoy some special statutory immunity from such judicial control. Thus we find proceedings by way of *prohibition* against the Minister of Health in respect of housing (*R.* v. *Minister of Health, Ex parte Villiers*, [1936] 2 K. B. 29; [1936] 1 All E. R. 817). A most striking instance of its applicability to modern administrative persons or bodies exercising judicial or quasi-judicial functions is in the case of *R.* v. *Electricity Commissioners*, [1924] 1 K. B. 171, the facts of which merit detailed description.

The Commissioners were empowered by statute to formulate schemes for effecting improvements in the existing organisation for the supply of electricity in an electricity district, and were directed to hold inquiries upon the schemes. Any decision to which they came as a

Marginal notes:
What is a Court?

Judicial and quasi-judicial functions.

R. v. *Electricity Commissioners.*

result of an inquiry might be embodied in an order and presented to the appropriate Minister for confirmation, but would come into operation only if, after such confirmation, it were approved by resolution of both Houses of Parliament. The Commissioners proceeded to hold an inquiry, whereupon opponents applied for a *prohibition* to restrain them from so doing on the ground that the scheme formulated was *ultra vires*. The Commissioners argued *inter alia* that no *prohibition* would lie, since they were in effect exercising not judicial but legislative functions, and no order from them could take effect until it had been approved by both Houses of Parliament. The Court of Appeal rejected this contention, holding that the Commissioners were entrusted with power to make a decision which might affect the rights of existing electrical undertakers, and, as Atkin, L.J., said:

> " I think that in deciding upon the scheme, and in holding the inquiry, they are acting judicially in the sense of the authorities I have cited, and that as they are proposing to act in excess of their jurisdiction they are liable to have the writ of prohibition issued against them."

Limitations of *prohibition*.

The limits to the applicability of *prohibition* are not yet evident ; but some limitations have already been set to the remedy. Thus it will *not* issue to restrain the exercise of *legislative* functions (*R. v. Church Assembly Legislative Committee, Ex parte Haynes Smith*, [1928] 1 K. B. 411). So, also, it will not issue to a mere private tribunal exercising a consensual jurisdiction, such as the committee of a club or the domestic tribunal of a nonconformist chapel or trade union ; though the Courts are not without other means of compelling such tribunals to observe the elements of justice. *Prohibition* will issue only to a *public* authority.

Yet, although the Courts acknowledge the existence of certain specific limits to the applicability of the remedy, their tendency is always to extend its range of usefulness, and the words of Brett, L.J., in *R. v. Local Government Board* (1882), 10 Q. B. D. 309, at p. 321, are still a safe guide :

> " My view of the power of *prohibition* at the present day is that the Court should not be chary of exercising it, and that wherever the Legislature entrusts to any body of

persons other than to the superior Courts the power of imposing an obligation upon individuals, the Courts ought to exercise as widely as they can the power of controlling those bodies of persons if those persons admittedly attempt to exercise powers beyond the powers given to them by Act of Parliament."

A fairly recent case, however, shows that the Court is reluctant to allow *prohibition* if there is a right of appeal from the inferior court which has not been exercised (*Queen Anne's Bounty (Governors of)* v. *Pitt-Rivers*, [1936] 2 K. B. 416 ; [1936] 2 All E. R. 161).

3. *Certiorari.* The name implies that the procedure is a means of " certifying " or informing the Court. As Scrutton, L.J., said of the process in its old form :

> " *Certiorari* is a very old and high prerogative writ drawn up for the purpose of enabling the [High] Court . . . to control the action of inferior Courts and to make it certain that they shall not exceed their jurisdiction ; and therefore the writ of *certiorari* is intended to bring into the High Court the decision of the inferior tribunal, in order that the High Court may be certified whether the decision is within the jurisdiction of the inferior Court " (*R.* v. *London County Council, Ex parte Entertainments Protection Association, Ltd.*, [1931] 2 K. B. 215, at p. 233).

The review by the High Court may sometimes take place even before the inferior tribunal has come to its decision.

The purpose of the remedy may be (*a*) to make better provision for the fair conduct of a case. A familiar example, made less frequent by provisions in the Criminal Justice Act, 1925, is the transfer by *certiorari* of a case from the local to a more distant place of trial if because of local sympathy or prejudice a fair trial is otherwise unlikely ; but here let us note that an assize is not an inferior Court and cannot therefore be reached by *certiorari* except as a result of statutory authorty ; (*b*) to quash a decision that goes beyond the competence of the inferior tribunal. Thus, in the case last cited, *certiorari* was used to restrain the London County Council, as the proper licensing authority, from permitting the licensees of cinemas to open on Sundays in defiance of the Sunday Observance legislation then in force ; on the ground that " laws cannot be dispensed with by the authority of the London County Council, when they cannot by royal authority " ; (*c*) to ensure observance of the requirements of natural

Purpose of certiorari.

justice (see Chap. 2, *ante*, p. 279).   Thus, in *R.* v. *Hendon R. D. C., Ex parte Chorley*, [1933] 2 K. B. 696, the decision of a Local Authority to allow the development of premises, even in an area covered by a proposed town planning scheme, was quashed by *certiorari* on the ground that one of those concerned in the decision was "biased in the sense that he had such an interest in the matter as to disqualify him from taking part or voting."

Overlap of remedies.

It will be noticed, even from these illustrations, that *certiorari* and *prohibition* are remedies which overlap, and the reports of decided cases will show that *certiorari* is usually sought, not alone, but side by side with *prohibition* or perhaps *mandamus*.   The purpose—and the only purpose—of *prohibition* is prevention, but though *certiorari* can serve the dual purpose of prevention or cure, the latter purpose is predominant.   This difference of purpose leads to a practical difficulty in the use of the two remedies, which is simply resolved by "shooting down both the barrels at once."   An aggrieved party may not be certain if and when a pending decision of which he complains has become, or is likely to become, a decision proper.   It would be unsafe for him, therefore, to rely on *prohibition* alone, as will be seen by comparing the two cases of *R.* v. *Minister of Health, Ex parte Davis*, [1929] 1 K. B. 619, where the local housing scheme in dispute had *not* yet been confirmed by the Minister of Health, and *R.* v. *Minister of Health, Ex parte Yaffe*, [1930] 2 K. B. 98 ; *reversed*, [1931] A. C. 494, where a similar scheme had already been so confirmed.   "An application for *prohibition* is never too late so long as there is something left for it to operate upon" (*per* Wright, J., in *Re London Scottish Permanent Building Society* (1893), 63 L. J. Q. B. 112, at p. 113).

It is to be observed, however, that just as the High Court will not use the process by *mandamus* to instruct an authority how to exercise its discretion, so as a rule *certiorari* will not issue for the purpose of exercising an appellate jurisdiction, even though the authority has jurisdiction to decide points of law and the Court is of opinion that it has decided erroneously.

The general principle is that *certiorari*, like *prohibition* and *mandamus*, will lie unless expressly taken away by statute. Decided cases, especially of the last two decades, have revealed the difficulty of framing a statute in language that is powerful enough to set this principle aside (see *R*. v. *Minister of Health, Ex parte Yaffe, ante,* pp. 326, 580). This is a great safeguard of the citizen against the arbitrary exercise of power by administrative bodies.

Statutory exclusion of prerogative remedies.

Though there is still considerable uncertainty as to the exact extent within which the orders *in lieu* of prerogative writs can be used to control the acts of government authorities, the effect of modern decisions is to show that the Courts will, unless they are absolutely forbidden by statute from so doing, exercise their controlling jurisdiction wherever they consider it necessary, and will not be readily restrained by considerations of a technical character.

Tendency to extend scope.

Section V. LIMITATION OF ACTIONS AGAINST PUBLIC AUTHORITIES

We must conclude with a brief notice of the Public Authorities Protection Act, 1893, and the Limitation Act, 1939.

It had long been the practice, when conferring powers or imposing duties on public authorities, to limit a time within which actions might be brought in respect of acts done under the statute in question. In 1893 the Public Authorities Protection Act was passed to supersede these scattered provisions and furnish a code of general application.

In cases where the defendant is a "public authority" the Act of 1893 limits the period during which *criminal* proceedings (*e.g.* for a public nuisance) may be begun to only *six months* next after the act, neglect or default complained of, and as re-enacted in s. 21 of the Limitation Act, 1939, curtails the normal six years of grace for the beginning of *civil* actions to only *one year* from the date on which the cause of action accrued. To this curtailing provision, however, some specific exemptions were made in 1893, and these now apply under both Acts.

The Act of 1893 also confers certain privileges in the matter of costs and tender of amends. The interpretation of the Act bristles with difficulties and is continually causing trouble in the Courts. It is therefore of peculiar importance to know the case-law on the subject. But any discussion of this would be beyond the scope of the present work, and we shall conclude with a few general observations :

(1) The term "public authority" is not confined to Local Authorities, and a large variety of bodies have been allowed the protection of the Act, *e.g.*, the Wheat Commission, the visiting committee of a mental hospital, and the managers of an elementary school ; but *not* commercial undertakings, even though they are public utilities. Nor does the protection of the Act, as we have previously said (p. 422), cover the newly created public corporations now operating the "nationalised" industries, though the creating statutes do themselves contain special provisions dealing with the limitation of actions, *e.g.* the Coal Industry Nationalisation Act, 1946, s. 49, and the Transport Act, 1947, s. 11.

(2) The period of limitation is strictly enforced, but the possibility of resulting hardship (*e.g.* in cases of illness delaying a plaintiff's action) is likely to be far less frequent after the reform of 1939, which lengthened the period for litigation from six months to one year. And, as we explained when dealing with remedies in tort (See Vol. II, Book II, Chap. 18), the Act of 1939 also prevented this lengthened period from running against an infant or person of unsound mind not in the custody of a "parent" as defined in s. 31, and provided that where the act, neglect or default is a continuing one, the cause of action is not deemed to accrue until the act, neglect or default has ceased.

(3) Though the statutory time-limit has been held inapplicable to *certiorari*, it has also been held that this remedy, lying in the discretion of the High Court, may be refused in cases of undue delay. The same would seem to be true, in this respect, of *mandamus* and *prohibition*.

BOOK II

CONSTITUTIONAL AND ADMINISTRATIVE LAW

PART VII

THE
COMMONWEALTH AND EMPIRE

SUMMARY

PAGE

CHAPTER 27. THE COMMONWEALTH AND EMPIRE   585

THE COMMONWEALTH AND EMPIRE

SUMMARY				PAGE
Section I. *The British Islands*	...	...	...	... 585
Section II. *Colonies*	...	...	...	... 588
Section III. *Protectorates and Protected States*		...	...	... 595
Section IV. *Trust Territories* ...	...	...	...	... 596
Section V. *The Dominions* ...	...	...	...	... 596
Section VI. *The Unity of the Empire*		...	...	... 600

Section I. THE BRITISH ISLANDS

Since the sixteenth century Wales has for most legal *Wales.* purposes been identified with England, and until quite recent times the tendency has been to draw still closer the bonds between the two countries. Thus they have the same legal system, and for more than a century Wales has been within the jurisdiction of the superior courts in London. An Act of Parliament which mentions England only is deemed to apply to Wales. Thus " England " really means England and Wales ; it is only for the sake of brevity that the full title is not employed. It should, however, be noted that when special legislation is passed for Wales, the English county of Monmouth is regularly included with the Principality (see *ante*, p. 501).

But there has been of late years a tendency to accord Wales separate treatment, so far at least as certain matters are concerned. Thus the existence of the Welsh language and of other national peculiarities has made it necessary to establish special Welsh Departments of the Ministries of Education and of Agriculture. The work *Education.* of the Ministry of Health is also, to some extent, " decen- *Agriculture.* tralised " in the creation of a separate Welsh Board of *Health.* Health. Moreover, since 1920, the Church in Wales has *Church.* been disestablished. Its government is now completely separate from that of the Church of England, though it remains episcopal and in communion with the Church of England (see, further, *ante*, pp. 355, 512, 523).

Scotland was, by the Act of Union, 1706, united into one kingdom with England by the name of Great Britain. Ever since there has been one Parliament for the two countries ; and an Act of Parliament extends to Scotland, unless it is expressly excepted or the intention of the Legislature to except it is otherwise sufficiently indicated. Moreover, from the end of the last century, a special Department, now under a Secretary of State for Scotland, has been established partly in London and partly in Edinburgh to conduct Scottish business (see *ante*, p. 415). But there are important matters in which Scotland retains independent institutions.

Scotland has its own courts of justice, and is out of the jurisdiction of the English Courts. The principal civil court, which sits in Edinburgh with a recently increased maximum of fifteen judges, is the Court of Session, consisting of an Outer House, composed of Lords Ordinary who sit at first instance, and an Inner House, composed of the Lord President, the Lord Justice Clerk and Lords Ordinary, sitting as a court of appeal in two divisions. The Lords Ordinary also exercise criminal jurisdiction, in Edinburgh and on circuit, under the designation of Lords Commissioners of Justiciary. An appeal lies from the Inner House of the Court of Session to the House of Lords in civil matters ; but there is no appeal to the House of Lords from the fairly recently created Court of Criminal Appeal for Scotland. Besides these Courts, there are subordinate courts presided over by the sheriff or the sheriff-substitute, with both criminal and civil jurisdiction, the latter unlimited as to the amount at stake. Scottish solicitors are known as " law agents," and many of them have the titles of Writers to the Signet, Solicitors of the Court of Session, and Procurators of the Sheriff-court. Scottish local government, again, though it has followed, or anticipated, the main lines upon which English local government has developed, differs from it in many material points.

The Scottish legal system is not that of England, being in part based directly on Roman Law, and it is only where the Common Law of the two countries happens to be the same, or in the interpretation of a statute applying throughout Great Britain, that the decisions of a Scottish

Court are of value to an English lawyer. It is, however, easy to exaggerate the differences between the two systems. Such fruitful sources of litigation as Income Tax, Patents, and Company Law are regulated identically in the two countries, and the voluminous enactments of modern social legislation are much the same for both countries. Their commercial law is the same, as are large portions of the law of contract and of tort. The main differences are to be found in the law of property and of the family ; and the form of the criminal law is different, though it would be very dangerous for anyone to assume that he could commit with impunity on one side of the Border what is an offence on the other.

By the Government of Ireland Act, 1920, Ireland was divided into two states, Northern Ireland, consisting of six of the nine counties of the Province of Ulster, and Southern Ireland, consisting of the rest of the island. By the Irish Free State Constitution Act, 1922 (Session 2), a new written constitution was adopted for the whole island, together with the name of the Irish Free State, but subject to the right of the Government of Northern Ireland to contract out of the Act. This right was immediately exercised, and the Irish Free State (Consequential Provisions) Act, 1922 (Session 2), was passed to confine the earlier and more limited " Home Rule " experiment to Northern Ireland. The result was that Ireland became composed of two States, each with a constitution of its own. *Northern Ireland.*

As regards Northern Ireland, the governing statute is the Government of Ireland Act, 1920, as amended by the Irish Free State (Consequential Provisions) Act, 1922 (Session 2), and the subsequent Northern Ireland (Miscellaneous Provisions) Acts. Under these Acts there is a separate Parliament, whose legislative power is limited to domestic affairs, consisting of the King, represented by the Governor of Northern Ireland, the Senate of Northern Ireland, and the House of Commons of Northern Ireland. Northern Ireland also continues to send representatives to the House of Commons at Westminster, thus furnishing an instance of true federalism within the United Kingdom. Legislation of the Imperial Parlia- *Government of Ireland Act, 1920.* *Parliament.*

ment extends to Northern Ireland unless it is expressly
excepted, but in practice such legislation will only concern the matters lying outside the powers of the Northern
Ireland Parliament, *e.g.*, the royal succession and property
of the Crown, peace and war, the armed forces, treaties
and foreign affairs, dignities and honours, nationality,

Executive. coinage, patents and copyright.   The executive power is
vested in the Crown, and is exercised by the Governor
with the aid of an Executive Committee composed of the
Ministers, who unlike our own have the useful right of

Judiciary. addressing *either* House.   The judiciary is framed upon
the model of the English Supreme Court ; and there is
an ultimate appeal to the House of Lords.

Eire. Not only has the former Irish Free State (called Eire
and now to be known as the Republic of Ireland) long
ceased to be a part of the United Kingdom, but by the
Ireland Act, 1949, has ceased to be part of His Majesty's
Dominions, though it is not for most legal purposes a
" foreign country " (see *post*, p. 601).

Law. The Common Law of Ireland is the same as that of
England ; and decisions of the Irish Courts are not
infrequently cited in English Courts, not as binding
authorities, but as showing the results that have been
reached on similar questions in a parallel jurisdiction.

Channel
Islands and
Isle of Man. The Channel Islands and the Isle of Man, since they
enjoy separate legislatures with full competence, are
not parts of the United Kingdom.   Legislation of the
United Kingdom Parliament does not affect them unless
they are expressly mentioned, *e.g.*, the National Service
Acts, 1948, can be made applicable to the Isle of Man by
Order in Council.   Nor are they generally included among
the Colonies, though this is done by the British Nationality Act, 1948, for its own purposes.   This Act, however,
permits a citizen of the United Kingdom and Colonies,
if on the ground of his connection with the Channel
Islands or the Isle of Man he so desires, to be known as a
citizen of the United Kingdom, Islands and Colonies.

Section II. COLONIES

Traditional
division. *Settled and Conquered Colonies.*   Among lawyers the
traditional division of colonies has been into settled

colonies and ceded or conquered colonies. It was originally the law that when British settlers went into a country which was uninhabited, or at least not under the control of any civilised power, they took their own law with them, together with all the rights which an Englishman has against the Crown. This meant that the Crown had no more right to legislate for them by virtue of the Prerogative than it had in the case of British subjects at home. It was therefore generally necessary to establish a Colonial Legislature, and this the Crown could do by virtue of the Prerogative ; the legislature comprised in all cases a Governor and at least one elected House. Ceded or conquered colonies, on the other hand, retained their existing legal system until it was changed by the Crown, but the Crown had absolute power over them. Thus there was no need to establish an elected legislature in a ceded or conquered colony, but once such a legislature was in fact granted, the Crown lost its autocratic power over the colony.

To this distinction between settled colonies and ceded or conquered colonies we owe the diversity of systems of private law in the Empire. Thus Quebec retains the French system, and the law of the Cape of Good Hope and of Ceylon is Roman-Dutch. But, from the point of view of government, the distinction has long become meaningless ; many of the settled colonies which once possessed elected legislatures surrendered them—usually because of difficulties or adversities—and received from Parliament Constitutions conferring on the Crown powers of the most extended kind. In particular, the Crown generally acquired the power to legislate for them by Order in Council, and in such colonies it became extremely rare to find a legislature which was " representative " in the sense that at least half the members were elected by the local inhabitants. Moreover, under the British Settlements Act, 1887, the Crown was given power to legislate either directly by Order in Council or indirectly through a nominated legislature, or by both means, for any British settlement in which a legislature had not otherwise been established. The old immunity, therefore, of a British settlement from autocratic government

Diversity of systems of private law.

British Settlements Act, 1887.

by the Crown disappeared. On the other hand, many ceded or conquered colonies acquired that immunity through the grant of representative institutions.

Parliament supreme. There is thus no uniform subjection of colonies to the Royal Prerogative, but *all* colonies—in the absence of Dominion status—are subject to the sovereignty of the Imperial Parliament, sitting at Westminster. But the legislation of the Imperial Parliament is held not to operate outside the United Kingdom unless the contrary is stated by express words or by necessary implication in the legislation itself. Yet, without doubt, Imperial legislation *can* operate beyond these shores, and in this it is unlike colonial legislation. A colonial legislature legislates only for the territory in which it is established. **Extra-territorial legislation.** It cannot give to its legislation extra-territorial operation, except where such operation is necessary for the government of the colony.

Apart from this exception " of somewhat doubtful extent," the relations between the Imperial Parliament **Colonial Laws Validity Act.** and colonial legislatures were fixed by the Colonial Laws Validity Act, 1865, which provides that

> " Any colonial law which is or shall be in any respect repugnant to the provisions of any Act of Parliament extending to the colony to which such law may relate, or repugnant to any order or regulation made under authority of such Act of Parliament, or having in the colony the force and effect of such Act, shall be read subject to such Act, order, or regulation, and shall, to the extent of such repugnancy, but not otherwise, be and remain absolutely void and inoperative."

The Act goes on to state that

> " No colonial law shall be or be deemed to have been void or inoperative on the ground of repugnancy to the law of England, unless the same shall be repugnant to the provisions of some such Act of Parliament, order, or regulation as aforesaid."

It follows that a colonial legislature has full power to change not only the rules of Common Law and Equity but even Statute Law, provided it is not Imperial legislation enacted for the colony.

But, from a constitutional point of view, it would be unwise to lay too much stress on this feature. The

Imperial Parliament does not, as a general rule, legislate for a colony without its consent, and, apart from certain Imperial statutes, such as the Merchant Shipping Acts, which are of general interest and are applied uniformly throughout the Empire, practically all the Imperial legislation which operates outside the United Kingdom consists of Acts prescribing the Constitutions of individual colonial legislatures. In these, the general rule has been, *either* to give full powers of legislation in *internal* affairs, a grant usually followed by the concession of responsible government on the same lines as that exercised in the United Kingdom, *or*, where that has not been done, to reserve power to the Crown to legislate for the colony by Order in Council.

Colonial Constitutions.

We shall later give some account of the steps whereby the Dominions have been elevated, first only by convention but ultimately even by law, high above the class of colonies ; so high, indeed, that in their external as well as their internal affairs they are as completely free— legally no less than politically—from all control by the Imperial Parliament and the Home Government as if they were independent states like, say, France or Brazil. The list now comprises Canada, Australia, New Zealand, the Union of South Africa, India, Pakistan, and Ceylon, the last three being recent additions to a list that has ceased to include either Eire or Newfoundland and still excludes Southern Rhodesia, to whose unique constitutional position we later refer (p. 593). Except for the purposes of the British Nationality Act, 1948, it is still to be classed as a colony as distinct from a dominion, and it is in fact the only remaining example of a *colony* with not merely a representative legislature but also an executive that is " responsible " to it ; in other words, a colony that is as close as possible to being a dominion without actually being one. Even if this one remaining example of such a colony should prove to be the last of its kind—and we do not presume to foretell how far the future lines of colonial constitutional progress will follow those of the past—even so, there will still be much historical and some practical interest in the old question, once the lively concern of all colonies with free institutions

Colonies distinguished from Dominions.

of their own, namely, whether a Colonial Constitution can be changed by the Colonial Legislature.

Constitutional amendment.

In so far as it is contained in an Act of the Colonial Legislature, a Colonial Constitution can *prima facie* be changed by that Legislature. If, however, it has been conferred by an Act of the Imperial Parliament, *prima facie* it can only be changed by an Act of the Imperial Parliament, for any Act of the Colonial Legislature which purported to alter it would be repugnant to Imperial legislation affecting the colony. But another section of the Colonial Laws Validity Act extends the powers of a Colonial Legislature which is " representative," *i.e.*, composed to the extent of at least a half of locally elected members. It enacts that

> " Every representative Legislature [*i.e.* one of the type described above] shall, in respect to the colony under its jurisdiction, have, and be deemed at all times to have had, full power to make laws respecting the constitution, powers, and procedure of such Legislature ; provided that such laws shall have been passed in such manner and form as may from time to time be required by any Act of Parliament, letters-patent, order in council, or colonial law for the time being in force in the said colony."

Accordingly, a Colonial Legislature of a *representative* character is empowered, subject to the provisions of the Act, to change, not only a Constitution contained in one of its own Acts, but even the provisions of a constituent Act of the Imperial Parliament. It is interesting to observe, in passing, that a representative Colonial Legislature can do what even the Imperial Parliament itself cannot do, that is to say, bind its own successors in respect of the manner of effecting a constitutional change (see *A.-G. for New South Wales* v. *Trethowan*, [1932] A. C. 526).

It may be remarked that it has been extremely unusual to withhold from a *representative* Colonial Legislature any power necessary to the fullest *internal* self-government, nor has the Imperial Parliament generally made any provision which fetters such a legislature in respect of the manner in which it shall effect a constitutional change. On the other hand, *non*-representative Colonial Legislatures, in the sense described above, have rarely, if ever, had constituent powers.

Even a colony with a representative legislature is sub- ject to the royal veto. In *all* colonies there is, in fact, a *double* veto, for not only may the Crown's representative in the colony veto colonial legislation, but it may be vetoed by the Crown itself acting on the advice of the Secretary of State for the Colonies. Both of these vetoes, unlike the royal veto in the United Kingdom, are in active use.

The *executive* government of a colony differs according as it possesses responsible government or is one of the class officially termed colonies not possessing responsible government, but usually known as Crown Colonies. (Of the former class the only present example is Southern Rhodesia, whose unique position as a colony—on the fringe of Dominion status but still not quite within it— is emphasised by the fact that for the purposes of the British Nationality Act, 1948, it is to count with the Dominions.) In Crown Colonies, the executive power is in the hands of the Governor or other representative of the King, subject to the control of the Secretary of State for the Colonies and (in most cases) to the terms of the Constitution of the Colony.

There are a great number of Crown Colonies—far too many to enumerate here—and the variety of their Constitutions is very wide. But two classes of Crown Colonies are clearly distinguishable, namely, (*a*) those in which the Crown has *not* full control of legislation, and (*b*) those in which it *has*.

(*a*) To this class belong only four Crown Colonies, namely, the Bahamas, Barbados, and Bermuda, and— quite recently—Jamaica. Each of these is governed by a Legislature consisting of a Governor—whose veto is by no means obsolete—a nominated Legislative Council, and a House of Assembly *entirely elected*. Legislation for the colony can be effected *only* by the Colonial Legislature *or* by the Imperial Parliament. The judges, in these *and all other* Crown Colonies, are appointed not by the Governor but by the Colonial Office, so that they are independent of the Colonial Executive, and can restrain it within the bounds of law without jeopardising their judicial positions.

Colonies where Crown *has* full control of legislation.

(b) In all other Crown Colonies the Crown can *either* legislate by Order in Council *or* procure whatever colonial legislation it desires by means of a nominated or official *majority* in the Colonial Legislature, bound to vote in accordance with the instructions of the Governor, and, through him, of the Colonial Office. In some of these Crown Colonies both methods are still open to it, and as long as this is so, this class of Crown Colonies may therefore be sub-divided as follows :

    (i) Those in which there is no provision for a nominated or official majority in the Legislature, but . for which the Crown *can* legislate by Order in Council ;

    (ii) Those in which there *is* provision for a nominated or official majority, but for which there is no power to legislate by Order in Council ;

    (iii) Those in which there *is* provision for a nominated or official majority, and for which there is *also* power to legislate by Order in Council. To this class the greater number of the Crown Colonies used to belong, but the number is now only a minority and decreasing fast ;

    (iv) Those in which there is still no Colonial Legislature but only a Governor, and for which the Crown may legislate by Order in Council.

Because throughout the Empire the surge of constitutional changes has already been so fast and furious since the ending of the war and seems likely to go on unabated, we have decided reluctantly to refrain from naming any particular colonies in illustration of the sub-divisions above-mentioned.

Law.

In most of the Crown Colonies, the Common Law is English, but reasonable native customs are fully enforced. In Ceylon, very recently made self-governing, Roman-Dutch Law is in force ; and in Mauritius and the Seychelles Islands, the system of law is that of the French Codes as promulgated in 1809.

Section III. PROTECTORATES AND PROTECTED STATES

The distinction between protectorates and protected Variety. states does not befit this elementary treatise ; nor need we dwell upon the power of the Crown under the British Nationality Act, 1948, to apply the Act to certain territories " as if they were protected states." Here it must suffice to say that Protectorate Constitutions are as various as those of Crown Colonies. The rein of control by the Imperial Government may be tight or loose. It may amount to nothing more than a prohibition of foreign relations with any but the protecting power ; on the other hand, in some protectorates the Crown exercises absolute control. There is indeed only one thing which differentiates a protectorate from a colony. A protectorate is not part of the King's dominions. It is foreign Foreign territory, though not so counted for the purposes of the territory. British Nationality Act, 1948. Two consequences follow from this : Acts of Parliament only expressed to be enacted for British Possessions do not apply to protectorates ; Parliament must legislate expressly for a protectorate if the legislation is to have effect within the protected territory. In the second place, their government is carried on by the Crown under the Foreign Jurisdiction Acts, 1890 and 1913, which provide for the administration of government and justice in foreign parts. It is interesting to notice an overdue provision of recent years whereby non-British subjects belonging to a protectorate, with no foreign nationality of their own, are to be known as British Protected Persons and as such to receive passports and diplomatic protection for the purpose of travel in foreign countries. They are specified in a recent Order made under the British Nationality Act, 1948, the provisions of which have been officially declared to " constitute a first step in assimilating the legal position of British protected persons to that of British subjects." Already they do not count as aliens under the Act, which stops short of permitting them British nationality except by naturalisation.

The protectorates are governed—so far as they are governed at all by the British Government—through the

38*

Colonial Office. Outside the Union of South Africa, much
of the British control of the continent of Africa is exercised through protectorates, such as the Uganda and the
Bechuanaland Protectorates, and—pending further expected post-war changes—there are other illustrations of
this form of government in the Federation of Malaya and
elsewhere.

Section IV. TRUST TERRITORIES

Several of the territories comprised in the Empire,
e.g., Palestine (until 1948) and Tanganyika, are really
protectorates of the former League of Nations, which
after the first World War entrusted the control of them
to certain of its member states, three of the Dominions
as well as the United Kingdom then becoming mandatory powers. The intention was that, so far from
governing as they liked or to their own advantage, the
mandatory states should abide by certain conditions laid
down in the mandate and should give an annual account
of their stewardship to the League.

The future status of some of these territories (hitherto
known as *mandated territories*) has been recently agreed
upon by the United Nations in accordance with the new
system of "trusteeship," and territories administered
under this system are now being known as *trust territories*.

Section V. THE DOMINIONS

We have already said that representative colonial
government has matured in certain cases into government that is "responsible" in the sense in which that
term is understood of our own Government. This means
that the responsibility is to the *local* legislature, and *not*
to the Secretary of State for the Colonies and through
him to the House of Commons at Westminster. Speak-

Convention
the source of
"responsible"
government.

ing generally, the transition from representative to responsible government is a process regulated by convention and not by law ; for it is unusual to find Constitutions making any express reference to the "responsibility " of the colonial administration. Again, not all
colonies with representative institutions have been able

to make good their claim to responsible government ; on the contrary, in some cases, bad finance or other factors have forced a colony even to surrender its representative constitution and accept another of a non-representative character, as happened in recent years both in Newfoundland and in Malta. The reason, then, for the emergence of responsible government is to be found not in the existing state of the law but in considerations of policy ; and its sanction is not legal but conventional or customary.

The majority of colonies which did acquire responsible government came to be known as Dominions, and though this term was formerly a loose one unknown to the law, and though it seems already to be falling into political disfavour, it was the term applied by the Statute of Westminster, 1931, to the Dominion of Canada, the Commonwealth of Australia, the Dominion of New Zealand, the Union of South Africa, the Irish Free State, and Newfoundland. (In the case of Newfoundland, however, the Constitution was later suspended in pre-war adversity, and after intervening years of prosperity Newfoundland has recently become a tenth province of Canada.) By 1931 the Irish Free State (called Eire and now the Republic of Ireland) had ceased to be part of the United Kingdom, but it had not by then abandoned the Dominion status which had come to it a decade earlier. *Statutory definition of Dominion.*

That status has, by very recent legislation, been conferred upon India (Hindustan), Pakistan, and Ceylon.

Most of the Dominions, in the years before 1931, as a result of their economic and political importance, became free *in political practice* from the control of the Home Government ; but there was not, however, any alteration of their *legal* status as colonies. Before the first Great War they had already become politically independent in all their *internal* affairs ; but *foreign* affairs still remained mainly a matter for the Home Government, and in 1914 it committed them to participation in the war. But their voice was not ignored either in the conduct of the war or afterwards in the making of the peace. Later, the control of their foreign affairs from Westminster was so far relaxed that, after some out-of-date hesitation, it *Dominion status.*

was laid down at the Imperial Conference of 1923 that the Dominions had independence in the making of treaties with foreign powers, and in the appointment of their own diplomatic representatives in foreign capitals. This process of *political* emancipation culminated in the insistence by certain of the Dominions upon such adjustment of their *legal* status as would bring it into line with the full freedom that constitutional convention allowed. Attention was given to their wishes by the Imperial Conference of 1926, the report of which includes the oft-quoted resolution as to Dominion status. The Dominions, it was resolved, are "autonomous Communities within the British Empire, equal in status, in no way subordinate one to another in any aspect of their domestic or external affairs, though united by a common allegiance to the Crown, and freely associated as members of the British Commonwealth of Nations." This resolution, though true in the political sense, was then untrue in the legal sense, and after the legal difficulties had been reviewed and resolved by a committee of lawyers reporting to the Imperial Conference of 1930, the Statute of Westminster was passed in the following year to ensure that political equality should be consummated as equality in the eyes of the law.

Imperial Conferences of 1926 and 1930.

Statute of Westminster, 1931.

Very little can here be said about this outstanding enactment and the host of varied and interesting problems that both the Act itself and its Preamble have created for the constitutional lawyer.

By section 2 the Dominions are relieved of the restrictions put upon all colonial legislation by the Colonial Laws Validity Act, 1865 (see *ante*, p. 590). Section 3 removes all doubt as to their full power to legislate with extra-territorial effect in the fashion of independent states (see *ante*, p. 590). Section 4 withdraws each of the Dominions from the scope of any subsequent Act of the Imperial Parliament which does not expressly declare that the Dominion "has requested, and consented to, the enactment thereof." Perhaps the most interesting part of the Act is its Preamble, which recites (1) that it would be in accord with the established constitutional position of all the members of the Commonwealth in relation to

Preamble.

one another that any alteration of the law touching the Succession to the Throne or the Royal Style and Titles should hereafter require the assent as well of the Parliaments of all the Dominions as of the Parliament of the United Kingdom ; (2) that it is in accord with the established constitutional position that no law hereafter made by the Parliament of the United Kingdom shall extend to any of the said Dominions as part of the law of the Dominion otherwise than at the request and with the consent of that Dominion. The student will notice a close parallel between these words of the Preamble and those of Section 4 of the Act, and the explanation (see also *ante*, p. 290) would seem to be that by reciting these conventions in a Preamble the equality of status could be made compatible with the supposed sovereign right of the Imperial Parliament to repeal even the Statute of Westminster itself. No more interesting illustration of the working of these conventions could be found than in the conduct of the constitutional affairs preceding the passing of His Majesty's Declaration of Abdication Act, 1936. It is recited in the Preamble to that Act that " the Dominion of Canada, pursuant to the provisions of section four of the Statute of Westminster, 1931, has requested and consented to the enactment of the Act, and the Commonwealth of Australia, the Dominion of New Zealand, and the Union of South Africa have assented thereto." The explanation of the puzzling discrimination between the four Dominions is that, whereas in the case of Canada there had to be a precise compliance with what was enacted in 1931, it was otherwise sufficient to comply with convention ; for neither Australia nor New Zealand had by then adopted (as they have since done) the Statute of Westminster as the law of their land, while in South Africa the constitutional position was complicated by the Union's own legislation.

We must add that the Imperial Conference of 1926 sanctioned the convention that the King's representative should not exercise his veto in a Dominion, and that he should act *only* on the advice of his responsible Ministers in the Dominion, so that no longer should he be in any sense a representative of, or even a channel of communi-

Governor-General.

cation with, the Home Government. A later Imperial Conference was emphatic that even the appointment of a Governor-General is no concern of the Home Government, and is to be made by the King exclusively on the advice of the Dominion Government.

Crown Proceedings Act, 1947.

Significant, in this context, is the explicit exclusion from the Crown Proceedings Act, 1947, of any Crown liability " otherwise than in respect of His Majesty's Government in the United Kingdom." The line is to be drawn by a Secretary of State, who is empowered to certify conclusively.

Section VI. The Unity of the Empire

We must now review in turn those factors that still effect some measure of unity within the Commonwealth. First in *political* importance has been the Imperial Conference, an institution of pre-war years that now seems dead in name and form but still alive in purpose, namely, the discussion of matters of common interest between the Dominions and the Mother Country. All the really important of such matters—whether they relate to defence or trade or currency or what not—are now likely to be of such pressing urgency that their discussion cannot await a next triennial meeting of Premiers in London but must instead be done promptly as occasion should arise, perhaps quite informally by consultations from day to day between the Governments concerned, perhaps more formally at *ad hoc* conferences of Ministers or even Prime Ministers.

Imperial Conference.

The King

Until only a few years ago it would have been possible to say that the King was, from the *legal* point of view, the great unifying factor, in that all legislation, passed by any legislature in the Empire, required his assent, whether given directly by him or indirectly through one of his representatives. Likewise, all executive acts were done, and all judicial functions exercised, in his name. Moreover, the status of a British subject implied a common allegiance to the same King. But there could be no denying that, in all these matters, the power of the King, and the unity of the Empire, were often more formal than real.

Even in a formal sense, however, the Crown has not been unaffected by recent constitutional changes, notably in Eire (now the Republic of Ireland) and in India and to some extent also in South Africa. In the first country, indeed, the Crown was replaced a decade ago by an elected President, who—in all internal affairs—was in effect Head of the State. Yet, in external affairs, though neutrality was successfully protested throughout the recent war, there was said to be an unbroken " association " with the British Commonwealth, the extent of which, as symbolised by the Crown, was from time to time pronounced upon somewhat vaguely and evasively during the years immediately before Eire's ultimate secession. But secession has not been the result of the similar decision of India to become a Republic. On the contrary, the Government of India, at the end of a successful conference in London of Commonwealth Prime Ministers, " declared and affirmed India's desire to continue her full membership of the Commonwealth . . . and her acceptance of the King as the symbol of the free association of its independent member nations and as such the Head of the Commonwealth." Moreover, it was made known at the same time that " the Governments of the other countries of the Commonwealth, the basis of whose membership is not hereby changed, accept and recognise India's continuing membership in accordance with the terms of this declaration." Thus, in the view of this recent assembly of statesmen, membership of the Commonwealth does not necessarily require allegiance to the Crown, and the King (the word used being not the Crown but the King) is " as such the Head of the Commonwealth " even though in India there is to be no royal function however formal. We must here resist the temptation to seek the legal meaning of all this ; for, in the words of a learned commentator, " the Commonwealth Prime Ministers produced a declaration which may well prove to be one of the great constitutional documents of modern times, but which is certain to prove the despair of constitutional theorists." And he adds this unflattering warning to lawyers : " The evolution of the Commonwealth has perhaps been the highest achieve-

Eire and India.

ment of the British genius for politics, and the politicians can say with some justification that this sphere of politics is too serious a matter to be left to the lawyers " (Modern Law Review (1949), Vol. 12, p. 351).

Judicial
Committee of
the Privy
Council. So, with befitting humility, we pass on to a third factor, this time legal rather than political, that still makes for some measure of unity, namely, the Judicial Committee of the Privy Council. The jurisdiction of this body (which sits in Downing Street) is regulated by a series of statutes beginning in 1833, but the historical foundation of the jurisdiction is to be found in the remnant of autocratic control that was left to the Crown in respect of its possessions beyond the seas (see *ante*, p. 296).

Composition. It is a body of very miscellaneous composition and includes the following elements : all privy councillors who hold or have held high judicial office in the United Kingdom, in particular the Lords of Appeal in Ordinary ; certain judges and ex-judges of the superior courts of the Dominions ; and certain other persons specially appointed, under statutory powers, on the ground of their knowledge and experience of *non*-English legal Relation to
House of
Lords. systems. The greater part of the work of the Committee is in fact done by persons competent to hear appeals in the House of Lords, and so the two final courts of appeal, though theoretically distinct and having different places of assembly, tend more and more to become identical in composition. The Committee delivers a single written judgment, which takes the form of reasons for humbly advising His Majesty to allow or to dismiss the appeal. By convention such advice *must* be followed.

Extent of
jurisdiction. In the absence of express legislation to the contrary, the King in Council has jurisdiction to hear appeals from all portions of the Empire, inclusive of the Protectorates and Trust Territories, but exclusive of the United Kingdom itself, where jurisdiction is confined to appeals from Ecclesiastical and Prize Courts. Appeal in civil cases is sometimes " as of right," which means that the Court appealed from cannot refuse leave to appeal on compliance with whatever the local procedural demands may be ; sometimes, on the other hand, it is a matter for the discretion of the local Court to give or refuse its leave. Not to be confused are the " prerogative appeals," which can only be brought by petition for the " special leave " of the Judicial Committee itself. This is even more exceptional in criminal than in civil matters, and it has to be shown that the conviction has been a gross disregard of the essentials of justice, as in a fairly recent case where a member of the trial jury could not understand the language spoken in the Court. This procedure by way of special leave from London could not, broadly speaking, be cut down or ousted even by a Dominion before 1931, though a Dominion might interfere at pleasure with the ordinary procedure " as of right " or with the discretionary power of its own Courts. Since 1931, however, Dominions have been able, under the Statute of Westminster and the India and Ceylon Independence Acts, to abolish entirely appeals to the Privy Council, including even the prerogative right of granting special leave to appeal ; and appeals from the Republic of Ireland, Canada and India are now a thing of the past.

It is appropriate to end with the power of the Crown to refer any matter for the opinion of the Judicial Committee—a power of little use except in Imperial affairs, but of especial convenience when the Crown is, so to speak, divided against itself, *e.g.*, in a boundary dispute between different parts of the Empire.

Special reference.

INDEX

The contents of this volume will be found indexed in the GENERAL INDEX to the whole work, which is printed at the end of Volume IV.

PRINTED IN GREAT BRITAIN BY WILLIAM CLOWES AND SONS, LIMITED, LONDON AND BECCLES